CYPRUS

Society and Culture
1191-1374

THE
MEDIEVAL MEDITERRANEAN

PEOPLES, ECONOMIES AND CULTURES, 400-1500

EDITORS

HUGH KENNEDY (St. Andrews)
PAUL MAGDALINO (St. Andrews)
DAVID ABULAFIA (Cambridge)
BENJAMIN ARBEL (Tel Aviv)
MARK MEYERSON (Toronto)
LARRY J. SIMON (Western Michigan University)

VOLUME 58

TUTA SUB AEGIDE PALLAS
· 1683 ·

CYPRUS

Society and Culture 1191-1374

EDITED BY

Angel Nicolaou-Konnari and Chris Schabel

BRILL
LEIDEN · BOSTON
2005

Cover illustration: Famagusta, St George of the Greeks. Photo: Gerald L. Carr.

This book is printed on acid-free paper.

Library of Congress Cataloging-in-Publication Data

A C.I.P. record for this book is available from the Library of Congress.

ISSN 0928–5520
ISBN 90 04 14767 5

PRINTED IN THE NETHERLANDS

CONTENTS

PREFACE

When Dr Andreas Pittas of Medochemie approached us to discuss the possibility of a book on the social and cultural history of Cyprus from Richard the Lionheart's conquest in 1191 to the death of Peter I in 1369, we thought about various options until we realized that his general parameters were more or less perfect for a volume. The only work that approaches the subject somewhat comprehensively is the two-volume history of Frankish and Venetian Cyprus published here in Nicosia in 1995–96 as volumes IV and V of the Archbishop Makarios III Foundation's *Ιστορία της Κύπρου*, edited by Theodoros Papadopoullos. Not only is this inaccessible to non-Greek speakers, however, but some of the chapters of this great achievement were composed several years prior to publication, and the explosion of Cypriology over the past ten to fifteen years has made significant changes to the field. The main work in English, volume II of Sir George Hill's *A History of Cyprus* (Cambridge 1948), focused on political history and is in any case out of date. Two recent books in English cover well the two areas where source material is both plentiful and spread out over the period in question, Peter Edbury's *The Kingdom of Cyprus and the Crusades 1191–1374* (Cambridge 1991), dealing with political and military matters, and Nicholas Coureas' *The Latin Church in Cyprus 1195–1312* (Aldershot 1997), treating the internal affairs of the Latin secular and regular clergy (soon to be accompanied by a second volume treating the period down to 1378). Thus what is needed is a new synthesis, in English, of the social and cultural history of the island in this period.

Since the topic of this book is so broad, and the source material is so varied, we decided that it would be impossible to do the job alone. Having fixed upon a structure, we enlisted the collaboration of four internationally recognized experts on various aspects of Frankish Cyprus. Peter Edbury's knowledge of the Frankish nobility of Cyprus is unparalleled, so he was the obvious choice to write on the Franks. Few people are equipped to deal with both Byzantine and Western art on Cyprus, the subject of Annemarie Weyl Carr's chapter. Gilles Grivaud and Nicholas Coureas are among the most prolific authors on Frankish Cyprus, having touched on a variety of themes. Since

Grivaud composed a mammouth 345-page 'chapter' on the intellectual life of Cyprus in 1191–1571 for the Ιστορία της Κύπρου, we asked him to draft an updated and abbreviated version for our period, which we have translated into English. Over the past decade Coureas has penned a great number of studies concerning commercial aspects of Frankish Cyprus, so the task of treating the island's economy fell to him. The remaining subjects—the Greeks and religion—we claimed for ourselves, although we had some pertinent background.

Initially we planned to direct the book at a broad, popular audience, so for example it was to include just a few endnotes. The preliminary results were so encouraging, however, that we reached the conclusion that the volume could also satisfy the needs of the scholarly community at the same time. Accordingly, we gave new instructions to the contributors and contacted Julian Deahl at Brill, who was enthusiastic. The editors of Brill's *The Medieval Mediterranean* series, the ideal place for this book, approved the proposal. Since all six authors are experts on Frankish Cyprus, to ensure the highest standards each author read every other chapter and gave written comments, sometimes extensive, to the other contributors, as did an anonymous reader for Brill.

We wish to thank our collaborators for their own chapters and for their assistance with the other chapters. Working with Julian Deahl and Marcella Mulder at Brill has been a great pleasure. We also express our gratitude to Brill's reader, to the series editors (especially Benjamin Arbel, who gave comments) for accepting the book, and to William O. Duba for providing computer, historical, and linguistic advice in the later stages. Our colleagues in the Department of History and Archaeology of the University of Cyprus have, as always, been very supportive. Above all, the people at Medochemie, led by Dr Andreas Pittas, without whose enthusiasm, generosity, and patience with inevitable delays this book would not exist in any form, deserve our warmest thanks.

A.N.-K. and C.D.S.
University of Cyprus
Nicosia, April 2005

The idea for this book was conceived in early 2002 during a visit to Cyprus of my late friend Johnny Stuart, the Scottish icon specialist, and Olga Popova, the vivacious sexagenarian Russian professor of Byzantine art. Johnny, an Orthodox Christian (in fact one of the very few Orthodox Scotsmen) gifted with an unparalleled charisma for languages, exhibited the enthusiasm of a child, with an eye 'specially' made to spot Byzantine masterpieces on wood or painted 'al fresco'. It was the first visit to the island for Olga, who has always been equally enthusiastic irrespective of personal pain, health problems, restrictive budgets, or adverse climatic conditions, dedicating her entire soul to Byzantine art and at the same time constituting the Byzantine 'snob' *par excellence*: 'Icon painting, dear Andreas, and I mean the real icon painting, stopped in 1453', with the fall of the City. *Basta.*

Conversing in English with Johnny and in German with Olga (the two of them in Russian), we set out on a week of explorations/excursions to the painted and other magnificent churches and monasteries of, mainly, the mountainous parts of Cyprus. The result: enthusiasm, love, and genuine feelings of excitement when we discovered each new thirteenth-century icon—and all this in a landscape truly medieval, Byzantine in places, attractive and slightly chilly, but enormously seductive and provocative. What was the reality then? How was Cyprus? Were these tough times, or 'Dark Ages', as they say? Were the people suppressed and poor? And what languages were spoken around Nicosia or Limassol? Were the Churches really at loggerheads, and if so, why? Most of these questions addressed to me went unanswered. My knowledge was limited to the tantalizing stories of Leontios Makhairas, the man who both spurred my interest in and directed my intellect toward this great time.

As soon as my friends departed, I contacted the Western medievalist at the University of Cyprus, Chris Schabel. Schabel immediately connected me with a visiting professor at the university, Angel Nicolaou-Konnari, the young scholar who has written an exciting thesis about the ethnic mix of the time, a thesis reading like a fairy tale. The three of us sat down together and came up with the plan for this book. My thanks go to Angel and Chris and the team of distinguished scholars they put together who contributed to the book: Annemarie Weyl Carr, Nicholas Coureas, Peter W. Edbury, and Gilles Grivaud. I find it superb that Brill has decided to publish it.

Somehow, Johnny and Olga are a part of it. Ultimately they have been the stimulus to reminisce and think about these bygone times.

Dr Andreas Pittas
Limassol, 24 December 2004

LIST OF CONTRIBUTORS

ANNEMARIE WEYL CARR (Southern Methodist University) specializes in Byzantine and Crusader art. Her work on Cyprus has centered on manuscript, mural, and icon painting and its contexts of use. Aside from her many articles on medieval Cyprus, some of which have now been reprinted in *Cyprus and the Devotional Arts of Byzantium in the Era of the Crusades* (Aldershot 2005), she has published *Byzantine Illumination 1150–1250* (Chicago 1987) and (with L.J. Morrocco) *A Byzantine Masterpiece Recovered, the Thirteenth-Century Murals of Lysi, Cyprus* (Austin 1991).

NICHOLAS COUREAS (Cyprus Research Centre) works on all aspects of the history of Frankish Cyprus, especially ecclesiastical and economic history. Besides his *The Latin Church in Cyprus, 1195–1312* (Aldershot 1997), the sequel to which he is currently writing, he has published many articles on Lusignan Cyprus, co-edited (with J. Riley-Smith) *Cyprus and the Crusades* (Nicosia 1995) and (with C. Schabel) *The Cartulary of the Cathedral of Holy Wisdom of Nicosia* (Nicosia 1997), and translated several volumes of source material, all noted in the bibliography.

PETER W. EDBURY (Cardiff University) is a specialist on the history of the Crusader Kingdoms of Jerusalem and Cyprus, notably with his *The Kingdom of Cyprus and the Crusades 1191–1374* (Cambridge 1991; Greek translation 2003) and his critical edition of *John of Ibelin, The Livre des Assises* (Brill 2003). He has published widely in the history and historiography of the Latin East in general, including (with J.G. Rowe) *William of Tyre, Historian of the Latin East* (Cambridge 1988), *John of Ibelin and the Kingdom of Jerusalem* (Woodbridge 1997), and texts in translation.

GILLES GRIVAUD (University of Rouen, formerly of the French School at Athens) focuses on the Eastern Mediterranean and the Balkans. He has published numerous volumes and articles on all aspects of the history of early Frankish Cyprus, as noted in the bibliography, but also on later periods, such as *Excerpta Cypria Nova: Voyageurs occidentaux à Chypre au XVème siècle* (Nicosia 1990) and *Villages désertés à Chypre (fin XIIe–fin XIXe siècle)* (Nicosia 1998).

ANGEL NICOLAOU-KONNARI (University of Cyprus) studies Hellenism under Latin rule. She is co-editor (with Michalis Pieris) of the diplomatic edition of the *Chronicle of Leontios Makhairas* (Nicosia 2003), editor of the historical treatise of Giorgio de Nores (Nicosia 2006), and she is currently revising for publication her PhD thesis, *The Encounter of Greeks and Franks in Cyprus in the Late Twelfth and Thirteenth Centuries. Phenomena of Acculturation and Ethnic Awareness.*

CHRIS SCHABEL (University of Cyprus) specializes in medieval intellectual history and the ecclesiastical history of the Latin East. Besides the studies noted in the bibliography, he has written *Theology at Paris 1316–1345* (Aldershot 2000).

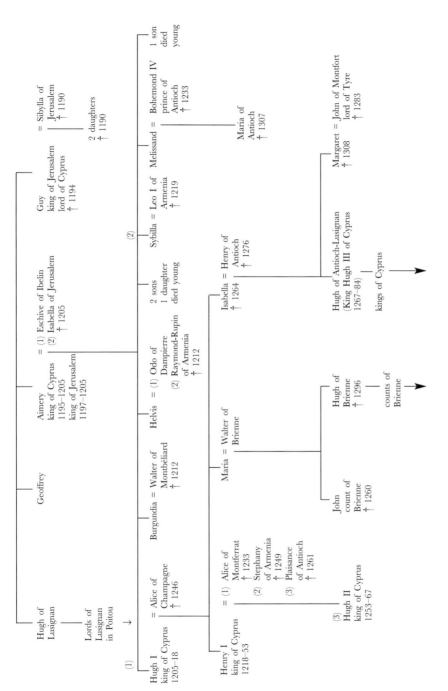

Figure 1. The Lusignan dynasty to 1267

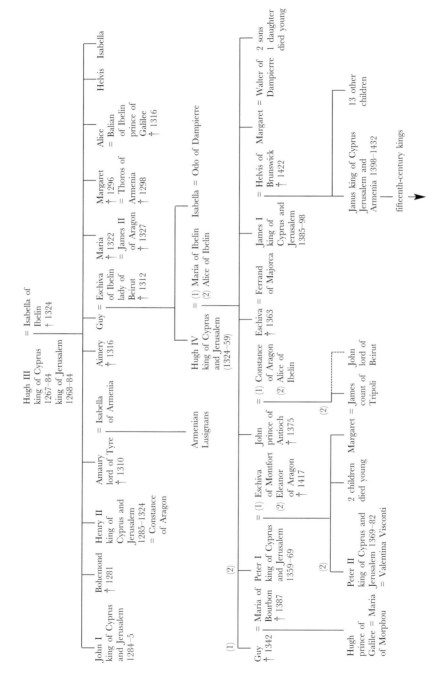

Figure 2. The Lusignan dynasty, 1267–1398

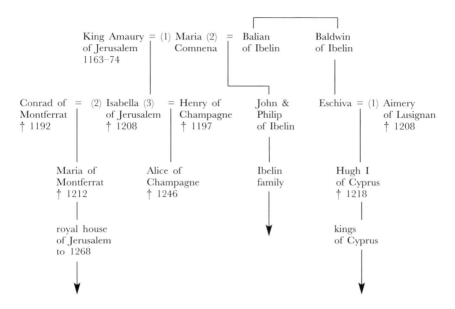

Figure 3.   The Relationship of John and Philip of Ibelin to the royal families of Jerusalem and Cyprus.

Note: After the death of Eschiva of Ibelin, Aimery of Lusignan married Isabella of Jerusalem whose fourth husband he was. Hugh I of Cyprus married Alice of Champagne.

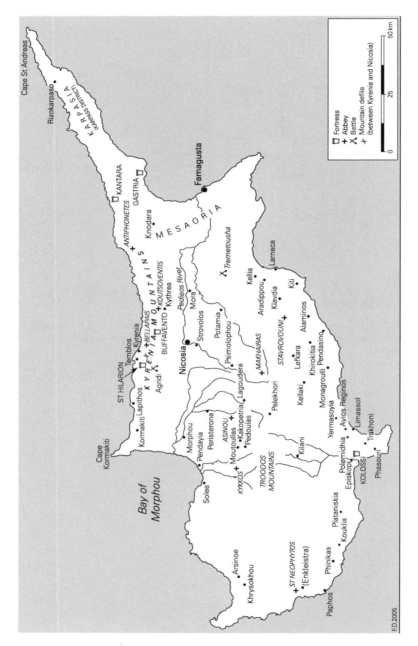

Map 1. Cyprus

INTRODUCTION

This volume is concerned with the cultural and social history of Cyprus from 1191 to 1374 when a French-speaking aristocracy ruled a largely Greek-speaking population. The political and military history of Frankish Cyprus, especially up until 1374, has been well served since the mid-nineteenth century, when Count Louis de Mas Latrie produced three volumes of narrative and sources in 1852–61. By the end of the century he and his son René de Mas Latrie had published editions of the main chronicles in Western languages and much of the documentary evidence, and Constantine Sathas had done the same for the main Greek sources. With the publication of much of the papal registers and other pertinent documents by the mid-twentieth century, Sir George Hill was able to treat the topic rather exhaustively in volumes two and three of his four-volume *A History of Cyprus* published in 1940–52. By 1991 other scholars, most notably Jean Richard, had more or less completed the foundations on which Peter W. Edbury constructed his new narrative, *The Kingdom of Cyprus and the Crusades 1191–1374*, which is unlikely to require a replacement in the foreseeable future.

The outlines of the political history of later-medieval Cyprus are, therefore, well known. In 1191 Isaac Comnenos was ruling Cyprus as self-proclaimed emperor, having usurped authority from Byzantium. On his way to Syria during the Third Crusade, King Richard the Lionheart of England defeated Isaac and conquered the island in May. Richard's forces held the island in the early summer of 1191, and then, after a brief uprising, he sold Cyprus to the Knights Templar, who promptly returned it to him in May of 1192 following a more serious revolt. Richard then sold the island to a Frenchman from Poitou, Guy of Lusignan, who had been king of Jerusalem by marriage. Guy began installing a feudal system on Western models, but in a purer form. After his death, his brother Aimery began negotiations with the Holy Roman Emperor, Henry VI of Hohenstaufen, for the creation of the Kingdom of Cyprus, and with Pope Celestine III for the establishment of a Latin ecclesiastical hierarchy on the island. Bishop Conrad of Hildesheim crowned Aimery in 1197, and 'officially' Cyprus remained a client kingdom of the German Emperor

until 1247, when Pope Innocent IV, in the context of the long struggle between Papacy and Empire, formally dissolved the political ties
between Cyprus and Henry VI's son, Frederick II. Thus in 1247
the actual independence of Cyprus, except for the period of the Civil
War, was made legal.

Cyprus retained this status until 1374, when after a punitive expedition the Genoese annexed Famagusta and the surrounding area.
With that the period of complete independence came to an end.
King James II was able to end the island's *de facto* partition in 1464,
but only with the help of the Mamluks, to whom Cyprus had been
paying tribute since the Egyptian forces invaded the island and captured King Janus in the mid-1420s. Gradually the Venetians came
to control the much-weakened state of Cyprus. This arrangement
was made official in 1489 when Venice relieved Queen Catherine
Cornaro of her nominal control, although the last Lusignan king had
died in 1474. The Venetians continued to rule Cyprus until the
Ottoman conquest of the island in 1570–71.

The period before 1374 represents not only an era of political
independence but also of peace and rising prosperity for Cyprus.
Only two serious internal disturbances interrupted this peace. First,
the dissolution of the bonds with the Holy Roman Empire did not
occur without a struggle. Frederick II himself came to Cyprus in
1228 and tried to make good on his claims during the regency of
Alice of Champagne, setting off the lengthy Civil War lasting until
1233, described in fascinating detail by one of the participants, Philip
of Novara, in *The Wars of Frederick II against the Ibelins in Syria and
Cyprus*. Then in 1306 Amaury of Lusignan usurped authority from
his brother, King Henry II, ruling as governor until his assassination
in 1310 and Henry's return. To these two troublesome events we
may add the Black Death of 1348, which hit Cyprus as hard as it
did most other areas of Europe and the Mediterranean.

Otherwise we can conveniently divide the period from 1191 and
1374 into two phases, before and after 1291 when Acre (the present Akko in Israel) and the other remaining crusader cities in Syria-
Palestine fell to the Muslims. The first phase is marked by close
political ties with the Crusader States and military activity on the
mainland, with Cyprus taking on the supporting role that King
Richard probably envisioned when he captured the island. Cyprus
had an important part in the Fifth Crusade of 1217–21 and, especially,
in the first crusade of King Louis IX of France, which began in

1248, both of which focused on Egypt. Moreover, at various times the kings of Cyprus also claimed the throne of Jerusalem, their claim becoming permanent in the 1260s.

The fall of Acre in 1291 ushered in a new era for Cyprus. The kingdom was now the front line against the Muslims, but resources could be kept at home rather than expended on the mainland. In addition, although refugees from Syria and Palestine had been coming to Cyprus since 1191, they came in waves in the last decades of the Crusader States and in a great flood in 1291. Many of these new settlers were nobles or bourgeois, and after an initial period of crisis, they showed themselves to be a benefit to the island, especially economically. Moreover, when the pope imposed an embargo on trade with the Muslims, Cyprus profited immensely as a middleman in the commerce between the Islamic and Christian worlds. The relocation to Cyprus of the headquarters of the main military orders, the Templars and Hospitallers, did cause tension with the crown and led in part to Amaury's usurpation, but this temporary instability ended around 1310 with Amaury's death, the removal of the Hospitallers to Rhodes, and the trial and suppression of the Templars. Thus despite worries about the Muslim threat and even about designs on Cyprus by other Western powers, such as the Aragonese and Angevin rulers of Sicily and Naples, the period before the relaxation and, in 1344, complete lapse of the papal ban on trade with the Muslims was to be the zenith for medieval Cyprus.

Afterwards Cyprus experienced a gradual decline as an entrepôt in the East-West trade, a decline exacerbated by the Black Death. It was probably in part to reverse this trend that the romantic King Peter I (1359–69) led the last great victorious crusade in 1365, taking and sacking Cyprus' main commercial rival, Alexandria. The dramatic events of the following decade left a profound imprint on the final two centuries of Latin rule. Peter's behaviour became erratic, and in 1369 he was murdered. Perhaps because of the disruption of Genoese (and Venetian) trading interests in the area that resulted from the sack of Alexandria, the Genoese invaded Cyprus a few years later. The immediate cause of the invasion stemmed from the latest in a series of incidents involving Genoa or Genoese citizens. Genoa nearly went to war with Cyprus in 1343–44 and 1364–65. In October 1372 violence broke out between Venetians and Genoese after the coronation of Peter II (1369–82) as king of Jerusalem in Famagusta. During the chaos, in which Cypriots took the Venetians' side, Genoese property was destroyed and lives were lost, but since Peter blamed the Genoese for the incident, they received no redress. From there things escalated rapidly: the Genoese invaded, the war dragged on to the detriment of Cyprus, and the negotiated settlement was harsh for the Cypriots, who agreed to pay a huge indemnity in install-ments, offer many important hostages to Genoa, and cede Famagusta to Genoa as further security for payment. Cyprus was *de facto* par-titioned in 1374, exactly 600 years before the most recent invasion and partition.

The war with Genoa did not destroy the island, but it had a profound effect on all aspects of Cypriot society. Thus not only did 1374 pro-vide the terminus for Edbury's book, but it marks a natural break for the present volume as well. But whereas it was possible for one person to master the political and military history of Cyprus in 1191–1374, the nature of the topic, source material, and secondary biblio-graphy makes it unlikely that a single scholar could provide a solid synthesis for the history of Cypriot society and culture in these years.

Although narrative political history is returning to popularity, social history broadly construed has a much more important place in schol-arship than it did a half century ago. Indeed for a while it seemed as if social history would practically eclipse all other forms. At the same time, with globalization and the increasing diversification of Europe and North America, the academic focus on multicultural societies has increased dramatically. In the context of medieval history, this often means an emphasis on areas on the borders between cul-tures. In a certain sense, at a time when language changed over short distances, long-distance travel was limited to a small section of the population, and mass media were confined to religious and political decrees, all areas were borders between cultures. In Western Europe, moreover, wherever Jews dwelt society was *ipso facto* multicultural. Nevertheless, it is the places where radical differences existed that attract our attention most of all. In the specific period with which this book deals, this means above all Spain, Ireland, Eastern Europe, Sicily and Southern Italy, the Crusader States, Latin Greece, and Cyprus.

What groups lived in early Frankish Cyprus? What was their func-tion in society? How did they identify and express themselves? How did they view others? How did these groups interact? These are some of the questions this volume attempts to answer. Approaching all of these issues requires training and experience that no one author is likely to have. Beyond the basic undergraduate and postgraduate education of a medievalist, this synthesis demands close familiarity with topics as disparate as feudal law and the *Filioque*, icon production and import duties, public notaries and passion plays. The result is that a synthesis of this sort has to be a collaboration. Until now the only such work that approaches the present book constitutes volumes IV and V of the *History of Cyprus* edited by Theodoros Papadopoullos. This work, however, is only available in Modern Greek, treats the entire period from 1191 to 1571, deals with political history as well, and is already a decade old.

A further obstacle to such a synthesis is the nature of the source material. Whereas the narrative of the political history of Cyprus in these years can be pieced together with the major chronicles, using the more fragmentary documentary sources to supplement, explain, verify, or nuance the story, with social history it is the fragmentary sources that often lead the way. Of course, we do not speak only of written sources, but of archaeological finds, works of art, pieces of parchment, etc. Just gathering these sources together is a huge task. Moreover, much of the written material is still in manuscript form, and it goes without saying that the scholar has to deal with Byzantine Greek, Latin, French, Italian, and other languages without benefit of translation. To the disparate nature of the source material we add the equally disparate—and more massive—secondary bibliography as a hindrance to a synthetic work on the society of Cyprus in these years. While Edbury's secondary bibliography contains some 300 entries, no small number, even our restricted bibliography for social history contains twice as many lemmata.

It is at this point that we must acknowledge our debt to the pioneering studies of scholars dealing with particular aspects of the social and cultural history of early Frankish Cyprus. The work of Camille Enlart in art and John Hackett in religion around 1900 are splendid examples of what could be achieved in cultural history with the sources then available. Since then, however, much more has come to light. Jean Richard, whom we have already mentioned, figures in every chapter in this volume; besides his many studies, he has provided a great deal of new source material from the Vatican over the past half century. In the last couple of decades Michel Balard has led a group of scholars—Balletto, Lombardo, Otten-Froux, Pavoni, Polonio—publishing many volumes of notarial sources from the Genoese and Venetian archives, while the prosopographical information that

Count Wilpert H. Rudt de Collenberg provided in his many arti-
cles has proven valuable. The patchwork of Greek sources has become
clearer through the efforts of Spyridon Lampros, R.M. Dawkins,
Constantine Chatzipsaltes, I.P. Tsiknopoullos, Jean Darrouzès, Peter
Schreiner, Costas Constantinides, and others. Rupert Gunnis, George
Jeffery, A.H.S. Megaw, Doula Mouriki, David Metcalf, Demetra
Papanikola-Bakirtzis, Athanasios Papageorghiou, and Andreas and
Judith Stylianou, not to mention the current staff of the Department
of Antiquities of Cyprus, are among those who have been instrumental in making the physical remains of the Frankish period—cas-
tles, churches, icons, paintings, coins, seals, pottery—more accessible
and understandable. One must not forget the many contributions of
Theodoros Papadopoullos, Costas P. Kyrris, Benediktos Englezakis,
Benjamin Arbel, David Jacoby, and Anthony Luttrell, besides the
legion of younger scholars too numerous to mention. Finally, the
journals and publications of the Cyprus Research Centre, the Society
for Cypriot Studies, the Archbishop Makarios III Foundation, the
Cypriot Society for Historical Studies, and the monasteries of Kykkos
and Neophytos have greatly enriched the field. It is to these scholars and institutions that we owe this volume, for if the general political narrative can be constructed with sources largely available before
1950, the social history of early Frankish Cyprus depends mostly on
what has been published since then.

This book is divided into six chapters with one-word titles, on Greeks,
Franks, Economy, Religion, Literature, and Art. The decision to
begin with the Greeks was a democratic and therefore modern one:
they represent the vast majority of the population in this period. On
medieval criteria the Franks might have come first, since they included
the aristocracy that held power. The other groups were less numerous than the Greeks and less powerful than the Franks, and for information on Syrians, Armenians, and other minorities, the reader is
directed to the chapters on the economy and religion, and to a lesser
extent on the Greeks and art. Naturally the four thematic chapters
on economy, religion, literature, and art focus on the contributions
of the Greeks and Franks.
    The opening chapter on the Greeks explores the nature and extent
of the social and demographic changes that the takeover of the
Lusignan regime meant for the majority of the population and their
identities. Although their rule was established by conquest, the social

system that the Lusignans introduced was not one of colonial exploitation from the outside, nor did it cause a sharp discontinuity with the past. Based on the medieval belief in social inequality, which assured the optimum economic and social advantages for the Frankish ruling class, the system nevertheless created conditions of peaceful cohabitation that avoided ethnic conflicts and allowed social mobility for the Greeks. Thence, a long-lasting pattern of social discourse between the two groups began in the thirteenth century. The enforcement of a strictly stratified system based on a legal system that defined ethnic and social differentiation in terms of religion offset the demographic superiority of the Greeks and fixed the social and ethnic boundaries, yet the Greek urban population was able to penetrate this social frontier through their economic and professional development. While the situation for unfree Greek peasants largely remained as it was under the Byzantines, in the thirteenth and fourteenth centuries members of free Greek families could follow careers as ecclesiastical dignitaries, notaries, and scribes and/or as officials in royal and seigneurial administration. They gradually acquired the necessary social and economic importance for the formation of a new kind of Greek aristocracy, allowing some of them to climb the ranks of the Frankish nobility in the fifteenth century. They thus assumed the role of an intermediary group between the Frankish aristocracy and burgesses, on the one hand, and the Greek lower classes, on the other, which facilitated cultural exchanges. Following the initial destruction of the Greek nobles—the *archontes*—the lower strata cooperated with the Frankish rulers as a means of survival. This, together with the fair administration of the Lusignans, helps explain both the absence of uprisings against the regime throughout the Frankish period and the formation of the identity of the *Kypriotis*.

The second chapter traces the origins and activities of the Frankish ruling class. Throughout the period of Lusignan rule in Cyprus (1191–1489) the Frankish settlers and their descendants never comprised more than a small minority of the population. These settlers were people of Western European extraction, distinguishable from the rest of the inhabitants as Latin-rite Christians, accepting the spiritual jurisdiction of the pope. The Lusignan kings of Cyprus, who established themselves after the conquest of the island during the Third Crusade, came originally from western France, but the knights, clerics, and townsmen who made up the Frankish community were of diverse backgrounds. Like any ruling elite they exploited the subject population for their own advantage, but as it was in their interest to ensure peace and stability, the population as a whole was able to benefit from the long periods of prosperity their rule entailed. The Lusignan regime exhibited many of the trappings of Western European kingship, but behind this façade much of the routine of government and much of the law as it affected the non-Frankish population harked back to Byzantine times. The monarchy proved durable with no damaging succession crises until the second half of the fifteenth century. Eventually the legitimate branch of the dynasty faded out, and it was this failure of heirs that ushered in the period of Venetian rule (1489–1571). The nobility, at least until the end of the fourteenth century, was reasonably homogeneous, dominated by a comparatively small number of knightly families. The nobles provided the kings with advisers and military commanders, but, as no nobleman possessed a fortress of any consequence, they were rarely able to challenge royal authority. Some nobles were extremely wealthy, famous for their enthusiasm for hunting.

Although Cyprus' role in the international carrying trade has received the most attention from historians, the chapter on the economy shows that under the Lusignans it retained its agricultural base, while becoming more export oriented and diversified—in both agriculture and manufacturing. Salt, sugar, and cotton in particular constituted important additions to the traditional production of wheat, barley, wine, and oil. Nevertheless, from the late thirteenth century to the mid-fourteenth century Cyprus was important in commerce between the Near East and Western Europe. The Mamluk conquest of Latin possessions in the coastal areas of Syria and Palestine between 1265 and 1291 and the consequent migration to Cyprus of Latins and Syrians were preconditions for Cyprus' participation in this trade. The pope responded to these losses in 1292 with an embargo on visits by Latin merchants to Muslim lands, and as a result merchants from Western Europe frequented Cyprus to obtain spices and other luxuries, as well as to sell textiles, timber, and iron. The immigrants contributed to urban life, not only in Famagusta, the main beneficiary of the above developments, but also in Nicosia and Limassol. The former became a centre for moneylending, while Limassol played a significant role in the export of Cypriot agricultural products. With royal encouragement Famagusta developed institutionally as well as commercially, becoming to some extent a replica of the lost Latin Kingdom of Jerusalem on Cypriot soil and welcoming merchants from smaller trading nations, such as Ragusans and Anconitans, along with the Venetians, Genoese, Pisans, Florentines, Provençals and Catalans. Long-distance trade between Cyprus and Western Europe coexisted with short to medium-distance trade, often run by Greeks, with Cilician Armenia, Hospitaller Rhodes, Venetian Crete and Euboea, and the Genoese colonies of Chios and Pera. Notwithstanding the decline of Cyprus' importance in the international carrying trade following the relaxation of the papal embargo in 1344, Cyprus continued to play an active part in international trade on account of the demand for its agricultural products, especially sugar, and for its salt and camlets.

Most historians have viewed the history of religion in Cyprus between 1191 and 1374 as a clash, or even war, between Latins and Greeks. The chapter on religion argues that the spiritual history of the island in these years was more colourful, more multicultural, and more complex, especially in cosmopolitan Nicosia and the emporium of Famagusta. Rather the period is characterized *both* by the jurisdictional dominance of the Latin clergy over the other, subordinate, Christian groups, and by peaceful coexistence, considerable toleration, and a degree of autonomy for non-Latin Christians and non-Christians. Despite some seizures of property and the installation of a Latin Church hierarchy in 1196, for the first three decades of Frankish rule Greeks and other rites were mostly left alone. In 1220 the Latin Church and Frankish aristocracy began to take steps to control and subordinate the clergy of the other groups, but for the most part the Westerners simply applied in Cyprus the same policy that was followed in the West and elsewhere in the Latin East. Indeed the non-Latin clergy enjoyed a more favourable position in Cyprus than elsewhere under Latin rule, while the non-Latin laity was not directly affected by the subordination of their clerics. This was, however, small consolation for the Greek and Syrian clergy, and the next four decades are characterized by the resistance, exile, protest, and even martyrdom of Greek priests and monks. Still, many of the Greek and Syrian clergy were willing to cooperate with the Latins and accepted the new *status quo*, and by 1260 this group had requested and received a permanent constitution, the *Bulla Cypria*, which was to regulate ecclesiastical affairs for the remainder of the Frankish period. Some Greeks and Syrians continued to resist the Latins and struggled with their co-religious who accepted the *Bulla Cypria*, but by 1300 they resolved to live with the new situation. In the fourteenth century the various Christian rites found that they had much in common, for example worshipping at the same shrines, participating in the same processions, and even intermarrying. Of course, there were internal tensions in the Latin regular and secular clergy, between Church and State, and among the Greek clerics, but monks and priests generally enjoyed a period of flourishing.

The history of the written culture of the Kingdom of Cyprus, the focus of chapter five, has received much less attention from specialists than the political and institutional history of the island; indeed the first works devoted to this subject only began to appear in the 1980s. Thus it constitutes a relatively new field of research, still lacking some of the tools that are indispensable for a systematic study of the material (catalogues of French or Latin manuscripts, for example), and requiring an examination of religious writings for a more complete understanding. Moreover, because of the emphasis placed on studies of political history, the secular written culture is often viewed from one-sided perspectives (Franks/Greeks), which deprive literature of its internal dynamism and minimize the spectrum of exchanges between the different systems of thought. In fact, the research has thus far shown that the Lusignan kingdom was very receptive to intellectual and spiritual trends that began both in the Latin West and in Byzantium—and even in the Arabic East, whether Muslim or Christian. In the intellectual realm the resulting situation is quite close to what art historians have observed.

The final chapter, on visual art, endeavors to weave together the histories of both the Latin and the Orthodox artistic production of the thirteenth and fourteenth centuries, and to find a coherent narrative in the two stories. Few fields can have seen so dramatic an expansion in the number of newly published monuments as medieval Cyprus has in the past decade. This rich volume of material needs to be integrated not so much into a history of Byzantine art on Cyprus, or of Crusader art, or even of an encounter of Orthodox and Crusader traditions, but rather of artistic production and consumption on Cyprus as a coherent social whole, with its distinctive geographic, social, residential, and intellectual patterns. The chapter inventories the artifacts that have been gathered, reviews current scholarly approaches to them, and proposes a broad historical shape in which to place them. This shape retains the traditional two phases, a thirteenth- and a fourteenth-century one. It distinguishes these phases less by a changing relation of Greek to Latin on the island, which is intermingled throughout, than by a shift in the artistic traditions upon which both draw. The thirteenth century is dominated by norms formulated on the Syro-Palestinian mainland. Already in the early decades of the century, beneath the lingering afterglow of Comnenian hegemony in the monumental cycles of 1190–1220, Cypriot icon painting reflects Syro-Palestinian conventions, and it is the Syro-Palestinian mainland in all its cultural complexity that dominates the work of Cypriot and immigrant Latin patrons alike in most media when artistic production escalates once again on Cyprus in the late thirteenth century. The fourteenth century, by contrast, is dominated by the impact of the high styles of Byzantium and the Gothic West. Though regional Cypriot traditions emerge in fourteenth-century painting, prominent Cypriot patrons—both Greek and Latin—turn to the high styles of the contemporary international courts. Both alike define their status by the courtliness of their art, not by its religious origin, thus opening the way to dramatic combinations of Gothic and Palaeologan. Facilitated by this meeting of articulate traditions, Cyprus reenters the international discourse of dominant styles, its regionalism giving way to what is recognized as Byzantine in painting, its architecture shaped by Gothic ashlar structures. Durable traditions then grow from the internalization of these international conventions, some initially Latin like the architectural sculpture of Cyprus, some inherently Greek—it is at this point that the icon of Kykkos assumes its distinctive form—and others, like the *vita* icon or the funerary icon, inherently hybrid.

Taken as a whole, these chapters show that the sharp dividing lines between ethnic and social groups that existed in 1192 became blurred over time, whether we look at art, literature, religion, economics, or ethnicity itself. Rather than clear categories and convenient boxes in which we can place people of different nationalities, what we have is a more confused spectrum, with individual people and works of art and literature sometimes fitting into a specific niche—say a Greek Orthodox peasant in the Troodos Mountains—and sometimes crossing supposedly impermeable boundaries—for example the splendid Gothic and Byzantine cathedral of St George of the Greeks in Famagusta. It is in the stunning richness of its blended multiplicity that Cypriot society in 1191–1374 captivates our attention.

GREEKS

Angel Nicolaou-Konnari

The establishment of a conquest state in the Middle Ages usually meant more for the local military and landowning aristocracy, which was often replaced by a new victorious nobility, than for the bulk of the populace, whose lives were less affected. Accordingly, the political and military control of Cyprus during the brief English and Templar governments did not cause a significant social disruption, aside from confiscations affecting the wealthy Greeks, all the more so because it operated from the outside and did not involve demographic changes. However, with the establishment of the Lusignan regime, the introduction of a new ruling class of Frankish knights that replaced the Greek *archontes*, and the settlement of Latin families on the island from 1192 onwards, a complex new social system was implanted that regulated relations between the native Greek population and the Frankish settlers. Although this system did not cause an immediate rupture with the pre-existing Byzantine social and institutional structures, especially in the rural areas, social stratification was now primarily based on inclusion or not in the ruling ethnic and religious group. Two other factors determined the nature of the new social system: first, the high pre-conquest population density and overall ethnic homogeneity, as well as the uniformity, antiquity, and complexity of the culture of the indigenous population; second, the fact that the introduced social system was not one of colonial exploitation from the outside by a parent state governing from a distant metropolis, but one of administration from within, based on the permanent settlement of the incoming group and their cooperation with the native population. Naturally, this system aimed at the optimum economic and social advantages for the Frankish ruling class, but it simultaneously entailed conditions of peaceful coexistence and therefore the well-being of their Greek subjects. Despite its apparent rigidity, which initially maintained the impermeability of the social and cultural frontiers, this social context preserved for the Greeks a certain continuity with their past and allowed them to rise in the economic and social ranks. Consequently, within the Greek community, group solidarity

was often outweighed by class considerations and social mobility
determined the processes of cultural interaction and redefinition of
identity for the two ethnic groups.

Population Estimates and Ethnic Composition

Evidence suggests that, despite natural disasters, by the end of the
twelfth century the population of Cyprus was sufficiently large and
wealthy to fulfill heavy fiscal obligations and to sustain an agricultural
production important enough to supply other countries as well. The
island seems to have witnessed a stable demographic trend, but, at
the time of the Lusignan establishment, the population of the island
is not thought to have exceeded 100,000.[1] The close insular space
of Cyprus allowed conditions of geographical isolation that facilitated
the creation of a culturally homogeneous population. At the time of
the Frankish settlement, the overwhelming majority of the population
were Greeks, who perceived themselves and were perceived by the
Latins as members of the Byzantine *oecumene*. This meant active participation in the Byzantine ideology of the time, which involved those
aspects of culture that defined the cultural identity of the *Romaioi*,
namely loyalty to the emperor, the Greek rite, and the Greek language (spoken on the island with some local particularities).
    Within the geographical and cultural space of Cyprus, foreign eth-
nic elements were usually assimilated or tolerated. Although before
1192 the percentage of the non-Greek ethnic element was most probably not very high, the society of Cyprus in 1192 when the Lusignans
arrived on the island and, especially, the society that was formed
after the crusader settlement were made of multinational fabric. The
presence of non-Greek groups in the pre-1192 period contributed to
the creation of a mentality of cultural tolerance on the island, and in
the Lusignan period, when their numerical presence was more prominent, their role as an intermediary between Greeks and Franks was
instrumental. At the end of the twelfth century, the Armenians were
probably the largest minority group, followed by the Maronites and
the Christian Syrians of various rites, the Jews, and some Latin mer-

---

[1] Edbury (1991: 14–15); Cheynet (1994: 68).

chants.[2] The first important change in the ethnic composition and
the size of the population of the island occurred soon after the takeover by Guy of Lusignan and the influx of settlers of Latin, Christian
Syrian, Maronite, and Armenian origin of various free social strata.
The first wave of immigrants must be placed in the period immediately
following 1192 and the last and most important one after the fall
of Acre in 1291. In between the population movement continued
and incoming refugees must have been particularly numerous in the
second half of the thirteenth century, following each loss of a Christian-
held city in Syria and Palestine to the Muslims. The Lusignans
required a ruling class of knights, but they may also have been concerned about the demographic superiority of the Greeks in general.

Despite these demographic changes, the Greeks always remained
by far the largest ethnic group. The contemporary Greek Cypriot
Neophytos the Recluse speaks of the depopulation of Cyprus of its
indigenous ethnic element and of the multiplication of the Latins,
claiming that almost all of the large villages and rural centres and
houses were left deserted and uninhabited. This can hardly be interpreted in terms of a massive exodus of the Cypriots, however, for
St Neophytos most probably refers to the emigration of Greek noble
families in the years preceding and following the 1192 Lusignan
takeover.[3] Although it is difficult to assess the size of the Frankish
population, it must never have surpassed one fourth of the total population. With the coming of the Lusignans, the Maronites and Syrians
(Orthodox, Jacobite, or Nestorian) became the largest ethnic groups
after the Greeks and the Latins. The population of the Armenian
community must have increased as well. There were small Jewish
communities in the main towns (Nicosia, Famagusta, Paphos) and
some other areas, but they probably declined after their economic
destruction caused by the Genoese invasion of 1373. Stephen of
Lusignan alleges that the Jews abandoned Nicosia after a pogrom
during Easter festivities, probably in the second half of the fifteenth
century; at any rate, by the end of the fifteenth century all Jews had

---

[2] Mas Latrie (1861: 99–115); Sacopoulo (1975: 79–85); Galatariotou (1991: 55–7,
60–7); Dédéyan (1994); Nicolaou-Konnari (1999: 51–80, 158–64); Papacostas (1999b:
passim); Grivaud (2000: passim). On the other groups, see also Schabel in this
volume.
[3] Neophytos the Recluse, *De calamitatibus Cypri*, 11–12, *Enkomion for the Holy Cross*,
178–9, and *Homily Concerning the Holy Fathers at the Council of Nicaea*, 272.

gradually migrated to Famagusta. The presence of Muslim and black slaves as well as slaves from the South Russia steppes and the Black Sea area is also attested in the sources. The number of Italian and Provençal merchants was limited in the thirteenth century, but, following the Latin setbacks in Syria in the 1270s–1280s and the fall of Acre in 1291, the Italian, Provençal, and Aragonese trading cities relocated their business to Cyprus and the number of their nationals on the island increased considerably.[4] Until the middle of the fourteenth century, the island witnessed an upward demographic trend. In 1347–48, though, the Black Death struck Cyprus extremely hard and, as in the rest of the Mediterranean world, it is likely that the population was reduced by between one third and one fifth. Thereafter, epidemics continued to break out, notably in 1362 and 1363; recurrent outbursts of the plague, especially in 1438 and 1470, prevented a recovery of the population in the fifteenth century. The Genoese invasion in 1373 and the Mamluk invasions in the first quarter of the fifteenth century must also have contributed to the decline of the population.[5]

The evidence indicates that rural areas were predominantly populated by Greek *paroikoi* (serfs) and *francomati* (free tenants), with a certain concentration of Maronites, Syrians, and Armenians in the coastal plains and the foothills of Pentadaktylos.[6] According to the 1260 *Bulla Cypria*, issued by Pope Alexander IV, the rural locations of Solea, Arsinoe, Karpasia, and Lefkara were designated as the episcopal sees of the four remaining Greek bishops, and artistic evidence points to a prosperous Greek rural population that provided patrons and supported the Church. Even though some of these places had already been Greek episcopal sees, it does not seem that they were of any particular significance, and the Greek bishops spent a large part of their time in the respective towns as well, where they also had a cathedral church.[7] No non-royal castles survive, with the possible

---

[4] Étienne de Lusignan, *Description*, fol. 76r; Richard (1979); Arbel (1979: 23–5; 1993: 153–4 and app., table I); Jacoby (1984a); Nicolaou-Konnari (1999: 164–78); Grivaud (2000); and Coureas in this volume.

[5] Edbury (1991: 15, 153; 1995a: 115–34, 145–58); Irwin (1995).

[6] *Le Cartulaire du chapitre du Saint-Sépulcre de Jérusalem*, nos. 174, 178; 'Document relatif au service militaire', 430.

[7] *Cartulary*, no. 78 (pp. 198, 201); *Synodicum Nicosiense*, nos. X.25.11 and X.25.30; pp. 46–9 below; Gounarides (1986: 326) and Kyrris (1993: 177–8). See also Carr in this volume on rural art.

exception of the slightly fortified manor of Pyla, and most Frankish knights lived in Nicosia ('La cité où demourerent les chevaliers'), employing mostly Greek and Syrian *baillis* instead of Latin ones to run their estates (*casalia*).[8] Evidence from the fourteenth century, though, indicates that some may have lived in the other towns and that some definitely resided at times on their rural estates.[9] Not more than ten Latin parishes may be found in the rural areas in the thirteenth century,[10] while Latin bishops seem to have preferred to reside in Nicosia and not in their sees.[11]

In the urban centres, where the presence of the Franks and the other communities was more prominent, the population composition was less homogeneous than in the rural areas and it soon acquired a multi-ethnic character. In Nicosia, the capital and administrative centre, the Frankish component was certainly important, while in the ports there was a concentration of Italians. It is not known whether the various ethnic groups had separate quarters in the towns. Evidence from church location, especially from the important number of scattered Latin and Greek churches built in Nicosia and Famagusta in the fourteenth century, suggests that the two ethnic groups were not excluded from each other's religious space and that no real segregation existed.[12] There must have been, though, an ordinary population concentration based on social and ethnic affiliation. The Frankish nobility were apparently grouped on fashionable streets reserved for the aristocracy; in documents dated 1264 and 1292, expensive houses of knights and bishops are mentioned as situated in *vie publice* (probably the main streets) and the area around them in Nicosia. The Italian merchants definitely resided in specific quarters in the towns, but these were not walled quarters in which they exercised their own jurisdiction to the exclusion of the royal officers, like in Acre, but districts where they tended to congregate.[13]

---

[8] The Templar of Tyre, *Cronaca*, §278 (514); Mas Latrie, *Histoire*, III, 642; Ludolph of Sudheim, 215. Generally, Richard (1977a: 335; 1979: 161–2) and Edbury (1995c: 356). See also Edbury in this volume for the Franks.

[9] 'Amadi', 265, 325 and 238, 263, 272–3; Mas Latrie, *Histoire*, II, 186.

[10] Collenberg (1979); Richard (1979: 162); Fedalto (1995: 679–80).

[11] *Cartulary*, no. 51; *Documents chypriotes des archives du Vatican*, 33–4, 73; Richard (1950: 104).

[12] Enlart (1899, I: 68–77, 250–67); Edbury (1995b: 342–4, 353).

[13] *Cartulary*, nos. 51–2; Papadopoulou (1983: §8).

Resistance or Submission: the Greek Reaction to Frankish Rule

The Lusignan takeover must be associated with Richard the Lionheart's conquest of Cyprus and must be viewed in terms of the abolition of the island's Byzantine political frontier and its inclusion in a new geopolitical reality, a fact acknowledged by Byzantine historiographers who considered that the 'island was henceforth incorporated in the Palestinian territory'.[14] One version of the thirteenth-century chronicle from the Latin East known as the *Continuation of William of Tyre* alleges that Guy of Lusignan asked Saladin for his advice on the best way to control the island. The story, repeated by the Greek chronicler Leontios Makhairas two centuries later, reflects the concern of the Lusignans in view of the 1191 and 1192 revolts against Richard's garrison and the Templars respectively. It suggests that they believed that they needed a sizeable number of Latin settlers to offset the demographic superiority of the Greeks.[15] However, the thoroughness and swiftness of Richard's conquest and the brutality of the Templar government as well as the failure of the previous uprisings may have destroyed any will for resistance on the part of the population. Moreover, the partial disappearance through emigration and the socio-economic reduction of the remaining Greek landowning aristocracy rendered them unable or unwilling to lead any resistance against the new rulers. Without the leadership of an aristocracy with the incentive and the means to organize a rebellion, the lower classes, for whom the introduction of the new regime probably represented few changes in everyday life, would not risk any form of resistance.

    The combination of the above factors with the impressive presence of a Frankish aristocratic military class contributed to the calm takeover by the Lusignans, the successful implementation of new institutions, and the submission and cooperation of the Greeks. Consequently, the Lusignan settlement was peaceful and uneventful, since there were no frontiers to defend and no insurgent population to control, while the passive attitude of the Greeks must be viewed as a historically natural reaction, a *kat'oikonomian* compromise dictated by the events. Moreover, it must be stressed that the first Frankish settlers, a group composed of a close nucleus of old *Polain*

---

[14] Choniates, I, 418; Skoutariotes, 398; Ephraem Aenius, 215.6020.
[15] *Continuation de Guillaume de Tyr*, 138–9; Makhairas, I, §§22–5. See generally on the revolts Nicolaou-Konnari (2000a: 61–7, 98–101).

families (second and third generation Westerners in the Levant) and some newcomers, were already acclimatized to the realities of the East. They emigrated to Cyprus with the intention of permanent settlement and, whatever colonial aspects this settlement had at the beginning, these were gradually lost as Cyprus remained the only safe Christian territory in the East. These were conditions that also favoured peaceful cohabitation and social and cultural interaction between the two ethnic groups. A comparison with Crete may enhance our understanding as to why there were no revolts in Frankish Cyprus. Seven important revolts are attested on Crete in the thirteenth century alone and three in the fourteenth, and revolts with a social or national character, some of which involved Constantinople or Cretan Venetians, continued to break out until the end of the sixteenth century. All the above factors favouring peace on Cyprus did not exist on Crete. On the contrary, the island of Crete witnessed a delayed, long, and difficult implementation of Venetian rule, the existence of a powerful class of Greek *archontes* who had a vested interest in retaining the privileges they had gained under the Byzantines and had formed a class consciousness legitimised by a legendary genealogy, the abolition of Greek Church hierarchy, and a firm colonial control by the metropolis and its imported bureaucracy.[16]

It is thus not surprising that the 1191–92 revolts were the only uprisings of the Greek population against the Latins; throughout the Lusignan rule no insurrections with a clearly ethnic character are attested in the sources. Neophytos the Recluse's mention of 'searches' and 'imprisonment' of the nobles in relation to post-1192 'disorders and disturbances', 'upheavals', and 'lamentation and moaning' could be a veiled reference to some movement on the part of the remaining nobles, unless he refers to the 1191–92 revolts or, generally, to the unhappy situation of the Greek nobles.[17] Some scholars have interpreted the subversive activities of the Greek pirate 'Canaqui' during Aimery of Lusignan's reign as the isolated reaction of a desperate *archontas*, but the events concerning his person should not be given more importance than they deserve and they should certainly not be considered to represent a popular movement with national or social character; his abducting of the royal family was very likely dictated

---

[16] See Maltezou (1990: 22–52 and passim).
[17] Neophytos the Recluse, *De calamitatibus Cypri*, 11, and *Sixth Sunday Homily*, 329.

by his intention to draw the maximum profit he could from royal
hostages. The sources describe him as a 'malefactor' who was 'most
hated by the Christians' and on whose head the king had set a price;
he enjoyed no popular support and his activities against the people
of Cyprus are described as 'privateering around the island of Cyprus'.[18]

Similarly, the revolt of the peasants in 1426–27, which Greek
scholars have often viewed as a nationalistic movement of liberation,
does not seem to amount to more than unsystematic riots and pillaging by some Greek peasants and some Spanish mercenaries in
the king's army, who took advantage of the absence of firm political control that followed the Egyptian invasion of 1426 and King
Janus' captivity. Leontios Makhairas condemns the events and describes
them in their social dimension, contrary to the way he portrays the
revolt against the Templars. Also, an anonymous witness, a Greek
jurat (κριτής) of the Court of the Viscount, records the episodes in
terms of rioting and pillaging by 'many thieves and privateers [. . .]
Kypriotes and every sort of people' ('πολούς κλέπτες και κουρσάρους
[. . .] Κηπρήτας και [. . .] πασαλόγην ανθρώπους').[19] Two other minor
peasant uprisings are mentioned in the sources, but again they seem
to have been isolated events, aimed at economic advantage during
periods of political crisis. The first one took place during the Genoese
invasion of the island in 1373 and consisted of the refusal of the
peasants of Pendayia, Morphou, and the area of Solea to pay their
taxes and perform their duties; the affair was settled very quickly
after the intervention of the constable James of Lusignan. The second
rising took place some time in the summer of 1472 with the intention
of killing King James II and making Charlotte queen, and it is only
casually mentioned by James' constable, Peter Davila, in a letter of
suppliance to the Venetian authorities. The episode is not mentioned
in other sources and its importance was probably blown out of proportion by Davila, who wanted to take credit for saving the kingdom from danger.[20]

---

[18] *Continuation de Guillaume de Tyr*, 162–5. Generally, Kyrris (1985: 19, 213),
Galatariotou (1991: 220), and Papadopoullos (1995c: 553–4).
[19] Makhairas, I, §§696–7, 700; Darrouzès (1958: 242–4). See generally Kyrris
(1989–1993: 234–8, 255–6, 261–7).
[20] Makhairas, I, §445; Mas Latrie, 'Nouvelles preuves (1871)', 352; Hill (1940–1952,
III: 647). On revolts in Lusignan Cyprus in general, see Nicolaou-Konnari (2000a:
69–71).

Social Structure

The ethnic and cultural homogeneity of the Greeks facilitated the application of a clearly stratified social system. The Franks were able to balance the demographic difference, maintain the social and cultural boundaries, and achieve peaceful conditions through good administration and cooperation with the native population. From the very beginning, social discrimination was defined and described in terms of religion, a trait of both the Byzantine and the Crusader identity. In the first half of the fifteenth century, Leontios Makhairas stressed both the religious compatibility of the two ethnic groups and the importance of religion for the maintenance of their respective social and ethnic boundaries: Guy had to bring people of his rite to help him control the island and establish a Latin Church, but at the same time one of the main attractions for the new settlers was the saintly character of Cyprus and its rich relics as well as its proximity to Jerusalem.[21]

The Legal Framework: Pluralism or Uniformity

With the coming of the Franks in Cyprus a new legal system was introduced, which, however, did not exclude the survival of 'jural enclaves, islands of ethnic-legal particularism' for the Greeks and other minority groups.[22] The Western tradition of law as a personal attribute and as part of a person's national heritage benefited non-Latin ethnic groups and enabled them to maintain a certain continuity in the field of private law. Moreover, language as the expression of the personality of the law was respected, and this led to the almost exclusive use of the vernaculars (Old French and the Greek Cypriot dialect) as languages of secular law in the Lusignan Kingdom of Cyprus. The Lusignan regime most probably introduced the law of Latin Syria from the beginning of the Frankish settlement on the island in the late twelfth century. This legal system was described in the *Assizes*, an unofficial set of treatises in Old French—designed to explain what the law was or to advise people how to plead—that were based on the procedure and the decisions of the High Court

---

[21] Makhairas, I, §§25–40.
[22] Bartlett (1993: 206–7, 217–20, quotation on p. 219).

and the Court of Burgesses. Most of the books that comprise the
Assises de la Haute Cour described the law as administered in the Latin
Kingdom of Jerusalem, but they applied equally in Cyprus ('les assises
et [. . .] les bons usages et les bones costumes dou reaume de Jerusalem,
les queles l'on doit tenir ou reaume de Chipre');[23] they were all written in the thirteenth century.[24] Similarly, the *Assises de la Cour des
Bourgeois* also reflect a legal situation in the Latin Kingdom of Jerusalem.
However, the translation of the text into Greek, its presence in manuscripts copied in Cyprus, and the fact that the 'Abrégé' (or 'Livre
du Plédéant' and 'Livre du Plaidoyer') was written on the island in
the middle of the fourteenth century clearly indicate that it applied
in the Court of Burgesses of the Kingdom of Cyprus too.[25]

Crusader customary law, as recorded in the *Assizes*, assured the
maintenance of the social and ethnic boundaries of the dominant
group. Social hierarchy based on class and ethnicity determined legal
status and privilege in the eyes of the law. The class of the Frankish
liegemen were in an advantageous position vis-à-vis the other Frankish
classes. Ethnic discrimination and social stratification, though, were
clearly understood in terms of religious affiliation, which defined identity and thus inclusion in or exclusion from the dominant group. Only
Latins, 'law-worthy guarantors of the law of Rome' ('loiaus garans
[. . .] de la loy de Rome') could testify as bearers of warranty against
a Frank in the High Court or fight judicial duels; Latins who had
served the Byzantines against the Crusaders were probably excluded
as well.[26] The Armenians and the Syrians were grouped together
with the Greeks and were also socially differentiated from the Franks
on the basis of religion ('gres ne suriens ne ermins ne jacopins. Ne
gens de nassion qui ne sont obeissans a Rome ne pevent porter
garantie en la haute cort').[27] Moreover, the jurists make it clear that
legal order corresponded to a hierarchization of religions and rites;

---

[23] Geofrey Le Tor, 444; Philip of Novara, 'Livre', 478, 523; Edbury (1997d:
23–6), with examples from John of Ibelin. On the *Assizes*, see also Edbury and
Grivaud in this volume.

[24] Grandclaude (1923: 46–50, 80–1, 88, 89–90, and passim); Edbury (1996; 1997d;
1998a; 2001b); Grivaud (1996: 992–1002).

[25] Grandclaude (1923: 33–8, 51–3, 90–2; 1926: 458–9, 463); *Assizes*, 21–8.

[26] Philip of Novara, 'Livre', 482, 486, 492, 497, 501–2; John of Ibelin, 165, 167,
687; *Assises de la Cour des Bourgeois*, 209. Generally, Edbury (2002: 136–7).

[27] John of Ibelin, 167; *Assises de la Cour des Bourgeois*, 53–4; 'Bans et ordonnances
des rois de Chypre', 364–5.

next to the Latin Christians come the Orthodox Syrians (Melkites), then the Greeks, the other Eastern confessions, the Jews, and finally the Muslims. Of course, the jurists described a procedure that had come to Cyprus from the Crusader mainland, and we have no other evidence that indeed the testimony of a Syrian was to be preferred to that of a Greek in Cyprus; it seems more probable that the hierarchization of the various Eastern Christian denominations before the law probably reflected popular perceptions of the *Other* rather than the reality of a strictly stratified social system.[28] In the royal bans that reflect everyday reality more than legal treatises do, the Franks, the Greeks, and the other communities were often associated on an equal basis.[29] Furthermore, although a Greek was in an inferior position when in litigation with a Frank, the legislators were very sensitive towards the ethnic and social realities of the Kingdom of Jerusalem and consequently of Cyprus and took great care to avoid conflict between the various communities. For example, one could testify as bearer of warranty only against members of one's own ethnic group (Greeks, Syrians, and 'tous autres Crestiens qui ne sont de la ley de Rome, pevent porter garentie les gens de leur lei').[30] Often ethnic and social differentiation was also defined in terms of language; a ban issued in 1300 talked of 'Franc ni Grifon ni Surien, ne home de quelque lengage que il soit'.[31]

Consequently, from the very beginning the Franks realized that the wise thing to do in order to achieve a long, successful settlement was to abide by the realities of a society where the majority were Greeks and to reach a *modus vivendi*. Thus, in the Court of Burgesses, where not only Franks but also Greeks and other linguistic groups applied for justice, the principle of the respect of the language of the interested party found its full expression. The legislator, sensitive to the cultural realities of a multi-ethnic society, provided that one should take the oath according to one's religion and language ('jurer [. . .] sur les livres des Evangiles escrites de leurs lettres') and a similar concession may be found in the *Assises de la Haute Cour* in the

---

[28] Philip of Novara, 'Livre', 499, 546–7, and esp. 532–4; John of Ibelin, 149–51, 264–5, 670–3; *Assises de la Cour des Bourgeois*, 53–6, 209, 171–3. Generally, Edbury (2001b: 562–5; 2002: 137–8).

[29] 'Bans et ordonnances des rois de Chypre', 361 (in 1298, 'de quelque nacion que il soit'), 365 (in 1300, 'Franc ni Grisois ni Surien').

[30] Philip of Novara, 'Livre', 502; *Assises de la Cour des Bourgeois*, 54–6, 171–3.

[31] 'Bans et ordonnances des rois de Chypre', 365; John of Ibelin, 238.

case of testimony for legal delay or 'essoine' ('de quelque nacion que il soit [. . .] que il jure selonc sa loy').[32] Moreover, the Lusignans allowed the Greeks and the other groups some form of judicial autonomy. Both the Syrians and the Armenians enjoyed special legal and social privileges under the Lusignan regime, probably an inheritance of their social condition in the Latin East and a result of the ties of the Kingdom of Cyprus with that of Lesser Armenia. It is not known when a court of the Syrians was established on the island; a 'raicius' is attested in 1210 but most probably he was a seigneurial *bailli* rather that a *rays*.[33] The *paroikoi*, the Greek serfs, were under the jurisdiction of the lord, and the seigneurial *baillis* in the estates were assisted by Greek jurats, who represented the community but whose competence is not clear. In 1317 in Psimolophou, the 'juratus' was 'Basilios Bougas'; in 1367 in Limassol, the 'jurés' 'Yany tis Annousas' and 'Vasily' were employed by the Latin bishopric of the town.[34] No special body existed for the *francomati*, the Greek free peasants, and the *perpyriarioi*, the Greek burgesses, who were under the jurisdiction of the state tribunals.

Family law, though, was within the jurisdiction of the Greek church tribunals, which had an extended competence that covered cases of matrimonial and inheritance law and matters of faith. It was the 1260 *Bulla Cypria* that guaranteed that the Greek episcopal courts (one in every bishopric) and those parochial tribunals that had existed before would be maintained, thus making possible the ensuing survival of Byzantine family law.[35] These courts were presided over by a judge (κριτήν) or a representative of the bishop, both ecclesiastics; he was assisted by a notary and other auxiliary persons.[36] The semi-ecclesiastical office of the *nomikos* is also attested in various documents; his competence was probably the same as that of a notary and covered the drafting of all sorts of contracts and testaments, as seen from the description of his duties in a certificate for notaries

---

[32] *Assises de la Cour des Bourgeois*, 171–3; John of Ibelin, 149.

[33] Edbury (1978: 175, 179); Richard (1987: esp. 385–8; 1995b: 360–2); Coureas (1995a).

[34] Richard (1947: 130, 140, 148); *Documents chypriotes des archives du Vatican*, 106, 107.

[35] *Cartulary*, no. 78 (p. 199); *Synodicum Nicosiense*, no. X.25.18–19; Schabel in this volume.

[36] Documents from the bishopric of Paphos/Arsinoe, in Simon, 11–73, and Maruhn, 226–55; documents from the bishopric of Nicosia/Solea, in Chatzipsaltes (1955: 27–9). Generally, Svoronos (1976: 10–13, 17); Zepos (1976a); Papadopoullos (1984: 3–6).

(Γράμμα νομικό). Most importantly the Greek ecclesiastical courts reached their decisions after consulting with wise and prominent men ('βουλήν λογίμων ανδρών', 'αξιόλογοι άνδρες και μάρτυρες').[37] The presence of laymen as assessors assisting the presiding officer in ecclesiastical courts must have facilitated the subsequent access of the Greeks to the Court of Burgesses as jurats or assessors. The terms 'ορκομοσιάτης' ('jurat'), 'ομότης' ('jurat'), and 'κριτής' ('judge' or 'jurat')[38] that survive in various documents and manuscript notes indicate that the office of the jurat in the Greek ecclesiastical courts, the seigneurial administration, and the Court of Burgesses acquired importance amongst the Greeks. At the end of the fourteenth century, a family of priests, for whom *Orkomosiates* (Ορκομοσιάτης) was probably a hereditary office adopted as a family name, served at the church of the Virgin Hodegetria in Nicosia, probably already the cathedral of the Greek bishop in the town.[39] The participation of lay notables in the procedure gave the ecclesiastical courts the aspect of a secular court. Moreover, it seems that the extent of the competence of these courts was larger than usually thought; this is supported by the fact that besides model cases of legal procedure in matrimonial matters and the relevant Byzantine law, the compiler of a ca. 1300 manual of the episcopal court of Paphos/Arsinoe inserted a selection of Byzantine law that included articles on property transactions between spouses or individuals, loans, testaments, guardianship, the Farmer's law, and the Sea law, some of which cover aspects of penal law. The Greek ecclesiastical courts became thus a kind of arbitration tribunal for every kind of litigation between Greeks.[40] Their existence gave the Greeks a form of important judicial autonomy, similar to the one enjoyed by the Syrians, and allowed the Greek clergy to assume its ethnarchical role.

The translation of the *Assises de la Cour des Bourgeois* into the Greek Cypriot dialect at some time between the end of the thirteenth and the middle of the fourteenth century points to the fact that Greek

---

[37] Lampros (1921: 164–5); Simon, 19, 23, 43, and passim ('Index', 119); Chatzipsaltes (1955: 28).

[38] Lampros (1917: 18; 1921: 341); Chatzipsaltes (1955: 29, 32–3); Darrouzès (1958: 238, 243).

[39] Darrouzès (1953: 89–90).

[40] Constantinides and Browning, *Dated Greek Manuscripts*, 128–9; Svoronos (1976: 11–17).

was used from an early stage in the proceedings of the court for
cases involving Greeks and implies the employment of Greek officers
in the Court of Burgesses. 'Michael', the viscount of Famagusta, who
is mentioned in two acts dated to 1296 and 1300, may have been
Greek or Syrian, to go by his name. The presence of Syrian, Genoese,
and Venetian jurats during the period 1296–1301, mentioned by
Lamberto di Sambuceto, a Genoese notary working in Famagusta,
suggests that Greek jurats probably existed too. In 1427, a Greek
jurat of the Court of the Viscount of Nicosia condemned the riots
of the peasants in a manuscript note.[41] It is not clear if the Greek
translation was commissioned by the government or rather made by
practitioners in the Court of Burgesses (ενεπίσημοι άνδρες, 'the officials'),
as presumably was the original Old French treatise itself.[42] In either
case, the need for a translation stemmed from the fact that, from
the very beginning, the Greeks had to apply to the Court of Burgesses
for cases not within the jurisdiction of the Greek ecclesiastical courts.
This was intensified in the 1360s when, following the enfranchisements of Peter I, the number of the Greek burgesses who were given
exactly the same rights as the Latin burgesses had suddenly rose.
Furthermore, the vernacularization of law with the introduction of
Lusignan rule in Cyprus allowed the textualization of the Greek
Cypriot dialect and its movement into domains usually restricted for
a higher form of language, and it bears witness to the generalized
use of the dialect as a *lingua franca* on the island. The fact that Greek
ecclesiastics and laymen participated in both the Greek ecclesiastical courts and the Lusignan Court of Burgesses, and held at the
same time important offices in seigneurial and royal administration,
rendered them competent in every aspect of administration and facilitated their social mobility.

The Institutional Framework: Continuity or Discontinuity

The English and Templar experience made Guy of Lusignan realize that the new kingdom needed a solid social structure. This
demanded generous land concessions, or, as Saladin allegedly told

---

[41] Lamberto di Sambuceto, *1296–1299*, no. 13, and *1299–1301* (1884), no. 114;
Lamberto di Sambuceto, *1296–1299*, no. 13, *1301*, no. 36, and *1299–1301* (1884),
nos. 114–15; Darrouzès (1958: 243). Generally, Edbury (1997b: 89–91).
[42] Ασίζαι A, 3.

the Cypriot king, 'que il [Guy] la [l'isle] doigne toute', since the main attraction for the new settlers lay in their social privileges and the acquisition of property in view of the loss of their property in the mainland to the Muslims.[43] Guy generously distributed land and money fiefs to knights and the lesser nobility, other assignments and annuities to the burgesses, as well as liberties and securities to the lower classes and the Syrians of free professions who, although they had to pay heavy dues, did not pay as much as the Greeks. According to Leontios Makhairas, 'to the Syrians he granted that they should pay in all cases the half of the fees due for buying and selling, and whatever dues the natives paid they [the Syrians] were not to pay'. There is no way of knowing what land prices or annual incomes from land were, but it would seem that, because of the limited insular space of Cyprus, the price of land was very high. Of course, the anticipated annual revenue of an average fief is unknown. It may be that Byzantine central records undervalued rural properties and it was only later that the new owners realized their true value, as implied by the claim of the chronicle known as *Chronique d'Ernoul et de Bernard le Trésorier* that fiefs worth 1,000 white bezants in Guy's time were worth twice as much in the time of his successor, Aimery of Lusignan.[44]

Richard the Lionheart's experiment to allow the 'counts and barons and all the inhabitants of the island' to keep half of their possessions in spite of his right of conquest was not successful.[45] The 1191–92 revolts would have provided Guy with a good excuse not to respect Richard's treaty with the *archontes*, the Greek aristocracy, and to move to further confiscations. Seizures initially involved all state (δημοσιακή) and imperial (βασιλική) land, some ecclesiastical property, as well as some property that belonged to the *archontes*, especially that of the rebels, of those who refused to cooperate with the new regime, and of those who had abandoned the island.[46] Philip of Novara speaks of the king in possession of 'gaste ou terre que l'on apele *vaselico*', while John of Ibelin speaks of 'gaste que l'on apelle chemin reau'; it is not clear if 'gaste' (= waste) refers to uncultivated/

---

[43] *Continuation de Guillaume de Tyr*, 138–9; Makhairas, I, §25. See also Edbury in this volume.
[44] 'Estoire de Eracles', 192; Makhairas, I, §26; 'Ernoul', 287. Generally, Papadopoullos (1964: 98–109).
[45] 'Benedict of Peterborough', II, 168; Roger of Howden, III, 111–12.
[46] Svoronos (1976: 9); Richard (1995a: 5–7, 17; 1997: 125–8).

-able or abandoned land. Philip also refers to the fiefs in Cyprus that had belonged to the churches, the abbeys, and the 'artondes' (read 'arcondes').[47] In 1197, the archbishop of Tyre was given the *casale* of Livadi, the former property of Minas, a Greek. In September 1210, Hugh I granted the Hospitallers the *casale* of Monagroulli, which must have passed from the hands of the Venetian community. With the same act the king granted the Hospital land and houses in Limassol, property he possessed after having confiscated it from its apparently Greek owners, a certain 'Lambite Sabastos' (= Olympites Sevastos?) and his sister, Sevastos being either a family name or a Byzantine honorific title.[48] In the same year, the king confirmed the grant of a piece of land near Nicosia by a certain John La Baume to the Hospitallers; the alienation of feudal holdings by royal permission indicates that the vassal had already been granted confiscated land, but it is not known whether it had been confiscated from an individual or from the land of the imperial fisc.[49] The case of the Venetian community of Limassol constitutes a good example of redistribution of land. In a report dating to the early 1240s, the community complained over the expropriation of their property, which had been granted to knights, turcopoles, free professions, the Latin secular and regular clergy, other trade communes, the king himself, and some Greeks; at the time of the Lusignan takeover, the property might have been untenanted or leased to Greeks, or simply its owners could not prove ownership.[50] By analogy, one may presume that if the Venetians had to suffer confiscations, the ordinary secular Greek property owners could do even less to protect their property; nevertheless, as will be discussed later, some Greek owners who could prove property rights were probably respected.

The redistribution of land at the beginning of the century no doubt altered entirely the social structure and the distribution of wealth, but the dearth of documentation makes it very difficult to assess the extent of institutional changes and their impact on the everyday life of the indigenous population; at best the evidence is

[47] Philip of Novara, 'Livre', 533, 536; John of Ibelin, 672. Generally, Edbury (1991: 20, note 31; 1995c: 357; 1998a: 173, note 14). On Greek church property see Schabel in this volume.
[48] *Cartulary*, no. 46 and passim; *Regesta Regni Hierosolymitani*, I, no. 844; *Cartulaire général de l'Ordre des Hospitaliers*, II, no. 1354, 121–2; Papadopoulou (1983: §60).
[49] Edbury (1978: 175, 179).
[50] Papadopoulou (1983: §51, 321, and passim); also, see Papacostas (1999b). See also Schabel in this volume.

circumstantial and at worst it comes from later sources. The main problem is that we know very little of Byzantine institutions on the island in the eleventh and twelfth centuries. Moreover, the question of Byzantine social structures in the twelfth century is a controversial issue and must be understood in terms of the extent to which Byzantine society comprised a minority of landlords and a large proportion of *paroikoi*. Despite similarities in the domain of land exploitation, unlike Western societies, the Byzantine society knew no bonds of dependence similar to vassalage and no evidence survives concerning the existence of a category of land submitted to military obligations on the island. The system of *pronoia* is nowhere mentioned in connection with Cyprus, while, as inferred from Nicholas Mouzalon's account, the *strateia* existed in the form of a tax.[51] Although it has been overstated by some historians, it seems that Richard's promise to the Greek aristocracy to grant the laws and institutions they enjoyed under Manuel I Comnenos in return for half of their belongings found expression in the Lusignans' pragmatism and good sense that made them realize the necessity for the continuity of certain of these institutions. It is, however, difficult to assess how far the Byzantine institutional legacy structured the Lusignan social system and to what extent there occurred the superimposition of imported feudal institutional structures upon the preexisting Byzantine structures.[52]

Several examples survive that demonstrate what has been described as 'the decisive role of Byzantine institutions in the medieval Kingdom of Cyprus'.[53] The Lusignans inherited the *sekreton* (σέκρετον) of the Byzantine administration (the office that kept the cadastres where landowners and taxes were registered), which assumed the function of a central financial office that administered the revenues of the royal domain and government expenditure. The very name of the *secrète* is the transliteration of the Greek word; in thirteenth-century Greek documents, the form *sekreton* is used for the royal *secrète*, while the forms *syngriton/syngritikos* (σύνγκριτον/συνγκριτικός) are found in later texts.[54] The dearth of evidence for its workings during the thir-

---

[51] Mouzalon, 127.574. Generally, Svoronos (1976: 1), Papadopoullos (1995b: xi–xiii), and Grivaud (1998a: 37, 44–5, and passim).

[52] Cf. note 45 above; Svoronos (1976: 1, 3–4, and passim); Grivaud (1991: 117–20, 126–7).

[53] Grivaud (1993: 144; 1998: 35).

[54] Lampros (1917: 18, 20, 23, 48; 1921: 340–2) for *sekreton* and Makhairas, I, §§14, 157, 158, 311, for later forms; cf. Makhairas, *Diplomatic Edition*, 73, 147, 148, 239, for the manuscript spellings of the various forms.

teenth century means that it is impossible to tell how far the Lusignans
maintained the preexisting office or simply the name.[55] A model document of the royal secrète for the registration of taxes owed in a
parish, drafted at the lord's demand, and written in Greek, survives
in a manuscript datable to 1317–20; the rubric of the document and
the terminology remind one of the Byzantine cadastral register called
ἔκστιχος κώδιξ.[56] Although early evidence is lacking, it seems that
from the very beginning, apart from Latin and French, Greek was
also used by the officials of the secrète, as was the practice in the
fifteenth century.[57] This was necessitated by the nature of the work
conducted by the secrète, which involved the registration of acts and
contracts between individuals of various social strata and different
ethnic origins.[58] In the procedure explained in a ban issued in 1310
and in the 'Abrégé' of the *Assises de la Cour des Bourgeois* it is made
clear that the presence of multilingual notaries and/or interpreters
who would be able to communicate with the persons involved was
necessary.[59] From early fourteenth-century evidence, it appears that
the secrète kept registers for dues owed by the Greeks (δημοσιακοί
κώδικες) or registered acts of sales that involved Greeks in the Greek
language for use by Greek officials; the minutes of the relevant meet-
ings were also kept in Greek. Although the *baillis* of the secrète were
members of the Frankish nobility, it seems that from an early time
the rest of the staff were recruited among the indigenous population, the Greeks and later the Cypriots of Syrian origin as well, and
this tradition constitutes a further indication of the continuity of the
institution.[60]

Moreover, the institution of the *comerc*, a term that designated both
the royal office of commerce and the duties on export and import
and on the sale of merchandise, was the direct descendant of the
Byzantine *kommerkion* (κομμέρκιον). Until the war with Genoa in 1374
when new taxes had to be introduced, most of the taxes levied on
production and commerce were inherited from the Byzantine fiscal

---

[55] Grivaud (1991: 119); Edbury (1991: 191–2); Richard (1995b: 352).
[56] Lampros (1917: 18). Generally, Svoronos (1959: 57–8, 142) and Grivaud (1991: 117–19).
[57] *Livre des remembrances*, passim. Generally, Nicolaou-Konnari (1995: 381–2).
[58] Cf. the 'Livre des ventes, dons et guagières et autres', *Livre des remembrances*, x.
[59] 'Bans et ordonnances des rois de Chypre', 369; 'Abrégé', 287, 241, 243, 255.
[60] Lampros (1917: 18, 20, 23; 1921: 340–2); Edbury (1991: 192); cf. pp. 46, 54 below.

system, as attested by terminology.[61] The Lusignans maintained some of the characteristics of the Byzantine monetary system too. Until the late thirteenth century, they preserved a coinage entirely Byzantine in iconography and appellation, the white bezant, a base gold piece of scyphate fabric based on a familiar type at the time of the conquest; the Lusignan petty coinage, though, was Western from the beginning.[62] The structure of the rural economy also demonstrates institutional continuity; administration units (χωρία/casalia, variously meaning villages or estates; προάστεια/presteries/prastia, meaning hamlets) and forms of exploitation (direct exploitation involving corvées—the forced labour the serfs were obliged to perform on the lord's estate—and paid workers; indirect in the form of farming out land to free tenants) remained the same. Also, the validity of ancient land divisions was acknowledged and the force of law was conferred on local custom; according to the *Assises de la Haute Cour*, one had to rely on the testimony of the elders for litigation concerning domain borders.[63]

Social Stratification: Mobility or Rigidity

The Greek Peasantry—Paroikoi and Francomati: One may assume that for the Greeks social changes followed population distribution, although the small size of the island rendered the rural and urban communities easily accessible to each other and prevented striking differences. It is likely that not much changed in the rural areas, besides a change of the ideological, and probably vague, concept of the lord. A significant difference might be the importance the seigneurial estate acquired within the feudal regime (in 1317–18 it represented one seventh of the cultivated land in the *casale* of Psimolophou), but again we do not know how important estates were under the Byzantines.[64] The Lusignans did not proceed to a massive reduction of free peasants to serfdom and the number of the *paroikoi*, the class of Greek serfs the Lusignans inherited from the Byzantine regime, was probably already high as in the rest of the Byzantine world. In fact, according to the *Continuation of William of Tyre*, when Guy of Lusignan became lord of Cyprus, he gave assurances to the peasants regarding

---

[61] Grivaud (1991; 1993: 133–4, 142–3, and passim; 1994: 151; 1998: 35, 36–7).
[62] Metcalf (1995a: 177–98). See also Edbury in this volume.
[63] Philip of Novara, 'Livre', 532–4; John of Ibelin, 670–3.
[64] Richard (1947: 130); Svoronos (1976: 5).

their rights ('Quant il [Guy] ot la terre, il manda assegurer les vilains').[65] What changed was the personal condition of the *paroikoi* (also called *sers, vilains,* or *rustici*), practically equated to that of the serf. They were not free of their persons and they were regarded as part of the things that pertained to a *casale*, the lord having the right to demand from his vassal not only land or a sum of money, but also villeins: men, women, and their children.[66] Despite their attachment to the land, serfs often fled.[67] In a ban dated 1355 the authorities demanded that the Franks, the free peasants (*francomati*), or the members of the foreign communes who wished to travel away from their place of origin within the island should carry 'letters sealed by the seal of the viscount or that of the bailli of the district' so that they could prove that they were not *paroikoi* and avoid arrest; if this was only introduced in 1355, it might also be a reaction to the social pressures caused by the Black Death.[68] If a serf struck a knight, the law specified that he should lose his right hand.[69] Moreover, the movable belongings of the *paroikoi* were mainmortable, that is, disposable by the lord at their death. Philip of Novara specifies that if a serf died without heirs, the lord took two thirds of his effects and his widow one third; if she was unable to pay the taxes on the land, the lord could take her plough and donkey.[70] In 1300, the Hospitallers dismissed this practice for their serfs, provided that the wife and children of the deceased continued to perform the obligations of serfdom ('coustume del vilenage'), and this was probably the reason why serfs escaped to the Hospital in 1367.[71]

The importance of the seigneurial estate rendered necessary both the increase of the number of the *corvées* and the reduction of the size of the tenures. However, the number of the *corvées* (two to three days a week compared to twelve to twenty-four a year under the Byzantines) comes from later sources: Philip of Mézières, writing in

---

[65] 'Estoire de Eracles', 191. Edbury (1989: 148 and passim; 1995c: 356–7).
[66] Mas Latrie, *Histoire*, II, 53–4; Philip of Novara, 'Livre', 496, 519.
[67] Philip of Novara, 'Livre', 535–6; 'Bans et ordonnances des rois de Chypre', 375; 'Formules', no. XIX, 386; *Documents chypriotes des archives du Vatican*, 102, 104; Luttrell (1986: 164).
[68] 'Bans et ordonnances des rois de Chypre', 373, 375; Mas Latrie, *Histoire*, II, 231, 436.
[69] Philip of Novara, 'Livre', 547.
[70] Edbury (2001b: 564, 566); Richard (1947: 134, 146, 147).
[71] *Cartulaire général de l'Ordre des Hospitaliers*, III, no. 4515, 811; *Documents chypriotes des archives du Vatican*, 102, 104 and Luttrell (1986: 164).

the second half of the fourteenth century, is the only source that mentions three days and he may be wrong; in the first quarter of the sixteenth century, Francesco Attar mentions two days. In 1271, royal serfs served two days a week, while in ecclesiastical estates, such as the *casale* of Psimolophou in 1317–18, the number seems to have been smaller.[72] The *paroikoi* possessed chattel in the form of plough and domestic animals. The size of their tenures was proportionate to the number of their plough-team and was taxed accordingly. A Greek document dated 1232 and entitled *Apokope ton psomion* (Ἀποκοπή τῶν ψωμίων) gives precious information concerning the distribution of tenures to the *paroikoi* as well as the fiscal obligations involved. According to the document, the *paroikoi* of the plains were divided into *zeugaratoi* (ζευγαράτοι, owners of one pair of oxen), *monoibodatoi* (μονοϊβοδάτοι, owners of one ox), and *pezoi* (πεζοί, those not possessing any cattle), and were respectively attributed land of 40, 30, and 20 *modioi*. This practice rested upon the old Byzantine structure of the rural regime; in the Byzantine Empire, the average size of the respective tenures corresponded to 150, 100, and 75 *modioi*, one *modios* calculated to be the equivalent of approximately 840 square metres.[73] A similar practice is attested in the rural regime of Latin Syria where the expression *charuga* designated both the number of plough-team and the size of the land. The term found its way into the Franco-Cypriot rural economy; the dues in chickens of the peasants of Psimolophou in 1317 corresponded to the number of the *charugae*.[74]

The tenure obligations of the *paroikoi* were the result of their personal condition and their enfranchisement meant their release from these obligations; on 15 February 1300, Theodoros, a layman from Kolossi, was enfranchised 'from all services and forced labour'. After the 1220 and 1222 agreements regulating matters concerning relations between the Latin Church, the State, and the Greek Church, *paroikoi* who were ordained priests or entered a monastery and had been subject to servile obligations until then were automatically enfranchised, although the privilege was not transferred to their children.

---

[72] Philip of Mézières, *Songe*, 382; Francesco Attar, 520; 'Document relatif au service militaire', 430; Richard (1947: 134–5, 151). Generally, Svoronos (1976: 3–6) and Grivaud (1998a: 36).

[73] Lampros (1921: 345–7). Generally, Svoronos (1956: 331–2; 1976: 6) and Grivaud (1991: 120–2).

[74] Richard (1947: 131, note 1, 134, 147).

In order to prevent the loss of serfs from the estates (perhaps the
more educated and hence more useful ones) and control their change
of place of residence, the 1220 and 1222 agreements stipulated that
Greek candidates for the priesthood needed the consent of both their
lay lord and the local Latin bishop. In an undated letter in a manuscript of ca. 1317–20, the king gave his permission for a Greek
who wanted to enter the monastery of Neankomi, a house that was
situated on the royal estate just outside Nicosia. As evidence from
a 1468 document indicates, abandoned children were considered
free.[75] The *paroikoi* were also submitted to *formariage*, the lord's right
to control the marriage of his serfs; in 1297, a special ban was issued
concerning the female servants of the king.[76] Moreover, it seems that
the Greek Church itself, which possessed its own Greek *paroikoi*, tried
to prevent intermarriage between *paroikoi* and *francomati*, probably as a
way to exercise control over marriage across classes and thus to prevent the change of balance between the two classes, since the offspring
from such unions were reduced to the status of *paroikoi*. In undated
canons inserted in a treatise on the seven sacraments attributed to
the fourteenth-century Greek Cypriot scholar George Lapithes, there
is an interesting provision concerning the prohibition of a priest's
performing a wedding between members of different social classes
(*paroikoi* with *francomati, paroikos* of the king with one of a knight, *perpyriarioi* with *francomati*) without the consent of the Greek bishop.[77]

The class of the *francomati* also seems to have been inherited from
the Byzantine class of the *eleutheroi*, the free peasants, in which, as
inferred from sixteenth-century texts, enfranchised *paroikoi* and manumitted slaves were later included. The *francomati* were tenants who
leased land at a fixed sum (= *apauteurs*). *Francomati* did have personal
obligations, sometimes according to contract in the case of those not
born in that status, but unlike the *paroikoi*, they were free of their
persons and as *apauteurs* they could buy the right to operate a fran-
chise. In the relevant chapters in the Greek version of the *Assises de
la Cour des Bourgeois*, the term *pakton* (πάκτον) renders both the act of

---

[75] *Cartulaire général de l'Ordre des Hospitaliers*, III, no. 4488; *Cartulary*, no. 84, 220–1,
no. 82, 214–15, no. 83, 217–18, no. 95, 249–50; *Synodicum Nicosiense*, nos. X.6 and
X.11; Lampros (1921: 146–7); *Livre des remembrances*, no. 155. Generally, Richard
(1995b: 363, 365–7). See also Schabel in this volume.
[76] 'Bans et ordonnances des rois de Chypre', 360.
[77] Darrouzès (1979: 99–100); Kirmitses (1983: 49, 76, 78). On the Greek clergy's
paroikoi, see e.g. Neilos, 17.

apautage and the rented property, and the persons involved are called *paktonaris, paktonaria* or lord of the *pakton* (πακτονάρης, πακτοναρία, αφέντης του πάκτου).[78] Several examples of Greek *apauteurs* survive in the sources: in the *Apokope* in 1232, the rent of taverns and orchards is mentioned; in Psimolophou in 1317, the lord pays damage expenses to the *apauteur* of the mills of the village for the time they remain inactive for repairs; in Alsos in 1348, 'Nikolaos Ourris' is 'paktonaris' and his *pakton* finishes in 1352; in 1367, several *apauteurs* are mentioned in Limassol, Kilani, Sylikou, and Lophou, including 'Thodri Romannis l'apautor' of the tannery and 'Jorge l'arsediaque' and 'sire Nicolle Romain', holders of 'apaus des vignes franches' in Kilani. Unfortunately, no evidence survives as to whether there existed different kinds of *pakton*, depending on the duration of the lease, the heritability of the right to use the land, the possibility of cooperative exploitation of the rented property, etc., as was the case in Venetian Crete.[79]

It has been said that in the taxpaying society of Byzantium, real freedom was the freedom from heavy taxation. Although no comparison is possible, taxes under the Lusignans may have been heavy, but not necessarily heavier and, at any rate, there is ample evidence that the population suffered and was heavily taxed both under the Byzantines and the usurper Isaac Ducas Comnenos (1184–91).[80] The fact that Neophytos the Recluse's social commentary in his post-1192 writings bears similarities to his pre-1192 accusations against the Byzantine ruling class and Isaac points to a situation that may not have been better, but was not necessarily worse either. Neophytos accuses the authorities of exploiting the lower classes and reiterates the complaints concerning poverty and deprivation, slavery and oppression, unhappiness, and depopulation.[81] In works dated between 1209 and 1213, he mentions laments and mourning, burning and darkness, murders, grief and imprisonment, the greed of the rulers and the oppression of the ruled.[82] Although it is impossible to know

---

[78] Francesco Attar, 520; Ασίζαι, 10, 77–9, *B*, 256, 327–9.
[79] Lampros (1921: 345); Richard (1947: 135, 147, 151); Constantinides and Browning, *Dated Greek Manuscripts*, 207–8; *Documents chypriotes des archives du Vatican*, 67, 78, 79, 81, 85, 91. Generally, Svoronos (1976: 4–5) and Richard (1995b: 368). For Crete, see Gaspares (1997).
[80] Kazhdan and Wharton Epstein (1985: 59); Galatariotou (1991: 189–203); Nicolaou-Konnari (2000a: 58–9).
[81] Neophytos the Recluse, *De calamitatibus Cypri*, 10–12, *Enkomion for the Holy Cross*, 178–9, and *Typike Diatheke*, 37, 40, 58. Cf. p. 15 above and pp. 41–2 below.
[82] Neophytos the Recluse, *First Sunday Homily*, 307, and *Sixth Sunday Homily*, 329.

to what extent this picture reflects the actuality of the social conditions in early Lusignan Cyprus, we do know that the *paroikoi* owed
one third of their produce and paid various taxes to the lord in both
money and kind, collectively called *catepanagium* and related to their
personal condition.[83] In the *Apokope*, the three categories of the *paroikoi*
of the plains owed a poll tax of 60, 40, and 20 *hyperpyra* respectively,
while those who held tenures in the mountainous areas paid one
sixth of their produce, calculated on the basis of the average revenues of the last three years. The situation of the *francomati* was
clearly more favourable: they owed one fourth to one fifth of their
crop production or a fixed amount for the other cultivations, they
were not subjected to the poll tax or the *corvées*, and they paid taxes
to the state. According to the *Apokope*, the tenures not granted to
paroikoi and all the tenures of the royal domain were taxed on the
basis of the quality of the soil and the availability of water.[84]

A social system of inequality and a clearly demarcated dichotomy
between the dominant and the dominated class may well have been
considered natural by the former, but in practice the Lusignans
needed to treat the native population reasonably well if they were
to achieve cohabitation conditions of peace and prosperity for both
communities. As explained in a document in an early fourteenth-
century manuscript that lists the duties assigned to a *bailli* by his
lord, the former is responsible for the interests of the king and his
lord as well as for the fair administration and welfare of all the villagers, including the *paroikoi*. Several examples of royal and seigneurial benevolence are preserved: in the same manuscript there survives
a letter of suppliance addressed to the king, 'my benefactor [. . .]
charitable and merciful judge', by the 'poor Romaioi' and it is
specified that 'even the rocks praise his charitable acts'; in 1299 the
state paid indemnities to the victims of Genoese corsairs in Episkopi;
in the aforementioned document, it is specified that the *bailli* must
prevent the oppression of the poor and must protect them from
harm; evidence datable to 1358 suggests that the Hospital treated
its serfs well.[85] According to the *Apokope*, in 1232 special care was

---

[83] Richard (1995b: 365, 370–1).
[84] Lampros (1921: 345). See generally Svoronos (1959: 125), Grivaud (1991:
120–2), and Richard (1995b: 371–2).
[85] Lampros (1917: 19–20, 50); 'Bans et ordonnances des rois de Chypre', 363;
Luttrell (1986: 164–5).

taken of the priests, the widows, and the very young villagers who
owed considerably less taxes, something that points to the flexibility
of the social system. Similarly, in 1317 the poll tax ('chevage') owed
by a boy serf in Psimolophou was less than that owed by adult serfs.[86]

Moreover, it seems that villagers were allowed to take extra jobs.
In the *casalia* of Knodara, Morfittes, and Dichoria in 1354–56 we
find Greek 'hosteliers' and paid workers, and in 1367 Greek 'sergens
et guardiens' and other workers were employed by the Latin bishopric in the district of Limassol.[87] The earliest available evidence of
life in a village dates to the year March 1317–February 1318. To
the extent a Church-owned estate may be regarded as typical, in
the *casale* of Psimolophou, owned by the Latin patriarchate of Jerusalem,
various sorts of taxes were levied and only 24 *paroikoi* out of a total
population of 250–300 villagers were unable to pay their obligations.
The overall picture is one of a busy, well-organized community represented by a Greek jurat and administered by a *catepan*, who was
also in charge of the collection of taxes and was often Greek. The
villagers sold their products at the Sunday markets in the towns,
during the time of the *corvées* the *paroikoi* (including women and children) received their food and a bonus when the work was finished
and probably a daily salary as well, and the rest of the peasant population participated in the administration of the estate as minor
officers or scribes or worked as servants, artisans, and paid labourers.[88] This somewhat idyllic picture is not necessarily contradictory
to the one suggested by the refusal of the peasants of Pendayia,
Morphou, and the area of Solea to pay their taxes and dues and
serve their *corvées* during the Genoese invasion of the island in 1373;
the episode does not indicate that their dues were very heavy for
them to pay, but rather that the peasants took advantage of the
absence of political control, as their quick submission to the constable James of Lusignan demonstrates.[89]

The Slaves: The case of the slaves is more complex. In 1325–29,
Francesco Balducci Pegolotti declared that acts regarding the purchase of slaves and registered by notaries did not have to be legal-

[86] Lampros (1921: 345); Richard (1947: 134, 152).
[87] Poncelet (1934: 17, 18, 23, and passim); *Documents chypriotes des archives du Vatican*,
76–110.
[88] Richard (1947: passim; 1995b: 370–3).
[89] Makhairas, I, §445.

ized by a royal official, which indicates how common and frequent
such transactions were. The use of slaves increased after the Black
Death as a result of the shortage of labour. It is noteworthy that in
notarial documents drafted in Famagusta by the Venetian Simon,
priest of San Giacomo dell'Orio, between 1362 and 1371, a rise in
the number of acts concerning the sale of slaves may be observed
in comparison with earlier notarial collections, while acts concerning slaves in general constitute the overwhelming majority of Simon's
surviving acts.[90] Several chapters in the *Assises de la Cour des Bourgeois*
deal with various aspects of slavery, but they do not specify the
servile legal status. The problem becomes more complicated by the
confused use of the word 'sers' by the legislators and the editor of
the text, who use indiscriminately the terms 'parici', 'esclas', 'vilains',
and 'sers'.[91] It is thus difficult to determine how their social condition differed from that of the *paroikoi*. What is certain is that they
could be sold or transferred, contrary to the *paroikoi* who were attached
to the land, and they were not allowed to be involved in commercial transactions.[92] On the other hand, although theoretically manu-
missions gave ex-slaves the status of *francomati*, in both Latin and
Greek acts of manumission the freed slave is said to have regained
his status of 'Roman citizenship'.[93]

Slaves in Cyprus are mentioned not only as domestic servants in
towns, a widespread practice in Genoa, Venice, and elsewhere in
the Western Mediterranean, but also as rural servants. The slaves
mentioned in the acts drafted in Famagusta by the Genoese notary
Lamberto di Sambuceto in the early fourteenth century and by the
Venetians Nicola de Boateriis and Simon in the second half of the
same century were most probably domestic slaves; in 1325, Nicholas
Hasen, 'sclavo regis', was in charge of the Famagusta royal arsenal;
in 1317, in Psimolophou there were four slaves; in the late 1330s,
more than one hundred Muslim slaves worked in vineyards in the
district of Paphos; in 1354–55, the *casalia* of Knodara, Morfittes, and
Dichoria included in their personnel nineteen slaves (thirteen adult

---

[90] Francesco Balducci Pegolotti, 88; Otten-Froux (2003: 21, 27–32).
[91] *Assises de la Cour des Bourgeois*, 139, 191, and 'Abrégé', 259; 'Bans et ordonnances des rois de Chypre', 361. Cf. Richard (1995b: 370) and Arbel (1993: 159).
[92] Poncelet (1934: 24) and Richard (1950: 121, 133); 'Bans et ordonnances des
rois de Chypre', 362, 374–5.
[93] Lamberto di Sambuceto, *1301*, no. 107; Lampros (1921: 153); Darrouzès (1959a:
35). Cf. Arbel (1993: 159).

males and six women and children) and in 1356 another four slaves
were purchased; in 1367, in Kameno Prastio three slaves served as
herdsmen; also, in the accounts of the collector of the Roman Curia
for the years 1357–63 several slaves were mentioned, but their kind
of occupation was not specified.[94]

These slaves were soon assimilated with the native Greek population both culturally and socially; their tender age must have contributed to their assimilation. Consequently, there exist several examples
of Muslim slaves with Greek Christian names,[95] while in both the
Assises de la Cour des Bourgeois and a ban issued by the king in 1355
the term 'batié' is juxtaposed to 'esclaf' to designate the baptized
and sometimes liberated Muslim slave.[96] The existence of Christian
or Greek slaves from the Byzantine world (*Romania* in general, or
more specifically Constantinople, Morea, Negroponte, and Candia),
contrary to the practice in Western Europe and despite papal prohibitions, follows the Oriental usage the crusaders inherited.[97] The
Greek Cypriots, or at least some of them, express an ardent solidarity towards their fellow *Romaioi* and there are examples of their
efforts to liberate Greek prisoners or slaves of the Muslims, such as
diocesan circulars for financial assistance to that end and model letters of manumission from the beginning of the fourteenth century.
According to Leontios Makhairas, however, the overall attitude of
Cypriot society towards slaves in general and those from Romania
in particular was very hard-hearted and this was one of the sins that
caused the loss of Famagusta.[98]

The Greek Burgesses—Perpyriarioi: The urban population was affected
more by the change of regime, because they were submitted to more
institutional changes as a result of the multi-ethnic composition of

---

[94] Lamberto di Sambuceto, *1296–1299, 1299–1301, 1300–1301, 1301, 1302,
1304–1307*, passim, Nicola de Boateriis, passim, and Otten-Froux (2003); *Documents
chypriotes des archives du Vatican*, 43–6; Richard (1947: 141); Ludolph of Sudheim, 212;
Poncelet (1934: 16, 23, 27); Richard (1950: 125); Richard (1984–1987: 17, 19, 25).

[95] Lamberto di Sambuceto, *1300–1301*, nos. 256, 350; *Documents chypriotes des
archives du Vatican*, 42, 44; Richard (1950: 121); Otten-Froux (2003: 75, 77). For
slave age groups, see Arbel (1993: table I).

[96] *Assises de la Cour des Bourgeois*, 137–9; 'Bans et ordonnances des rois de Chypre',
374–5.

[97] Lamberto di Sambuceto, *1296–1299*, nos. 13, 30, 31, 38, 97, *1300–1301*, nos.
176, 269, 331, 332, 351; Richard (1947: 141; 1950: 121); Otten-Froux (2003: 63,
67, 68, 75, 76, 79, 93).

[98] Lampros (1921: 152–3, 155–6, 337–9); Darrouzès (1959a: 35–6); Makhairas,
I, §482.

the towns. The servile character of the fiscal obligations of the Greek
burgess class, the *perpyriarioi*, raises many problems as to their origin, but it seems to have been limited to the fiscal aspect only and
did not involve any of the personal limitations associated with the
paroikoi—indeed some burgesses were free.[99] Apart from the fact that
they were submitted to the *chevage*, the only other limitation was their
obligation to ask for the king's permission, in his capacity as their
lord, to sell immovable property. In 1298 some 'sers dou roi' were
allowed to possess 'borgesies' (urban grants of property or rights),
while in 1315 a special royal ban was proclaimed, forbidding the
royal servants to alienate their inheritance without the consent of
the king.[100] The burgesses paid rent for their houses and shops, since
we read that in 1367 in Limassol the 'ensenssives de maizons' and
the 'luage des estassons' were part of the revenues of the Latin diocese.[101] Some of the burgesses were workers and artisans; in documents dated 1317 and 1325–26, workers of Greek, Syrian, and
Frankish (from Cyprus or the Holy Land) origin travel from Nicosia
to Psimolophou or from Nicosia to the shipyards of Famagusta according to their professional needs.[102] Some of the Greek urban population must have suffered from poverty; in 1296 in his testament,
Nicholas of Balneo bequeathed various amounts of money to 'pau-
peribus', amongst them an unspecified Greek. The domestic servants
of the Frankish aristocracy and the 'famuli' of the Italian communes
probably belonged to this group of impoverished Greeks.[103]

In general, however, the professional activities of the *perpyriarioi* do
not seem to have been different from those of the Franks or Syrians,
and their employment in important positions in the royal administration, their success in commercial activities, and their wealth allowed
them to achieve social mobility and contribute to the prosperity of
the kingdom. According to Leontios Makhairas, by the middle of the
fourteenth century 'the majority of the people in Cyprus, most of
those who worked for the secrète and all the rich people of the
burgesses of Nicosia, were *perpyriarioi*'. They were able to buy their

---

[99] Svoronos (1976: 3–4, 10); Richard (1995b: 359–63, 372).
[100] 'Bans et ordonnances des rois de Chypre', 361, 371.
[101] *Documents chypriotes des archives du Vatican*, 77.
[102] Richard (1947: 136, 141); *Documents chypriotes des archives du Vatican*, 38–49.
[103] Lamberto di Sambuceto, *1296–1299*, no. 24 and *1300–1301*, 'Index' with
various examples.

freedom and enjoy personal liberty, like the Syrian and Latin burgesses in the second half of the fourteenth century under King Peter I, who was desperately in need of finding money to finance his military expeditions; nevertheless, although no examples may be traced in the sources prior to these massive enfranchisements, isolated cases must have existed.[104] Leontios also provides us with the information that James I (1385–98) appointed sons of burgesses as his squires instead of sons of knights, and probably Greeks were included too.[105] The social and economic prominence of the burgesses allowed them to form a new kind of Greek upper class that will be discussed below.

The Greek Archontes—Disappearance or Emergence of a New Class: The study of the presence of the class of the Greek *archontes* in post-1192 Cyprus is a controversial matter. First of all, some clarification of nomenclature is necessary because of the vagueness of the term *archontes*; it is used to designate all individuals of pre-1192 Byzantine Cypriot society who may be considered to have belonged to the local aristocracy: landowners, military and political or administrative dignitaries, and other notables. The gradual destruction of this class must have started soon after Isaac Ducas Comnenos had seized power on the island in 1184. Both the local saint Neophytos the Recluse and contemporary Byzantine and Western sources agree that Isaac persecuted the upper class, confiscated their property, and abolished privileges they had been granted by Manuel I Comnenos (1143–80). Isaac's attitude led to the emigration of a number of the nobles and the alienation of the remaining ones. It is thus not surprising that during Richard's expedition on the island the most dissatisfied of the *archontes* rallied around the king of England and the heads of the towns submitted to him in the hope that the change of regime would mean better conditions for them. The abortive insurrections of the Cypriots against Richard's garrison and the Templars must have contributed to the destruction of the local aristocracy, especially the first one in which there was most probably participation of the nobles.[106]

With the establishment of the Lusignan regime on the island in 1192 and the introduction of a new social system that depended on

---

[104] Translation based on Makhairas, *Diplomatic Edition*, 147–8, 180–1; cf. Makhairas, I, §§157, 215.
[105] Makhairas, I, §§97–8.
[106] Nicolaou-Konnari (2000a: 53–67).

the acquisition of fiefs by a new class of landowners, probably neces-
sitating further confiscations of land, the position of the remaining
Greek nobles must have been aggravated. Following the seizures of
their property discussed above and the loss of their class privileges,
it seems that soon after 1192 there was a new wave of emigration
of the landowning, administrative, and ecclesiastical aristocracy of
the island. The addressee of a letter on the misfortunes of Cyprus,
written by Neophytos the Recluse in ca. 1196, may have been one
of the people who had left under Isaac, while Basil Kinnamos, bishop
of Paphos, must have been amongst those who left after 1191/2.[107]
However, Neophytos' references to the emigration of the nobles are
very often problematic insofar as he does not always specify whether
the flights occurred under the Latins or before, whereas the uncertain dating of some of his works makes things even less clear. In
two of his works where references to flights and persecution of the
nobles may be safely attributed to the Lusignan period, Neophytos
asserts that the rich and powerful had abandoned their houses, fields
and vineyards, swine and cattle, rich belongings and families, and
left Cyprus in secrecy for Constantinople; those who stayed had to
suffer imprisonment, searches, and loss of their money. In another
work with uncertain dating, which, however, testifies to the dire situation of the nobles at the end of the twelfth century, Neophytos
claims that 'most of the rich and powerful [of Cyprus] are in chains'.[108]
What becomes clear from the Recluse's account is that the destruction of the native landowning and administrative aristocracy was not
solely the outcome of the Lusignan takeover but the result of all the
socio-political changes that affected Cyprus at the end of the twelfth
and the beginning of the thirteenth century.

The destruction of the local aristocracy did not, however, necessarily mean the disappearance of all Greek noble families. The fact
that in the first half of the fifteenth century Leontios Makhairas fails
to mention the presence of Greek *archontes* at the beginning of Lusignan
rule must not be interpreted as proof of the non-preservation of their
memory in local tradition because of their disappearance; Makhairas
very often keeps a meaningful silence over important events and his
treatment of the thirteenth century is very brief anyway. It seems

---

[107] Tsiknopoulos (1969: 342); Mango and Hawkins (1966: 205) and Mango (1976: 9).
[108] Neophytos the Recluse, *De calamitatibus Cypri*, 10–11, *Homily Concerning the Holy Fathers at the Council of Nicaea*, 272, and *Homily against the Jews*, 519.

that within the new social order, the remaining *archontes* wisely chose the safe and, in the long run, profitable attitude of compromise and collaboration in order to preserve some rights, even if this meant that they had to suffer a humiliating submission, loss of their class privileges, and dispossession of most of their property. On the other hand, in view of the fragility of the newly established kingdom, the Lusignans must have granted some liberty to those of the nobles who had stayed, because they had to rely on the old ruling Greek class to help them administer the island. In the rural areas where some *archontes* had probably retired, the Byzantine structure did not collide with the feudal system. Within the rural regime, they may have retained some non-feudal possession rights that did not involve military obligations, in the form of free tenures of small importance. They did not own important estates, exclusively granted as fiefs, but their land, which they possessed before 1192 or acquired later, could be inherited or alienated.[109] In the urban areas, however, the integration of the Greek aristocracy posed serious problems. The idea that the remaining Greek nobles were assimilated with the burgess class and held possession rights in the form of *bourgeoisies* until the end of the fourteenth century, when they were reintegrated in the nobility, is not satisfactory. Furthermore, it is not clear to what extent they were distinguished from the *perpyriarioi*, a class that was denied freedom. What is certain is that the Lusignans did not allow the survival of the Greek *archontes* as a social class, like in Venetian Crete, or the creation of a *special* class of Greek aristocracy, like in Frankish Morea, that might potentially threaten the stability of their regime. Consequently, the description of the old Greek nobility as a 'second-class aristocracy' is not satisfactory either.[110]

Therefore, cases that could be considered to represent feudal tenures by Greeks must be studied cautiously. Although according to the d version of the *Continuation of William of Tyre*, Guy gave 'rich fiefs, both to Griffons and to knights who came with him', there is no evidence that these fiefs involved feudal privileges and obligations. Moreover, the context of the phrase is not clear and the term 'Griffon' might designate people of Byzantine culture who came from the

---

[109] Papadopoullos (1964: 105–6; 1976: 21–3); Svoronos (1976: 2, 7); Richard (1997: 124, 127, 128); Grivaud (1994: 155).
[110] Hill (1940–1952, II: 8); Papadopoullos (1976: 21ff.); Svoronos (1976: 2, 6, 10); Grivaud (1994: 150–1); Richard (1995b: 354–5).

mainland, while the text, generally hostile to Guy, might be deliberately disparaging of him.[111] In 1197, a certain 'Minas turcopulus',
obviously a Greek by his name, was the former owner of the *casale*
of Livadi which was given to the archbishop of Tyre. It is not
specified if the *casale*, an important one, was the fief accompanying
the position of the turcopole or property previously owned by Minas
and confiscated. The fact that not only the king but also knights
hired their own turcopoles points to local recruitment and argues in
favour of the possibility that this is an example of an old Greek
noble family that was included in the lower Frankish military class
and that some Greeks were enfeoffed too, as the Continuator says.[112]
Whatever the case may be, his constitutes the unique example of
feudal tenure by a Greek that survives in the sources. No Greek
names may be traced amongst the vassals of the Lusignans or amongst
the officers of the crown in the thirteenth century, while the very
few Greek names that survive in family affiliations in the *Lignages
d'Outremer* are not Cypriot.[113] In his autobiography, George of Cyprus,
the future Patriarch Gregory II of Constantinople (1283–89), outlines the situation. He remembers from his early years on his native
island in the 1250s (he was born in 1241/2) that, amongst those of
the Greek ruling aristocracy who had lost their property because of
the Latins, some managed to preserve a life of relative prosperity,
although theirs could not be compared with that of the rich and
powerful. His family suffered equally with the other leading Greek
families, but George himself spent his time hunting and could afford
studying in the Byzantine centres of the time.[114]

It thus becomes clear that the continuity or discontinuity of the
presence of Greek noble families in the thirteenth century must be
studied within the context of the new social conditions created for
them and their ability to adjust to them. The existence of a Greek
upper class should be investigated in terms of their financial situation and social prominence, for which knighthood and enfeoffment
seem meaningless, insofar as feudal privileges and obligations are
concerned (fief tenure, office of the crown, participation in the mil-

---

[111] *Continuation de Guillaume de Tyr*, 139; Nicolaou-Konnari (2002b: 190–1).
[112] *Cartulary*, no. 46. Generally, Richard (1986b: 265) and Savvides (1993: 134–5).
[113] Richard (1976a: 16; 1979: 160); Collenberg (1977b: 105ff.; 1995: 788–800,
app., table A); 'Les Lignages d'Outremer', 463.
[114] George of Cyprus, 177–9.

itary and administrative duties of a liegeman).[115] Moreover, it is important to stress that social rise to the rank of enfeoffed knights usually required the adoption of the Latin rite. Although there might have been a number of cases, no evidence survives earlier than the fifteenth century, unless one considers a certain 'Theodoros the liegeman, called Avrar(tou?)', whose death on Tuesday 21 December 1367 is mentioned in a note in the margins of a manuscript, to be Greek, and 'Sir Thomas Barech, a Greek burgess who became a Latin knight' in the 1380s, to have adopted the Latin rite. Conversion to the Latin rite remained a relatively rare phenomenon, because it involved a complete change of cultural values and group attachment. If in the first half of the fifteenth century Leontios Makhairas condemned in very strong terms the fact that the Orthodox Syrian Thibald Belfarage (= Abul'l Faraj) changed his rite in order to achieve social rise under Peter I and Peter II, by analogy one may easily imagine what the popular reaction would have been in the thirteenth and fourteenth centuries.[116] Consequently, the existence of a Greek aristocracy in the thirteenth century must not be viewed either in terms of the old Byzantine nobility in reduced circumstances, who fought their way up and succeeded at some stage in regaining recognition as noblemen, or in terms of feudal noble status. Within the new social framework, a different kind of Greek upper class emerged that included wealthy, educated Greeks, some of whom may have belonged to the old noble families. This was a process of *kat'oikonomian* compromise and accommodation to the new system of social stratification on the part of some Greek families, who managed to use the new social realities to their own advantage.

The sources provide several examples of Greek landowners, some of whom seem to have been quite wealthy. Donations of land to Greek ecclesiastical establishments in the late thirteenth and first half of the fourteenth century suggest that Greek free peasants were allowed to possess alienable property. Evidence survives concerning donations to the monastery of the Priests in the district of Paphos and to the church of the Holy Cross in the town of Paphos. In 1245, a Nicosia family with apparently Greek Christian names ('Andronicus', 'Theodorus', 'Iohannis', and 'Nicolaus') were granted the house they

---

[115] Collenberg (1982b: 74, 78ff.); Arbel (1989: 181–5 and passim, esp. 184).
[116] The *praktoras* Nicholas Bili (end 14th c.) possibly converted. Darrouzès (1956: 57–8); Makhairas, I, §§599, 579. Generally, Richard (1995b: 355 and note 79).

had built on ecclesiastical property by Archbishop Eustorge of Nicosia.[117] In the early thirteenth century, property expropriated from the island's Venetian community was held by unspecified Greeks. In the town of Limassol, the property included land in the area of St Nicholas, land given to a 'Constantino Colocato', and houses granted to a Greek priest; in Nicosia, a house; and in a village with uncertain name that might be Sylikou in the district of Limassol, houses and vineyards granted to 'villani', probably Greek *francomati*. The nature of the property is not specified, but it probably involved *bourgeoisies* and free tenures.[118] The involvement of Greek priests and jurats in the registration in Greek and the collection of the taxes owed by the landowners of a parish points to the existence of Greek landowners, who paid taxes to the king and whose property was registered in the secrète. Some time in the late thirteenth century, a certain 'Georgios' from Lefkara who lived in Nicosia sold a vineyard he had inherited from his father to another Greek; the sale was registered in the secrète, more vineyards remained in George's possession, and the purchaser bought the land 'in perfect lordship and ownership to sell it, grant it, give it as dowry, exchange it, or do whatever he wants with it', a description that could apply to allodial land.[119]

Moreover, evidence suggests that the Greek churches must have been supported financially by some important families, whatever disruption of patronage resulted from the flight of Greek nobles and the new social and financial conditions of the remaining ones. As Neophytos the Recluse remarked in his *Typikon*, because of the dire economic situation after 1192 the Enkleistra was obliged to acquire property in the early thirteenth century (a small plot of arable land and a vineyard), while apparently it was supported by donations before.[120] According to the narrative *Martyrion Kyprion*, two of the thirteen Greek monks tortured and executed by the Latins in 1231, the Cypriots Ignatios/Gennadios and Gregorios/Gerasimos, were of noble parents, but it is not clear if the narrative refers to their social status before or after 1192. In the late thirteenth—early fourteenth century, an *anagnostes* gave lessons to the children of a 'lord' (αυθέντης).[121]

---

[117] Darrouzès (1951a: 99; 1951b: 42–3, 41, 30, 47, 37, and passim); *Cartulary*, no. 58.
[118] Papadopoulou (1983: §§7, 33, 44, 52, 93, 101).
[119] Lampros (1917: 18; 1921: 340–2).
[120] Neophytos the Recluse, *Typike Diatheke*, 37–8, 48.
[121] *Martyrion Kyprion*, 328; Lampros (1917: 17; 1921: 147).

The anonymous authors of late thirteenth- and fourteenth-century manuscript notes preserve the evidence of generous donations to monasteries, such as the monastery of the Priests in the district of Paphos.[122] In his very old age in ca. 1214, Neophytos mentioned that he borrowed books from 'truly rich' people and commemorated their names in Mass.[123] Also, in his *Foundation Rule* of the monastery of Makhairas which was confirmed in 1210, Neilos, the bishop of Tamasia and former abbot of the monastery, appealed to the '*archontes* of the island' to assist financially the monastery; the term probably refers generally to the 'authorities' of the island at the time (i.e. the Latin rulers), but, contextually and linguistically, one could also attribute the meaning of 'Greek notables' to the word.[124]

Relative artistic discontinuity in mural painting in the thirteenth century compared with the bloom of the twelfth century might be interpreted in terms of the impoverishment of the Greek upper class and the diversion of funds away from the rural centres into the hands of the new Frankish aristocracy in the towns. However, artistic production, albeit reduced, never ceased, and in the late thirteenth century testimonies of patronage reappear and suggest a strong financial situation for part of the Greek population as well as religious and artistic continuity. This was particularly obvious in the rural areas, which were less affected by earthquakes and where life had been less disrupted.[125] At least two important monasteries were founded in the thirteenth century (Trooditissa and Christ Antiphonetes at Kalogrea) and an impressive number of churches, the Enkleistra included, were built, renovated, and/or decorated.[126] Surviving names of patrons include Leo tou Authentou (= lord), who installed a rich cycle of paintings in the church of the Virgin of Arakou at Lagoudera in 1192 and whose name suggests noble origin (although it is not clear if he was a Cypriot or a Byzantine official); John Yerakiotes, son of Moutoullas, and his wife Irene, who sponsored the foundation and decoration of the church of the Virgin at Moutoullas in 1280; Michael, son of Katzouroubes, his wife, and children, through whose

---

[122] Darrouzès (1951b: 42, 49, 47, and passim); p. 45 and note 117 above.
[123] Neophytos the Recluse, *Homily Concerning the Presentation of the Virgin*, 236–7.
[124] Neilos, 61; Neilos, *Rule*, 122, chapter 161.
[125] Carr (1995a: 241ff.). On art see also Carr in this volume.
[126] Papageorghiou (1972); Stylianou and Stylianou (1985: 43, 323, 354, 158, 349, 295, 65, 51, 448, 470, 241, 52, 407, 467); Carr and Morrocco (1991: 99–113).

donation the church of St Demetrianos at Dali was renovated and
painted in 1317; Anastasia Saramalina some time in the late thirteenth
century and a couple and their son (dressed in the Western manner)
in ca. 1300, who sponsored some of the paintings in the narthex of
the Virgin Phorviotissa at Asinou.[127] Unfortunately, we do not know
how expensive the decoration would have been and, by analogy,
how rich these patrons were. It seems, though, that patrons shifted
away from mural cycles to other, less expensive forms such as icons
and manuscripts.

A study of icon painting in Cyprus in the thirteenth century points
to a prolific output of icons produced on the island and intensive
private Greek patronage. The existence of some 20 large icons, designed
for public use in churches, reflects a context of Greek patronage rich
and powerful enough to maintain both the activity of artistic workshops and the development of a 'self-sustaining local manner', the
maniera Cypria; eight thirteenth-century icons survive from the district
of Limassol alone. There survive also instances of communal patronage; the church of the Holy Cross at Pelendri, which was built in
1176, was redecorated in the fourteenth century, probably under
communal patronage as the important number of donor portraits
and the plural form used in the dedicatory inscription indicate.[128]
Furthermore, the continuity of manuscript production (fourteen dated
Cypriot manuscripts have survived from the eleventh/twelfth centuries, six from the thirteenth, and 35 from the fourteenth), especially of the luxurious illuminated manuscripts of the *decorative style*
family still produced until 1240, also suggests the existence of Greek
patronage.[129] Examples of communal patronage are attested in the
sources as well; in 1193, the priests and householders of the village
of Sevouris sponsored a Gospel lectionary; in 1204, the Greek flock
of the parish of St Epiphanios at Kouklia, in the district of Paphos,
also sponsored a luxurious and expensive Gospel lectionary.[130] The

---

[127] Nicolaides (1983: 685–6); Mouriki (1984: 172–3; 1985–1986: 13); Stylianou
and Stylianou (1985: 134–40, 158–9, 167, 178–9, 323, 425–7); Carr and Morrocco
(1991: 92–3).
[128] Mouriki (1985–1986: 58–61 and passim); Sophocleous (1993a); Christoforaki
(1996: 215).
[129] Constantinides and Browning, *Dated Greek Manuscripts*, 49–226 and 'List of
Manuscripts'; Carr (1987–1988).
[130] Darrouzès (1956: 34, 42); Constantinides and Browning, *Dated Greek Manuscripts*,
95, 103–4.

quality of the manuscripts produced as well as the non-religious contents of some of them point to artistic and social continuity and indicate the existence of a class of wealthy, educated Greeks, an intellectual and social elite that would include rich men of letters, such as George Lapithes, in the first half of the fourteenth century.[131]

Only the Christian names of these Church donors and sponsors or owners of manuscripts survive with specification of place of origin, kinship relation, or 'ἐπίκλην' (by-name or nickname). This suggests that there was a new class of wealthy Greeks who were not necessarily the descendants of the old noble families. It would seem that from relatively modest beginnings in the thirteenth century, members of these families succeeded in acquiring economic and social prominence and eventually noble status sometime in the fifteenth century. However, this process of social mobility that started in the thirteenth century was slow and complex and it also involved families that may never have entered the Frankish nobility. Family names that are included in the Frankish nobility at the end of the fifteenth century may be traced from the end of the thirteenth century, but it is difficult to establish family lineage and there is no way of knowing whether persons with identical or similar names belonged to the same family. Furthermore, the identification of Byzantine names found in later sources, and especially of names that go back to the Comnenian aristocracy, is a dangerous endeavour, while the Byzantine names in Stephen of Lusignan's late sixteenth-century list of noble families refer most certainly to latecomers. This is why some of the names that may be traced in earlier sources appear on sixteenth-century lists of nobles and some not.[132] On the basis of whether a family was included in the ranks of the knights or not, Benjamin Arbel believes that families that may be identified with relative certainty as both noble and Greek in lists of nobles of the second half of the sixteenth century are the Synglitico, the Capadoca, the Condostefano, the Podocataro, the Sozomeno, and the Bustron; none of these names are included in Leontios Makhairas' lists of *kavallarides* of the 1370s.[133] It is worthwhile to study in detail all the available

---

[131] Constantinides and Browning, *Dated Greek Manuscripts*, 142–4, 165–7, 187–9, 171–3, and passim; Constantinides (1995: 15–21); Grivaud (1994: 153–4; 1996: 939–41, 1049–54). See also Grivaud in this volume.

[132] Étienne de Lusignan, *Description*, fols. 82v–83v; Arbel (1989: 185–7) for the various lists.

[133] Arbel (1989: 184–5, 187–90); Makhairas, I, §§542, 563.

information concerning members of these families, because tracing the course of their career will allow a better understanding of the processes of Greek social mobility and cultural interaction between the two ethnic groups and of the close association between the two phenomena.

The family names of Kappadokas/Capadoca, Boustronios/Bustron, and Sekretikos/Synkritikos/Syngritikos/Synklitikos/Syngritico/Synglitico may be traced as early as the thirteenth century. In 1318, 'Georgius Capadoca' was the scribe of the royal secrète, competent in Greek, French, and Latin. In 1367, 'Phelipe' and 'Lion Capadoca' were 'apautours', tenants who leased land in Kilani and Lophou. In the late fourteenth/early fifteenth century, 'Loze', wife of 'Lambertos Kontostephanos', was the daughter of a 'Sir Kapadoka'. In 1411, a 'Georgius Capadocius' was 'consiliaris regni'. The family was included in the Frankish nobility in the late fifteenth century and is mentioned in Stephen of Lusignan's list.[134] It has been suggested that the Bustron family was of Syrian or probably Maronite origin, and came to Cyprus after 1291, but historical evidence is in fact lacking.[135] What could be the earliest mention of the family may be traced in Vat. Palat. gr. 367, a manuscript datable to 1317–20; the *bailli* (?) of the village of Knodara was 'ζωαν πουτρ(ου)' (= Jean Boustrou?), a spelling of the name that survives in the fifteenth century as one of the variants of the chronicler George Boustronios' name (Τζώρτζης [Μ]Πουστρούς).[136] Later names and terms of address indicate that the family included both Greek and Latinized members; in 1423, a 'Quir Dimitri Boustron' is mentioned, while in the early fifteenth century an address to the knight 'messire Thomas Boustrou' survives. The family is included in Stephen of Lusignan's list.[137]

The Synglitico family was probably originally one of those families who had traditionally staffed the Byzantine *sekreton/syngriton* and subsequently the Lusignan secrète. Thus, the name most probably had a professional origin, designating an officer of the secrète

[134] Richard (1947: 124, 127, 140); *Documents chypriotes des archives du Vatican*, 79, 81; Darrouzès (1956: 47–8); Collenberg (1982a: 636, 692; 1984: 528); Étienne de Lusignan, *Description*, fol. 82v. Collenberg (1977b: 121, 123; 1984: 542, 627–9) and Arbel (1989: 188) for later references.
[135] Grivaud (1996: 1089); Boustronios, 'Introduction', 253*–7*, 262*.
[136] Lampros (1917: 23); Boustronios, 'Introduction', 35*, 247*–62*, 266*–7*.
[137] *Documents chypriotes des archives du Vatican*, 30; Darrouzès (1950: 176; 1959a: 34); Étienne de Lusignan, *Description*, fol. 82v. Collenberg (1983: 41–6; 1984: 654–5) and Grivaud (1992: 533–41) for later references.

(*sekretikos/sekretarios*) and often attached to the Christian name of such an officer to be gradually adopted as a family name. This is attested by the way its spelling evolved; the thirteenth-century name Sekretikos follows the early form *sekreton*, while the later forms Synkritikos/ Syngritikos/Synklitikos agree with *syngriton*.[138] The earliest surviving mention of members of this family goes back to 5 April 1261 from the obituary of Constantine Sekreticos.[139] Vat. Palat. gr. 367, rich in information on thirteenth-century Cyprus, provides the following names of members of the family: in 1305/6, Theodora, daughter of Constantine Sekretikos, received a dissolution of her engagement from a Greek ecclesiastical court; a 'Ioannis', son of Constantine Sekretikos, bought a vineyard in the village of Lakkoi; a mention of the 'eminent lord' Constantine Sekretikos might refer to the same person as the one(s) before; the names of Nikolaos and Constantine Sekretikos also survive, but it is not not clear if theirs is a family name or an office.[140] In 1317, a 'domino Constancio Singritico' (the same as the one before?) sold a vineyard in 'Piscopio'. On 29 March 1397, the name of a certain George Syngritikos (κήρης ο σηρ Τζόρτζου ο Σηνκγριτικός) was registered for the annual donation of a candle to the monastery of the Priests in the district of Paphos. A 'sir Nikolaos Syngritikos' is mentioned in 1398 in a manuscript marginal note. The physician 'μάστρε Τζουάν Συνγκριτικός'/'mastro Gioan Synglitica' is mentioned by Leontios Makhairas and Florio Bustron in ca. 1425; this is probably the same person as the burgess 'mestre Johan Singritico' mentioned in 1423. The colophon of one of the two manuscripts of the Greek version of the *Assises de la Cour des Bourgeois* was signed by the scribe 'Antonios Sinkritikos' in 1469; in a note, Antonios also mentioned the birth of his son 'Chris(t)ophis' in February 1457.[141] Stephen of Lusignan includes them amongst the most important noble families of the sixteenth century.[142]

---

[138] Lampros (1917: 23); Banescu (1913: 14, 15.6); cf. p. 29 above.
[139] Darrouzès (1950: 170); Chatzipsaltes (1955: 32).
[140] Lampros (1921: 340–2, 348–9; 1917: 48–9, 18); Chatzipsaltes (1955: 27–9, 31–2).
[141] Richard (1947: 129, 151); Darrouzès (1951b: 40; 1958: 238); Makhairas, I, §665, Florio Bustron, 360, Darrouzès (1950: 186); *Documents chypriotes des archives du Vatican*, 30; Darrouzès (1950: 187), Constantinides and Browning, *Dated Greek Manuscripts*, 239, 240.
[142] Étienne de Lusignan, *Description*, fol. 83v. Generally, Collenberg (1977b: 122) and Arbel (1989: 187) and, for later or undated references, Collenberg (1984: 667–8), Arbel (1989: 187, 190 and note 195; 1995: 328ff.), and Constantinides and Browning, *Dated Greek Manuscripts*, 239, note 4, 300.

The well known families of Kontostephanos/Condostefano, Apo-
dehatoro/Apodicator/Apodocator/Podocataro, and Sozomenos/
Sozomeno, identified as noble in the sixteenth century and included
in Stephen of Lusignan's list, seem to have achieved social importance later or are simply not mentioned in the extant thirteenth-century sources.[143] In 1368, the bilingual scribe of the secrète of the
Latin bishopric of Limassol was 'Thodre Condostefano'. In the late
fourteenth–early fifteenth century, 'Lambertos Kontostephanos, son
of the late Stylianos Kontostephanos', who probably came from
Sylikou, is mentioned in several manuscript notes.[144] The earliest
mention of the Podocataro family dates to the year 1367 when a
'Michel Apodicator' is mentioned as the 'apautour' of Vavla. Most
probably, members of the family started out as wealthy town merchants to acquire later important administrative offices; Sir John
Apodehatoro was a rich merchant at the time of King Janus
(1398–1432), and he was probably charged with supplying the Cypriot
army with wine in 1426.[145] A 'Sava Sozomeno' from Limassol is
mentioned in 1367. At the end of the fourteenth century, the sister
of Sir John Sozomenos married Nicholas Bili who later married
Leontios Makhairas' sister. The *praktoras* 'sir Nicol Bili' may have
entered the Frankish nobility in the 1370s according to the testimony of Leontios Makhairas, but the Bili family is not present in
thirteenth or sixteenth-century sources.[146] The Kinnamos family may
have been one of the old Byzantine noble families. The bishop of
Paphos until ca. 1192, when he left for Constantinople, was Basil
Kinnamos. In 1367, 'Johan Quinnamo' was 'apautour' in Sylikou.
A 'Τζουάν Κίναμος' (the same?) is mentioned in two undated notes
of a thirteenth-century manuscript. Another John Kinnamos was
probably a candidate for the episcopal throne of Paphos/Arsinoe in
the second half of the fourteenth century. According to W.H. Rudt
de Collenberg, the family rose to nobility in the second half of the

[143] Étienne de Lusignan, *Description*, fols. 82v–84v; Arbel (1989: 187–90).
[144] *Documents chypriotes des archives du Vatican*, 61, 88, 94, 99, 101, 102; Darrouzès
(1950: 169; 1956: 47–8). Collenberg (1977b: 121, 123) and Arbel (1989: 187) for
later references.
[145] *Documents chypriotes des archives du Vatican*, 80; Makhairas, I, §§661, 678. Collenberg
(1977b: 121, 124; 1984: 650–3; 1993: 135–41) for later references.
[146] Richard (1950: 132); Makhairas, I, §§563, 620, 630, 633. Generally, Arbel
(1989: 184–5) and Pieris and Nicolaou-Konnari (1997: 84) and, for later references,
Collenberg (1983: 32–7).

fourteenth century, but evidence is in fact lacking.[147] The family name Strambali may also derive from the name of a profession, with possible etymology *estrange bailli*; this is suggested by the various spellings of the name in contemporary sources (Stranbailli/Stranbaily/Stranbali/Strambali) and by the intense presence of members of the family in important administrative positions in the fifteenth/sixteenth centuries. It is, however, very doubtful whether the family, first mentioned in the middle of the fifteenth century, was of Greek origin.[148]

The investigation of the lives and careers of members of the above families reveals the existence of a group of educated Greeks, who participated in the royal and seigneurial administration, who achieved social and economic prominence in virtue of their education and linguistic abilities, and some of whom were gradually included in the Latin aristocracy. The new realities created by the 1192 social and political change caused the emergence of this new class of wealthy Greek bureaucrats. The Lusignans had to rely on the old Greek bureaucracy to administer the island, and this necessity was dictated by the lack of Latin human resources and implied the continuity of a Byzantine administrative tradition and probably the survival of some of the old noble families. It is interesting to note that, although most of the members of these families are qualified as κυρ/*quir*, σιρ/*sire*, μεσίρ/*messire* or αυθέντης (lord) in Greek, French, and Latin texts of the thirteenth and fourteenth centuries, they probably belonged to the classes of *francomati* or *perpyriarioi*, since these terms of address suggested social and economic prominence and not nobility. Onomastics and biographical data imply that the family name of these eminent Greek Cypriots derived from and/or was confused with their profession. This is very indicative of the importance attributed to a person's social function in thirteenth- and fourteenth-century Lusignan Cyprus, since any other way of breaking up the social boundaries and achieving social rise (enfeoffment, knighthood, or intermarriage) was largely excluded.

Within this social context, several examples of these Greek bi- or multilingual administrators and bureaucrats may be traced in the sources. Seigneurial administration in the rural areas remained in the hands of specialized Greek officers experienced in Byzantine and

[147] P. 42 and note 107 above; *Documents chypriotes des archives du Vatican*, 79; Darrouzès (1950: 182–4; 1951a: 99–100, 102); Collenberg (1977b: 121).
[148] Nicolaou-Konnari (2002a: 290, 298–301, and passim).

local practices. In 1237, Pope Gregory IX complained that the lords
of the kingdom replaced their Latin *baillis* in their *casalia* with Greeks
and Syrians. In 1317, two of the officers of the *casale* of Psimolophou
were Greeks, the notary 'Georgios Panaguiri' and the jurat 'Basilios
Bougas'. During 1354–56, the administrator of the estate of Walter
of Brienne that included Knodara, Morfittes, and Dichoria was
'Cosmas from Athens, the so-called doctor' and the *catepan* (tax collector) of Morfittes, 'Niquifore Limbiti tis quiras'.[149] Similarly, several
examples of Greeks participating in the royal administration survive
and include the '*apokrisiarios* Zacharias', who most probably worked
in the chancery and was sent as a royal envoy to the Seljuk sultan
in 1216. The fact that Greek continued to be the international language for the kingdom's correspondence and diplomatic contacts with
the Byzantines and non-Latin princely courts and ecclesiastical dignitaries in the Eastern Mediterranean, a practice that was carried
into the fifteenth century, points to the presence of an important
number of Greeks in the chancery. The case of Zacharias mirrors
the identical one of Leontios Makhairas two centuries later, when
the latter was sent on a mission to Asia Minor in 1432.[150] Ample
evidence indicates that Greek *escrivains* staffed the royal secrète as
well. A document of the royal secrète that is written in Greek is
confirmed by the Greek priests, jurats, and landowners of the parish
and witnessed by the Greek *sekretikoi* and the liegeman of the king.
The moral poem *Spaneas* is attributed to 'Georgios, *grammatikos* of the
royal *sekreton*'. In a note datable to 1345/6, a 'Sir Nikolaos, *grammatikos* of the *syngriton*' is mentioned. More examples of the presence
of Greeks in the secrète and the Court of Burgesses have been discussed before.[151] It would appear that gradually these bureaucrats
came from the same group of families of Greek burgesses and thus
formed a tradition of professional civil servants who were competent
in both French and Greek and perhaps Latin and staffed the secrète
in particular and the Lusignan administration in general.

   Furthermore, it must be stressed that the role of Greek clerics in
the Frankish lay administration was instrumental for the creation of

---

[149] Mas Latrie, *Histoire*, III, 642; Poncelet (1934: 14, 16, 24, 28); Richard (1947: 130, 140–1, 148); pp. 24–5 above.
[150] Lampros (1908: 43–54; 1917: 39–41; 1921: 151–2); Mas Latrie, *Histoire*, III, 64–6; Bertrandon de la Broquière, 106.
[151] Lampros (1917: 18, 359.5–6); Constantinides and Browning, *Dated Greek Manuscripts*, 204; pp. 26, 30 above.

those conditions necessary for the social mobility of the Greeks. The fact that the Greek Church was allowed to retain administrative and judicial autonomy on the basis of the 1260 *Bulla Cypria* created the right framework for the existence of various ecclesiastics who were educated and knowledgeable enough to participate in both the Greek ecclesiastical administration and the royal and seigneurial administration. During 1354–56 in Knodara and in 1367 in Limassol, the *catepans* were Greek priests.[152] A certificate for ecclesiastical notaries that survives in a manuscript datable to 1317–20 indicates that this professional group had to be trained for a career in both ecclesiastical and secular administration, which involved competence in a wide range of administrative activities (*taboullarios* and notary, *nomikos* and drafter of contracts).[153]

It would also seem that, as a result of the progressive reduction of the number of the Greek bishoprics and the amalgamation of the old dioceses with the four remaining ones that started in the 1220s, ecclesiastical dignitaries acquired a new-found importance as diocesan *archontes*.[154] A list of these ecclesiastical offices with a description of their duties may be found in the Cypriot versions of the *offikia* of the Byzantine Church, and individuals serving as ecclesiastical and semi-ecclesiastical dignitaries are mentioned in the sources: *protohiereus* or *protopapas, deutereuon, hiereus, chartophylax, anagnostes, protonotarios, notarios, sakellarios*.[155] The fact that most contemporary obituaries written in the margins of manuscripts mention only the names of priests may be the result of the nature and ownership of the manuscripts, but it also points to the social importance of these ecclesiastics as leaders of the community and to a family tradition in the holding of these offices.[156] In several notes in Paris. gr. 1129 there survive the names of such a family of *protopapades, nomikoi, taboullarioi,* and *anagnostes* from Myrianthousa from the second half of the fourteenth century, the *pater familias* and sponsor of the manuscript in 1353 being 'Michael, *hiereus* and *nomikos* of Marathasa and *taboullarios* of the bishopric of Solea'; around 1400 the manuscript was in the possession

---

[152] Poncelet (1934: 16, 21, 24); *Documents chypriotes des archives du Vatican*, 77, 101, 106, 107.

[153] Lampros (1921: 164–5, 342).

[154] Darrouzès (1970: 236; 1979: 20, note 52, 29–30, 36–7).

[155] Darrouzès (1970: 235–6, 556–63; 1979: 90); Lampros (1917: 24–5; 1921: 156–9).

[156] Darrouzès (1956: 55–6) (obituaries dated to 1238, 1268, 1286, and 1287).

of another '*papa* Michael', who was also castellan of Marathasa.[157] At the end of the fourteenth century, a family of priests who served at the church of the Virgin Hodegetria in Nicosia ('Georgios', 'Vasilis', and 'Stylianos') had probably held the office of the jurat in the local ecclesiastical court in a hereditary fashion, and thus adopted *Orkomosiates* as a family name. A tradition in the holding of the post of *nomikos* of Alsos is also attested for another family of priests mentioned in Paris. gr. 1093 between 1382 and 1410; we may assume that this was the practice earlier too. In the second half of the fourteenth/first half of the fifteenth century, evidence survives concerning a family from Letympou that included priests, *anagnostes*, and *nomikoi*.[158]

The cases of Romanos/Romanites, Chartophylax, and Anagnostes constitute good examples of those Greek families that included priests and ecclesiastical or semi-ecclesiastical notables who held offices in the royal and seigneurial administration at the same time and must have played a prominent role among the rural Greek population in particular. It is difficult to identify persons bearing the surname Romanos/Romanites as members of the same family. The name may derive from the Greek word for *porter* (ο ρομανήτης του μοναστηρίου), but it might also indicate origin from Byzantine territory (*Romania*) with the meaning of a *non-Cypriot Greek*; a scribe from Thrace is called 'a *xenos* (foreign) Romanites' in the colophon of a 1251/2 manuscript and a Byzantine slave is described as *Romanites*.[159] The death of a certain 'John Romanites' on 27 April 1294 is mentioned in a manuscript note. On 23 April 1348 and 25 February 1382, donations to the monastery of the Priests in the district of Paphos by Maria and Kali 'Romanito-poulli' are recorded. In the first half of the fourteenth century, the scribe 'Dimitrios anagnostes and romanites' was active on the island. The names of 'Theodoro', 'Georgio', 'Coste', 'Micheli', 'Nicolao', and 'Manoli' 'Romanitis'/'Romathi', inhabitants of Nicosia, are mentioned in 1325 and those of 'Nicolle', 'Pierre', and 'Thodri' 'Romannis'/'Roumain'/'Romain' from the district of Limassol in 1367. The family belonged to the upper echelons of Cypriot society in the fifteenth–

---

[157] Darrouzès (1953: 88, 96–9); Constantinides and Browning, *Dated Greek Manuscripts*, 213–16.

[158] Darrouzès (1953: 87, 89–90, 95–6; 1959a: 39).

[159] Darrouzès (1951b: 39; 1953: 95; 1956: 39; 1957: 135); Constantinides and Browning, *Dated Greek Manuscripts*, 53, 121, 158, 197; Lampros (1921: 337).

sixteenth centuries, but it does not seem to have entered the Frankish nobility.[160]

The name Chartophylax most probably originally designated the ecclesiastical officer described as 'representative of the bishop' in the *offikia* of the Byzantine Church. 'Romanos Chartophylax' was a scribe active from 1315 to 1324. In 1359, 'Ser Michaeli hartofilacha' was the scribe in the preceptory of the Hospital in Cyprus and a tenant of the order's vineyards. The names of 'Nicolle Hartofilaca' from Kivides and 'Jorge Hartofilaca' from Limassol survive in documents dated to the year 1367. According to Leontios Makhairas and 'Amadi', in 1377 a 'messer Thomaso Cartofillaca' was appointed *bailli* of the estates of Queen Eleanor of Aragon; the King of Aragon Peter IV addressed him a letter in 1382, in which he was called 'Thomas Archophileta'.[161] The surname Anagnostes (= lector) creates much confusion because it very often indicates an ecclesiastical office rather than a family name.[162] Scribes and notaries known under this name include the Romanos anagnostes Chartophylax and Demetrios anagnostes Romanites mentioned before, a Michael anagnostes in 1268 and a Basil anagnostes in 1303, Constantine *euteles* Anagnostes, the chief notary of Cyprus (ο πριμμικήριος των κατά Κύπρον ταβουλαρίων), who was active in the second half of the thirteenth century (he already held the office in April 1259), Leon anagnostes (beginning of the fourteenth century), and Gabriel anagnostes, the owner of a Gospel lectionary completed in 1345/6; also, a certain John anagnostes and his nephew Mark anagnostes are mentioned sometime after 1235.[163] The donors in an inscription dated to 1356 on a panel from Chrysaliniotissa church in Nicosia are 'Manuel anagnostes of Xeros' and his wife Euphemia.[164]

---

[160] Darrouzès (1951b: 42, 38); Constantinides (1984–1987: 631–4, 636–8), Constantinides and Browning, *Dated Greek Manuscripts*, 196–7, 204; *Documents chypriotes des archives du Vatican*, 41, 42, 44, 45, 78, 83, 85, 86. Collenberg (1977b: 122, 124; 1984: 647) for later references.

[161] Darrouzès (1970: 556–8, 561); Chatzipsaltes (1955: 27–9); Constantinides and Browning, *Dated Greek Manuscripts*, 144–7 and 'Index of Scribes'; Luttrell (1986: 165, 180–1); *Documents chypriotes des archives du Vatican*, 83; Richard (1950: 132); Makhairas, I, §581, 'Amadi', 487; Mas Latrie, *Histoire*, III, 765.

[162] Lampros (1917: 17; 1921: 147).

[163] Constantinides and Browning, *Dated Greek Manuscripts*, 144, 147, 196–7, 159, 143, and 'Index of Scribes'; Darrouzès (1956: 55–6; 1979: 30–1, 90).

[164] Talbot Rice (1937: 100–3); Carr (1995b: 340–1).

Intercommunal Relations and Ethnicity

The degree of *Romanity*, or participation in the Byzantine *oecumene*, and the reality of the cultural identity of the Cypriots at the end of the twelfth century when the Latins settled on the island must be viewed in terms of both the prevailing Byzantine ideology of the time and their regional particularities. Geographical isolation from the Byzantine centres and proximity to the Crusader States differentiated them from the Constantinopolitans and favoured cultural adaptability and exchanges as well as an attitude of *kat'oikonomian* submission and cooperation when facing incoming foreign ethnic groups. Negative or positive, pre-1192 contacts with the Latins demystified them as the *Other* and allowed the Greeks of Cyprus to acknowledge the compatibility of the two cultures. The post-1191/2 political, social, and demographic changes determined the nature of the encounter between Greeks and Franks on the island and, therefore, the relationship between each group's self-perception. The perception of the *Other*, on the one hand, and culture change and ethnicity, on the other, should be investigated in the context of these changes.[165]

No sharp social discontinuity resulted from the 1192 Latin settlement insofar as the Greeks maintained their demographic superiority and the Lusignans adopted some of the preexisting Byzantine institutions and social structures. From the beginning of the establishment of the Lusignan regime, a long-lasting pattern of social discourse began between the two ethnic groups: the Lusignans balanced the demographic difference and maintained the social and ethnic boundaries through the enforcement of a strictly stratified social system, while the Greeks gradually achieved the penetration of the social frontier through their economic and professional rise, profiting from their participation in seigneurial and royal administration and the enfranchisements of the Greek burgess class in the 1360s. This led to the formation of a new kind of Greek aristocracy, some of whom climbed

---

[165] Cypriot identity defined with relation to the rest of the Greek world and the *Other* is currently an issue of major interest amongst scholars; see indicatively Maltezou (1995), Nicolaou-Konnari (1999; 2000–2001; 2002b: 187–8, 190–4; forthcoming a), the proceedings of a Round Table organised by the Association 'Histoire au présent' in 1995 and meaningfully entitled *'Kyprios character. Quelle identité chypriote?'*, published as vol. 43–44 of the Association's review *Sources Travaux Historiques*, and those forthcoming of the conference 'Identités croisées en un milieu méditerranéen: le cas de Chypre', held in Rouen in March 2004, eds. S. Fourrier and G. Grivaud.

the ranks of the Frankish nobility in the fifteenth century. The destruction of the class of the Greek *archontes* completed soon after the settlement of the Franks on the island meant that there were no leaders to form a resistance against the Lusignan regime, while the fact that the Greeks achieved social rise by means of cooperation with the Franks implied that the Greek upper class never assumed a role of national leader that would create the necessary conditions for uprisings against the Lusignans. This Greek elite assumed thus the role of an intermediary group between the Frankish aristocracy and the Latin burgesses, on the one hand, and the Greek lower classes, on the other, that facilitated cultural exchanges.

Ethnic and social groups are traditionally mutually exclusive insofar as they are consistently endogamous. Therefore, although the Franks always remained a minority, no specific example survives from the thirteenth and first half of the fourteenth centuries of intermarriage between the Frankish nobility, for whom data is available, and the Greeks. But lack of specific evidence concerning mixed marriages, especially at the lower strata, should not be interpreted as proof that such cases did not exist. A regulation of 1251 is directed at 'all Greeks who have received the sacraments of confirmation and marriage' according to the Latin rite, which probably refers to Greeks marrying Franks in Latin churches rather than Greek converts to the Latin rite. Likewise, although there are no stipulations in the *Assises*, the *Bulla Cypria*, or the manuals of family law of the Greek episcopal courts concerning mixed marriages, it seems that many marriages between Latins and Greeks were also celebrated according to the Greek rite, as implied by the fact that they were prohibited by the Latin synod of Nicosia twice, in the 1280s and in 1353. In the *Constitutions of Ranulph*, it was stipulated that marriages between Latins and Greeks had to be celebrated in Latin churches, which may suggest that the contrary had been taking place; as reference was also made to secret marriages, one may infer that probably in some cases Greek priests were willing to marry Latins whom the Latin Church had refused to marry or Latins and Greeks. In 1353, Archbishop Philip of Chamberlhac had to issue restrictions against mixed marriages under certain conditions and to threaten clergy who celebrated clandestine marriages, which again indicates that the Greek rite was followed in many cases of mixed marriages, otherwise the Latin archbishop would not have minded. The archbishop instructed that mixed marriages should be celebrated in Latin churches, the banns should

be read three times according to the customary Latin manner, the
Greek party should first be confirmed according to the Latin rite,
and the children of such marriages were to be brought up in the
Latin Church. It was also forbidden to clergy of both denominations
to administer the sacrament of marriage to members of the other
denomination, and lay persons participating in such marriages were
to be excommunicated. But, gradually, the demographic superiority
of the Greeks together with the drastic reduction in Frankish immigration must have favoured mixed marriages. In the fifteenth century, the papacy was obliged to sanction intermarriage between
Greeks and Latins as well as marriages and funerals for the Latin
population celebrated in accordance with the Greek rite.[166]

Language and religion constituted two of the most important criteria of identification for the Greeks and influenced ethnic awareness
and determined *Otherness*. The study of the different ways in which
the linguistic forms were organized in the multi-ethnic Cypriot society of the thirteenth and fourteenth centuries reveals that sponta-
neous linguistic interaction took place from an early time. To a large
extent this was the result of the fact that the Lusignans did not
exclude either language from any domain of use. The social and
economic advantages involved in language acquisition provided the
Greeks with the necessary motivation to learn French and/or Latin
while the new social and demographic reality of the Franks demanded
the adoption of the local form of Greek as a means of communication with the native population. Although it is difficult to assess
the population proportion and stratum involved, these phenomena
facilitated linguistic diffusion and interaction and, to this effect, the
role of the intermediary group of Greek bureaucrats was very important. Linguistic exchanges also led to the emergence of the Greek
Cypriot dialect as a *lingua franca* for the entire population. The dialect
was formed under the action of French influences that mainly concerned the domains of administrative lexicon and phonetics; it was
used as a textual language in authoritative domains, such as law and
administration and later historiography and literature, thus integrat-
ing cultural and social changes.[167]

[166] *Synodicum Nicosiense*, nos. B.14, C.6, M.I. Generally, Emilianides (1938: 200–7),
Hill (1940–1952, III: 1080–1), Kirmitses (1983: 51), Richard (1995b: 355, note 79),
and Coureas (1997: 308). See also Schabel in this volume.
    [167] Nicolaou-Konnari (1995; 2000b). See also Grivaud in this volume.

The ethnic and sacred nature of religion meant that it was more resistant to change and influences than language. It is thus not surprising that in Lusignan Cyprus religious affiliation defined ethnic and social differentiation and, consequently, inclusion in or exclusion from the Frankish ruling class. Change of rite involved a change of ethnic identity and was a very rare phenomenon; as mentioned above, even cases of converted Greeks by reason of social mobility are hard to trace in this first period of the encounter between Greeks and Franks in Cyprus. For both groups, religion remained the most important criterion of cultural identity, group affiliation, and social differentiation.

In the period under study, a separate ethnic affiliation still existed for each group, but the process of the redefinition of identity towards the formation of a common identity or common traits of identity for at least part of the Cypriot population was well under way. The characteristics of the identity of both groups were not static, but underwent dynamic change related to the close association between national identity and historical and social change and the political choices contingent upon them. The Greeks of Cyprus always considered themselves to be *Romaioi* (= of Byzantine culture, Greek rite, and Greek language), and the ethnic name *Kyprios* conveyed both place of origin and cultural identity, describing them in terms of their Romanity and their particularities. It is, however, difficult to determine when exactly the name *Kypriotis* emerged on the island as an ethnic name that denoted all the inhabitants of Cyprus, both Greeks and Franks, and one that inherited all the national connotations involved in the French *Chiprois* or the Latin *Cyprius* or *Cipricus*. It is attested for the first time in a Greek text from Cyprus in the fifteenth-century chronicle of Leontios Makhairas, but it is very likely that the widespread use of the name, with all the ideological correlations involved, coincided with the culmination of the processes of social and cultural interaction between the Greeks and Franks and the generalised use of the Greek Cypriot dialect by the entire population of the island, phenomena that marked the second half of the fourteenth and the fifteenth century. The name *Kypriotes* defined the Cypriots in terms of their relation to Cyprus as a geographical and political entity; in other words, they were the group occupying the particular space delineated by the island's geographical frontier and forming the kingdom of the Lusignans. Consequently, the name expressed group affiliation and ethnic consciousness, but the identity traits it conveyed did not involve religion, ancestry, or social status, whereas language in the form of the Greek Cypriot dialect seems to have been a condition of ethnic affiliation associated with it.[168]

It is, however, difficult to determine to what extent this national meaning of the name incorporated a linguistic and ethnic reality (the way the entire population of the island perceived themselves in relation to the formation of a *nation* of Cypriots) or simply reflected the attitude of a particular milieu (the Frankish ruling class and the Greek upper class to which Leontios Makhairas belonged), since the extent of the presence of this group in the extant sources is probably misleading.[169] It would thus seem safer to speak of a diversity of identities, corresponding to different social and cultural groups within the Cypriot society. It is still interesting, however, to repeat the incident described by the Breton Lord of Villamont, who visited the island in 1589. Even if one allows for exaggeration, Villamont being a Frenchman, the fact that his Greek Cypriot host is reported to have embraced him in joy when he realized he was from France, 'saying in Italian much in praise of the French, and how since they had lost the Kingdom of Cyprus, the Cypriots had never been well treated, and had lost their liberty', and showing him with pride tombstones of Frankish knights, adding 'that even today the Cypriot Christians availed themselves of the privileges granted to them by the French', is indicative of the positive souvenir that the Lusignan rule had left on the collective memory of the Greeks and of the existence of common group bonds for the Greeks and Franks of Cyprus.[170]

---

[168] Nicolaou-Konnari (2000–2001; forthcoming a); Grivaud (1995: 112–13); Golubovich (1906–1927, II: 200–14).
[169] Nicolaou-Konnari (1998).
[170] *Excerpta Cypria*, 174.

FRANKS

Peter W. Edbury

The inhabitants of the Greek-speaking world had been using the word *Φράγκοι*—Franks—to denote people of Western European origin well before the Frankish conquest of Cyprus in 1191. Typically a Frank would have spoken a Western language and would have been identifiable as coming from one of the kingdoms of the West, but what *defined* a Frank was not language or place of origin so much as religious adherence. A Frank was a Latin-rite Christian who accepted the spiritual jurisdiction of the pope. Writing in Cyprus around the middle of the thirteenth century, Philip of Novara could speak of a *Franc de la lei de Rome*—a 'Frank of the law of Rome'[1]— and it was their confessional allegiance, or *lei*, that the Franks themselves saw as the essential characteristic of their community. That was what set them apart from the other peoples—mostly Greeks, but also some Syrian Christians, Armenians, Jews and Muslims—who lived under their rule in Cyprus.

The Frank therefore was not necessarily a Frenchman. Whereas it is true that many of the Frankish elite in Cyprus belonged to families that originated in France, there were plenty of exceptions. Philip of Novara, for example, had arrived from Novara in Italy in the early years of the thirteenth century, and his heirs were still active as members of the ruling elite in Cyprus in the third quarter of the fourteenth. On the other hand, the infrequency of people of English or German origin is indicated by the presence on Cyprus of families with the surnames L'Englés (= L'Anglais) and L'Aleman. Evidently, when their first ancestors came to the island, these appellations had been sufficient to identify them.

It is also clear that members of the Frankish ruling class spoke French among themselves, and that French was the language of government and the courts. There is a story, which probably originated with Philip of Novara, of a Tuscan knight in Cypriot service killed

---

[1] Philip of Novara, 'Livre', 533.

by some other Cypriots at the battle of Nicosia in 1232 as a result
of a misunderstanding thanks to his poor pronunciation of the French
battle cry.[2] Philip himself, despite his Italian background, wrote in
French and stands out as one of the most accomplished literary figures
of the thirteenth century among the Frankish population; he was also
a highly-regarded pleader—in French—in the High Court.[3] Much
later, in 1396, Oger lord of Anglure, a visitor to Cyprus, commented
that the king, James I, spoke 'good enough French' ('assés bon
françois').[4] It was only in the fifteenth century that the dominance
of French as the language of the ruling class came to an end. By
then it would appear that many nobles were using Greek among
themselves for everyday conversation, but the final eclipse came about
as a result of the influx of Italians and Catalans at the time of James
II's seizure of power in the 1460s and then as a consequence of the
Venetian takeover—*de facto* from the mid-1470s, and *de jure* from
1489. But even in the first two centuries of Frankish rule, there were
sizeable communities of Italians in the ports who presumably would
have spoken their own languages among themselves, and there is
also evidence for a sort of commercial *lingua franca* in use among the
ordinary people in the towns in which Greek, French and Italian
vocabulary and syntax were employed indiscriminately. By its very
nature such usage was not normally committed to writing and so
remains little known, although Professor Jean Richard did find a
commercial account from Cyprus datable to 1423 which appears to
preserve an example of this speech.[5]

Monarchy

Today Lusignan is a sleepy town a few kilometres southwest of Poitiers
in western France. There is a fine twelfth-century church, but little
remains of the castle, which in the fifteenth century was depicted
for the month of March in the *Tres Riches Heures* of the Duke of Berry.
In the twelfth century, however, Lusignan was the centre of a power-

---

[2] 'Amadi', 172.
[3] John of Ibelin, 756, cf. 759. On Philip see also Grivaud in this volume.
[4] Oger of Anglure, 84.
[5] *Documents chypriotes des archives du Vatican*, 22–30. The existence of a commercial
and nautical *lingua franca* influenced by Greek and Italian was a phenomenon experienced by all Eastern Mediterranean peoples; see Kahane, Kahane, and Tietze (1958).

ful lordship where the lords could trace their ancestry in a direct line
of succession back to the tenth century. Ambitious and assertive, in
the 1160s, 1170s and 1180s they frequently crossed swords with their
overlord, King Henry II of England, and his son Richard, to whom
Henry had entrusted the duchy of Aquitaine. What was more, by
the end of the twelfth century successive generations of the family
had acquired an impressive record as crusaders. Hugh VI of Lusignan,
who in the 1080s had fought the Muslims in Spain, had taken part
in the Crusade of 1101 and had been at the battle of Ramleh of
1102. Hugh VII had come to the Holy Land on the Second Crusade
in 1147–48. Then in 1164 Hugh VIII fell captive in Syria and died
a prisoner of the Muslims. The lords of Lusignan were well connected
and could number the counts of Tripoli among their kin in the East.[6]
It should therefore come as no surprise that two of Hugh VIII's
younger sons, both of whom had managed to get on the wrong side
of Henry II, should travel out to the Kingdom of Jerusalem to make
careers for themselves. Aimery of Lusignan had arrived there in about
1170. He speedily rose to prominence in royal service and married
Eschiva of Ibelin, the daughter of a prominent nobleman. His younger
brother Guy did even better. He came out in 1180 and almost immediately wed Sibylla, the widowed sister of King Baldwin IV.

The story of what happened next has been told many times. In
1186 Guy and Sibylla became king and queen of Jerusalem. Guy's
accession had been controversial, and he lacked the support of many
of the nobility. A year later, in July 1187, Saladin, the Muslim ruler
of Egypt and those parts of Syria not in Frankish control, invaded
the kingdom. Guy, who presumably took the view that a resounding
victory over the Muslims would silence his critics for good, accepted
the challenge, but at Hattin, in the battle that followed, the Christian
armed forces in the East suffered their most catastrophic defeat ever.
There were few survivors, and Guy and Aimery were among those
leaders taken captive. Saladin followed up his victory with a rapid
campaign which culminated in October 1187 with the surrender of
Jerusalem. By the end of the year he controlled the whole of the
Kingdom of Jerusalem with the exception of Tyre and some isolated
fortresses. Contemporaries were divided as to whether or not Guy
was to blame for these disasters. When in 1188 he was released, his

[6] Riley-Smith (1995: 31, 39–40).

surviving supporters from before the collapse of the kingdom rallied to his side, while his opponents kept their distance.

In the meantime the pope had called for a new crusade to win back what had been lost. Some of the smaller contingents in what came to be known as the Third Crusade had arrived by the early months of 1189, but the armies led by the kings of England and France and the emperor of Germany were slower to set off. In the summer of 1189 Guy, with the support of many of the crusaders already in the East, began his campaign to regain conquered territory by laying siege to the port-city of Acre. It was a bold attempt to wrest the military initiative from the Muslims and, at the same time, steel a march on his detractors. Had the operation met with early success, Guy might yet have been able to efface the memory of his defeat at Hattin and reassert his leadership of the Christians in the Holy Land. In the event the siege turned into a protracted struggle which only ended two years later, in July 1191, after the arrival of King Philip Augustus of France and King Richard the Lionheart of England. So the glory went instead to the kings and the crusaders from the West, and Guy, whose wife had died in the meantime, had failed to win over the local Franks. Initially Richard was prepared to give Guy his support, but he soon came to realize that leaving him in charge of what remained of the Kingdom of Jerusalem after the crusade was over was not going to work and that he would have to be provided for elsewhere.

In the spring of 1192 Richard imposed his settlement. The throne of Jerusalem and the territories along the coast that the Christians had managed to recover were to go to Guy's leading opponent, Conrad of Montferrat, whose wife, Isabella, was descended from the pre-1187 kings of Jerusalem. Guy was to receive the island of Cyprus, which Richard had conquered on his way to the East the previous year. In May 1191 Richard had seized Cyprus from the Byzantine usurper, Isaac Ducas Comnenos, in a brief campaign which, so far as we can tell, had not been accompanied by any large-scale destruction.[7] It must have seemed a good solution. Cyprus was prosperous and secure behind its natural frontier, the sea. The Byzantine emperor, who would be seen by many as the rightful ruler, was far away, preoccupied by problems nearer home, and in any case he lacked

---

[7] Nicolaou-Konnari (2000a).

a fleet. On the other hand, the Christian possessions along the coast of Palestine and Syria had suffered four years of war and devastation, and, with the ending of the crusade later in 1192, they were held subject to the terms of a truce with the Muslims that would be of limited duration. Jerusalem itself remained under Muslim control. What is remarkable is that Guy was not satisfied and wanted the mainland territories as well. What is perhaps even more extraordinary is that the Christians managed to keep their precarious control of the coastal regions of Palestine and Syria for another hundred years.

So Guy and his brother Aimery arrived in Cyprus in 1192. Their elder brother, Geoffrey, had been in the East during the Third Crusade and had acquired a reputation as one of the heroes of the expedition, but he had returned to the West where his nephew, whom he had looked after during his childhood, was now lord of Lusignan. Guy and Aimery brought with them many of the knights and nobles who had supported them during the siege of Acre, and together these men formed a nucleus for the Frankish regime that now took control. On Guy's death, which apparently occurred towards the end of 1194,[8] Aimery was accepted as his successor. The new ruler was understandably anxious to establish a legitimate basis for his rule, and to this end he made overtures to both the pope and the Western emperor, Henry VI of Hohenstaufen. What the pope did was to institute a Latin ecclesiastical hierarchy in the island with an archbishop at Nicosia and bishops at Paphos, Limassol and Famagusta. This was in 1196.[9] With the island now organized as a province of the Latin Church, it was open for the Western emperor to raise Cyprus to the status of a kingdom with Aimery as the first king. This Henry did without further delay. The kingdom henceforth would be under the suzerainty of the Western empire, and, to emphasize this point, in 1196 Henry sent two of his own bishops to the East to take Aimery's homage. Then, in September 1197, his chancellor, Bishop Conrad of Hildesheim, arrived to crown Aimery king, using regalia that the emperor had provided for this purpose.[10]

---

[8] After 15 August 1194, the date of his sole surviving charter issued in Cyprus; see Mayer (1996: 917–18).

[9] *Cartulary*, nos. 1–4, 8; *Synodicum Nicosiense*, nos. X.1–4. See also Schabel in this volume.

[10] Naumann (1994: 43–6, 167–8).

What all this amounted to was that a younger son of a long-estab-
lished, middle-ranking French aristocratic house had succeeded in
founding a royal dynasty on Cyprus (see genealogical table above,
pp. xiii–xiv). After Aimery's death in 1205 the throne passed through
three more generations until in 1267 his great grandson, Hugh II, died
at the age of about fifteen, and the line of his direct male descendants came to an end. The next king was Hugh II's cousin, another
Hugh, the son of his father's sister who was the wife of the younger
brother of the previous prince of Antioch. Hugh III, or Hugh of
Antioch-Lusignan as he is often known, could trace his paternal
ancestry to another, greater, French aristocratic house, the dukes of
Aquitaine of the early twelfth century. His descendants were to hold
the throne until 1458 when there was a failure of legitimate male
heirs. What happened then was that King John II was succeeded
by his daughter, but she was ousted by her bastard half-brother,
who reigned until 1473 as James II. The dynastic and political crisis brought about by the death of James' infant son in 1474 led
directly to intervention from the Venetian government. For a number of years the Venetians used James' widow, Catherine Cornaro,
as their puppet, but in 1489 they ended the pretence and took direct
control for themselves. No longer was Cyprus an autonomous kingdom. From the 1470s it was one of Venice's overseas possessions
and then, from 1570–71, a province of the Ottoman Empire.

In the course of time the kings of the Lusignan dynasty came to
obtain other royal titles. Soon after his coronation as king of Cyprus,
Aimery of Lusignan married the widowed heiress to the throne of
Jerusalem, and from the end of 1197 until his death in 1205 he
ruled the two kingdoms as king of Cyprus and as king-consort of
Jerusalem. On his death the truncated Kingdom of Jerusalem passed
to his wife's daughter by an earlier marriage. Eventually the rights
to the crown of Jerusalem were acquired by the imperial Hohenstaufen
family with the result that from the late 1220s onwards the kings
were absentees, fully occupied with problems in Germany and Italy.
The kingdom was largely left to its own devices until 1268, when,
with the demise of the last legitimate Hohenstaufen descendant, King
Hugh III of Cyprus came forward to claim the throne of Jerusalem
as the rightful heir. His rights did not pass unchallenged, and in any
case he and his sons can have derived little advantage from them
as the last vestiges of the Christian possessions in Syria and Palestine
were to fall to the Egypt-based Mamluk sultanate in 1291. Nevertheless

the Lusignan monarchs continued to style themselves kings of Cyprus and Jerusalem until the extinction of their dynasty. In 1393 they acquired a third crown, that of Cilician Armenia, although here again the title was purely nominal as Cilicia had been conquered several years earlier.

In Cyprus the Lusignan dynasty headed an alien, Frankish regime. The kings governed the island in a manner designed to suit their own interests and those of the Frankish knights and clerics who surrounded them. But the majority of these people were at least resident in the island, and that meant that most of the agrarian and commercial wealth produced in Cyprus remained there and was not siphoned off for the benefit of outside interests. Similarly it was much to the Lusignans' advantage to put the well-being of their kingdom at the top of their agenda, and that meant that for as long as their island kingdom retained its autonomy, the population's well-being would not be sacrificed to satisfy the demands of an external power. Broadly speaking, what was good for the regime was good for Cyprus as a whole. Admittedly the regime could be harsh and exploitative and many Greeks found the presence and actions of the Latin Church deeply galling, but the Lusignans were able to give Cyprus long periods of peace and stability. Partly this can be attributed to the biological accident that until 1458 there was always a male heir to the throne ready to step into the shoes of his predecessor. Unlike the Kingdom of Jerusalem or the Frankish principality of Achaea and the duchy of Athens, the twin states set up in Greece in the early thirteenth century after the Fourth Crusade, Cyprus was not afflicted by political crises arising from the failure of male heirs. True, there were civil wars in 1229–33 and 1460–64, and clearly the foreign wars of Peter I in the 1360s and perhaps the efforts of Henry II between 1287 and 1291 to defend the last strongholds in the Latin Kingdom of Jerusalem placed a considerable strain on the island's resources. Much more serious were the Genoese war of 1373–74, which deprived the regime of control of Famagusta and left Cyprus under tribute with the result that there was a significant haemorrhage of bullion from the island, and then the Mamluk invasions of the mid-1420s which left the kingdom tributary to Egypt and put the royal finances in serious disarray for a generation. But against these disasters can be set the long periods of relative tranquillity, especially in the first half of the fourteenth century when commerce flourished and the island prospered.

So what were the kings like? No royal portraits or tombs and no crowns or other regalia survive from the thirteenth or fourteenth centuries. We do, however, have royal seals and coins. Until late in the thirteenth century the Lusignans issued a Byzantine-style scyphate electrum coin known generally as the 'white bezant'. It belongs in the tradition of the Comnenian third-hyperpyra, and its name arises from the fact that whereas its Byzantine prototype was originally about eight carats (i.e. one third) gold, the gold content of the Cypriot coins was approximately half that with the result that they have a distinctly pale appearance.[11] The coins show a Byzantine-inspired image of Christ enthroned on the obverse and the king standing, wearing a crown and holding an orb and staff on the reverse. The royal vestments are Byzantine. The earliest coins show the king wearing the chlamys, but from the second decade of the thirteenth century they have the loros. (Henry I is also shown wearing the loros on his seal.)[12] It is open to question whether these representations can be taken as an indication that the kings dressed in Byzantine-style garments on formal occasions. However, at the end of the thirteenth century the mints ceased producing the white bezants and instead began issuing a silver coin with a design modelled on the French *gros tournois*. The *gros* showed the king in Western attire seated on a throne with, on the reverse, the lion rampant that was the Lusignans' heraldic device (Figs. 10–11). A few years later the lion rampant was replaced by the heraldic symbol of the kings' other kingdom, the Cross of Jerusalem.[13] If the iconography of the white bezant proclaimed the king as the rightful successor in Cyprus of the Byzantine emperors, the new silver *gros* asserted that he was a king in the European tradition of St Louis.

There is no doubt that that was how the kings wanted to be seen. At the beginning of each reign they underwent a Western-style coronation ceremony, normally presided over by the Latin archbishop of Nicosia. In the fourteenth century Hugh IV, Peter I and Peter II each had separate coronations, this time in Famagusta, as king of Jerusalem. The kings appointed officers bearing the traditional Western titles of Seneschal, Constable, Marshal, Butler and Chamberlain, and, although the Kingdom of Jerusalem was lost, in the four-

---

[11] Metcalf (1995a: 180–1).
[12] Metcalf (1995b: 369).
[13] Metcalf (1995a: 199–204).

teenth century they also appointed titular officers for that kingdom as well. It is difficult to know how far these officers actually fulfilled the functions that their titles denoted, or whether they simply played a ceremonial role on state occasions. But the fact that they surrounded themselves with princes of the blood-royal and senior members of the nobility bearing these titles is further evidence that the kings were anxious to project a Western European image for their regime. What they did not do was appoint people with Byzantine titles. Their formal charters similarly belonged in the European tradition that the Lusignans would have brought with them from the Kingdom of Jerusalem. There was never any attempt to emulate the Byzantine chrysobull.

So if the monarchs wanted to show that they belonged squarely in the Western tradition of kingship, it is worth considering what sort of attitudes people in the West had towards them. In 1247, at the height of his dispute with the Emperor Frederick II, Pope Innocent IV declared the dependence of Cyprus on the Western empire at an end with the result that the kings could now been seen as fully autonomous.[14] On the other hand, later popes refused to recognize the Lusignans' claim to be kings of Jerusalem and were careful to avoid addressing them with that title in their diplomatic correspondence. In 1302 Pope Boniface VIII, in ratifying the treaty of Caltabellotta which had suggested the possibility of placing an Aragonese prince on the throne of Cyprus, had even shown himself prepared to countenance the idea of dispensing with the Lusignans altogether.[15]

Some idea of the international standing of the monarchy can be gained from noting whom the members of the Lusignan family were able to marry. In the thirteenth century the kings married locally. Aimery had married the queen of Jerusalem, and his son, Hugh I, also married into the Jerusalemite royal family. Hugh's son, Henry I, married the sister of the king of Cilician Armenia and then into the family of the princes of Antioch. Hugh II had been betrothed to the Ibelin heiress to Beirut at the time of his death, and Hugh III, long before his accession and at a time when he was probably not considered a likely heir to the throne, had also taken a member

---

[14] *Les Registres de Innocent IV*, no. 2441.
[15] *Les Registres de Boniface VIII*, no. 5348 at col. 853.

of the Ibelin family as his bride. We have to wait until the fourteenth century before we find the Lusignans marrying Western royalty. In 1315 King Henry II's sister Maria married King James II of Aragon. Two years later Henry himself married Constance, the daughter of James' brother, King Frederick of Sicily. In 1330 Guy of Lusignan, the eldest son and thus heir-presumptive of King Hugh IV, married the French noblewoman Maria of Bourbon. Maria's father, Louis of Bourbon, was a second cousin of the then king of France and a leading proponent of crusade planning at the French court. Guy predeceased his father, and in 1353 the new heir to the throne, the future Peter I, married Eleanor, the daughter of Peter of Ribargoza, a younger son of James II of Aragon. Earlier one of Peter's sisters had married Ferrand, the younger brother of the king of Majorca. In the 1370s Peter II married Valentina, the daughter of the lord of Milan, Bernabo Visconti. Of these unions that of Maria of Lusignan and James II of Aragon stands out as the most distinguished, yet even here James was a widower and his heir was a child by an earlier marriage. In the event Maria bore him no children and may anyway have been past child-bearing age at the time of the wedding. Henry II and Peter I both married into junior branches of the Aragonese royal house, and, though a descendant of St Louis, Guy of Lusignan's bride was even more distantly related to the then king of France. Clearly the Lusignans were not perceived as appropriate marriage partners for the highest rung of Western European royalty; at best they were seen as being on a par with cadet lines.

Traditionally kings were the leaders of their people in war, but here the Lusignans' record was distinctly patchy. Aimery (1196–1205) and Hugh I (1205–18) both engaged in warfare against the Muslims, although in each case their reigns coincided with substantial periods of truce. Henry I (1218–53), whose minority ended in 1232 at the time when Cyprus was in the middle of the Civil War of 1229–33, seems not have gone on campaign in person except for a brief period with St Louis at the start of his ill-fated Egyptian campaign of 1249–50. Hugh II (1253–67) never reached his majority. Hugh III (1267–84), on the other hand, does seem to have been prepared to take an active role in the defence of Latin Syria, so much so that in 1271, after a series of expeditions in the 1260s to defend Acre from the attacks of the Egyptian sultan, Baybars, his vassals refused to serve outside Cyprus. The dispute was settled by compromise, but never again did Hugh lead Cypriot troops on campaign against the

Muslims, and the latter part of his reign was dominated by his futile attempts to recover Acre from the partisans of his rival, Charles of Anjou. At the start of his reign Henry II (1285–1324) was confronted with the need to defend first Tripoli (1289) and then Acre (1291), but, although he was present at the siege of Acre, he left before the final assault. For the rest of his reign, the longest of any Cypriot king, he avoided any personal involvement in warfare. With Hugh IV (1324–59) we are faced with a problem. We know that during his reign Cyprus was heavily involved in naval leagues directed against the Turks in the Aegean and that the rulers of the Turkish emirates of southern Anatolia paid the king tribute. What we do not know—and this is largely down to the lack of any detailed narrative account of the reign—is how far Hugh himself took the lead.

The next king, Peter I (1359–69), stands out as by far the most martial of any of the Lusignan monarchs. His campaigns to Antalya and Alexandria and his other raids on the coasts around the Eastern Mediterranean impressed contemporaries[16] but overburdened the island's resources. Peter evidently set much store by being able to attract Western nobles into his service. As if to emphasize his military intent he was shown on his coins holding a drawn sword instead of a sceptre, and in an attempt to appeal to contemporary chivalric values he founded his own secular order of knighthood, the Order of the Sword.[17] Ultimately the strain on the royal finances coupled with the prospect of military failure in his war against the Mamluk sultanate were to lead to his murder. His son, Peter II (1369–82), had barely come of age when Cyprus was invaded by the Genoese.

The kings were of course responsible for the defence of their realm, and to this end they spent what we can assume was a significant proportion of their income on maintaining their armed forces and keeping their castles in a state of readiness. As we shall see the nobility had military obligations, and it would seem that they and their retinues continued to form a major element in the royal army: writing of the events of 1373 the historian Leontios Makhairas told how the king summoned his knights and vassals 'to come with their horses, weapons and men to do the service they owed for their fiefs'.[18] We

---

[16] For example, Guillaume de Machaut, *La Prise d'Alixandre*, and Geoffrey Chaucer, *Canterbury Tales*, 17, 194.

[17] Metcalf (1995a: 207); Boulton (1987: 241–8).

[18] Makhairas, I, §418.

know less about those troops that kings retained on a permanent footing. There are a number of references to 'stipendary knights' in the account of the events surrounding the rule of Amaury of Tyre between 1306 and 1310, and many of these men would appear to have belonged to families headed by feudatories.[19] Evidence for tur-copoles—men who were armed and equipped as mounted archers in the Turkish fashion—and foot soldiers is even more elusive. We also have scant information about the kings' naval resources. It looks as if what normally happened was that they would lease ships and their crews from the Italians when required rather than maintain a permanent navy of their own. There was a naval arsenal at Famagusta which acted as a depot for naval stores and where small boats could be built, and also a military store there known as the *zardehané*.[20]

The kings did not possess castles of a scale to rival the greatest Crusader fortresses of Syria and Palestine. They enlarged the mountain-top castles of St Hilarion, Buffavento and Kantara that they inher-ited from the Byzantines, and rebuilt the castles at Nicosia, Limassol, Famagusta and Kyrenia (Figs. 2–5). No trace now remains of the castle at Nicosia, and even the line of the medieval walls is largely a matter for conjecture, but at Famagusta and Kyrenia substantial remains of the Lusignan fortresses remain encased in the later Venetian masonry. At Paphos the Lusignans built a small castle soon after their acquisition of the island, but it was thrown down in an earth-quake in 1222 and never rebuilt.[21] At Nicosia, Famagusta and Kyrenia there were town walls, and we know that at Famagusta these were being built, or at least strengthened, in the first decade of the four-teenth century.[22] In Nicosia the castle doubled as the royal palace. Kyrenia Castle, which from the narratives of the civil wars of 1229–33 and 1460–64, as well of the Genoese invasion of 1373–74, would seem to have been one of the strongest points in the whole island, was used as a prison. Among those incarcerated was a certain John le Miège who in 1343 whiled away his time making the sole sur-viving copy of the enormously informative history of the Lusignan regime known to posterity as *Les Gestes des Chiprois*.[23] Buffavento was

[19] 'Amadi', 259, 264, 266, 269, 275, 294, 337.
[20] John of Ibelin, 801; *Documents chypriotes des archives du Vatican*, 40–9.
[21] Megaw (1994). I am not persuaded by the author's suggestion that the castle at Paphos was built by the Hospitallers.
[22] Edbury (1995b: 339).
[23] Philip of Novara, *Guerra*, §§139–40 (235–6). See also Grivaud in this volume.

also used as a prison; it was there, for example, that a knight named Anseau of Brie was confined when in about 1308 he first learnt of the charges against the Templars.[24] St Hilarion, or to give it the contemporary name, *Deudamor*, was of particular strategic importance as it lies close to the pass through the mountains linking Nicosia to the coast at Kyrenia; it contains what appear to have been substantial residential quarters (Fig. 6), and it is assumed, though on no very sound documentary evidence, that it served as a summer retreat for members of the royal family. It was certainly used by both sides as a place of refuge during the war of 1229–33.[25]

In keeping with Western ideas of monarchical government the kings surrounded themselves with noble counsellors. Taking advice was an essential element in rulership. The monarch could draw on the collective wisdom of his men, but he would also need to secure their support in major decisions. The kings of Cyprus were not despots, and the ideal to which they aspired entailed ruling in cooperation with their senior vassals. They also needed to be able to delegate responsibilities. It was only to be expected that the kings would rely on members of their own family and on the wealthiest of their nobles, but, if they wished, they could also pick and choose their advisers from among the lesser members of the knightly class, from the clergy and also from people from outside Cyprus. Indeed, in the fourteenth century the kings regularly included an Italian trained in Roman Law among the men who comprised their retinue, and Peter I employed his Italian physician, Guido of Bagnolo, in a position of trust as a counsellor and diplomat.[26]

Kings could take advice from whom they wished, and no king would want to have counsellors forced upon him. The royal council should therefore not be confused with the High Court. Every royal vassal had the right and, when summoned, the duty to attend the High Court. It was there that the formal legal business of government was conducted, and it operated on the principle that what was done there was committed to the collective memory of its members for future reference. So, for example, it was at the sittings of the High Court that the king would take the homage and fealty of

[24] *Processus Cypricus*, 160.
[25] Philip of Novara, *Guerra*, §§34 (130), 49 (145), 73 (169), 81 (177); 'Estoire de Eracles', 369, 377.
[26] Livi (1918).

his vassals and that he would make grants of property, ratify treaties and issue laws. The other function of the High Court was as a judicial tribunal for the king and his vassals. It was there that the vassals could engage in litigation among themselves and try to enter claims against the king if they believed he was depriving them of something that was rightfully theirs. The laws and procedures that operated in the High Court copied those used in the Kingdom of Jerusalem.[27] Customs governing tenure and inheritance were clearly conservative and remained in force throughout the centuries of Lusignan rule and on into the Venetian period. Those having to do with criminal matters were more problematic. Once set in motion the procedures in cases of murder, homicide, treason, assault and disputes over property worth more than a mark of silver (the equivalent of 25 white bezants or 50 silver *gros*) would end in trial by battle and the death of one of the litigants. It has to be assumed that in most instances either the parties would reach an out-of-court settlement before the case came to its natural conclusion, or the presiding officer would stop the trial. As a judicial procedure, its operation seems antiquated, even by the standards of the thirteenth century, and it may well be that claimants increasingly sought redress by petitioning the king for trial in accordance with Roman Law principles.

In Cyprus, as in other kingdoms, there was plenty of opportunity for service. The kings needed knights on whom they could rely to act as castellans and as provincial governors. A knight with the title of viscount or *bailli* would preside in the burgess courts, the tribunals that dealt with non-noble Cypriots, and would be generally responsible for safeguarding the king's interests in the locality. Kings expected their vassals to take the lead in military activities and also to act as envoys and administrators. The royal secretariat or chancery as it was known was headed by a chancellor who certainly until well into the fourteenth century was a member of the Latin clergy. Royal finance was a matter for the secrète. The name of this department of state betrays its Byzantine origin, and, although the staff were Greek Cypriots, its head was a Frankish knight.

---

[27] Philip of Novara, 'Livre', 478; John of Ibelin, 755. See also Grivaud in this volume.

Nobility

In the thirteenth century it was believed that Saladin had counselled Guy of Lusignan that if he wanted to keep control of Cyprus he should give it all away.[28] In other words, Guy should share the island's resources with as many supporters as he could find so that, by maximizing the number of Frankish settlers with a vested interest in keeping his regime in being, he would have the necessary manpower to overawe the indigenous community and defend his realm against attack. Whether Saladin actually gave Guy that advice or whether, as is likely, it is simply an example of historical myth-making is open to question, but there is no doubt that Guy and Aimery brought with them to Cyprus significant numbers of settlers from Latin Syria. In common with the Lusignans themselves, many of these people were men and women who had been dispossessed by Saladin's conquests. The dominant group were those knights and nobles who had backed Guy of Lusignan during and after the siege of Acre. Some would have been members of his household, and, of these, some, like the Lusignans, had origins in Poitou.

Not surprisingly these settlers brought with them the legal and social customs that had developed during the previous century in the Kingdom of Jerusalem and with which they were familiar. By the late twelfth century knightly society in Latin Syria was underpinned by a system of feudal tenure.[29] The knight's principal source of income would be a fief—perhaps a landed estate, perhaps an annuity assigned against a particular source of royal or seigneurial revenue, or perhaps a combination of the two—and he would hold this fief in return for performing specified services. It was thus a conditional grant, and, if the holder failed to fulfil his side of the contract, the lord could, with the agreement of his court, revoke the grant and expel him from his property. The knights were by definition a military elite, and their services were essentially military. Before taking possession of his fief, a knight would have to perform homage and swear fealty. That meant that in addition to being the king's subject in a general sense, he was specifically the king's vassal, a man who in a public ceremony had indicated his personal subordination

---

[28] *Continuation de Guillaume de Tyr*, 138–41.
[29] Edbury (1998b).

to the king and had sworn to defend him and his interests come what may. The king could, if he wished, grant a fief free of services, but the recipient would still be expected to do homage and fealty and so show the same degree of loyalty.

By the time of the Frankish settlement of Cyprus in the late twelfth century, the knight had evolved from being simply a man who served in his lord's army as a mounted warrior to someone whose rank placed him in the social elite. Being a knight had always implied a military vocation, but, combined with wealth and descent from ancestors of comparable standing, it had now acquired a status that conferred nobility. Holding a fief, serving as a knight in the lord's host, performing homage and fealty, going through the initiation ritual of being 'dubbed a knight', and being able to claim 'gentle' birth set this elite—this nobility—apart from other men. Among other things it meant that knights were conscious of their own social superiority with the result that it is rare to encounter any upward mobility into their class from below. On the other hand, knights from outside Cyprus, whether from mainland Syria or from Western Europe, were acceptable, not least because they shared the same chivalric ethos. To preserve their exclusivity knights would find their marriage partners in those families they considered their equals, and this resulted in the emergence of a fairly small group of closely interrelated families that dominated noble society.

Within this fief-holding elite there were of course social gradations related to wealth or kinship. Most knights held their fiefs from the crown, and even those who did not still owed liege homage to the king. In theory the act of liege homage by the vassal of a lord meant that should the lord rebel against the king, the vassal was to side with the king against him. In actuality this sort of situation did not occur in Cyprus. However, what liege homage did do was give the rear vassals the right to engage in litigation in the High Court and to share in that court's deliberations. Indeed, for all vassals participation in the business of the High Court was just as much a requirement of vassalage as participation in the royal army. The vassals would sit in judgement, would take collective responsibility for the decisions of the court, and would be expected to recall what they themselves had witnessed being done there in the past.[30] They might

---

[30] For example, Philip of Novara, 'Livre', 496–7.

be called upon to act as summoners or take part in a delegation from the court sent to investigate a particular claim, and those with a thorough understanding of court procedures and the substance of the law would act as counsel for litigants or as *avantparliers* for witnesses. To the extent that all vassals had both a duty and a right to take part, there was a measure of equality between them. In Cyprus this sense of egalitarianism was heightened by the fact that no nobleman held a fortified town or a fortress of any military significance as part of his fief, and no nobleman had a court of his own in which his own vassals could be judged or in which public justice could be dispensed. So although wealth and family connections together with the prominence of individual members in military affairs or in government service might give a particular family greater distinction and greater influence, with the result that lesser men could be readily overawed, in theory at least no noble enjoyed any special legal privilege.

These last points indicate a significant difference between Cyprus on the one hand and the Kingdom of Jerusalem and the Frankish principalities in southern Greece on the other. In Cyprus there were wealthy nobles but no militarized lordships. All the fortresses belonged to the king, with the exception of the small castles owned by the Templars at Gastria and the Hospitallers at Kolossi (Figs. 7–8: the present structure at Kolossi was built in the mid-fifteenth century, and, although solidly built, was not of any major military significance; there is no reason to believe that the previous fortress on the same site was any more substantial). In the Kingdom of Jerusalem and in the Principality of Achaea, as in Western Europe, lords commonly held important castles which might on occasion serve as bases for rebellion or civil war. But in Cyprus, without the security offered by privately owned fortifications, armed resistance to the king on the part of a noble was virtually unheard of. At most a lord would have had a fortified tower or country residence that would offer security against marauders, but no more. A concomitant to the absence of seigneurial castles was the absence of juridical franchises. In Cyprus no lord controlled the administration of public justice in his locality. All courts for freemen and all courts in which penalties of death or mutilation could be imposed belonged to the crown. (The one major inroad into this royal monopoly of justice was, as in Western Europe, that cases of heresy and matrimonial or testamentary matters belonged to the Church courts.) By contrast, in the Kingdom of Jerusalem the greater lords all had responsibility for defence within their lordships—

hence the control of the castles—and also responsibility for justice. They controlled the local burgess courts and also had courts for their vassals in which they could impose the death penalty should the occasion demand.[31] In Cyprus nobles did not have these rights. They or their stewards could discipline the unfree peasants on their lands. Otherwise justice was the prerogative of the crown.

Feudal tenure and vassalage were the preserve of the Franks. Kings and lords did not give fiefs to members of the indigenous popula-tion—at least not before the fifteenth century. The two earliest exam-ples known to me of Greeks or Syrians becoming knights and receiving fiefs date to the late fourteenth century, and it is significant in this respect that the individuals concerned, Thomas Barech and Thibald Belfarage, were both converts to the Latin rite.[32] So fief-holding was an exclusively upper class affair. The terms and conditions under which fiefs were held, the rules of inheritance, the position of heiresses and widows and the residual rights that a king or lord had over the fiefs of his vassals were of interest only to the Franks. The vassals came to regard the customs governing their fiefs and their relation-ship with their lords as privileges to be defended against encroach-ments from the king or from any third party. So for example, when in 1369 the vassals murdered King Peter I, it is clear that a major reason, or at least a major justification, for their action was the per-ceived threat to their privileged status. As we have seen, the High Court was the king's court for his vassals. It was there that the Frankish vassals would take their disputes over the inheritance of fiefs, and there that the king would deal with men who had failed to perform feudal service or had behaved in ways that might seem to constitute a breach of fealty. It was also in the High Court that vassals accused of murder, assault, theft or other crimes would be arraigned. But here again the vassals had a significant advantage: no one who was not himself a Frank—a man *de la lei de Rome*— could bear witness in the High Court against a Frank.[33] Those who were not vassals, whether Franks or Greeks, would normally find justice elsewhere, in one of the burgess courts established in each of the principal towns.

---

[31] Edbury (1997a: 155–62).
[32] Makhairas, I, §§568, 579, 599.
[33] Philip of Novara, 'Livre', 501.

Many fiefs consisted of rural estates. Thus for example, in the early fourteenth century the titular lord of Beirut held Lapithos, the count of Jaffa, Peristerona in Morphou and Episkopi, the prince of Galilee, Akaki, and a knight named Raymond Viscount, Nisou.[34] Other lands belonged to the Latin Church and religious corporations—bishoprics, monastic foundations and the military orders—but the largest single land holder was the king. Whereas there is evidence for Greek churches and monasteries keeping at least some of their endowments, there is no certain evidence for major Greek lay landowners retaining their rural estates after the initial Frankish settlement in the 1190s and being absorbed into the feudal structure of society as happened in parts of Frankish Greece after the Fourth Crusade.[35] Some Frankish knights had fiefs comprising an income assigned against a specified source of royal revenue such as a royal estate or the taxes levied on trade from a particular town. Many vassals owned urban properties which they either used to accommodate themselves and their families or rented out, but whether they held them as part of their fiefs or had full rights of ownership appears to have varied.

In the second quarter of the fourteenth century a German pilgrim, Ludolph of Sudheim, stated that the nobility lived in Nicosia.[36] But evidently not all of them, or at all times. The principal narrative for the political crisis of 1306–10 speaks of knights of Paphos and Limassol, although it is not clear whether they actually resided in these towns or in nearby rural residences, or had simply been stationed there as part of the local garrison. But at least some nobles definitely had residences on their rural estates. For example, in 1302 the count of Jaffa, Guy of Ibelin, was staying at his house at Episkopi when he and members of his family were captured by pirates, and in 1308 Philip of Ibelin, the seneschal of Cyprus, was banished to his estate at Alaminos. A generation later we hear of Hugh IV's daughter going to stay with her aunt at the village of Colota to the north of Famagusta.[37]

---

[34] 'Amadi', 267, 295 (Lapithos); Edbury (1975–1977: 50) (Peristerona); 'Amadi', 238 (Episkopi), 384 (Akaki), 285 (Nisou).

[35] For a review of the evidence suggesting some tenurial continuity from Byzantine times, see Grivaud (1994). On Greek church property, see Schabel in this volume; for the landed class, see Nicolaou-Konnari.

[36] Mas Latrie, *Histoire*, II, 215.

[37] 'Amadi', 238, 263, 265, 272–3, 325; Mas Latrie, *Histoire*, II, 186.

Just as the Lusignan kings were keen to present an image of themselves that conformed to the ideas of monarchy prevalent in the West, so too the nobles were anxious to adopt the European chivalric ethos. Young nobles learnt requisite etiquette through serving their elders. Philip of Novara recounts how as a young man he was in the service of a Cypriot knight named Peter Chappe at the siege of Damietta in 1218–19. He was required to read romances aloud to Peter and his guests, and it was his skill in reading that ultimately was to be responsible for Ralph of Tiberias, the leading legal expert of his day and a veteran of the Third Crusade, instructing him in the laws of the Kingdom of Jerusalem.[38] What those romances were we can only guess, but there is reason to believe that a few years earlier Robert of Boron, the author of the *Roman de l'Estoire dou Graal*, had been in Cyprus in the entourage of Walter of Montbéliard, the brother-in-law of King Hugh I and his regent in the years 1205–10.[39]

The Arthurian theme turns up again on Cyprus a few years later, in 1223. In that year John of Ibelin, lord of Beirut, one of the most powerful nobles in the Latin East and brother of the then regent of Cyprus, held a celebration to mark the knighting of his two eldest sons. It was clearly an extravagant affair with feasting, gift-giving, jousting, and enactments of the story of Brittany and the Round Table. Unfortunately it is not entirely clear from the description whether this was a stage-play, in which case it appears to be the earliest known instance anywhere of the performance of an Arthurian story, or whether it was the participants in the jousts who dressed as characters out of the Arthurian cycle, in which case that too is a first.[40] Philip of Novara, to whom we are indebted for this detail, later alluded to the story of Guillaume d'Orange in a way that assumes that his readers would be familiar with it, and he also satirized his political opponents in verse as characters out of the tale of Renard the Fox.[41] These insights into the cultural world of the Cypriot nobility are all too few. But clearly the nobles were accepted by their counterparts in the West as equals. Philip of Novara's treatise on knightly behaviour, *Les quatre ages de l'homme*, circulated in the West, and, writ-

---

[38] Philip of Novara, 'Livre', 525. On literature in general, see Grivaud in this volume.
[39] Nicholson (2001: 151 and note 105).
[40] For alternative views, see Keen (1984: 93) and Jacoby (1986a: 163, 166).
[41] Philip of Novara, *Guerra*, §§16 (112), 46–8 (142–4), 54–7 (150–3), 64 (160).

ing of the events of 1250, John of Joinville, who as the hereditary seneschal of Champagne was well placed to comment, described Guy of Ibelin, the constable of Cyprus and another of John of Ibelin's sons, as the 'most accomplished knight I have ever seen'.[42]

It is clear that many nobles were enthusiasts for falconry and hunting. In his description of the siege of St Hilarion Castle in the winter of 1229–30, Philip of Novara noted that many of the knights had left the fighting to go to their estates and fly their falcons. In his history of the Civil War of these years, Philip's sole reference to the Greeks of Cyprus is to a falconer in a context which would seem to mark his respect for their expertise in this field.[43] Writing ca. 1340, Ludolph of Sudheim described how the nobles and knights, whom he claimed were the richest in the world, spent their entire income on hunting: the count of Jaffa had 500 dogs, and another noble employed ten or eleven falconers; some would go off hunting in the woods and hills for a month at a time, when they would live in tents and have their food and other necessities brought up on camels and other beasts of burden. Maybe Ludolph exaggerated this obsession with hunting, just as he presumably exaggerated when he spoke of daily tournaments, but we know from other sources that even the nobly-born bishop of Limassol in the 1360s had three falconers in his household, and that it was a quarrel over a pair of Turkish greyhounds involving the future Peter II and the son of one of the nobles that was one of the incidents that led to the murder of Peter I. Not long after Ludolph's visit the count of Jaffa incurred the wrath of King Hugh IV, and the king had his property, including his falcons, greyhounds and hunting dogs, sold off for a fraction of their value. Contemporaries also mention hunting wild sheep with trained leopards, and in the 1280s Archbishop Ranulph found it necessary to issue a prohibition on monks hunting or possessing hounds or falcons.[44] In the 1220s a knight named Gauvain of Chenichi went to Europe and, as someone who knew much about falcons, was honoured at the court of the Emperor Frederick II whose own book on the subject, *De Arte Venandi cum Avibus*, is justly famous. In the second half of the fourteenth century treatises on falconry were composed in Cyprus,

---

[42] John of Joinville, ch. 66.
[43] Philip of Novara, *Guerra*, §§52–3 (148–9), 57 (153) line 179.
[44] Mas Latrie, *Histoire*, II, 201, 215; Makhairas, II, 133, note 3; *Synodicum Nicosiense*, no. B.16.

although sadly these have not survived.[45] Henry II and Hugh IV
both issued ordinances on the recovery of lost hawks or hounds. The
penalties for keeping escaped falcons or hunting dogs were severe,
but on the other hand the owner was obliged to make generous
compensation to the finder for his trouble; the owner of a fully grown
falcon would pay the finder exactly half what he would have had
to pay the man who had apprehended his runaway adult male slave.[46]

We are left with an impression of a nobility that was wealthy, cul-
tured and keen to conform to the norms of chivalric behaviour current in the West. What was missing was military might. No castles
and, so far as can be ascertained, no appreciable military retinues
meant that the nobles had to work with the kings rather than against
them. The king was the greatest source of patronage. That meant
that there was much to be gained by loyal service, whilst, as the
surviving supporters of Amaury's coup of 1306 were to discover to
their cost when Henry II returned to power four years later, kings
could be vindictive to those who opposed them. It is arguable that
the Arthurian cycle of medieval romances in certain respects provided a model for the relationship between the king and his nobility. In the fictional narrative, Arthur is largely content to sit back
and allow the heroes of his Round Table to achieve feats of arms
and perform deeds of honour that redound to his praise and to the
renown of his whole court. In the real world of Cypriot high politics,
where reputation in the eyes of the West counted for much, the
kings wanted men of distinction around their throne whose prowess
would add lustre to the regime. It is no exaggeration to say that the
Frankish kings needed Frankish nobles so that they could bask in
their reflected glory. A king who was king only of poor knights, serfs
and artisans would cut a very poor figure in the eyes of contemporary observers. Far from being a threat to the king, the aristocrats
of Frankish Cyprus played an essential role in the projection of the
kingdom's image to the world. As we have seen, writing of the events
of the mid-thirteenth century, John of Joinville spoke highly of the
constable of Cyprus, Guy of Ibelin. He was also impressed by the
conspicuous display exhibited by Guy's cousin, John of Ibelin count
of Jaffa, both at the start of Louis IX of France's Egyptian cam-

---

[45] Richard (1963: 898–9); Jacoby (1986a: 164).
[46] John of Ibelin, 795–6.

paign in 1249 and later when the French king came to Jaffa.[47] When
in 1328 King Hugh IV granted the Venetians a new commercial
privilege, the document was witnessed by his chancellor, who was
the archdeacon of Nicosia, along with some other cathedral dignitaries
and a no doubt intentionally impressive list of lay witnesses:
the constable of the Kingdom of Jerusalem, the lord of Arsur (a
direct descendant of the men who had held that lordship in the
Kingdom of Jerusalem until the 1260s), the marshal of Jerusalem,
the marshal of Cyprus, the admiral of Cyprus, the *bailli* of the royal
secrète, the butler of Jerusalem and three other royal counsellors,
one of whom was the *marescalcus hospicii regii*, the controller of the
king's household. Fourteenth-century visitors to Cyprus such as
Ludolph of Sudheim were impressed by the wealth and display of
the aristocracy.[48]

In 1374, however, the old nobility suffered a major blow when
the Genoese carried off into captivity over seventy knights, most of
them from families long established in the island.[49] It would seem
that many of these men never returned. James I (1382–98) deliberately
set out to make good the losses, giving chosen vassals either
high-sounding but largely meaningless offices such as that of marshal
of Jerusalem or chamberlain of Armenia, or awarding them
titles to long-lost lordships in Syria or Palestine, including the principality
of Galilee and the lordship of Bethsan.[50] Cyprus was clearly
impoverished by the war with Genoa of 1373–74 and by the subsequent
demands for ransom and tribute, but at least the king could
now give the impression that once again there was a lustrous aristocracy
around his throne.

The Franks of Cyprus produced no saints who were recognized
throughout Western Christendom. Peter Thomae, the papal legate
on Peter I's crusade to Alexandria, who was buried in the Carmelite
church in Famagusta in 1366, was beatified, but he was an outsider.
The cult of St John of Montfort only seems to have become prominent
in Nicosia in the fifteenth century and commemorated a French
nobleman who had come to Cyprus on Louis IX's crusade of 1249–50
and had died there before the ill-fated expedition had embarked for

---

[47] John of Joinville, ch. XXXIV, C.
[48] Mas Latrie, *Histoire*, II, 143–4, 215.
[49] Mas Latrie, 'Nouvelles preuves (1873)', 80–4; Makhairas, I, §542.
[50] Edbury (1995a: 140–1).

Egypt.[51] The Franks endowed Latin churches and founded a wide range of religious establishments. The impression is left of a community whose religious beliefs and activities, despite the crusading ethos that was laid upon it, were decidedly conventional. Anecdotes that illustrate Frankish spirituality on Cyprus are rare: one of the lay witnesses at the trial of the Templars in 1311, a knight named Raymond of Beirut, told the inquisitors how, as a guard, he had attended Mass celebrated by a Templar chaplain after the arrests and, at the elevation of the Host, the Host in the hands of the priest appeared greatly enlarged; he later considered this to have been a miracle intended to teach him that the brothers of the Temple were innocent of the charges against them and that it was all right for him to associate with them.[52]

In the mid-fourteenth century we hear of complaints that the Frankish nobles were not paying tithes, that they were preferring to hear Mass, marry and have their children baptised in private chapels in their houses rather than attend the divine office in Nicosia Cathedral, and that their women were attending Greek-rite or other Eastern churches.[53] Fear that the beliefs of individual Franks might be affected by un-Roman ideas and practices taken from the Greek community or from the other Eastern churches seems to have been commonplace, but, although the compilation of texts known as the *Synodicum Nicosiense* includes a number of references to heresy, none of the conciliar decrees it contains alludes to specifically Western heresies.[54] These decrees also have provisions, mostly dating from the mid-thirteenth century, forbidding Christians from seeking help from Jewish or Muslim physicians and from consulting sorcerers and diviners.[55] Belief in sorcery may have been widespread. According to Ferrand of Majorca, whose diatribe against his father-in-law, King Hugh IV, is highly coloured, in 1340 the king accused Ferrand's mother, Isabella of Ibelin countess of Jaffa, of having accomplished the death of the king's daughter by sorcery. It is impossible to know whether Hugh actually made this allegation, but the fact that in his legal treatise

---

[51] Edbury (2001a: 29). For religion and the Franks, see also Schabel in this volume.

[52] *Processus Cypricus*, 157–8.

[53] *Cartulary*, nos. 128–9, 131.

[54] For example, *Synodicum Nicosiense*, nos. B.6–7 and 18.

[55] *Synodicum Nicosiense*, nos. A.XIII–XIV, B.10, C.11–12, G.IV.g; cf. no. X.26.5 and *Cartulary*, no. 79, 206.

of ca. 1266 John of Ibelin recorded that it was forbidden for participants in judicial duels to carry a charm or *sorcerie* about their persons on the field of battle is further clear evidence that such things
were taken seriously.[56]

The Ibelins

For much of the thirteenth and fourteenth centuries the Ibelin family maintained a dominant position within the Cypriot nobility. The
founder of the family's fortunes in the East was a certain Barisan
who by 1115 had been appointed castellan of Jaffa (Tel Aviv). Nothing
is known for certain about his background, although his name suggests that he may have originated from Genoa or somewhere nearby
on the Ligurian coast of Italy. He was clearly a man of considerable political skill, and in 1141 King Fulk of Jerusalem gave him
the newly built castle at Ibelin (the modern Yavne), which he had
constructed as part of his strategy to contain the Muslims who still
held Ascalon. Barisan and his sons made good marriages and soon
added the neighbouring towns of Ramleh and Mirabel to their patrimony. By the time Guy of Lusignan arrived in the East in 1180,
Barisan's sons, Baldwin lord of Ramleh and Balian (a modified form
of the name 'Barisan') lord of Ibelin, were prominent members of
the nobility in the Kingdom of Jerusalem. Indeed, Balian was married to King Amaury's widow, the Byzantine princess, Maria Comnena.
Aimery of Lusignan had wed Baldwin of Ramleh's daughter, but
this link did not prevent Baldwin and Balian coming out strongly in
opposition to his brother Guy's accession to the throne of Jerusalem
in 1186. Baldwin seems to have died soon afterwards, but Balian,
one of the few Christian leaders to escape death or captivity at
Hattin, remained implacably opposed to Guy after the collapse of
the kingdom. In 1190 he and Maria were instrumental in arranging for Guy's leading rival in the East, Conrad of Montferrat, to
marry Isabella, Maria's daughter by King Amaury, who was now
the heiress to the throne of Jerusalem. So when Guy and Aimery
began organizing the Frankish settlement of Cyprus, there was certainly no place there for Balian of Ibelin or the two sons and two
daughters that Maria had born him. However, in 1197 Aimery of

---

[56] Mas Latrie, *Histoire*, II, 188–9; John of Ibelin, 237, 243.

Lusignan married Queen Isabella, who by then had been widowed twice, and so became ruler of the Kingdom of Jerusalem while being king of Cyprus. There was now something of a reconciliation between Aimery and the new generations of Ibelins—Balian had died around the end of 1193—and Aimery arranged for John, the elder son, to acquire the lordship of Beirut. Isabella and Aimery both died in 1205, whereupon in the Kingdom of Jerusalem John became regent for the new queen, his half-sister's unmarried daughter. It was then that Hugh I, the new king of Cyprus, married another of Isabella's daughters, Alice of Champagne. So John and his brother, Philip of Ibelin, were henceforth to be the half-uncles of the queen of Cyprus as well as being the first cousins of King Hugh's late mother (see genealogical table above, p. xv).[57]

It was only after Hugh's marriage that the Ibelin brothers came to prominence in the island. In 1217, when they appear for the first time in royal charters from Cyprus, they headed the witness lists, taking precedence over all the other vassals.[58] Then, at the beginning of 1218, King Hugh died leaving an heir, Henry I, who was aged only eight months, and his widow, Queen Alice, appointed Philip of Ibelin her deputy to govern the kingdom. Royal minorities in the Middle Ages were almost invariably times of political trouble, but in the case of Henry's minority the situation was aggravated by the fact that the Ibelins had only recently arrived on the scene. While they shot to power, so the sons of the original settlers—men who had supported Guy before 1192 and therefore regarded the Ibelins as their opponents—were squeezed out. As the 1220s progressed, the Ibelins and their supporters came under attack from Alice, who tried unsuccessfully to dislodge Philip from his position of authority, and from the Western emperor, Frederick II, who as suzerain of Cyprus considered the regency arrangements a matter for him to decide. In these circumstances some knights, who felt excluded from the influence and the rewards of office that their fathers had enjoyed only a few years before, conspired to topple the Ibelin-dominated regime. Their moment came when in 1228 the emperor turned up in the East as the leader of a crusade. He immediately showed his own antipathy to the Ibelins, and when in 1229 he returned to the West he left a group of their opponents in con-

---

[57] Edbury (1997a: 4–32 passim).
[58] Edbury (1997a: 33–4).

trol of Cyprus with instructions to put an end to Ibelin power there. The result was the Civil War which lasted until 1233 and which ended with a total victory for the Ibelins.

By now Henry I had come of age, and it is clear that henceforth he had little choice but to allow his kinsmen to take a leading role in noble society in the island. Philip of Ibelin had died in 1227 or 1228, but his son John soon came to acquire an influential position in royal circles. Henry I and John 'the Younger', as he is sometimes called in the documents to distinguish him from his uncle and namesake, married sisters, members of the royal house of Cilician Armenia, and in about 1246 Henry arranged for John to take charge of his mother's former dower, the county of Jaffa. As count of Jaffa, John henceforth occupied a position of great prominence in the Kingdom of Jerusalem until his death in 1266.[59] He is chiefly remembered now as the author of the largest and most comprehensive treatise on the laws and customs of the High Court to have been written in the East. Jaffa itself was lost to the Muslims in 1268, but John's descendants continued to use the title 'Count of Jaffa' and lived on in Cyprus for another century. John of Ibelin, lord of Beirut, died in 1236. He had five sons who grew to manhood, of whom only one died before he could marry and have children of his own. His eldest son, Balian, succeeded him as lord of Beirut and held the office of constable of Cyprus until his death in 1247, when he was followed in that office by his younger brother, Guy. John's second son, Baldwin, became seneschal of Cyprus, while the other son, another John, received the lordship of Arsur (or Arsuf) in Palestine.

What this meant was that from the second quarter of the thirteenth century there were no less than five branches of the Ibelin family in Cyprus: four descended from John's sons and one, the family of the counts of Jaffa, descended from Philip. The senior branch, the lords of Beirut, failed in the male line in 1264, but the others prospered. From the 1240s until the 1360s they monopolized the office of seneschal, although without making it hereditary in any one line, and from the 1230s until about 1300 they monopolized the office of constable. Their first serious setback occurred in the aftermath of Amaury of Tyre's coup d'état of 1306. King Henry II resumed power in 1310 and saw to it that several of the Ibelins, erstwhile supporters

---

[59] Edbury (1997a: 65–101).

of Amaury, ended their lives in prison. Even so, the family retained its prominence for another generation. Like Aimery of Lusignan and Hugh III, who had each married Ibelin women, though in both instances long before their accession, King Hugh IV took both his wives from the family. In the mid-thirteenth century John II of Beirut had married a daughter of the duke of Athens, but in the fourteenth a granddaughter of Guy of Ibelin, the mid-thirteenth century constable of Cyprus, outdid this achievement by marrying Ferrand, the son of King James I of Majorca, while her sister later married Duke Henry of Brunswick-Grubenhagen.[60]

It is odd therefore that all the remaining branches of the Ibelin family should have died out during the third quarter of the fourteenth century. In any generation there is always the possibility that a son will not live to have children of his own or that he will marry and have only daughters or that his sons will predecease him, and so the extinction of noble families is to be expected. But the disappearance of the Ibelins, who seem to have been present in significant numbers as late as the 1360s, is striking. After 1375 not a single male member of the family is known. It might be noted that the Lusignans were to die out similarly. In the fourteenth century both Hugh IV and James I had had several sons who grew up to have children, but, although there were plenty of Lusignans on Cyprus in the early 1400s, by the time of the death of King John II in 1458, there were no male Lusignans of legitimate descent left.

Philip of Novara's history of the Civil War of 1229–33 is an unashamed *apologia* for the deeds of the Ibelins written by one of their supporters. But even Philip cannot conceal the fact that his hero, John of Ibelin, lord of Beirut, used strong-arm tactics to secure his aims and retain power, and it is possible to see beyond Philip's eulogy to gain a picture of a 'godfather' figure, surrounded by his sons and other relatives and employing a large network of dependants and clients both in Cyprus and in the Kingdom of Jerusalem to ensure the continuance of his position of power. How people were related to the Ibelins clearly mattered, and in the 1270s the compendium of genealogical information known as the *Lignages d'Outremer* was put together in Ibelin circles. By the early fourteenth century the family was pretending to be descended from the counts of Chartres,[61]

---

[60] Collenberg (1977–1979).
[61] *Lignages d'Outremer*, 97; Nielen-Vandevoorde (1995: 110–13, 118–19). On Philip's *History* and the *Lignages*, see also Grivaud in this volume.

but, although in fact it was almost certainly of humble origins, by the middle of the thirteenth it already had connections throughout Europe. John count of Jaffa (died 1266) was a great-grandson of Barisan, the founder of the family's fortunes. His wife was the sister of King Hetum I of Cilician Armenia (1226–70). His grandmother had been a member of the Byzantine imperial dynasty of Comnenos—she was a great-niece of the Emperor Manuel I—and his mother was a member of the Burgundian Montbéliard family. Through his mother he was related to many of the aristocratic families of Burgundy and Champagne, including John of Joinville, the seneschal of Champagne, who had no hesitation in noting that the count of Jaffa was his kinsman and describing the lavish display of his armorial bearing—a red cross *paté* on a gold ground—when they met while Joinville was in the East with King Louis IX of France. John of Jaffa was of course the nephew of John of Ibelin, lord of Beirut, the man who had successfully opposed the Emperor Frederick II and prevented his officers from taking charge in both Cyprus and the Kingdom of Jerusalem. Among his cousins were the lords of Sidon and Caesarea and also, as the son of his father's sister, Philip of Montfort lord of Tyre. Philip for his part was the first cousin of Simon de Montfort earl of Leicester (died 1265), the brother-in-law and great opponent of King Henry III of England. Simon's wife's sister had been married to the Emperor Frederick II.

The eastern branch of the Montfort family eventually inherited the title to the lordship of Beirut as well as an unfulfilled claim to the duchy of Athens. After the loss of their Syrian possessions the family was to remain in Cyprus until the line failed in the second quarter of the fourteenth century.[62] The Montfort and also the Dampierre family—similarly descended from a sister of John of Ibelin, lord of Beirut—clearly came close to the Ibelins in terms of wealth though not of numbers. But there were many other families in Cyprus that, though they may have lacked kinship with royalty, nevertheless had links with the Ibelins and continued to play a significant role in noble society over many generations. The Mimars and Brie families, both of which supported the Ibelins in the struggle against Frederick II, had been related to the Ibelins since well before the Frankish acquisition of Cyprus.[63] Other nobles in Cyprus included

---

[62] Edbury (2001a: 23–4).
[63] *Lignages d'Outremer*, 60, 63, 122, 124.

the heirs to the Latin Syrian lordships of Bethsan and Jubail (or Gibelet). Yet others are known—for example, the Babin, Le Tor and Montgisard families—who similarly could trace their ancestry to knights in the twelfth-century Kingdom of Jerusalem.[64] On the other hand, the earliest evidence for a member of the Norès family in Cyprus dates from 1217.[65] They were royal vassals who only emerge from the obscurity of our sources at the beginning of the fourteenth century when Louis of Norès was one of those knights who remained faithful to Henry II at the time of Amaury of Tyre's seizure of power in 1306. In the next generation Baldwin of Norès was marshal of the royal household under Hugh IV, and then in the 1360s James of Norès held the post of turcopolier of Cyprus under Peter I. What is remarkable is that, unlike every other family that is known to have been established in Cyprus during the first thirty years of Frankish rule, it did not die out. Indeed, it was to come to even greater prominence in 1529 when John of Norès bought the title of count of Tripoli from the Venetian authorities, and his family remained in Cyprus to take part in the island's defence against the Ottomans. They are later found living in Italy.[66]

King and Vassals

There was a fundamental difficulty confronting the Frankish rulers of Cyprus. Their regime owed its existence and its justification to the Crusades, and from 1268 the kings proudly proclaimed themselves kings of Jerusalem and numbered among their vassals the princes of Galilee, the counts of Jaffa, and the lords of Arsur, Bethsan, Tyre and Jubail. In the fourteenth century it became the practice to give the princes of the blood-royal the titles of prince of Antioch and count of Tripoli, while other titles redolent of the crusading past were revived for members of the nobility. In theory at least the kings of Cyprus should therefore have been spearheading the quest to recover the Holy Places for Christendom. The problem, however, was that Cyprus, a comparatively small island supporting a com-

---

[64] Edbury (1990: 4295–6); Edbury (1997a: 142, 146, 154).
[65] *Regesta Regni Hierosolymitani*, I, no. 896.
[66] *Lacrimae Nicossienses*, 123–9, 172. On the later Norès, see Giorgio de Norès, *Discorso*, and Nicolaou-Konnari (forthcoming b).

paratively small population, had limited resources for military ventures, and the Muslim world of the Near East, situated rather close,
was much larger and much more populous. To an extent the Cypriots
were fortunate in that Muslim rulers normally gave little attention
to naval warfare, and so, although there are two Egypt-based raids
recorded in the thirteenth century, there was no serious Muslim invasion until the 1420s.

We do not know how many vassals the kings could call upon for
military service, or how many other mounted warriors were available
for hire in time of need. Hugh III is said to have brought 250 mounted
men to Tyre in 1283 and Henry II 200 mounted men and 500 foot
soldiers to Acre in 1291. In 1374 the Genoese took over 70 noble
prisoners from Cyprus, many of them men who had answered a feudal summons to come to Famagusta only to be arrested on their
arrival.[67] What these figures tell us is that, however distinguished individual nobles may have been, there were not very many of them—
certainly not enough to challenge the military might of the Mamluk
sultanate which from 1260 ruled both Syria and Egypt, expelled the
Franks from their last strongholds in Syria in 1291, and then continued to rule this extensive empire until the early sixteenth century.

The idea that there were few Frankish nobles on Cyprus was used
repeatedly as a justification in petitions to the pope for licences to
marry within the prohibited degrees of consanguinity. After the Fourth
Lateran Council of 1215 the Latin Church attempted to enforce the
rule that no one should marry a relative who was a third cousin or
nearer, and in addition that no one who wished to remarry could
marry a third cousin or nearer relative of their first husband or wife.
The Lateran Council's decree forbade marriage with a far wider
range of relations than were excluded by contemporary incest taboos,
and, with the nobility firmly committed to the principle that its members should take their marriage partners from the limited number
of families of comparable social standing, it became common for
them to request the pope for a relaxation of the rules.[68]

The reaction of the nobles to the underlying assumption that the
Holy Places in Jerusalem and elsewhere should be recovered for
Christendom seems to have been a mixture of realism and willing

[67] Edbury (1991: 99, 208).
[68] Collenberg (1977a).

acceptance. In the thirteenth century Cypriot nobles participated in crusading expeditions including the siege of Damietta during the Fifth Crusade (1217–22) and St Louis' campaign in Egypt of 1249–50, and both Hugh III and Henry II used their military resources to reinforce the defenders of Latin Syria from the 1260s onwards. After 1291 we find members of the nobility involved in some small-scale Cyprus-based naval raids on the coasts of Syria and Egypt, and in the 1360s there were plenty of Cypriot knights prepared to take part in the campaigns initiated by King Peter I. On the other hand, in 1271, not long after an unsuccessful Egyptian naval raid on Cyprus, the nobles challenged the right of the king to demand that they perform feudal military service in the Kingdom of Jerusalem—the real issue seems not to have been so much that they did not owe such services but that the king had been making excessive demands—and in 1306 it would appear that there was a widely held opinion that the king had not done enough to prepare the defences of Cyprus against a Mamluk fleet that was then believed to be in preparation.[69] The murder of Peter I by a group of nobles in 1369 took place against a growing realisation that Peter had overstretched the island's resources in his war on the Mamluks, and that there was a genuine danger that the Muslims would wreak revenge.

So the nobles seem to have adopted an ambivalent attitude to foreign war. On the one hand, there was the duty that stemmed from their Christian and chivalric ethos that demanded that they should help see to it that Jerusalem should once again come under Christian rule, and this from time to time meant following the commands of their king. On the other, there was the need to look to the security of Cyprus and that could well mean establishing a *modus vivendi* with the Mamluks. There was always the added fear that, if a crusade from the West did arrive, it could prove inconsequential and short-lived, and then Cyprus would be left vulnerable to the retaliation the expedition had provoked, once the crusaders had returned to Europe.

These last considerations may help explain an otherwise rather puzzling fact. At an unknown date sometime in the thirteenth century the Templars and Hospitallers both stopped allowing members of noble families in the Latin East to join their orders. The military orders, of which the Templars and the Hospitallers were the largest

---

[69] 'Document relatif au service militaire', 427–34; Mas Latrie (1888: 535).

and most famous, had extensive properties on Cyprus, so much so that after the suppression of the Templars in 1312 and the transfer of most of their assets to the Hospitallers, the Hospitallers were by far the largest landholder on the island apart from the crown.[70] In the early twelfth century the Templars had begun as a group of men who took quasi-monastic vows of chastity, poverty and obedience and had the vocation of protecting pilgrims to Jerusalem. The Hospitallers had begun as a religious order in the Holy Land caring for sick and dying pilgrims. Both orders came to accept wider roles in the defence of the crusader conquests, and by the late twelfth century they had acquired fortresses of major strategic significance and were playing an important role in the political and military life of the Latin East. They had a reputation for their commitment to war on the enemies of Christendom and for their military effectiveness. With the fall of Acre in 1291 both orders transferred their headquarters to Cyprus. Then, in the first decade of the fourteenth century, the Hospitallers conquered the Byzantine island of Rhodes which they ruled as a sovereign power until 1522, while at almost exactly the same time and as a result of the policy adopted by King Philip IV of France, the Templars were dissolved.

To be a brother of either military order, a man had to be a member of a knightly family. But apparently not a member of a knightly family on Cyprus. It may be that few Cypriot nobles would have wanted to become brothers of these orders anyway, but that does not explain why none of them did. Back in the twelfth century nobles from Jerusalem had joined, and as late as about 1233 the Jerusalemite nobleman Garnier L'Aleman had entered the Templars, as had John of Ibelin, lord of Beirut, on his death-bed in 1236.[71] These are, however, among the last known examples. The rules of neither order specifically forbade recruitment in the East, but it is likely that at some point the orders made a conscious decision to refuse to accept candidates from the Frankish territories in the Levant. The only explanation that comes to mind is that they feared that such recruits would suffer from a conflict of interest. The orders were committed to a crusading strategy against the Muslims, and such a policy could well have turned out to be incompatible with the priority

---

[70] Luttrell (1972: 167–9).
[71] Edbury (1997a: 50–1, 64).

of ensuring the freedom of Cyprus from Muslim attack. Add to that the likelihood of political tensions between the military orders and the Cypriot crown—relations between successive kings and the Templars in particular were poor from the 1270s onwards[72]—and the undesirability from the orders' point of view of having Cypriot brothers who might rise to prominence within their organization becomes clearer.

There were of course other outlets for members of Cypriot knightly families who wished to pursue a religious vocation. Comparatively few examples are known of them following a career in the secular church, although it can be noted that in the mid-thirteenth century Guy of Mimars became bishop of Paphos, and that Guy of Ibelin, a brother of the lord of Arsur, held the bishopric of Limassol from 1357 to 1367.[73] Occasionally we find members of noble families serving as cathedral dignitaries such as Henry of Jubail (Gibelet), archdeacon of Nicosia and royal chancellor at the close of the thirteenth century and in the opening years of the fourteenth, or John of Norès, treasurer of Nicosia at around the same period. Others nobles could join Latin monasteries. Thus for example Henry Chappe was abbot of the Cistercian monastery at Beaulieu in Nicosia in the early fourteenth century, and Plaisance of Jubail (Gibelet) was abbess of the Cistercian nunnery of St Theodore in Nicosia around the same time. Maria of Ibelin, the sister of John count of Jaffa, was St Theodore's first abbess in the mid-thirteenth century, and John's daughter, Margaret of Ibelin, was later abbess of the Benedictine house of Our Lady of Tyre in Nicosia.[74]

With the end of Frankish rule in Syria and the Holy Land at the close of the thirteenth century, the kings of Cyprus and their advisors seem to have adopted a generally circumspect attitude towards the Mamluk sultanate. However, their policy was certainly not one of craven appeasement. Some Cyprus-based naval raids took place around 1300, and King Henry II paid at least lip-service to the idea of maintaining a commercial blockade in the hope of weakening the

---

[72] Claverie (1998).
[73] Edbury (1983: 129–30); Richard (1950).
[74] Henry: Mas Latrie (1888: 541), 'Amadi', 299, Schabel (2004a: 82–96); Maria: *Lignages d'Outremer*, 100; Margaret: *Lignages d'Outremer*, 100, 'Amadi', 296, 350, 387; Plaisance: current excavation of Cyprus Department of Antiquities under Eftychia Zachariou.

sultanate. But there was never any serious possibility of the Cypriots engaging in full-scale warfare against the Mamluks unaided. All this changed with the reign of Peter I (1359–69). Peter realized that he would have to get military support from the West, and right from the start he seems to have employed mercenary forces from outside his kingdom.[75] Between 1362 and 1365 he toured Europe—he was the only reigning king of Cyprus ever to travel to the West—trying to recruit men for the crusade that in 1365 captured and then immediately abandoned the Egyptian port of Alexandria. Peter plainly reckoned that news of a major military success would inspire more Western nobles to come to Cyprus and join in the subsequent campaigns. He hoped to appeal to widely-held chivalric ideas in the West that included viewing crusading against the Muslims as both a religious duty and a matter of personal honour. It was a gamble, not least because the attack on Alexandria meant that Peter had now committed Cyprus to a full-scale war against the Mamluks. What happened was that a good number of Western nobles did respond to news of the Alexandria Crusade, but it was not long before the momentum began to flag. The Mamluks seemed unable to launch a counterattack, but the cost of the war and the obstructive behaviour of the Italians whose trading activities had suffered as a direct consequence of the crusade hampered Peter's war effort.

Another problem was the commitment of Peter's own vassals. There is good reason to suppose that many of them were keen to participate in the fighting, but it is clear that they shared a growing sense of unease. In particular they were concerned at the lengths Peter was prepared to go to win the support of the westerners. Western knights who would turn up for a period of campaigning and then go home were not a problem. What worried the Cypriots was Peter's preparedness to make generous grants of property in Cyprus to newcomers to secure their continued service. For example, it was almost certainly during his reign that the Venetian Cornaro family obtained the valuable village of Episkopi, and one of Peter's Western captains, Brémond de la Voulte, received Polemidia and Ayios Reginos.[76] Retaining credibility and respect was another problem. In the summer of 1367 Peter quarrelled with another westerner who had come

---

[75] For references to mercenaries at the beginning of the reign, see Makhairas, I, §§103, 109.

[76] *Documents chypriotes des archives du Vatican*, 80, 84.

to Cyprus in the aftermath of the Alexandria campaign, Florimont
of Lesparre. According to Leontios Makhairas the dispute had started
over a row between one of Florimont's associates and a possibly base-
born officer prominent in Peter's service named John of Moustry.[77]
Exactly what happened is unclear, but evidently Florimont considered
that Peter had dishonoured him and challenged the king to a duel
at the court of the king of France to satisfy his honour. Peter accepted
the challenge, and at the end of 1367 set off once more for the
West. The histories of the reign gave the affair considerable attention,
and Pope Urban V wrote to express his disapproval. In the event
the affair ended in Florimont's apology and a reconciliation brokered
by the pope.[78] It is difficult to know what the Cypriot nobles would
have thought about this episode, but they may well have thought
Peter had acted unnecessarily in accepting the challenge and that
his reaction showed that he placed an undue value on his standing
in the eyes of these European volunteers. The accounts of the closing
weeks of Peter's life strongly suggest that his judgement generally
was sadly awry. Peter was murdered by a group of his own vassals
in January 1369, and there is little doubt that the king's increasing
irascibility towards the Cypriot nobles as a class was a major cause.
The failing fortunes of war and the fact that the island's resources
were unable to sustain it were also important for understanding what
happened, but it is also clear that resentment over Peter's partiality
for the westerners had a significant part in his downfall.

Burgesses

By comparison with the nobility, the non-noble Frankish population
of Cyprus remains somewhat elusive. We are told that Guy of
Lusignan brought burgesses to Cyprus, but how many of these were
Franks and how many were indigenous Levantine Christians (or
Suriens as they are known in the sources) is unclear.[79] Similarly the
ethnicity of the sergeants—the word is derived from the Old French

---

[77] Makhairas, I, §206. For John, see Edbury (1980: 229).
[78] Makhairas, I, §§206, 214, 216–17; Guillaume de Machaut, *La Prise d'Alixandre*,
lines 7357–922.
[79] *Continuation de Guillaume de Tyr*, 139. For this section, see also Coureas in this
volume.

sergenz meaning a 'serving man'—is not usually specified, although those whose livelihood was derived from property or rents held in feudal tenure would have been Frankish. Philip of Novara refers to burgesses who were skilled pleaders in the High Court. However, the one man he mentions by name, Raymond of Conches, belonged to a family that from the beginning of the fourteenth century if not earlier was accepted as being of knightly status.[80] The fact is that there is very little evidence for the fabric of non-noble, urban society in Cyprus before the fourteenth century, and there is no evidence at all to suggest that the Lusignan regime ever attempted to establish Frankish *villes neuves*—rural settlements of Western European farmers—in the Cypriot countryside as had happened in the Kingdom of Jerusalem in the twelfth century. Thanks to the survival of two versions of a Greek translation from Cyprus of the Frankish *Livre des Assises de la Cour des Bourgeois*, which had been composed in Acre in the mid-thirteenth century, and the fourteenth-century French *Livres du Plédéant et du Plaidoyer*, which originated in Cyprus, we have a lot of information about the law as administered in the burgess courts in Cyprus.[81] These texts have much to say about property held in burgess tenure—the *borgesie*—but the law governing this category of real estate applied equally to Franks and non-Franks. They also described procedures for dealing with criminal cases that came before the burgess courts, but these too affected the population as a whole and not just the Frankish element.

It is only as we come to the end of the thirteenth century that the veil of silence is lifted and, thanks to the survival of several of the registers of the Genoese notary Lamberto di Sambuceto, we can see something of the Frankish burgess community resident in Famagusta. Sambuceto's registers, however, give a necessarily lop-sided view. For a start, he is largely concerned with commercial affairs, and many of his clients were merchants who were passing through Famagusta on their way to or from their home ports in the West. Then again, although he is by no means solely concerned with the affairs of the Genoese, there can be little doubt that his compatriots feature to a disproportionately large extent. But it nonetheless true that his registers

---

[80] Philip of Novara, 'Livre', 515. For his namesake and presumed descendant as a knight in the early fourteenth century, see *Cartulary*, no. 113.

[81] For the first, see Greek text, Ασίζαι, and English trans, *Assizes*. The second is edited as 'Abrégé du Livre des Assises de la Cour des Bourgeois'.

are a veritable gold-mine for the historian and tell an enormous amount about urban society at the time. Sambuceto himself lived in Famagusta from around 1294 until 1307 when he returned to Genoa. In the late 1290s he held an official position as 'notary and scribe of the commune of Genoa in Famagusta', but he then worked as an independent notary, using as his base the shop of a Florentine spicer named Bertozzo *Latinus*, although towards the end of his sojourn in Famagusta he transferred his activities to the premises of a Genoese called Peter *Pelleterius* (or Peter the Skinner). Precisely where these shops were is not known, although we may assume that they were located conveniently for the harbour and the Genoese *loggia* which at that period was situated on the water front.

Famagusta at the beginning of the fourteenth century was enjoying a commercial boom. Partly this had been brought about by the fall of Acre and the other Christian-held ports on the coast of Syria and Palestine, and it seems to have been stimulated by an influx of refugees from the mainland. Some of these people still bore sobriquets indicating their place of origin, such as Acre, Sidon, Beirut or elsewhere. Sambuceto also indicates the presence of long-term residents who, like him, were Genoese nationals. Some of these, such as Ianuino de Murta, had money to invest and owned houses that they rented out; others, for example, Allegro Fateinanti, were notaries; yet others, such as Pellegrino the shoemaker, were artisans. Some people, among them Pellegrino and Lanfranc of Romea, both of whom were careful to state that they were 'Genoese inhabitants of Famagusta', even remembered to include in their wills a legacy to the civic charity back home in Genoa.[82] It should be noted that, in contrast to the situation in Acre before 1258, the Genoese did not have a quarter in Famagusta in which they had extra-territorial rights. Indeed, in 1301 it would appear that they did not yet have their own church.[83] There were other people of Western origin with links to other cities in the West such as the barber Hugh of Toulouse. Pellegrino's associates included tailors, leather workers, tanners and skinners, all of whom have names that suggest that they too were men of Italian origin. Elsewhere we hear of tavern-keepers named Bartholomew and Gerard. Vivian of Ginembaldo was a banker, money-changer

---

[82] *Lamberto di Sambuceto, 1300–1301*, nos. 366, 415.
[83] *Lamberto di Sambuceto, 1300–1301*, no. 349.

and businessman whose premises were in the heart of the commercial area in Famagusta and whose activities resulted in him being placed under a sentence of excommunication for illicit trade with the Muslims. He had come to Famagusta from Acre and seems to have known Arabic.

On a few occasions Sambuceto indicates that particular individuals held public office as jurats (or assessors) in the burgess court at Famagusta. Such people would be well-regarded members of the community who were well acquainted with the law and who would be called upon to decide both criminal and civil cases as well as deal with a considerable body of routine business including the conveyancing of real estate. Five men are mentioned by name. Two of them, Riccobuono Ocelli and Liacius Imperiale, were members of the expatriot Genoese community, and one, Pellegrino de Castello, may have been a member of a family that had previously lived in Acre and that had links with Venice. A fourth, Abraynus, sounds from his name as if he was of Syrian origin. None have names that suggest they were members of the Greek community, and indeed people with Greek names rarely appear in Sambuceto's registers. So being a Genoese did not prevent a man from accepting public office under the Lusignans, despite the frequent disputes between the government and the Genoese merchants, and it would appear that these long-term Genoese residents participated fully in the life of the community as a whole.[84]

Famagusta was clearly a busy, cosmopolitan port. Some of the nobles lived there, although the evidence suggests that most maintained town-houses in Nicosia. The town also contained many Western merchants and artisans living alongside refugees from Syria and Greeks. Some of these westerners, like Sambuceto himself who remained in Famagusta for around thirteen years, were not permanent settlers but eventually moved on or returned to the West. Others no doubt did see themselves as permanent, and in some cases belonged to families that had been living there for several generations. Admittedly, it is difficult to track such families, but in various ways they must have contributed to Famagusta's prosperity and to the tangible memory of the Frankish community there preserved in the surviving churches, of which the magnificent early fourteenth-century cathedral church of St Nicholas is the most striking.

---

[84] For fuller discussion with references, see Edbury (1995b; 1997b; 1997c).

ECONOMY

Nicholas Coureas

The economy of Lusignan Cyprus exhibits continuity with that of Roman and Byzantine Cyprus in that land was the basis of economic and social relations. Most of the population were peasants engaged in agriculture, the ruling class' wealth was mainly in the form of landed estates and the majority of exports consisted of primary produce. What did change radically was the importance of commerce within this agricultural framework, as well as the new role Cyprus began to assume, from the latter half of the thirteenth century onwards, as an entrepôt in the carrying trade between Western Europe and the lands of the Eastern Mediterranean and the Middle East. Cyprus prospered on account of this role, while the increased external demand for Cypriot agricultural produce—wheat, wine, oil, carobs, pulses, salt and above all sugar—led to the evolution of an economy that remained agricultural but became highly export orientated. The main towns, Nicosia, the capital, and Famagusta, the island's easternmost harbour, developed impressively, and the monuments of Gothic architecture that excite the wonder of visitors to the present day attest to the wealth drawn by the Church, the island's rulers and the merchants, local and foreign, from their agricultural estates and commercial enterprises.

The other towns of Cyprus, Limassol, Paphos and Kyrenia, did not develop to anything like the same extent, but they too participated to some degree in the new economic patterns created partly by the Latin conquest and partly by political and economic developments in Europe and the Near East. This is particularly true for Limassol, serving as a port for the export of agricultural products such as wine, sugar and carobs and as a stopover for pilgrims travelling to the Holy Land, although the floods, plagues and earthquakes that ravaged it in the fourteenth and fifteenth centuries harmed its economic progress. These developments in conjunction with the Latin conquest also encouraged migration to Cyprus, from both Western Europe and the lands of the Near East. The immigrants, whether transitory or permanent, originating from Latin Syria, Genoa, Venice, Provence,

Catalonia and elsewhere, participated to a very great extent in Cypriot international commerce, primarily as merchants but also as artisans, shipwrights, tavern keepers, sailors and ships' captains, playing a role out of all proportion to their numbers. Although various immigrants had settled on Cyprus in the late Byzantine period, under the Lusignans immigration acquired a momentum and an economic importance that were unprecedented.

Another development was the emergence of new industries on Cyprus, enabling its economy to diversify without altering its agricultural foundation. From 1220 onwards kilns in Paphos, Lemba, Lapithos and Engomi near Famagusta were producing pottery that developed its own distinct characteristics over time. Until the final expulsion of Latins from Syria in 1291, Cypriot glazed pottery was also exported to Acre and its hinterland.[1] From the late thirteenth and early fourteenth centuries onwards textile industries in Cyprus produced samite and camlets that were in increasing demand not only in Western Europe but also in the Near East. Workshops for dyeing such textiles came into being in Nicosia, while shipbuilding also developed in the harbour of Famagusta. The main Florentine banking houses of Bardi, Peruzzi and Mozzi all had representatives on Cyprus by the early fourteenth century, something that points towards the development of new service sectors in the Cypriot economy, while contemporary documents attest to the existence of money-lenders and merchants in Nicosia, Famagusta and the other towns. The presence of a major slave market in Famagusta and of another in Nicosia likewise betokens a growing service sector, for most of the slaves worked in an urban setting, although many were also employed in agriculture, particularly in capital- and labour-intensive industries such as sugar and viticulture.[2] This chapter shall outline and describe how and why the Cypriot economy developed and diversified in these centuries. It shall also examine and discuss the internal and external factors that set these far reaching changes in motion.

---

[1] Pringle (1986: 458–60, 465–70); Stern (1995).
[2] In addition, manuscript and icon production were specialised areas of artistic activity with an economic dimension that developed on Cyprus in the thirteenth and fourteenth centuries; see Mouriki (1985–1986); Carr (1987–1988); Constantinides (1991); Constantinides and Browning, *Dated Greek Manuscripts*, 11–18.

The Natural Resources of Cyprus

Writing in the 1070s, over a century before the Latin conquest, the Byzantine historian Kekaumenos stated that Cyprus along with Crete produced wheat, barley, pulses, cheese, wine, meat and olive oil, while the twelfth-century Arab geographer Edrisi referred to Cyprus' timber and copper.[3] A description of the natural resources of Cyprus in the period of Latin rule is an essential prerequisite for understanding its economic and commercial activity. Cyprus has two main mountain ranges, the Pentadaktylos or Kyrenia Mountains running along the northern coastline and the Troodos massif, located in the centre of the island and branching out eastwards towards Larnaca. Between them lies the central plain of Mesaoria, a dry bed through which run seasonal rivers of the *wadi* type that fill with rainwater in winter. This plain is suitable for cereal cultivation, and through irrigation orchards and market gardens can be cultivated, the water for such irrigation usually coming from wells. The plains between the Kyrenia Mountains and the sea are among the most well watered and fertile in Cyprus, while the deep valleys to the north of the Troodos massif in the Marathasa, Solea and Khrysokhou areas, to the west in the district of Paphos and to the south in the district of Limassol, are well watered on account of retaining rainfall and have lush vegetation. The forests of the Troodos range were a rich source of timber for the shipyards in Famagusta, and the pine trees, the trunks of which formed excellent masts for sailing ships, were in great demand in the early part of the fourteenth century. The salt lakes near Limassol and Larnaca, the so-called *salines*, yielded rich deposits of salt, especially at Larnaca, and their revenues were lucrative enough for the extraction and sale of salt to be a royal monopoly. Furthermore, the salt lake at Limassol contained fish farms under royal control, from which, according to the accounts for the years 1367–68, the Latin bishop of Limassol received an ecclesiastical tithe of 537 bezants annually. This indicates that they brought the crown over 5,000 bezants in annual revenue. The pilgrim Dietrich von Schachten observed that good quality fish was to be found in Limassol when visiting the place in 1491, while the sixteenth-century chronicler

---

[3] Galatariotou (1991: 52–3).

Florio Bustron mentioned the great number of fish, chiefly giltheads, caught in the salt lake.[4]

The cultivation of cereals was the most important agricultural activity practised on Cyprus, barley and wheat being the main staple crops. Carobs, beans, lentils, oats, flax and flaxseed were also harvested. Among other products, some of which will be discussed in greater detail below, are sugar, molasses, cotton, olive oil, fleeces, wax, honey, wine, camlets, samites and silk. Other leguminous plants grown on Cyprus, which figure less conspicuously in the written records, were vetches, whose cultivation at Psimolophou is recorded, and lobster seed, four hogsheads of which were purchased at the village of Knodara for feeding the slaves there. Wheat, barley, pulses, sugar, camlets, wine and cotton were all export crops, as were onions, large quantities of which were produced in the Paphos district as well as in villages of the Mesaoria plain, such as Psimolophou. Olives were more important for the oil they produced than for the fruit itself. The oil was used in the manufacture of soap, another Cypriot export by the first half of the fourteenth century. Sesame oil was also produced on Cyprus.[5]

Wine was an important item of agricultural production, and then as now the vineyards were concentrated in the districts of Limassol and Paphos in the southwestern part of the island. As early as 1300 Genoese in Cyprus were sending money to Limassol to buy wine as an investment, and a notarial deed of 1307 mentions the export of wine by two Genoese to the island of Rhodes, which the Hospitallers were then in the process of conquering. Although the ship sailing to Rhodes departed from Famagusta, it had previously loaded on board six butts of wine at the port of Limassol, and one notes that the wines of Pelendri and Kilani were especially prized among those of the Limassol district.[6] Ludolph of Sudheim, who visited Limassol between the years 1336 and 1341, mentioned the extensive vineyard at an unidentified location called Engaddi, possibly in the hills north of Limassol. It was two square miles in extent, had belonged to the

---

[4] Richard (1985: 267–8); *Documents chypriotes des archives du Vatican*, 38–9, 78–9 and note 11; *Cartulary*, no. 50; Florio Bustron, 28; *Excerpta Cypria Nova*, no. 40.

[5] Richard (1985: 275 and note 100). Later Venetian figures are in Mas Latrie, *Histoire*, III, 494–7, 534–6.

[6] Lamberto di Sambuceto, *1300–1301*, no. 165, *1304–1307*, nos. 148, 152; Richard (1985: 276).

order of the Templars, and at the time of Ludolph's visit there were over one hundred Muslim captives working there as slaves. Viticulture is a labour-intensive enterprise, which explains the use of slave labour, employed to an even greater extent in the cultivation of sugar, as shall be seen below. An ordinance of 1355 prohibited serfs suspected of abandoning their lands from seizure during the grape and sugar harvests, or even during the months of March and April when the vines needed tending.[7]

An account from the *casale* of Porchades (Parsata) near Lefkara listed the various stages involved in maintaining the vines, two periods of ploughing followed by pruning, cultivating, cutting off the shoots, layering the runners, and finally picking and trampling on the grapes. Once pressed, the juice extracted from the grapes was stored in the *pitharia*, the great earthenware vessels kept in the cellars of the *casalia*, which could hold 55 gallons or more. The wine was transported in goatskins, and certain casks for this purpose called *boutes* held over 65 gallons. The officers of King Louis IX of France purchased considerable quantities of wheat and wine long before the arrival of the king's crusading forces on Cyprus in September 1248, a fact illustrating Cyprus' significant agricultural resources at this time. When explaining the high mortality rate experienced by King Louis' forces whilst on Cyprus, the anonymous author of the *Directorium* maintained, with considerable exaggeration, that when drunk undiluted Cypriot wines could burn and destroy one's intestines and bowels. Ludolph of Sudheim concurred, stating that the red wine became white after six to nine years in the *pitharia* and had to be drunk diluted, with nine parts of water to one of wine.[8]

Salt was an important Cypriot product, and when the Venetians began exploiting various sources of salt in the Mediterranean basin from the late thirteenth century onwards, the deposits on Cyprus were also included. Such deposits were generally located on small islands and in coastal areas, facilitating the export of salt by ship to Venice, and from 1270 onwards Venice began to import salt from Ibiza, Sardinia, Alexandria, the Crimea and Cyprus. The Venetians made use of the Cypriot deposits in the salt lakes of Limassol and

---

[7] Ludolph of Sudheim, 212; 'Ordenemens de la court dou vesconte', 422, no. 385; Richard (1985: 276).

[8] Ludolph of Sudheim, 216; Hill (1940–1952, II: 140–6); Richard (1985: 276); Forey (1995: 71, 73).

Larnaca more regularly than those situated elsewhere, and one notes
that the locality of Larnaca is already mentioned as 'Salines' in Latin
documents of the thirteenth and fourteenth centuries. In September
1236 King Henry I of Cyprus, short of money after the Civil War
of 1229–33, received a loan from Archbishop Eustorge of Nicosia, to
be repaid from the revenues of the royal salt pan at Salines. The terms
of the agreement imply, although they do not explicitly state, that the
exploitation of salt was already a royal monopoly, and that the incomes the crown drew from its exploitation were easily in excess of
2,000 white bezants. At that time the salt extracted was sold to private merchants, and from 1280 onwards Venetian merchants in particular began purchasing it in great quantities. A Venetian commercial
edict of 26 April 1286 fixed a price of six pounds and five *sous* for
every *modius* of salt imported to Venice by bulky Venetian ships that
journeyed from Cyprus, Sardinia and Ras al Makhbaz. New prices
were fixed in the subsequent edicts of 1287 and 1292, but in 1301
King Henry II decided to increase the export duties that Venetians paid
on Cypriot salt from six to fifteen percent. Despite Venetian protests,
the ruling remained, and Cypriot salt, which the Venetians prized
highly and described as *bianchissimo et fortissimo*, continued to be sent
to Venice until the Ottoman conquest of Cyprus in 1571.[9]

The coastal plains of Cyprus, notably those of Kyrenia and Limassol,
abound in carob trees, and carobs were a staple Cypriot export crop
throughout the medieval period and beyond. The Genoese exported
carobs from the beginning of the fourteenth century, as appears from
two deeds of the period. The first, from 1300, states that a Genoese
ship owner hired his ship to a certain Girard Galee, who undertook
to sail to Constantinople via Limassol, where he was to load 300
sacks of carobs. In the second deed, from 1302, Balthazar de Quarto
of Genoa rented a ship to two other Genoese merchants, who on
sailing forth from Famagusta would likewise stop off at Limassol to
have 400 sacks of carobs loaded on board for sale in Tunis. Balthazar
was to be paid four bezants for every sack of carobs.[10] The export
of carobs from Limassol continued into the later fourteenth century.
A notarial deed of 1361 states that a certain Mafiolus bought 200
sacks of carobs, undertaking to sail from Limassol to Venice or

[9] *Cartulary*, no. 50; Hocquet (1979, I: 98–9, 100–1, 141; II: 204–5, 210); Mas
Latrie, *Histoire*, II, 99–100; Jacoby (1995: 398).
[10] Lamberto di Sambuceto, *1300–1301*, no. 29, *1302*, no. 266.

another Adriatic town and to sell them. Even after the war of 1373 with Genoa, as a result of which the Genoese occupied Famagusta and forced the crown to have all major exports sent through this port, the export of carobs, like that of cereals, was not harmed, for the peace treaties of 1374 and 1383 allowed cereals to be loaded on board ship for export along any part of the Cypriot coastline, since these were low-value products. Their export continued into the fifteenth century and beyond, as various pilgrims stopping off at Cyprus while journeying to the Holy Land attest.[11]

The cultivation of cotton, the prime Cypriot export during the Venetian and early Ottoman periods, possibly began on Cyprus at some point in the thirteenth century. No records attest to it before the fourteenth century, although from 1301 onwards numerous notarial deeds refer to the export of cotton, often in conjunction with other products such as grain, pulses, salt and carobs, to Western Europe and other destinations in the Aegean and the Black Sea, and especially to Venice and Ancona. Marino Sanudo the Elder, writing in the early fourteenth century, states for the year 1307 that Cyprus produced cotton in abundance. A note of caution must be sounded here: Egypt, Syria and Cilician Armenia as well as Cyprus cultivated cotton in this period, and so it is not always certain whether the cotton exported from Cyprus was indigenous or brought there from elsewhere. From 1370 onwards, however, and especially following their conquest of Famagusta, the Genoese ceased purchasing large amounts of cotton from Alexandria in Egypt. Instead they bought it from other localities, especially Cyprus, although Sicily, Malta and parts of Southern Italy likewise supplied Genoa with cotton in this period. Hence in the Genoese custom registers for the years 1376–77 one finds numerous entries on the import of cotton from Cyprus and Syria, but only one on the arrival of Egyptian cotton. The entries referring to the arrival of bocasine, a by-product of cotton, from Cyprus likewise far outnumber those concerning its import from Beirut or Egypt. By the end of the fourteenth century the Aegean island of Chios, under direct Genoese rule from 1356, had also become a major market for cotton originating mainly from Turkey, but also from Cyprus and Syria in those instances when such cotton was not shipped

---

[11] Nicola de Boateriis, no. 91; Jacoby (1995: 431); *Excerpta Cypria*, 68, 72; *Supplementary Excerpts on Cyprus*, 35, 41–2, 46; *Excerpta Cypria Nova*, nos. 28, 36, 43, 48.

directly to Flanders. Like sugar and the vine, the cultivation of cotton was both capital and labour intensive, and so could only be done by major landowners with large reserves of cash. The crown, the Hospitallers—who following the dissolution of the Templars in 1312 acquired their estates and became the largest landowners in the district of Limassol—and, from 1360 onwards, the Venetian Cornaro family were among them. Most of the cotton fields were located on the southwest coast in the area between Lemba and Limassol, as were the sugar-producing areas of Cyprus.[12]

Sugar was Cyprus' most profitable export crop from the fourteenth to the early sixteenth centuries. It is not clear whether sugar was introduced to Cyprus before the Latin conquest of 1191 or shortly thereafter, given the numerous Latin sugar plantations in thirteenth-century Syria. A clause in an agreement of 1228 with the bishop of Acre stated that the Hospitallers had to continue paying tithes on lands that had been turned over to sugar cultivation, although these lands were normally exempt from tithes. The Hospitallers may have been practising a form of tax evasion, and although there is no conclusive evidence, this may have occurred on Cyprus as well. Among the properties King Hugh I awarded the Hospitallers in 1210 was the *casale* of Kolossi.[13] If sugar was not already cultivated there the Hospitallers introduced it shortly after acquiring the *casale*, although the first explicit mention of sugar production there dates from 1343, in the Catalan merchant Joan Benet's purchases from Cyprus during his journey to Famagusta. This sugar constituted over a third of Benet's imports by value. Sugar refining was a complex process, and archaeological excavations of refineries near Kouklia in the district of Paphos illuminate its workings considerably. The earliest evidence for its cultivation comes from the castle of Saranda Kolones behind Paphos harbour, where archaeologists have unearthed fragments of the pottery moulds fashioned for collecting the cane juice and retaining it while it crystallised into conically-shaped sugar lumps. These basins were destroyed in the earthquake of 1222, but their existence proves the cultivation and refining of sugar on Cyprus from the early thirteenth century onwards, if not earlier. The earliest physical traces

---

[12] Jacoby (1995: 420 and note 44); Ashtor (1976: 686–7); Balard (1978, II: 741–2); *Documents chypriotes des archives du Vatican*, 67–8, 111–13.

[13] Jacoby (1995: 417); Hamilton (1980: 302); *Cartulaire général de l'Ordre des Hospitaliers*, II, no. 1354.

of a refinery are in Stavros near Kouklia, dating from the late thirteenth century.[14]

By the end of the thirteenth century Cypriot sugar was exported
to Europe, and the trade was important and lucrative enough to
attract the interest of important Genoese. In 1299 Simon Rubeus,
a member of a prominent Genoese noble family, offered as security
for a loan Cypriot sugar that was to be brought to Genoa on board a
ship belonging to Andrew Spinola, who likewise belonged to the
Genoese nobility. In around 1320 Marino Sanudo the Elder observed
that enough sugar was produced on Cyprus for the satisfaction of
Western European requirements, though whether this was true or
simply a claim he forwarded to discourage Latin Christians from
purchasing sugar produced in Muslim lands cannot be established.
Following the demise of Latin Syria with the conquest of Acre and
Tyre by the Muslims in 1291, Syrian sugar production fell. The
papal embargo on trade with the Muslims, moreover, applied from
1292 to 1344, discouraged the purchase of sugar from Muslim lands
while encouraging the production and sale of Cypriot sugar. This
explains the partial restructuring of the Stavros refinery in the fourteenth century.[15]

The kings of Cyprus knew how profitable sugar was, encouraging
its cultivation on their estates. The reacquisition of land King Aimery
undertook a few years after the Latin conquest of 1191 ensured that
the royal domain included a large portion of the most fertile areas,
especially the well-watered plains. Documents of the fourteenth and
fifteenth centuries show that the royal estate included the sugar producing *casalia* of Lefka and Morphou in the western end of the fertile
plain of Mesaoria and that of Potamia southeast of Nicosia. There
is no record of sugar cultivation on the royal *casalia* of Sigouri,
Palaikythro, and Aradippou, or on those of Kanakaria and Lapithos
in the Karpass and Kyrenia districts, but it was cultivated at those
of Kouklia, Emba, Lemba and Akhelia in the Paphos district and
that of Akanthou in the Karpass peninsula. By the mid-fourteenth
century the Lusignan crown had invested heavily in their sugar plantations at Kouklia, southeast of Paphos, as had the Hospitallers at
Kolossi and the Venetian Cornaro family at Episkopi. At Kouklia

---

[14] Plana i Borràs (1992: 117–18); Wartburg (1995: 127 and passim); Megaw (1982: 215–16); Luttrell (1996: 165).
[15] Lamberto di Sambuceto, *1296–1299*, no. 138; Luttrell (1996: 165).

and Episkopi far more pottery moulds for making crystal sugar have
been found than for making the more expensive sugar loaves, indicating that sugar was produced primarily for export, with the cheaper
type being considered more competitive. Episkopi appears to have
become a centre of sugar production relatively late, in the later fourteenth century. Formerly belonging to the Ibelin family, the Venetian
Fantino Cornaro had acquired it by 1367. In 1378 the Venetian
senate gave Fantino's brother Frederick permission to export powdered sugar refined at Episkopi to Venice, and the Cornaro family
produced sugar into the fifteenth century and beyond, despite losing water rights to the Hospitallers in 1401 and suffering a renewed
water loss in 1468.[16]

Excavations at Episkopi and Kouklia show that waterpower was
utilised to the utmost, revealing the installation and use of the new
type of water-powered mills with horizontal wheels and vertical mill-
stones. The Episkopi excavations have found part of the water conduit,
the whole of the compression chamber for the sugar cane, an arched
underground chamber containing a horizontal wheel forming part
of the water mill complex and a partly excavated arched corridor
southwest of the chamber whence the water exited with the rota-
tion of the wheel and irrigated the adjoining sugar plantations. One
of the areas for boiling the pulp, with eight pairs of heating cham-
bers, has also been unearthed. Excavations at Kolossi are still at a
preliminary stage, and so far the mill, located to the south of a stone
aqueduct and in excellent condition, has been exposed along with
the compression chamber and the underground arched hall containing
a horizontal water wheel, likewise in an excellent state of preservation. The placement of the hall directly under the compression chamber is a feature common to the three sugar refineries of Episkopi,
Kouklia and Stavros excavated on Cyprus.[17] The importance of water
in establishing and maintaining agricultural enterprises also comes
across in the excavations of the thirteenth-century agricultural grange
of the Cistercian monks near Pyrgos, a village north of Amathus in
the district of Limassol. The Cistercians, who developed extremely
advanced hydraulic and sanitation systems for supplying piped water
to their monasteries and the mills and fishponds pertaining to them,

---

[16] Wartburg (1995: 126, 151, note 4); Grivaud (2001a: 363); Luttrell (1996: 165–7),
using Jacoby (1977).
[17] Wartburg (1995: 128 and figs. 4, 5, 9); Solomidou-Ieronymidou (2001).

built two cisterns and a mill for their grange at Pyrgos, fine structures
still standing today. The water mill constitutes the earliest example
of pre-industrial technology for the post-classical period in Cyprus.
The sophistication of Cypriot agriculture is perhaps best seen in the
Lusignan plantations around Potamia south of Nicosia. The recently
excavated system of wells, water wheels, canals, and mills irrigated
the fields and processed the produce of the royal estate (Figs. 12–13).[18]

In Cyprus as elsewhere in the Mediterranean the village, the main
unit of agricultural production, was an economic as much as a social
unit. The two prevalent types of village in Cyprus were the *casale*, a
nucleated village of several dozen households, and the smaller *prastio*,
a hamlet that was often dependent on the *casale*. In all villages except
the smaller *prastia* there were two kinds of land, that of the feudal
lord worked by the serfs or *paroikoi* two or three days every week
and the land cultivated by the peasants in general to raise their own
crops. Both serfs and free tenants also had to make crop payments
from their own harvests, in the case of the serfs around one third
of the annual crop. Most villages had a cluster of buildings belonging to the lord, which rarely attained the dimensions of a manor
house and, even when they did, remained unfortified, although a
few villages such as Kiti and Pyla in the present Larnaca district
had towers (Fig. 9). The buildings were constructed in the traditional
manner practised right up to the twentieth century, consisting of
stone foundations rising up to approximately one metre above ground,
mud brick walls and terraced roofs with joists and lathes supported
by 'French columns' called 'βολίτζια', a word deriving from the
Provençal French *volige*. Other than granaries, stables, and wine cellars
the villages had an oven, a bakehouse and a wine press in the lord's
buildings, and on occasion a sugar mill or an olive press. Certain
villages, examples being Kythrea, Palaikythro and Psimolophou,
boasted flourmills powered either by water or animals, and numerous
casalia had a *canute*, a word of Armenian origin denoting a tavern
that also served as an inn, as the legislation of the *Assises de la Cour
des Bourgeois* makes clear.[19]

---

[18] Schabel (2000b: 353, 356–8); Rizopoulou *et al.* (2002: 384–5, 388–90); Lécuyer
(2004 and forthcoming). The Potamia remains date to ca. 1348–73.
[19] Richard (1985: 269–70); *Cartulary*, no. 62; *Assizes*, Codex One, arts. 101, 103–4,
Codex Two, arts. 101–3. See also Nicolaou-Konnari in this volume.

The larger villages, whether exploited directly by the feudal lord or rented out to someone else, would have had, other than the *bailli* who exercised the overall supervision of the economic activity, a scribe assisting him, a person responsible for the granary, an innkeeper, a blacksmith, a carpenter and some bakers, as well as landless labourers and slaves who were fed, shod and lodged at the lord's expense. Solely the lord's overseer and some landless labourers and slaves, however, would live in the smaller *prastia*. Such slaves were often Muslims captured in raids against the coasts of Egypt and Syria, and the *Assizes* mentioned above have legislation on such slaves who escaped. Villages practising sugar cultivation, such as Episkopi and Kolossi in the Limassol district and Lemba and Emba in the Paphos district, would have many slaves.[20] Livestock were extremely important in agriculture, for their labour as well as for consumption. Cows, goats and sheep were all raised, and their milk used in cheese production. There were many horses, mules and donkeys in the towns and villages throughout the island.[21] At Psimolophou the Latin patriarch of Jerusalem, who owned the *casale*, lent the peasants 868 white bezants to buy these animals for carting and ploughing purposes, while camels were also used in Cyprus as pack animals. Smaller animals included pigs, poultry and bees, and according to a letter of Pope Innocent III dated February 1200 the feudal lords were defrauding the Latin Church of Cyprus of its tithes by paying them only on such animals, while livestock were not tithed in the accounts of the diocese of Limassol for 1367. The mention of all the animals stated above, especially horses, in the *Assizes* itself testifies to their significance.[22]

The crown, the nobles, and the Church, especially the Latin military orders, were the main owners of land, and the Venetian Cornaro family can be added to them in the later fourteenth century. Greek monasteries also practised agriculture, and the foundation rules of the monasteries of Makhairas and St Neophytos' Holy Cross near

---

[20] Mas Latrie, *Histoire*, III, 30–4; Ashtor (1983: 294); Richard (1985: 270); Balard (1995: 417–20, 449–51); *Assizes*, Codex One, art. 240, Codex Two, art. 238. See also Nicolaou-Konnari in this volume.

[21] *Lettres de Jean XXII*, no. 43118; Mas Latrie, *Histoire*, III, 496, 535–6, for late figures.

[22] *Documents chypriotes des archives du Vatican*, 62–3, 78–86; *Papsturkunden*, 371–2; Richard (1947: 135); *Assizes*, Codex One, arts. 31, 34, 37–8, 53, 72, 81, 92–3, 149, 210, 218, 226, 237, 242–3, 295–7, Codex Two, arts. 35, 38–9, 54, 74, 83, 93, 95, 109, 146, 208, 216–17, 224, 235, 240–1, 296–8.

Paphos, dating from 1210 and 1214 respectively, contain allusions to arable land, vineyards and livestock, and numerous regulations on the gathering of crops and its supervision. Monks were appointed as stewards and had assistants, including a cellarer and the keepers of the grange and the warehouse.[23] The feudal lords and the crown made much money through selling grain, pulses and wine to the merchants, as when for example on 14 October 1300 a Genoese paid 600 white bezants for 130 jars of wine from John of Ibelin, the titular lord of Arsur, visiting his storehouses for this purpose. The Augustinian nunnery of St Mary and All Saints at Acre in Palestine owned an estate in the diocese of Paphos, which included a cistern and a well, from which according to a letter of Pope Gregory IX of November 1237 it drew foodstuffs and produce consisting of corn, pulses, rice, oil, wine, cheeses, sugar, candlesticks and soap, a product made from olive oil, and its annual revenues totaled 1,092 white bezants. This range of products indicates how the island's agricultural wealth, the mainstay in the revenue of the crown, the nobles and the Church, was both considerable and diversified.[24]

From Byzantine Province to International Entrepôt: 1191–1291

Although at the time of the Latin conquest Cyprus' economy had an agricultural base, the Byzantine emperor, the Byzantine aristocracy—originating mainly from Constantinople—and the Church being the major landowners, developments of the twelfth century provided a foretaste of what was to come. In 1126 the Byzantine Emperor John Comnenos extended to Crete and Cyprus the trading privileges that his father Alexios had awarded in 1082 to the Venetians in other areas of the Byzantine Empire, and in 1147 his successor Manuel Comnenos confirmed these privileges. The first notarial deeds recording Venetian trading activities in the ports of Limassol and Paphos date from 1139 and 1143, and a third charter of 1189 records how an unnamed man at Paphos charged a Venetian resident of Tyre 30 bezants for the drawing up of a testamentary deed. The commercial

---

[23] Neilos, *Rule*, ch. 83, 85, 91, 104–5, 132, Neophytos, *Rule*, ch. 10, 13. On church income, see also Schabel in this volume.
[24] Lamberto di Sambuceto, *1299–1301 (ROL)*, no. 364; *Les Registres de Grégoire IX*, II, no. 4013; *Regesta Regni Hierosolymitani*, I, no. 1085; Richard (1985: 282–3).

dealings of the Venetians with Byzantine Cyprus were conducted
from Paphos, the island's westernmost port, and Limassol, the island's
major port in the late Byzantine period.[25]

Just how extensive these commercial activities were is indicated
by a Venetian report drawn up around 1243 that lists formerly
Venetian properties that were most likely confiscated before 1200,
although the precise reasons and dates are unclear. The report lists
Venetian urban properties and lands in the Cypriot countryside.
Most urban and rural properties were in the town and district of
Limassol, with far fewer in Nicosia and Paphos, and none at all in
Famagusta. The Venetians owned several churches, many shops and
houses, gardens, flourmills, pastures, and even a few *casalia*. In Nicosia
they had a house that proved suitable for the king of Cyprus' needs.
The owners included members of prominent Venetian families, such
as the Querini, Venier, Zancaruol, Zeno, Da Canal, Sabatini and
Michel.[26] Accordingly, when King Richard I of England came to
Cyprus in 1191, he received a delegation of Latin merchants on
board his galley in Limassol, and they informed him of the usurper
Isaac's flight from the city. Richard sent them back with assurances
that the lives and properties of the local populace were in no danger from his forces.[27] Thus by the time of the Latin conquest Cyprus
was already a society undergoing Western economic penetration.

The conquest wrought no radical change on the system of land
tenure in Cyprus, other than through the introduction of feudal obligations on the fiefs granted by the king. The lands previously belonging
to the Byzantine emperor and to those aristocrats who left the island
after 1191 were taken over by Guy of Lusignan, as well as some of
the property of the remaining Greeks and the Church. The scale of
confiscations cannot be quantified, although Benedict of Peterborough
states that the Byzantine lords ceded one half of their lands to King
Richard. Some lands were granted as fiefs to incoming Latin nobles and
burgesses, some were granted to the crown, and some to the Latin
clergy, enough that around 1195 Guy's elder brother and successor
Aimery had to recover some for the crown. A considerable portion

[25] Richard (1986a: 70–3); Grivaud (1994: 150–1, 155); Galatariotou (1991: 56
and note 75); *Documenti del commercio veneziano*, I, 77–8, 85–6, 366–7.
[26] Papadopoulou (1983: 308–15); Papacostas (1999b); Schabel (2002: 404); Schabel
in this volume.
[27] 'Estoire d'Eracles', 163–4; Nicolaou-Konnari (2000a: 43, 55).

of the arable land on Cyprus must have been kept for the royal domain. There is no thirteenth-century documentation on how many of Cyprus' villages, probably numbering over 800, formed part of the royal estates, but Venetian statistics compiled before 1531, perhaps in around 1500, list 260 royal *casalia*, to which another 60 can be added on account of an absence of heirs, for such estates were incorporated into the royal domain. This amounts to roughly one third of all Cypriot villages. Given the fluctuations caused by confiscations, redistributions and the absence of heirs from the thirteenth to the sixteenth century, this proportion cannot be considered constant throughout the Lusignan period. Nonetheless, royal estates must have formed a large part of the total land area under cultivation.[28]

The Lusignan kings encouraged commerce but maintained a tight control on economic activity within the kingdom, and the centralised fiscal administration they had inherited from Byzantium helped them in realising this aim. They ensured that they had estates in many of the most fertile and well-watered parts of Cyprus, encouraged the cultivation of profitable export crops like sugar, and maintained control over the salt lakes, which yielded valuable exports in the forms of salt and salted fish. They also drew revenues from customs imposts and from the movement of goods within Cyprus, ensuring in these cases that royal officers weighed and measured such goods, but they did not create a merchant fleet for moving such goods themselves, allowing instead the ships of the Venetian, Genoese, Provençal, Catalan and other overseas merchants to transport these commodities both to and from Cyprus and around the island. Nonetheless, they granted far fewer concessions to the Italian and other communes than those granted in Latin Syria. Not until the fourteenth century did some of these communes have their own bonded warehouses in Cyprus, unlike Acre in the thirteenth century, where the Genoese and the Venetians had their own warehouses coexisting with the royal depot. Indeed, the crown itself could determine the location of such markets, and in May 1199 King Aimery established the Limassol market on confiscated lands. Nor, as in Latin Syria, did the communes have extensive holdings throughout the Cypriot countryside, except for the Venetians early on in the Limassol district. Later, the only *casale*

---

[28] *Cartulary*, nos. 1–4, 8, 78 (esp. p. 200), 83, 95; Richard (1986a: 68, 70–1); Edbury (1991: 16–18); Grivaud (2001a: 362). See also Nicolaou-Konnari in this volume.

recorded as belonging to a commune proper was Despoyre, which King Henry I granted in 1232 to the Genoese.[29]

Royal control over economic activity was pervasive. The crown kept exclusive control over public highways, which meant that estate owners could not levy tolls on the traffic using them, and likewise monopolized the minting of coins, unlike the situation in the Kingdom of Jerusalem, where some of the major nobles struck their own coins and where various foreign currencies circulated alongside the local ones, royal or noble. Imported foreign currency was melted down and re-struck in the royal mints, one of which was situated in Nicosia in the thirteenth century and another possibly at a coastal location, such as Limassol or Paphos.[30] A series of royal bans and ordinances dating from the late thirteenth and early fourteenth centuries shows how the quality of certain items, such as gold, silverware, drapes and camlets, was subject to royal supervision, and the textiles had to obtain a royal stamp of approval. Royal supervision was also extended in the area of prices so as to prevent speculation in times of scarcity, the ordinance of 1296 regulating the price of bread being a good example.[31] The bread sold in Nicosia was itself made from flour from the royal flourmills in Kythrea, a village northeast of the capital. Fixed dues were payable for the sale of foodstuffs, the operation of shops, especially those on the covered way in Nicosia, and, at city gates, for goods about to enter the town, particularly on wine.[32]

In economic terms the incoming Latins did not completely displace the indigenous Greeks and Syrians of Cyprus. The Byzantine institution known as the *syngritikon* seems to have continued as the secrète throughout the Lusignan period. It corresponded to an inland revenue department, and its officials managed the royal domain and the finances of the crown until the Venetian annexation of Cyprus in 1474, probably applying traditional Byzantine methods in registering properties, determining customs dues and receiving statements of account from the viscounts, other royal officials, and persons to whom the royal estates had been farmed out. Pensions, annuities and other items of expenditure were disbursed from these revenues. Although

---

[29] Grivaud (2001a: 363–5).

[30] Edbury (1991: 185); Metcalf (1996–2000, I: 1–3, 11–13).

[31] 'Ordenemens de la court dou vesconte', 408–10, nos. 360, 362–3 and 413–16, nos. 369–74.

[32] *Cartulary*, no. 62; Richard (1995b: 350).

not until 1318 was one of the officials, George Cappadoca, mentioned by name, Greeks appear to have staffed it by tradition. A bull of Pope Gregory IX of 1237 makes it clear that Greek and Syrian *baillis* were being appointed to administer crown lands and noble estates, often in place of Latin ones, and we have specific examples from the fourteenth century. Moreover, even some Greek and Syrian landowners remained, as the accounts of the *casale* of Psimolophou and the autobiography of George of Cyprus, later Patriarch Gregory of Constantinople, demonstrate.[33]

Where a change from Greek to Latin landowners occurred, however, it did not substantially alter the conditions of the rural peasantry forming most of the population, and who depending on their legal status owed to varying degrees labour service and rents payable in cash or in kind, in the form of crops, to their lords.[34] They did not deal directly with the feudal lords, for the latter employed *baillis* or *appaltores* for the administration of their estates and they were often Greeks or Syrians able to speak the language of the peasantry.[35]

Trade with Western European and particularly Italian merchants increased considerably following the Latin conquest, when the pre-1191 dominance of the Venetians over other Western traders on the island was ended. On arriving in 1192, Guy of Lusignan promised grants and exemptions to Pisan merchants in Cyprus.[36] In 1207 Pisan and Venetian merchants travelling from Beirut to Egypt alighted on Cyprus to land some commodities, and by 1210 Girard of Maske, possibly belonging to the noble Pisan family of Masca, is attested as owning a house in Limassol. According to the Venetian report of around 1243, in Limassol the Pisans possessed a courtyard, the Pisan Hugh of Clara possessed a house, and another Pisan, Lobardus, possessed a garden, a quarry and a graveyard. The allusion to a courtyard indicates that the Pisans in Limassol were organised as a corporate entity and were not simply resident there as individuals. Limassol remained the most important and possibly the only centre of Pisan mercantile activity in Cyprus throughout the thirteenth century. Even after the fall of Acre and Tyre in 1291, and despite Famagusta's

---

[33] Edbury (1991: 191–2); Mas Latrie, *Histoire*, III, 641–2; Grivaud (1994: 152, 154); Richard (1947: 129). See also Nicolaou-Konnari and Edbury in this volume.
[34] Richard (1985: 270–3); Edbury (1989: 147–9).
[35] Edbury (1998b: 146–8). See also Nicolaou-Konnari in this volume.
[36] *Continuation de Guillaume de Tyr*, 150–3.

increased importance, it continued to be the official centre of the Pisan community, and in 1293 the Pisan consul in Cyprus was attested as the official representative of the Pisan commune throughout the island, not simply of Pisans in Limassol. His court and administration were located in the *loggia* of the Pisan commune, situated near the *commercium regis*, the royal customs house near the harbour area. The consular staff included a *sensarius*, the official middleman of the commune, a notary who served as the scribe of the commune, and a *platearius* or sergeant. Even in 1307 the respective functions of the notaries attached to the Pisan consuls at Limassol and Famagusta still favoured Limassol. In Famagusta the Pisan notary assisted Pisan merchants in a semi-official capacity, but his colleague in Limassol still bore the title 'scribus atque notarius Pisani communis in Cipro', on account of which he acted in an official capacity.[37] Limassol's good mooring facilities and relatively westerly location made it, along with the harbour of Paphos to a lesser extent, the natural port of call for Western merchants visiting Cyprus in the late Byzantine period and the first century of Lusignan rule. The island's main port until the end of the thirteenth century, its lucrative trade is illustrated by the contract that King Aimery of Cyprus negotiated with a consortium of merchants as early as May 1199, in which he granted them the right to levy customs in Limassol for two years and received 28,050 white bezants in return.[38]

The organization of the Pisan commune was found, broadly speaking, in the other communes set up in Cyprus, Latin Syria and Latin Greece by overseas colonies of Venetian, Genoese, Catalan or Provençal merchants. Provençal as well as Italian merchants began to trade with Cyprus shortly after the Latin conquest, although not quite as early as has been claimed. The document dated October 1198 in which Aimery offers merchants from Marseilles trading privileges and a *casale* is a forgery, although it may have been modelled on trading rights awarded them in the twelfth and thirteenth centuries, the texts of which have been lost. Provençal trade with Cyprus was established in the early thirteenth century. Mas Latrie claims that from 1225 onwards the citizens of Montpellier enjoyed trading privileges with Cyprus similar to those acquired by merchants from

---

[37] *Cartulaire général de l'Ordre des Hospitaliers*, II, no. 1354; Jacoby (1984a: 155 and note 49, 158–9); Papadopoulou (1983: 310, lines 55–6 and 312, lines 107–8, 138–40).
[38] *Regesta Regni Hierosolymitani*, II, no. 755a.

Marseilles. This is possible when one considers that around 1233, shortly after the Civil War, Raymond of Conches was admitted as a witness for King Henry I in deliberations initiated by the nobles' court on Cyprus, the *Haute Cour*. The king's poverty as a result of this war is explicitly referred to in these deliberations, and in March 1236 he tried to attract merchants from Marseilles, Montpellier and other Provençal towns trading in the area by reducing customs duties.[39]

According to the relevant document, drawn up in Nicosia at the request of Raymond of Conches and Giraud Oliver, the consul of Marseilles in Acre, transactions concluded in Cyprus were facilitated, duties payable on goods imported to and sold in Cyprus were reduced to four percent, and unsold goods could be freely transported and sold elsewhere without payment of duty. Goods purchased in Cyprus would be subject to local duties only, while goods imported from the Sultanate of Konya or other places in the region would be subject to a four percent duty if sold in Cyprus. If they were re-exported then a duty of one bezant would be payable on every *quintar* of alum exported, two bezants on every *quintar* of wool, one bezant for every hundred goatskins, half a bezant on each *rotulus* of silk, and one bezant on every hundred bezants' worth of silk drapes and other merchandise. Later sources also allude to the import of unrefined silk and silken fabrics from Konya and Syria to Cyprus, as well as alum, wool and goat hides.[40]

The Provençal merchants owned real estate on Cyprus by this time. According to the Venetian report of ca. 1243 the commune of the Provençals acquired property in Limassol, possessing a house and two shops. Nonetheless, Provençal merchants probably just visited Limassol at this time and did not reside there, using it like the Italians as their chief operational base. Provençal trade with Cyprus was boosted in 1248 by King Louis IX of France's crusade against Egypt and the logistical preparations involved, for he used Cyprus and particularly the port of Limassol as his headquarters. Hence the notarial registers of a certain Amalric from March to July 1248 contain a total of 462 *commendae* contracts, 184 of which, that is nearly 40 percent, concern trade with Syria, Acre and Cyprus, even if only

---

[39] *Regesta Regni Hierosolymitani*, I, no. 747; Mas Latrie, *Histoire*, I, 315 and notes 2, 4, II, 24–32; Mayer (1972: 186–8); Philip of Novara, 'Livre', 515–16.
[40] *Regesta Regni Hierosolymitani*, II, no. 1071; Mas Latrie, *Histoire*, I, 315 and notes 2, 4; Mayer (1972: 193–5); Jacoby (1995: 395–6).

nine of the *commendae* explicitly mention Cyprus as a destination. Two Marseillais ships, the *Cygnus* and the *Sicardus*, are mentioned as sailing to Cyprus for trading purposes, and King Louis chartered other ships from Marseilles to transport troops and supplies to Cyprus.[41] More ships from Marseilles frequented Cypriot ports during the crusade and the king's subsequent sojourn in Cyprus, which explains Pope Innocent IV's confirmation at this time of the privileges enjoyed by Marseillais merchants in Cyprus. This confirmation formed part of a series of documents drawn up for reducing the tolls payable on the goods these merchants transported.

The pope wrote several letters in March 1250. He assured the commune of Marseilles that he had confirmed the privileges that King Aimery had allegedly granted them in Cyprus 1198, as well as their possession there of the *casale* of Flacie, not knowing that the charter was forged. He instructed the Latin patriarch of Jerusalem and the archbishop of Nicosia to uphold the privileges that the kings of Cyprus had granted to Marseilles. He informed King Henry I that the commune of Marseilles had complained of unjust imposts and exactions that the king and some of his nobles had demanded, asking him to desist from such practices henceforth. Then the pope wrote again to the commune of Marseilles assuring them that he had confirmed the various privileges, incomes and properties that the kings of Cyprus and Jerusalem had granted them at different times. The commerce between Marseilles and Cyprus, however, slackened in the wake of King Louis IX's departure, for in 1257 the people of Marseilles petitioned Charles of Anjou, Louis' brother, to assist them in recovering 'the rights and possessions that they had once enjoyed in Ancona, Cyprus and other places'. A letter of Pope Clement IV dated 9 June 1267 to the commune of Marseilles proves that the merchants there continued to maintain trade with Cyprus. Clement confirmed the privileges that the people of Marseilles claimed to have received from King Aimery and which Pope Innocent IV had subsequently ratified. King Hugh III of Cyprus began his reign in 1267, and perhaps the commune of Marseilles felt the need to have their privileges reconfirmed by the new ruler. It was in this period, in 1272, that a delegation of Anconitan merchants first visited Cyprus,

---

[41] Papadopoulou (1983: 311, lines 95–7); Pryor (1984: 397–400); Abulafia (1987c: 22, 27, 29–32).

bringing with them letters of commendation from their magistrate and from their lord, King Charles of Anjou, who had by then conquered Southern Italy and Sicily.[42] No recorded exchange of goods took place during their visit, the earliest occurring in the fourteenth century.

Genoese trade with Cyprus began soon after the Latin conquest. Genoese merchants resident in Cyprus are recorded as early as 1203 and in 1218 Queen Alice, the widow of the recently deceased King Hugh I, granted them several privileges, including the freedom to buy, sell, export and import by land and sea throughout the kingdom, with neither tolls nor the customary payments attached to such tolls being imposed upon them. The Genoese also acquired the right to be tried in their own communal courts for all cases other than robbery, treason and homicide, over which the royal courts had exclusive jurisdiction. Furthermore, they were given two tracts of land in Nicosia and Famagusta on which they could build houses, while Queen Alice undertook to compensate any Genoese ship that was wrecked off the coasts of Cyprus for the loss of its crew and cargo. She made this concession with the consent of her counsellors, among whom was Philip of Ibelin, the *bailli* of Cyprus and the leading representative of what was to become the island's most powerful noble family, with which the Genoese were to forge extremely close links. One observes that Famagusta was included in the grant of land made to the Genoese, indicating their early involvement there and their appreciation of its future commercial potential at a time when neither the Venetians nor the Pisans appear to have exhibited corresponding interest in this port.[43]

Genoa acquired additional commercial privileges in Cyprus during the Civil War of 1229–33. Genoese ships helped King Henry I and the nobles led by the Ibelins take the harbour fortress of Kyrenia from the Cypriot adherents of the German Emperor Frederick II. The king, who had recently attained his majority, rewarded them in a new treaty of December 1232. It renewed their legal rights, their immunities and their commercial privileges mentioned above, although Genoese merchants purchasing commodities needing to be weighed and measured, such as wheat, barley, pulses, wine or oil, had to pay various duties to the royal officers, who were obliged to measure the

---

[42] Mayer (1972: 198–201, 204–5, 211–12); Aristeidou (1978: 50).
[43] Mas Latrie, *Histoire*, II, 39; Jacoby (1984a: 159 and note 72). On the Ibelins, see Edbury in this volume.

goods on request. Additional lands were granted to the commune and people of the city of Genoa in their corporate capacity. In Nicosia they obtained the houses near the Pedieos River in which the consuls and vice consuls of Genoa had long been resident, as well as their own public baths. In Limassol they received some houses and a tower by the seashore close to the public highway and the royal customs house, which placed them near the harbour. The consul of Genoa was also granted the *casale* of Despoyre with its appurtenances in the district of Limassol. In Famagusta the commune acquired some houses near the public highway with their backs to the sea, and in Paphos houses in the Karmi district. These were described as suitable as residences for the Genoese consuls and vice consuls, who were also allowed ovens within their premises in all Cypriot towns. This enabled the Genoese communities to bake their own bread and acquire independence from outside suppliers, a privilege subsequently extended to individual Genoese. King Henry also promised to protect the persons and properties of subjects of Genoa within his realm on both land and sea, including those shipwrecked. Relations between Cyprus and Genoa were further cemented by the five-year defensive alliance concluded in December 1233. By 1243 the commune of Genoa had acquired an additional house in Limassol, formerly owned by a Venetian.[44]

The Venetian report of ca. 1243 records an impressive amount of property owned by the Venetian community on the island but confiscated at some point. Since it is certain that some of these possessions were lost decades before 1243, most scholars assume that all of it was seized before 1200. The expropriations, regardless of when they occurred and for what reason, must have harmed the Venetians greatly, for none of the prominent Venetian families mentioned in the report appears subsequently. Despite the losses, Venetians continued to conduct trade involving Cyprus. Already in 1201 a Venetian merchant named John Mençulo de Baffo, whose surname suggests that he lived in Paphos, undertook a joint venture with his nephew Peter Rambaldo, who entrusted him with 71 bezants while they were at Paphos. Mençulo's trading activities encompassed Syria and Alexandria in Egypt, whence he exported alum.[45]

---

[44] Mas Latrie, *Histoire*, II, 51–8; Hill (1940–1952, II: 125); Jacoby (1984a: 159 and note 77).

[45] Jacoby (1984a: 165–6); Papacostas (1999b); Schabel (2002: 404); *Documenti del commercio veneziano*, I, nos. 454–5.

Venetian sources also confirm Limassol's continuing importance for them in the late thirteenth century. An incomplete Venetian portolan possibly compiled around 1270 follows the course of an itinerary from Acre to Europe via Cyprus, with specific mention of Limassol but not Famagusta or Paphos. An observation in the Venetian commercial handbook of Zibaldone da Canal, a member of the prominent da Canal family, also indicates such links between Acre and Limassol. This handbook states that prior to 1291 similar weights and measures were used in both Limassol and Acre, and refers to Limassol as the main port of Cyprus. The trade between Limassol and other Mediterranean ports covered short rather than long distances. Saffron, nutmeg and other spices like pepper, described as 'minor' because they were sold in small quantities, were imported from Acre, while pine resin and indigo were exported. In the later thirteenth century the Venetians developed a lively commerce in Apulia in Southern Italy, importing grain along with olive oil to Limassol.[46]

A resolution of 1302 adopted by the Venetian senate states that the crown of Cyprus had granted judicial privileges to the commune of Venice in the thirteenth century. The first grant under King Henry I was not implemented because the king lacked the requisite power, and he later offered the Venetians a large sum of money for privileges promised but not given. Mas Latrie considers the grant to have antedated 1233, the king's minority at the time explaining his inability to implement it. Jacoby has suggested that the Venetian ambassadors visiting Cilician Armenia in 1246 may have tried unsuccessfully to reverse the expropriations of Venetian property taking place before 1243, but his arguments are inconclusive given that there is no evidence that they also came to Cyprus. According to the Venetian senate's resolution, the Venetian ambassador Mark Barbo was also offered money following King Henry's death, during the regencies of Queen Plaisance of Antioch (1253–61) and her successor Hugh of Antioch-Lusignan (1261–67), who later became King Hugh III (1267–84). During the 1280s ships sailed regularly between Venice and Cyprus, and Venetian ambassadors visited Cyprus three times, in 1285, 1286 and 1288, in order to uphold and promote Venetian interests there, the resolution of 1302 representing a continuation of this policy. It also alluded to possessions, jurisdictions and privileges that the Venetian merchants and commune enjoyed in Byzantine

---

[46] Jacoby (1986b: 410, 412; 1995: 397–8).

Cyprus, especially in the Nicosia and Limassol districts. Through their ambassador the Venetians now requested from King Henry II that their merchants should trade throughout the island without paying tolls, should be granted churches, a square and a *loggia* in which to reside in Nicosia, Limassol and Famagusta, and should be allowed to buy them if they were not granted. They also wished disputes between Venetians and cases where a Venetian was the defendant to be settled in their own courts. Their requests were largely satisfied in the treaty concluded with Henry in June 1306.[47]

Genoese merchants developed trade between Cyprus and the Christian Kingdom of Cilician Armenia by the later thirteenth century, as appears from the deeds of Federico di Piazzalunga and Pietro di Bargone, both Genoese notaries resident in Laiazzo, the kingdom's chief commercial port. The acts drawn up by Bargone in 1277–79 provide much detailed information. The will of the Genoese Otto Blanchard refers to a ship that he had owned with John of Quarto, a resident of Famagusta, stating that this ship had undertaken three voyages up until then. Blanchard resided permanently in Famagusta and had a house there. In a notarial deed of April 1279 the Genoese merchant Peter of Giusulfo appointed procurators to act for him, and among the witnesses was a certain Arancio of Limassol, who must have been a merchant resident in Limassol with business in Laiazzo. In an act of October 1279 a master of medicine named Roland appointed a procurator to recover a debt from William *di Addone sive Cypro*, who must have resided in Cyprus, although the particular town is not stated. A transaction of November 1277 records how Rici di Noli sold between 35 and 40 *quintars* of iron to John Camarlengo, undertaking to have it transported to Nicosia at his own risk. The agreement even provided for the transportation of the fodder required for the horses that would transport the iron. The deed does not state the port of unloading, but Famagusta or Kyrenia would be likeliest, both being nearer Nicosia than Limassol was.[48] The fact that the iron was destined for Nicosia suggests, moreover, that the purchaser resided there and had a warehouse in the capital.

Piazzalunga's deeds for the year 1274 record the grant of loans,

---

[47] Mas Latrie, 'Nouvelles preuves (1873)', 46–8 and 47, note 1; Mas Latrie, *Histoire*, II, 102–8; *Délibérations des assemblées vénitiennes*, I, nos. 66, 81, 87, 115–16, 122, 126, 151; Jacoby (1984a: 165–6).
[48] Pietro di Bargone, nos. 46, 72, 118, 128.

the repayment of debts and money transfers between merchants operating in Armenia and Cyprus, and two members of the noble Genoese Rubeus family, Guy and Lanfranc, appear prominently as procurators. The notarial acts do not state in which town they lived, but by the middle of the thirteenth century Nicosia had become a centre for money lending. Hugh of Fagiano, the archbishop of Nicosia, stridently and unequivocally condemned the capital's usurers in 1257. He accused them of amassing considerable interest in the guise of notional sales, whereby the borrower 'purchased' goods at a price much higher than their actual worth from the lender and then 'sold' the goods back to him at a lower price amounting to hardly one half of the original purchase price. Furthermore, interest over and above the legal limit, which the archbishop unfortunately does not specify, could be obtained through the imposition of an imaginary 'penalty', or by making the borrower declare falsely that he had borrowed a sum far greater than that received and compelling him to repay the declared as opposed to the actual sum. Archbishop Hugh stated that these subterfuges practiced so as to obtain interest had spread like a cancer throughout Cyprus 'and especially in the city of Nicosia', and that since the prohibitions he had declared against them had hitherto been ineffectual, he was not simply repeating the prohibitions but also declaring excommunicate all involved in such transactions. The fact that borrowers were clearly prepared to go along with such subterfuges, however, despite their unethical character and the high rates of interest they had to pay, shows that there was a strong demand for capital that was to be used to finance commercial ventures.[49]

The Genoese trade in iron may also have caused problems. During the mid- and late thirteenth century the Muslims imported timber and iron to an increasing extent from Western merchants for fashioning galleys, siege engines and weapons in general. In 1251 Archbishop Hugh condemned such exports and those engaging in them, something repeated by his successor, Archbishop Ranulph, around 1280, as well as in the *Assizes* of the *Cour des Bourgeois*, drawn up in

---

[49] Federico di Piazzalunga, nos. 42, 54–5, 65, 68–9; *Synodicum Nicosiense*, nos. C.8, B.16b, A.XXIX.

[50] *Synodicum Nicosiense*, 154–5, no. 8, and 136–7, no. 15b; *Assizes*, Codex One, art. 45, Codex Two, art. 46.

Acre in the mid-thirteenth century.[50]

The gradual loss to the Muslims of the castles and cities still held
by the Latins on the Syrian coastline between 1263 and 1291 encouraged Famagusta's development as a international entrepôt in the carrying trade between Western Europe and the lands of the Near East.
Although before 1291 refugees had the option of fleeing to Acre and
Beirut, they often came to settle in Cyprus. Moreover, refugees from
Antioch settled in both Cyprus and the Kingdom of Cilician Armenia.
Most of those going to Cyprus probably left after Sultan Baybars'
forces had captured their cities, settling chiefly in Famagusta, although
others settled in Limassol and Nicosia. Famagusta was nearer both
to Syria and to Cilician Armenia, so from Famagusta it was easier
for settlers to keep trading with their fellow refugees in Cilician
Armenia.[51]

In 1291 the forces of the Muslim Sultan Kalawun, Baybars' successor, captured Acre and shortly afterwards the remaining Latin
coastal cities in Syria, which were destroyed to prevent their use as
bridgeheads by Latin invaders. The refugees heading for Cyprus
joined previous settlers in Famagusta, further boosting its commercial life. Sometimes only the wealthy could flee to Cyprus, Tyre
being a case in point, for the poor lacked boats. The abrupt influx
of numerous refugees in 1291 inevitably caused short-term economic
dislocation. On their arrival, foodstuffs suddenly shot up in price,
causing a massive depreciation in value of whatever possessions the
refugees sold, and thereby impoverishing them further. Rents sky-
rocketed and their former friends spurned them now that they were
poor, although King Henry II employed some dispossessed knights
and sergeants and along with the queen provided alms on a regular
basis. Refugees from Tortosa formed their own quarter in Famagusta,
which indicates that many had settled there.[52]

The refugees who migrated to Cyprus in the later thirteenth century included Italians and Syrian Christians. Pisan refugees from
Acre settled in Famagusta, although it is uncertain whether they
acquired Pisan nationality before or after reaching Cyprus, while
other Pisans arrived directly from Italy. Some were artisans, others
were merchants, including members of prominent Pisan families, and

---

[51] Jacoby (1984a: 153–4 and note 41).
[52] Richard (1972: 221); Jacoby (1984a: 154 and note 47); The Templar of Tyre,
Cronaca, §§268 (504), 280 (516).

some were Tuscans with Pisan nationality. The Genoese in Cyprus increased from 1285 onwards. Genoese refugees from the fortress of Marqab and the cities of Tripoli and Botrun settled mainly in Famagusta after those places fell between 1285 and 1289. Additional Genoese refugees from the captured cities of Sidon, Tyre, and Tortosa settled there in 1291, while the Genoese of Jubail were brought to Cyprus in a Genoese galley in 1300. The term 'Genoese', moreover, encompassed citizens of Genoa, residents of the Ligurian cities under Genoese control and Latins and Syrians in the Eastern Mediterranean who had been awarded Genoese nationality without full citizenship rights. Among the latter were refugees from Jubail settling in Cyprus, who were numerous and important enough to be included among the Genoese subjects acquiring privileges in the commercial treaty of 1365 between King Peter I of Cyprus and the Commune of Genoa.[53] The loss of the final Latin possessions in Syria and Palestine and the arrival of Latin and Syrian refugees fulfilled the third precondition required for Cyprus to perform an important role in the international commerce of the fourteenth century, the other two having been the establishment of a Latin feudal administration and the attraction of Western merchants. A new chapter in its economic and commercial development now opened.

Cyprus as a Hub of International Commerce: 1291–1374

The Rise of Famagusta

The development of Cyprus in general and of Famagusta in particular as an international trading centre forced both the Lusignan crown and the Western trading communities to upgrade their institutional presence in Famagusta, now the island's chief commercial port and, together with Alexandria and Laiazzo, one of the three great emporia of the Eastern Mediterranean. Under King Henry II Famagusta acquired a new judicial status with the establishment of a burgess court there sometime between 1285, when the king began his reign, and 1296. After the loss of the cities of Latin Syria the king had Famagusta linked institutionally to the defunct Kingdom of Jerusalem

---

[53] Mas Latrie, *Histoire*, II, 257; Jacoby (1984a: 156–61); The Templar of Tyre, *Cronaca*, §378 (614).

with the offices and privileges pertaining to it, and the Lusignan
kings of Cyprus retained the title to the former kingdom. The seals
of the customs house and of the mint in Famagusta, founded under
Henry II and minting silver *gros* coins from 1310 onwards, bore the
arms of the Kingdom of Jerusalem, and clearly the king was bestow-
ing not only the commercial but also the institutional privileges of
the now destroyed coastal cities of the Kingdom of Jerusalem on
Famagusta, in effect reconstituting the lost kingdom on Cypriot soil.[54]
This reconstitution along with the rapidly burgeoning commercial
activity and population of Famagusta led to the extension of its judicial institutions. By the early fourteenth century it had acquired a
marine court subject to the castellan of the city, the Court of the
Chain mentioned in the *Livre des Assises des Bourgeois* probably being
the same as this, a court for the large Syrian population presided
over by a *rais* who was a Latin knight, and a commercial jurisdiction presided over by the *bailli* of the *commercium* or customs house,
dealing mainly with customs duties. The *Livre des Assises des Bourgeois* also
mentions a market court, but whether one functioned as a distinct
entity in Cyprus cannot be ascertained, and the Court of Burgesses
or the *bailli* of the *commercium* mentioned above may have fulfilled its
functions.[55]

After 1291 the Western communes in Cyprus likewise upgraded
their institutions in Famagusta. Whereas previously the Genoese in
Cyprus were subject to consuls and *vicecomites* residing in Latin Syria,
from 1292 onwards they came under direct Genoese supervision in
the person of a *podestà et vicecomes Januensis* resident in Cyprus, the
first one being Matthew Zaccaria. For the first few years this *podestà*
was resident in Nicosia, where from 1297 onwards there also existed
a Genoese *loggia* so as to keep in close touch with the royal court.
However, a consul subordinate to the *podestà* headed the Genoese
communities existing in Limassol, Famagusta and Paphos, a hierarchy modelled on that of the Genoese colony at Pera from the 1260s

---

[54] Richard (1972: 222–5); Metcalf and Pitsillides (1992: 13); Metcalf (1996–2000,
II: 5). On the Kingdom of Jerusalem's continuation in Famagusta, see Edbury in
this volume.
[55] Lamberto di Sambuceto, *1296–1299*, no. 155, *1302*, no. 278, *1299–1301 (AOL)*,
no. 118; 'Bans et ordonnances des rois de Chypre', ch. 32, 377–8; Francesco Balducci
Pegolotti, 83–9; *Assizes*, Codex One, arts. 41, 43, 45–6, 230, 274, 288, 290–4, 297,
Codex Two, arts. 42, 44, 46–7, 272, 287, 289–93, 296, 298; Richard (1972: 223–5;
1987: 388); Grivaud (1993: 133–45; 1996: 1007 and note 173); Pietro Valderio, 8.

onwards. But the war between Venice and Genoa beginning in 1293 also affected Cyprus. A Venetian fleet sailed in 1294 to Limassol, destroying the Genoese tower and *loggia*, and when it sailed to Famagusta the royal castellan there, Philip of Brie, advised Genoese merchants in the town to seek refuge in Nicosia.[56] This is the context of the 48 Genoese notarial deeds that the Genoese notary Lamberto di Sambuceto drew up in Nicosia between March and December 1297, an invaluable source for the structure and commercial activities of the Genoese commune there.

Prominent Genoese families such as the de Mari, Rubei, de Porta and Clavaro in Nicosia engaged in lending or borrowing money for commercial ventures and held important offices on occasion. Paschal de Mari appears in 1297 as the Genoese *podestà* in Nicosia. Other Genoese officials mentioned are the *platearii*, court officers of the commune entrusted with gathering tolls, the *bacularius* or bailiff and the *serviens domini potestatis*, a sergeant of the court of the Genoese commune in Nicosia. A notarial deed of 1297 alludes to the clerkship of Nicosia, which the captain of Genoa granted for one year to the notary Nicolinus Binellus, who in turn leased it to Bonaiuncta de Savio. The captains of Genoa were officers with wide-ranging military, financial and judicial powers appointed by the doges of Genoa for one year to administer overseas colonies, while the scribes of Genoese overseas communes held the clerkship. Besides the clerkship of Nicosia there was a similar office in Famagusta, and notaries normally held both positions. In 1299 Sambuceto was either appointed the scribe of the Genoese commune in Famagusta or was acting in this capacity informally. The office of distrainer, who seized the goods of debtors unable to repay, is also mentioned in the Genoese notarial deeds of Nicosia. Two Genoese mentioned in a document confirming the repayment of a debt to Percival de Mari allude to the debtor Nicholas and his brother Leo Pignatarius, who repaid this debt on Nicholas' behalf. The surname Pignatarius, meaning distrainer, probably alludes to this office.[57]

King Henry II apparently favoured Venice in its war with Genoa, and following the Genoese victory at Curzola in 1298 relations between Cyprus and Genoa worsened steadily. In 1299 the Genoese

---

[56] 'Amadi', 232–3; Jacoby (1984a: 159 and note 79, 161–2); Hill (1940–1952, II: 208–9); Edbury (1986: 112–13; 1991: 111–12).
[57] Lamberto di Sambuceto, *1296–1299*, nos. 37–85.

nationals not resident in Cyprus along with the *podestà* and the consuls
of the seaside towns left the island, and in March 1299 the Genoese
ambassador to Henry had Octolinus Rubeus appointed as vicar for
the *podestà*. When Octolinus himself left Cyprus shortly afterwards,
the Genoese assigned two rectors in his place, Octolinus' brother
James Rubeus and Paschal de Mari, mentioned above as the *podestà*
in 1297. By 1301, however, normal relations had been restored.
Although members of these prominent Genoese families were still
residing in Nicosia in the fourteenth century—Paschal's brother
Percival de Mari and Octolinus Rubeus and his brother Simon
testified at the trial of the Templars in 1310–11—the rupture provided the Genoese with the opportunity to move their headquarters
to thriving Famagusta.

Famagusta, Limassol and Paphos each had a rector aided by a
scribe to represent the interests of the Genoese residents. The rector of Famagusta was more important than the others, having two
sergeants at his disposal rather than one. James of Signano, the Genoese
rector of Famagusta in 1299–1300, also had two *platearii* and the
guardian of the Genoese *loggia* to assist him. The Genoese acquired
a *fondaco* or bonded warehouse in Famagusta at this time, possibly
contiguous to the *loggia*. By April 1301 the Genoese were deliberat-
ing the erection of a church in Famagusta dedicated to St Lawrence,
their patron saint. A church of St Lawrence already existed in Nicosia
and possibly served the Genoese community there, and so plans to
construct a new church of St Lawrence in Famagusta indicate its
new significance for the Genoese in Cyprus. Thus when the Genoese
reestablished the office of *podestà* in September 1301, they abolished
the position of rector in Famagusta and appointed Thomas Panzanus
'*podestà* of the Genoese in Famagusta and Cyprus', rather than Nicosia
and Cyprus. signalling Famagusta's now pre-eminent position as the
administrative centre of the Genoese communes on the island.[58]

The Venetians likewise remodelled their institutional presence in
Famagusta after 1291. The text of the Venetian claims submitted in
1302 refers to Limassol and Nicosia but not Famagusta when allud-
ing to the past, precisely because of limited Venetian interests there
in the thirteenth century. But Venetian families recorded in Acre

---

[58] Lamberto di Sambuceto, *1296–1299*, no. 83; Jacoby (1984a: 162–4); Edbury
(1991: 110–11); *The Trial of the Templars*, 67–70.

before 1291 were later present in Famagusta, while some families had members resident in both Famagusta and Venice itself. Although unlike their Genoese counterparts, until the later fourteenth century members of Venetian noble families who were engaged in commerce did not reside in Cyprus, but simply visited Famagusta, by 1302 Venice had focused her presence in the city. Some time between 1291 and 1296 Angelo Bembo is mentioned as the consul of the Venetians in Famagusta, and a document of 1302 referring to Nicholas Zugno as the *consul Venetorum in Cipro* six years or more earlier shows that he had held this office by 1296. Several notarial deeds of 1296–1300 record his exercise of judicial powers over his Venetian fellow nationals, and significantly some of them allude to him as *baiulo*. This title, held by the officers heading all the important Venetian communities in the Eastern Mediterranean, Constantinople and Euboea, was higher than that of consul. By May 1300, moreover, Zugno and his successors were described as the *baiuli* of the Venetians throughout Cyprus. These *baiuli* in Famagusta included among their staff a *platearius*, a *cridator* or town crier attached to the court of the Venetian commune and a *bastonerius* exercising police powers. Furthermore, in Famagusta the Venetian *loggia* was close to the royal *commercium* or customs house. It should be noted that the Venetian presence in towns other than Famagusta was also upgraded, for in 1308 Limassol was important enough to have a Venetian *baiulo*, James Mora.[59]

Trade with the Western Mediterranean and the Adriatic

The presence in Famagusta of other trading communities active on Cyprus intensified after 1291, in some instances establishing communities for the first time. By 1299 the Marseillais, the Montpellerins and the Narbonnais all had consuls in Famagusta, and there was a *fondaco* or bonded warehouse specifically assigned for the Marseillais traders at the port of Famagusta.[60] King Henry II granted the Catalans trading privileges in 1291, and by May 1299 there was a Catalan consul in Cyprus based at Famagusta, although Catalan embassies that were sent to the king in 1293 and in 1316 to obtain a *fondaco*

---

[59] Jacoby (1984a: 167–71).
[60] Lamberto di Sambuceto, *1296–1299*, nos. 103–5, 146, 159–60; Jacoby (1984a: 172).

for the Catalans in Famagusta, the abolition of the *commercium* and
a reduction of the dues on goods undergoing transshipment were
unsuccessful.[61] A notarial deed of July 1300 records two Anconitan
consuls in Famagusta.[62] Florence and Ragusa (Dubrovnik) were two
mercantile communities with no recorded consular presence on
Cyprus, although trading there. The Florentines had close relations
with the Pisans, and on Cyprus many Florentines passed themselves
off as Pisans so as to pay lower customs duties. Therefore it would
have been natural for Pisan consuls to represent them, and by
February 1301 there was a Pisan consul at Famagusta, although he
was subordinate to his counterpart in Limassol.[63] The city of Ragusa
was politically dependent on Venice from 1205 to 1358, albeit enjoying a considerable measure of internal autonomy,[64] and so Ragusans
trading with Cyprus had recourse to the Venetian *baiulo* or *rectores*
resident in the various towns of the island. Besides, there is no record
of Florentines or Ragusans residing permanently in Cyprus, which
in itself obviated the need for a consular presence.

Despite the long-standing Pisan presence on Cyprus, it was Henry
II who in 1291 first conferred a royal diploma promising them security throughout the kingdom and its harbours and recognising their
right to have their own judicial officer in civil cases. Pisans paid a
two percent duty on the value of goods imported and one percent
on goods transshipped elsewhere, while duties payable for chartering
a ship were reduced from one fifth to one tenth. Pisans paid the same
taxes as the burgesses of Nicosia for purchasing victuals. The Pisan
commune possibly requested these formal privileges after the loss of
Latin Syria. Limassol continued to be the commune's administrative
centre, but there was also a *loggia* in Famagusta, and by 1367 it also
possessed a garden in Limassol and a church in Nicosia, dedicated
to St Peter like the Pisan churches in Acre and Constantinople.[65]
When the notarial deeds, chiefly those of Sambuceto, describe the
Pisans as *habitatores* or *burgenses* of Famagusta or, more occasionally,
of some other Cypriot city, this is proof that they resided in Cyprus
and were not simply visitors. Some came to Cyprus from Latin Syria,

---

[61] *Memorias Historicas*, II, nos. 31, 45; d'Olwer (1926: 164).
[62] Lamberto di Sambuceto, *1299–1301* (*AOL*), no. 169.
[63] Francesco Balducci Pegolotti, xx and 84; Otten-Froux (1986: 137).
[64] Krékič (1980b: 25).
[65] Otten-Froux (1986: 128–30).

others from Pisa and its Italian territories, but for most even this information is lacking. The notarial deeds provide a few names of noble Pisans but most originated from the *popolo*, as in the case of the Venetians and the Genoese.

The notarial deeds mention Pisan consuls, court officers, notaries, bailiffs and most of all people engaged in commerce, such as Siger Nucius Porcellus who furnished planks of wood for shipbuilding in Famagusta in 1325. Also mentioned are artisans, tailors, a dyer, a haberdasher and sailors, such as Hugolino and Bernard of Pisa who in 1326 steered ships to Cilician Armenia. Especially interesting is the mention of John de Rau, a Pisan originating from a family later prominent as bankers, whose will of 1333 bequeathed sums to the Latin churches of Famagusta and Nicosia, to the four main mendicant orders and to the hospital of St Stephen in Famagusta. As the commune of Pisa showed less interest in the Pisans of Cyprus in the fourteenth century they gradually disappeared. Some became subjects of the Lusignan crown, such as one involved in a brawl with the Genoese in 1364 along with some Cypriots. He was sentenced by the Genoese *podestà* to have his tongue cut off. Many of the Pisans engaged in trading ventures were party to the *in commendam* contracts, obliging the borrower to repay the capital and three fourths of the profits, although in areas less at risk from the evils of piracy and warfare he sometimes repaid only two thirds or one half. They concluded such contracts with other Pisans, Venetians, Tuscans and notably Genoese merchants, for both Pisans and the Genoese traded frequently with Cilician Armenia. Other destinations mentioned in deeds involving Pisans included Venice, Ancona, the Adriatic littoral, the Aegean area and Clarentza in two instances and Provence in one instance. Textiles, wine and grain were sent to Cilician Armenia, sugar and cotton to Venice, carobs to the Aegean area and drapes to Clarentza, while pepper was also traded. Cotton and ginger were imported from Cilician Armenia, yet paradoxically no notarial deed mentions Pisa as a destination.[66]

Some of Sambuceto's notarial deeds indicate a lively trade between Cyprus and Florence in the early fourteenth century. The Florentine banking houses of the Bardi, Peruzzi and Mozzi were involved in the importation of grain to Cyprus from Apulia, a region in the

---

[66] Otten (1986: 130–7, esp. 136, note 87, 140–3).

Angevin Kingdom of Naples, and practised large-scale moneylending. Cyprus and other lands of the Near East experienced several years of drought at the close of the thirteenth century, and the Lusignan crown promulgated legislation in 1296 to control bread prices. Representatives of the Bardi arranged for consignments of wheat to be despatched to Cyprus on ships setting sail from the Apulian ports of Manfredonia and Barletta in 1299–1300.[67] Those deeds recording loans show that representatives of the Bardi, Peruzzi and Mozzi banking houses lent or borrowed impressive sums in transactions involving Anconitans, Sicilians, Majorcans, Genoese and Latin Christians. Moneylenders of Nicosia advanced sums to representatives of the Peruzzi, while the Piacenzan banking house of Cavazoli also executed money transfers in Cyprus.[68] The Peruzzi appear even more prominently as bankers in the notarial deeds of 1307–10, drawn up by Sambuceto and his colleague Giovanni de Rocha, arranging for pepper to be shipped to Genoa and transporting grain to Rhodes. The Hospitallers had recently conquered Rhodes from Byzantium and it lacked grain on account of the fighting. A deed of March 1310 records that the Peruzzi also chartered ships in Cyprus.[69] By the fourteenth century there were more Florentines than Pisans in Cyprus and the Eastern Mediterranean. Michel Balard has cautiously estimated that there were 46 Florentines and 97 Pisans trading in Famagusta shortly after 1300, but in the deeds of the Venetian notary Nicholas de Boateriis, resident in Famagusta between 1360 and 1362, five Florentines appear as opposed to one Pisan.[70]

As financiers, the representatives of such banking houses enjoyed enhanced social standing, witnessing contracts signed by Genoese, Venetians, Piacenzans, South Italians, Catalans, Sicilians and Christians originally from Latin Syria. The contracts concerned diverse matters, such as wills, the appointment of proctors, dowries, debt repayments, loans and currency exchanges involving Armenian *daremi*, *livres tournois* and Cypriot bezants. A number of contracts specify that the

---

[67] Mas Latrie, *Histoire*, II, 97–8; Lamberto di Sambuceto, *1299–1301 (AOL)*, no. 109, *1300–1301*, nos. 57, 64, *1296–1299*, nos. 10, 36; Richard (1967–1968); Jacoby (1995: 409).

[68] Lamberto di Sambuceto, *1296–1299*, no. 111, *1300–1301*, nos. 102, 142, 178, 248, 343, 262–3, *1302*, no. 64.

[69] Lamberto di Sambuceto, *1304–1307*, no. 98; Giovanni de Rocha, nos. 61, 80, 85.

[70] Balletto (1998: 261–3).

gold or Saracen bezant of Cyprus equalled three and a half white bezants. One must bear in mind, however, that by the early fourteenth century the Cypriot bezants appearing so often in notarial deeds of the time are units of account rather than actual currency, for by then the *gros grands* and the *gros petits* had displaced the bezant as the standard currency struck under King Henry II.[71] The Latin clergy in Cyprus also had dealings with the Bardi and the Peruzzi in effecting money transfers to Rome, as appears in papal letters. Such bankers regularly lent money to Latin prelates, as we learn from ensuing problems. For example, in 1336 a dispute arose between merchants of the Bardi resident in Cyprus and Bishop Gerard of Paphos over the restoration of money assigned to him from the papal treasury for the defence of Cyprus against the Muslims. Gerard had not spent the money for the purposes intended, but for the expenses of his church, and had mortgaged the goods of his church to the Bardi for up to 25,000 gold florins, so that his successor Bishop Eudes was unable to repay the sums owed to them.[72]

Francesco Balducci Pegolotti, whose trading manual *La pratica della mercatura* is an invaluable guide to the commodities, prices, weights and measures in use throughout the Mediterranean area in the early fourteenth century, was himself first employed by the Bardi in 1310. Coming to Cyprus in 1324, he persuaded King Hugh IV to reduce the import duties payable by all Florentine merchants from four to two percent, in line with their Pisan, Provençal, Anconitan and Catalan counterparts. Prior to this only Florentines employed by the Bardi and the Peruzzi banking houses paid a two percent duty. Pegolotti secured successive extensions of this privilege, and in 1327 he convinced King Hugh to grant it on a permanent basis. Previously many Florentines had passed themselves off as Pisans so as to pay less duty, but following the king's grant the *bailli* of the *commercium* in Famagusta decreed that the proctor of the Bardi residing there would constitute the sole court of appeal whenever an individual's Florentine citizenship was contested. Pegolotti also assisted in despatching large sums of money from the papal treasury in 1329. Some time after 1329 he left Cyprus and returned to Florence, coming back to Cyprus around 1335–36. He was probably in Cyprus when

---

[71] Lamberto di Sambuceto, *1301*, nos. 7, 153, *1302*, nos. 13, 45, 58, 64; Metcalf (1996–2000, II: 6–12).

[72] *Lettres de Jean XXII*, no. 64264; *Lettres de Benoît XII*, no. 3872.

he obtained a charter from the king of Cilician Armenia exempting the Bardi from paying customs dues in Armenia, for he himself wrote that he received this privilege 'while on Cyprus during that time for the said (Bardi) company'. The Florentine Giovanni Boccaccio's *Decameron*, written in the mid-fourteenth century, refers several times to merchants travelling to Cyprus and to Cypriot merchants, including one journeying from Cyprus to Armenia.[73]

Following the relaxation of the papal embargo on trade with Muslim lands in 1344 and the collapse of the Bardi and Peruzzi banking houses in 1345, Florentine trade with Cyprus declined, although Florentine merchants continued to visit. The notarial deeds of Boateriis indicate that they dealt mainly with Venetians and Greeks from Venetian Crete, exporting capes from Famagusta and Limassol to Rhodes, selling slaves in Famagusta, and recovering sums owed for the purchase of cheese sent to Alexandria, which may have come from Venetian Crete, a major producer and exporter of cheese in this period. Early in 1365, four Florentine merchants acting as proctors for their fellow citizen, Barna Luce Alberti, appeared before King Peter I for the recovery of a debt.[74] After 1350, however, Florentine trade and banking relations increased with Alexandria and Damascus. By 1391 only three Florentines appeared in the lists of the *massaria* enumerating the creditors and debtors of the treasury of Genoese-occupied Famagusta, the war of 1373 having dealt a heavy blow to a trade already in decline.[75]

The Provençals and Catalans traded intensively with Cyprus around 1300. Both worked closely with the island's Templars, who like the Hospitallers had moved their headquarters to Limassol after the fall of Acre in 1291, as well as with the Genoese and the Florentine and Piacenzan banking houses. The war at the end of the thirteenth century between the houses of Anjou and Aragon temporarily hindered Marseillais trade with Cyprus by blocking the sailing route through the straits of Messina. Following the fall of Acre, however, Marseillais *commenda* contracts continued to serve for trading ventures involving Cyprus.[76] Notarial deeds illustrate the varied activities of

[73] Francesco Balducci Pegolotti, xx, 60, 84; Giovanni Boccaccio, *The Decameron*, xli.
[74] Ashtor (1983: 65–6); Nicola de Boateriis, nos. 14, 101, 113, 118, 143; *Documenti sulle relazioni delle città toscane coll'Oriente*, no. lxxxiv, A and B.
[75] Ashtor (1983: 137–8); Balard (1995: 290).
[76] Pryor (1984: 402).

Marseillais and other Provençal merchants. These included the advance
of loans, involving naturalised Marseillais who originated from Acre
or descendants of Marseillais who had originally settled in Latin
Syria, who witnessed transactions involving the Templars.[77] One of
them, Gratian of Acre, witnessed an agreement involving the repayment of 16,350 silver *tournois* by Count Bernard Guillelmi to his creditor Theodore, a Templar doctor, for a consignment of Cypriot corn.
Other transactions concerned Templars, Catalans, and the Piacenzan
banking house of Pietro Diani. Some notarial deeds from 1300–01
show Pisan, Genoese and Piacenzan participation in the passage of
goods between Provence and Cyprus, sometimes via Cilician Armenia
and with the involvement of the Scotti and the Pietro Diani banking houses.[78]

The goods transported in these transactions are typical of East-
West trade in the period. On board the Templar ship *Falconus* bound
for Marseilles were powdered sugar, cotton, silk, one measure of red
dye and one board of camlet, all standard export articles from Cyprus
or the adjoining Near Eastern lands. Another ship going to Marseilles,
the *Santa Maria de Cesso* belonging to the Marseillais Geoffrey de
Cervera, likewise carried sugar, cotton, pepper and ginger, the last
two products probably originating from Mamluk Egypt and Cilician
Armenia respectively. A Genoese ship called *Santa Maria*, which
Piacenzan merchants had hired, carried sugar, cotton, red dye, cinnamon, ivory tusks, ginger, gum-lac, incense and indigo. These products originated from Cilician Armenia where the *Santa Maria* had
gone before returning to Famagusta to undertake its journey to
Marseilles. Its itinerary illustrates the importance of Cyprus as a
transshipment centre in this period. Other commodities sold or
acquired by Marseillais and Montpellerin merchants on Cyprus
included cowhides, soap, saffron, beef tripe, gowns and felt hats. The
cowhides probably came from Mamluk Syria or Egypt, the felt hats
from Cilician Armenia and the soap from Cyprus, which manufactured and exported it, notably to Turkey and Pera opposite Constantinople.[79] Catalan merchants in Cyprus transported similar goods.

[77] Lamberto di Sambuceto, *1299–1301 (AOL)*, nos. 73–4, *1300–1301*, nos. 221,
240–1; Jacoby (1984a: 172).
[78] Lamberto di Sambuceto, *1300–1301*, nos. 148, 246–7, 413, *1301*, nos. 18,
102–102a.
[79] Lamberto di Sambuceto, *1300–1301*, nos. 121, 246–7, *1301*, no. 18; Jacoby
(1995: 409–10, 438–9).

Imports included linen, garters, cloth of gold, French cloths, silk, saffron and olive oil, the last import suggesting that Cyprus was experiencing a shortage, or that extra oil was required for manufacturing soap. Exports from Cyprus and the Mamluk lands or Cilician Armenia included sugar, cotton, sugar powder, cinnamon and pepper, with pepper and sugar being most in demand. In February 1301 the merchant William of Orto delivered to James Andrea of Narbonne in Cyprus cloths, wool and salted meat worth 800 Barcelona pounds, which James Carbona of Barcelona then purchased. The Catalans also shipped grain and pulses from Cyprus to Cilician Armenia, where they bought Armenian cotton and forwarded it to Catalonia via Cyprus.[80]

Catalans and Provençals cooperated in Cyprus, having maintained commercial links since the early thirteenth century, when the Provençals had helped the Catalans re-conquer Majorca from the Muslims. Under King James I of Aragon Montpellier and Barcelona had developed close commercial relations.[81] James Andrea and James Carbona, both mentioned above, cooperated on several occasions, while on 27 February 1301 two trumpeters, the Catalan William of Barcelona and Peter Seguer of Marseilles, witnessed the repayment of a loan. Both the debtor and the creditor were Genoese, and the debtor had borrowed money to purchase cotton at Famagusta and to resell it at Bougie in Tunis, a destination hardly mentioned in the deeds of Sambuceto. In June the Catalan Borras Taliada witnessed the appointment of three procurators, all from Narbonne, by Bernard Inardus of Narbonne for the recovery of some debts. A number of notarial acts, moreover, record Catalan imports of wheat and olive oil and their dealings with the Templars on Cyprus, while the appearance of witnesses from Tarragona and Tortosa in Spain indicates that the Catalans in Cyprus did not originate exclusively from Barcelona.[82] Cyprus was suffering a grain shortage at this time due to a prolonged drought. The grain imported may have come either from Aragonese Sicily or the Kingdom of Naples, and in 1300 the Florentine banking house of Bardi was involved in grain imports from Apulia.

[80] Lamberto di Sambuceto, *1300–1301*, nos. 226–7, 257, *1301*, no. 56; Ashtor (1983: 43).
[81] Abulafia (1994: 114–16, 180–6).
[82] Lamberto di Sambuceto, *1300–1301*, nos. 235, 251, 408, 148, 166, 171.

Catalan ship owners also transported people, and in February 1301
Bernard Marchettus undertook to transport some Templars to Majorca
in a transaction concluded at the Templar house in Famagusta.[83]

The Hospitallers on Cyprus also had commercial links with
Provençals and Catalans. In August 1301 the Hospitaller Fernand
Rodriguez gave goods valued at 136 *sous tournois* to a Montpellerin
agent of Raymond of Conches, himself a citizen of Montpellier,
receiving in return 683.75 white bezants. Pere de Soler, an Aragonese
Hospitaller, was active in organising exchanges of currency between
Cyprus and Aragon in 1305, but with the transfer of the Hospitaller
headquarters to Rhodes by 1310 and the dissolution of the Templars
in 1312 these business relations ceased.[84] Provençals and Catalans
on occasion conducted business with the Genoese, and several notarial deeds record Catalans lending to them or witnessing transactions
between them. In September 1301 Raymond Barratam of Marseilles
appointed a proctor to recover money lent to a Genoese merchant,
while Anselm Guidonis of Genoa sold the *Sant'Antonio*, formerly purchased for 2,400 white bezants from a consortium of Marseillais
merchants.[85] The Catalan trader William of Ginabreda conducted
business with Pisans, Venetians and Genoese. Not all partnerships,
however, were harmonious. In June 1299 the Catalan consul Bartholomew Basterius and several Catalan merchants accused the galley master William Carato of Barcelona of damaging the cotton—from
Aleppo—, sugar, and cloths that they had on board his ship and
demanded compensation. All the commodities were standard Cypriot
exports and imports.[86]

Catalan trade with Cyprus continued to be brisk in the mid-fourteenth century, although there were also recorded instances of Catalan
violations of the papal embargo, as well as their acts of piracy in
Cyprus against Genoese, Venetians and Provençals in the early to
mid-fourteenth century.[87] The surviving account book of Joan Benet,

---

[83] Lamberto di Sambuceto, *1299–1301 (AOL)*, no. 109; Lamberto di Sambuceto,
1300–1301, nos. 219, 258.
[84] Lamberto di Sambuceto, *1301*, no. 6; *Assegurances a Barcelona*, nos. 26–8.
[85] Lamberto di Sambuceto, *1300–1301*, nos. 203, 209, 251, 267–8, *1301*, nos.
77, 130.
[86] Lamberto di Sambuceto, *1300–1301*, nos. 354–6, 410, *1296–1299*, no. 150.
[87] *Memorias Historicas*, II, nos. LXV, CCLVI; Mas Latrie, *Histoire*, II, 111, 170–1,
203–5, III, 707–8, 720–2, 728–36; Nicola de Boateriis, nos. 59, 155, 159; Ashtor
(1983: 21–2, 66).

a Catalan from Majorca, records the goods he was importing to and exporting from Famagusta in 1343. It mentions imports of saffron and olive oil and exports of cotton, sugar and various spices, but new imports not encountered before are rice, kohl—a mineral extracted from the mines around Falset in Tarragona—and silver, which formed 88.5% of the total value of Benet's imports. Silver used for minting coins was greatly in demand in Cyprus, Cilician Armenia and the Near East.[88] The 27 *commandas commerciales* given in May 1349 by a number of persons, including Jews of Barcelona, to the merchant Nicholas Sermona of Barcelona likewise mention silver more than any other export, frequently cloths, oil, honey and rice, and less often saffron, blankets, tin, enamel, lead, salted meats, cumin, *cofoll*, almonds and chestnuts. Besides Venetian Crete, the new destinations mentioned in the itineraries of Catalan ships bound for Cyprus after the lifting of the papal embargo in 1344 include Beirut, Syria and Rhodes, under Hospitaller rule since 1310 and assuming increasing importance in Catalan trade. In the *commandas commerciales* for the years 1363–79 Crete is no longer a destination for ships travelling to Cyprus, while Rhodes and Beirut appear several times. By the end of the fourteenth century Catalan ships sailing to Syria were using Venetian Crete or Hospitaller Rhodes as a stopover, bypassing Cyprus altogether. Nonetheless, Catalans and Provençals continued to visit Cyprus up to the end of the century and beyond to purchase native Cypriot produce such as sugar and cotton.[89]

Unlike the Catalans, numerous Provençals are recorded as actually living in Cyprus, and in their wills of the years 1300–01 some, like Bernard Faixie, expressed their desire to be buried in the Latin churches of the island and bequeathed sums to Latin institutions in these towns as well as in their native cities such as Narbonne. One of Faixie's creditors, Bernard Inardus, was resident in Narbonne but had commercial interests encompassing Cyprus, Venice, Crete, Cilician Armenia and possibly Cherson in the Crimea, an illustration of Cyprus' integration in trading networks spanning the whole Mediterranean region. Provençal trade with Cyprus continued well into the fourteenth century, and prominent among the Cypriot merchants resident in Montpellier at this time was Joseph Zaphet of Famagusta,

---

[88] Plana i Borràs (1992: 112–20).
[89] *Comandas Commerciales Barcelonesas*, nos. 99, 102–4, 106, 135, 140–1; Balard (1995: 432).

who originated from Latin Syria and obtained Montpellerin citizenship after trading for many years with this and other Provençal towns.[90] A prominent Provençal merchant in Cyprus was Raymond Sarralher of Narbonne, who arranged the currency conversion and transfer of papal taxes from Cyprus to the West. These taxes were used to finance the defence of Smyrna, captured from the Turks in 1344. In 1355 Pope Innocent VI asked King Hugh IV to intercede for Raymond because Venetian merchants had plundered his goods, an illustration of how rivalries between Western merchants in Cyprus could erupt in violence.[91]

In the later fourteenth century the Marseillais, whose main export was coral, traded directly with Alexandria and like the Catalans used Crete and Rhodes as stopovers, bypassing Cyprus, or else exported to Cyprus on Genoese or Luccan ships, which meant that their cargoes were not declared as coming from Marseilles. Peter Auriac's letter of appointment as the Montpellerin consul for Cyprus in 1345 illustrates that he had wide-ranging jurisdiction over his fellow merchants like that of the Venetian, Genoese and Pisan consuls. King Hugh's correspondence with the consuls of Montpellier between 1352 and 1354, however, shows that Montpellerin merchants were angry over the increased customs dues and tolls they paid the royal officers to weigh their goods, increased perhaps because royal revenues from the international carrying trade had fallen after the relaxation of the papal embargo in 1344. Before 1345 Venetian galley lines to Cyprus and Cilician Armenia consisted of six to ten galleys, but by around 1350 the number had fallen to between three and five.[92] Under King Peter I, the Montpellerins complained to Pope Urban V of the doubling of the *commercium*, the traditional four percent duty on goods carried to and from Cyprus, and the king agreed to reduce it to its initial level. In the charter the king granted the Montpellerins in 1365 duties were lowered to two percent. He granted extended powers of criminal as well as civil jurisdiction—including the right to inflict corporal punishment—to the Montpellerin consuls, like those he had granted the Venetian *baiuli* in 1360, undermining the hitherto

---

[90] Lamberto di Sambuceto, *1300–1301*, nos. 145, 389, 408, *1301*, nos. 14, 24, 33, 178, 178A–179, 218–19; Jacoby (1995: 428–9).

[91] *Lettres d'Innocent VI*, nos. 1760–1, 1765; *Lettres de Clément VI*, no. 5070.

[92] Ashtor (1983: 37, 52, 65–81, 85, 114, 137, 144–6); Mas Latrie, *Histoire*, II, 208–10, 219–20.

exclusive right of the royal court to try criminal charges brought against members of the mercantile communities.[93] From 1356 onwards, however, the Hospitallers granted the merchants of Narbonne and Montpellier extensive privileges on Rhodes because they benefited from the financial services they performed for the papacy. Provençal trade with Cyprus declined after 1350 and by 1391 there were hardly any among the recorded foreign residents in Famagusta.[94]

Ancona and Ragusa were the two Adriatic towns besides Venice trading with Cyprus in the fourteenth century. The Anconitans transported chiefly cotton from Cyprus, or Syrian and Armenian cotton via Cyprus, to Ancona and other destinations, with 28 notarial deeds from July 1300 to October 1301 regarding such shipments.[95] During this period Ancona was a major distribution point for imports to central Italy's thriving cotton industry. Fifteen of the deeds record consignments of cloth forwarded to Ancona and other destinations on Anconitan ships, with Baronus Pellegrinus de Galante forwarding twelve of them between October 1300 and October 1301.[96] Baronus also cooperated with Italian merchants, who exported various products. An Anconitan merchant he worked with sent a consignment to Ancona consisting of sugar, cotton, pepper, cloth and a quantity of gold in October 1301, and two counterparts of his sent similar shipments at this time. With his Florentine partners, both associates of the Peruzzi bankers, another Anconitan trader exported salt from Cyprus for sale in Venice or Ancona. Other Anconitan merchants imported hemp and cloths to Cyprus, as well as lard, cheese, salted meat and sardines. A deed of April 1302 records two merchants, one from Padua and another from Ancona, appointing a proctor to receive some nuts in Armenia.[97] Anconitan ship owners also carried goods to Cyprus from places other than Ancona, such as Pera, the Genoese colony opposite Constantinople.[98] The Anconitans, moreover,

---

[93] *Lettres d'Urbain V*, nos. 115, 185; Mas Latrie, *Histoire*, II, 250, 268–72; Hill (1940–1952, II: 317); Jacoby (1995: 414, 428–9).

[94] Luttrell (1986: 170 and notes 77–9, 81); Balard (1995: 286–8).

[95] Lamberto di Sambuceto, *1299–1301 (ROL)*, no. 274, *1300–1301*, nos. 48, 54, 59, *1301*, nos. 181–2, 185–6, 188, 192–6, 198–200, 202–8, 220–2, *1304–1307*, no. 153.

[96] Lamberto di Sambuceto, *1301*, nos. 188, 192–3, 195–6, 198–200, 202, 208, 220–2; Abulafia (1993b: 202).

[97] Lamberto di Sambuceto, *1300–1301* no. 64, *1301*, nos. 181, 220–2, *1302*, nos. 37, 159, 164.

[98] Giovanni de Rocha, nos. 28, 69.

transported goods for the Hospitallers, and one such transaction was recorded at the court of the castellan of Famagusta, the *commercium*.[99] Cyriac of Ancona was especially prominent as a lender or borrower of money, dealing with Florentines, Genoese, Pisans, Manfredonians and persons originating from Latin Syria. The Anconitan merchant Ivan de Galvano, mentioned as a debtor and as a witness in two notarial deeds, was possibly of Slavic origin. Only two deeds refer to the Anconitans selling slaves on Cyprus, for they could buy slaves more easily from the Slavic hinterland of Dalmatia on the eastern Adriatic littoral.[100]

Anconitans, notably the Paternani family, appear in several deeds as lenders, borrowers and moneychangers in transactions involving Genoese, Florentines and merchants originating from Latin Syria.[101] Anconitans also frequently witnessed transactions involving Genoese, Ragusans, Venetians, Provençals, Florentines, inhabitants of Messina in Sicily and Cretan Jews.[102] Pegolotti's *La pratica della mercatura* gives both Cypriot and Anconitan weights and measures in its section on Famagusta, for spices, cotton, cotton canvas, honey, as well as silver marks, items transported between the two places. The section on Ancona states the products that unarmed Anconitan galleys brought to Cyprus: wine, oil, oakum, goat's hair, grains and pulses, wax, hooked and unhooked oars, sandalwood, Florentine cloths and silks, French cloths, coarse cloths, canvasses and soap. Unarmed galleys returning from Cyprus to Ancona and Apulia in general also transported goods originating not solely from Cyprus but other lands in the Near East.[103] High-value spices, sugar and precious metals were generally transported on armed galleys in this period, and bulky low-value cargos such as salt, grain and pulses went on unarmed private merchants ships. Anconitan and Cypriot merchants also cooperated outside Cyprus, as when in August 1359 a Cypriot and an Anconitan merchant exported 50 *modii* of Ragusan grain as feed for the horses on board

---

[99] Lamberto di Sambuceto, *1299–1301 (AOL)*, no. 118.
[100] Lamberto di Sambuceto, *1300–1301*, nos. 98, 103, 225, 270–1, 342, 360, *1301*, nos. 2, 16, 130, 239, *1302*, nos. 13, 37, 46, 52, 81, 84; Abulafia (1993c: 553).
[101] Lamberto di Sambuceto, *1300–1301*, nos. 58, 337, *1302*, no. 185, *1299–1301 (AOL)*, nos. 58, 81.
[102] Lamberto di Sambuceto, *1300–1301*, nos. 14, 23–4, 58, 70, 82, 158, 191, 204, *1301*, nos. 16, 38, 130, 203–7, *1296–1299*, no. 158, *1302*, nos. 13, 33, 49a, 65, 88, 101, 131, 140, 187a, 267, *1299–1301 (AOL)*, nos. 141–2, 181, 195–6, *1299–1301 (ROL)*, nos. 462, 470; Abulafia (1993c: 526–8, 534, 545–6).
[103] Francesco Balducci Pegolotti, 83–4, 93–4, 157–8.

their ship. Furthermore, Anconitans appear in five deeds of the Venetian notary Nicola de Boateriis in 1360–62. One records the purchase at Limassol of carobs going to Venice, proof that Anconitan merchants did not trade solely with Famagusta. They appear more frequently in the notarial deeds of Simon, a priest of San Giacomo dell'Orio, covering 1362–71, as buyers of Cypriot agricultural products such as sugar. In 1405 they chartered a Catalan ship to bring cotton from Syria and sugar from Cyprus back to Ancona. During the late fourteenth and early fifteenth centuries, however, Ancona intensified trade with Egypt and Syria rather than Cyprus.[104]

The Ragusans trading with Cyprus, like the Anconitans, sold a few slaves, sometimes exporting them from Serbia and Bosnia and selling them on Cyprus or else, as happened in 1283, in Ragusa to visiting Cypriots. Two deeds record trade between members of the prominent Genoese de Mari family and Ragusans. In April 1300 Lanfranc de Mari emancipated a female slave originating from Sclavonia, whom he probably bought from Ragusans, and in November 1300 Nicholas de Mari lent 100 white bezants to Francis and Anthony, two Slav brothers residing in Famagusta probably coming from Ragusa or the surrounding area.[105] Most deeds of Sambuceto mentioning Ragusans concern the ship owners Lawrence and Marino de Gozo, possibly related and whose surname is a corruption of the Serbo-Croat Gucetic. Lawrence de Gozo dealt with merchants from Barletta, Florence and especially Venice. In Cyprus as elsewhere merchants from major mercantile communities like Venice, Genoa, Pisa and Florence formed partnerships with those from smaller communities who undertook to transport their goods. Ragusans and Anconitans in Cyprus performed this function, and various acts show Lawrence de Gozo transporting such goods for Venetians and Florentines, as well as purchasing cotton to transport himself.[106] The second Ragusan ship owner, Marino de Gozo, appears in some fourteen notarial deeds dated 7 and 8 October 1301, involving the shipment of cotton, possibly of Syrian provenance, from Cyprus to 'Venice or any bet-

---

[104] Stöckly (1995: 133–6); Krékič (1961: no. 240) and Nicola de Boateriis, nos. 85, 91, 93, 145, 177; Ashtor (1983: 241) and Otten-Froux (2003: nos. 29–30, 34, 62, 124, 126, 166).

[105] Krékič (1961: no. 34); Lamberto di Sambuceto, *1299–1301 (AOL)*, no. 110, *1299–1301 (ROL)*, no. 405; Abulafia (1993c: 553).

[106] Krékič (1961: no. 273); Lamberto di Sambuceto, *1300–1301*, nos. 76, 84, 164, 191, 201; Abulafia (1993b: 187; 1987b: 206); Jacoby (1995: 411).

ter destination' on behalf of the creditors, mainly Greek merchants originating from Laodicea in Latin Syria.[107] Commerce between Cyprus and Ragusa continued into later periods. In 1343 George Zadar, a resident of Ragusa, is mentioned as planning to depart on the galleys bound for Cyprus in the place of another Ragusan who had undertaken to pay him, the galleys being either Venetian or those sent every year by the Ragusan government to Egypt and Syria, which could stop off in Cyprus on their way. Even after Venice ceded Ragusa to the Kingdom of Hungary in 1358, commercial contacts were maintained, and Ragusan trade with Cyprus, although always limited in scale, continued right into the nineteenth century.[108]

Trade with the Eastern Mediterranean and the Black Sea

The commerce between Cyprus and the lands of the Eastern Mediterranean and the Black Sea differed in several respects from that with the lands of the Western Mediterranean and the Adriatic. It involved short to medium-distance as opposed to long-distance trade, and so the smaller cargo vessels known as *gripariae* figured in it more prominently than the galleys. It was also far more tightly controlled by the Venetians and Genoese. The Venetians had annexed Crete in 1211 and assumed increasing control over Euboea from the mid-thirteenth century onwards, while Genoese assisted the Hospitaller conquest of Rhodes around 1310, founded trading colonies at Pera opposite Constantinople and Caffa in the Crimea in the thirteenth century and placed Chios under their control in the fourteenth century. Cyprus became integrated in both the Venetian and the Genoese trading networks established in the Eastern Mediterranean and Black Sea regions. These overlapped significantly in Hospitaller Rhodes and Lusignan Cyprus, both areas not under direct Venetian or Genoese control. Another important difference was the inclusion of Cretan and Rhodian Greeks in this commerce. Although Greeks were involved in long-distance trade, as the fourteen documents involving Marino de Gozo noted just above indicate, as owners of *gripariae* ideally suited for covering more limited distances Greeks could participate more easily in such intra-regional trade than in the

---

[107] Lamberto di Sambuceto, *1301*, nos. 203–7, 210–16, 218–19.
[108] Krékič (1961: nos. 207, 273, 284; 1980c: 260); Ashtor (1983: 108–9, 143–4); Aristeidou, *Ragusa*, 67–186; Aristeidou (1987).

trade between Cyprus, Italy and Western Europe. Yet Pisans, Spaniards, Sicilians, Provençals and Cretan Jews also played a part, albeit less conspicuously than the Venetians, Genoese and Greeks of Rhodes and Crete. In addition, Cypriot harbours other than Famagusta figured more prominently because of the short to middle-distance nature of this trading network.

The notarial deeds of Sambuceto, Rocha and Boateriis are the main sources for this trade. Three deeds from around 1300, concerning loan repayments and the hiring of a ship, illustrate how Sicilians, Pisans and native Cypriots as well as Venetians and Genoese took part in the trade between Cyprus and Rhodes prior to the Hospitaller conquest of that island in 1306–10.[109] The Genoese freebooter Vignolo de Vignolo assisted in the conquest, and henceforth the Genoese assumed greater prominence, figuring in virtually all the deeds of Sambuceto concerning Rhodes for early 1307. Two of them drawn up at the Genoese *loggia* in Famagusta concerned 400 white bezants borrowed by the Genoese citizen Marino della Porta, whose family were among the Genoese trading aristocracy, and the repayment of 50 white bezants borrowed *in commendam* by Simon Falipanus, a Genoese burgess of Famagusta, from his fellow burgess Linardus. Two deeds concern the sale of a slave girl by her Genoese owner to a Florentine spice merchant for 30 bezants, and one a loan of 400 white bezants that a Genoese advanced to a compatriot for a trading venture in Rhodes and Turkey. Another records how the Hospitallers sold ships to the Genoese, indicating that after the Genoese supplied the Hospitallers with galleys for the conquest of Rhodes, the Hospitallers then sold those that were considered superfluous. In May 1307 a certain Manuel Scarlatinus borrowed 120 white bezants from a compatriot so that they could jointly transport a consignment of wine from Cyprus to Rhodes. Incidentally the deal highlights the continuing importance of Limassol, since the wine was loaded on board Manuel's ship in the harbour there.[110]

The Genoese Zaccharia family ruling Chios from 1304 to 1329 exported the mastic produced there to Cyprus among other destinations, and sometimes it arrived there via Rhodes, as certain notar-

---

[109] Lamberto di Sambuceto, *1300–1301*, no. 272, *1301*, no. 235, *1296–1299*, no. 155; Luttrell (1975: 283).

[110] Riley-Smith (1967: 215); Luttrell (1972: 164–5; 1975: 283–4); Ashtor (1983: 43); Lamberto di Sambuceto, *1304–1307*, nos. 29, 36, 64, 84, 103, 110, 148, 152.

ial acts indicate. A deed of November 1309 records the purchase of cloth of Chalôns and of mastic from the lords of Chios by Ansaldo de Grimaldis. Megollo Lercari, who belonged to another prominent Genoese family, exported mastic to Cyprus between 1318 and 1333, although Lusignan royal galleys impounded some of his shipments bound for Egypt, a forbidden destination under the papal embargo. Nevertheless, the Genoese lords of Chios in 1320, 1322 and 1325 obtained papal indulgences to export mastic to Alexandria.[111] Pegolotti's *Pratica della mercatura* mentions mastic on sale in Famagusta, indicating that some of the mastic bound for Egypt was sold in Cyprus. The import of mastic to Cyprus via Rhodes continued into the 1320s, and from 1360 onwards it was sold and distributed from Famagusta throughout Cyprus, Egypt and Syria, as proven by the fact that mastic sent to Syria and Egypt was defined by Cypriot weights.[112]

The commercial contacts between Cyprus and Rhodes figure even in Boccaccio's *Decameron*, which alludes to a Cypriot merchant from Paphos visiting Rhodes on business. Furthermore, several contracts in the deeds of 1360–62 indicate a trade triangle made up of Cyprus, Rhodes and Crete, in which Venetians and Greeks from Crete, Genoese, and Greeks from Constantinople and the Peloponnese took part. A deed dated 1361 records how the Venetian citizen Sir Dardi Bon appointed a Venetian from Crete as his procurator for recovering money a sailor had stolen, authorising him to begin legal proceedings in Famagusta, Rhodes, Crete or elsewhere. A Venetian based in Crete as opposed to Venice could commence such proceedings in Rhodes more easily. The Hospitallers were hostile to Venice and had supported Genoa against her in the war of 1351–55, but the commerce binding Crete and Rhodes made them friendlier to both Venetians and Greeks from Crete. Indeed, Cretan insurgents found refuge and assistance in Rhodes when rebelling against Venice in 1363–65.[113]

As stated above, this regional trade involved the Cypriot harbours other than Famagusta to a far greater extent. Two deeds of 1361 involving George Mirodi (Mavroides?) of Crete, the owner of a small *griparia*, and his creditor, the Venetian Sir Paul Colonna, who was

---

[111] Lamberto di Sambuceto, *1304–1307*, no. 18; Giovanni de Rocha, no. 23; Balard (1978, I: 120; II, 745, 747); Edbury (1991: 150).
[112] Francesco Balducci Pegolotti, 77, 313; Donato di Chiavari, nos. 47–8, 50; Balard (1978, II: 744, 748–9).
[113] Giovanni Boccaccio, *The Decameron*, lxii–lxiii and 141–2 (day II, novel 7); Nicola de Boateriis, nos. 28, 39, 98; Luttrell (1974).

from Crete, specify journeys from Famagusta via Limassol and Paphos to Rhodes. In one case the cargo was silk, the transport of which is mentioned in another deed of 1361. Manulius Verigo, a Venetian from Crete, would take silk from Cyprus to Rhodes, with Miletus, Theologo or Palatia on the Turkish coast mentioned as alternative destinations. He was to sell the silk and purchase other merchandise for sale either in Famagusta or, with his creditor's consent, in Antalya on the coast of southern Turkey. He would sell any pieces not sold there in Kyrenia, Paphos or Limassol, where he intended to stop off before his final return to Famagusta.

Paul Colonna financed other trading ventures from Cyprus to Rhodes and Crete, advancing money to Demetrios, the Cretan Greek owner of a *griparia* captained by the Rhodian Greek George Cappari, and he was repaid in full when this vessel reached Kyrenia. George may have sailed there directly from Rhodes as opposed to Crete, for ships sailing from Crete were more likely to make port in one of the southern harbours of Cyprus. Kyrenia, moreover, was a port of embarkation for travellers journeying to Rhodes or Turkey, and so would also be a natural destination for ships from Rhodes bound for Cyprus. Two more deeds involve the repayment of money owed by a Cretan Greek to a Greek from Constantinople, due to take place in Alexandria, Rhodes, Crete or Famagusta, and the sale of a Greek slave on Rhodes or Cyprus by the proctor of Sir Mark Quirino, a Venetian resident of Crete. Trade between Rhodes and Cyprus continued down to the end of the fourteenth century and beyond. In 1376 the Venetian brothers Mark and Frederick Cornaro had sugar-refining factories in Rhodes to which Cypriot sugar originating from their estates at Episkopi in the district of Limassol was sent and refined, and in 1381 the Greek burgess John Sozomenos of Rhodes employed an agent named Michael Conderato in Cyprus for transferring money from Cyprus to Rhodes on the Hospitallers' behalf.[114]

Trade between Cyprus and Crete was especially important in the early fourteenth century, when galleys setting out from Crete to Famagusta carried grain, cereals, pulses, cheese and olive oil to Cyprus, purchasing salt and sugar there for their return journey. Besides the Venetians, Genoese and Anconitan merchants resident in Candia and the other principal Cretan towns were involved in this

---

[114] Nicola de Boateriis, nos. 98–9, 114, 125, 139–40, 174, 176; Jacoby (1995: 430, note 61, 451); Nepaulsingh (1997: 20); Luttrell (1993b: 200–1).

trade, and in 1332–35 ships travelling from Europe to Cyprus via the Venetian possessions of Modon, Euboea and Crete loaded and unloaded both goods and merchants in the course of their journey prior to reaching Cyprus itself.[115] According to a deed of 7 June 1300, a Venetian living in Crete, Iofredus Lupinus, sold a vessel he owned jointly with the Ragusan Bontempus to a Genoese purchaser. The mention of the Ragusan Bontempus illustrates the involvement of others besides Genoese and Venetians in the trade between the two islands. Cretan cheese was a famous export, and its despatch to Cyprus appears in a deed of August 1301. In another deed of August 1301 George Galimar and Andrew Bozatus, a Venetian burgess of Famagusta, declared before Nicholas Zugno that his ship containing the cargo of a fellow Venetian was about to sail to Crete. The cargo consisted of Provençal canvasses, Chalôns cloths and 1,200 white bezants.[116] Two deeds of September 1301 involving the lease and sub-lease of a ship belonging to the Genoese citizen Lombard Sardena make it clear that slaves from Cyprus were transported to Egypt for sale there, and that the ship, after purchasing spices at Alexandria or Damietta, would return to Cyprus via Crete, selling the spices in Crete at a handsome profit and apparently circumventing the papal embargo on trade with Muslim countries. In 1311 the Venetian grand council promulgated a decree stating that 200 *staia* of pulses and 100 *staia* of wheat should be sent every year from Crete to Cyprus for the requirements of the Venetian *baiulo* in Famagusta, and demand for Cypriot sugar expanded in both Venice itself and Venetian Crete during the fourteenth century. Pegolotti's trading manual records the Cypriot equivalents of the Cretan measures used for grain in the Cretan towns of Candia and Canea, which indicates the export of Cretan grain to Cyprus in the second quarter of the fourteenth century.[117]

Several deeds from after 1350 concern the sale of slaves between merchants resident in Crete or Cyprus. Some of the purchasers or vendors mentioned were Venetians from Crete subsequently residing in Famagusta. Other parties included a Pisan physician living in

---

[115] Thiriet (1959: 329–30); Ashtor (1983: 38); Blijnuk (1991–1992: 446, 448).
[116] Lamberto di Sambuceto, *1299–1301 (AOL)*, no. 134, *1301*, nos. 39, 48; Jacoby (1999).
[117] Lamberto di Sambuceto, *1301*, nos. 95, 148; Thiriet (1959: 330); Francesco Balducci Pegolotti, 93.

Famagusta, a Spaniard from Saragossa likewise living there and
Missauth the son of David, a burgess of Famagusta, whose name
suggests that he belonged to Famagusta's Jewish community. The
slaves sold were invariably Greeks from the Aegean area, for Turkish
piracy in the Aegean increased from the early fourteenth century
onwards and after 1425 Aegean Greeks displaced Muslims as the
slaves most frequently sold in the slave markets of Famagusta and
Nicosia in Cyprus. The prices for slaves given in the notarial deeds
of Boateriis later in the century are on average double those paid
in the earlier deeds of Sambuceto and Rocha near the beginning,
for the Black Death of 1348 created a labour shortage that pushed
up the price of slaves.[118]

Several deeds of Sambuceto, Rocha and Boateriis concern the
lending and exchange of money by parties involved in commerce
between Cyprus and Crete, including Cretan Jews, for Crete had an
important Jewish community dating back to Byzantine times, and
Cyprus likewise had Jewish communities in Nicosia and Famagusta,
as well as in the *casale* of Psimolophou, where they worked as tanners. On 16 September 1352 a Jew living in Crete received a sea
loan to embark on a trading venture to Rhodes and Famagusta, and
in 1361 the Jewish physician Isaac, normally resident in Candia but
then present in Famagusta, acknowledged certain debts in Cretan
hyperpera that he had incurred to purchase some cloths and hides,
promising to repay his creditor Sambatius—a rabbi living in Candia—
the debt along with possible damages in connection with it.[119]

Deeds of Sambuceto involving loans, the parties to which had
commercial interests in Cyprus and Crete, mention Venetians living
in Venice or Crete, Cretan Greeks and Anconitans. Fewer nationalities
appear in the deeds of Boateriis concerning loans by parties with business interests in Crete and Cyprus. The lenders are mainly Venetian
and the borrowers chiefly Greeks from Crete, although Greeks from
Chios and Coron in the Peloponnese as well as a Sicilian from
Messina are recorded.[120] These transactions illustrate both the par-

---

[118] Nicola de Boateriis, nos. 60, 80–1, 122–4, 172, 176; Arbel (1993: 146–7);
Coureas (1995b: 107–10).
[119] Makhairas, I, §§397, 453; 'Amadi', 469; Florio Bustron, 327; Lamberto di
Sambuceto, *1300–1301*, no. 8, *1299–1301 (ROL)*, no. 323; Nicola de Boateriis, no.
126; Starr (1942); Jacoby (1977: 171–2); Richard (1947: 145).
[120] Lamberto di Sambuceto, *1300–1301*, nos. 82, 213, *1301*, no. 29, *1301–1307*,
no. 151; Nicola de Boateriis, nos. 69, 84 and 175.

ties and the small-scale loans characteristic of the short-distance trade between Cyprus and Crete. In both short- and long-distance trade procurators were important, for traders with interests in various places could not deal with them all at once. Several deeds of Sambuceto record how Nicholas Zugno, the Venetian *baiulo* of Cyprus, and the prominent Narbonnese trader Bernard Inardus appointed fellow nationals as procurators for recovering sums of money or goods they were owed in Crete. In September 1301 the Genoese resident of Famagusta Gerard Banel appointed a Venetian resident of Crete to recover goods owed to him there by the Pisan Pucci Bercedani. In the deeds of Boateriis of 1360–62 Venetians resident in Crete, Venice or Cyprus appointed fellow Venetians resident in Crete to recover money owed to them.[121]

It was in this period that trade between Crete and Cyprus changed when a branch of the powerful Venetian Cornaro family, possessing estates in Crete around Candia in which viticulture, silviculture and cereal cultivation were practised, moved to Cyprus. From its Cretan estates it exported wheat and wine to nearby Karpathos and Cyprus, developed the cultivation, refinement and export of sugar from its Cypriot estates—located at Episkopi in the district of Limassol—and established a virtual monopoly over the import of Cypriot salt and sugar to Crete. The family increasingly controlled trade between the two islands and it also had a sugar-refining factory in Rhodes.[122] The above developments illustrate how a powerful family could exploit the unified trading area the three islands formed by the end of the fourteenth century.

Despite the important colony of Venetian citizens that had developed by the early fourteenth century in Euboea, which they called Negroponte, lack of firm political control there prevented Cyprus from developing intensive trade with it. Only three deeds of Sambuceto allude to persons from Euboea, all Venetians resident there, not indigenous Greeks.[123] Things changed after the consolidation of Venetian influence in Euboea after 1317: in the 1360s, of the 185 published deeds of Boateriis concerning Cyprus, eighteen deal with

---

[121] Lamberto di Sambuceto, *1300–1301*, nos. 69, 408, *1301*, no. 176, *1302*, nos. 56, 105; Nicola de Boateriis, 7, 27, 38, 64, 89, 97.
[122] Thiriet (1959: 330, 333); Luttrell (1993b: 200–1).
[123] Lamberto di Sambuceto, *1299–1301* (*AOL*), nos. 127, 137, *1302*, no. 100; Zachariadou (1983: 14–15, 95–6); Topping (1975: 108, 114–15).
[124] Nicola de Boateriis, nos. 3, 18, 36, 71, 103.

Euboea, five of them the advancement of loans.[124] Eleven documents of Boateriis referring to slaves from Euboea in Cyprus are of particular interest, for all but one concern their manumission, not their sale. The earliest such document mentions a public auction in Nicosia, in which the highest bidder, the Venetian ambassador, liberated the slave purchased. An officer of King Peter I of Cyprus conducted the auction and this deed, the only known reference to slaves being sold in Nicosia, alludes to a slave market there as well as in Famagusta. In five out of the ten cases of manumission, the slaves themselves purchased their freedom, while in the other five instances the slaves' owners had them freed without payment. In two of these cases the slaves, manumitted on their masters' death, were also left sums of money.[125] Brisk trade between Cyprus and Negroponte continued in later years. Of the 199 published acts of the priest Simon of San Giacomo dell'Orio, covering the years 1362–72, one tenth refer to persons from Euboea, owners of *gripariae*, merchants and slaves, who were either sold or manumitted on Cyprus.[126]

Trade between Cyprus and the Genoese colonies of Pera and Caffa in the Black Sea region developed from the close of the thirteenth century, and Lamberto di Sambuceto was himself employed in Caffa in the years 1289–90. Prominent Genoese trading families found in Cyprus, such as the de Mari, della Volta and de Camilla, promoted commerce between Cyprus and these colonies. The earliest deed of 1 May 1297 alludes to a loan financing a trading venture to Cilician Armenia, Sebasteia in Turkey and Tabriz, while two deeds of 1299 and 1300 concern money transfers.[127] Several deeds of early 1307 record the Genoese citizen Henry of Travi as a borrower of money and a carrier of goods to Pera, including cotton. The creditors and witnesses, all Genoese, included members of the de Mari and della Volta families. In March 1307 a Genoese resident of Famagusta sold a Greek slave girl aged twelve to Philip of Messana, a resident of Pera whose name suggests a Sicilian origin. The de Mari, de Camilla and della Volta families appear more often in the trade between Pera and Cyprus from 1309 onwards, in the notarial deeds of Giovanni

---

[125] Makhairas, I, §482; Nicola de Boateriis, nos. 2, 52, 60, 77–8, 100, 123–4, 152, 157, 167; Zachariadou (1983: 56); Setton (1975: 196); Arbel (1993: 157–8, 184–90).
[126] Otten-Froux (2003: nos. 3–4, 13–15, 21, 45, 70–1, 76–7, 87, 92, 95, 97–8, 119, 155, 159, 184).
[127] Lamberto di Sambuceto, *1300–1301*, no. 2, *1296–1299*, no. 94; Balard (1995: 280–1).

de Rocha. Deeds of this period, sometimes drawn up at the Genoese *loggia* in Famagusta, refer to money transfers between Cyprus and Pera, and one of the ships bound for Pera also stopped off at Rhodes to take cargo on board.[128] The cargo that arrived in Famagusta in November 1309 via Laiazzo in Cilician Armenia, on the ship of the Anconitan Maioranus, illustrates what goods reached Cyprus from Pera. They included silk, untanned russet-coloured hides, one hundred capes of black lamb's wool, carpets and corn 'in the measures of Romania', as the Aegean area was called. The notarial deed states that these goods were now on board another ship, indicating that they had reached Cyprus in transit, perhaps *en route* to Genoa.[129]

Pegolotti's *La pratica* states that sacks of soap from Cyprus and Crete were sold in both Pera and Constantinople. Cypriot resin and buckrams were also sold there by weight in sacks, although the buckrams may have originated from further east. Cypriot carobs were sold in Pera, one sack of Cypriot carobs amounting to 1.75 *modii* in measures of corn, while Cypriot camlets were also sent to Pera and Caffa. The de Mari family also appears in the notarial deeds of Boateriis concerning commerce between Cyprus and Pera, as for instance in a loan advanced in August 1360, and these deeds record persons from Pera and Caffa, both free and slaves, residing in Famagusta.[130] Trade between the Genoese colonies of Pera and Caffa and Famagusta, itself under Genoese occupation from 1373 until 1464, continued into the fifteenth century. Cypriots resided in both colonies from 1381 onwards, and in May 1390 one of them, the slave George originating from the Zarbatori family, obtained a conditional manumission from his owner Anthony de Casteliono, a notary in Pera. But the commercial networks of the inhabitants of Pera suffered on account of the Ottoman advances, the decline of Byzantium and the closure of trade routes passing through Persia, and by the mid-fifteenth century relations between Cyprus and these Genoese colonies were minimal.[131]

---

[128] Lamberto di Sambuceto, *1304–1307*, nos. 17, 37–9, 49, 92, 174 and 2, 43–4, 77, 79, 86, 88.

[129] Giovanni de Rocha, no. 28.

[130] Francesco Balducci Pegolotti, 33, 35–6, 93; Fleet (1999: 24); Nicola de Boateriis, nos. 1, 113, 129, 168.

[131] Balard (1978, I: 271–2, 288, 305 and notes 308, 851; 1987: no. 113).

Conclusion

In the first two centuries of Frankish rule the traditional economy of Cyprus became diversified without abandoning its agricultural foundation, while commerce flourished. With the increased penetration by Western merchants and immigrants from both Western Europe and the adjoining lands of Syria and Palestine, and the establishment of Venetian and Genoese commercial colonies in the Eastern Mediterranean after the Fourth Crusade of 1204, Cyprus fulfilled the requirements for participating in the international carrying trade. This involved the despatch to Western Europe of silks, spices, salt and cotton, and agricultural produce such as wine, grain, pulses, oil, carobs and above all sugar, in exchange for textiles, timber, iron, silver and other goods from Western Europe. Cyprus participated in this trade throughout the Lusignan and Venetian eras as a primary producer, and, especially after 1292, following the imposition of a papal embargo on trade with Muslim lands, as a middleman. This particular role was seriously undermined when the papal embargo ended in 1344, and the war with Genoa in 1373–74 along with the Mamluk invasion of 1426 dealt further blows to Cypriot commerce. As a primary producer, however, Cyprus remained fully integrated in the patterns of East-West trade throughout the medieval period and beyond.

RELIGION

Chris Schabel

The case of the papal legate Peter Thomae, titular Latin patriarch of Constantinople and Carmelite friar, reveals much about the history and the historiography of religion in Cyprus in the early Frankish period. As legate, Peter was sent to the East to work for Church union, promote crusading efforts, and fight heresy.[1] In 1360, toward the end of the period covered by this book, and not long after his arrival in Cyprus, Peter summoned to Nicosia Cathedral the Greek bishop of Solea, who was the leading Greek cleric, and as many Greek priests as possible, perhaps including other bishops and abbots. All the doors of the cathedral were shut, to prevent a riot of the Greeks. Then, accompanied by the Latin clerics, and sitting in front of the high altar, Peter called the Greeks before him and preached to them, trying to bring them back to obedience to the Roman Church. One Greek priest, a certain Mantzas, protested loudly and stirred up the others. The Greek townpeople heard the commotion and ran to the cathedral, but were at first barred from entering. The crowd turned violent, but when King Peter I was informed he sent his brother John, prince of Antioch, to restore order.[2]

A year or two later, probably late in the summer or 1362, an outbreak of plague hit Famagusta. Away in the capital, Peter Thomae arranged for a procession to protect the city. Fasting on bread and water, the king, the royal family and household, the nobles, the burgesses, and the people proceeded barefoot from the royal palace to the cathedral, where they joined the legate and all the clergy of the various Christian nations. After leading the kneeling congregation in song, the legate led the procession through Nicosia to the cemetery, and ascending the pulpit he preached an inspiring sermon to the multitude. Thus comforted, the crowd followed the legate back to the cathedral to hear Mass. Nicosia was spared. But the plague in

---

[1] Philip of Mézières, *Peter Thomae*; Boehlke (1966).
[2] Philip of Mézières, *Peter Thomae*, 92–3; Makhairas, I, §101; 'Amadi', 409–10; Florio Bustron, 258. For another source for Peter Thomae's stay, see Gonis (1986).

Famagusta was taking 30 to 40 victims daily, so Peter Thomae
decided to go himself to the 'furnace of pestilence and death' and
lead another procession. In the even more cosmopolitan coastal city,
all the sects of Christians again joined in their own groups, singing in
their own languages: 'Greeks, Armenians, Nestorians, Jacobites,
Georgians, Nubians, Indians, Ethiopians, and many other Christians',
we are told, 'each of whom had a different rite and a different
tongue, as well as the Latins'. Barefoot, fasting on bread and water,
they all gathered in the cathedral and then walked in procession,
and the legate 'provoked the people to such devotion that, at God's
command, many infidel Saracens, Turks, and Jews living there burst
into tears and walked barefoot with the Christians' procession'. After
another inspiring sermon, the plague ceased.[3]

Peter Thomae's stay in Cyprus is representative of the history of
religion in the Frankish period in several ways. It reflects the tension
between newly arrived Latins, a minority in a position of power,
and the established majority of Greeks, who were reduced in status.
It shows that the spirited Greek clergy and populace would not tolerate threats to their religious identity. It also exemplifies how the
Greeks in the Frankish period had the confidence and even the security to express themselves without fear of severe reprisals. On the
other hand, Peter Thomae is the personification of the Franks as a
whole in his gradual change of attitude: he grew to understand and
to tolerate the Greeks over time, and the two groups were able to
find not only a *modus vivendi*, but much religious common ground.
They were, after all, Chalcedonian Christians in a sea of non-
Chalcedonians, Jews, and Muslims. And that is the final part of our
theme that the legate's story relates: there were not just two groups,
but religion in Frankish Cyprus was characterized by a great variety of practices, liturgical languages, rites, and even faiths.

The example of Peter Thomae is also paradigmatic of the historiography of religion in this period in Cypriot history, both before
and after the Ottoman conquest in 1570–71. We have two main
sources for the episode in the Cathedral of Holy Wisdom, or St
Sophia, in Nicosia: the fifteenth-century chronicle of the Greek Cypriot
Leontios Makhairas, and the chancellor of Cyprus Philip of Mézières'
hagiographical *vita* of his contemporary, St Peter Thomae.[4] Not sur-

[3] Philip of Mézières, *Peter Thomae*, 97–100.
[4] Philip of Mézières, *Peter Thomae*, 92–4, 97–100; Makhairas, I, §101.

prisingly, there are significant differences between these versions. Makhairas contends that the legate intended 'to make the Greeks Latins' and 'to confirm them by force', implying that Prince John blamed Peter Thomae, whereas Mézières relates that Peter Thomae merely explained to them their schismatic 'error' using Scripture, and that Greek priests actually opened the cathedral doors to the mob, who ran in shouting 'death to the legate', and were only prevented from harming the stoic Carmelite by the timely arrival of the prince. Mézières adds that, afterwards, the legate actually did confirm the bishop of Solea, the other Greek bishops, and all the Greek priests of Cyprus, thus bringing them back to obedience to the Roman Church. Moreover, Makhairas never mentions the processions at all.

In many ways the modern historiography follows Makhairas' lead, although often Makhairas himself presents a more balanced view.[5] Most historians have reduced the religious history of Frankish Cyprus to the first two themes mentioned above, which are then characterized as Latin coercion and the heroic Greek defence of their religion. In their works the representative events are the three famous episodes of violence: the execution of the thirteen Kantara monks in 1231, the riot provoked by the papal legate Peter of Pleine-Chassagne in 1313, and the incident of 1360 described above—accompanied by a particular interpretation. In recent decades a few scholars, among them all the contributors to this book, have begun to modify this picture in different ways, but the overwhelming majority of articles and textbooks touching on this subject remains unchanged.[6] This chapter will take a different approach to religion in Frankish Cyprus. It will reduce the focus on conflict and the higher clergy and increase the emphasis on practice. It will treat the various themes mentioned above in roughly reverse order. In the end, it will address the traditional issues, in the hopes that a different approach will prove fruitful.

---

[5] Grivaud (2001b: 8–23); *Synodicum Nicosiense*, 36–44.

[6] For revisionist views, see especially Richard (1996), Coureas (1997), Nicolaou-Konnari (1999: chapter 9), Grivaud (2001b: part III, chapter 2), *Synodicum Nicosiense*, 'Introduction', Carr (1998–1999), Schabel (forthcoming b), Carr in this volume. To save space, this chapter will focus on sources. For earlier works, see Sathas, II, 'Introduction', Philippou (1875), Frankoudes (1890), Duckworth (1900), Hackett (1901), Hackett-Papaioannou (1923–1932, I), Kourites (1907), Zannetos (1910–1912, I), Hill (1940–1952, III: 1041–104), Magoulias (1964), Gill (1977), Englezakis (1980), Kirmitses (1983), Efthimiou (1987), Kyrris (1990–1991; 1993), Papadopoullos (1995c), Coureas (1995c).

A Multiplicity of Rites and Faiths

Peter Thomae's processions were neither the first nor the last in which the great variety of religious groups of Cyprus participated. By the fourteenth century, against a common enemy, whether natural or man-made, the entire population found common cause and common modes of expression, in battle or in procession.[7] During a drought in 1308, Amaury, who had usurped power from his brother King Henry II, led a procession 'of all the nations through the island'. The opposite problem occured in 1330, when the Pedieos River rose to unprecedented levels and flooded the capital. The Dominican archbishop of Nicosia, John of Conti, led processions of 'Franks, Greeks, Armenians, Nestorians, Jacobites, and Maronites' for 40 days. Afterwards the procession was made an annual affair on the anniversary of the great flood, stopping at the monasteries of the various sects. In 1392–93 the enemy was again the plague, and King James I ordered a barefoot procession, this time led by the Greek clergy with their icons.

If we can judge from later witnesses, these common events also occurred on an annual basis during religious festivals. For example, in 1313 the papal legate Peter of Pleine-Chassagne decreed that the feast of Corpus Christi should be celebrated on the Thursday after the Octaves of Pentecost.[8] The Dominican Cypriot Stephen of Lusignan provides this description of the Corpus Christi procession as it was in the mid-sixteenth century, and it may apply to earlier periods:

> The spectator can see at first the Greek cross, and the crowds of people go around it without any order. Then the Greek priests follow, then the image of the Holy Virgin, followed by crowds of women. This is the usual way in which Greeks always organize their processions. Then there are the Latin mendicants, arranged according to their order; then follow the Indian priests, who wear a turban on their heads (these turbans are made of turquoise or blue linen), and the bishop and his mitre; then come the Nestorians, the Jacobites, the Maronites, the Copts, and the Armenians, and almost all of them wear turbans. Also, all of them wear the chasuble, following the Latin custom, except for the Armenians, who wear round birettas with a white band. Then follow the Latin priests, accompanied by their archbishop

---

[7] On processions, see Grivaud (2001b: 302–7); cf. Coureas (1998: 83–4).
[8] *Synodicum Nicosiense*, no. H.XXXV.

or by a suffragan, then the regimento and the noblemen. It is really beautiful to see so many people belonging to different religions and so many groups of Christians with different denominations and rites.[9]

Unfortunately, because this sort of information usually comes from travellers and chronicles, we are not well informed about the thirteenth century, nor do we have solid evidence for the populations of the various religious groups in absolute or sometimes even in relative terms. Accounts of Richard's conquest mention Armenians in 1191 fighting for Isaac, and in 1211 Armenians were described alongside the Greeks as serfs of the Franks, which may indicate a mainly rural presence. The first document that makes a point of discussing religious groups on Cyprus other than Greeks and Latins is a papal letter of 1222 refering to 'Syrians, Jacobites, Nestorians, and others', and the rubric applied a century later in 1322 adds 'Maronites', although they were on Cyprus even before 1191. Thus we may be able to state that in the first phase of the Frankish period, in terms of numbers, the Greeks were followed by Greek-rite Syrian Melkites, then Syrian Nestorians and Jacobites, while Armenians and Maronites perhaps figured less because they were predominantly outside the cities.[10]

The new influx of refugees from Syria in the latter half of thirteenth century changed the demographics, increasing the overall proportion of the non-Greek sects. If we consider the above-mentioned lists of 1330 (for Nicosia: Armenians, Nestorians, Jacobites, and Maronites) and of the early 1360s (for Famagusta: Armenians, Nestorians, Jacobites, Georgians, Nubians, Indians, Ethiopians, and many other Christians), together with the Augustinian James of Verona's 1335 report (for Famagusta: Jacobites, Armenians, Georgians, Maronites, Nestorians) and the Provincial Council of Nicosia of 1340 (Maronites, Armenians, Nestorians and Jacobites),[11] we may be able to put together a picture of the relative numbers of these groups in the fourteenth century. In what follows, for the most part the groups will be treated briefly in roughly reverse order of importance.[12]

[9] Étienne de Lusignan, *Chorograffia*, fol. 35r, and English trans., *Chorography*, §179; cf. *idem, Description*, fols. 75r–76v.
[10] Hubatsch (1955: 295); *Excerpta Cypria*, 13 (Oldenburg, with Cobham mistranslating 'servi' as 'slaves'); *Cartulary*, no. 35; *Synodicum Nicosiense*, no. X.9; Grivaud (2000: 53); Coureas (2001a: 349). See also Nicolaou-Konnari in this volume.
[11] *Excerpta Cypria*, 17; *Synodicum Nicosiense*, no. L.1.
[12] For this section, see also Richard (1979), Grivaud (2000), Coureas (2001a), Coureas *et al.* (forthcoming) and Nicolaou-Konnari in this volume. It should be

Muslims, Jews, and Minor Groups of Christians

Muslims: In about 1252 and about 1280 Latin archbishops of Nicosia warned Christians against seeking Jewish or Muslim doctors, and in 1298 Archbishop Gerard declared that having sex with a Jewish or Muslim woman was a major crime, subject to his jurisdiction. It is not known whether there were 'Saracen' doctors on Cyprus in the thirteenth century, but learned Muslims did visit King Hugh IV's court in the mid-fourteenth century for philosophical and theological debates, and Hugh patronized Arab artists. Certainly many captive Muslim slaves worked in agriculture—over 100 on one estate—and as domestics, and sexual contact would have been possible in the cities. The owners of Muslim slaves sometimes kept them from baptism, partly fearing that it would mean emancipation, so these slaves would probably have practiced their religion. Notarial records from around 1300 in Famagusta show that merchants freed slaves with Arabic names. Nevertheless, Philip of Mézières could also have been refering to Muslim merchants in Famagusta, in which case their legal standing—and their right and duty to swear on the Quran—was spelled out in the *Assizes*.[13]

Jews: Despite the prohibition against Jews on Cyprus following the massacres in the Jewish revolt in 116 AD, Jews had returned to the island by the sixth century and by the middle Byzantine period were represented by two groups, the Orthodox and the Kaphrossin, considered heretics by the former for observing Sunday rather than Saturday. Perhaps St Neophytos' *Treatise against the Jews*, written in 1186, reflects the size of the community on the eve of the Frankish conquest. If so, then we may be able to apply to the thirteenth century the information we have for the fourteenth, when Jews were living in Famagusta, Nicosia, and Paphos, near Neophytos' monastery, where they had a synagogue. Jews engaged in trade, tanning, dyeing, and medicine. Jewish doctors had in addition a religious education, which probably made their employment by Franks especially upset-

---

noted that the *Livre des Assises des Bourgeois* covers the legal status of Muslims, Jews, Jacobites, Nestorians, Armenians, Syrians, Latins, and Greeks, but since it reflects the realities of the Crusader mainland where it originated, it is difficult to use it to determine the relative importance of these groups in Cyprus, or even to be certain of the *Livre*'s complete applicability in all cases.
    [13] *Synodicum Nicosiense*, nos. A.XIV, A.XXVII.2, B.10, B.18d, G.IVb; *Syntagma*, no. 98.6; Lamberto di Sambuceto, *1296–1299, 1299–1301, 1300–1301, 1301, 1302, 1304–1307*, passim; Coureas (2000a); *Assizes*, Codex One, art. 291, Codex Two, art. 291, and passim. See also Coureas and Nicolaou-Konnari in this volume.

ting to the Latin clergy. Some Jews on Cyprus in the thirteenth century were probably curing and sleeping with Christians, considering the decrees mentioned above. In the 1250s Archbishop Hugh likened the 'words and incantations' of the professional mourning women who wailed at funerals to those of pagan and Jewish rituals. Although the *Assizes* afforded Jews some legal protection, since they were able to swear on the Torah and Greeks filing suits against Jews had to produce Jewish witnesses, there were ominous signs in the early fourteenth century. In 1310 the papal envoy Raymond of Piis is said to have taken a great deal of money from the Jews of Nicosia and Famagusta, and a few years later Archbishop John of Conti 'ordered that the Jews and Jewesses must wear a yellow sign on the head to be recognized', the first such occurrence in the former Greek lands and a century before the Venetian territories adopted the measure. Unfortunately, the events of 1373–4 and of the fifteenth century were disruptive for the Jewish community, so that the interesting information we have from the Jewish traveller Elias of Pesaro from just before the Turkish conquest is not accurate for the earlier period.[14]

Ethiopians, Indians, Nubians, and Copts: Mézières mentions the first three as being in Famagusta, and among the 'other Christians' of Famagusta, he included Copts, whom he mentions elsewhere. These groups, different in race but with shared doctrines, were small enough before 1374 that the papacy did not deal with them. The only other information we have for the Copts in the early period is that the Dominican Alfonso Buenhombre visited their monastery of St Anthony in Famagusta. This institution, together with the church of St Anthony, perhaps existed from the early fourteenth century. Later a Coptic cathedral of St Anthony is attested in Nicosia, but it is unknown whether it existed before 1374. At first the Copts were joined with the Ethiopians, or Abbyssinians, who supposedly arrived in Cyprus from Jerusalem just before Richard's conquest. After the groups split, the Ethiopians managed to gain possession of a church of St John Chrysostomos in Nicosia, near the royal palace. Of the Indians and Nubians in this period we know nothing. Until the Genoese invasion, all these small groups were no doubt concentrated in Famagusta.[15]

---

[14] *Excerpta Cypria*, 73–6; *Synodicum Nicosiense*, nos. A.XIV, A.XX, B.10; 'Amadi', 327 and 406; Florio Buston, 194; *Assizes*, Codex One, arts. 289 and 291, Codex Two, arts. 289 and 291; Starr (1949: 102–3); Grivaud (2000: 57–8).
[15] Grivaud (2000: 49–50); Grivaud in this volume.

Georgians: The fact that independently James of Verona in 1335
and Philip of Mézières over a quarter century later refer to Georgians
in Famagusta suggests that they had a community in that town,
although it must have been small because the papacy did not worry
about them doctrinally. Beyond James' assertion that they were baptized like Latins but performed the liturgy in Greek, we know nothing
about them, but it is likely that they had arrived from Syria with other
refugees toward the end of the thirteenth century. Strangely, on the
opposite end of the island, a few kilometers from the coast near Polis
tis Khrysokhou, and apparently unrelated to the Famagusta community, the Georgians possessed the monastery of Yialia, probably
founded before 1000, restored around 1200 by the Georgian Queen
Thamar, and still active during the thirteenth century. Upon hearing the report that a Georgian and two Greeks, without consent,
called themselves abbots of Yialia and of two Greek monasteries,
and were running them into the ground, in 1306 Pope Clement V
ordered Bishop Peter of Montolif of Paphos to investigate and to
reform them with Latins, if necessary. Since St Nicholas Davli visited Yialia in the 1310s, the reform was probably not carried out,
although the local tradition is that it was a Latin house. Ruins with
thirteenth- and fourteenth-century paintings can still be seen.[16]

Arabic-Speaking Syrians: Maronites, Jacobites, and Nestorians

At the Nicosia Provincial Council of 1340, there was an 'interpreter
between the Latins and the Maronites, Jacobites, and Nestorians', who
were all significant enough to be summoned. Given that James of
Verona reported that these three groups were present in Famagusta in
1335, and that the residents of that city 'understand well the Saracen
and Frankish tongues, but chiefly use Greek', we can conclude that
Arabic was the language of these three groups of Syrian Christians,
although there are inscriptions in Syriac, which may have been used
in the liturgy.[17]

Jacobites and Nestorians: In 1222 Pope Honorius III included the
Cyprus Jacobites and Nestorians among those who refused to be
subjugated to the Latin archbishop of Nicosia, but who were appar-

---

[16] *Acta Clementis V*, no. 6; *Synodicum Nicosiense*, no. X.34; Enlart (1987: 360); Gunnis
(1936: 468); Grivaud (2000: 48).
[17] *Synodicum Nicosiense*, no. L.14; *Excerpta Cypria*, 17; Enlart (1987: 215).

ently without a leader.[18] These sects were non-Chalcedonian Christians considered heretics by both Latins and Greeks. In 1326, after the great population increase from the arrival of the wave of refugees at the end of the thirteenth century, Pope John XXII wrote to the Dominican Patriarch of Jerusalem Raymond Bequini, acting bishop of Limassol, and complained about the activities in Cyprus of 'some sons of iniquity, called Nestorians and Jacobites, whose most wicked sects were once condemned and damned in the General Councils':

> The aforesaid Nestorians damnably profess that there are two persons in Our Lord, Jesus Christ, and that He is the adoptive son of God by an inhabiting Grace, and said Jacobites profess that there inheres in Christ only a single nature. They have their own separate churches, in which they publicly proclaim errors and heresies of this sort.[19]

The Jacobites of Cyprus, monophysites as the above description relates, are recorded as having a Bishop Athanasius in 1264, while the Nestorians may have had a bishop in Nicosia in the thirteenth century. If the 1222 and 1326 letters are anything to go by, these groups did not submit to the Latin Church in Cyprus, and perhaps this is why their leaders at the 1340 council in Nicosia are described as 'rectors' or 'elders': did Archbishop Elias of Nabinaux, who summoned them, not yet recognize their episcopal status?[20]

The apparent success of the 1340 synod may help explain why the existing Jacobite and Nestorian communities in Nicosia and Famagusta thrived so openly in the coming decades. We have few details about their establishments in Nicosia before the fifteenth century, when the Jacobites already possessed a monastery and two churches, although they probably at least had their cathedral churches there in the fourteenth century. From Leontios Makhairas we learn of the fantastic wealth of the Famagusta Nestorian merchants in the mid-fourteenth century; Francis Lakha used some of this money to build a Nestorian church, probably the still extant St George Xorinos or SS Peter and Paul, which are in the Gothic style but have Syriac connections. In the fifteenth century the Jacobites also had a church in Famagusta, which was probably constructed in the previous century. It is possible that the so-called 'Tanners Mosque', a Gothic church in the Syrian

---

[18] *Cartulary*, no. 35; *Synodicum Nicosiense*, no. X.9.
[19] *Acta Ioannis XXII*, no. 89; *Synodicum Nicosiense*, no. X.50.
[20] Grivaud (2000: 51); Coureas (2001a: 350–1); *Synodicum Nicosiense*, nos. L.1, L.13.

quarter of Famagusta near the Maronite and Nestorian churches, is the Jacobite church.[21]

Maronites: It is difficult to evaluate the Maronite presence on Cyprus, because some Maronites submitted to Rome even before 1191 and afterwards their orientation in Cyprus was rural, lasting to the present day, except for the displacement caused by the Turkish invasion and occupation in 1974. Maronites were on Cyprus from before the conquest, and since Maronite patriarchs appointed two monks as abbots of the monastery of St John at Kuzbandu in 1121 and 1141, it is probable that near the famous Greek abbey of St John Chrysostomos of Koutsovendis there existed a Maronite house in the first half of the twelfth century. After the conquest the silence of the Western ecclesiastical sources may be due to the Maronites' status as uniates, but it is probable that they only became numerous on Cyprus in the late thirteenth century, with the decline of the Crusader States. In the fourteenth century there were Maronite communities in both Famagusta and Nicosia. They are mentioned in a rubric of 1322, and they were important enough to be represented by a bishop, a certain George, at the 1340 Council of Nicosia, and before 1357 they also had a bishop named John. Although the Maronites likely spoke Arabic at the time, James of Verona says that in Famagusta their liturgy was in Greek and they performed baptism in the Latin way. In the fourteenth century the Maronites probably possessed the extant Gothic church of St Anne in Famagusta, and in the fifteenth century they are recorded as having a church of St James in Nicosia.[22]

Armenians

As is the case with the Maronites, the Armenian community in Cyprus has a history that goes back to the early Middle Ages and continues today. In 1136/7 the population of Tell Hamdun in Cilician Armenia was resettled in Cyprus by the Emperor John II Comnenos, and the Armenian Cypriots apparently had a bishop in 1179, fought for Isaac

---

[21] Makhairas, I, §§92–5; Enlart (1987: 215, 280–6, 299–302); Grivaud (2000: 51–2). See also Carr in this volume.

[22] *Excerpta Cypria*, 17; *Cartulary*, no. 35; *Synodicum Nicosiense*, nos. L.1, L.13, X.9; Hill (1940–1952, I: 305 and note 1; III: 1045, note 4); Enlart (1987: 274–9); Papacostas (1999a: II: 104–5); Grivaud (2000: 53–4). It is not known if or when the modern Arabic some Cypriot Maronites speak experienced a shift from Syriac: Borg (1985: 2–3, 150–1).

Comnenos in 1191, and were recorded as making up part of the servile population in 1211. Thus, they were probably well entrenched in Cypriot society from the beginning of Frankish rule. Again like the Maronites, the Armenians' absence from early papal correspondence is probably in part a reflection of their close relationship with Rome, or at least that of the Kingdom of Armenia. Despite some doctrinal differences, the papacy did not complain explicitly about the Cyprus Armenians as it did about the Jacobites and Nestorians, or even about the Syrian Melkites and Greeks. Ties between the Kingdoms of Armenia and Cyprus were very close from the beginning of the thirteenth century, even with much intermarrying among nobles and royals, as we learn from requests for papal dispensations for marriages within the prohibited degrees of consanguinity. Members of the Greek clergy used Armenia as a place of voluntary exile before 1250, while during his coup Amaury forcibly sent his brother King Henry II to Armenia. Later, in 1322, Henry created an Armenian garrison for Kyrenia, and henceforth Armenians constituted a permanent fixture in the army. These ties and the continuing influx of refugees from the Muslim advance in Syria and Cilician Armenia account for the fact that from Henry's time on the Armenians seem to be the most important religious group on Cyprus after the Greeks and Latins.[23]

One member of the Armenian royal house, the historian Hayton of Gorhigos, was of the Latin rite and became a canon at Premonstratensian Bellapais Abbey, going on a lengthy mission to the pope in the first decade of the fourteenth century. Unlike Hayton, the bulk of the Armenian population did not Latinize, of course, and around 1310 Armenian monophysite monks went into exile in Cyprus, most of them staying. By then the Armenians had a bishop in both Famagusta and Nicosia, possessing three churches in Famagusta, in addition to an important monastery with a scriptorium. One of these churches may have been the Gothic Armenian Church preserved in the northwest of the walled town, near the Syrian quarter. The church of St Mary of Vert, which an Armenian family restored, received papal support in the 1310s from both Clement V and John XXII, who offered indulgences to visitors and direct Latin Church donations. By

---

[23] See above; Hill (1940–1952, I: 305); Coureas (1995a: 33–41, 55–6); Grivaud (2000: 44–5); Coureas (2001a: 349–50).

the fifteenth century, when there was an Armenian quarter in Nicosia, they had two churches in the capital, including a cathedral, and we can probably project their existence back on the fourteenth century. They also possessed a miraculous Holy Cross in the sixteenth century, which again may have been in their hands much earlier.[24]

It is possible that the Armenian churches of Nicosia and Famagusta differed in their allegiances, because only one bishop, Gregory (a mistake for George?) was present at the 1340 synod, and at some time before 1342 Archbishop Elias appointed George Noreghes 'bishop and pastor' for 'the faithful Armenians living on the island of Cyprus', implying that there were still 'unfaithful' ones as well. George went to Avignon in person, where he was baptized in the Latin rite, confirmed in holy orders—since he 'had not received the sacrament and orders *properly* beforehand'—and consecrated by early 1344. Thus some of the Cyprus Armenians were true uniates after that date.[25]

Melkite Syrians

Although the Armenians were probably the most important religious group after the Greeks and Latins, they may have been outnumbered by the Syrian Melkites, who did not exactly constitute a separate religious entity. These Syrians were religiously Greek but linguistically—at least some of them—Arabic. After the fall of Acre Syrians had a privileged juridical position on Cyprus vis-à-vis the other non-Latin groups. This is not necessarily an exception to the rule that religion is the primary marker of identity in this period, however, because this was simply a transferal of the rights they enjoyed in the Crusader States where the Greek language population was minimal.[26]

Melkite Syrians were already prominent on Cyprus in 1222, when Honorius III complained of their insubordination, but they apparently did not have a special position yet. Perhaps the pope's suggestion that they had no religious leadership is in error, for in 1229 the Greek Patriarch Germanos II addressed a letter to both the

[24] *Acta Clementis V*, nos. 24 and 45; *Acta Ioannis XXII*, no. 7; *Synodicum Nicosiense*, no. X.35; Coureas (1995a: 65–6, 70); Grivaud (2000: 45–6); Enlart (1987: 286–8); Coureas *et al.* (forthcoming).
[25] *Acta Clementis VI*, no. 41; *Synodicum Nicosiense*, nos. L.1, L.13, X.54; Coureas (2001a: 352–3).
[26] Grivaud (2000: 52–3).

Greek and Syrian ecclesiastics on Cyprus, urging them to resist Latin pressures. Among the requests the Greek hierarchy presented Pope Innocent IV in 1250 was that they be given the tithes 'from the free Syrians and Greeks of the Kingdom of Cyprus'. Again in 1267, we read of 'the Syrians that work lands or other possessions', who were 'obliged to pay the tithes according to ancient custom and the decision once made [in 1220] between the prelates and the illustrious queen and other nobles of the Kingdom of Cyprus'. The Syrians' membership in the Greek religious community is confirmed in the *Bulla Cypria* of 1260, which Pope Alexander IV applied 'to the Syrians of the same kingdom who from ancient times have observed the same practices, rites, and the ecclesiastical justice of a common law as the Greeks'. The implication is that Syrian Melkites had been on Cyprus for a long time, were factors in the rural and urban economy, preserved a separate identity, and yet were united with the Greeks religiously.[27]

Although the two groups apparently shared the same higher clergy of Greek bishops, this does not necessarily mean that they attended the same services, since Patriarch Germanos referred to Syrian clerics in 1229. In 1263 Pope Urban IV lamented how, as he was told, 'some people, both ecclesiastics and seculars, namely Greeks and Syrians, go against [the *Bulla Cypria*] by their own rashness'. Rubrics of 1322 specify that Urban was talking about 'Greek and Syrian clerics'. Another letter of 1263 mentions 'a great many Greek and Syrian laymen of the Kingdom of Cyprus' opposing the *Bulla Cypria*, then refers to 'said priests and clerics from the aforesaid Greeks and Syrians' who are obedient to the Latins.[28]

No doubt the number of Syrian Melkite clerics on Cyprus grew substantially after the fall of the Crusader States toward the end of the thirteenth century. Writing in the 1280s, Archbishop Ranulph gives orders to 'bishops and priests, ephors, master chaplains, and laymen, Greek and Syrian', and mentions 'all Greek and Syrian monks and priests'. By 1313, we hear of 'abbots of the Syrians who had come to that kingdom from parts of Syria after this arrangement and who stay in the kingdom', so they had more than one monastery

[27] Germanos II, 'Letter 2'; *Syntagma*, no. 80; *Acta Innocentii IV*, no. 24; *Cartulary*, nos. 35, 78, 106; *Synodicum Nicosiense*, nos. X.9, X.18.3, X.25.32, X.29.
[28] Germanos II, 'Letter 2'; *Syntagma*, no. 80; *Cartulary*, nos. 11, 35, 75, 79; *Synodicum Nicosiense*, nos. X.9, X.26.4, X.27.2–4.

on Cyprus. We even have a suggestion that Syrians had important positions within the Greek hierarchy. At the same time, at least the refugee Syrians dwelling in Nicosia and Famagusta had special rights, and some of them even enjoyed the privileges of Venetian and Genoese citizens. But the Greek Bishops Leo of Solea and Olvianos of Lefkara, in the Latin dioceses of Nicosia and Limassol respectively, claimed in the 1310s that all such Syrians were subject to their jurisdiction, according to the *Bulla Cypria*.[29] They told Pope John XXII that the

> Greek pontiffs and their precedessors had been in peaceful possession or quasi [possession] of the right of the immediate subjection of the aforesaid abbots and other Syrians, and of confirming the election of these abbots, and of hearing the marriage cases which would occasionally arise among said Syrians or between them and the Greeks, from the time of said arrangement.[30]

The Latin bishops disagreed about the Syrians who arrived after 1260, and in the 1310s they were involving themselves in marriage cases and confirmations of abbots, and even filling vacant Syrian benefices and offices in the Greek cathedrals and churches. On the one hand, these Syrians did have a clergy and special rights, but on the other, the Syrians did not have their own bishops and the Latins and the papacy considered them to share the same rites as the Greeks, speaking of 'the clergy and populace of the Greeks and Syrians'. The papal legate Peter of Pleine-Chassagne initially found in favour of the Latin Archbishop John of Nicosia and Baldwin of Famagusta, but Pope John XXII asked for a new investigation. The dispute continued for decades in Famagusta, where the population of refugee Syrians was highest. In the early 1360s the legate Peter Thomae again found in favour of the Latin Bishop Leodegar of Famagusta and against the Greek Bishop John of Karpasia, although Popes Urban V and Gregory XI had to confirm the legatine decision in 1365 and 1373 respectively. The vague position of the Melkite Syrians between the Latins and Greeks would continue into the fifteenth century, but the dispute testifies to their numerical and economic importance in fourteenth-century Cyprus.[31]

---

[29] *Acta Ioannis XXII*, nos. 35–6; *Synodicum Nicosiense*, nos. B.7c, X.37.1–2, X.38.1–4.
[30] *Acta Ioannis XXII*, no. 36; *Synodicum Nicosiense*, no. X.38.1
[31] *Acta Ioannis XXII*, nos. 36–7; *Acta Urbani V*, no. 72; *Acta Gregorii XI*, no. 54; *Synodicum Nicosiense*, nos. B.22a, X.38.2, X.39, X.58.

The Latins

We are better informed about the Latins on Frankish Cyprus than about any other religious group, due to the survival of the *Cartulary* of the Cathedral of Holy Wisdom of Nicosia, the record of church legislation known as the *Synodicum Nicosiense*, papal letters, and numerous references in chronicles and charters. Nevertheless, this evidence is still patchy in comparison with areas of the West, and it is heavily focused on disputes, thus giving a skewed view of the subject. Nicholas Coureas has been treating the institutional history of the Latin Church in Cyprus in great depth, so this section will merely provide a broader portrait of the Latin rite on Cyprus.[32]

Latin communities existed on Cyprus before 1191, mainly Venetians, along with some Latin churches and a small number of Latin priests. After the conquest, the military order of the Knights Templar ruled the island for a short time in 1191–92 and retained large estates afterwards. Then, in the first years of the Lusignan period, Guy and Aimery gave shares of confiscated property and incomes of Venetian and Greek landlords to the nobility, the main military orders (Templars, Hospitallers, and Teutonic Knights), and various Latin ecclesiastical establishments in Syria-Palestine such as the archbishop of Tyre, the Cistercians of Syria, and the abbey of the Temple of the Lord in Jerusalem. It was only in 1196 that Pope Celestine III agreed to Lord Aimery's request for a Latin church hierarchy and established the Latin archbishopric of Nicosia with suffragan bishoprics in Paphos, Limassol, and Famagusta. A substantial amount of Venetian ecclesiastical and secular property was then given to the secular church, but most had been given elsewhere.[33]

It has become a cliché that the secular Latin clergy on Cyprus was wealthy. In fact it was relatively poor in absolute terms. Starting from nothing, the archbishopric was only given two villages as an endowment, along with the plot of land where the cathedral was to be built. Otherwise, it was to receive the tithes from the diocese (probably eight of the fourteen Greek dioceses) and whatever pious donations it could get. Only the Nicosia foundation document survives, but certainly the three suffragan bishoprics started with much

---

[32] See Coureas (1997) generally for the thirteenth century.
[33] *Cartulary*, nos. 1–4, 8; *Synodicum Nicosiense*, nos. X.1–X.3; Hubatsch (1955: 200); Richard (1969–1970: 69–70); Marsilio Zorzi; Richard (1997); Papacostas (1999b).

less.[34] The fact that the bulk of the population was not Latin, and did not pay tithes on land obtained before 1215, reduced the amount of tithes the Latin clergy was to receive, and the Frankish laity itself resisted payment from the very beginning. Add to this the competition for donations from the Greek clergy and the military and monastic orders in Cyprus and Syria, and the results cannot have been encouraging.

Nevertheless their needs were few, given the small Frankish population to serve and its concentration in the cities, especially in Nicosia at first. Even there, the legate Eudes of Châteauroux remarked in 1249 that there were 'few parishes of the Latins in the Nicosia diocese', and in the city itself the only parish church in 1253 was the cathedral. Not only were costs low, but in the beginning there were still few rivals in the Latin regular clergy. Each Latin suffragan bishop was assisted by a cathedral chapter, which depending on the diocese consisted of officers and several canons, usually totaling perhaps ten members, a small number compared to many Western chapters. Nicosia began with sixteen canons, but settled on twelve in the 1250s, so that the chapter still had fewer than 20 members. Since the Frankish nobility spent much of its time in Nicosia, the bishops also maintained residences there. Each bishop and chapter tried to increase its wealth through donation or investment, and their success is reflected in the cathedrals. The Cathedral of St Mark in Limassol was the former Venetian church, and it was not large. Paphos, whose bishop was often also the papal tax collector, never had a large cathedral either. The first St Nicholas Cathedral in Famagusta, which may also have been a Venetian church, was probably small, and it was only in the first decade of the fourteenth century with the radical economic growth of the town that the present cathedral was begun. Even this church and Nicosia Cathedral, while impressive by Levantine standards, are modest in comparison with those of European cities of similar size.[35]

Nicosia was by far the wealthiest diocese. The records of the frequent one-time donations of money or commodities that the cathe-

---

[34] *Cartulary*, nos. 8–9; *Synodicum Nicosiense*, no. X.2; Edbury (1975–1977); Richard (2001b).

[35] 'Amadi', 291; *Regesta Clementis V*, no. 8998 (*Bullarium Cyprium II*); *Synodicum Nicosiense*, nos. A.XXVIII.2, E.V, E.X; Enlart (1987: 355–6); Collenberg (1979); Marsilio Zorzi, 184, lines 9, 16.

dral received in alms, for burials or other services, have, of course, not been preserved, but we know some donations of property and incomes. In 1217 Philip of Ibelin gave a generous annual income in money, grain, and wine to the cathedral for a chaplain to say masses for his and his mother's souls, and Baldwin of Morphou made a similar donation of money in 1234, as did King Henry I twice in 1239, Hugh III in 1270, and Henry II in 1287. Queen Alice gave the cathedral free milling rights in Kythrea in 1220, and Henry I granted a *casale* and other property to the church in 1233 and 1234. With its resulting funds the cathedral was able to purchase important properties in 1222, 1233, and 1247, and to make substantial investments in 1236 and 1248. By the middle of the thirteenth century the cathedral provided an income for the archbishop; a chapter that had about seventeen members, including the dean, archdeacon, treasurer, cantor, and master chaplain; and ten priests, ten deacons, ten subdeacons, and ten acolytes. Eventually permanent altars were established for the Virgin, St George, St Nicholas, St Francis, and others, and the cathedral had a substantial collection of relics. More visibly, there was money to build the cathedral church itself.[36]

It is fortunate that the archbishop and chapter were able to make significant progress on the cathedral and in their investments in the first part of the century, because afterwards the competition for pious donations grew fierce. From the beginning some funds were diverted to private chapels, sometimes approved and sometimes opposed by the Church hierarchy. The only significant local rival before 1250, however, besides the two main military orders, was Episcopia Abbey, better known as Bellapais. It was probably established under Guy, but by 1206 King Hugh I had granted in alms 'the place Raylos, in which your monastery is situated, and the place that is called Episcopia, with everything contained within them, to the prior of the church of St Mary of the Kyrenia Mountains, of the Order of St Augustine', and Archbishop Alan gave the canons exemption from tithes. By 1211 it had switched to the Premonstratensian Order, and by 1224 it was an abbey. It obtained a *casale* called Prestia by 1225, it certainly had a house in Paphos, perhaps with a priest, by 1246, and even the priory of St James in Nicosia at a later date. Hugh

---

[36] *Cartulary*, nos. 16, 31–4, 40–1 (contrary to the English summary, Baldwin was not dead), 54–7, 62; Enlart (1987: 82–130).

III, later in the thirteenth century, and Hugh IV, in the fourteenth century, would further endow the abbey so that it became the splendid gem of Gothic architecture we see today. Thus it was successful in drawing away funds from the cathedral, but more than that, like the military orders, it was effectively independent from the secular church, a powerful rival that Archbishop Eustorge was already labouring to control in 1232.[37]

After 1250 there was a radical reduction in the relative importance of the Latin secular hierarchy on Cyprus. First, by then the mendicant orders of the Franciscans and Dominicans, founded in the 1210s, had established themselves in Cyprus. Francis himself visited Cyprus during the Fifth Crusade, and his order and the Dominicans both had convents in the capital by about 1230, probably with the help of Philip of Ibelin's wife Alice, and the friars' preaching attracted crowds and money. Already in 1254 Archbishop Hugh of Fagiano was complaining that the people were going to the regular clergy, meaning primarily the mendicants, for confession, Mass, and burial, which took away revenues from the secular clergy. They were so successful in Nicosia that while the cathedral was the main place of burial for important persons in the thirteenth century—most people were buried in the Great Cemetery—after 1314 the Franciscan convent was the favourite, and with King Hugh IV's death it became the Dominican house. By the end of the thirteenth century the Franciscans and Dominicans had expanded, and a snap-shot for the Latin community of Famagusta around 1300 gives a similar picture: about half of those who drew up wills were choosing burial either in the cemetery or the church of St Michael 'deforris', owned by the bishop and chapter, while the other half were more or less evenly divided between St Nicholas Cathedral itself, where some of the richest were buried, and the mendicant orders, first the Franciscans and then the Dominicans—but they often received donations even from those who chose burial elsewhere.[38]

A second factor is that, around mid-century, Latin monks and

---

[37] Étienne de Lusignan, *Description*, fols. 31v, 89r; *Cartulary*, nos. 8–9, 36–7, 42, 109, 131; *Synodicum Nicosiense*, nos. G.IVa, X.2.9, X.60; *Regesta Honorii III*, nos. 5156, 5376 (*Bullarium Cyprium I*); *Livre des remembrances*, no. 214; Enlart (1987: 174–200).

[38] *Cartulary*, no. 38 (cf. no. 68); Lamberto di Sambuceto, *1296–1299, 1299–1301, 1300–1301, 1301, 1302, 1304–1307*, various documents; Otten-Froux (2003: 32–4 and passim); Nicola de Boateriis, passim; Edbury (1997c: 237–9); Imhaus (1998); Coureas *et al.* (forthcoming).

nuns began to arrive from Syria in the wake of the Muslim advances. Cistercian monks had settled at Pyrgos near Limassol around 1240, but in the early 1250s they moved to a spot just outside the walls of Nicosia, founding Beaulieu Abbey. Probably in the 1240s, Benedictine monks from the abbey of St Paul of Antioch were installed in the monastery of the Holy Cross at Stavrovouni, directly or indirectly replacing Greek monks. Together with the leaders of the military orders and of the Franciscans and Dominicans, the abbots of Bellapais, Beaulieu, and the Holy Cross became powerful figures in Cypriot religious affairs, and their establishments attracted patronage.[39]

By the mid-fourteenth century, while the number of the Latin secular clergy must have grown to meet the needs of the Latin refugees of Syria, the growth of Latin monasticism seems to have far outpaced that of the seculars, who probably still had only a handful of parish churches in Nicosia and Famagusta and perhaps less than a half dozen outside the cities. Not only were there Franciscan and Dominican convents in Nicosia, Famagusta, and Limassol, with a Franciscan house in Paphos and a Dominican convent in a village, but by 1300 the Carmelites and Augustinian hermits had also arrived on the island, supposedly eventually founding houses in all cities except Paphos. In and around Nicosia there were also two houses of Franciscan nuns, two convents of Cistercian nuns (both founded before 1250), a Cistercian priory, a house of Benedictine monks, and no less than five Benedictine nunneries. If one adds the military orders and the known hospitals, the capital probably contained in excess of 20 Latin religious houses. That such a staggering number was possible is due not only to the religious vitality of the Latins but also to the fact that the Frankish population was largely free, since Latin monks and nuns came from the non-servile classes.[40]

Many of these establishments competed with the cathedral for donations, congregations, and burials. For example, after an earthquake King Henry II gave 18,000 bezants for the reconstruction of the Benedictine convent of Our Lady of Tyre, and Pope John XXII granted an indulgence to visitors to the abbey, to encourage further donations. Boniface VIII offered a similar indulgence to donors to the Benedictine convent of Our Lady of Tortosa, whose church still

---

[39] *Cartulary*, no. 68; *Bullarium Cyprium*, various documents; Schabel (2000b).
[40] *Cartulary*, nos. 63–4; Otten-Froux (2003: no. 175); Nicolaou-Konnari (1999: 314); Coureas *et al.* (forthcoming).

stands. This convent possessed a miraculous icon of the Virgin brought
over from Tortosa, which explains the abbey's name. A few Latin
monasteries were exempt from tithes, or at least reluctant to pay
them, and some avoided the jurisdiction of the archbishop of Nicosia.
In the 1250s and 1260s, for example, the archbishop had to negotiate
with the military orders over jurisdiction, tithes, and burial rights.
Thus, not only did the construction of the regular clergy's often
sumptuous buildings require large sums of money that might otherwise have gone to the archbishop and chapter, but the secular church
did not always benefit directly from their presence.[41]

Besides the military orders' commandaries, the mendicant convents in Limassol and elsewhere mentioned above, the abbeys of
Stavrovouni and Bellapais, and a house of Augustinian canonesses
in Paphos (St Mary the Egyptian), the Latin monasteries were concentrated in Nicosia and in Famagusta. A recently discovered document from the 1360s seems to state that four of Nicosia's Benedictine
nunneries, a Cistercian convent, and a house of Franciscan Poor
Clares all had sister institutions with the same names in Famagusta.
The house of Poor Clares may be identified with the ruins known
as Ayia Photou. Surely established after 1291, these six would bring
the total of known Latin monasteries in the second city of the realm
to ten. The wealth of Famagusta allowed the construction of spendid
Latin churches there in the fourteenth century. In the first decade
of the century, the old cathedral of St Nicholas the Confessor proved
too small to accommodate the recent increase in population. In spite
of certain financial abuses, the bishop and chapter of Famagusta
managed to construct the present edifice, dedicated to the same saint,
with papal encouragement. This was achieved despite competition
from the religious orders, especially the mendicants. Dominicans and
Franciscans had important churches, and by 1361 the Augustinians'
church of St Anthony in Famagusta had become a favoured place
of burial and the local Carmelites were obtaining gifts.[42]

In addition to the three big abbeys of Bellapais, Beaulieu, and
Stavrovouni, and the cathedrals of Nicosia and Famagusta, the mendicant convents in those two cities were the greatest examples of

---

[41] 'Amadi', 292, 349–51; *Les Registres de Boniface VIII*, no. 309 (*Bullarium Cyprium II*); *Lettres de Jean XXII*, nos. 8533–4; *Cartulary*, nos. 89, 91; Richard (2001a).
[42] 'Amadi', 291; Nicola de Boateriis, nos. 157, 168; *Regesta Clementis V*, no. 8998 (*Bullarium Cyprium II*); Otten-Froux (2003: nos. 175, 185, 195); Enlart (1987: 222–45, 293–4); Richard (1999: 12–16).

Latin church architecture on Cyprus, the direct products of the pious generosity of the Frankish population. In Nicosia, the Augustinian, Dominican, and Franciscan convents, all fourteenth-century constructions, each had two cloisters, although the Carmelite convent also boasted 'large buildings'. The most magnificent was the Dominican house, whose greatest patron was Hugh IV, while Henry II had favoured the Franciscans, supporting for example the altar of St Francis in Nicosia Cathedral. Only the Augustinian church remains today. In Famagusta the mendicants had to make do with one cloister each, but the substantial remains of the Franciscan and Carmelite churches reflect their former glory.[43]

The business of religion was lucrative in the Middle Ages, and the scattering of tombs of wealthy Latins around the medieval churches of Nicosia illustrates how successful the regular clergy was in attracting laymen. As in the West in the 1250s, a struggle erupted in Cyprus between the secular and regular clergy. In 1253 Archbishop Hugh complained that some of the regular clergy of Nicosia were applying 'their scythe to the harvest that belongs to others' and stealing the cathedral's parishioners, who attended Mass in the churches of the regular clergy, contrary to canon law. Hugh then wrote to Pope Innocent IV, who in 1254 instructed the Latin patriarch of Jerusalem to stop the regular clergy from receiving confessions, absolving sins, celebrating public services, and encouraging bequests and burials in their cemeteries. As elsewhere in Europe, the Latin secular clergy on Cyprus had to learn to live with the new reality, although it was not easy: in 1298 Archbishop Gerard related that one's parishioners could opt for burial elsewhere, but he remarked that secular clerics and regulars were sometimes arguing over corpses.[44]

Other factors in the weakness of the Latin secular clergy are the absence of leadership, clerical abuses, and the lack of lay cooperation. A large percentage of the Latin higher clergy throughout our period was foreign, which meant that many bishops spent little or no time in their sees. Nicosia was often without a resident archbishop. Sometimes this was due to problems with the crown and nobility, who prevented the archbishops from exercising their religious authority. For

---

[43] *Cartulary*, no. 57; *Excerpta Cypria*, 23–4, 26, 43–4, 51–2, 120; Enlart (1987: 146–50).
[44] *Synodicum Nicosiense*, nos. A.XXVIII.2, G.XVIIa; *Cartulary*, no. 38 (cf. nos. 89, 91); *Lacrimae Nicossienses*; Imhaus (1998).

this reason, Archbishop Eustorge was in exile around 1230 and Hugh in 1253, and Hugh and Ranulph actually died in exile in the 1260s and 1280s respectively. From the 1250s to the 1330s there were long periods when Latin patriarchs of Antioch and Jerusalem drew the revenues of the vacant bishopric of Limassol. Later in the thirteenth century the election process broke down more and more frequently in every diocese, with disputes causing further periods of vacancy and long and costly appeals to the pope, which rarely resulted in the success of the applicant. Finally, already in the thirteenth century but with increasing frequency in the fourteenth, the popes appointed prelates directly, and since their candidates were usually in the West, there were often long delays before the appointees reached their sees.[45]

There was also frequent bickering among the clergy, usually over issues related to money, the cause of much clerical abuse. Papal letters often relay accusations of financial irregularity against the higher clergy who abused their offices, while the *Synodicum Nicosiense* details the abuses of the lower clergy, although many of them are perennial—general laxity, scandalous appearance and behaviour, ignorance, drinking, sex, gambling, business dealings—especially in societies where the clerical vocation has fringe benefits. The most interesting abuse is greed, especially surrounding funerals. Archbishop Hugh asserted that some priests and clerics showed up at services for the dead in order to get wax candles, sometimes just grabbing them during the funeral from the laymen who carried them to the altar, and then these clergymen would leave even before the service ended. They desired the valuable candles so much that when they went and joined the procession to the deceased's house, instead of following one cross, they all carried crosses, 'not because of God or any devotion, but for the sake of the candles'. The clerics would cry out for candles and in the commotion the crosses would collide. The papal legate Eudes of Châteauroux added that clerics often demanded money deposits in advance for funeral processions, ringing the bells, and digging the graves, as well as candles for engagements, marriages, and baptisms. The Latins—and the Greeks—were ordered to offer these services for free, unless the laypeople insisted and specified what was being paid for. In 1320 the Dominican Archbishop John of Conti decreed that no payment was to be made until the body was in the grave, and he actually ordered priests to refuse voluntary offerings for confession, baptism, and extreme unction.[46]

Despite the severity of the abuses in Cyprus, it appears that the situation in Syria was even worse, as Eudes of Châteauroux related in 1254. Eudes remarked that 'in some churches of Outremer clerics transgress against the ecclesiastical sacraments by putting them up for sale', and detailed how the greedy members of the clergy extracted fees from the faithful for every imaginable service. Decades later, in his poem about Acre written after the fall of that city, the Templar of Tyre lists the sins of the secular clergy in Syria: 'Now I want to tell you about the clergy', he begins, before commenting on their devotion to 'Lord Money' above all things. Luckily the Dominicans and Franciscans were there to keep things from 'getting a great deal worse', since 'they restrain many men from evil deeds'. But he concludes, 'The perverse behaviours of this time, which you have heard me recounting, were not the custom in Cyprus at all'.[47]

Another reason for the Latin secular church's relative weakness is the lack of secular cooperation. It has often been suggested that the crown and nobles opposed the local Latin clergy out of a desire to protect the Greeks and avoid strife. It would be more accurate to say that the Frankish aristocracy was often uncooperative generally when it came to paying tithes, avoiding marriage with relatives, and reforming morals, although they were willing to make donations for the salvation of their souls. The *Cartulary* of Nicosia Cathedral abounds with complaints from archbishops and popes about the kings' and regents' failure to assist in the enforcement of canon law and the collection of tithes, problems that plagued the church during the entire period covered by this book. One should not forget that the crown also quarrelled with the Templars from 1279 until the coup of 1306. After the trial and suppression of the Templars, which could be seen as a pan-European defeat for the Latin Church, the resulting transfer of property to the Hospitallers made them the second largest landowner on Cyprus after the king.[48]

---

[46] *Synodicum Nicosiense*, nos. A.XXV, A.XXX, E.XVII, I.X–I.XI; Coureas (1997: 111–17); Schabel (2004a: 87, 91, 95, 99, 108–9).

[47] *Synodicum Nicosiense*, no. F (cf. nos. A.XXVII.2, B.18d); The Templar of Tyre, *The Deeds of the Cypriots*, §530, lines 165–211; The Templar of Tyre, *Cronaca*, §294 (530), verses 43–54; Kedar (1985).

[48] *Cartulary*, nos. 10–11, 27, 29, 69–70, 75–77, 79, 81, 87–108; cf. *Synodicum Nicosiense*, nos. G.XVI, L.I, X.12, X.26–X.30; Coureas (1997: 121–72); Claverie (forthcoming). See also Edbury and Coureas in this volume.

These difficulties not withstanding, the life of the Frankish nobility was closely intertwined with that of the Latin clergy, although few local nobles or knights actually made a career in the Church. All religious festivals had what we would call a secular element in the Middle Ages, but what we would call secular festivals also had a religious element. The very establishment of the Kingdom of Cyprus in 1196 assumed the existence of a Latin Church, and it was an ecclesiastical representative of the Emperor Henry VI who crowned Aimery of Lusignan in 1197. Again in 1247 Pope Innocent IV released King Henry I from his subordination to Frederick II, and Cyprus became a client kingdom of the papacy. The military orders were an important element in the island's defence in the thirteenth century, although after 1291, when the Hospitallers and Templars moved their headquarters to Cyprus, relations with King Henry II were tense. In the early 1310s, however, after his brother Amaury's coup had ended, the Templars had been suppressed with a famous trial, and the Hospitallers had decided to move their centre to Rhodes, Henry could breathe easier. Within the kingdom clerics often played other important roles in the government: at least until the 1330s the chancellor of the kingdom was apparently always a Latin cleric, as for example the archdeacon of Nicosia Cathedral Henry of Jubail (or Gibelet), who served as chancellor for several decades.[49]

The most visible connection between Church and State was in public ceremonies. Royal weddings, funerals, entrances, triumphs and other festivals all officially involved the Latin clergy. Coronations will serve as an example. The coronation of the kings of Cyprus took place in Nicosia, and three of them—Hugh IV, Peter I, and Peter II—were also crowned kings of Jerusalem in Famagusta, following the 1295 unification of the see of Famagusta with that of Tortosa in Syria. Since the ceremony was often held during a major feast day such as Christmas or Easter, one can imagine that the clergy of all nations was involved. The coronation ceremony in Nicosia started with a procession from the royal palace to the cathedral, led by the future king. The Latin archbishop, or another high-ranking Latin such as a papal legate, received the procession and gave blessings. Then the future king swore on the Gospels to protect the Church, to preserve

---

[49] 'Estoire de Eracles', 209; *Les Registres d'Innocent IV*, no. 2441; Edbury (1991: 189); *The Trial of the Templars in Cyprus*; Schabel (2004a: 82–96). See also Edbury in this volume.

the freedoms and privileges granted by his predecessors, to render justice to widows and orphans, to keep the laws and customs of the kingdom, and to govern his people justly. In case the king was not of age, the regent had to take similar oaths. The archbishop then asked the prelates, barons, knights, liegemen, burgesses, and representatives of the people who were present for their approval. After the *Te Deum* and a Mass, the consecration began when the king was anointed and given the symbols of his office: ring, sword, crown, sceptre, and orb. The crowd acclaimed the new king, then the king kissed the prelates, took his seat on the throne, and received communion. At the end, the archbishop blessed the standard and gave it to the king. Once the religious ceremony was completed, a procession returned to the palace where a banquet was held, with barons acting as the servants.[50]

It is important to remember that, although personally they adhered to the Latin rite, the kings of Cyprus were the political leaders of all Cypriots. It should not come as a surprise, then, that the royal family was an important patron for the Greek churches, especially from the reign of King Hugh IV (1324–59). Hugh followed the advice of the Greek Patriarch Ignatios of Antioch to have an icon of three Greek saints painted to fight a plague of locusts, and after its consecration the locusts desisted. The famous story of the cross of Tochni in the chronicle of Leontios Makhairas provides the best illustration, however. A Latin priest stole from a church in the village of Tochni a jeweled cross that contained a piece of the True Cross, brought by Constantine's mother Helen. After failing to escape by sea, the priest threw it into a hollow tree, where it remained for 18 years until about 1340. Then a Greek slave boy named George was led to the tree and found the cross, which performed miracles. In the end a monastery was built to house the cross, but along the way we find the royal family visiting the Greek monastery of Makhairas (which seems to have been a summer refuge for them), supporting the cult of the cross, only reluctantly obeying the Latin hierarchy, building a Greek church, tacitly accepting the Greek bishop of Solea's blessing, and transforming the church into a Greek monastery. Finally, Patriarch Ignatios had a cross containing relics made, to be used in processions around the new church against locusts, drought, or plague.

---

[50] Richard (1972); Grivaud (2001b); Coureas *et al.* (forthcoming); *Cartulary*, no. 79; *Synodicum Nicosiense*, no. X.26.8.

Many other examples could be given of the support that Henry II, Hugh IV, and Peter I gave to the Greek clergy in the fourteenth century.[51]

Frankish patronage of non-Latin churches was not restricted to the royal family, of course. Although in the 1360s a Venetian of Famagusta stipulated in his will that 'not a penny' should go to Greeks, there is considerable evidence of Frankish donors in Greek ecclesiastical art and architecture, especially after the fall of Acre in 1291. Written records are scarce, but an interesting case that does survive is the 1307 bequest of the Genoese Peter of St Donatus: he left money in his will to several Latin churches and convents in Famagusta and also 'ad altare Griffonorum Sancti Georgii', that is, St George of the Greeks, no doubt the predecessor of the present ruined Greek cathedral, under construction in 1363. In addition, Latin lords helped maintain the churches and monasteries situated on their fiefs, as did Walter of Brienne in 1354, who also gave to a Greek church in Nicosia. This should not surprise us, when we recall that even the Latin regular clergy employed Greek *baillis*.[52]

As we shall see, besides mixed donations there was considerable mixing of rites in fourteenth-century Cyprus, but there were also mixed marriages and eventually a tendency for Latins to move to the Greek rite. The Latin hierarchy frequently denounced 'clandestine marriages', starting around 1250 and continuing to the end of our period, and these pronouncements probably involved mixed marriages. Thus around 1280 Archbishop Ranulph repeated the prohibition against 'clandestine marriages' and those who assisted in them, just after requiring that mixed marriages between Latins and Greeks be announced according to the Latin observance. Likewise, in 1353 Archbishop Philip linked mixed marriages with clandestine marriages and specified that the Greek bride or groom should first be confirmed in the Latin rite, the banns should be announced in the Latin manner, and the children should follow the Latin rite. Philip was not making new policy, however, for already in the early 1250s Archbishop Hugh ordered 'Greeks who have received the sacraments of confirma-

---

[51] Makhairas, I, §§40, 67–77; Grivaud (2001b); Carr in this volume. On Hugh IV see Schabel (2004b).
[52] Lamberto di Sambuceto, *1304–1307*, no. 82; Poncelet (1934: 10, 16, 18); Carr (1995a); Nicolaou-Konnari (1999: 309); Otten-Froux (2003: nos. 4, 16, 16). See also Carr in this volume.

tion and marriage in the way of the Roman Church' and their children to continue following the Latin rite. Some of these Greeks may have been 'converts', but most were probably married to Latins.[53]

Since in our period Franks had a higher legal status than Greeks, spouses in mixed marriages and their children probably never officially went over to the Greek rite. Rather they would have done so unofficially, and it is probably in part for legal purposes that Archbishop Philip also specified that Franks should not administer the sacraments to Greeks, and Greeks should not administer them to Franks. Philip said that these things were frequently causing 'many scandals between Franks and Greeks', but the evidence suggests that it was the Latins going to Greek services that occurred most often. In 1368 we learn that King Peter I had complained to the pope that 'a great part of the noble and plebean women of [Nicosia], attacking the Catholic faith that they orally profess with ways and deeds contrary to it, frequent the churches of Greeks and schismatics, hearing the divine offices according to their rite'. Since women are specified, perhaps the Frankish men avoided such trouble by receiving the sacraments privately. Accordingly, Peter lamented that 'many barons, knights, and burgesses' of Nicosia stayed away from St Sophia and 'now have their sons and daughters baptized and contracts of marriage solemnized in their own and profane houses, and they have masses and other divine offices celebrated in their houses and in their rooms'.[54]

Thus at Peter's death in 1369, the secular Latin Church of Cyprus was 'orphaned of its spiritual children and empty on Sundays and feast days', losing its congregation for three reasons: private chapels, the regular clergy (especially the mendicant orders), and the Greeks. With the Great Schism of the West (1378–1417), the Latin clergy became more Cypriot, the foreign clerics often remained absent, the monasteries gained some independence, and the crown controlled the local church.[55] Under these conditions of increased separation from the West, the Greek language and rite further influenced the 'Latin' laity.

---

[53] *Synodicum Nicosiense*, nos. A.XVI, B.14c and 15l, C.6 and 18, G. Ivk, IX, L.II, M.I–II. See also Nicolaou-Konnari in this volume.

[54] *Cartulary*, no. 131; *Synodicum Nicosiense*, nos. M.II, X.60; *Assizes*, Codex One, art. 58 and Codex Two, art. 59. For a different approach to Greek-Latin integration and segregation, see Coureas (2000c).

[55] Collenberg (1982a: 667–72).

The Greeks

The traditional approach to the religious history of Frankish Cyprus narrowly focuses on the Greek clergy and its relationship to the Latins, ignoring the other communities and the populace. It is also ahistorical, because it is seen from a modern perspective, with the Latins portrayed in dark colours. Indeed, a recent treatment simply bears the title 'The Church in the Dark Ages: Latin Rule'.[56] Briefly, we have a depressing picture of a Latin clergy that stripped the Greek clergy of its property, forced it into submission, abolished its independence and rights, refused to tolerate its beliefs and practices, attempted to Latinize it, and persecuted those who would not yield. The strength of the Cypriots' Orthodoxy and Hellenism helped them to survive intact and preserve their identity. Aside from some factual errors, this is a logical interpretation based on the modern ideals of democracy, freedom of religion, and the self-determination of peoples, perhaps sometimes with a slight dose of Greek Orthodox chauvinism. From a medieval perspective—with very different ideals—the history of the Greek rite in early Frankish Cyprus appears to be merely the natural result of the Frankish conquest. This section tests the main elements of the traditional view from the perspective of a medieval historian.[57]

Economy

Let us begin by asking what the economic status of the Greek ecclesiastical institutions on the island was during the early Frankish period. Obviously, the Greek Church was not stripped of *all* its possessions after Richard the Lionheart's conquest in 1191, for Greek churches and monasteries continued to function without apparent pause throughout the period, and we hear of Greek clergymen deriving their living from their possessions. On the other hand, the Greek Church did not survive the conquest unscathed. The question is to what degree the Greek Church suffered economically. Even here, one has to distinguish between the direct and the indirect negative

---

[56] Aristeidou (2004).
[57] This section is a condensed version of Schabel (forthcoming a), inspired especially by the pertinent chapters in Coureas (1997), Nicolaou-Konnari (1999), and Grivaud (2001b).

economic effects on the Greek Church. Indirectly the Greek Church was deprived of its largest benefactors. The richest landowners of Cyprus who possessed estates elsewhere seem to have left the island at the conquest, while whatever imperial patronage could perhaps have continued to flow from Constantinople after 1191—as in the case of Makhairas Monastery—would have dried up after would-be crusaders conquered that city in 1204.[58] The remaining potential donors were a smaller number of Greeks—with fewer possessions— who were not of servile status, and the Franks themselves.

Directly, the impact is hard to gauge. Some of the former lands of the emperor and of the Greek landlords no doubt found their way into the hands of the Latin Church via royal or other donations, something which would have lessened the need for seizures of Greek ecclesiastical property for the Latin Church. But there were other potential sources of wealth. A substantial number of Venetians lived in pre-conquest Cyprus, and they possessed a great number of estates. Many of these estates were seized, probably soon after the conquest, and we have a crucial document of ca. 1243 recording the fate of some of these confiscated Venetian properties. In at least four cases Greeks are mentioned as being in possession of formerly Venetian property in the early 1240s, an indication that Frankish policy was not uniformly anti-Greek. A much greater portion, however, was given to the military orders, the Cistercians, and the secular Latin Church, which means that at least a part of its buildings and estates did not derive from Greeks at all, let alone the Greek Church.[59]

Among the possessions of the Venetians before 1191, moreover, we find a considerable number of churches, including two in rural areas. In Nicosia, Paphos, and perhaps Limassol the Venetians had possessed churches of St Nicholas. Since the compiler of the document was probably relying on his imperfect and incomplete memory decades after the fact, the original cathedral of St Nicholas of Famagusta may have been a Venetian church of that name. Much of the recorded Venetian property was in and around Limassol, and the Latin bishopric of Limassol was one of the greatest beneficiaries, perhaps receiving enough to meet most of its needs. Among other

---

[58] Neophytos the Recluse, *De calamitatibus Cypri*, 10–11; *Syntagma*, no. 73; Neilos, *Rule*, 73.

[59] Marsilio Zorzi, 184–91; Papadopoulou (1983); Richard (1986a; 1997); Papacostas (1999b).

things, it obtained the church of St Mark, which became the Latin cathedral, because it is described as the 'maiorem ecclesiam' or 'great church', the usual way to refer to a cathedral.[60]

What then is the evidence for confiscations of Greek ecclesiastical property? The only Greek documents of the first couple of decades of Frankish rule that allude to the Greek clergy's economic status give the impression that things were not so bad. St Neophytos relates that his monastery was untouched, but that the monks were forced to purchase land for cultivation. Likewise, it was reported in Nicaea in 1209 that the churches and the clergy 'remained in their usual order' after the conquest. In the early 1220s, Greek Cypriot prelates vaguely reported that 'our situation had been up till now very distressing, but we were able, however, to bear our misfortunes, because only our bodies had to suffer'. The only specific example of a confiscation is for Kykkos Monastery: two or three of the villages it is said to have possessed before 1191 are listed later as royal properties. Even in this case, however, our information that the villages had belonged to Kykkos comes from a very late source.[61]

That Kykkos may have lost property to the king should remind us that the Latin Church was not in a position to take any of its property over directly. Indeed, the Latin secular hierarchy, that is the archbishop, bishops, parish priests, and their staffs, was not even established until 1196. Whatever it did obtain was either through the generosity of the Frankish laity or through purchase; the Latin Church did not seize Greek clerical wealth. As we have seen, the Latin secular hierarchy was not even in a position to control the Latin religious orders, which were to varying degrees independent from the local Latin secular church's jurisdiction and attracted a substantial amount of patronage in their own right.[62]

The little that we actually know about what the Greek clergy lost confirms this picture of a somewhat helpless Latin Church. In his legal treatise dated more than sixty years after the conquest, Philip of Novara makes an oblique reference to some confiscated Greek church

---

[60] Marsilio Zorzi, 184–91; Papadopoulou (1983); Richard (1997); Papacostas (1999b).
[61] Magoulias (1964: 80); Richard (1986a: 68); Chatzipsaltes (1964: 141–4); Germanos II, 'Letter 1'; *Syntagma*, nos. 78–9; *Greek Texts*, 142; Nicolaou-Konnari (1999: 308); Englezakis (1995: 165, 183–4); Neophytos the Recluse, *Rule*, 142, 158.
[62] *Cartulary*, nos. 36–38, 63–4, 68, 89, 91; *Synodicum Nicosiense*, nos. A.XXVIII.2, G. XVIIa; Richard (1969–1970: 69–70).

property: it ended up in secular hands to constitute fiefs. This accords with what is stated in a Latin document that is, ironically, the only direct, positive, and nearly contemporary evidence for the seizure of Greek ecclesiastical property in the early years. The famous agreements of 1220 and 1222 between the queen and nobles, on the one hand, and the local Latin archbishop and bishops, on the other, state that the Latin hierarchy will no longer dispute the Frankish nobility's claims to any 'possessions and lands or places' formerly owned by the Greek clergy that had ended up in secular hands. After the first agreement Pope Honorius III asked Queen Alice to grant to the Latin churches some of the seized 'possessions that the churches, cathedrals, and monasteries of the Greeks are known to have had'.[63] The answer was negative, and in the 1222 agreement the following was appended:[64]

> Except for the cathedrals and other churches of the Latins, all *casalia*, *prestarias*, and the collective possessions that they hold at present or which they will be able to acquire in the future with royal consent from the donation of kings or of others, with which, along with the tithes and other things mentioned above, the [Latin] churches must be content.

The agreements are noteworthy; the sources of the Latin Church's income and property are thus specified: donations and tithes, not Greek ecclesiastical property—and the erroneous claim of certain writers that the tithes were taken away from the Greeks ignores the fact that the Greeks had not collected tithes. There is no mention of any previous seizure of Greek churches or monasteries, just possessions and estates. The possessions and estates that the Greek Church did lose ended up in the hands of the Frankish crown and nobility, not the Latin Church. Finally, it should be remarked that the same agreement actually secures the Greek clergy's rights to property that had not been seized or that had been granted after 1191, which 'they shall similarly have and possess free and exempt from this time forward, peacefully and quietly'.[65] The overall picture, then, is of a Greek Church that lost some, but by no means all, of its possessions to the Frankish nobility, but none of its churches or monasteries.

---

[63] Philip of Novara, 'Livre', 536; *Cartulary*, nos. 80 and 82–4, cf. no. 95; *Synodicum Nicosiense*, nos. X.6.10 and X10, cf. no. X.11.10a; Edbury (1995a: 355–7; 2001b: 557, 565).

[64] *Cartulary*, no. 95; *Synodicum Nicosiense*, no. X.11.10a.

[65] *Cartulary*, nos. 82–4, 95; *Synodicum Nicosiense*, nos. X.6.8, X.11.8; Richard (1992a).

The Latin Church received some of the Venetian churches and properties, tithes for further income, and donations from the Frankish nobility with which more churches could be built, donations that could have come from former imperial or Greek noble estates just as easily as from the Greek clergy.

But in three cases it has been claimed that a Greek church or monastery at least ended up in Latin hands: Hagia Sophia, Bellapais, and Stavrovouni. By 1196, the archbishopric of Nicosia possessed the 'Nicosia church' and the plot on which it stood. The cathedral of Nicosia came to be known as *Sancta Sophia*, and it is assumed that the name was taken from the old Greek cathedral, which was therefore taken over from the Greeks. If this assumption is correct, it is still more reasonable that Hagia Sophia was the name of the Byzantine church—the so-called Bedestan—adjacent to the present cathedral to the south, but in this case the Latins must have returned it to the Greeks afterwards.[66]

In the Middle Ages the present abbey of Bellapais was known in Latin as 'Episcopia', from the Greek word for 'bishop'. For this reason it is assumed that the abbey was a Greek church of some sort when it was given to the Augustinians around 1200. But, again, there is no positive evidence, and there are other possible explanations. At any rate, as in the case of Nicosia Cathedral, the land was not taken by the Latin Church, but given to it by the crown. Moreover, it was a religious order and not the secular Latin Church that was the beneficiary.[67]

The same can be said for Stavrovouni, which became Benedictine, although the Latin Church may have had something directly to do with this. It is assumed that there was an active Greek Orthodox monastery at Stavrovouni at the time of the conquest. In 1211 Wilbrand von Oldenburg reported that 'the life of its inmates, if they will allow me to say so, is very unlike that of monks', which may be an indication that they were not Latins. By 1254 it was in Benedictine hands. How the transfer occurred is uncertain, but it seems that this exception might prove the rule. Just before 1240 Greek monks were among those who went into voluntary exile in Armenia. Pope Gregory IX ordered Archbishop Eustorge of Nicosia to 'assign [to Latins] the

---

[66] *Cartulary*, nos. 8–9; *Synodicum Nicosiense*, nos. X.2.3–5; Willis (1986); Papacostas (forthcoming).
[67] *Cartulary*, no. 36; *Regesta Honorii III*, no. 5156.

monasteries of the Greeks fleeing Cyprus because of heresy'. Again in 1246 Pope Innocent IV instructed Eustorge to reform lax, corrupt, or heretical Greek monks. Perhaps the monks had left Stavrovouni or were accused of heresy, and Eustorge gave the abbey to Latin refugee monks from the Syrian mainland. If this scenario is true, then it exemplifies how a Greek church could have come into Latin hands without being forcibly seized during the early years after the conquest.[68]

So the Latin Church does not seem to have been the beneficiary of the seizure of Greek churches or Greek ecclesiastical property, let alone the perpetrator, at the conquest, nor do actual churches or monasteries seem to have been taken. The Greek Church did lose both benefactors and property as a direct result of the conquest, in each case due to the Frankish nobility. But how much did it lose and how poor was it? This is hard to say. We know that some Greeks continued to make donations to Greek ecclesiastical establishments, and eventually Latin donors are attested as well. We actually possess considerable information about monastic property that suggests that the regular clergy thrived, even in the decades just after the conquest. The *Typika* of the monasteries of Makhairas and St Neophytos, completed in 1210 and 1214 respectively, speak of considerable property, daughter houses, dependent serfs, substantial incomes, and even expansion in terms of numbers of monks and purchases of land. In 1216 and 1217 Pope Honorius III confirmed an impressive array of Cypriot properties owned by the monasteries of St Theodosios of Palestine and St Catherine of Mount Sinai. The fact that they requested papal confirmation may indicate that they were having difficulties, but St Catherine did manage to acquire even more property in the fourteenth century. This worked in reverse, for Pope John XXII, who also protected St Catherine, wrote King Leo V of Armenia in 1326 demanding that he restore to the abbey of St George of Mangana, near Nicosia, its daughter house of St George Lampron in Armenia. Nor was Mangana the only Greek abbey to own property abroad, since Koutsovendis possessed the monastery of St Sabbas in Palestine after 1334.[69]

---

[68] Hubatsch (1955: 296); *Excerpta Cypria*, 14; *Les Régistres d'Innocent IV*, no. 8001; *Cartulary*, nos. 71–4; *Synodicum Nicosiense*, nos. X.13, X.16; *Acta Honorii III et Gregorii IX*, no. 262; *Acta Innocentii IV*, no. 30; Pavlides (1992: 75a).

[69] Neilos, *Rule*, 49–53 and Neophytos the Recluse, *Rule*, 135, note 12; *Acta Honorii III et Gregorii IX*, nos. 1, 17; *Acta Ioannis XXII*, no. 85; *Synodicum Nicosiense*, no. X.49; Richard (1986a); Coureas (1994; 1996). See also Nicolaou-Konnari in this volume.

Greek clerics did claim to be poor. For example, during the protracted negotiations that led to Pope Alexander IV's promulgation
of the *Bulla Cypria* in 1260, the pope related that the Greek Archbishop
Germanos 'humbly begged us to consider the poverty of the Church
of the Greeks' and to hurry up the proceedings. But the fact that
Germanos and his suffragans were able to journey to Rome for such
proceedings suggests that their poverty was not crushing, as does the
description of the damage done to the houses and vineyards of the
Greek priests who obeyed the *Bulla Cypria* in the years just following.
Likewise, around 1320, when Bishop Leo of Solea was in Avignon on
other business, he complained that his estate was too poor to support
him. Nevertheless, Leo claimed on another occasion that his Greek,
Syrian, and Latin enemies, clerical and lay, had made off with movable and immovable goods from his estate, including 'serfs, various
sums of money, many herds of various species, and no small quantities of wheat and barley'. Afterwards a Latin knight was still able
to extort 1,000 silver bezants and ten gold florins from Leo. Later,
however, we hear from Abbot Germanos of Mangana what seems
to be the truth of the matter: Leo lied and was in fact quite rich,
with an annual income of 1,500 gold florins. Nor should this surprise us, given the splendid—and expensive—Greek churches of the
era, such as the Cathedral of St George of the Greeks in Famagusta,
constructed near the end of our period.[70] Whatever the exact economic
state of the Greek clergy in general, it does not seem to have been
destitute, and at times certain members appear to have been well off.

Jurisdiction

It is noteworthy that almost a quarter century passed after the installation of a local Latin ecclesiastical hierarchy on Cyprus before the
first recorded attempt to control the Greek clergy. In the meantime,
as upsetting as it was to the likes of St Neophytos, the mere establishment of the Latin clergy cannot have been considered completely
uncanonical, for not only did Latins have churches that were active
on Cyprus before 1191, but Georgians, Maronites, and Armenians
did as well, as we have seen. What eventually made the coexistence

---

[70] *Cartulary*, nos. 75, 78; *Synodicum Nicosiense*, nos. X.25.8, X.27.2, X.38.3–5, X.42,
X.46; *Acta Ioannis XXII*, nos. 36, 39a, 62; Otten-Froux (nos. 4, 6); Nicolaou-Konnari
and Carr in this volume.

of the Greek and Latin hierarchies problematic was that the Latins did *not* view the Greeks as heretics, but rather as lost orthodox sheep who had strayed from the fold. Moreover, recent events had sealed the schism and created a hostile atmosphere, notably, for the Latins, the massacres of Latins in Constantinople in 1182 and the Greeks' failure to support the Third Crusade, and, for the Greeks, the Fourth Crusade and its aftermath. One would thus expect both the Latin subjugation of the Greek clergy on Cyprus and the Greek clergy's active resistance.

We must look now at the 1220–1222 agreements. It is striking that the main purpose of the documents, even according to the rubric inserted in the *Cartulary* exactly one hundred years later in 1322, is to reach an agreement between the Latin clergy and the Frankish nobility concerning tithes. That is, the documents are mainly about a financial compromise that does not involve most Greeks. But the Greek clergy was subjugated. There were so many Greek priests and deacons that, until their number decreased sufficiently, they would have to stay in their villages. The ordination of Greek serfs could only be done with the assent of their lords. Greek serfs ordained in this way could move about freely, with the Latin bishop's permission, although not with their wives or children. The 1222 agreement added two new clauses. First, admission to monasteries was to be restricted to a certain number, so that when one died or was transferred, only then could another join the monastery, if he were a serf of the lord on whose land the monastery lay. Second, the number of Greek bishops was to be reduced to four, and they were to reside in four small towns and be obedient to the Latin bishops.[71]

There is no doubt that this is the subjugation of the Greek clergy, but why was this done? This requires an understanding of the immediate context and of the context in the West. It is rarely mentioned that the restrictions on Greek priests, deacons, and monks concern serfs, not all Greeks, and free Greeks continued to join monasteries without obstacles. In the West entry into monasteries was restricted to freemen, usually those who had property for an endowment, and in some regions and monastic orders only nobles could be admitted. Likewise, entering the priesthood was not possible for just anyone. In all cases permission from the lord was required.[72] Since serfs were

---

[71] *Cartulary*, nos. 82–4, 95; *Synodicum Nicosiense*, nos. X.6.2 and 4–6, X.11.2, 4–6, 9, and 10b.

[72] See, for example, Lodge (1903) and Pijper (1909). Even in the 1220s, free Greeks joined Kantariotissa without hindrance: *Martyrion Kyprion*, 320–4.

property of a sort, after the conquest of Cyprus, when many Greek
nobles fled, the bulk of the Greek population was servile according
to Western tradition and could not join the clergy. It appears from
the agreement that, in the first decades of Frankish rule, Greek serfs
were joining the clergy anyway and in large numbers, but that the
crown and nobility continued to demand that they fulfill their servile
obligations.

This situation was not ideal for the nobles, the Latin clergy, or
the Greek clergy. Greek priests were needed to administer the sacraments to the large Greek-speaking majority, but the Latin Church
could not accept a servile priesthood: this would fly in the face of
Western tradition, especially after the Gregorian Reform. This is why
in the third clause in the agreements Queen Alice had to grant freedom from manorial obligations to all Greek priests and deacons who
were so obliged beforehand. But since many Greek serfs probably
joined the Church in order to avoid servile obligations, the parties
decided on a logical compromise that allowed for a controlled number
of Greek serfs to become monks, and even for some Greek serfs to
join the priesthood under certain circumstances to administer to the
Greeks. If the Latin bishop ordained a serf without his lord's consent, however, the bishop had to supply a replacement serf. Likewise,
if the bishop allowed such a priest to transfer to another village, the
bishop had to find a replacement priest. Complicating matters was
the fact that Greek priests, although not monks, could marry and
have children, which was frowned upon in the West. The children
of former serfs were to retain their servile status.[73] On these points
the solution adopted in Cyprus did not differ markedly from that in
Norman Sicily, Frankish Greece, or the West in general.[74]

It is important to stress that, as in similar circumstances elsewhere,
it was not the nobility, but the Latin clergy that won these concessions for the serfs. But in return, the Latins required obedience in
all spiritual matters from the Greek priests and deacons, and the
reduction of the status of the Greek bishops to assistants. From the
standpoint of the Latins, this last item was simply enforcing a regulation of the Fourth Lateran Council of the 'Universal Roman
Church', just held in 1215, which stipulated that no two bishops

---

[73] *Cartulary*, nos. 82–4, 95; *Synodicum Nicosiense*, nos. X.6.3, 5, X.11.3, 5, 9.
[74] *The Assizes of King Roger*, clause 10; *Acta Honorii III et Gregorii IX*, nos. 48, 115;
Pijper (1909: 689–90).

could occupy the same see, but that in cases where there were different language groups, assistants could be appointed. If they were to be assistants, then there would only be need for four of them, and the Latins took advantage of the existence of the remote sees of Solea, Arsinoe, and Karpasia—perhaps Lefkara, the home of St Neophytos and a royal fief, already had a bishop too—to provide titles for these four assistants, although they probably did not always reside in those villages. It was implied that the position of Greek archbishop would be abolished, and we learn from a letter of the Greek Patriarch Germanos II that Archbishop Neophytos went into exile as a result. The arrangement was similar to what had happened in Latin Syria, although the status of the Cypriot bishops seems to have been higher than that of their Syrian counterparts, while in the Morea the Greeks did not retain their bishops at all. Not only did the 1222 agreement preserve a Greek episcopacy in Cyprus, but according to Germanos' letter the Greeks also kept their ecclesiastical courts, although the Greek clergy and laity had the right of appeal to the Latins.[75]

Despite these concessions, from the perspective of much of the Greek clergy at the time the situation was almost intolerable. For one thing, the Greek upper clergy were accustomed to a degree of independence and had come to view their church as a separate entity in terms of common language and liturgy, not in terms of the legal jurisdiction of a universal church. Whether or not the Greek Church of Cyprus enjoyed 'autocephalous' status is somewhat immaterial, because Latins could and eventually did claim that this status had been transferred to the Latins. Thus just as before 1191, in 1209, and in the early 1230s the Greeks asserted their ecclesiastical independence except for the emperor's rights to nominate or appoint the archbishop, the Latin archbishops after 1196 maintained their independence except for the pope's rights.[76] The Greeks were prepared, or forced, to accept the existence of an independent Latin clergy on Cyprus, but the Greeks demanded that their independence be respected too. Here was a true difference in belief, but there was to be no real compromise

[75] *Cartulary*, no. 86; *Acta Honorii III et Gregorii IX*, no. 87; *Synodicum Nicosiense*, nos. X.7.1, X.8.3; Germanos II, 'Letter 1'; *Syntagma*, no. 79; Hubatsch (1955: 292–3); Galatariotou (1991: 13).
[76] Chatzipsaltes (1964: 141–4); Lampros (1917: 41–3); *Syntagma*, nos. 78, 81; *Greek Texts*, 142, 153; Schabel (2002–2003: 342).

on this matter from the Latins, who were in the position of power, although it seems that *de facto* a small compromise was reached: the Greeks were able to remain in their sees until death.

As bitter as this pill was to swallow for the Greek upper clergy, with their long traditions, there was more required of them. Since the 1220–22 agreements contain only clauses that were in some way of interest to the crown and nobility, they do not give us the specifics of properly ecclesiastical matters. We know from Germanos' letter, however, that the Greek bishops were to swear oaths of fidelity and, apparently, homage, to their Latin counterparts.[77] Despite the outrage that writers have expressed concerning the oath, this needs to be seen in the Western context. Taking an oath of fealty, at least, did not constitute a special requirement for the Greek bishops. Historians have sometimes seen the oath as an added burden for the Greeks, a kind of special punishment, but this is untrue. Oaths were normal for all levels of all hierarchies in the West, both lay and clerical, and there are several examples of these in thirteenth-century papal letters to Cyprus. In the case of bishops, they included a promise of fidelity and obedience to the pope. For the Greek bishops in Cyprus, who were also subordinate to their Latin counterparts, this element was in the oath as well. Otherwise, the oath was the same verbatim as that taken by all bishops of the Roman Church.[78]

The Greeks objected to the oath and the Latins insisted upon it not because it was something the Greeks in particular had to do, but simply because it meant formal incorporation into the Roman Church and acceptance of the Latin bishops as the only true hierarchy on the island. As far as we know the Greeks were prepared to accept other churches on the island, including that of the Latins, and they did not insist on the unity of all churches. For the Latins, however, the hierarchy of the Church of Cyprus was one, the higher prelates were now Latins, and since the Greeks were orthodox like the Latins, they too had to take the pertinent oath for their positions. Each side understood the oath as an elimination of the separate existence of a Greek Church; they simply disagreed about whether that was a Good Thing.

---

[77] Germanos II, 'Letter 1'; *Syntagma*, no. 79.
[78] Cf. Pope Gregory IX's *Decretales*, liber II, tit. XXIV 'De iureiurando', cap. 4 (vol. II, col. 360); *Bullarium Cyprium* (forthcoming).

Doctrine

Many theologians maintained that the only essential doctrinal difference between the two sects concerned the *Filioque*, the Latin assertion that the Holy Spirit proceeds from the Father *and the Son*. Nevertheless, the *Filioque* never caused strife on Frankish Cyprus, nor did most other differences. Around 1220, calling the Latins 'unorthodox' and charging them with 'wrong belief', the Cypriot St Neophytos listed ten of the 27 Latin errors he knew of, but only two issues seem to have caused tension.[79]

Although not on Neophytos' list, perhaps because he was not yet aware of it, the first issue was obedience to the pope, as we have seen. This was becoming for the Latins a question of doctrine, and in the early fourteenth century Pope Boniface VIII's bull *Unam sanctam* would state that obedience to the pope was absolutely necessary for salvation.[80] The Greek bishops did not know exactly how to react to the 1220–1222 agreements, so an embassy was sent to Nicaea to consult with Patriarch Germanos. In a letter dated late 1222 or 1223, Germanos told the Greek Cypriots to accept the jurisdictional requirements and even the right of appeal to the Latin ecclesiastical courts. Persuaded by refugees from Constantinople, however, Germanos advised the Cypriots not to take the oath. The result was that the Greeks of Cyprus were split between those who submitted and those who did not, as we learn from a second letter of Germanos, dated July 1229 and this time addressed to both Greeks and Syrian Melkites of Cyprus. Germanos urged the faithful to avoid all contact with the Greek clergy that had submitted. Unfortunately we have no way of knowing how many had given in, but in the early 1230s Archbishop Neophytos remarked that he had submitted, only to seek and receive forgiveness from Germanos himself afterwards. Probably in 1229 Neophytos was still outside the Church, in Germanos' eyes.[81]

The second issue of contention, the most important for Neophytos, concerned the use of leavened and unleavened bread, or enzymo and azymo, in performing the sacrament of the Eucharist. Here the reverse occurred: the Latins did not consider the issue important, and although they used unleavened bread, they accepted the Greek

---

[79] Meyendorff (1983: 90–4); Englezakis (1995: 163, 167, 175, 186, 190–3).
[80] Tierney (1964: 188–9).
[81] Germanos II, 'Letter 1' and 'Letter 2'; Lampros (1917: 41–3); *Syntagma*, nos. 79–81; *Greek Texts*, 153.

use of leavened bread as valid. For the Greeks, however, not only was it very significant, but they considered the Latin practice erroneous and even heretical. When Germanos wrote his letter in 1229, thirteen Greek monks of the monastery of Kantara had already been in prison and exposed to torture for more than a year over this issue, and in 1231 the monks were brutally executed in public in Nicosia, an event marking the low point in Greek-Latin relations on Cyprus.[82] The normal view has been that the martyrdom of the thirteen monks is indicative of Latin attitudes toward the Greeks in the Frankish period and that it was a Latin attempt to force the Greeks to adopt the Latin practice. Without justifying or condemning the event—for this is not the historian's task—we can still see that these assertions are incorrect.

It cannot be indicative of Latin attitudes in the Frankish period, since such a thing happened only once in three centuries of Frankish rule. Moreover, it occurred in a time of chaos in Cypriot history: a civil war, a child king, an archbishop in exile, an era of fear of heresy. Indeed, the person who provoked the event and called for the monks' execution, a certain Andrew, was apparently a member of the new Dominican Order, which was created specifically to fight heresy. Probably, then, the deadly episode was never repeated because it happened under unique circumstances and it is not indicative of Latin attitudes in general. The issue did not go away, but the Latins stopped executing Greeks.

But the Greeks also gradually changed their tactics. That they were able to do so is because the assertion that they had to adopt the Latin practice is erroneous. Even our main Greek source, the *Martyrion Kyprion*, indicates that the Greeks were executed or martyred not because they used leavened bread, but because for years they refused to stop calling the Latins heretics for using unleavened bread. The Latin sources repeatedly state this. They never question the validity of the Greek practice, and indeed often they expressly state that the Greek practice is acceptable. What the Latins would not tolerate is the Greek accusation that they were heretics for their practice.[83]

---

[82] *Martyrion Kyprion*; *Cartulary*, no. 69; *Synodicum Nicosiense*, nos. X12.3–4; Anonymous, *Contra Graecos*, col. 518D; *Acta Gregorii IX*, no. 179a; Banescu (1913: 11–14); Mercati (1920–1921); *Syntagma*, no. 83.3; *Greek Texts*, 158; Englezakis (1995: 176, 190, 195). I am currently working on a book-length study of the issue.

[83] *Martyrion Kyprion*; *Synodicum Nicosiense*, nos. B.6a, B.18g, L.10, X.12, X.13; *Cartulary*, nos. 69, 71–4; *Acta Honorii III et Gregorii IX*, no. 262.

Archbishop Neophytos, who had apparently returned from exile at some point, seems to have understood the Latins' perspective better than Patriarch Germanos. The Greek monks would not change their stance without permission from Germanos, who had urged them to resist and who, after the execution, complained to Pope Gregory IX about their deaths. Around the same time, Archbishop Neophytos complained to Emperor John Vatatzes in Nicaea about Germanos' interference in Cypriot ecclesiastical affairs, encouraging resistance with his letters. Neophytos added that the monks went to their execution willingly, without his involvement, after having gravely insulted the Latins' faith.[84] Then Pope Gregory wrote to the Latin prelates in the East, including Archbishop Eustorge of Nicosia, on 9 March 1238, demanding that Greek priests swear an oath of obedience to Rome and abjure the 'heresy . . . whereby they falsely claim that the Latins are heretics because they celebrate Mass with unleavened bread', and a Greek source records that the Cypriot Greeks did submit on 22 July 1238. By 1240, however, Neophytos, his suffragan bishops, and many other Greek clergymen had changed their minds, although they chose exile in Armenia rather than the path of the thirteen monks of Kantara.[85] There is circumstantial evidence that the dispute continued into the early 1280s during the reign of Archbishop Ranulph of Nicosia. He complained about Greek 'obstinacy' on the azymo issue, related that some Greeks had gone into hiding because of it, and imprisoned Bishop Neophytos of Solea—not to be confused with St Neophytos or Archbishop Neophytos. Finally, before the turn of the century, when yet another Dominican, Bishop Berard of Limassol, made a visitation of the Greek Bishop Matthew in his cathedral in Lefkara, we find Matthew and his priests refusing to say anything at all about unleavened bread. Enraged, Berard successfully pursued Matthew's excommunication, but to Berard's chagrin, Matthew was able to seek protection with the Latin Archbishop of Nicosia, John of Ancona. Archbishop John was a Franciscan, a member of an order much more favourably disposed toward the Greeks.[86]

---

[84] Lampros (1917: 41–3); *Syntagma*, no. 81; *Greek Texts*, 153; *Synodicum Nicosiense*, no. X.12.3; *Cartulary*, no. 69; *Acta Honorii III et Gregorii IX*, nos. 179, 179a.

[85] *Cartulary*, nos. 71–4; *Synodicum Nicosiense*, no. X.13; *Acta Honorii III et Gregorii IX*, nos. 230, 262; *Syntagma*, no. 83.3; *Greek Texts*, 158.

[86] *Synodicum Nicosiense*, nos. B.18.f–g, X.31, X.32; *Acta ab Innocentio V ad Benedictum XI*, nos. 119–20; Schabel (2004a: 82–6).

Although in the Council of Nicosia in 1340 the Greek bishops apparently agreed voluntarily that unleavened bread—and even the *Filioque*—was acceptable, it is doubtful that the Greeks completely changed their opinion. Rather the Franciscan Archbishop Elias was probably able to persuade them to swear to Roman beliefs in bulk, with the qualifier that the Greeks could follow their rites as long as they did not contradict the 'Catholic faith'.[87] We hear nothing else of the issue that caused so much tragedy in the thirteenth century. Thus once the Greeks accepted the oath and stopped calling the Latins heretics,[88] the Latins stopped asking, and the remainder of Greek beliefs were tolerated.

Practice

We have seen, then, that the Greek 'doctrines' that the Latins would not tolerate were the Greeks' refusal to take an oath to the Roman Church, that is their denial of the Roman interpretation of papal primacy, and the Greeks' accusation that the use of unleavened bread was heretical. In both cases these 'doctrinal' issues were connected to actions, to practice. What the Latins thought about Greek practices in general is revealed in Pope Innocent IV's letter of 1254 to his legate, Cardinal Eudes of Châteauroux.[89] The Latin Archbishop Hugh of Fagiano had been arguing with the Greek bishops about their different practices. Repeating the words of previous popes, Innocent says that he wishes to tolerate the harmless differences of the Greeks in ritual, but not those 'that appear dangerous to their souls'. In most cases the pope either approves the Greek practice or calls for a minor modification. On only a small number of points does the pope request a real change: widows should be allowed to remarry as often as they are widowed; the Greeks should henceforth confer seven clerical orders instead of just four; and, perhaps most important, the Greeks should adopt the term 'Purgatory', although here the pope clearly thinks that the Greeks already share the Roman belief in a vague way.

Innocent's requirements are rather mild, something that should

---

[87] *Synodicum Nicosiense*, nos. L.3, 10, 12.

[88] Aside from Pope John XXII's mumbling about Purgatory in 1326: *Acta Ioannis XXII*, no. 89; *Synodicum Nicosiense*, no. X.50.2.

[89] *Cartulary*, no. 93; *Synodicum Nicosiense*, no. X.23.

not be attributed to the pope's friendly attitude toward the Greeks, for Innocent followed the expressed intent of earlier popes and he was the first pope who chose to speak out on these matters in the Cypriot context. In the 1280s Archbishop Ranulph of Nicosia would repeat Innocent's proclamations, with one or two harsher interpretations, and we see much of the discussion again in the Greek Cypriot scholar George Lapithes' treatise on the sacraments from the mid-fourteenth century. As scholars have commented, the treatise supports the Greek position in cases where the Latins and Greeks differ. But Pope Innocent himself obviously never demanded much ritual conformity. Rather than viewing Lapithes' treatise as an example of Greek resistance, we could see it as reflective of the tolerance of what the Latins considered non-essential ritual differences. The *Taktikon* of the Karpasia-Famagusta bishopric, perhaps from the fourteenth century, also suggests this tolerance.[90]

Certainly there was no question of Latinization. The one case where a serious problem with Greek practice occurred bears this out. When the papal legate Peter of Pleine-Chassagne came to Cyprus in the 1310s, he observed that at one point during the divine office, before the consecration of the Eucharist, the Greeks and Syrians would prostrate themselves before the raised host. Since it was not yet the body of Christ, the legate reasoned, this practice constituted idolatry and implied heresy. Pope John XXII's solution was mild. He ordered the Greek bishops to 'instruct the people' and to 'illuminate their cloudy—perhaps, in this matter—understanding', so they would not worship the unconsecrated host. But John hastened to add that 'we do not intend by this' to prohibit them from showing fitting reverence and devotion to the celebrating priest at that point, 'in accordance with the custom of the aforesaid Greeks and Syrians'. He concluded his letter even more cautiously: 'Of course, we do not wish by this will of ours to diminish the arrangement of Alexander IV'. In the end the only ritual modification that was required was that the non-Latin clergies 'settle on a certain sign which can be known to all those hearing the divine office at the hour when they complete the body of Christ', so that they would avoid idolatry, according to Archbishop Elias' council of 1340.[91]

---

[90] *Synodicum Nicosiense*, no. B; Darrouzès (1979: 92–121); Papaioannou (1912–1913); Coureas (2000b).

[91] *Acta Ioannis XXII*, no. 35; *Synodicum Nicosiense*, nos. L.IV, X.37.9–10.

In treating the liturgical freedom of the Greeks in Frankish Cyprus, one should not overlook monasticism. About 40 Greek monasteries functioned at some time in the middle Byzantine period (965–1191), maybe less than 30 at the conquest in 1191, but by the 1560s there were perhaps close to 60. A Venetian report of 1562 mentions 52 active Greek monasteries, and Stephen of Lusignan refers to 24 by name, adding that there were more, including 18 small houses in the Troodos Mountains alone. Our sources are so limited that there may have been many more, such as the monastery of St Gerasimos in Famagusta mentioned in 1363 in a newly discovered document. In any event, with the Latin and Oriental Christian houses, there were at least one hundred monasteries at one point, an indication of the favourable conditions for monasticism under Frankish rule.[92]

The Frankish authorities did interfere, however. It appears that in the first decades of Frankish rule the numbers entering monasteries grew, perhaps because servile Greeks wished to avoid their manorial obligations. For example, the numbers were increasing in Makhairas Abbey and St Neophytos' Hermitage. In the case of smaller houses located on lands owned by nobles and coming under their authority, the problem would have been particularly acute. Hence in 1222 the nobles and the Latin bishops agreed on a compromise: as we have seen, the number of monks in the Greek monasteries would be limited, but serfs could become monks, with the permission of their lords. Supposedly they were then free, for Archbishop Ranulph later specified that Greek monks should not perform servile labour. After 1222, the papacy considered the Greek monasteries as part of the Roman Church, in the Order of St Basil, which meant that the popes subjected monasteries—just as the Latin ones—accused of laxity and heresy to investigations for possible reform. Of the houses founded before 1191, there is no evidence that any were suppressed, but as noted above it appears that Stavrovouni may have been 'reformed' with Latin monks in the 1240s. In most cases, however, the investigations did not result in such drastic measures.[93]

Some Greek monasteries deliberately sought papal projection. In

---

[92] Mas Latrie, *Histoire*, III, 540, 543; Étienne de Lusignan, *Description*, fols. 84v–85r; Otten-Froux (2003: no. 6); Papacostas (1999a: I, 106, 123). See also Carr on monasticism.

[93] Neilos, *Rule*, 50–1; *Cartulary*, nos. 71–4 and 95; *Synodicum Nicosiense*, nos. B.15, X.11.9, X.13, X.16, X.34, X.35; *Les Régistres d'Innocent IV*, no. 8001; *Acta Innocentii IV*, no. 30; *Acta Clementis V*, nos. 6 and 24.

the 1240s the monastery of St Margaret in Agros and its depen-
dency of St Mary of Stilo on the Acrotiri Peninsula, both ancient
foundations, submitted to the pope directly and continued to enjoy
good relations with the papacy until the end of our period. St George
of Mangana was heavily involved with the papacy throughout the
fourteenth century, receiving guarantees for its property in Cyprus
and in Cilician Armenia. The fact that Greek churches and monasteries were often exempt from tithes explains their general absence
from fourteenth-century documents recording payments to Rome for
crusade subsidies.[94] Several important houses developed friendly relations with the Lusignans. The early thirteenth-century portions of
the *Typika* of St Neophytos and Makhairas monasteries, founded in
the twelfth century, specifically ask the Lusignan king for protection.
Later in the thirteenth century Neankomi Monastery outside Nicosia
came under the crown's umbrella, as did Kykkos by 1365, when
Peter I made repairs after a terrible fire. A traveller in 1344–45
remarked how King Hugh IV 'supports the monks of his realm from
his fisc'. Makhairas seems to have been a favoured mountain retreat
for the royals in the fourteenth century. The story of the Cross of
Tochni describes the royal establishment of a Greek monastery near
Nicosia in the mid-fourteenth century. When we consider all examples of Latin patronage, contrary to a monastic crisis in Frankish
Cyprus, what we find is a period of flourishing.[95]

The Bulla Cypria

Let us return to the question of the legal position of the Greek clergy,
which had not yet been settled when Innocent IV treated Greek
practices in 1254. After Archbishop Neophytos and many other members of the Greek clergy went into exile around 1240, the year of
Patriarch Germanos II's death, Pope Gregory IX died in 1241 and
Innocent IV succeeded him in 1243. Innocent's goals were the same
as Gregory's, but, as we have seen, the new pope was more tactful
and perhaps more intelligent. Almost immediately we learn that some
Greeks had professed their loyalty to the Roman Church, if only for

---

[94] *Cartulary*, nos. 107–8; *Synodicum Nicosiense*, nos. X.14–15, X.56, X.59, X.61; *Acta Innocentii VI*, no. 131; *Acta Urbani V*, no. 120; *Acta Gregorii XI*, no. 26; Coureas (1994).

[95] Neilos, *Rule*, 122; Makhairas, I, §§74, 76, 624; Lampros (1917: 16–17); Englezakis (1995: 182–3); Grivaud (2001b: 288–9).

papal protection from grasping laymen, as did the monks of the monastery of St Margaret of Agros. In 1246 Innocent told his legate Lawrence of Portugal to try to entice Greeks back into the fold of the Roman Church by offering them immediate subordination to the pope without any Latin bishops as intermediaries. What some historians have not noticed is that the offer of immediate subordination was not to be extended to Greeks already subject to Latins. Perhaps because he was a Franciscan, Lawrence overstepped his orders and offered the same deal to all Greeks. Neophytos and the others returned to Cyprus as a result, but Innocent rebuked Lawrence for his failure to follow orders. Eventually he was removed and the legate of King Louis IX's Crusade, Eudes of Châteauroux, took his place.[96]

The Greek Cypriot clergy, however, had already come back and proceeded as if Lawrence's offer still stood. Putting Innocent in a difficult position, Archbishop Neophytos and the Greek bishops submitted directly to the pope via Eudes, and as obedient sons they had Eudes send Innocent some requests in 1250. Logically, they desired a return to their status before the agreements of 1220 and 1222, which they wanted annulled: they asked to have fourteen bishops again, independence from the local Latin hierarchy, free ordination and entry into monasteries, and unrestricted jurisdiction over their subjects in spiritual matters. And since all landlords now had to pay tithes to the Latin Church, the Greek bishops asked for the tithes paid by the free Greeks and Syrians as well as the Greek monasteries.[97]

The situation was delicate, and Innocent made no decision. He asked Eudes to investigate further and to protect the Greek bishops from abuse in the meantime. But before a decision was made, Archbishop Neophytos died, and in 1251 the Greek bishops asked Innocent to be allowed to elect a successor. Without agreeing to anything broader, Innocent gave his permission. Perhaps this was made easier by the death of the Latin archbishop of Nicosia, Eustorge, around the same time, but with the accession of Hugh of Fagiano the struggle began again. Moreover, unlike Eustorge, if we are to judge from Eudes' damning description of the state of the Latin clergy on the island under Eustorge's leadership, Archbishop Hugh was a zealous reformer. Like Eudes, Hugh was a scholar, with university training in canon and civil law. He was not about to let slip by what he

---

[96] *Cartulary*, nos. 107–8; *Synodicum Nicosiense*, nos. X.14, X.15, X.17; *Acta Innocentii IV*, nos. 31, 35.

[97] *Acta Innocentii IV*, no. 74; *Synodicum Nicosiense*, no. X.18.

took as irregularities of any sort. The Greeks elected a certain George to succeed Neophytos, but Archbishop Hugh complained to Innocent about the election and, as noted above, about the Greek practices that he found too un-Latin. We have already seen that Innocent largely sided with the Greeks on the matter of their practices, and he did not go back on his word about the election of the Greek archbishop either. In 1254 George was confirmed and took the name Germanos.[98]

Innocent died soon afterwards, however, before having settled the crucial matter of the status of the Greek hierarchy. Innocent's successor, Alexander IV, reaffirmed the authority of the Latin Archbishop over both the Latin and Greek bishops. In this state of ambiguity, Archbishops Hugh and Germanos quarreled over their respective roles until Germanos decided to go to Rome for a final solution. By then there were, apparently, only four Greek bishops left, as stipulated by the 1222 agreement, and with Arsinoe vacant the other three bishops went to Rome as well.[99]

The result was the *Bulla Cypria*, a true Constitution of the Greek Cypriot higher clergy, issued by Alexander in 1260.[100] As with every other important document in Cypriot ecclesiastical history, scholars disagree about its production and its significance. Most maintain that the Latins imposed it upon the Greeks, while others see it, more plausibly, as the result of negotiations. Most regard it as the complete subjugation of the Greeks, while others view it, more correctly, as a compromise. All admit that it was a temporary compromise that Archbishop Germanos was allowed to keep his title, his independence, and most of his power until his death or resignation. In general the 1220 and 1222 agreements were repeated, but with some significant clauses in favour of the Greeks, who obtained some of what they had sought in 1250. The bishops still had to take an oath to the pope and local Latin bishop, but if the earlier oath was both homage and fealty, now it was only fealty. The Greeks would elect their own bishops, although confirmation would come from the Latins. Only the pope could depose Greek bishops; the local Latin prelate could not. The Greek bishops were assured ordinary jurisdiction over the Greeks and the Syrian Melkites in their dioceses. As in 1222, legal cases on church matters between Greeks were to be decided by the

[98] *Acta Innocentii IV*, nos. 79–80, 102–3; *Synodicum Nicosiense*, nos. E, X.19–X.20, X.22.
[99] *Cartulary*, nos. 7, 78; *Synodicum Nicosiense*, nos. X.24, X.25.2–4, 10.
[100] *Cartulary*, no. 78; *Synodicum Nicosiense*, no. X.25.

Greek bishops, although the parties had the right of appeal to the Latin bishop and finally to the pope. Greek bishops were exempted from attending provincial councils, so as not to burden them. The Latin bishops' visitations of the Greek bishops were limited out of similar financial considerations for the Greeks. In short, rather than abolishing the independence and rights of the Greek clergy, the *Bulla Cypria* guaranteed the existence of a separate, partially independent, but also subordinate Greek ecclesiastical hierarchy after 1260.

Still, just as after the Council of Florence much of the populace back home opposed the uniate Greek representatives, in Cyprus the first few years after the publication of the *Bulla Cypria* were characterized by conflict, even violence, between the Greek and Syrian laymen and clerics who rejected the new arrangement and those who accepted it. Moreover, some of the Greeks and Syrians who rejected it insulted, plotted against, and undermined the rights of the Latin churches. Archbishop Hugh had always had a stormy relationship with the secular authorities, and now the regent, Hugh of Antioch-Lusignan, would not even aid the archbishop in dutifully prosecuting Latins and Greeks guilty of 'religious' crimes such as blasphemy, sorcery, gambling, and sodomy, let alone punish the Greeks and Syrians who refused to have contact with the Greek clergymen— presumably Germanos and his followers—who were loyal to the Roman Church and to the Latin archbishop. Instead, the rebellious Greeks and Syrians were allowed to exclude the others 'from their society, proclaim them heretics and schismatics, withhold' their income, 'demolish their houses and uproot their vines', 'strip them of their goods and rights, and otherwise afflict them and their churches and families with serious injuries and pressures'. Archbishop Hugh was powerless to do anything other than offer the loyal Greeks food and lodging in his own home, since the regent would not assist him against the other Greeks and Syrians and even asserted that the archbishop had no jurisdiction over the other crimes except for his power over his own clerics and serfs. Perhaps in frustration Archbishop Hugh pronounced sentences of excommunication against various high-ranking Latins. But those who were thus excommunicated ignored their sentences, even to their deaths, and so the archbishop complained that he was reduced to the level of 'a simple priest'.[101]

---

[101] *Cartulary*, nos. 11, 75–77, 79, 81; *Synodicum Nicosiense*, nos. X.26–X.28.

It is important to stress four things that are often overlooked or misunderstood in the historiography. First, as with the 1220–1222 agreements, the dispute over the *Bulla Cypria* was as much between two different groups of Greeks and Syrians as it was between Latins and Greeks. Second, some of the Greek clergy, at first a minority, obeyed the *Bulla Cypria* and were loyal to papal Rome. Third, there is no reason to assume that Germanos was one of those who opposed the *Bulla Cypria*. Indeed, since he is not mentioned as being against it, and since he accepted it in the first place, it would be logical to assume that Germanos was no longer one of Archbishop Hugh's enemies. Fourth, Latins did not agree amongst themselves on the *Bulla Cypria* either, since the secular authorities, Latins, were in no rush to enforce it. Possibly this was partly out of fear of popular unrest, especially just after the Byzantine reconquest of Constantinople in 1261, but clearly the lack of enforcement of the *Bulla Cypria* was only one of Hugh's many complaints against the regent and the nobles. In short, the whole period needs to be seen within the context of a struggle between Church and State, and not simply between Greek and Latin.

The *Bulla Cypria* was promulgated in the summer of 1260, but before the end of 1262 Hugh saw no point in staying on Cyprus as a figurehead, and he left for the papal see. In letters dated Orvieto, January 1263, Pope Alexander's successor, Urban IV, warned the 'regent, barons, and nobles' to comply with Archbishop Hugh's requests, uphold the archbishop's rights, compel the Greeks and Syrians opposing the *Bulla Cypria* into peaceful obedience, protect those showing loyalty, and punish the Latins and Greeks committing the abovementioned crimes, or else be held accountable for the sins of others. Later, when Archbishop Hugh's vicars asked the regent to take measures against an excommunicated noble, the regent claimed to have taken an oath not to do so. Urban's efforts apparently had no effect, and the pope sent other letters from Orvieto in the spring of 1264, reminding Hugh of Antioch-Lusignan of the more important oath he had taken to 'maintain and defend the rights and honours of the churches'.[102] As we learn from a letter from the Latin patriarch of Jerusalem to the treasurer and the vicar of Nicosia dated January 1267, it appears that Hugh of Fagiano never returned to

---

[102] *Cartulary*, nos. 11, 75–77, 79, 81; *Synodicum Nicosiense*, nos. X.26–X.28.

Cyprus, but that the problems between the secular and ecclesiastical
authorities on the island continued and at least some 'Greek abbots,
monks, and priests' still failed to obey the *Bulla Cypria*.[103] Moreover,
there is evidence that during the reigns of Archbishop Hugh's successors relations among the various Latin clergy of Cyprus were once
again strained.

Documents from the tenure of Archbishop Ranulph (1278–ca. 1284)
show how these issues remained two decades after the *Bulla Cypria*.
It seems that Ranulph's reign was unhappy from the start, and there
are several parallels to Hugh of Fagiano's archiepiscopate: Ranulph
quarreled with the local Latin clergy; the secular authorities would
not help him, and in fact caused him further problems; he became
powerless and went into exile, never to return; he had trouble with
the Greeks.[104] A large section of the *Synodicum Nicosiense* consists of
Ranulph's 'Regulations Concerning the Greeks and Others'. Except
for the opening statements stressing the friendship and the unity of
the faith among the various rites of Cyprus, and calling for mutual
respect, the tone is negative toward the Greeks. Ranulph blames the
higher clergy of Greeks for endangering the souls of the Greeks and
Syrians through their 'ignorance, simplicity, and what is worse, misdeeds'. Ranulph asserts that many members of the Greek clergy are
ignorant of proper ceremonial and penitential procedures, for example concerning the canonical hours or offering the Eucharist to those
who have not confessed. Ranulph considers the four remaining Greek
bishops to be merely 'tolerated' on Cyprus, which implies that
Germanos had died and Neophytos had succeeded him as bishop
of Solea. Using a clause from the Fourth Lateran Council of 1215,
Ranulph suggests that the Greek bishops, rather than simply independent and elected prelates, are viewed as appointed by their Latin
counterparts as assistants for the non-Latin population, which is a
harsh interpretation of the *Bulla Cypria*. In fact Ranulph reminds the
Greeks that, according to the agreements of 1220 and 1222, ordination of Greeks requires the permission of the Latin bishop and,
for serfs, of the temporal lord. Judging from this document, relations
between Greeks and Latins were still strained in the early 1280s.[105]

---

[103] *Cartulary*, no. 106; *Synodicum Nicosiense*, no. X.29.
[104] See Schabel (2004a: 82–7).
[105] *Synodicum Nicosiense*, no. B.

By the end of the thirteenth century, however, things had settled down. From then on we can speak of the peaceful coexistence of the Greek and Latin clergies on the island. The *Bulla Cypria* functioned as it was designed, and the only episodes of strife between Greeks and Latins on religious matters occurred either because the *Bulla Cypria* had been vague or because outsiders threatened the *status quo*. The two most famous such events occurred in Nicosia in 1313 and 1360. In both cases, newly arrived papal legates, both named Peter, promulgated new legislation for the Greek bishops or attempted to change their practices and beliefs by decree, and each time the Nicosia populace rioted and the *Bulla Cypria* was reaffirmed, although in 1313 the Greek bishops were imprisoned for encouraging the mob to attack the legate.[106] Contrary to the claims of some writers, these episodes were not popular rebellions against general oppression. Rather two short outbreaks of violence, lasting only a matter of hours and directed—successfully—at the actions of a single outsider, punctuated the otherwise peaceful religious history of Cyprus in the fourteenth century.

More often the sources tell of the implementation of the terms of the *Bulla Cypria*. As Pope Alexander arranged, from 1260 down to 1571 there were only four bishops, and after the death of Germanos the archiepiscopal office was indeed abolished. Nevertheless, the bishop of Solea was *de facto* head of the Greek clergy and was allowed to retain the Church of St Barnabas in Nicosia as his base in the capital—an arrangement that may have held from early on for the other Greek bishops too. By 1300 the popes and other Latins indirectly recognized St Barnabas as a cathedral church, since they referred to its dean and canons. A Latin document for 1363 mentions the works on 'the Church of St George of the bishopric of the Greeks' in Famagusta. Sometimes in Greek texts these bishops also claimed the titles of the suppressed bishoprics within the Latin diocese in which they presided, and sometimes they did not, but there seems to have been no attempt to revive the old bishoprics as independent entities.[107]

---

[106] Philip of Mézières, *Peter Thomae*, 92–3; Makhairas, I, §101; 'Amadi', 395–6, 409–10; Florio Bustron, 247–8, 258; *Acta Ioannis XXII*, no. 35; *Synodicum Nicosiense*, nos. X.37.2–3; texts in Schabel (forthcoming a).

[107] *Cartulary*, no. 52; *Synodicum Nicosiense*, no. X.33.2; Schabel (2001–2002); Otten-Froux (2003: nos. 4 and 6). On the bishops' titles, see Kyrris (1990–1991; 1993) and Nicolaou-Konnari (1999: 332–4).

Several sources report that, upon the death of the Greek bishop, the *Bulla Cypria*'s procedure for the election of the successor was carried out. Around 1300, for example, after the death of Bishop Matthew of Lefkara (or Amathus), according to 'the arrangement of the most holy Pope Alexander', on the instructions of the Latin Bishop Berard of Limassol, the dean, canons, and other clerics of the cathedral (numbering 29 in the sixteenth century) invoked the Holy Spirit and, on the advice of trustworthy men, elected Olvianos, presenting the election to Berard for approval. Olvianos indeed became bishop, no doubt after taking the oath of fealty recorded in the same manuscript, Vat. Palat. gr. 367. The full election procedure and oath prescribed in the *Bulla Cypria* continued to be in use until the Turkish conquest, when Stephen of Lusignan gave a detailed eyewitness account for Lefkara. Numerous copies of the oath survive in Latin, Greek, French, and Italian.[108]

The *Bulla Cypria* also had stipulations for the deposition of Greek bishops by the pope and for the provisioning of unfilled sees by the Latin bishop, but it seems that the need never arose. In general, the arrangement warned the Latin bishops not to interfere with the Greek bishops' normal jurisdiction over the Greek monasteries, churches, and populace. Thus when Pope John XXII wrote to the Cypriots to reserve for himself the appointment of the archbishop, he expressly stated that his reservation did not pertain to 'the churches that the Greeks hold in the city and diocese of Nicosia'.[109]

Greeks were obliged to attend annual synods of the Latin bishop, although they were exempt from the provincial councils. Elias of Nabinaux did succeed in getting them to attend a provincial council in Nicosia in 1340, but this was supposedly voluntary. The Latins retained the tithes, and the Greek bishops were compelled to pay a limited sum for the visitation of their Latin counterparts. Stephen of Lusignan describes the payment. We have an interesting example of such a visitation in the late 1280s, when Bishop Berard of Limassol visited the cathedral of Bishop Matthew of Lefkara. The results were

---

[108] *Cartulary*, no. 78; *Synodicum Nicosiense*, nos. X.25.12–14, 24–26; Chatzipsaltes (1958: 14–18); Darrouzès (1979: 84–5); Ioannides (2000: 361–2, 369–71); Étienne de Lusignan, *Chorograffia*, fol. 32r; idem, *Description*, fols. 87v–88r.
[109] *Cartulary*, no. 78; *Synodicum Nicosiense*, nos. X.25.15–17, X.51.2; *Acta Ioannis XXII*, no. 93.

unhappy for both of them, as we have seen, but the example shows that the terms of the *Bulla Cypria* were carried out here as well.[110]

According to the *Bulla Cypria*, the Greeks were to have their own ecclesiastical courts for suits between Greeks, with the right of appeal through the Latin hierarchy. Hence the text of the 'Greek Laws' of Cyprus, describing the implementation of Byzantine marriage and family law after the *Bulla Cypria*, states that for the Paphos bishopric the authority was 'the bishop of Arsinoe, president (πρόεδρος) of the city and diocese of Paphos', but the litigants had the right of appeal within a certain time limit to a 'greater judge', 'to the Latin bishop, or to the archbishop of Nicosia, or to the pope'. For a concrete example, after the death of Bishop Neophytos of Solea, perhaps around 1286, the election was disputed between Dean Leo of the Church of Solea, Dean Theodore of the Church of St Barnabas—the bishop's church in Nicosia—and Abbot Joachim of St George of Mangana. The three claimants took their case to the vicar of the archbishop of Nicosia, and the losers, Theodore and Joachim, appealed to the pope. Leo, Theodore, and Joachim's representative, a monk named Germanos, journeyed to Rome. There Pope Boniface VIII pronounced in favour of Leo, and the ruling was enforced. On other occasions Greeks appealed to the pope against the abuses of Latin, Greek, and Syrian laymen and clerics, as did Bishop Leo of Solea himself in 1321. Examples of the internal functioning of the Greek ecclesiastical courts survive, as in 1306 when a charge of adultery was brought before Bishop Leo. The case was between Theodora, daughter of Sir Constantine Sekretikos, and Thomas, son of Sir Zak David. Perhaps 'Zak David' is the name of a Syrian Melkite, in which case the *Bulla Cypria*'s stipulation that these Syrians would be subject to the jurisdiction of the Greek hierarchy was also implemented. However, a long controversy did occur concerning the Syrian refugees who arrived after 1260, since it was unclear whether they were included in the *Bulla Cypria*. This issue was particularly acute in Famagusta, with its high population of Syrian Melkites, and the Greek bishops of Karpasia appealed to the pope against the Latin bishops of Famagusta on various occasions, as we have seen.[111]

---

[110] *Cartulary*, no. 78; *Synodicum Nicosiense*, nos. X.25.21–22; Étienne de Lusignan, *Chorograffia*, fol. 32r.
[111] *Cartulary*, no. 78; *Synodicum Nicosiense*, nos. X.25.18 and 32, X.33, X.37–X.38,

Thus the *Bulla Cypria* constituted and came to be looked upon as the Magna Carta of the Greeks. With justice Archbishop Elias of Nicosia referred to it in 1340 as 'the *agreement* between Latins and Greeks in the Kingdom of Cyprus, observed for so long, which Lord Alexander of happy memory, the Roman pontiff, produced'. More than once Greek texts also called it an 'agreement' (συμφωνίαν). Around 1320 the Greek bishops Leo of Solea and Olvianos of Lefkara described it as having solved the problems between Greeks and Latins and as having been 'observed peacefully afterwards' until the intervention of the papal legate in 1313. In the latter case, as in others, the Greeks expressly and successfully used the *Bulla Cypria* against the legate to defend their rights. In fact, it seems that Leo and Olvianos convinced Pope John XXII of its utility, and in 1322 the pope tried to apply the Cypriot model of Greek-Latin church relations to the newest Latin conquest: Rhodes.[112]

Greek Orthodoxy survived the Frankish period not so much because of a successful national struggle against complete absorption as because the Greeks always remained the majority and neither the Franks nor the Latin Church ever attempted any Latinization. The Latin Church required what it thought was the bare minimum from the Greek clergy—nothing from Greek laymen—and the Greek clergy gave the Latin Church what was required, including, by the end of the thirteenth century, an oath of obedience from the bishops and an end to active opposition concerning unleavened bread. Almost all other particulars of the Greek rite, what we now call Greek Orthodoxy, were allowed to remain the same. There was no schism, no heresy.

The security of Greek Orthodoxy is indicated by the ease with which the Greek clerics maintained ties with Constantinople, in the realm of art, for example. Patriarch Germanos II was in close contact with the Cypriots in the 1220s. George of Cyprus, who, even before the *Bulla Cypria* was issued, was admitted for studies in a Latin clerical school in Nicosia—ironically our only evidence for their early functioning—, later became Patriarch Gregory of Constantinople

---

X.58; Sathas, VI, 519, lines 16–17, 30–1; Otten-Froux (2003: 19); Chatzipsaltes (1955: 27–9); *Acta ab Innocentio V ad Benedictum XI*, no. 132; *Acta Ioannis XXII*, nos. 35–6; *Acta Urbani V*, no. 72; *Acta Gregorii XI*, no. 54; Nicolaou-Konnari in this volume.
[112] *Synodicum Nicosiense*, nos. L.12, X.37.1–2; Ioannides (2000: 368); *Acta Ioannis XXII*, no. 35; Luttrell (2003: 103 and 201–2), with a papal bull of 1 March 1322.

(1283–89). As patriarch, Gregory took an active interest in the welfare of his countrymen, corresponding with King Henry II on their behalf and praising Henry's predecessors for their enlightened attitude toward the Greeks of Cyprus. In 1326 Pope John XXII still complained that some Greeks were actually importing the Eucharistic host from Constantinople, and a traveller remarked in 1344–45 how they followed the Church of Constantinople and the 'errors' of the Greeks, whom the pope considered schismatics. Most importantly, Cyprus and Cypriots played a significant role in the Hesychast controversy in the middle decades of the fourteenth century, with the Greek Cypriots and even King Hugh IV supporting the anti-Palamite cause and offering the anti-Palamites shelter when things did not go their way. Barlaam and Gregory Akindynos corresponded with the Cypriot George Lapithes, and his and King Hugh's activities were well known to Nicephoros Gregoras. The anti-Palamite archbishop of Thessalonike was the Cypriot Yakinthos. It is even possible that the Greek bishops' agreement to the Roman profession of faith in 1340 is related to the controversies in Constantinople.[113]

With their close connections to the Oecumenical Patriarchate it was natural that three of the Greek bishops turned to Constantinople again during the chaos of the Great Schism of the West at the beginning of the fifteenth century, wishing to be recognized as part of the Greek Church, although it seems the fourth bishop, of Lefkara/Limassol, was Latin-minded and wanted to remain loyal to Rome. For the Patriarchate, Joseph Bryennios refused their request, because they had taken an oath to the pope and the local Latin hierarchy and participated in common processions and ceremonies with them. The Greek Cypriot bishops replied, basically, that the oath was just superficial. They even interpreted the clause 'salvo ordine meo' in the oath as 'except my faith', a completely unjustified translation, given that the same clause is also found in some oaths taken by Latin abbots and bishops. In any case, Joseph Bryennios insisted that no such oath could be ignored. Despite what some historians have said, it is improper for us to call any of these views 'incorrect': the Latins were satisfied with the oath; the bishop of Lefkara represented a group that was content with the situation; the other three bishops

---

[113] George of Cyprus, 177–9; *Syntagma*, nos. 88–9, 97–107.7; *Greek Texts*, 156–7; *Acta Ioannis XXII*, no. 89; Luke (1924: 9); Kyrris (1961; 1962); Gonis (1986). See also Carr and Grivaud in this volume.

represented another group that considered themselves Greek Orthodox
in every way, resented the separation from the Byzantine *oecumene*,
and downplayed the oath; Bryennios, the outsider, saw them all as
uniates.[114]

Conclusion: Christianity as Unifier of the People

The members of the general populace were generally free to follow
their own rite, although the Latin clergy preferred that children of
mixed marriages involving Latins adhere to the Latin rite. The Greek
clergy may have felt the same way, but we have little documentation. Beyond the differences in language and liturgy, however, the
various groups of Christians on Frankish Cyprus had a good deal
in common. Professor Carr discusses the ubiquity of Gothic architecture in her chapter. One might also mention the common worship of Cypriot saints or saints who died in Cyprus, especially
Barnabas, Hilarion, and Epiphanios, which the Latin Church supported from the mid-thirteenth century. In the early fifteenth century King Janus requested and received papal approval for an office
for St Hilarion, which was otherwise Western with Cypriot content.
The result is preserved in a famous Torino manuscript and constitutes a unique example of Western polyphony in the East. And whatever the exact nature of the equally famous Greek-language *Cyprus
Passion Cycle* dating from before 1320, it seems that it represents an
important cultural synthesis. If this was a Western import into Cyprus,
it appears that in the 1370s, after hearing the office in Cyprus, Philip
of Mézières exported the Feast of the Presentation of Mary in the
Temple to the West where is became part of the Roman calendar.[115]
In short, one could as easily stress shared elements as separate ones.

As in the case of most areas of Christendom, Cyprus had its own
pilgrimage sites, which were shared by the Christian population. By
far the most famous destination for pilgrims was Stavrovouni, the
mountaintop monastery between Nicosia, Limassol, and Larnaca
which housed the Cross of the Penitent Thief, a relic attracting vis-

---

[114] *Syntagma*, nos. 109, 112; Katsaros (2000).
[115] *Cartulary*, no. 130; *Synodicum Nicosiense*, nos. E.XXI, X.55; *The Cyprus Passion Cycle*; Hoppin (1968: 12–13, 99); Cattin (1995: 251–3); Kügle (1995: 151, 155, 160, 165, passim); Puchner (2004: 182–5); Grivaud in this volume. For this section, see especially Grivaud (2001b).

itors already long before the Frankish conquest. The mountain sits
alone not far from the coast, and so, although it is not anywhere
near the highest on the island, it was often described as such because
of its location and isolation. Wilbrand von Oldenburg climbed the
mountain in 1211, at which time the convent was small and contained a small chapel in which the cross hung. He remarks that the
monks, presumably Greek, did not live like monks, but Wilbrand
may have been unfamiliar with Greek monasticism. The medieval
tour guides informed him that Helen, the Emperor Constantine's
mother, had brought the cross from Jerusalem in order to stop the
devil, who had been preventing the burial of the dead.[116]

As we have seen, by 1254 Stavrovouni was in the hands of the
Black Monks, Benedictines from Antioch, perhaps replacing the Greeks
after the exile of much of the Greek clergy around 1240 or as a
result of a forced reform of the monastery after 1246. This apparently caused no disturbance in the tourist trade, for almost all travellers comment on the Benedictine monastery with the 'cross of the
good thief' or claim to have visited it, although this may have become
a topos. Around 1333 Wilhelm von Boldensele remarked that the
monks had managed to obtain other relics, including a nail from the
Passion. In 1394 Niccolò Martoni catalogued the relics as follows:
'a large piece of St Anne'; St Blaise's arm; the nail; St George's rib;
'a stone with which St Stephen was stoned'; a piece of the True
Cross—and apparently another piece embedded in the larger cross.
The Augustinian James of Verona visited in 1335, at which time it
was a popular pilgrimage goal, visited by 'a vast multitude', and
invoked by local sailors in danger. In noting that Peter I, while pray-
ing before the cross on Good Friday, heard a voice urging him to
crusade, Guillaume de Machaut translated 'a vast multitude' into
real terms: 100,000 pilgrims have seen the cross. Martoni describes
his pilgrimage in great detail, but as he went in cold December, in
low season, when the monks were unprepared for the tourists, his
experience was somewhat unpleasant. The following December the
lord of Anglure made it his first stop on Cyprus, traveling with a
group up the 'very high and painful climb'. At that point, and probably earlier, 'fair' conventual buildings surrounded the 'fair' church,
which had a main altar and another altar in the chapel of the cross.[117]

---

[116] *Excerpta Cypria*, 14.
[117] *Excerpta Cypria*, 16, 18, 27–9; Luke (1924: 7–8); *Excerpta Cypria Nova*, no. 14;
Guillaume de Machaut, *The Capture of Alexandria*, 24; Richard (1986a: 66–7).

A word should be said about the main attraction, the miracle of the cross, noted as early as 1106. In 1211 Wilbrand wrote that 'it hangs and swings in the air, they say, resting on no support. But it is not easy to see this', he adds, as if to express his doubts. James of Verona asserted that he actually touched the cross, which was hanging between two rocks. Martoni noted that it was 'raised and suspended, and nowhere attached, which seems a great miracle', but the following year the lord of Anglure wrote that 'this holy cross is a thing wonderful to be seen, for it is very great and thick, and is borne in the air, yet you shall not be able to see that anything bears it', concluding strangely that 'when one touches it it shakes much'. The monastery was sacked in the Mamluk invasion in the 1420s, at which time the Benedictines seem to have left, although they retained the property. Mamluk sources relate that they discovered that the cross was suspended by springs, which explains the shaking. By 1553 the miracle was said to have ceased on account of an earthquake, and the cross was attached at the ends and could swing, 'in token that it did once hang in the aire'.[118]

Although they could not compare to Stavrovouni, there were other pilgrimage sites. Famagusta boasted the church of St Mary of la Cava, just outside of the city. From 1328 it was the property of the Greek monastery of St Catherine of Sinai, but 'many people, Latins and Greeks', went to pray there, sailors asked for the Virgin's protection, and Latins gave donations. According to James of Verona, who celebrated Mass there, it was 'two bowshots' from the city in a cave 36 steps below ground level. It was nicely decorated but small, although its popularity required the services of three chaplains—one wonders if they were from different rites. St Catherine's tomb was housed in a chapel 'to which the people of Famagusta go with great devoutness and frequency'. St Catherine seems to have been popular enough to have her own pilgrimage route in and around the city, featuring her place of birth, the spot where she learned to read, and a church on a small island 'two bowshots' from the city near the harbour, on which an angel 'betrothed Catherine' to Christ. Relics and miraculous icons abounded. The royal family kept the body of St Hilarion in the castle that today bears his name, and in Nicosia the royal chapel, the cathedral (for example, the head

---

[118] *Excerpta Cypria*, 14, 18–19, 27, 29, 38–41, 71–2; *Excerpta Cypria Nova*, no. 23.

of Epiphanios), and the chapter of the Hospitaller commandery of
St John boasted important relics, as did the church of St Stephen
and the Carmelite convent in Famagusta. St Mamas was already
working miracle cures from his tomb in Morphou in the 1330s, emit-
ting a special oil by the early fifteenth century. At that time St
Mamas and the body of the thirteenth-century knight St John of
Montfort were drawing crowds, as were places associated with St
Paul in Paphos, although whether these were popular destinations
before 1374 is not known for certain.[119]

The various groups seem to have had common rituals as well.
Marriage ceremonies shared non-Western particularities. In 1335 in
Famagusta James of Verona saw a bride led on horseback 'with her
eyebrows and forehead painted' to the groom's house, both proceeded and followed by large lit candles, in this case 20 in front and
20 behind. 40 women trailed, dressed in long black cloaks and showing only their eyes, a tradition adhered to since the fall of Acre, James
was told. In 1394 Martoni still recorded the same custom of wearing black veils in mourning for the loss of Syria over a century
before. James of Verona also attended a funeral of a rich Famagustan,
in whose house James found two women singing in Greek by the head
of the corpse, and two women 'piously wailing' by his feet, 'and
these are the flute players'. There is no way to discern the rite of the
deceased, because the ritual was common: Latin priests were invited,
but the singing was in Greek, praising 'the dead man for his beauty
and thrift and other virtues', James was informed.[120] Already in the
early 1250s the Archbishop of Nicosia complained that

> In the funeral rites for the dead, in houses, churches, and cemeteries,
> they summon flute players who play the mourning tune, whom they
> call 'singing women'. These women not only disturb the divine ser-
> vice, but, with words and incantations that are vain and in agreement
> with the ritual of pagans and Jews, they even provoke or excite other
> women to wail and to beat and wound themselves.[121]

Hugh prohibited all clerics from being present where such women
were performing, and all people from summoning or paying them

---

[119] Makhairas, I, §33; *Excerpta Cypria*, 16, 19–21, 24–5, 30, 35, 45, 51–4, 57–9;
Luke (1924: 8); Richard (1986a: 61–5); *Excerpta Cypria Nova*, no. 3; Otten-Froux
(2003: nos. 19 and 175). Kykkos may have been important after 1365.
[120] *Excerpta Cypria*, 17, 24, cf. 60.
[121] *Synodicum Nicosiense*, no. A.XX.

to come to houses and funerals. He even threatened the women with capture, beating, and torture, fearing an increase in infidelity. Obviously his prohibition failed, but infidelity does not seem to have increased as a result.

Of course the visiting Latin prelates did attempt to 'correct' a few of what they considered the religious errors of simple folk, as in the case of worshipping the unconsecrated host. Usually this was without local support, however, and had little effect. For example, in 1301 the famous Franciscan Raymond Lull wished to perform as missionary in Cyprus itself to preach to 'infidels and schismatics, namely Jacobites, Nestorians, and *Momminas*', but King Henry II prevented it. Likewise, when St Brigitte visited in 1372, it was in vain that she warned the Greeks that they would be doomed to be ruled forever unless they 'conformed totally to the Roman Church's holy regulations and rites'. The Council of Nicosia of 1340, however, was the successful culmination of efforts to coax non-Latins into conformity at least with the elements of Roman practice and doctrine that, according to the pope, were at that time considered necessary for salvation. The papacy always declared its willingness to tolerate the practices and beliefs of the Greeks and other Oriental Christians. In the 1220s, after three decades of waiting and seeing, the first goal of papal policy became obtaining the spiritual and ecclesio-political submission of these groups to the pope and to the Latin archbishop of Nicosia. In 1222 Honorius III remarked that the Nestorians and Jacobites were not submitting, whereas the Armenians and Maronites were perhaps less problematic. Many of the Greeks resisted for a further three decades, but in 1254 Innocent IV was ready to examine Greek practices, approving and disapproving according to the traditional criteria, although he added the doctrinal issue of purgatory. By the early fourteenth century, when the numbers of Oriental Christians had grown, the papacy moved to place doctrinal differences more squarely on the agenda. Thus in 1326 Pope John XXII was concerned about Jacobite and Nestorian heresy, and the attitudes of some of the Greeks toward purgatory. However, in 1338 Benedict XII wrote Archbishop Elias to applaud his efforts at 'inducing the various nations of Greeks, Armenians, Jacobites, and other Easterners living in the Kingdom of Cyprus' to adopt even the rite of the Roman Church.[122]

---

[122] Golubovich (1906–1927, I: 368–9); *Acta Ioannis XXII*, nos. 89, 93, 96; *Cartulary*, no. 35; *Synodicum Nicosiense*, nos. X.9, X.50, X.53, X.54; Pilzt (1986: 56).

We have seen that Elias was successful with some of the Armenians, but what is most impressive is Elias' Provincial Council held in the archiepiscopal palace in Nicosia in January 1340. All the bishops of the Latins, Greeks, Maronites, and Armenians, the rectors of the Nestorians and Jacobites, and a 'great multitude' of other clerics of all these rites gathered in the hall of the archbishop's palace. Elias had compiled a detailed 'Confession of Faith' according to the Roman doctrine in every aspect—even the *Filioque*, purgatory, the beatific vision, and papal primacy—although he made sure to exempt the Greek rites 'which are not opposed to the Catholic faith', which were guaranteed by the *Bulla Cypria*. This document was read out to the assembly and translated into Greek, Arabic, and Armenian. Afterwards, we are told, all the bishops and elders of the non-Latin sects voluntarily consented, for themselves and their flocks, to each item of the Confession, asking Elias to relay their consent to Pope Benedict XII.[123]

Even if Elias exaggerated his success, the council does indicate that relations among the various Christian sects on Cyprus were not usually hostile, and friendly communication was possible. And although liturgical separation was still maintained, both for practical linguistic reasons and chauvinism—hence the policy of 'separate but *almost* equal'—there is evidence that Elias' achievement had some real effect, if only local and short-lived. Over the next quarter century the Armenian Bishop George Noreghes went to Avignon for papal confirmation, the Latin Archbishop Philip strengthened the feasts of the local saints Barnabas and Epiphanios that the legate Eudes of Châteauroux had established for Nicosia Cathedral a century before, Pope Urban V granted Archbishop Raymond the right to absolve schismatic or heretical clerics arriving on Cyprus from elsewhere, and the Greek abbey of St George of Mangana was described as 'obedient to the Roman Church'.[124]

By the time Peter Thomae died in 1366, after his initial hostile reception in 1360, it appears that some Cypriots of all types had grown to appreciate him. As his body lay ready for burial in the Carmelite church in Famagusta, whose evocative ruins are still extant:

---

[123] *Synodicum Nicosiense*, nos. L.1–14. See also Schabel (1998; 2000a).
[124] *Acta Clementis VI*, no. 41; *Acta Urbani V*, nos. 45a, 120; *Cartulary*, no. 130; *Synodicum Nicosiense*, nos. X.54, X.55, X.57, X.59.

The church was filled with men and women, catholics, schismatics, and infidels, who unanimously and very devoutly venerated the legate's body as holy. Wondrous to say, for the schismatic nations of Christians, namely the Greeks, Armenians, Georgians, Jacobites, Copts, Maronites, and others divided from the Catholic Church (especially Greeks and their monks, who when the legate was alive had freely drunk his blood in sacrifice of oblation)—because he had confuted their errors with clear proofs and had inspired them that they must come back to the bosom of the Holy Roman Church, [although they were] now polluted by many injuries, but quasi converted from their errors or devoted sons of the legate—with heads bare, contrary to their habit, they kissed the feet and hands of the holy legate with profound reverence . . .[125]

In 1368 Pope Urban would not characterize the Cypriot Greeks as schismatics, but Philip of Mézières was notoriously anti-Greek, considering them 'rotten apples': in order to exaggerate Peter Thomae's holy mission, Philip used 'schismatics' for hagiographical propaganda. What is important is that the groups could mourn together the death of a supposedly hated man. Among those who testified or had someone testify that the legate's body worked miracles were a Greek slave named Costas, a Nestorian woman named Elizabeth, and a Syrian Melkite named George, 'of the Greeks' sect'. When Philip of Mézières had the tomb opened, several Greek priests were present.[126] Peter Thomae's experience in Cyprus shows why there is no simple way to portray religion in early Frankish Cyprus, except that it was devoutly Christian.

---

[125] Philip of Mézières, *Peter Thomae*, 155–6.
[126] *Cartulary*, no. 131; *Synodicum Nicosiense*, no. X.60.2; Philip of Mézières, *Peter Thomae*, 173–4, 180. 182; Petkov (1997).

LITERATURE

Gilles Grivaud

In the history of cultural exchanges between East and West, the Latin East certainly did not play the role of mediator on a level comparable to that played by the Spain of the *Reconquista*. Nevertheless, its literary production and intellectual life show that Outremer provided fertile soil for exchanges between cultures foreign to one another.[1] Cyprus participated in this movement on its own level, becoming a natural crossroads of cultures of the Eastern Mediterranean. Indeed, far from detaching the island from its natural hinterland, the conquest of 1191 accelerated the establishment of nuclei of Western culture in the heart of the ancient Byzantine province. Consequently, the texts produced in the Lusignan kingdom before 1374 testify to the reception and transmission of currents of thought and of literary trends emanating from both the East and the West.[2] From this perspective, art historians have been the avant-garde, revealing the complexity of outside influences in a state that, if it belonged to the political and cultural sphere of the Latin East, remained profoundly imbued with the Byzantine heritage.[3]

Writings composed in Cyprus, by definition polyglot, stem from a great variety of genres. First, there is an impressive collection of Greek manuscripts of hagiographical, homiletical, and liturgical content confirming the integration of the native culture with the Orthodox world. Frankish letters are, for their part, marked by their secular content, affirming a juridical culture, the development of a historical and moral tradition, and a hint of a philosophical thought different from the proselytism that is linked to crusader ideology. Latin religious literature, little known and barely studied, appears to be composed mostly of canonical texts. With regard to the Eastern Christians,

---

[1] Cf. the recent synthesis by Minervini (2001; 2002).
[2] This essay is a shorter, revised, and updated version of Grivaud (1996), where one can find a fuller bibliography.
[3] For an account of the bibliography produced by art historians, see Carr's chapter in this volume.

the little information we have confirms the attachment of the minority groups to their original confessional practices.[4] This mosaic of literary expressions—one of the original traits of the literary production of the kingdom—accounts for the provisional character of the present analysis: it depends on the survival of manuscripts, it privileges the lay production over the religious, and, for practical reasons, it divides into separate categories works that deploy at the same time several codes of expression.

Modes of Written Expression

Languages and Education

Under the Lusignans Greek remained the main language of communication of the kingdom, but one encounters heterogeneous linguistic pockets, since the ports hosted merchants coming from the entire Mediterranean basin who conducted business in French, Italian, or Arabic, using Latin to draw up their contracts. In Nicosia, where the machinery of state was concentrated, the language mix seemed normal for everyday exchanges. In contrast, in the countryside the foreign elements were limited to the coastal plains and the lower slopes of the Pentadaktylos, where groups of Maronites, Syrians, and Armenians dwelled. This distribution of populations suggests that contact zones between communities were unequal.

Unlike the regions open to large-scale trade, the Troodos massif formed the conservatory of insular traditions, at a time when the mountains supported a population that was much denser than after 1600.[5] The educated class there appears to have been initially clerics, especially monks, whose communities stimulated the demand for liturgical and theological manuscripts. Compared to this religious culture, the activities of the peasants remain unknown, whatever the vitality of the Akritic epic poetry in the oral tradition until the modern era may have been. Elsewhere, educated Greeks were concentrated in the urban centres, the residence of the notaries and secretaries of

---

[4] The written production of these minorities is not examined here; on the topic, see Schabel in this volume, Grivaud (2000), and Coureas (2001a).
[5] Grivaud (1998b: 424–6).

the royal and ecclesiastical administrations, the authors or copyists of most of the surviving texts.

Parallel with their authors, the Greek texts present distinct levels of language. The most prevalent was the Byzantine *koine*, the language of religious manuscripts. The Atticising Greek of Constantinopolitan intellectuals was not much in evidence on the island, with the exception of George Lapithes, to the extent that by the end of the fourteenth century Cyprus was considered a cultural desert.[6] Instead of the classical scholarly expression, the Greeks opted for a vernacular language, in its dialectal form. Thus the *diglossia* pertaining to medieval Cypriot culture, broadly speaking, followed the evolution of linguistic and literary practices of medieval Hellenism, since the Cypriot *diglossia* opposed the language of religious manuscripts to the dialect, not a learned culture to a popular literature.[7] Of these two levels of language, the vernacular form has attracted the most attention. These studies show that, just as the other Greek dialects, Cypriot acquired its traits from the eighth to the thirteenth centuries.[8] After an initial phase of cultural and political isolation following the Arab expansion, the Latin conquest marks the start of a new period of change for the *koine*, which is distinguished by phonetical transformations and the enrichment of the vocabulary with French, Latin, or Italian words. In this way the dialect progressively acquired new traits, even if one has to wait until the fifteenth century for it to obtain the status of a literary language. Nevertheless, the slow formation and the late fixation of the dialect's traits provoke endless discussions about the origin of the texts. Thus, while Pierre Breillat attributes, with reservation, the poem of Branor le Brun to a Cypriot of the beginning of the fourteenth century, Roderick Beaton opts for a wider dating, from the end of the thirteenth to the middle of the fifteenth century, in a place where Greeks and Franks form lasting contacts.[9]

Within the Frankish community, quite naturally French dominated as a language of administration, culture, and communication, undoubtedly reaching a large portion of the Latin-rite population, the Italians in particular, both those who were completely integrated in the local

---

[6] Manuel Palaeologos, *Letters*, 44–5.

[7] Kriaras (1967); Beck (1974); Browning (1978a); Beaton (1989: 11–12); Asdraha (1994); Nicolaou-Konnari (2000b).

[8] Kahane and Kahane (1982: 135–40); Aerts (1986); Nicolaou-Konnari (1995; 1999: ch. 8; 2000b).

[9] Breillat (1938); Beaton (1989: 140–2).

society, like Philip of Novara, and those who were only temporarily on the island, as attested by the will of the Venetian merchant Obertin of Saint Antonin, written in French in Famagusta in January 1294.[10] Nevertheless, it is still hard to determine the original characteristics of the French spoken in Cyprus. Employed by Franks coming from different regions, it progressively incorporated Italianisms and local variances that accompanied the gradual hybridisation of the urban society. This interpenetration of linguistic systems led to a weakening of the French literary expression, much more evident after 1374.[11] Literature in Latin remains poorly known; religious literature seems to have been flourishing, especially of a legal nature, if one considers the constitutions promulgated until 1354.[12] The sources show that if Latin—along with Greek—was the diplomatic language, it was replaced by French for the drawing up of charters.[13] The pillar of religious life, Latin was not a vehicle of literary expression for the Franks, except for clerics coming from the West, like Raymond Lull, who used the most widespread language for the texts they wrote on the island. At the same time, around 1300, we find that the mendicant orders, concerned with understanding Eastern spirituality, made translations from Arab and Greek into Latin. The decay of true Latin culture was obvious in 1313 according to the legate Peter of Pleine-Chassagne. In the fourteenth century, Latin was hardly ever used outside institutions of the Latin rite, with the exception of the Italian notaries who always employed Latin for drawing up documents.[14]

Through this layering of linguistic practices, more profound developments appear. The period during which French declines corresponds to the emergence of Italian as a language of communication, while the Greek dialect remained the language used by the majority of the population. This linguistic overlapping is more complicated in the towns, where the Oriental minorities had to use several languages; thus, during their stays in Famagusta in 1335/40, James of Verona and Ludolph of Sudheim noted the simultaneous use of Greek, French, and Arabic.[15] Their remarks pose the question of the

---

[10] Bertolucci Pizzorusso (1988); Minervini (1999: 159–60).

[11] Minervini (1996a: 244–8).

[12] Richard (1991–1992: 241–2); *The Trial of the Templars in Cyprus*; Schabel (2000a); *Synodicum Nicosiense*.

[13] Lambros (1908: 48–51); Richard (1986c: 83).

[14] For a recent overview on editions of Italian notaries working in Cyprus, see Otten-Froux (2003: 15–16).

[15] Ludolph of Sudheim, 216; James of Verona, 176–9.

influence multilingualism exercised on literary activity, a situation that is difficult to evaluate outside the towns. The Frankish aristocracy offers few clear examples of bilingual persons. Little solid proof exists that any of the Lusignans were bilingual, although some members of the Ibelin family spoke or wrote French, Arabic, Greek, and Latin.[16]

The sources are silent about the linguistic abilities of the Franks, even if one can assume that in the fourteenth century the growing political and commercial presence of the Italians facilitated the penetration of their language in noble society; thus, the citizenship privileges granted by Venice act as paths for the Italicisation of the elite. In 1328, Marshal Thomas of Montolif acquired this privilege, and Peter I followed his example, proclaiming on his arrival in Venice in 1364: 'Mo' son io ben Veniçiano'.[17] The Hellenisation of the aristocracy is very difficult to grasp; it is impossible to determine the sponsors of the sumptuous Hamilton Psalter, which was composed in Cyprus ca. 1300.[18] We find closer contacts in the middle of the fourteenth century with the marriage of Isabella (Maria) of Lusignan and Manuel Cantacuzenos of Mystras in 1355. Finally, we should not forget the place of Arabic in the island's multilingual society following the immigration of refugees from Syria. The Bibi, the Audeth, the Salah, and the Urry, to mention only the most famous families, were absorbed into the Latin society of the kingdom without abandoning their cultural or confessional origins: in 1361 in Famagusta marriage contracts were still drawn up in Arabic.[19]

This state of multilingualism must be understood with all its imperfections: speaking Greek, French, Italian, or Arabic did not entail correct expression in these languages, and Leontios Makhairas would later emphasize the 'barbarisation' of Greek when people learned 'Frankish', so that no one knew what their language was anymore: '. . . και απο τότες αρκέψαναμαθάνουν φράγκικα, και βαρβαρίσαν τα ρομέκα, ως γίον και σήμερον και γράφομεν φράγκικα και ρομαίκα, ότι εις τόν κόσμον δεν ιξεύρουν ήντα συντύχάννομεν'.[20] Indeed, in a society where education was not widely available, multilingualism provoked a barbarisation of the languages through the multiplication of linguistic

---

[16] Collenberg (1977–1979: 119–20, 157–8, 178–9, 203; 1979–1980: 289).
[17] *I libri commemoriali*, II, 28; Carile (1970: 110).
[18] Havice (1984); Carr in Evans (2004: no. 77).
[19] Nicola de Boateriis, no. 70; Collenberg (1979–1980: 229–30); Richard (1991–1992: 244).
[20] Makhairas, *Diplomatic Edition*, 148 (ms. V).

interferences, a phenomenon that individuals belonging to culturally homogeneous milieux did not experience.

The process of the barbarisation of the languages is explained in part by the poor foundations of the educational structures. The auto-biography of George of Cyprus reveals that a rudimentary Greek instruction existed, outside Nicosia, and that higher education was only available in Latin.[21] Afterwards, until the Renaissance, learning Greek was probably limited to the monasteries. Undoubtedly it is within this context that Lapithes taught the Scriptures, ca. 1340. Moreover, when young Greeks wished to pursue studies above the elementary level, they went to Constantinople, where George of Cyprus opened his classes to his compatriots.[22]

We know more about instruction in Latin. With the establishment of the Latin bishoprics and the decisions of the Fourth Lateran Council (1215), each cathedral church was to set up a school for training deacons. In Cyprus, this ruling became reality only after the visit of the papal legate Eudes of Châteauroux, who in 1249 ordered Archbishop Eustorge of Montaigu to open two schools, one of gram-mar for beginners and one of theology for a higher degree. He also obliged the suffragan bishoprics to maintain a grammar school.[23] This introduction of Latin religious education was reinforced with the arrival of the mendicant orders, with the Franciscan and Dominican convents possessing their own *studia* in Nicosia and perhaps in Famagusta and Limassol as well. The Dominicans showed themselves to be particularly active, enjoying a direct connection with Thomas Aquinas, who may even have come to Nicosia around 1267.[24] After 1291, the Dominicans of Cyprus were permitted to send two or three friars to Italy every year to complete their theological studies.[25] The Franciscans also maintained instruction in theology, as revealed by isolated references to their masters in Nicosia—Raymond of Albaterra

[21] Lameere (1937: 176–9); Schabel (1998: 37); Georges' words should be mod-erated, according to Pérez Martín (1996: 2–3).

[22] Constantinides (1982: 108).

[23] Schabel (1998: 38–9); *Synodicum Nicosiense*, no. E. II.

[24] Richard (1991–1992: 241), who refers to the testimony of Fr. Nicholas of Marsilly in *Acta sanctorum*, VII Martii, 707; the Dominican doctor's stay in Cyprus does not appear in the biographies dedicated to him, which, generally, barely men-tion Thomas' travels in Italy between 1259 and 1269; see Walz (1962: 118–20) and Weisheipl (1974: 141–239).

[25] Loenertz (1937: 28).

1338, John Carmesson 1366—and Famagusta—Peter Frumenti ca.
1340/42.[26] Although we lack information for the other orders in this
era, the Cistercians, Carmelites, Premonstratensians, and Augustinians
surely had their own *studia* on Cyprus. The quality of the instruction
provided in these schools is poorly documented, but seems to have
been on the level of their counterparts in the West. For example,
Matthew of Cyprus sat on a commission in Rome in September
1321 to evaluate the treatise of Marino Sanudo Torsello.[27] The standards appear to have been lower in the episcopal schools, since, in
June 1313, Peter of Pleine-Chassagne criticized the level of learning
of the lower clergy.[28] Certainly the educational structures of the kingdom could not compete with the Italian universities. The attraction
the Paduan masters had for the Cypriots is already apparent in 1353,
when the faculty of canon law accepted a Cypriot student, Giovanni
di Guglielmo.[29]

Usages and Forms of Written Culture

From the above information on the educational system it becomes
obvious that true centres of education were concentrated, on the one
hand, in the Greek monasteries and, on the other, in Nicosia and
Famagusta. The geography of education does not by itself provide
a complete picture of the diffusion of reading and writing. The royal
chancery and secrète, which employed numerous secretaries, scribes,
notaries, and accountants of different languages, testify to this.[30] Besides
the central administration, other offices employed a staff of notaries
and scribes, like those of the courts of justice, of the viscounts, and
of the castellans, as well as the commercial court of the *commercium*
of Famagusta and those of various minor regional administrations.
On the local level, the management of fiefs by an aristocracy largely
residing in Nicosia depended on a small bureaucracy attached to the
estates. From the 1220s *baillis* were recruited from among the Greeks

[26] Golubovich (1906–1927, I: 398; III: 349; IV, 244, 316).
[27] Marino Sanudo Torsello, 1–2, and general remarks in Schabel (1998: 39–40)
and Minervini (2001: 613).
[28] *Synodicum Nicosiense*, no. H. VI.
[29] Fabris (1942: 124).
[30] *Livre des remembrances*, xiii; Lampros (1908: 48–51); Richard (1986c: 77–9); Edbury
(1991: 188–9); Grivaud (1992: 542, 561; 2001b: 238–51); Nicolaou-Konnari (1999:
223–7; 2000b: 9).

and Syrians, who were more competent than the Latins previously employed. Thus at Psilomophou, in 1318, the administrative staff of the estate belonging to the Latin patriarchate of Jerusalem included seven persons knowing how to read, write, and calculate.[31]

Private notaries provide fundamental evidence for this written culture. According to royal legislation, only acts recording dowries, wills, freight agreements, and the purchase of slaves could be drawn up by a notary, all other acts having to be validated by royal officers. The destruction of private archives in 1426 and 1570 explains the small number of acts preserved in comparison to the abundant registers and minutes of the Italian notaries of Famagusta. Apart from revealing the extent of the notarial practice in the kingdom, the acts of Italian notaries suggest that, outside the world of transactions, an intense production of documents regulated public life. This phenomenon included the Greeks, if one can believe the palaeographic studies that confirm the role of the notariate in the development of the culture of the fourteenth century.[32]

It is thus hardly surprising that many authors belonged to the world of notaries and secretaries, such as the Templar of Tyre, the copyist of Paris. gr. 1391, and the compiler of Vat. Palat. gr. 367. Indeed, the notarial profession and relative profusion of bureaucracies requires us to approach the level of literacy in the kingdom from a different angle. Cyprus, like Frankish Syria, lacked higher instruction, but this seems to have been compensated for by a network of schools and by the transmission of techniques and practices within specialized bodies for the drafting of charters. Consequently, the situation in Cyprus seems close to the Byzantine imperial bureaucratic model, where the use of writing implies a broad diffusion of functional literacy, to use Robert Browning's expression.[33] The Byzantine institutional legacy would thus condition the transmission of a technical training among notaries and scribes.

The Role of Patrons

As the seat of noble families, of numerous administrations, and the main schools, Nicosia possessed everything necessary to become a

---

[31] Mas Latrie, *Histoire*, III, 641–2; Richard (1947).
[32] Canart (1987–1988); Constantinides and Browning, *Dated Greek Manuscripts*, 13–14.
[33] Ševčenko (1974: 70–6); Browning (1978b).

real cultural centre, a role that Famagusta played in a more modest way. In both cities, the stimulus for literary and artistic production follows the models observed in the medieval Christian world, where one distinguishes between products of the patronage emanating from the learned aristocracy and those destined to satisfy the needs of the religious communities.

Patronage for religious purposes is amply documented in Greek manuscripts. Around 1200, commenting on the flight of the *archontes*, Neophytos the Recluse expressed his dismay at seeing the disappearance of the patrons supporting the Enkleistra.[34] His assertions used to be interpreted in the sense of an almost complete disappearance of the Greek aristocracy, a view that has recently been modified. Among the Greeks, clerics formed the majority of those commissioning manuscripts. Incipits, colophons, or marginalia confirm this starting in 1193, when the clergy of the village of Sigouri obtained a Gospel produced at their expense. Many other testimonies verify that the copying of religious texts remained constant throughout the thirteenth and fourteenth centuries.[35]

It is harder to pin down the patronage of the Frankish nobility. The Lusignans have left few traces of their supporting literature. It seems that around 1267 Thomas Aquinas addressed his *De regno* to the king of Cyprus, undoubtedly Hugh II, and Master Peter of Paris dedicated a philosophical treatise to Amaury, lord of Tyre. Still, no reign rivals that of Hugh IV, whose splendor radiated from Constantinople to Italy. During his visit to Cyprus around 1347/49, a learned Byzantine using the pseudonym Agathangelos drew a flattering portrait of the royal court, which George Lapithes and other erudite Greeks, Latins, and Arabs frequented. Hugh IV's reputation reached Constantinople, where Nicephoros Gregoras composed a encomium to the glory of the king.[36] Gregoras praised the virtue of a prince devoted to justice, concerned with fostering an atmosphere of benevolent peace, and endowed with intellectual acuity. King Hugh, an avid follower of theological and philosophical discussion, initiated, among other things, an ambitious policy of patronage, commissioning Boccaccio to compose a repertory of mythology around

---

[34] Galatariotou (1991: 172–7).
[35] Darrouzès (1950: 172–3; 1957: 141); Galatariotou (1991: 175–6); Constantinides and Browning, *Dated Greek Manuscripts*; Nicolaou-Konnari (2000b: 10–11).
[36] Leone (1981); Nerantzi-Varmazi (2001); Schabel (2004b).

1350. Hugh died before the completion of the first version (of 1360), but Boccaccio was proud of his princely patronage and dedicated to him this redaction of the *Genealogia deorum gentilium*.[37] After 1359, Peter I continued in his father's footsteps, applying the policy to his own political projects. He surrounded himself with personalities like Philip of Mézières and Guido of Bagnolo, the king's personal physician but also a philosopher with Averroist leanings, an astronomer, a historian, and Petrarch's adversary in a discussion in Venice in 1368.[38]

Among the Frankish nobles traces of patronage or of literary activity are rare, although their sponsorship is more illustrious in the Kingdom of Jerusalem with respect to the production of illuminated manuscripts.[39] On the island, the Ibelins are individually distinguished by their juridical activities, such as those of John and James in the 1260s. Above all they display a favorable attitude toward chroniclers, historians, jurists, or men of letters, for all the important names of the thirteenth and the beginning of the fourteenth century figured in their entourage (Philip of Novara, Geoffroy Le Tor, the Templar of Tyre). For more than a century, the family surrounded itself with the writers who constructed the history and the law of the Frankish kingdom. Afterwards, in the fourteenth century, examples of the literary patronage of the nobles become quite rare. Is this proof of disinterest in literary culture, a consequence of the private devotion that caused a multiplication of religious foundations? Leontios Makhairas recalls the memory of Queen Alice (of Ibelin) who, a little after 1340, founded the monastery of Stavros o Phaneromenos, had it decorated with paintings, and donated βιβλία to it.[40] This example suggests that spiritual preoccupations exceeded more profane considerations, absorbing the donations of noble houses, a tendency already mentioned in a letter of Pope Honorius III to Archbishop Eustorge of Montaigu in December 1221.[41]

The Latin ecclesiastical dignitaries acted similarly in the period up to 1340. The Hospitaller Simon le Rat, commander of Cyprus between 1299 and 1310, received the dedication of a French translation

---

[37] Zaccaria (2001: 91, 111). See Giovanni Boccaccio, *Genealogia*.
[38] Iorga (1896: 109, 144–5); Livi (1918: 51–68); Kristeller (1952).
[39] Minervini (2001: 612–15).
[40] Makhairas, *Diplomatic Edition*: 106–7; for a similar contemporary example in Lefkara, see Constantinides and Browning, *Dated Greek Manuscripts*, 203–4.
[41] *Cartulary*, no. 66.

of a psalter, made by Master Peter of Paris, a translation that was possibly finished in France.[42] Later, Florio Bustron praised the patronage of Archbishop John of Conti, who completed the decoration of St Sophia around 1330, then proceeded to compile the *Cartulary* of the cathedral church.[43] Undoubtedly absenteeism explains the silence concerning the activities of other prelates. In sum, the investigation of literary patronage suggests that Frankish sponsorship was little developed, except during the reign of Hugh IV.

Reception, Diffusion and Transmission

Whether Franks or Greeks, the authors circulated in a society that was subject to multiple influences, a reflection of controversies and spiritual quests that were originally foreign to the kingdom but penetrated and participated in local culture. The intellectual trends did not affect men of letters in a uniform manner. Their reception results from phenomena that belong to the theoretical framework of acculturation since they all stem from the interaction of heterogeneous cultural systems. At the present state of research, it is premature to try to discern the different degrees of reciprocal cultural assimilation. One example will suffice to show that we should be prudent with regard to the general orientation of the Greek religious literature of the thirteenth century: does it tend toward the utter rejection of the Latin rite, as the narrative of the martyrdom of Kantara in 1231 would have us suppose, or rather is it along the lines of a uniate perspective, as the *Cyprus Passion Cycle* would suggest? Far from envisioning a global response, one should insist on the heterogeneity of individual behaviours within each social group and within each community, where the actors of cultural history are reflections of the political and social tensions that surround them.

In this respect, the progress of intellectual trends is measured in connection with the figures known for their intellectual activities. The thirteenth century and the beginning of the fourteenth, an era of incessant crusading, witnessed the influx of the Westerners. From 1191, troubadours accompanied Richard the Lionheart, such as Guiraut de Bornelh, *maître des troubadours*, and the Toulousan Peire Vidal, who

---

[42] Thomas (1923: 29–30); Minervini (2002: 340).
[43] Florio Bustron, *Historia*, 254–5; *Cartulary*, 48–54; Bacci (2000: 361–8).

completed a pilgrimage to Jerusalem and upon his return to Genoa
had himself proclaimed emperor on the basis of a marriage contracted
in Cyprus with the niece of the emperor of Constantinople.[44] However
legendary, Cyprus and the daughter of Isaac Ducas Comnenos entered
straight into the imagination of the troubadours. During the same
time, Robert of Boron, who seems to have accompanied Walter of
Montbéliard to Cyprus, was inspired by Byzantine and Syriac traditions to compose his *Roman de l'Estoire dou Graal*.[45]

If the circumstances of the visit of Frederick II in 1228/29 were
not very favourable to allow the emperor to exercise any influence
on the local culture, the arrival of King Louis IX marked a decisive
stage. During his sojourn on the island between September 1248 and
May 1249, the king was accompanied by his family, an army of some
25,000 men, and his chronicler, John of Joinville.[46] The eight months
of contact between the courts of Louis IX and Henry I reinforced
the Frankish identity of the island's aristocracy. A marked influence
on legal literature is apparent: when Louis arrived in Acre, in February
1250, a discussion took place on the keeping in French of the *Livres*
of the Haute Cour and of those of the Cour des Bourgeois; this led
in 1252/53 to the creation of the post of the scribe of the Cour des
Bourgeois.[47] Is it by chance that, at about this time, Philip of Novara
began writing his *Livre de forme de plait*? In the entourage of Louis IX,
Hugh of Fagiano, dean of the metropolitan chapter of Rouen, left
Normandy for Cyprus, where he took the habit of the Premonstratensians before being elected archbishop in 1250. Louis IX was
still in the East when Hugh began promulgating the constitutions of
the Church of Cyprus in 1252 (to 1257), thus sharing the preoccupations of the legislators of the Kingdoms of Jerusalem and Cyprus.[48]

Parallel to this, the Crusades consolidated Cyprus' role as a crossroads between East and West, notably with the missions to the
Mongols. In 1245 Pope Innocent IV's embassies to the Great Khan
put the Mongols in contact with Louis IX who, in Cyprus, received
two letters from the Khan, immediately translated into Latin and
French, in December 1248. At the same time the king of Cyprus

---

[44] Boutière and Schutz (1973: 51–2, 351–5); Hoepffner (1961: 53–5, 146).
[45] According to the thesis of Gallais (1970), followed by Ciggaar (1993: 152–6;
1994: 91–2; 1996: 146).
[46] Richard (1983a: 208–16); Le Goff (1996: 187–9).
[47] 'Abrégé', 246, 249; Folda (1976: 13, 21).
[48] *Synodicum Nicosiense*, no. A.

received a letter from Constable Sempad of Armenia who, from Samarkand, observed the life of the Christians under Mongol rule. To maintain the first contacts, a new embassy was assigned to the Dominican Andrew of Longjumeau, who left Cyprus for Central Asia in January 1249. Other voyages followed, such as that of the Franciscan William of Rubrouck, who reached Karakorum in 1253 and who, on his return, after a stay in Nicosia, wrote up his account in Acre in 1255/57. Thanks to these missions, the news circulated in the Levant and Cyprus, spreading factual or imaginary information that coloured the narrative of the Templar of Tyre, Riccold of Monte Croce, Hayton, and Marino Sanudo Torsello, when they reported the customs of the Mongols. But merchants were other bearers of information, as the Templar of Tyre relates.[49]

After the fall of St John of Acre, the withdrawal of religious foundations, the military orders, and 'bourgeois' Syrians to the island encouraged the development of a Latin and Oriental Christian culture in an urban setting. Henceforth Cyprus was an indispensable observation point for those who wanted to launch new crusades. Hayton, Marino Sanudo Torsello, and Raymond Lull stopped in Famagusta in search of information and support for their projects. From a missionary perspective, Alfonso Buenhombre, an Arabic-speaking Spanish Dominican, stayed in Famagusta between 1339 and 1342, translating texts from Arabic into Latin; in 1341 he translated the *Vita* of St Anthony found in the manuscript of the library of the Coptic monastery of St Anthony. In Cyprus Buenhombre pursued the career of interpreter and commentator that he had begun in Egypt. He complained that the mendicant friars living in Cyprus were ignorant of Arabic, that Arab Christians had no knowledge of the teachings of the doctors of the Roman Church, and that the Latins were unable to draw from the lessons of the study of the life of the anchorites of Egypt, of the work of Ephraem the Syrian.[50] Twenty years later the dialogue that the Dominican provoked found an echo in the merchant Athanasios Lepantrenos, who mentions the trilingual interpreters active on the island, among them George Lapithes.[51]

---

[49] Guillaume de Rubrouck, 118, 168, 240, 243; Marino Sanudo Torsello, 238; The Templar of Tyre, *Cronaca*, §§345 (581)–348 (584); Riccold de Monte Croce, 79–115; Golubovich (1906–1927, I: 229; II: 383); Richard (1977b: 70–80); Guéret-Laferté (1994).
[50] Meersseman (1940); Halkin (1942).
[51] Gregoras, *Epistulae*, no. 18.

Buenhombre participated in this climate of interconfessional exchanges and reinforces the image of a society enlivened by an intense dialogue among communities in the reign of Hugh IV, a dialogue that was probably enriched—as Chris Schabel had clearly demonstrated—by the presence of major Dominican theologians, like Raymond Bequini and Peter of Palude, in the 1320s, or Franciscans such as Elias of Nabinaux, appointed archbishop of Nicosia in 1332 and serving until 1342.[52]

Connections with Byzantium appear to have been loose during the thirteenth century. Thus one finds hardly any influence of George of Cyprus—Patriarch Gregory II from March 1283 to June 1289—on the letters of his native island, even though traces remain of his correspondence with King Henry II.[53] Nevertheless the figure of George of Cyprus marks a turning point in the history of the Byzantine intellectual renaissance, since he reestablished higher education in Constantinople, attracting students from Cyprus.[54] George linked them to the debates of the capital of the Palaeologans, as we learn from letters addressed to Leo, a Cypriot living in Constantinople at the beginning of the fourteenth century. A philosopher inspired by ancient thought, Leo refers to classical authors, his passion for astronomy, and his collection of manuscripts, acquired in Italy and, perhaps, in Cyprus.[55] Certainly George of Cyprus blazed a trail that other scholars from the island would follow. George is without doubt also an actor in the rapprochement with the Frankish kingdom, for among his disciples figures John Glykys who, before becoming patriarch in 1315, was charged with an embassy to Cyprus and Cilicia in 1294. Accompanied by a young Theodore Metochites, who was also obsessed with theology, Glykys hoped to obtain a Lusignan princess worthy of marrying the son of the Emperor Andronicos II. The effort ended in failure, but an increase in exchanges between the Palaeologans and the Frankish kingdom was assured.[56]

The relations we observe between Cyprus and Constantinople are confirmed in the course of the fourteenth century. The contents of

---

[52] Schabel (1998: 44–52; 2000a).

[53] Lampros (1921: 151–2); Lameere (1937: 23, 193–4). On George generally, see Constantinides (1982: passim), Papadakis (1997), and Hinterberger (1999: 354–8).

[54] Constantinides (1982: 108).

[55] Rein (1915: 9, 57–9, 97, nos. 8, 9, 11, 12, 55, 56, 81, 82, 90–92, 124, 125, 135, 137, 147, 151).

[56] Laiou (1972: 54–5); Constantinides (1982: 98).

Vat. Palat. gr. 367, composed around 1317/20, resemble a collection of disparate pieces copied by a family of notaries connected to the Greek chancery of the Lusignans. Besides administrative or fiscal documents and formulae for correspondence, one also find texts of a religious inspiration and—something quite rare—a profane work (the *Spaneas*).[57] The history of Vat. Palat. gr. 367, the subject of a forthcoming study by Alexander Beihammer assuring that part of the material copied dates to the 1230s, verifies links with Byzantine savants, from Nicaea before 1261 and from Constantinople afterwards.[58]

The volume of exchange between Constantinople and Cyprus was undoubtedly reinforced with the arrival of Greek scribes leaving Asia Minor as it fell under the domination of Turkish emirs.[59] Striking confirmation comes a few decades later during the Palamite quarrel. This debate, which opposed Barlaam the Calabrian and Gregory Palamas, starting in 1341, mobilised Cypriot men of letters who lived on the island, in Thessalonike, or in Constantinople. George Lapithes played a significant role in the controversy. Before it even erupted, Lapithes was already maintaining a regular correspondence with Barlaam in 1335/36, with Nicephoros Gregoras before 1341, and with Gregory Akindynos beginning in 1342.[60] During the controversy, Lapithes and other known Greek Cypriot monks and dignitaries defended the anti-Palamite cause. Lapithes' role is expressed in treatises refuting the theses of Palamas and in letters of a polemical content exchanged with the scholars of the Empire.[61]

With the victory of the Hesychasts in Constantinople, Cyprus became a place of refuge for those who feared persecution. If Gregory Akindynos considered going into exile there, Cyril, the metropolitan of Sidon, actually came to Cyprus as a refugee in 1355. Around 1359 Patriarch Ignatios II of Antioch also resided in the island, frequenting the court of Hugh IV. The philosopher John Kyparissiotis, also threatened, stayed in Cyprus during the summer of 1371, before converting to the Latin rite. In the case of Kyparissiotis, as in that

---

[57] Description of the manuscript in Constantinides and Browning, *Dated Greek Manuscripts*, 153–65.

[58] Beihammer (forthcoming).

[59] Constantinides and Browning, *Dated Greek Manuscripts*, 12.

[60] Gregoras, *Epistulae*, nos. 14–16; Sinkewicz (1981: 152–4); Karpozilos (1981–1982: 493–8).

[61] Akindynos, *Letters*, nos. 42, 45–6, 60; Mercati (1931: 187, 223, 260–1); Darrouzès (1959b: 9); Meyendorff (1959: 87, 107, 116, 126–7); Kyrris (1961; 1962: 28–30); Tsolakis (1964); Gonis (1986).

of George Cydones, their relations with the Dominicans of Nicosia remain unknown. A bastion of anti-Palamism, Cyprus even provoked the reaction of the monk-Emperor John-Joasaph Cantacuzenos, who wrote to Bishop John of Karpasia, around 1369/71, in order to assure him of the orthodoxy of Hesychasm. Cantacuzenos sent to Cyprus copies of his *Antirhetorica*, in which he refuted the positions of Prochoros Cydones.[62] If one cannot evaluate the success of this policy, the flow of anti-Palamism and then of triumphant Hesychasm passed from Constantinople to Nicosia without obstacle. They probably took the same paths taken by the Persian astronomical manuscripts that were translated into Greek in the Byzantine capital and used by George Lapithes.[63]

In this concert of visits and correspondence, the role that Hugh IV played does not appear very clearly, but, with Peter I, the reactivation of the politics of crusading casts a shadow on the previous atmosphere of concord. Peter surrounded himself with Western thinkers (Philip of Mézières, Guido of Bagnolo) and sought grand diplomatic alliances in the West. Is it by chance that the long poem in praise of Peter was born in France, after the king's assassination, with the pen of Guillaume de Machaut, who also composed for him the *Dit de la Marguerite*, a complainte, and, perhaps, musical works?[64] In Cyprus St Brigitte of Sweden strengthened the spirit of the crusade. Her prophecies at Famagusta left a long-lasting impression, down to Stephen of Lusignan, and reveal the climate of intolerance that accompanied the arrival of the papal legate Peter Thomae.[65] The philosopher George Cydones, a convert to the Latin rite, had to leave Nicosia to escape the fate in store for him because of his proposals that were hostile to the legate; in 1362 we find him in Mystras at the court of Cantacuzenos.[66]

Until 1373 the Kingdom of Cyprus was never separate from the currents of thought circulating in the Eastern Mediterranean, although

[62] Makhairas, *Diplomatic Edition*, 88, 107; Gregoras, *Correspondance*, no. 159; Cydones, nos. 31, 35; Mercati (1931: 52, 194, 197–8, 215–16, 223, 228, 338–40); Meyendorff (1959: 152); Darrouzès (1959b: 9, 11, 15–21); Dentakis (1977: 20–2); Karpozilos (1981–1982: 493, 495); Gonis (1986: 335–6).
[63] Tihon (1977: 279–80; 1981: 107–9); Constantinides and Browning, *Dated Greek Manuscripts*, 13.
[64] Guillaume de Machaut, *La Prise d'Alixandre*; Poirion (1978: 24, 195).
[65] Étienne de Lusignan, *Description*, fols. 231v–234v; Golubovich (1906–1927, V: 171–2, 175–8); Piltz (1986: 51); see also Schabel in this volume.
[66] Loenertz (1948); Gonis (1986: 337–50).

it is not possible to evaluate the reception of 'foreign' ideas and their incorporation into insular traditions. The processions organized during natural catastrophes or important political events illustrate, for example, how the Latin elites followed the pilgrimages and devotions linked to Greek cults.[67] In contact with their subjects, the Franks drew near to Greek piety, but they remained fully imbued with the ways of Western culture, for diplomatic alliances tightened the bonds between the Lusignan court and those of European princes. In this respect, an analysis of the circulation of manuscripts provides an index for the diffusion of ideas among Cypriot authors, or at least in their libraries.

A few secure testimonies illustrate the penetration of ideas and the literary styles of the Cypriots. Among the Greek manuscripts of a secular bent, one finds a thirteenth-century selection of classical authors that appears to be intended for training students. A century later one counts as follows: a collection comprising the verses of Michael Grammatikos and the *Spaneas*, copied around 1316/20; a fragment of the *Romance of Alexander*; a disparate collection consisting of a dictionary of political verse; sermons; the poems of the rhetor Michael Holobolos; the prologue of the *Alexiad* of Anna Comnena;[68] and finally, among the ten volumes copied by Romanos Anagnostes are philosophical texts of Aristotle and Michael Psellos, the *Physics* of Nicephoros Blemmydes, and lexicographic works.[69] These indications hardly attest to an extensive penetration of classical thought or of Byzantine chronicles in the island's culture, compared to the mass of religious manuscripts that have been preserved: one need only mention that a rather modest sanctuary as that of Prodromos, at Argaki, possessed a rich library of 30 volumes in 1363.[70]

For the Franks it is possible to approach the issue through the inventories of two libraries, those of a Dominican bishop of Limassol, Guy of Ibelin, and of the physician Guido of Bagnolo. Of these two inventories, Guy of Ibelin's was drawn up on the island before the dispersion of his legacy (1367). It shows that the Dominican had amassed 52 works, for the most part philosophical and theological texts, collections of sermons, hagiographical accounts, and volumes

---

[67] Grivaud (2003); see also Schabel in this volume.
[68] Darrouzès (1950: 162, 175); Gamillscheg and Harlfinger (1989: no. 294); Constantinides and Browning, *Dated Greek Manuscripts*, 153–65.
[69] For a complete list of Anagnostes' works, see Constantinides and Browning, *Dated Greek Manuscripts*, 12.
[70] Couroupou and Géhin (2001: 157–8).

of canon law. Together these volumes, produced in the West, prove that the Dominicans of Cyprus followed developments current in the order's Western convents.[71] Guido of Bagnolo's library, taken from Cyprus to Venice in 1368, just a year before the Emilian humanist's death, is known through an inventory dated 1380, and so the collection of 60 volumes it records underwent alterations after his departure. The interest in medicine and philosophy is not surprising for Guido—indeed he had 38 medical manuscripts, mainly medieval treatises, many of them translated from Arabic, seven works of Galen and one of Hippocrates, twelve of philosophy (Aristotle, Avicenna, Averroes, John of Damascus), seven of astronomy (among them Claudius Ptolemy's *Almagest*), and three of geometry.[72] This is an important collection, revealing Guido's erudition, drawing on the Greek, Latin, and Arabic traditions. As fragmentary as it is, the information for private collections of manuscripts indicates that the diffusion of texts occurred without hindrance in the kingdom.

Despite the lack of studies on the process of transmission of traditions from the Greek *oecumene* to Cyprus, some hypotheses allow us to believe that the island also played the role of mediator within the Greek world. Thus, the Akritic tradition arrived, surely from Asia Minor, in the eleventh and twelfth centuries, and it was adapted to its new environment and preserved until our days. When in the composition of his *Teseida* Boccaccio was inspired by a version of Dighenis Akritas, was it a Cypriot tradition that had reached Italy? There is nothing to substantiate this, but in the *Decameron* Boccaccio asserts that he is employing Cypriot legends: 'just as we have already read in the ancient histories of the Cypriots' ('si come noi nell'antiche istorie de' Cipriani abbiam già letto'). This confession and, more especially, the relationship that Boccaccio maintained with Hugh IV, suggest a connection to the epic narratives that circulated on the island, although Boccaccio could also have been inspired by Cretan traditions.[73] The question of the composition of the *Lament of the Virgin* also appears uncertain. According to Samuel Baud-Bovy, this funeral chant was born in Cyprus around 1300, when a chanter was inspired by an episode in the *Cyprus Passion Cycle* in writing a poem put to music with a melody using a rhythm of Frankish origin.[74] As hypo-

---

[71] Laurent and Richard (1951); Schabel (1998: 43–5).
[72] Livi (1918); Schabel (1998: 43).
[73] Giovanni Boccaccio, *The Decameron*, day V, 1; Pertusi (1962; 1970: 533–7).
[74] Baud-Bovy (1959: 362–7).

thetical as they are, the theories concerning the Akritic songs and the *Lament of the Virgin* bring up the problem of the diffusion of Greek culture in the Greco-Latin world after 1204 and the place that Cyprus might have held in these exchanges.

Cyprus also played the role of mediator between civilizations through translations done on the island, but in a spirit different from those done in the other states of the Latin East, since Cyprus remained principally a land of Greek culture.[75] As Jean Richard remarks, from the beginning of the thirteenth century the donations of Frankish lords to Greek churches indicate some knowledge of the local hagiographic literature, which could only have been accessible through translations.[76] After 1291, the Lusignans attracted scholars and men of letters, transforming their court into a setting open to Westerners, Greeks, and Arabs. It is during the reign of Hugh IV that signs of activity increase dramatically: Buenhombre made a Latin version of a Coptic *Vita* at the very moment that George Lapithes was translating an astronomical treatise from Latin into Greek and adapting Latin manuals to compose his treatise on the seven sacraments.[77] This vitality, as art historians have concluded, shows that the Frankish kingdom was a melting pot of exchanges between the autochtone and allochtone cultures, even if, in volume, the translation movement appears to have been less developed than in the Kingdom of Cilician Armenia, above all in texts of a religious nature.[78]

The Maturity of Historical and Legal Writings

In the history of the literature produced on Cyprus, the period up to the reign of Peter I constitutes a flowering that is without parallel before the Renaissance. Frankish letters—with origins in the other states of the Latin East—very quickly made their appearance with the stabilisation of political life, when the jurists produced the treatises making up the *Assizes*. From Acre, a philosophical movement took shape, developing in the reigns of Henry II and Hugh IV. Moral literature flourished in Philip of Novara, who brilliantly embodies

---

[75] On translations in the Latin East, see Minervini (1996b; 2001: 634–48).
[76] Richard (1991–1992: 241).
[77] For other hypotheses on relations between the culture of the Frankish kingdom and the West, see Ciggaar (1994: 94–7).
[78] Mahé (1996: 60–1); Ter-Vardanian (1996); Weitenberg (1996).

the secularisation of the contents, since the works in the Latin language remained restricted to the religious sphere. In the young kingdom the clerics immediately lost their monopoly on writing.

The literary production of the Greeks follows a similar evolution, with a time-lag of a half century. After 1191, one sees no notable rupture in the contents of texts that are written or copied in the religious tradition. Neophytos the Recluse continued to produce the same variety of writings he had begun in the 1170s, completing his final work around 1214; the political changes did not affect the volume or nature of his works. In the same period Neilos composed the *Diataxis* that founded the monastery of Panayia of Makhairas (1201).[79] The first two decades of Latin rule left the Greeks to cultivate their traditional religious inspiration. Quite logically, to tell the tale of the martyrdom of the monks of Kantara, those recording the event chose the genre of hagiography over the chronicle.[80]

It is probably the secular institutions of the Frankish kingdom that opened the breaches in the Greek religious culture. The Byzantine juridical heritage is apparent in manuscript Paris. gr. 1391, composed ca. 1300, and the Greek translation of the *Assises des Bourgeois* and the collection of Vat. Palat. gr. 367 date to this period. By itself this last manuscript encapsulates Greek culture, linking acts of the chancery, religious poetry in learned language, the long moral poem of *Spaneas*, and the liturgical drama of the *Cyprus Passion Cycle*. From Neophytos the Recluse to George Lapithes, the Greek literary production resounds with the echoes of discussions associated either with the Franks of the realm or with the Byzantines of the Empire.

The Historical Tradition

Born with the Crusades, the Kingdom of Cyprus owed many of its institutions and much of its history to the Kingdom of Jerusalem. Consequently, the historical writings of the thirteenth century found their models in the previous narratives composed in Outremer. Until 1359, Cypriot historiography treated the destinies of the two kingdoms together and borrowed, to varying degrees, from the *Historia* of William of Tyre, through the *Continuations*, to the collections of *Annales* of the

---

[79] Neilos, Τυπική Διάταξις; Galatariotou (1991: 18–19, 261–81); Nicolaou-Konnari's chapter in this volume.

[80] *Martyrion Kyprion.*

Holy Land. Another notable characteristic of Cypriot historiography is its wealth, for all genres that make up medieval historical literature are represented: chronicles, histories, annals. Moreover, Cypriot historiography, Frankish or Greek, was written in the vernacular.

The Continuations of William of Tyre and the Chronicle of Ernoul: The *Continuations* of William of Tyre met with a reception that was greater than that of the narrative that they continue, since more than 40 manuscripts have been found.[81] One can discern four groups: 1) the French translations, abridged or not, of William of Tyre's work; 2) the *Continuations* (known under the titles *Livre dou Conquest* or *Estoire de Eracles*, *Livre d'Eracles*, *Roman d'Eracles*); 3) the chronicle of Ernoul and Bernard the Treasurer; and 4) the *Estoires d'Outremer*.[82] If two of these groups are of particular interest for Cyprus—the *Continuations* and the *Chronique d'Ernoul*—there is no indication that any was composed or copied in Cyprus, at a time when the military and political destiny of the Latin East was common to all the Franks of Outremer.

Studies of the circumstances of the composition of the *Continuations* and of the *Chronique d'Ernoul* have reached contradictory conclusions, especially with respect to the identity of Ernoul and the relationship among the manuscripts, essential for distinguishing the original text from later versions.[83] The debate, which is still open, largely concerns the method of the compilers, who recast pre-existing material in new combinations, intervened by following other sources or their own experience, and completed the narrative of events down to different dates (from 1228 to 1277). These difficulties—amplified by the flow of copies from Outremer to the West, then the reverse—do not change the fact that the texts inspired by the work of William of Tyre introduced into Cyprus a historical tradition coming from the Kingdom of Jerusalem. Nevertheless, unlike the case of the *Historia*, the continuators used the vernacular language and neglected to borrow from the classical and Christian authors that were so dear to the archbishop of Tyre.[84]

The role of the Franks of Cyprus in the composition of these compilations remains difficult to determine. The intervention of witnesses who had participated in the conquest of the island seems obvious in

---

[81] Folda (1973); Morgan (1973: 1–6).
[82] See *Continuation de Guillaume de Tyr*, 'Ernoul', and 'Estoire de Eracles'.
[83] Morgan (1973); Edbury (1997e).
[84] Edbury and Rowe (1988: 32–43).

some versions, but otherwise it is hard to tell. It is more important
to note that the historical thought that William of Tyre had begun
disappeared in the *Continuations*, which can be considered works of
popularisation intended for a large readership. Yet their literary content permits us to discern society's tastes, for certain texts show the
characteristics of lay culture present in Philip of Novara and the
Templar of Tyre. Thus they reveal the use of proverbs, the defense
of the feudal code of ethics, the current use of discourse for drama-
tising the account, the direct intervention of the author by way of
criticism or advice, and the recourse to rhymed verse to amplify the
expression of emotions. In the thirteenth century their composition
evolved in the direction of narrative accounts, close to annals. From
then on, the texts lost their moral and aesthetic ambitions and the
creative stream of the *Continuations* ran dry after 1261. Nevertheless,
despite these reservations concerning their documentary authentic-
ity, the *Continuations* are among the sources historians of the Kingdom
of Cyprus use for the period until the Renaissance.

The Annales of the Holy Land: Along with scholarly history and the
chronicle, a third historical genre developed, that of annals. At least
three French manuscripts, one of which exists in a Spanish translation,
preserve a chronicle summarizing the main facts of the history of the
Holy Land from 1095 to 1291. Battles, alliances, peace treaties, and
other events of political and military life are registered without special commentary, and the history of Cyprus has a minor position.
The place of composition for the annals has not been determined.
Covering two centuries of the history of the Kingdom of Jerusalem,
perhaps they were written in Cyprus, or at least completed in Cyprus,
before passing to the West, since the copies in the vernacular seem
to have been made in France after 1291. The intervention of Cypriot
annalists belongs to the realm of hypothesis. Still, the annals circulated in Cyprus, since they were used by historians active in the
kingdom before and after 1291 (the compiler of the *Gestes des Chiprois*,
the *Chronique d'Amadi*, some continuators of William of Tyre, and
even a little anonymous chronicle of the fifteenth century).[85]

The Gestes des Chiprois: The work known as the *Gestes des Chiprois*
combines three chronicles compiled in the 1310s.[86] The first of these

[85] *Annales de Terre Sainte*; *Anales de Tierra Santa*; Grivaud (2001b: 319); Edbury (forthcoming).
[86] Complete edition of *Les Gestes des Chiprois* by G. Raynaud in 1887 and by

chronicles, the *Chronique de Terre Sainte*, traces the history of the Holy Land from the creation of Adam until 1224; the second, adapted from the memoirs of Philip of Novara, covers the years 1218–1242; the third, the *Chronique du Templier de Tyr*, deals with the following period, ending in 1309. By collecting, modifying, or composing the three accounts, the compiler began an unusual work in the context of the local historiography, since he constructed a history of the King-doms of Jerusalem and Cyprus over a long duration, thus consciously putting together a synthetic work. The text of the *Gestes des Chiprois* survives in a single, incomplete exemplar (the beginning of the account down to 1132 is missing), copied by John le Miège, a prisoner at Kyrenia, on 9 April 1343, at the request of Aimery of Milmars.[87]

The attribution of this compilation to Gerard of Monréal is a hypothesis that is still unverifiable, resting exclusively on the assertion of Florio Bustron.[88] Gerard of Monréal remains a figure whose public life is limited to a few scraps of information and whose name is not present in the manuscript of the *Gestes*. Perhaps Gerard is the author of the first text (*Chronique de Terre Sainte*), but the responsibility for the other accounts cannot be ascribed to him. Thus, as was men-tioned, the second chronicle is taken from the memoirs of Philip of Novara (see below) and the third and longest is the work of a Templar from Tyre who, without giving his identity, reveals some information about his life in his text. One finds that he was a page of Margaret of Lusignan, the wife of John of Montfort, lord of Tyre; from Tyre, as a youth he next went to Acre, where he lived until 1291; he became the secretary and then the squire of the grand master of the Temple, William of Beaujeu, for whom he drew up official acts and did trans-lations from Arabic. After 1291 the squire reached Cyprus where he seems to have obtained a position in the king's household, before joining the service of the senechal, Philip of Ibelin, the king's uncle. After 1300 the chronicler left the Temple and joined the Hospital. We lose track of him after the year 1309.[89] Thus he was a chronicler

R. de Mas-Latrie, G. Paris, and C. Kohler in 1906. Only two chronicles have received a recent edition: Philip of Novara's *Guerra* and The Templar of Tyre's *Cronaca*; unfortunately, these editions, far better than the previous ones, deprive the original text of its consistency as a whole.

[87] Philip of Novara, *Guerra*, §140 (236).
[88] Florio Bustron, *Historia*, 8.
[89] Cf. Mivervini in her introduction to the edition of The Templar of Tyre, *Cronaca*, 1–2.

who was active in a setting that allowed him to gather information
at its source. His position as secretary predisposed him to studying
correspondence and gave him access to archival documents. His environment thus permitted him to observe political life at the turn of
the fourteenth century.

The main problem raised by the *Gestes* revolves around the difficulty
of assessing the intervention of the compiler—the hypothetical Gerard
of Monréal—in the organisation of the original material and in the
redaction of the final manuscript, transmitted by the copy of John
le Miège. The three chronicles are unified and structured by a narrative that is based on a rigorous chronological principle, with the
wording obsessively following the yearly course of events. Anxious
to justify his method, the author explains that 'it is fitting to speak
one after the other concerning the things that happened' ('covient a
parler, des choses quy avyenent, l'un an aprés l'autre').[90] For this
reason, he borrows copiously from the *Annales* of the Holy Land, especially in the section devoted to the period before the Civil War
(*Chronique de Terre Sainte*). The compiler also interpolates annalistic
notes in the memoirs of Philip of Novara, but in the two last sec-
tions he progressively departs from the style of annals to privilege
the written or oral sources that he has at his disposal. Sometimes,
to cope with his evidence, the historian hesitates, admits his disor-
der, and limits his interference to the insertion of transitions, in a
manner that improves the coherence of the work.

The compiler's mediation indeed seems reduced with the texts he
uses (*Livre dou Conquest* or *Estoire de Eracles*, the memoirs of Philip of
Novara, the chronicle of the Templar of Tyre). The third chronicle
of the collection exhibits formal qualities and political ideas that are
novel in the context of the Kingdom of Cyprus and therefore belong
to the Templar himself. This author, who composed his text in the
1310s, understood the result of previous wars and grasped the island's
new place in the Eastern Mediterranean. Up until 1291, the narrative focuses on Syria, but afterwards Cyprus takes on a determining
role, which demands a brief geographical description of the island,
the first in a historical work written within the kingdom.[91]

From then on the Templar chronicler, an eyewitness to events,
employs the first person in the narrative, completing his text with

[90] The Templar of Tyre, *Cronaca*, §309 (545).
[91] The Templar of Tyre, *Cronaca*, §278 (514).

data gathered in Syria, Cyprus, or from merchants who informed him, both on the customs of the Mongols and the trial of the Templars in Paris. He reconstructs the commercial and political relations that determine the island's future: the history of Cyprus depends on the resolution of the conflicts between the Mamluks and Mongols, on the result of the second war between Venice and Genoa, and on the success of the Spanish *Reconquista*. The chronicler's horizons encompass the events from the Mediterranean to Central Asia. The Mongol presence in Syria provides material for a long exposé on the Tatars, which seems to rest on descriptions of merchants or missionaries frequenting Cyprus.[92]

This subtle political analysis accompanies strongly held positions, for his testimony to the fall of Acre holds nothing back. Very rapidly, he follows the path of Philip of Novara (see below) in reporting the twists of Frederick II.[93] He repeatedly defends the memory of William of Beaujeu, then criticises the government of Amaury of Lusignan, the usurper of the throne.[94] Finally, he writes superb verses against the egoism of the wealthy and powerful of Cyprus when confronted with the influx of refugees from Syria in 1291. His reproaches, which spared the king and queen, were addressed to all members of the island's society, formerly the friends of the Christians of Syria: the bourgeois profiteers who raised the rent on houses; the regular clergy, accused of simony; the mendicant orders, for their pride and poor guidance; the crown, princes, and barons, to blame for bad government.[95] The chronicler expresses his disappointment and attacks head-on the various actors from the feudal class, who increasingly opposed the faith in word and deed. In conformity with Christian morality, the chronicler interprets the fall of Acre as divine punishment for the evil ways of the crusader knights.[96]

The coming of the refugees from Syria to Cyprus provokes violent emotions in the Templar chronicler, tied to the solidarity that he felt toward the expatriots. His suffering and his disgust led him to compose a long poem incorporated into his narrative so that this rhyme 'would always be found and remembered' ('seit tous jours trovee et

---

[92] The Templar of Tyre, *Cronaca*, §§296 (532), 300–09 (536–45), 345–78 (581–614), 461–2 (697–8).
[93] The Templar of Tyre, *Cronaca*, §10 (246).
[94] The Templar of Tyre, *Cronaca*, §§147 (383), 466 (702).
[95] The Templar of Tyre, *Cronaca*, §§280 (516), 294 (530).
[96] The Templar of Tyre, *Cronaca*, §293 (529).

remembree').[97] As in the memoirs of Philip of Novara, the poem serves to strengthen the rhetoric. Thus the chronicler, now poet, laments the disappearance of chivalrous and Christian ideals in Cyprus more than he mourns the loss of Acre. The poet takes up his argumentation, deploring the fact that the idea of crusading chivalry is disappearing to be replaced by values in which money acquires the crucial role. He inveighs against usurers who conduct their trade with complete impunity and gain the public's respect. He rants against those who accumulate goods and wealth in disregard for the poverty-stricken. From now on, the simple spirits learn humiliation and the old lineages are no longer respected. Corruption pollutes human relations and the simony of the Church. His quatrains express the despair of a spectator viewing the mutilation of the Latin East and of Cypriot society. Undoubtedly he was profoundly affected by the political crisis following the deposition of Henry II and by the division of the aristocracy of the kingdom. The chronicler's verses constitute more acerbic critiques than those contained in the prose narrative. Their virulence does not escape the author who, to exonerate himself, affirms that his public defends his point of view. By employing a more literary form, the author loses the historian's reserve in order to adopt the empassioned style of a witness, for the Templar of Tyre reports with emotion the state of collapse of the crusade ideal.

Preserved in just one manuscript, the compilation of the *Gestes des Chiprois* attests, by itself, to the level of maturity that historical thinking reached at the beginning of the fourteenth century, a maturity that appears to be the fruit of the dramatic unfolding of events that weakened Frankish power in the Holy Land. Following the example of the *Gestes*, other chronicles would preserve the memory of the political life of the Lusignan kingdom in the course of the fourteenth century. Thus, the *Chronique d'Amadi*, known via a single manuscript from the Venetian era,[98] displays several similarities with the *Gestes*, to such a degree that it suggests a conscience attempt to maintain, or rather prolong, the pioneering work of the historian that Florio Bustron named Gerard of Monréal.

---

[97] The Templar of Tyre, *Cronaca*, §294 (530).
[98] 'Amadi'.

Notes and Small Greek Chronicles

Compared to the voluminous historical literature in the French language, the meagre Greek production turns out, at first sight, to be disappointing. Despite this, an examination shows that the zest for the chronological recording of events inspired monks, scribes, and notaries, who have left an abundant series of notes, colophons, and small chronicles in the manuscripts. Certainly, these sparse writings, written on account of local circumstances or for personal reasons, always anonymously, offer no general coherence with respect to their contents, but one can put them into categories.

One group consists of obituary notices. Their formulae follow specific protocols and the models are repeated without notable variations. Some monasteries, like the Iereon, record the notices connected to the monastery in one single manuscript; thus Paris. gr. 1588 lists 157 deaths of monks and abbots, those of a few kings and nobles, and of the faithful who gave donations to the convent, between 1203 and 1458. Added to this we find elections of abbots, visits, pilgrimages, donation acts, and notes on catastrophes. With this patient compilation the monks constructed the collective memory of their institution.[99]

A second group collects the acts of donations of lands or rents to chapels, churches, or monasteries. These acts employ the formulae of private law in following the donation clause with a ritual curse against violators, then a clausula on the redactor of the act, which precedes the signatures of witnesses. These acts of donation are, as a general rule, entered in Gospel lectionaries, because their sacred character sanctions the donation to the establishment. Nevertheless, unlike Paris. gr. 1588, the notaries do not copy these acts in a single volume, so the property of the sanctuaries receives less attention. Obviously, these notices stem from the wish to protect a decision of private law more than a desire to preserve the memory of the community.

A third group of notices is more illustrative of the scribes' interest in the history of their island. These notices are spread out wherever there is empty space, on endpapers or dividing sheets, and take on the look of small chronicles.[100] This type of recording displays striking similarities to that of the *Annales* of the Latin East. Six small chronicles are known. Of the two contained in Vat. Palat. gr. 367, one

---

[99] Darrouzès (1951b); Constantinides and Browning, *Dated Greek Manuscripts*, 76–80.
[100] *Byzantinischen Kleinchroniken*, I, 21.

tells of five outstanding events between May 1191 and June 1222, and the other records twelve occurrences of significance in the life of the kingdom from 1209 to 1310.[101] Paris. gr. 546 preserves, on the recto of folio 324, three notices without any connection between them, dated 1330, 1347, and 1479, but whose character evolves from the style of annals to a more developed exposé.[102] As a general rule, these notices concern crucial events in political life or catastrophes that visited the island.

This microhistory, individual and local, reveals the care that monks, secretaries, and notaries took to preserve the memory of important events. Their motivations are never expressed and all of them have been buried by the sands of time. They are anonymous transmitters of a memory deprived of emotion and of commentary. Greeks, and Franks to a lesser extent, participate in this writing, thus exposing a relative diffusion of historical consciousness.

Legal Writings

With the creation of the Kingdom of Cyprus by Aimery of Lusignan, the young monarchy was endowed with legislative and juridical institutions that from the beginning were modeled on those of the Kingdom of Jerusalem. This transfer of practices that had been defined in the Latin East resulted in a superposition of distinct regulations on the same soil. According to the various social or ethnic communities, feudal customary law, canon law, Greco-Roman law—above all in its Byzantine expression—and Syrian customary law were applied, although we cannot forget the legal privileges granted to merchants of certain nationalities, which permitted their communities to be governed according to their own laws. Each group developed its legal definitions, procedural rules, and organs of jurisdiction, which sometimes overlapped or complemented each other, leading to an undeniable confusion of coexisting juridical systems. In this respect, the example of Syrian customary law applied in Famagusta illustrates the complexity of the question, because if the tribunal of the *cour du raïs* rendered judgments, no one could evaluate the laws on which they depended,

---

[101] *Byzantinischen Kleinchroniken*, I, 198–204; Constantinides and Browning, *Dated Greek Manuscripts*, 161–3.
[102] *Byzantinischen Kleinchroniken*, I, 205–6.

or even determine if the judges had access to a written corpus of Syrian customary law.[103]

The debate over the kingdom's legal structures was not limited to aristocratic circles, for the young Latin Church was also endowed with statutes and regulations. In September 1257 Archbishop Hugh of Fagiano collected the disciplinary statutes and the regulations of the Church of Nicosia that had been promulgated since 1252. Other disciplinary canons were passed in the Limassol diocese in September 1298, with Archbishop Gerard of Langres presiding. Afterwards, until 1354, the synods that gathered in Nicosia continued to add to this legislation. Gradually conciliar decisions increased the volume of the constitutions of the Church of Cyprus, while parallel to this the blossoming of canon law prompted John of Ancona (perhaps the same John of Ancona who was archbishop of Nicosia in 1288–95) to pen his *Summa iuris canonici*—a *summa* of the rubrics of Pope Gregory IX's *Decretals* (composed in 1234)—in the Latin East in the years 1265–68.[104] The 1250s and 1260s marked the convergence of the legislative and juridical preoccupations of the various institutions of the kingdom, since the initiatives of the clergy were contemporary with the efforts of Philip of Novara, who composed his *Livre de forme de plait* in the 1250s.[105] In fact, the thinking of the clerics and the lawyers developed at exactly the same time. As testimony we have the *De regno*, written by Thomas Aquinas.

The Treatise of Political Philosophy of Thomas Aquinas

Uncertainty about the circumstances that led to the composition of Thomas Aquinas' treatise raises a number of questions, first concerning the Dominican master's actual presence on Cyprus, and then concerning the identity of the King Hugh of Cyprus to whom the work was addressed, since King Hugh II, still a child, died toward the end of 1267, leaving his throne to Hugh III, who was crowned on Christmas day that same year. Claude Roguet argued that this treatise, as with Giles of Rome's work addressed to the young King Philip the Fair (ca. 1279), was written for a young monarch open to advice—Hugh II—, which suggests a composition before Christmas of 1267.[106]

---

[103] Richard (1987: 385–8; 1995c).
[104] Bertram (1977: 52–8); Schabel (2000a); *Synodicum Nicosiense*.
[105] Edbury (2001b: 557).
[106] Roguet in his preface to his edition of Thomas Aquinas, *Du gouvernement royal*, viii.

This hypothesis would explain why the treatise is incomplete, since Thomas abandoned the writing of *De regno* after chapter 4 of book II. The opuscule was completed after 1300 by a disciple of the master, Ptolemy of Lucca, the author of the definitive title, *De regimine principum*.[107]

In this work Thomas adopts a position that is distinct from the one he outlines in his other writings where, when he approaches questions of political philosophy, the Dominican often follows Aristotle's precepts to praise a mixed government, consisting of a king assisted by a council of aristocrats elected by the whole of the citizenry. In contrast in *De regno* Thomas defends a concept of power organised on the principle of a kind of absolute monarchy. This novelty would be justified, according to Maurice Grandclaude, by the concern to develop a theory adapted to the problems linked to Hugh II's minority.[108] On the other hand, for other historians of medieval political thought—who pass over in silence the address to the king of Cyprus—the treatise would reflect preoccupations connected to the troubled situation in Italy in the 1260s.[109]

The incomplete nature of *De regno* implies that the text did not circulate in the kingdom, but Thomas Aquinas' ideas could have spread from the Dominican *studium* of Nicosia. Indeed, why not draw a connection between the positions of Thomas and those of John of Ibelin, who, in the same years, battled against the theory of the absolute power of the monarch? Of course the count of Jaffa did not formulate his ideas in the shape of a treatise on political philosophy, and his response is given through a work of jurisprudence following the model of Philip of Novara's treatise. Nevertheless, the work of the Dominican master lies just below the surface of the juridical writings of the 1260s, opening a debate on the nature of power, since it is closer to the ancestral conception of monarchy that inspired the *Livre au Roi*. Alien to the legislation of the Kingdoms of Jerusalem and Cyprus, Thomas Aquinas' treatise participates in its development by approaching it via a theoretical discourse that remains the only work of political philosophy concerning the institutions of the

---

[107] The treatise appears in all complete editions of the philosophical opuscula of Aquinas and was also published independently and translated; see Thomas Aquinas, *De regimine principum* and *Du gouvernement royal*.

[108] Grandclaude (1929); Gilson (1974: 354–71); Weisheipl (1974: 189–95).

[109] Catto (1976); Hamilton Bleakley (1999).

kingdom. In fact, the Cypriot nobles' mode of expression in structuring their political and juridical organisation never departs from the framework of the treatises on jurisprudence that would form, little by little, the corpus of the *Assizes*.

The Assizes of the Kingdom of Jerusalem and of the Kingdom of Cyprus

The enterprise to codify laws that occurred in the Latin East from the end of the twelfth to the fourteenth century is called improperly the *Assizes of Jerusalem*. Far from constituting a corpus of official law of the Kingdoms of Jerusalem and Cyprus, the *Assizes* bring together the recollections of law-givers, the writings of jurists, and the procedures of the High Court or the Court of the Burgesses established in the two realms. This disparate character contradicts the hypothesis that it was a composition organised methodically by the crown. The development of legislation in the kingdom did not result in the creation of a homogeneous code of law, as is attested by the variety of the collections, all written in French.

Maurice Grandclaude has explained how the word *assise* designates a decision of legislative nature adopted by the king and his liegemen gathered in a council where jurisconsults were regularly present and, sometimes, bourgeois members attended in the case of jurisdiction for commoners (such as the Court of the Viscount) when non-feudal assizes were passed. Besides the assizes there were *espéciaux commandements*, decisions taken by the king without the assistance of his council of liegemen. To abuses of the monopoly of royal power the nobles responded with *remèdes*. In addition to these various acts there were *ordonnements de cour* passed by the Court of the Viscount to settle the cases of the commercial or municipal police. Finally, uses and customs, also redacted in the form of assizes, completed the legislative apparatus. The collection of the assizes thus includes both decisions emanating from distinct courts and measures passed down through oral tradition.[110]

The compilation of this legislative and juridical apparatus took place after Jerusalem fell to Saladin, despite the legends concerning an earlier compilation known as the *Lettres du Sépulcre*.[111] After 1187 the jurists of the Latin East began putting the law into writing, and a first codification was completed, without doubt, at Aimery of

---

[110] Grandclaude (1923: 9–26).
[111] Edbury (1996).

Lusignan's instigation. Thus John of Ibelin reports the quarrel between the king and the jurist Ralph of Tiberias, in which they evoked their ability to draw on the memory of assizes that had disappeared. Many important jurists participated in the long process of stabilizing the law, a process involving the members of the aristocracy and, perhaps, some bourgeois. Besides Ralph of Tiberias, Philip of Novara, John of Ibelin, Balian of Sidon, Ranier of Giblet the Elder, Rostain Aimar, Giles Viconte, Hernois of Giblet, Geoffrey Le Tor, and James of Ibelin distinguished themselves in this school of jurists.[112] The first surviving text, the *Livre au Roi*, was composed around 1200. It was then complemented by five treatises written in the second half of the thirteenth century, all devoted to customary law (the *Livres* of Philip of Novara, John of Ibelin, Geoffrey Le Tor, and James of Ibelin, and the *Clef des Assises*), around the time when the codification of laws pertaining to the bourgeoisie occurred (*Assises de la Cour des Bourgeois, Livres du Plédéant et du Plaidoyer*); only the first of the codes proper to the bourgeoisie would be translated into Greek.

The Livre au Roi: this is a collection of 52 chapters, perhaps composed in Acre at the end of the twelfth century.[113] Probably put together for Aimery of Lusignan, it clarifies the king's prerogatives over the vassals and their reciprocal obligations. Defending the principle of royal authority over the aristocracy, the work is a throwback to a conception of the monarchy which the actual practice of legislation contradicted at the very time of the *Livre*'s composition. Undoubtedly intended to reestablish the juridical tradition of the kingdom after the battle of Hattin, the *Livre au Roi* inaugurated an early tradition of drawing up medieval customary law in the vernacular. There is no indication that jurisconsults based on Cyprus participated in its creation, since it is ignored in the treatises of the second half of the thirteenth century, even if a new copy of the *Livre au Roi* was made in Cyprus around 1315/17.[114]

The Livre de Jean d'Ibelin: This is considered the most important of the *Assizes of Jerusalem*. It is also the most voluminous, comprising 239 chapters.[115] Composed by the count of Jaffa during the last years of his life, between 1264 and 1266, the text does not survive in the

---

[112] Grandclaude (1923: 110–11).
[113] *Le Livre au Roi*.
[114] M. Greilsammer in her introduction to *Le Livre au Roi*; Greilsammer (1999).
[115] John of Ibelin, *Le Livre des Assises*.

autograph, but in five other manuscripts, the oldest of which was copied in Acre in the beginning of the 1280s. With small additions and in conjunction with other treatises making up the *Assizes*, the *Livre de Jean d'Ibelin* would constitute the core of the official code of the Kingdom of Cyprus after 1369.[116]

John of Ibelin conceived his treatise in three parts. The first (chapters 1–126) focuses on the procedures that had to be followed before the tribunals. Here John offers much advice on the forms of the *plaid*, providing proof, and the quality of testimonies, analysing the various punishments for criminals and the process of the judicial duel. John complements this section with explanations regarding specific cases governed by assizes, defined as established customs of long usage. The second part of the treatise (chapters 127–217) is dedicated to the law of fiefs and to vassalage. Here John offers a sophisticated analysis of possible disputes opposing lord and vassal as regards fiefs and their transmission. It is in this context that John clarifies his position at great length, in envisioning the cases where the vassal can sever the bond of obedience to his lord without breaking the oath of fealty. The third part (chapters 218–239), undoubtedly appended to the original text, consists of a series of chapters treating more precisely the institutions of the Kingdom of Jerusalem.

Without being a work of juridical theory, John of Ibelin's treatise constitutes an imposing *summa* on the customary law of the Latin East, one that would never be surpassed. Conceived at the end of the 1260s, it defends an ideology that privileges the feudal nobility at a time when, as Peter Edbury emphasizes, customary law was confronting the rationalism of Roman Law, which was undergoing a complete renaissance in Italy in the twelfth and thirteenth centuries.[117]

The Livre de Geoffroy Le Tort: This is the third work written about the *Assizes* of the High Court. A member of a noble family of the Holy Land, Geoffrey—like Philip of Novara and John of Ibelin—dedicated the last years of his life to composing juridical treatises, ca. 1265–70. In the series of books of assizes, Geoffrey's two treatises hold a secondary place, one containing 32 chapters, the other 19, devoted to questions of feudal law. Geoffrey complements Philip of

---

[116] Grandclaude (1923: 81–8); Richard (1952: 116–7); Edbury (1980; 1998a); Edbury's introduction to his edition of John of Ibelin, *Le Livre des Assises*.

[117] Greilsammer (1999: 243–5); Edbury in his introduction to John of Ibelin, *Le Livre des Assises*, 43–4.

Novara on some points and adds a few remarks that are more developed. As a whole it has the appearance of a collection of notes.[118]

The Livre de Jacques d'Ibelin: Of minor importance, this also discusses questions of feudal law. James of Ibelin, the son of John, dictated his book on his deathbed, in May-June 1276. The treatise resembles that of Geoffrey Le Tor in its conciseness and its methodical exposition, the two jurists having been inspired by John of Ibelin, whom they summarize, adding corrections concerning the secrecy that must surround the king's council and the ceremony of homage.[119]

Clef des Assises de la Haute Cour du royaume de Jérusalem et de Chypre: This is the title of a gathering of rubrics summarizing and, sometimes, correcting the *Livre de Jean d'Ibelin*. An anonymous author composed the work between 1286 and 1291. The treatise in summary form defends a conception of the law close to that of Geoffrey Le Tor and James of Ibelin, explaining it in a more analytic and synthetic style.[120]

Assises de la Cour des Bourgeois: This is a work on the law applicable to the bourgeoisie. Since its anonymous author was a member of the bourgeoisie of Acre, it is not a Cypriot production. M. Grandclaude dates the composition of the *Livre* to between 1229 and 1244, which J. Prawer prefers to narrow to 1240 and 1244, although according to C. Cahen and J. Riley-Smith the text only obtained its definitive form later, in the 1260s.[121] This *Livre* is the sole legal treatise on the practice of the courts of the viscounts and on the laws specific to the bourgeoisie, contemporary with similar texts produced in the West. It deals with judicial organisation, procedure, property, contracts, and the status of populations not of the Latin rite. Far from being a descendant of the customary law of the Latin East, the *Assises des Bourgeois* derive from *Lo Codi*, a treatise of Roman Law composed around 1150 in Arles. For more than half of the *Assises*' 297 chapters, *Lo Codi* is the inspiration for the author, who probably employed a Latin version of the Provençal treatise, adapted to the judicial practice of the Kingdom of Jerusalem. Thus in a roundabout way

---

[118] Geoffrey Le Tor, 'Livre de Geoffroy Le Tort'; Grandclaude (1923: 89–90, 148–9); Edbury (1990: 4291–7).

[119] James of Ibelin, 'Livre de Jacques d'Ibelin'; Grandclaude (1923: 148–9).

[120] 'La Clef des Assises'; Grandclaude (1923: 148–9).

[121] *Assises de la Cour des Bourgeois*; on the author and his work, see Grandclaude (1923: 50–70, 123–7); Richard (1953); Cahen (1963); Riley-Smith (1973: 85, 268); Prawer (1980: 358–72, 408–9).

the Greco-Roman juridical tradition acquired the force of law without borrowing directly from Byzantine law.[122]

The date of the introduction of the *Assises de la Cour des Bourgeois* in Cyprus has not been documented, but it would not have been much later than the date of its composition. Nor do we know the conditions that led to its translation into Greek. Three manuscripts of the text in Greek translation have been located so far.[123] The late date of these copies provides no clue for dating the translation, which logically appears nearly contemporary with the collection of the 'Greek Laws' of Paris. gr. 1391 and compilation of Vat. Palat. gr. 367, manuscripts composed between 1300 and 1320. The Greek translation follows the French text faithfully, and the terminology particular to the Latin institutions forced the translator to create neologisms that would pass into the Cypriot dialect ('αβαντάτζια', 'βισκουντάτον', 'προβελίτζια').[124] For the Greek subjects of the Frankish kingdom, this translation permitted the reconciliation of Greco-Roman and Byzantine law with the law of the *Assizes*. The Greco-Roman influence is felt in family and inheritance law in particular and applied to regulations for property ownership. The example of the assize on disinheritance, attributed to Baldwin II (1118–31), shows characteristics similar to Justinian's *Novellum* 115. One finds other borrowings from the *Procheiron*, the *Ekloge* of the Isaurians, and Syrian regulations.[125]

The Saterian of William of Saint-Étienne: The mania for codifying the law in Cyprus also infected the military orders, notably that of St John of Jerusalem. Relocating to Limassol after the loss of Acre, the Hospitallers obtained from William of Saint-Étienne a voluminous collection in which statutes and various documents on the history of the order are put together. William had begun the treatise in Acre in 1282, and in Limassol, while preceptor of the commandery of Cyprus, he took up the task again, recasting and enlarging the work. William finished his collection in September 1296, giving it the title *Saterian*, a French adaptation of *lex Saturiana* (a term used to designate laws refering to a variety of subjects).[126] Since it was composite and novel

---

[122] Grandclaude (1923: 123–7); Prawer (1980: 366–90).
[123] Nicolaou-Konnari (1999: 229–30, 232); Coureas in his introduction to his translation of the *Assizes*, 15–19.
[124] Sathas in his introduction to his edition of the Ασίζαι, 100–5; Chatziioannou (1964); Nicolaou-Konnari (1999: 229–33, 275–9).
[125] Zepos (1976b); Prawer (1980: 439–57); Papadopoullos (1976: 33–4).
[126] Delisle (1906); Riley-Smith (1967: 272–3).

in its overall form, William's text stands at the crossroads of legal, historical, and philosophical literature. As a historian, William borrowed from a *Continuation* of William of Tyre that he supplemented with other sources, scrupulously developing his collection. In the juridical section, he adopted a philosophical stance to explain the different origins of the laws (law of nature, law of custom, law of right understood as canon law). He illustrated his conception with quotations from the Church Fathers, from Gratian's *Decretum*, and finally from Cicero, whose *De inventione* William follows in the French translation of John of Antioch.[127] On the whole, the *Saterian*, despite flaws in internal organisation, allowed the Order of St John to fix its juridical and historical traditions in the aftermath of 1291. It also shows how William of Saint-Étienne shared his contemporaries' concern for preserving the memory of the institutions of the Latin East.

The Juridical Tradition after 1300

In the fourteenth century one finds both a long silence in legislative activity surrounding the High Court and a constant evolution in the defining of the law of the *bourgeois* and of the law of the Greek population of the kingdom. In the first case, after the *Livre de Jacques d'Ibelin*, we have no treatise that adds to the thinking on the *Assizes* of the High Court. The jurists, remaining anonymous, adapted the old treatises to the practice of the institutions and cultivated the tradition, copying or translating it, without moving forward in the definition of customary law. The troubled political conditions and the drift of the exercise of royal power toward absolute monarchy explain the silence concerning legislative activities and the decline in the elaboration of the law.[128] Just as significant for the evolution of institutions, the preservation of the laws that pertained specifically to the Greek community reveals the elevation of its status in the society of the Frankish kingdom.

The 'Greek Laws' and Vat. Palat. gr. 367

In the first two decades of the century the law specific to the Greeks was officialised. At the turn of the century the famous *Greek Laws* of

---

[127] Delisle (1906: 34–40); Ciggaar (1994: 95); Minervini (2002: 340).
[128] Grandclaude (1923: 17–18, 153–68); Edbury (1980: 227–9).

Paris. gr. 1391 were gathered together; a little later, around 1317/20, an officer of the chancery collected some texts in Vat. Palat. gr. 367; finally, the *Assises de la Cour des Bourgeois* was translated into Greek. This conjunction of dates does not prove that it was only around 1300 that the Greeks reached the point where they could legislate in matters of religious, commercial, or private law, but rather that the process of associating the Greeks in the affairs of the Latin kingdom was accelerated and fixed in written form. From May 1191 Richard the Lionheart granted the *archontes* the possibility of retaining the regulations and privileges that governed them in Byzantine times. The indications agree that the enterprise of translation and of defining the law of the Greeks should be attributed to the reigns of Henry II and Hugh IV.

The work contained in Paris. gr. 1391, composed for the bishop of Arsinoe/Paphos, belonged to the episcopal tribunal of that see and is certainly the work of a jurist. It contains a complete collection of laws intended for the practical use of the tribunals and includes a series of models of procedure. The book brings together extracts from Byzantine law collections (*Procheiron*, *Synopsis basilicorum major*, Michael Attaleiates, and the *Ekloge* of the *Novella* of Leo VI). It also contains a Greek translation of the *Constitutio* or *Bulla Cypria*, a poem dedicated to Michael Psellos, and a manual relating to the family and inheritance law of the Greeks. This manual, composed by an anonymous jurist, gives a series of detailed ordinances by presenting six booklets concerning engagement or marriage. Two series of booklets stand out, regarding rulings that are properly Cypriot, with extracts of the *Epitome legum* compiled ca. 920. The manual's originality lies in its development of certain aspects of Cypriot family law without immediate reference to Byzantine models, while still respecting the Greco-Roman conception of family law. Overall, the organisation reveals the intent of a jurist who is faithful to an ancient tradition and a purist who goes back to Justinian's *Code*.[129]

The compilation of Vat. Palat. gr. 367 provides a different example, showing the emergence of a Franco-Byzantine culture. The manuscript gathers together various documents, Greek or taken from Frankish/Latin models, profane or religious, offering a rather vast panorama of the interests and tastes of members of the Greek chancery of the

---

[129] Simon; Maruhn.

Lusignans. An analysis of the juridical documents reveals the care taken to reproduce known formulae for the establishment of notarial acts and official letters. One finds formulae for wills, privileges, or inventories mixed with models of correspondence between the magnates of the kingdom or of the Orthodox world. Other letters and acts done by the Greek religious officials or monks attest to the participation of the ecclesiastical hierarchy in the election of Greek bishops and, more generally, to the juridical arrangements regarding the Greek population of the realm. The gathering of heterogeneous documents displays the practical concerns of the scribe, who classifies notarial formulae or official letters.[130] This taxinomical effort is combined with a desire to clarify procedure, a tendency that the scribe shared with the Latin jurisconsults in their *Livres du Plédéant et du Plaidoyer*.

The Livres du Plédéant et du Plaidoyer

Attributed to the same anonymous author, the *Livre du Plédéant* and the *Livre du Plaidoyer* were written in the middle of the fourteenth century and are collectively known as 'Abrégé du livre des Assises de la cour des Bourgeois'. The two books both tackle questions of private law and clarify the measures in the *Assises de la Cour des Bourgeois*. The *Livre du Plédéant* devotes its 40 chapters to the organisation of the bourgeois courts, while the *Livre du Plaidoyer* treats the rules of procedure, reproducing formulae and extracts from the treatises of jurisconsults. Constructed according to a logical scheme, the two treatises explain the procedure of bourgeois jurisdictions and testify to a progression in the definition of points of law. The discussion follows the method of the jurisconsults of the previous century, since the subjects of dispute are discussed by making references to earlier works.[131]

The Aftermath of the Revolution of 1369

By shunning the law of the *Assizes*, King Peter I incited the wrath of the liegemen, who carried out his assassination. Very quickly, the regicide was presented as the vassals' response to the arbitrary rule of the king. A few hours after his death, the nobles gathered in coun-

---

[130] References in Constantinides and Browning, *Dated Greek Manuscripts*, 153–65.
[131] 'Abrégé', 229–92 ('Le Livre du Plédéant'), 293–352 ('Le Livre du Plaidoyer'); Grandclaude (1923: 90–2, 168–70).

· cil and issued their grievances in an ordinance that demanded the strict application of the regulations of the *Assizes* and that decreed that the *Livre de Jean d'Ibelin* would be the official code of the kingdom. A committee of six liegemen was set up on 16 November 1369 to establish a new redaction of the treatise, intended to be the official text. To accomplish this task, they collected the different manuscripts to determine the more complete reading, then they collated the text, appending various acts.[132] Nevertheless this updating of certain rulings was done from a conservative perspective, since a reformulation of written law was not considered, but only the immutability of tradition, in spite of the paradox of establishing as the code a treatise of jurisprudence composed a century before.[133]

Genealogical Literature

Complementary and contemporary with the codification of feudal custom, genealogical literature took shape, ca. 1268/70, in the form of a catalogue of notices devoted to the great families of the Kingdom of Jerusalem, gathered under the title *Lignages d'Outremer*.[134] The different versions of the first compilation, set down in the circle of the Ibelins in order to complement the juridical treatise of John of Ibelin, created an original genre that developed afterwards in the form of new lists, all retaining the title *Lignages d'Outremer*, with supplementary notices. Thus an inventory that is rather different from the first was composed around 1305/06, serving as the nucleus for the versions that would enrich it down to 1458. In total, more than a thousand people are mentioned in the successive versions.

Conceived in order to clarify the chapters on the transmission of fiefs contained in the treatises on the *Assizes* of the High Court, and often attached to the *Livre de Jean d'Ibelin*, the *Lignages d'Outremer* established kinship ties, making an inventory for each family, a list of names without philological pretension. The text sometimes pays particular attention to persons dying without heirs and to successions through the female line, but it omits reference to the case of the revolt against royal power and passes over in silence the juridical activities of the

---

[132] Cf. Edbury's conclusion in his edition of John of Ibelin, *Le Livre des Assises*, 18–19, and the texts in 'Appendix 7' of the same edition.
[133] Grandclaude (1923: 161–2, 165–6); Richard (1952: 108–11, 115–18).
[134] *Lignages d'Outremer*.

jurisconsults. Despite these silences, genealogical literature emerges at
the moment the Kingdom of Jerusalem suffers serious military rever-
sals. This historical context explains the urgency to fix the order of
succession for each line. For the compiler, the only thing of importance was the blood of crusading families. No Greek line is mentioned,
although there is an Armenian version of the text deriving from the
original French one.[135]

Philip of Novara

Philip of Novara was born at the end of the twelfth century, no doubt,
and under unknown circumstances he left his native Lombardy and
headed to the Latin East. He then became a vassal of the Ibelins,
with whom he maintained a close relationship until the end of his
life, particularly during the Civil War between the Ibelin family and
their supporters and Frederick II. In his memoirs, Philip presents
himself as a man of action, who played a decisive role during the
events. His life after 1243 remains obscure because that year ends
Philip's narrative of the 'War of the Lombards', which he began
writing in 1247.[136] It seems that he devoted the end of his life to the
composition of his autobiography or memoirs and of his manual on
jurisprudence. Finally, at the age of 70, Philip wrote a moral treatise.
Thus, Philip of Novara wrote three separate works: the first one is
presented in the form of an autobiography, in which poems, love songs,
a narrative on the 'War of the Lombards' accompanied by more
poems and songs of religious inspiration are included; the second book
contains his legal writings; and the third is the moral treatise *Des.IIII.
tenz d'aage d'ome*. Consequently, Philip's writings encompass different
literary genres and establish him as a universal spirit of his time.

The Literary Works

Only a fragment survives from the first collection, the narrative of the
war between the Ibelins and Frederick II. This fragment comes down
to us in a copy made in 1343 from the modified version included

---

[135] Nielen in her introduction to the *Lignages d'Outremer*.
[136] For a recent survey on his life, see Melani in his edition of Philip of Novara,
Guerra, 36–45.

LITERATURE 259

in the *Gestes des Chiprois* after 1310. Thus, the global conception of Philip's first book would have escaped us completely if Michel Zink had not reconstituted the initial project.[137] It seems, thus, that Philip composed a volume divided in different parts, the main unifying principle being his subjective point of view and a monodic narration. With variations in form (prose/verse) and in narrative perspective (autobiography/chronicle), Philip relates the principal events of his life from different approaches: the autobiographical section traces his education and his youth, while the memoirs give an account of his age of maturity, when the man confronted his world, and the religious songs illustrate the concerns of the old man.

Philip's life provides the material for the first book, in which he gives an account of his acts and deeds, passions and fears, without once attempting to be objective. Given this perspective, the fragment of his memoirs on the Civil War tells us more about Philip's feelings than about the actual situation during the years 1229–33;[138] Philip's *vérité* explains his commitment to the Ibelins, something which confers an apologetic character to his narrative. Philip builds his narrative on a detailed chronology of the events that led to the conflict. The memorialist uses the notes he took during the conflict, sources he found in the local archives, and letters which are sometimes wholly reproduced. The discussions are presented in the form of passionate dialogues, the use of the direct discourse intensifying the dramatic character of the context. The meeting between Philip of Ibelin and Frederick II in Limassol demonstrates how Philip of Novara translates antagonisms into a Manichean portrayal of the *dramatis personae*. He does not understand the quarrel in terms of the political oppositions, but he interprets it as a power struggle between two men, one symbolising justice and legitimacy, the other the pretensions of a tyrant.[139] For Philip, this war is the expression of the fight between good and evil, his conception of history founded on Christian and chivalrous values. The narrative abounds with cases where respect for institutions is celebrated against the law of arms imposed by the emperor. He praises the honour of knightly lineage, both for the dignity acquired through acknowledged merits and for the capacity to maintain a transferable landed patrimony. Finally, the renunciation of the material

[137] Zink (1985: 207–21).
[138] Last edition by Melani, see Philip of Novara, *Guerra*.
[139] Philip of Novara, *Guerra*, §31 (127).

life is conceived as a first step towards repentance preceding the taking of orders before death; this is how John of Ibelin behaves, an example of moral and religious integrity, while Frederick II is excommunicated for his misdeeds.

In relating his memoirs, Philip reveals original literary qualities that go beyond the simple genre of the epic poem.[140] With regard to previous chronicles, Philip breaks from the narrative style in prose by interpolating five poems (*rimes*) in various episodes.[141] This versification shows his ability to use octosyllable, sometimes the Alexandrine or the decasyllable, and even the *sirventois*. Evidently, Philip was in the process of developing his poetic techniques, and one may doubt his natural aptitude for the art of poetry. To the extent that these *rimes* cover themes and episodes already treated in prose, Philip confers a higher value on poetic language than on epic narration, while also introducing a playful and burlesque dimension in a narrative glorifying knighthood.[142]

Indeed, French literature provides Philip with ample material to produce an allegory that constitutes a ferocious satire of his enemies: his source of inspiration is the *Roman de Renart*.[143] The two opposing factions in Cyprus are defined according to the French prototype: the *bailli* Aimery Barlais, condemned for his wicked acts, becomes *Renart*, his cousin Amaury of Bethsan, *Grimbert*. In the Ibelin party, the wolf *Ysengrin*, the enemy of *Renart*, incarnates the lord of Beirut, and the wolf-cubs, the Ibelin sons; as far as Philip of Novara is concerned, he keeps for himself the role of the cock *Chantecler*, a herald distinguished 'both by his song and by his prowess on the field of battle' ('à la fois par son chant et par ses prouesses sur le champ de bataille').[144] The battle locations are also placed in the framework of the imaginary geography of the *Roman de Renart* and the island's castles are transformed into *Maucreux* or *Maupertuis*.[145] On three occasions Philip casts the animals of the *Roman de Renart* in the role of the narrator who relates in verse the events of the war: before the castle of St Hilarion, where the narrator is blessed; at the siege of Kantara, where the narrator is present; and, finally, in the 220-octosyllable

---

[140] Bromiley (1998).
[141] Philip of Novara, *Guerra*, §§47 (143), 51 (147), 54–5 (150–1), 57 (153).
[142] Zink (1985: 208); Aslanoff (1997).
[143] Philip of Novara, *Guerra*, §§47 (143), 57 (153), 111 (207).
[144] Flinn (1963: 163–4).
[145] Philip of Novara, *Guerra*, §§54 (150), 57 (153); Flinn (1963: 160–4).

burlesque poem entitled 'C'est la rime de Renart, come Yzengrin le desconfist', in which the chronicler claims that he has written a new branch of the *Roman,* thus revealing his talent. Henceforth, the animals act on their own and become protagonists. The endless dispute between *Renart* and his enemies allows Philip to expose the qualities and the flaws of the various characters, condemning *Renart*'s wickedness, jealousy, and hypocrisy, praising *Yzengrin's* wisdom, perspicacity, and loyalty. The transposition of the intrigues of the *Roman de Renart* into the Cypriot historical context demonstrates the *érudition renardesque* of Philip, who draws from various branches of the *Roman.*[146]

The Cypriot knights are also imbued with the *renardesque* tradition, as shown by John of Ibelin's answer to the bishop of Sidon in Acre in the spring of 1233, when the latter asks John to recognize the emperor's authority. John of Ibelin makes use of a long parable based on a story drawn from the fabliaux of *Renart,* in which the emperor is associated with the wolf and John with the stag.[147] Philip borrows two more examples from the French literary tradition that bear similarities with the Cypriot reality, one from the *Chanson de Roland,* when *Renart* is compared to the traitor Ganelon, and the other from the Arthurian Cycle, when the chronicler stresses that the Ibelin family organised a feast during which one 'contrefait les aventures de Bretaigne et de la Table Reonde'.[148]

The Legal Writing

The *Livre de forme de plait* is available in only one edition, that of 1841, and Maurice Grandclaude and Peter Edbury have pointed out its main shortcomings.[149] The published text is a version reviewed and corrected by Philip, who intended to recast definitively the original material, a task that was never carried out. Philip left us two works of jurisprudence: first, the *Livre de forme de plait,* composed of 89 chapters and concerning the Cypriot institutions, the first draft of which was written between 1252 and 1257 and revised a few years later; second, the text of ten answers to various plaintiffs seeking legal advice from him.

---

[146] Philip of Novara, *Guerra,* §57 (153); Flinn (1963: 172); Jacoby (1984b: 626).
[147] Philip of Novara, *Guerra,* §111 (207); Flinn (1963: 173).
[148] Philip of Novara, *Guerra,* §§16 (112), 54 (150); Loomis (1939: 79–80); Jacoby (1984b: 626–8).
[149] Philip of Novara, 'Livre'; Grandclaude (1923: 70–6); Edbury (2001b).

In both cases, Philip's goal is to restore the spirit of the old assizes
lost after the disappearance of the mythical *Lettres du Sépulcre* in 1187.
He inaugurates the kingdom's juristic school by composing a treatise whose example other jurisconsults would recall for many years
to come. Philip conceives the *Livre de forme de plait* as a private treatise aimed at teaching the profession of pleading to a friend, most
probably John of Ibelin, count of Jaffa.[150] In the first section, he
gathers the procedural rules on how to initiate proceedings and to
conduct a lawsuit. Philip then attempts to recover the principal assizes
from past memory, indicating for each one the points of litigation
and the solutions proposed by the main jurisconsults of the time. He
concludes with the moral and intellectual qualities rightly claimed
by the profession of the advocate. In the ten answers he gives on
the occasion of legal consultations, Philip continues his traditionalist
approach by dealing with the assizes or offering executory formulae.

The practical guidebook that Philip assembled can be considered
a success. The jurist knows how to start from specific cases in order
to extract rules of procedure and to explain the meaning of the
assizes, before examining the difficulties encountered in their application.
His ability to set forth and analyse the various arguments does not
involve an original appreciation of the legal material, because Philip
solves the litigation problems by systematically taking recourse to the
opinions of his peers, to whom he pays his highest compliments. The
Livre de forme de plait's lack of originality reveals the place that Philp
wishes to hold in the legal history of the Latin kingdom: he revives
the *Assises de Jérusalem*, reestablishes usages, and restores the memory
of his contemporary jurisconsults to maintain the continuity of a tradition threatened, if not with disappearance, at least with profound
changes. Not once does Philip envisage a modification of the ancient
principles of jurisprudence. He sees himself as the guardian of a customary practice that he wants to pass on to future generations by
reproducing the ancient models.

Undoubtedly, the clarity of his intent is blurred by a heavy style
which is at times confusing, probably because his treatise was partially rewritten towards the end of his life, when the author showed
obvious signs of senility. The principles of certain arguments that
Philip put forward were also contested, notably by John of Ibelin,

---

[150] Philip of Novara, 'Livre', 475–6; Edbury in his introduction to John of Ibelin,
Livre des Assises.

and the *Livre de forme de plait* would, in the end, have only a weak echo in subsequent legal works.[151]

The Moral Work

The ethical concerns that sustained Philip in his autobiographical and legal works prepared the way for the author to devote the last years of his life to the composition of a moral treatise, *Des .IIII. tenz d'aage d'om*.[152] As early as the *Livre de forme de plait*, two chapters containing thoughts on wisdom and science already announced the treatise. Philip's aim is strikingly simple and coherent: he intends to present the moral precepts that should guide a man through the four periods of his life—*anfance, jovent, moien aage, viellesce*—, each period counting twenty years, according to a tradition that goes back to Pythagoras and Bede, but which may also be found in an Arabic text, the *Secret of Secrets*, a text that was widely available in its Latin translation by Philip of Tripoli, active in the Latin East between 1225 and 1267.[153] The treatise concludes with three parts given *postscriptum*; they comprise a chronological scale adjusted to the preceding remarks, a long passage giving advice on the four values common to the four ages of life, and a general summing up of the rules stated before. The entire work ends with a short poem of mediocre quality.

The treatise opens with thoughts on childhood. In the introduction, Philip recalls the Christian model of education. From the most tender age, a child should be taught obedience to God and his parents, and love for his fellow men. He must be given a profession, preferably a worthy one—a cleric or a knight—with the prospect of attaining the rank of master. Naturally, a young knight's education involves the principles of high and noble culture, aiming at the acquisition of generosity, *cortoisie*, and a taste for rhetoric. In order to achieve this, the young knight should learn 'the histories and the books of authors in which there is much that is well said, and good advice, and great sense' ('les estoires et les livres des autors ou il a mout de biaus diz, et de bons consaus, et de granz senz '). Philip advises that children should not be allowed to play and that young girls should be kept under tight control: 'One should not teach a woman to read

---

[151] Florio Bustron, *Historia*, 8; Grandclaude (1923: 134–5).
[152] Philip of Novara, *Les quatre âges de l'homme*.
[153] Minervini (1995: 166); Paravicini Bagliani (1999: 9–12).

or write' ('A fame ne doit apanre letres ne escrire'). Philip demonises
women who, through carnal contact, bring dishonour upon a house;
does not the proverb declare that 'one cannot give venom to a snake,
because it already has too much' ('au serpent ne puet on doner
venin, car trop en i a')?[154]

Youth, from 20 to 40 years of age, is considered to be the most
dangerous period in a man's life. Lack of judgement and consciousness
as well as the temptation of sins threaten to ruin the young man.
Philip condemns insulting behaviour towards the poor and preaches
obedience to the suzerain and respect for hierarchy, since adults are
in possession of power and wisdom. A young man's aim should be
the achievement of exploits and the acquisition of wealth in order to
secure his old age and build a transferable patrimony. A man's most
valuable wealth, however, 'is to marry a woman to whom God has
given the grace of good repute and of bearing good children' ('est
de fame espouser, a cui Dieus a doné grace de bone fame avoir, et
des bons anfanz engendrer'). Young girls were in a disadvantageous
position because of the morals of the era, since one had to prevent
a woman from committing adultery; 'It is different for men, because
with regard to the sin, it is the great one of vain glory, so that it
might be or might be said that they have pretty girlfriends, or young
ones, or rich ones' ('Autrement est des homes: car, comment qu'il
soit dou pechié, il ont une grant vainne gloire, que l'an dit ou seit
que il ont beles amies, ou jones, ou riches').[155] Compared to the disgrace that befalls the family of an immoral woman, a young man
can atone for his carnal sins by repentance. Thus, Philip conforms
with the rule according to which society punishes women, while religion saves men.

During adulthood, that is to say from 40 to 60 years of age, a man
has to consolidate and expand his possessions, a necessary condition
if he wants to feed his children; he also has to procreate a line of
descent and live honourably, giving alms to the poor. *Moien aage* brings
a man wisdom and he becomes an example of courtesy, justice, and
humility for those around him. Three rules open the doors of par-
adise: acquire one's wealth honestly, serve God, and respect every-
one else's life and feelings. An adult must use his mind to distinguish
good from evil and must reject presumptuousness, arrogance, and

---

[154] Philip of Novara, *Les quatre âges de l'homme*, 13, 16, 17.
[155] Philip of Novara, *Les quatre âges de l'homme*, 46, 50.

treachery. Moreover, Philip gives a long, often repetitive list of the qualities and flaws one has to take into consideration. Consequently, the moral obligations Philip preaches are those of his century and allow very little room for personal elaboration. In his set of exhortations, Philip adds long paragraphs intended for women; their condition should not make them neglect their duties of abstinence, honour, their children's education, and simplicity in everyday life. Those who prefer lust will be abandoned by their lovers when their beauty fades and will be spurned by God and society.

Old age is placed within the context of penitence and repentance, because the elderly man should think about saving his soul, even if it entails despising mundane things. He must be very careful to avoid sin, especially lust, arrogance, and greed if he is poor, because old age renders men imperfect and then detestable. Philip emphasises the shame that befalls lustful old men who take young wives, and the disgrace that follows lustful old women who apply make-up to conceal their decrepitude.

Considered as a whole, Philip's moral treatise is rich in lessons. Nevertheless, it remains difficult to understand fully because the chapters devoted to the *moien aage* and the *viellesce* do not possess the structural clarity of the first parts. Philip displays signs of senility when he multiplies repetitions. The *post-scriptum* parts contribute nothing to his argumentation, but only show how, 'with one foot in the grave' ('sor l'orle de sa fosse'),[156] Philip is no longer in a position to master either reason or expression.

Could this treatise be considered a personal work? Charles-Victor Langlois answered affirmatively, arguing that Philip did not borrow from the usual sources employed by medieval authors of moral treatises.[157] This is a valid argument in so far as Philip does not refer to Christian or Latin authors. On the other hand, his treatise abounds in extracts from romances, citations of proverb, and references to the values of his era. Again, one discerns a peculiar lack of originality in words that aim at perfect harmony with the morality of feudal Christian society.[158] Both in his treatise and in the *Livre de forme de plait*, Philip appears to be very conservative with respect to the traditions and principles that governed the Frankish kingdom.

---

[156] Philip of Novara, *Les quatre âges de l'homme*, 35, according to Philip's own words.
[157] Langlois (1908: 188–9, 219).
[158] Charpentier (1989).

In the name of a conventional Christian morality, the only criticisms expressly stated are directed against the rich burgesses who harass the poor, the powerful who are described as donkeys, and the lust that invaded Cypriot society.

Another interesting aspect of this treatise is the way Philip makes use of the cultural references of his time to construct his discourse. The frequent proverbial formulae are treated as proofs of further authority that reinforce the words. Philip draws from this popular wisdom, transmitted through the proverbs: 'Cuidier n'est pas savoir', 'De jone saint, viel diable', 'Qui tout covoite tout pert', 'Mesure dure'. Philip further illustrates his text using allegories, parables, or examples borrowed from tales or medieval romances; the material for his *exempla* derive from romances (*Lancelot, Alexandre le Grand, Roman de Troie, Barlaam et Josaphat*) and from oral tradition.[159]

Philip of Novara's moral work does not contribute anything new to our understanding of the author. Conservative at heart, he adhered to the values of the society to which he belonged. He defended its moral tenets and its cultural referents. In developing the precepts that must guide a man in his life, Philip intended to compose a work of reference, always from a didactic perspective and at a moment when philosophical debates made their appearance in Cypriot literature. Until his death, Philip was a spokesman for Frankish noble society, both in terms of its preoccupations and its means of expression.

Moral Literature and Philosophy

A concern with the life of man and the individual's place in society was one thing that Latin and Greek authors had in common. Philip of Novara began this trend, for his moral treatise found an echo in John of Journy twenty years later. In contrast, the Greeks derived their sources from the Byzantine capital, proof that the intellectual currents between Constantinople and Cyprus were reinforced. Although intended for distinct publics, the two moral systems met in the court of Hugh IV.

---

[159] Ciggaar (1994: 93).

John of Journy's Dîme de pénitance

The author of the longest poem written in French in the Kingdom of Cyprus (3296 verses) left no mark either on medieval literature or on political history. John of Journy belonged to a family originating in Artois that took up the cross in the twelfth or thirteenth century and, according to the *Lignages d'Outremer*, acquired a certain renown, forming marriage alliances with noble houses. Thus John of Journy wed Euphemia, daughter of John of Soissons, and another member of the family, Enguerran of Journy, played a prominent role in the 1270s, representing Hugh III at the Second Council of Lyons (1274). We have no further information about the person of John of Journy, who completed his poem, *La Dîme de pénitance*, in Nicosia in 1288.[160]

The subject of John of Journy's poem is the penance that humanity must perform for God, the 'tithe' that John wishes to pay. For illustration, John uses—and misuses—allegory, comparing God to a fountain that washes away the filth of sin, in particular sin from carnal pleasures. One obtains redemption by cultivating humility, a virtue allowing a person to acknowledge his sins and reach salvation and grace, overcoming evil with good works. The only path of justice is through penance, and John launches into long discussions on the regular practice of contrition, confession, and atonement. Contrition is compared to a detergent that brushes painfully the dirty linen, leading the sinner to confession, an aspect that receives more attention. One must confess to the local parish priest frequently. John describes how to confess, specifying that the sinner must admit his faults spontaneously, rather than reply to the priest's interrogation. To help the sinner identify his offences, Journy lists the various capital sins, arguing that it is best to evaluate sins according to their gravity rather than their nature. Thus he shares Philip of Novara's opinion when he declares that, for the sin of lust, the older the culprit the more serious the sin.[161] Journy tries to elucidate what motivates a person to commit a crime, to determine the degree of premeditation in each act and to understand the circumstances of the sin. Having made his confession, the sinner receives his penance from the priest, which allows him to atone.[162]

---

[160] John of Journy, *La Dîme de pénitance*; Payen (1967: 569–76).
[161] John of Journy, *La Dîme de pénitance*, lines 1705ff.; Philip of Novara, *Les quatre âges de l'homme*, 95–6.
[162] Payen (1967: 569–74).

Having instructed his reader about the sacrament of penitence, John of Journy returns to the issue of man's struggle against the Enemy, flesh and the world. The poem ends with a long prayer inspired by the desperate state of the Holy Land. John of Journy admires Henry II's war effort, but the precarious military situation in the Latin East leads him to pray for the pope, the emperor and the Western rulers, the king of Armenia, the prince of Antioch, the lord of Tyre, and King Henry.[163]

A work written for Franks, the *Dîme de pénitance* exhorts the reader to practice confession. This sacrament, which was imposed on the West after the Fourth Lateran Council (1215), seems to have been gaining ground in the Latin East as well, and John of Journy attempts to render the penitent capable of appreciating the gravity of his acts through self-conscious effort. In the context of Cypriot culture, John illustrates the degree that high religious culture had penetrated the laity, using traditional sources of the time, such as the *Summae* of Thomas of Chobham and Raymond Peñafort.

Other elements, this time drawn from a secular tradition, also emerge in the poem, for example, proverbial quotations, as when John of Journy repeats the saying that Philip of Novara favoured, 'Mesure dure'. A taste for courtly life and beautiful speech is also evident.[164] To this lay culture, John adds a deep knowledge of the Bible, quoting patristic sources and referring to Cicero and Proclus. Nevertheless, despite his wish to place his poem in a scholarly tradition, John seems to have a secondhand knowledge of literary works, something that renders his poem only superficially learned. Instead of quoting classical writers, Journy borrows heavily from a popular work, the Pseudo-Augustinian treatise *De vera et falsa paenitentia*.[165] He is also inspired by the prayers contained in a French parish ceremonial book, reproducing its sequence of arguments and exhortations and adjusting the liturgical text to his literary needs.

In the next century, moral literature would expand to include works that approach more the spirit of didactic models developed by ecclesiastical writers, as is attested by an anonymous manual of confession, inspired by the *Somme du Roi*, a work composed by the friar Lawrence of Bois in 1279.[166] We cannot follow the evolution of this

---

[163] John of Journy, *La Dîme de pénitance*, lines 2985–3265.
[164] John of Journy, *La Dîme de pénitance*, lines 2828, 3100.
[165] Payen (1967: 572–3).
[166] Brayer (1947).

literary tradition after 1300. Nevertheless, after 1291 Cyprus became a substitute destination for those obliged to undertake an expiatory pilgrimage. The island welcomed penitent pilgrims, but there is no written testimony that would illustrate the evolution of the practice of penance.

Between Religion and Philosophy

Although following the progress of moral literature in Cyprus is relatively easy, tracing the course of philosophical thought on the island is a much more difficult task. This is because, on the one hand, evidence is lacking and, on the other, it is difficult to trace the borderline between religious production and pure philosophical thought.

The Catalan thinker and poet Raymond Lull stayed in Cyprus between August and December 1301, when the Franciscan was 60 years old. The news that the Mongolian army had arrived in Syria caused his departure for Cyprus, and his arrival in the East must be placed in the context of his numerous projects for a crusade against Islam, projects that Lull never ceased planning until the end of his life. As soon as he arrived in Cyprus, the Franciscan was informed of the failure of the alliance with the Mongols. He then attempted to convince Henry II to implement a project involving the conversion of the kingdom's heretics and schismatics (Jacobites, Nestorians), a proposal that the king discarded. Ill, or perhaps poisoned, Lull was hospitalised at the monastery of St John Chrysostomos, where he composed a rhetorical treatise, completed in September. He was then cordially received by the grand master of the Temple in Limassol, only to move on to Famagusta, where, in December, he composed a philosophical treatise. In January 1302, Lull proceeded to Ayas and finally returned to Majorca.[167]

The two works that Lull authored on the island are part of a literary production born in Cyprus by merely accidental circumstances. The Franciscan confirms that his treatise on logic is part of his *Arte general*, but this treatise, entitled *Liber de natura*, owes to its Cypriot background peculiarities of thinking related to a debate with monophysite Christians. These exchanges allowed Lull to formalise the differences between the divine and human natures of Christ in order

---

[167] On Lull's visit in Cyprus: Golubovich (1906–1927, I: 368–9); Delaville Le Roulx (1886: 27–32); Llinares (1963: 112–5); Platzeck (1964, I: 30–1).

to refute opposing errors.[168] In the second treatise, the *Rhetorica nova*, written in Catalan, Lull applied himself to explaining the art and technique of persuasion.[169] These two treatises, of minor importance in Lull's huge literary production, most probably did not circulate at all in Cyprus. Nevertheless, the Catalan master supplied enough material to sustain discussions justifying the undertaking of new crusades or the conversion of the island's monophysites.

Making the acquaintance of the kingdom's powerful men, Lull received the support of the Templars, a proof that his projects were welcomed by the military orders. In this respect, the role played by the Hospitallers seems to have been very important, since several members of their commandery in Cyprus wrote or urged others to write philosophical works. William of Saint-Étienne, a knight in Acre in 1282, incited the Hospitaller John of Antioch in Acre in 1282 to translate into French two works, grouped together under the title *Rettorique de Marc Tulles Cyceron*, of which only the *De inventione* belongs to the Latin philosopher. Considered to be an exemplary translation for its respect of the original text, this *Rettorique* marks the beginning in the Latin East of a translation movement into vernacular languages, a movement that originated earlier in Italy but that appears to be very new in the context of French-language literature. William of Saint-Étienne used this translation for his *Saterian*, including in it extracts in order to support his thesis on the nature and origin of laws (see above).[170]

Simon le Rat, a Hospitaller who lived on the island from 1299 to 1310, commissioned the French translation of a Latin psalter to Master Peter of Paris, probably a Venetian citizen. Peter of Paris seems to have enjoyed a certain renown since three of his translations have survived; apart from the Psalms, Peter of Paris translated Aristotle's *Politics*, again from Latin into French, and then, a little later, the *Consolatio Philosophiae* by Boethius, which he completed with comments. There exists some uncertainty as to the place where the translation was executed. It may have been Cyprus, but evidence suggests that it was probably France or Genoa, where the manuscript was

---

[168] Ramon Lull, *Liber de natura*.
[169] Ramon Lull, *Rhetorica Nova*; Golubovich (1906–1927 I: 369); Llinares (1963: 431); Platzeck (1964, II: 40).
[170] Delisle (1906); Monfrin (1964: 224–6); Riley-Smith (1967: 32–3, 36, 272–3); Minervini (1995: 167; 2002: 340).

copied in 1309. This translation, which was strongly criticised for its
poor linguistic qualities, contains notes according to which Peter of
Paris was also the author of a philosophical treatise dedicated to the
lord of Tyre, undoubtedly Amaury of Lusignan, King Henry II's
brother. The content of the treatise remains unknown, but the notes
of the translation of the *Consolatio* inform us that in the treatise Peter
discussed man's free will, the nature of marriage, and the relation
between *littera* and *expositio*.[171] Thus, at the beginning of the fourteenth
century, a philosophical tradition emerged in Cyprus combining a
translation movement with the writing of original treatises, and hence
preparing the ground for the discussions that would enliven Hugh IV's
court.

The Cypriot Spaneas

At the beginning of the fourteenth century, Greek men of letters
also demonstrated a vivid interest in moral, religious, and philosophical
issues. A didactic poem in the vernacular, included in the compilation
that survives in Vat. Palat. gr. 367 and known in the literary tradition
under the title *Spaneas*, bears witness to these intellectual tastes.[172] The
anonymous author presents himself as an elderly man whose public
life has ended in failure in exile. From the place where he is banished,
the old man writes a long poem in the form of a moral treatise for
his son, in which the author includes many exhortations aiming at
the young man's education and instruction. His advice concerns the
crime of blasphemy, the dangers involved in criticising the emperor,
the meaning of friendship, controlling one's tongue, prayer, virtue,
wealth, poverty, and the respect owed to one's superior. The poem,
composed in the twelfth century and of dubious literary quality, is
divided into three parts, drawing its arguments from Scripture or
from Pseudo-Isocrates. Easy to understand, the instructions of *Spaneas*
are addressed to a large audience and so it enjoyed uninterrupted
public success down to modern times. In the fourteenth century the
text was copied and reworked and several versions survive in Southern
Italy, Serbia, and Cyprus.[173]

---

[171] Thomas (1923); Ciggaar (1994: 94–5); Minervini (2002: 340).
[172] The Cypriot version was edited by Lampros in 1917; see 'Spaneas'.
[173] Danezis (1987).

Within the *Spaneas* tradition, the Cypriot version is considered complete, without significant deviations from the original.[174] The Cypriot version is marked by the use of learned expressions and archaic grammatical forms, a conventional style using affected and rare terms. The classicising aspect of the Cypriot *Spaneas* does not preclude the phonetic transcription of certain words according to the pronunciation of the Cypriot dialect. These features demonstrate that the author of the Cypriot version reconciled the fidelity to the Byzantine text with a demotic expression concealed beneath a certain literary pretention. The *inscriptio* of the Cypriot *Spaneas* reveals that the authorship of the poem is attributed to a certain George, 'γραμματικόν του ρηγικού σεκρέτου'. This reference to an official of the secrète shows the diffusion of Byzantine culture amongst the Greek personnel of the Lusignan chancery. Consequently, by appropriating a Byzantine model, at the beginning of the fourteenth century Cyprus participated in the vernacular medieval Greek literary tradition. There can be no doubt that this admonitory literary genre enjoyed an important success in learned circles since it had a direct impact on George Lapithes.

George Lapithes

We possess only fragmentary biographical information on George Lapithes, gleaned from his correspondence with Byzantine scholars between 1336 and 1351. Gregory Akindynos, Barlaam the Calabrian, Nicephoros Gregoras, Yacinthos, metropolitan of Thessaloniki, and Irene-Eulogia Choumnaina praised his knowledge and his depth. An important epistolizer and a teacher of Scripture, Lapithes was also a rich landowner with a beautiful residence where he enjoyed entertaining philosophers and people of every religion and of every tongue. He himself knew Latin, discussed Latin beliefs, and frequented the royal court where he participated in philosophical and theological debates.[175] A respected and influential figure, George Lapithes became involved in the Hesychast controversy, siding with the anti-Palamites of Thessalonike and Constantinople, giving them unreserved support

---

[174] Spadaro (1986); Danezis (1986–1987).

[175] Gregoras, *Correspondance*, 344–6 and *Epistulae*, 406–11; Akyndinos, *Letters*, nos. 10, 42, 44–7, 60; Loenertz (1957: 90–1); Meyendorff (1959: 67, 126–7); Kyrris (1962: 23–4); Tsolakis (1964); Pingree (1976); Darrouzès (1979: 39–41); Sinkewicz (1981); Karzopilos (1981–1982); Danezis (1986–1987).

from Cyprus. Being an accomplished scholar, Lapithes possessed several talents that allowed him to translate or compose texts, of which few have survived. We know that he wrote several treatises against Gregory Palamas and against the Latins that have been lost. There survive three letters to Nicephoros Gregoras, three fragments of theological works, a translation of a Latin astronomical treatise adapted from Arabic, a treatise on the seven sacraments, and a long didactic poem.[176]

Unconnected to the anti-Palamite controversy, George Lapithes composed a poem in the form of a spiritual guide in 1490 political verses. These *Στίχοι πολιτικοί αὐτοσχέδιοι εἰς τὴν ἀκοήν* offer a number of practical rules on how one should behave in private and in public, thus following the tradition of *Spaneas*. *Spaneas* inspires Lapithes, since he reproduces almost 140 of its verses, even if he does not borrow verbatim. The way he uses *Spaneas*, paraphrasing the Byzantine text or translating vernacular expressions into the learned language, is exceptional in the Cypriot literary tradition. The resemblance is not limited to linguistic and stylistic modifications, which have an affected result and add no real literary value to the poem. Lapithes' moral exhortations, like those in *Spaneas*, concern respect for authority and the virtuous life according to the spirit of Orthodoxy, as well as more general issues, such as the nature of man, justice, family, and friendship.[177]

George Lapithes also translated religious and scientific texts from Latin into Greek. David Pingree has identified him as the astronomer who, using a Latin manuscript, was responsible for the Greek version of the *Toledan Tables*, based on a now-lost Arabic original composed in the eleventh century, providing the necessary data for calculating the movements of the planets. The extant Greek text is an autograph penned in Cyprus in the 1330s. Apart from the translator's technical competence, it displays the scientific culture of a scholar who himself comments on various passages and compares his text with other astronomical treatises, such as Claudius Ptolemy's *Almagest*, a famous work in the medieval world, and the *Alphonsine Tables*, which became known in the West thanks to the different versions established by

---

[176] *PG*, CXLIX, cols. 1010–46; Gregoras, *Epistulae*, 406–11; Tsolakis (1964: 85, 94–6); Pingree (1976); Darrouzès (1979: 97–113).
[177] Danezis (1986–1987).

Parisian astronomers in the 1320s.[178] Although the attribution of this translation is not completely certain, that of the *Treatise on the Seven Sacraments* has been definitely established by Jean Darrouzès.[179] The latter treatise is a work of vernacularisation, very similar to the summaries made especially for the Greek bishops from Latin manuals on the seven sacraments. The work reveals once more Lapithes' linguistic and theological abilities. It also demonstrates his attachment to Greek teachings, since he retains Greek formulae that are strange to the spirit of the Latin rite.

Lapithes' written works are characterised by a willingness to translate, to comment, or to develop a way of thinking rather than to create a work *ex nihilo*. As in the case of Philip of Novara, fidelity to religious and moral traditions induced Lapithes to avoid deviating from the models that formed medieval Greek identity. An interesting aspect of Lapithes' thought is the principle according to which the best guidance for one's conscience comes from reading old stories. This rule—praised in similar terms by Philip of Novara[180]—confirms that a learned Greek culture flourished in Cyprus during the first half of the fourteenth century. We have no way of knowing the identity of the authors used by George Lapithes and his contemporaries to develop their thinking, but in his correspondence with the monk Barlaam the Calabrian, when they discuss classical thought they refer to Plato and Aristotle and to the possibility of reconciling the two schools of thought from a Christian perspective.[181] Undoubtedly, the above evidence argues against the thesis that learned Greek culture disappeared on Cyprus during Frankish rule. A number of Greek manuscripts verify that scholars in Cyprus followed Byzantine intellectual trends closely; Nicephoros Blemmydes' *Physics* enjoyed a relative success, copied three times between 1314 and 1332;[182] at the same time, Romanos Anagnostes copied in 1323/24 a miscellaneous collection, including Aristotle's *De caelo*, a treatise by Michael Psellos, and various maxims.[183] A little earlier in the same century, Leo the

---

[178] Pingree (1976); Poulle (1984: 3–4); Constantinides and Browning, *Dated Greek Manuscripts*, 209–12; Pedersen (2002: I, 11, 43, 180).

[179] Darrouzès (1979: 38–48, 97–113).

[180] Philip of Novara, *Les quatre âges de l'homme*, 23–4.

[181] Sinkewicz (1981: 154–65).

[182] Canart (1977: 312, no. 2, 314, no. 21, 315, no. 22); Constantinides and Browning, *Dated Greek Manuscripts*, 142–3, 165–7, 187–9.

[183] Canart (1977: 312, no. 1); Constantinides and Browning, *Dated Greek Manuscripts*, 185–7.

Cypriot's exchange of letters reveals his passion for books: he was an avid collector of volumes containing works by Plato, Aristotle, Proclus, Simplicius, and Gregory of Cyprus, as well as astronomical works that could be purchased in Cyprus.[184]

The first half of the fourteenth century thus marked a revival of interest in the Greek philosophical tradition, at a moment when a trend for translating Latin texts into French made its appearance. No Frankish Cypriot of the time seems to have been in a position to rival George Lapithes' erudition. In this respect it is noteworthy that, without the descriptions provided by the Byzantine Agathangelos, one could doubt that Greeks and Latins actually conversed on matters inherited from classical thought. These debates during the reign of Hugh IV were most probably part of more general discussions, focusing on doctrinal questions. Aristotelianism provided the scholars of the Frankish kingdom with the necessary arguments, as it did for those in Paris or Constantinople.

Other Forms of Literary Expression

Although literature in the Lusignan kingdom seems to be dominated by the major genres—history, law, morals—, the accidental survival of certain manuscripts permits us the reasonable hypothesis that other genres were also produced on the island. The scarcity of these works and lack of other information prevent us from understanding the circumstances of their composition and the public to which they were addressed. Nevertheless, if we appreciate them globally, these texts affirm that, as the meeting point of cross-cultural influences, Cyprus functioned as a receptacle of heterogeneous traditions, which were assimilated and reproduced in many combinations within the framework of medieval Greek culture.

The Enigmatic Cyprus Passion Cycle

Back in 1916, Spyridon Lampros published a play of the Passion of Christ included in Vat. Palat. gr. 367, a codex datable to around 1320.[185] This text has provoked lively discussions concerning the

---

[184] Rein (1915: 57–9, 97 and nos. 8, 81).
[185] Constantinides and Browning, *Dated Greek Manuscripts*, 159. Lampros (1916: 381)

existence of religious drama in a Byzantine environment. Some historians consider the play to be irrefutable proof of such activities amongst the Greeks, while others reject this position, declaring that the Cypriot origin of the play implies that it is a Western work, conceived independently from a society that, ever since the canons of the Council *In Trullo*, forbade the development of dramatic art.[186]

The *Cycle of the Passion of Christ* contains ten scenes intended to demonstrate the Easter theme of the triumph of Christ's Resurrection over death. These scenes present successively the Raising of Lazarus, Christ's Entry into Jerusalem, the Last Supper, the Washing of the Feet, Judas' Betrayal, Peter's Denial presented together with the Trial of Christ, the Mockery of Herod, the Crucifixion, the Resurrection, and the Doubting of Thomas. For each scene, the scenarist reproduces dialogues and monologues from the Canonical Gospels, complementing them with stage and acting directions in order to facilitate its performance. In the main, these directions follow the Scriptures, but their vague character means that, surprisingly, many episodes are left without precise instructions.

In its present form, the scenario of the *Passion Cycle* cannot have been shown on the stage. The large number of the cast (six male and three female leads and about fifty minor or mute roles), the great number of *loci* that had to be represented on the stage, and the absence of concrete instructions render the material production of such a play in its extant manuscript form impossible, and no other contemporary source allows the assumption that the play was ever performed. It is thus perfectly legitimate to suggest that the scenario of the *Passion Cycle* was a first version of a text intended to be reworked. Unfortunately, the silence of the sources concerning the circumstances of its composition prevents us from understanding the aims of its author. For Samuel Baud-Bovy, the *Cyprus Passion Cycle* follows a Western model, adopting the form of the Latin religious plays and adjusting it to the tastes of the Greek public by means of the Byzantine *koine* and the Greek religious tradition. It seems that the author uses a model deriving from a *Passion* from Monte Cassino (twelfth century), adding scenes from the Apocryphal Gospels, and

---

and Vogt (1931) date the codex to the fourteenth and the middle of the fourteenth century respectively; Mahr gives a date between 1254 and 1260 in the introduction to his edition of *The Cyprus Passion Cycle*, 11.

[186] Baud-Bovy (1975); Puchner (1983; 2004).

completing his dialogues from a Homily on Holy Saturday or from another one by Pseudo-Chrysostomos, allowing for some improvisation for the part dedicated to the Lament of the Virgin.[187]

The Western origin of this text is of exceptional interest for our understanding of Cypriot culture in the second half of the thirteenth century. Liturgical drama, attested in various narrative forms from the eleventh century onwards in France and England, spreads to Italy before it reaches the Latin East, as shown by the Cypriot *Cycle*. The transmission of the model through Benedictine monasteries is a plausible hypothesis, even though the possibility of a secular original cannot be excluded. For example, the mid-thirteenth century *Passion des jongleurs*, from which the first religious plays in French derive, was composed in the form of a poem whose free style was half-way between a narrative and a play, thus allowing the jongleurs to interpret and even imitate several characters.[188] From this perspective, the Cypriot *Cycle* may be viewed as participating in contemporary experimental literary trends, using semi-dramatic techniques for a play that was conceived in a way that did not necessarily obey precise stage rules.

Regardless of whether it was ever performed, the *Cyprus Passion Cycle* bears witness to the relatively early appropriation by Greeks of a genre proper to Latin culture and of their desire to present it to a larger public. The *Cycle* represents a phenomenon of acculturation characteristic of a society that favoured discussions concerning forms of stylistic expression. Unfortunately, we do not know if the example set by the *Passion Cycle* found any imitators; its being a *unicum* prevents us from ascertaining whether religious plays existed within the framework of either the writings of the kingdom of the Lusignans or the Byzantine literary tradition.

Romance and Epic Narrative

It is difficult to evaluate the importance of romance, be it of Byzantine or Western origin, in the island's Greek or French compositions. Philip of Novara and the Templar of Tyre demonstrate that the Brittany Cycle had reached the Latin East. During the festivities that

---

[187] Vogt (1931: 45, 61); Mahr in his introduction to his edition of *The Cyprus Passion Cycle*, 34, 37; Baud-Bovy (1975: 341–5); Puchner (1983: 89–97).
[188] Joubert Amari Perry (1981: 75–92).

took place in Cyprus in 1224 on the occasion of the knighting of the
two elder sons of John of Ibelin, and then in Tyre in 1286 during
the coronation of Henry II of Lusignan, stage representations of the
adventures of the knights of the Round Table and of Brittany fea-
tured Lancelot, Tristan, and Palamedes. The diffusion of knightly
culture was made possible through the circulation of chivalrous
romances in Italy, France, and England, as well as in Frankish
Outremer, where authors like Philip of Novara borrowed extensively
from these romances.[189]

On the other hand, the sources remain silent on the diffusion of
Byzantine romances among the Greek public. We know that in the
thirteenth and fourteenth centuries Byzantine poets used models taken
from Western romances, such as the *Guerre de Troie*, the *Histoire du
très éprouvé Apollonius de Tyr*, or the *Achilléide*, which they translated or
freely adapted, turning them into political verse. Logically, Cyprus
could have played the role of intermediary in the transmission of
romances between Greeks and Franks. However, the examination of
the content of Greek manuscripts from Cyprus or found on the island
shows that it is too early to offer conclusive answers to this question
because the literary genre of the romance is very poorly represented.
The romance of *Barlaam and Joasaph* was of course copied or circulated on the island,[190] but, compared with the vogue this text of religious inspiration knew in both the East and the West, evidence is
too slim to indicate that the genre flourished in Cyprus. Similarly,
the fragment from the *Romance of Alexander* found in Oxon. Bar. 20
does not constitute sufficient proof that Cypriot society of the time
had developed a taste for romances.[191]

In view of the absence of concrete evidence, Pierre Breillat's study
of an extract from Vat. gr. 1822, containing a fragment of a knightly
romance, must be viewed with caution. The work consists of 307
political verses, lacking beginning and end.[192] It is inspired by an
episode that relates the exploits of the Vieux Chevalier Branor le Brun.
This episode constitutes the prologue of a French romance that

---

[189] Philip of Novara, *Guerra*, §16 (112) and The Templar of Tyre, *Cronaca*, §203
(439); Loomis (1939: 79–80); Jacoby (1984b: 627–32); Ciggaar (1994: 96; 1996:
148–9); Grabŏis (1997: 64–5); Agapitos (2004).
[190] Darrouzès (1950: 184; 1957: 140, 147); Gamillscheg and Harlfinger (1989: no.
285); Constantinides and Browning, *Dated Greek Manuscripts*, 181–3, 212–6.
[191] Gamillscheg and Harlfinger (1989: no. 294).
[192] Breillat (1938); Löseth (1890: 424–8).

enjoyed much success down to the Renaissance, the *Guiron le Courtois*, a long Arthurian romance in prose, sometimes also called *Palamède*, and most certainly composed around 1235–40. In Italy, this romance circulated as part of the compilation of Rusticien of Pisa, a work written between 1274 and 1298.[193] Branor le Brun's episode was translated several more times into Italian and there also exists a Greek translation. Opinions on the Greek translation diverge: on the basis of linguistic evidence, which must be treated cautiously given the scarcity of the dialectal traits, P. Breillat believes that the translation was executed before 1350 and probably in Cyprus.[194] Conscious of the weakness of the linguistic argumentation, A. Garzya and R. Beaton reject the possibility of a Cypriot translation, but accept that the text came from a milieu where Greeks and Franks were in contact, between 1204 and 1453. K. Ciggaar has suggested recently that the text could have been inspired by a manuscript brought to Acre around 1270 by Prince Edward, the future Edward I of England.[195]

The poet who translated into Greek the exploits of the Vieux Chevalier largely reproduced a French or Italian prototype. Textual divergences must be attributed to the fact that he either worked from memory or used a version with many interpolations. The original French work relates the story of the Vieux Chevalier who challenged the companions of the Round Table and the kings in Arthur's retinue. Branor le Brun took up the challenge against all his adversaries, including King Arthur. Thus, Branor le Brun asserted the superiority of the knights of the First Table over those of the Round Table. In the Greek version, the poet fails to render correctly the relationship amongst the different Arthurian heroes, giving Gauvain an imaginary kinship and inserting elements drawn from a version of *Tristan*, a romance that had circulated in the Latin East.[196]

Torn between fidelity to his French model and personal inspiration, the Greek poet expresses his respect for royal authority, on which he bestows divine investiture.[197] One never mocks royal authority, the Arthurian model suggests, because in the Greek version, Branor

---

[193] Löseth (1890: 423–32, 466–72).
[194] Breillat (1938: 324–5).
[195] Garzya (1983: 279–80) and Beaton (1989: 139–42), followed by Nicolaou-Konnari (2000b: 13, 18); Ciggaar (1996: 146–7).
[196] Breillat (1938: 313–7). On the presence of a *Tristan* in the Latin East, see Jacoby (1984b: 628–9).
[197] Breillat (1938: 327, line 25).

le Brun refuses to fight against his master and the poet praises the
knights' loyalty towards their suzerain. In the second part of the narrative, the poet diverges from the text of Rusticien of Pisa, indulging
his taste for irony and comedy. This has been interpreted as an
expression of nostalgia for the old Byzantine order (identified with
the First Table). The French or Italian model thus provided the
basic plot of the narrative, but the poet also used traits drawn from
his own Hellenic culture in order to enrich his text with images and
stylistic effects. His language is characterised by archaisms that are
almost anachronistic compared to contemporary written language in
Cyprus, and it is distinctively different from the language used in
the Byzantine knightly romances.

Incontestably, the poem of the Vieux Chevalier emerged from the
encounter of the Frankish and Greek cultures, since its model derives
from the knightly romances that circulated in the Latin East and in
Romania. The uncertainty surrounding the origin of the translation
and the difficulty in producing conclusive linguistic proof prevent us
from asserting that the text originated in the Lusignan kingdom. Of
course, this Greek text presents some similarities with the *Cycle of the
Passion of Christ*. Moroever, its theme resembles that of a Greek popular ballad from Cyprus, written down for the first time in the twentieth century, the *Song of Zografou* ('Τραγούδι της Ζωγγραφούς'). In this
song, a Greek knight, assisted by his brother, fights against a Frankish
lord for the love of a beautiful girl from Naples. The two texts present no similarity in form or style, but courtly love and knightly values seem to constitute the basic themes of the ballad, regardless of
the modifications effected by the *poiitarades* during the Ottoman era.[198]

A Continuous Poetic Tradition

Other popular songs can be dated to the Lusignan period with greater
certainty, even though they were collected and written down after
1850. The *Song of Arodaphnoussa* ('Η Αροδαφνούσα'), for example,
echoes the tragic love affair between Joan L'Aleman and King Peter I.
The story lines of the known versions differ in many points from
the events related in the chronicles of Leontios Makhairas and 'Amadi',

---

[198] Edited by Menardos (1921), repr. in Christodoulou and Ioannides, *Cypriot Folk
Songs*, 407–13; Lassithiotakis (1999: 201–2); Irmscher and Troumbeta (2002).

but even if the identification of the characters of the song with the historical persons remains problematic, there is no doubt that the song was born in the historical context of Lusignan Cyprus, as shown by Angel Nicolaou-Konnari and Michalis Pieris.[199]

In this respect, it is important to remember that Cyprus occupies an important position in the Greek tradition of oral epic poetry, or of Akritic songs. The collective memory of the Cypriots has preserved the remnants of several medieval poems, such as the *Song of Armouris* ('Το τραγούδι του Αρμούρη/Αζγουρή') and that of *Porphyris* ('Το τραγούδι του δεινού Πορφύρη'), which belong to a cultural legacy that has come down to us via oral transmission.[200] Within the context of the long presence of Byzantine culture on the island, there is no written evidence from the Frankish period that would help clarify the issues of the appearance and transmission of the epic tradition in Cyprus. Cyprus maintained the tradition of epic poetry without transferring it into written form, unlike Crete, the place of origin of the *Dighenis* of the Escorial, copied in the fifteenth century.

The common theme of these songs is the fighting between Greek heroes and the Arabs, during the frontier wars in High Mesopotamia in the ninth–tenth centuries. The problem of historical identification is of course of no consequence for the emergence of the Cypriot tradition, since it is impossible to specify the exact time when these songs reached Cyprus, although the arrival of populations from Asia Minor seeking refuge from the Seljuks after 1071 provides a plausible chronological framework. What is important to stress is that the Cypriots received and assimilated this non-Cypriot Greek tradition, producing new versions with a clearly Cypriot character.

The general story lines of the epic songs relate the personal prowess of the Greek leaders during their expeditions against the enemy and against death, and sometimes during their revolts against authority. There can be no doubt about the respect shown to the spirit of the original tradition; notably, in the *Song of Porphyris*, the Cypriot versions do not diverge from the initial models any more than their Cretan counterparts. This fidelity is accompanied sometimes by a liberty in the development of certain situations. For example, in the *Song of Armouris*, the Cypriot poets are inspired by Peter I's exploits, as shown

---

[199] Edited recently by Christodoulou and Ioannides, *Cypriot Folk Songs*, 413–21; Nicolaou-Konnari (1985); Pieris (2003).

[200] Edited by Christodoulou and Ioannides, *Cypriot Folk Songs*, 573–7, 620–7.

by the first lines of a version from Emba, a village near Paphos;
where the Moscow manuscript has 'Παφούτις εκουρσέψασιν Σαρακηνοί
τ' Αμούριν', the Cypriot variant states, 'Παφούτις εκουρσέψασιν οι
Φράντζοι τ' Ανεμούριν', thus presenting an undeniable affinity with
the chronicle of Leontios Makhairas: '[. . .] και απεζέψαν εἰστό ανεμούρην
και εκουρσέψαν το'.²⁰¹

The variant from Paphos of the *Song of Armouris* reverses the historical situation, making the Franks the protagonists instead of the
Muslims. Most importantly, by confusing Amorion, a town in Phrygia,
with Anamur, a port on the Cilician coast, the Cypriot poet links
two events of the war against the Muslims that are five centuries
distant from each other. He thus brings up to date the eternal fight
between Christians and Muslims through the crusades of Peter I,
whose exploits involve names that are more familiar to the ears of
the Cypriot poet than those of towns in Asia Minor. Undoubtedly
more traces of this opposition between Muslims and Franks may be
found in many other Akritic songs collected on the island, but studies of intertextuality are lacking and we cannot fully appreciate the
contribution the poets of the time made to these narratives that originated in Asia Minor. The direct filiation with Byzantine tradition
is made more evident in the case of songs that belong to the cycle
of narrative poems with animal characters. Three contemporary songs
demonstrate the end result of an oral process of elaboration that
began in the Middle Ages ('Διήγησις τετραπόδων ζώων', 'Συναξάριον
του τιμημένου γαδάρου', 'Γαδάρου, λύκου κι' αλεπούς διήγησις').²⁰²

Compared to the rich oral poetic tradition, the learned written
production seems very poor. It includes only some epigrams and two
poems included in Vat. Palat. gr. 367 and attributed to Constantine
Anagnostes.²⁰³ One of the poems is written in the form of an exhor-
tation Anagnostes addressed to one of his young disciples, urging
him not to be discouraged by his teacher's punishments. The poem
develops this common theme in moral literature in 46 political verses,
partially using the learned Greek and partially the vernacular. Although
they present only limited interest for the history of medieval Cypriot

²⁰¹ Grégoire and Lüdeke (1939: 239, lines 3–6 from version no. 5); Makhairas, *Diplomatic Edition*, 138.
²⁰² Eideneier (1987).
²⁰³ Banescu (1913: 11–18) with the corrections and studies of Mercati (1917; 1920–1921; 1922).

poetry, the poems of Constantine Anagnostes attest to the existence of a learned poetic expression within the circles of the Greek notaries at the Lusignan chancery.

Our understanding of literature in Cyprus during the early period of Lusignan rule is necessarily limited by the availability of texts. They testify to a large variety of genres, but they do not enlighten us about other areas of thought of which only traces survive. The absence of geographical texts, for example, a genre fairly well represented elsewhere in Outremer, demands further investigation.[204] The short description of the island in the *Chronicle* of the Templar of Tyre (see above) hardly betrays any particular interest in texts describing the different sites of the island; it certainly does not contribute to our understanding of the role the Cypriots might have played in the composition of guidebooks for pilgrims to the Holy Land, since they almost all stopped in Famagusta before reaching Jaffa.[205]

On the other hand, in spite of the silence of the sources regarding texts of a scientific nature, we know that treatises on falconry were composed in Peter I's entourage, such as a *Livre du Prince*, written by Molopin and Michelin. This text, which bears witness to the existence of an instructive cynegetic literature in Cyprus, later became a source of inspiration for John of Francières, who composed on Rhodes between 1458 and 1469 his own book on falconry, a very popular treatise in Renaissance France.[206] Most certainly, this type of treatise is related to courtly culture and the way of life of Frankish knights, and does not reveal any particular interest in zoology. It was probably in the same milieu that a taste for astronomy and astrology was developed. Suffice it to recall the passage from Leontios Makhairas where King Peter I comments on the conjunction of planets that determined the course of his life.[207] On the basis of the evidence provided by the existence of several manuscripts and by the activity of George Lapithes, astronomy seems to have flourished in the fourteenth century, even if it still remains impossible to discern the existence of a particularly Cypriot school of thought.

[204] Minervini (2001: 631–4).
[205] According to Cardini (2002: 220) three pilgrimage guides may have been written in Cyprus, during the thirteenth century.
[206] Richard (1963); Wistedt (1967: 20–5); Smets (forthcoming); Edbury in this volume.
[207] Makhairas, *Diplomatic Edition*, 200.

Undoubtedly, further research will clarify and complete our knowledge and understanding of the production of texts of either a literary or a scientific nature in the Frankish Kingdom of Cyprus. Moreover, in addition to this secular culture, it is necessary to consider the huge production of religious texts in order to reconstruct the dynamics of an intellectual life that saw no real distinction between the profane and the sacred. This will enable us to understand better how the literary production evolved in Frankish Cyprus, a production that originated within the framework of both the Outremer and the Byzantine literary traditions, but whose development after 1291 shows strong similarities with the situation in Greco-Latin Romania.

ART

Annemarie Weyl Carr

Few fields can have seen so dramatic an influx of newly published material over the past decade as has the art history of medieval Cyprus. Heralded by the re-edition of two complementary classics—the English translation of Camille Enlart's great volume on Frankish architecture, and the expanded edition of Andreas Stylianou and Judith Stylianou's handbook on the painted Orthodox churches—the volume of new publication includes a range of surveys and monographic studies, a brisk sequence of published symposia, lengthy articles on the arts in the medieval volume of Theodoros Papadopoullos' *History of Cyprus*, and compendia honouring Doula Mouriki and Peter Megaw. Four recent doctoral dissertations devoted to the island's art have yet to be published, and others are in progress.[1] But the expansion of new material is due above all to two shifts within the field of visual culture itself. One is the heightened attention to what are traditionally called 'minor' arts, seen in Costas Constantinides and Robert Browning's compendium on manuscripts, Demetra Papanikola-Bakirtzis' work on pottery, Sophia Makariou's on metalwork, and Michele Bacci's and Anna Muthesius' on embroidered silk.[2] The other is the pervasive effort on the part of the government, the Church, and private foundations to record, preserve, and develop museums for the icons of Cyprus, yielding a parade of well-catalogued exhibitions in Thessalonike, London, and Nicosia, visitors' guides to new museums,

---

[1] Enlart (1987) translating Enlart (1899); Stylianou and Stylianou (1997) significantly augmenting the earlier edition, Stylianou and Stylianou (1985); Papadopoullos (1996); Patterson Ševčenko and Moss (1999); Herrin *et al.* (2001). For the conferences: *Proceedings of the First International Symposium on Mediaeval Cypriot Palaeography* (Nicosia, 3–5 September 1984), published in *EKEE* 17 (1987–1988); Bryer and Georghallides (1993); Coureas and Riley-Smith (1995); Loizou-Chatzigabriel (1997); *ΠΓ΄ΔΚΣ*, published in 2001; Christodoulou and Perdikes (2001). For the dissertations: Christoforaki (1999); Papacostas (1999a); Leventis (2003); Schryver (2005). In progress for example is Christina Spanou, *L'art pictural du XIIIe siècle à Chypre: origines, influences, tendances. Le témoignage des icones* (Ph.D. Thesis, University of Paris).

[2] Constantinides and Browning, *Dated Greek Manuscripts*; Papanikola-Bakirtzis (1989; 1996a; 1996b); Makariou (2000); Bacci (2000); Muthesius (2004).

and regional volumes on Paphos and Kition.[3] The result has been
a veritable explosion of otherwise unpublished artifacts: the number
of Cypriot icons known in published literature has literally doubled
in the last ten years. This expansion has shifted our perception
significantly. With few notable exceptions, this is an expansion of
Greek art, dominated by painting and portable objects. A medieval
Cyprus defined largely by the imposing architectural monuments of
Latin immigrants and invaders is now countered if not virtually super-
seded by the vast legacy of Cypriot Orthodox painting, a shift deep-
ened by the events of 1974, which left Cyprus' major Gothic
monuments inaccessible behind the Green Line in the Turkish-occu-
pied North. The shift in dominant media has brought, in turn, a
more nuanced perception of patronage, requiring historians to examine not merely the ways built structures divided groups, but the ways
in which images, styles, and portable goods—all more volatile than
buildings—moved within and between groups. Our understanding
both of patronage itself and of the range of choices available to
patrons has become much more ramified as the evidence expanded.
Viewership, too, has assumed a more nuanced history: works made
to serve one group often lived out their useful lives under the gaze
of another, and acquired their shape in history from their viewers.
With this, finally, the old orientalist expectations of cultural dualism
have receded. Only rarely can one ever speak of an artifact as belonging 'purely' to one or another pole of cultural identity, be it Frankish
or Greek, Syrian or Armenian. An image of two cultures in rigid
opposition has been displaced by a dynamic one of multiple cultural
groups under constant mutual pressure.

These pressures played themselves out on Cyprus itself, but they often
did so with cultural traditions that were composite already before
reaching the island. One sees this in Cyprus' relation with Syria-
Palestine. Cyprus had been in cultural contact with the Syro-Palestinian
mainland throughout the eleventh and twelfth centuries. Thus, Kurt
Weitzmann pointed out the stylistic kinship uniting the frescoes at
Koutsovendis, Asinou, and Trikomo on Cyprus, the miniatures of
the Antiochene manuscript Athos, Koutloumousiou 61, and a cluster

[3] Papageorghiou (1995a); Papanikola-Bakirtzis and Iacovou (1998); Sophocleous
(2000); *Holy Metropolis of Morphou* (2000); Perdikes (1997); Papageorghiou (1996);
Spanou (2002); Eliades (2004b).

of icons on Mount Sinai.[4] Presumably, artists of common, probably
Antiochene training built their style simultaneously into the artistic
traditions of Syria, Cyprus, and Sinai in the decades on either side
of 1100.[5] A similar pattern emerges in the kinships of script, ornament, and iconography that unite manuscripts Princeton, Garrett 3
of 1136 from the Palestinian monastery of St Sabbas, Vat. Barb. gr.
449 of 1153 and the Kraus Gospels of 1156 associated with Cyprus
by John the Cretan's ownership of the latter, and the somewhat later
psalter, Athens, Benaki Museum, cod. 34.3, made for the overseer
of the Cypriot estates of the patriarchate of Jerusalem.[6] Palestinian
manuscripts certainly made their way to Cyprus in the Comnenian
period: Tassos Papacostas points out Paris. gr. 1590, containing notes
about Asinou, and Florence, Laurenziana, San Marco 787, with a
note about John the Cretan, probably both from Kalamon in Palestine.[7]
Such Middle Byzantine precedents make a similar commonality in
the Lusignan period readily imagined. In the interim, however, the
mainland institutions had been fundamentally affected by the cultural
displacements produced by the Crusades.[8] What reached Cyprus
from Syria-Palestine was more and more the product of this convergence of peoples. Thus the artifacts reaching Cyprus were mingled. Contact with Europe, meanwhile, was mediated repeatedly by
European visual traditions that were themselves affected by Orthodox
imagery. Anne Derbes' study on Siena and the Levant, Ioanna Christoforaki's elegant case-studies on the imagery in the church of the
Holy Cross, Pelendri, and my own article on Cyprus and Italy underscore the cross-cultural complexity of the very materials with which
Cyprus' own tensions were being formulated and expressed.[9]

   The materials of which Cyprus' medieval art was compounded,
then, are complex. More than they invite answers, they invite questions,
about where, and in what elements of a larger whole, the definitive
fulcra of group or personal identity should be sought; what situations
did and what situations did not call for clear boundaries; and what
media were employed to mark the boundaries of identity visibly: all

---

   [4] Weitzmann (1975).
   [5] See the discussion by Papacostas (1999a, I: 109).
   [6] Carr (1987–1988: 131).
   [7] Papacostas (1999a, I: 113).
   [8] As noted for the first time cogently by Papageorghiou (1972: 212); see also
Young (1983: passim) and esp. Hunt (1991).
   [9] Derbes (1989); Carr (1995b); Christoforaki (1996; 1997; 2000).

of these are questions raised by—not premises brought to—the analysis of Cyprus' medieval art. If the prodigal flood of new monuments has given us any challenge, it is to resist the temptation to read the art history of medieval Cyprus solely as the story of two cultures in confrontation, and to look instead for other and larger stories.

Among these larger issues, that of Cyprus' own cultural geography is surely primary. Thus the Paphos district—indeed, the west of Cyprus altogether—is generally dismissed as a likely site of artistic energy because travelers' reports continue for centuries to describe the devastating earthquake of 1222.[10] Yet surviving visual evidence suggests a powerful artistic tradition, challenging us to build a geography on the basis not of verbal but of visual testimony. Quite as important is the distinction drawn so often between the urban culture of the coastal plains and the village culture of the Troodos villages. As Tassos Papacostas brings out, it is only toward the end of the Byzantine period that the Troodos churches begin to play a role in the history of Cyprus' art.[11] Rather than being deeply rooted in the Byzantine past, the prominence of the Troodos villages seems to reflect the commercial energy brought to the coastal areas from the twelfth century onward, forcing the coastal communities to exploit their mountain resources. His analysis of the Troodos area suggests that the urban/village dichotomy should be read less as two disjunct worlds—an urban and coastal one of conquerors, a rural one of Cypriots—than as a symbiotic system distinctive to the medieval economy, a symbiosis that invites us to seek artistic as well as commercial reciprocity. How culture played across Cyprus' geography in the medieval centuries deserves closer attention.

Another story that needs to be written is that of the relation of monasteries to their lay populace. A majority of the surviving painting from the Lusignan period is in Orthodox monastic churches. Significantly, this is true of works of Latin as well as of Orthodox patronage: the famous icon of St Nicholas tis Stegis with a Ravendel knight from the narthex of St Nicholas, Kakopetria (Fig. 19), the Latin lady in the narthex at Asinou,[12] and the Latin shop-owners portrayed

---

[10] Challenging the stress on the earthquake of 1222, and with earlier bibliography, see Wartburg (2001).

[11] Papacostas (1999a, I: 51–5).

[12] Papageorghiou (1992a: pl. 32) and Folda (1995: 216–22) (Kakopetria); Hein *et al.* (1996: pl. 26) and Carr (1998–1999: 66–7) (Asinou).

at St Nicholas tis Stegis are all instances of Latin patronage in an Orthodox monastic setting. The presence of these works in Greek monastic contexts begs a better understanding of the monastery as an economic and cultural nexus. A third story, more fully played out in the fifteenth and sixteenth centuries, concerns the emergence of new types of village organization, manifested in the mounting numbers of jointly sponsored and decorated village churches. Powerfully rooted in the fourteenth century, on the other hand, is a fourth story awaiting its compilation, that of the forging of cultural icons in Cyprus' complex society. Both the cross-relics of Stavrovouni and Tochni, and the icons of Kykkos, Makhairas, and the churches in Nicosia assume unprecedented vitality in the mid- and later fourteenth century, as Gilles Grivaud and I have begun to show. Yet another story deserving its history is that of a Latin aristocracy aspiring to be the 'crossroads of excellence' that defined the Levantine court of eminence.[13] These are stories in which art plays effectively across multiple social, creedal, and economic categories.

The Thirteenth Century

No century is more significant to the story of medieval art on Cyprus than the thirteenth, but it is hard to know just when the thirteenth century should begin, much less when it ends. The radical contrast in quality between the murals of 1183 and those of 1196 at the Enkleistra is often treated as a symbolic summary of the catastrophic rupture caused in 1191, and it is true that St Neophytos' patron, Basil Kinnamos, seems to have fled the island in the wake of the Frankish invasion, for he was on a ship attacked by pirates in 1192.[14] The painters he had sponsored don't seem to have vanished, though; Neophytos may simply have been in no mood to retain them, seeking the solace in violent times of a more overtly ascetic manner. To the contrary, the years around 1200 are characterized by a veritable glut of monuments, making it hard to see an abrupt rupture, or even to sense whether 1184, 1191, or 1204 was the most catastrophic of the

[13] Carr (1995a; 2004b) and Grivaud (2001b).
[14] E.g. Wharton (1988: 90): 'The Crusader conquest of the island in 1191, however, marks a dramatic end to the Cypriots' participation in the commonality of the Empire'; Gioles (2003: 168) echoes her assessment. For Kinnamos, Young (1983: 384).

events associated with the turn of the century. Monasteries continued for several decades to compose handsomely penned *Typika* like those for Makhairas in 1210 and the Enkleistra in 1214; to receive grants of money, land, and privileges from the emperor in Constantinople, as Makhairas did from Isaac II Angelos (1185–95) and Alexios III Angelos (1195–1203); to found metochia like Makhairas' early thirteenth-century Blachernitissa convent; and to designate the Lusignan king as the institution's *epitropos*, as Neophytos did.[15]

Artifactual production, in turn, was stimulated by the Frankish occupation: Demetra Papanikola-Bakirtzis points out that the production of glazed pottery in the Paphos area flourished precisely from the early thirteenth century onward.[16] Architecture, spurred partly by repairs after earthquakes of 1160,[17] was copious and apparently ongoing at the end of the century; close to a sixth of the 112 surviving churches listed by Tassos Papacostas from 650 to 1200 were built or reconstructed in the late twelfth century, including complex structures like the domed octagon at Kalogrea, the domed cross-in-square church of St Kerykos and Ioulitta at Letympou, and a majority of the island's domed cruciform buildings.[18] These include the Chryseleousa at Emba, St Eustathios at Kolossi, St George at Choli, the Venetian church of the Holy Cross Mesokerou, the Chryseleousa church at Chlorakas, and St Theodosios at Akhelia.[19] Many of the late twelfth-century buildings received mural decoration, and a striking number of significant mural cycles are assigned to the generation following 1191. The cycle at Lagoudera, though it may have been

---

[15] See the *Typikon* of 1210 of Makhairas Monastery (preserved at the monastery), Neilos, *Rule*, 73, 124–5 (the Blachernitissa was founded by Neilos, Bishop of Tamassos and sometime hegumen of Makhairas, to be supported by an allocation of one-eighth of the revenues of Makhairas Monastery), and the *Typikon* of 1214 of the Enkleistra (Edinburgh, University Library, Laing, Ms. 811), Neophytos the Recluse, *Rule*, 139, ch. 7. For Church economics, see also Schabel in this volume.

[16] Papanikola-Bakirtzis (1996a; 1993: esp. 121–5).

[17] Earthquakes of 1160 are cited by Papacostas (1999a, II: 22) in dating the Chryseleousa at Emba and by Megaw and Hawkins (1977: 159) for the Panagia Kanakaria, Lythrangomi.

[18] On Kalogrea, see Stylianou and Stylianou (1996: 1230–1). On St Kerykos and Ioulitta, see Karageorghis (1990: 33).

[19] The late twelfth-century domed cruciform churches listed alphabetically by Papacostas (1999a, II) are the Chryseleousa at Emba, St Eustathios at Kolossi, St George at Choli, and the Venetian church of the Holy Cross Mesokerou. Stylianou and Stylianou (1996: 1232) add the Chryseleousa at Chlorakas and St Theodosios at Akhelia.

planned already before the Crusader conquest, surely followed the advent of Isaac Comnenos; the cycles of the Archangel church at Kato Lefkara, the church of Christ Antiphonetes at Kalogrea, St Themonianos at Lysi, the Panagia Amasgou at Monagri, and St Solomoni in Paphos,[20] to say nothing of the more fragmentary survivals published by Spanou at the Panagia Angeloktisti in Kiti, St Basileios at Xylophagou, and the Holy Cross in Pano Lefkara,[21] constitute an exceptionally rich concentration of work.

These wall paintings have consistently been regarded as Comnenian, implying their patrons' solid bond with the cultural conventions of Byzantium and its capital.[22] The cycles' notable iconographic inno-vations like the depiction—indeed, in St Solomoni the iteration—of Christ's person in the Eucharistic vessels on the apse wall, though responding to what St Neophytos suggests were points of particular sensitivity in Cyprus, continue to be innovations fed by developments in the capital.[23] The cycles' stylistic sophistication dwindles steadily, showing that the bond with the capital had been broken by the events around 1200. But to say that it was broken immediately in 1191, or even in 1204, is to miss the monuments' message. The most concerted barrage of Comnenian mural painting that survives on Cyprus comes *after* 1191. The very concentration of architecture and painting in the decade following Cyprus' conquest contrasts so sharply with the expectation of catastrophic disruption that it invites an alter-native interpretation. The escalation in patronage may in itself be evidence of crisis conditions, as wealth—rather than circulating—congeals in the form of sacred donations or investments. It is a pat-tern that would recur in the sixteenth century. Stella Frigerio-Zeniou has shown that a significant number of the sixteenth-century 'Italo-Byzantine' cycles of paintings associated with the Panagia Podithou, Galata, and the 'Latin Chapel' at St Herakleidios, Kalopanagiotis,

---

[20] Nicolaides (1996) and, most recently, Winfield and Winfield (2003) (Lagoudera); Papageorghiou (1990) (Kato Lefkara); Stylianou and Stylianou (1997: 469–85) (Kalogrea); Carr and Morrocco (1991) (Lysi), though dated here to the second half of the thirteenth century; Boyd (1974) (Monagri); Young (1978) (St Solomoni).

[21] Spanou (2002: 30–1, 34–5, 36–8, pls. 13, 17–18, 20–2).

[22] As will be seen, this was as true of medieval Cypriots as it is of modern scholars.

[23] Christ's image in the Eucharistic paten is described by St Neophytos, depicted in the apse of Kato Lefkara, Papageorghiou (1990: 211, pl. XXXIII, 1), and iterated at St Solomoni, where Christ is shown not only in the paten but in the chalice: Stylianou and Stylianou (1997: 349).

belong to the decades on the brink of or following the Ottoman conquest, presumably reflecting a freezing of assets in the face of foreign
conquest.[24] The blaze of productivity in Cyprus in the decades on
either side of 1200 may reflect a similar pattern of anxious investment.
Certainly the dense clustering of monuments after 1191 means in
essence that the thirteenth century either begins in the late twelfth
with a surge of resolute continuity, or begins only after that surge had
run its course around 1220.

That this pattern of feverish continuity among the Greeks should
contrast with the behavior of the newly installed Frankish regime is
only to be expected. To the extent that its artistic strategy remains
visible, the new Lusignan regime adopted a pattern of highly selective
but emphatic self-definition. Its coinage retained Byzantine types; in
fortification, too, A. H. S. Megaw concludes that the new rulers moved
into the still effective defences left by the Byzantines, modifying them
only at a deliberate rate and avoiding the fortification of either cities
or the residences of the king's vassals.[25] In the cathedral church of
Nicosia, on the other hand, the Lusignan regime spoke firmly and in
large scale (Fig. 14). The early history of the cathedral of St Sophia is
shrouded in complexity; it was likely begun by 1209, possibly incorporating an earlier Templar church in which Guy of Lusignan had
been buried.[26] It stands out sharply, however, for its novelty. It retains
in its north portal capitals and a lintel in the manner of the so-
called Temple Workshop in Jerusalem, but in other respects it abandons the building traditions of Crusader Jerusalem and turns instead
to the conventions of the European homelands of the royal family.
Its plan resembles those of west-central France;[27] the buttressing
copies that of Laon; most striking of all, the eastern end abandons
the square form frequent in the Holy Land in favour of a chevet of
thoroughly French design. Chevet and transept seem to have been in
use by 1228, displaying in the ambulatory four columns that modern
historians have suggested may have come from the Orthodox cathedral church.[28] If St Sophia's name and site were those of the Orthodox

---

[24] Frigerio-Zeniou (2000–2001; 1998).
[25] Metcalf (1983: 51–6) on Cypriot coinage to the introduction of the *gros* under
Henry II (1285–1324); Megaw (1977). See also Edbury in this volume.
[26] *Cartulary*, 48–54; Enlart (1987: 82–96); Boase (1977: 167).
[27] Coldstream (1987: 7), who parallels it with the plan of the church of Avénières
at Laval, and that of Cunault on the Loire near Fontevrault.
[28] Metcalf (1995b: 372–3, notes 30–1); Papageorghiou (1982: 218).

cathedral, the ideological thrust of its scale and language would have stood out all the more strongly. In fact, the site of the Orthodox archiepiscopal seat before 1191 remains uncertain, and it is not clear how it was related to the early Christian basilica beneath the present Bedestan, the metropolitan church of the Hodegetria cited in the fourteenth century, or the church of St Barnabas in which an archiepiscopal staff continued to function after 1260.[29] It is clear, however, that the Latin cathedral announced the rupture that the Orthodox mural cycles belied. Equally significantly, it modified the legacy of the Crusader mainland, too. It was French, not Frankish.

St Sophia poses key questions of Lusignan identity: its relation to the resident Orthodox; to the merchant populace, who were far more Italian than French; but above all to the mainland, worked out in the Lusignans' decades-long ambivalence to the Crusader States and their crown. Both local and mainland elements quickly made their way into the Lusignan mix. Already in 1211, Wilbrand von Oldenburg had said that the houses of Nicosia 'in their interior adornment and paintings closely resemble the houses of Antioch',[30] suggesting that if the Lusignans' cathedral looked to France, their fellow Franks looked to the Levant for their amenities. The tableware in these very houses, in turn, was probably of Cypriot manufacture. The more portable a medium, the more readily it seems to have been able to move into new contexts, and by the end of the century Cypriot glazed tableware—finding a ready market in the immigrant households— was rich with the imagery of Gothic romance.[31]

Central to thirteenth-century developments in the Lusignan and the Orthodox traditions alike was Cyprus' relation to the Syro-Palestinian mainland. The story on the Lusignan side must have been traced most visibly in the churches of the monastic orders, begun already in the century's first half and continued with mounting grandeur in the second. As communities and in many cases also artifacts and holy objects flowed into Cyprus from the Holy Land,[32] habits of construction and usage surely came, too. The churches of the orders

---

[29] Kyrris (1993: 164–5, 176–7); *Synodicum Nicosiense*, no. X.33; Papacostas (forthcoming).

[30] *Excerpta Cypria*, 14.

[31] Papanikola-Bakirtzis (1996a; 1988).

[32] Thus Imhaus (2001) and Richard (2001a) point out the miracle-working icon of the Virgin from Tortosa, installed in the convent of Notre-Dame de Tortosa in Nicosia.

gathered in Nicosia, especially at the western side of the city, where they were eventually obliterated by the building of the Venetian walls.[33] Thus their history is mute. Only the church at Bellapais remains from this period; its architecture has been seriously analyzed only relative to France, but one notes a square eastern end of a kind used by several of the orders in the Holy Land, and this points to what must have been a cardinal aspect of the orders' implantation: the heightened hold of mainland Crusader forms on Cyprus. One yearns to know what this implied for their painted decoration.

In painting, Cyprus' relation to the mainland was fundamental. This had both Latin and Eastern Christian dimensions. Orthodox Cyprus' long-standing bond with Syria-Palestine was surely affected fundamentally by the upheavals of 1191 and 1204. This is indicated by the surviving icons of the early thirteenth century. They contrast with the wall painting of this period. Where we view mural painting almost entirely in terms of continuity, we view icons almost at once in terms of change: of the icons assigned to the early thirteenth century only the double-sided Crucifixion from the church of St Luke, Nicosia, now in the Byzantine Museum there, displays recognizably metropolitan forms.[34] The others, with their pastiglia ornament, linear forms, simplified colour schemes, and red backgrounds, look unfamiliar, anticipating the later thirteenth-century icons of the so-called *maniera Cypria* far more than they recall those of the Comnenian era. Alien, often Western sources have been sought to explain them.

Thematically an icon like the double-sided panel of the Virgin Theoskepaste in the Byzantine Museum, Paphos, seems indeed to respond to the Crusading character of its era (Figs. 15–16). Its coupling of the Mother of God with a warrior saint is not attested earlier in Byzantine imagery and very probably responds to the militarization of society in the wake of the Crusades; Sharon Gerstel has discussed the burgeoning of warrior saints in the imagery of regions settled by Crusaders.[35] Formally, in turn, the icon displays many conventions that would become signature features of Cypriot painting in the later thirteenth century. They include the pastiglia ornament, the red and green colours, and the elaboration of the costume of the Mother and Child. Often it is the Child's garments that are

[33] Along with Enlart (1987: 34 and passim), see Coldstream (1993; 1998) and Schabel (2002).
[34] Papageorghiou (1992a: pl. 18).
[35] Papageorghiou (1992a: pls. 15a, 15b; 1992b); Carr (1998–1999: 62); Gerstel (2001).

elaborated, especially by a cloak falling in Latin fashion over his back,[36] but here the elaboration is Mary's red veil. These features have all been explained by Doula Mouriki as Western, as well.[37] How true this is remains moot. Red is a colour of preference in a number of regional traditions, including that of Cyprus itself if the apse of 1178 at Pelendri is taken into account, and Boyd is surely right to emphasize among them the Syrian, with which Cyprus had long contact already.[38] Pastiglia, in turn, is attested already in the mid-twelfth century in Constantinople: George Soteriou showed that it had been used in the mosaic icon of the Virgin from the Pammakaristos church there. Though pastiglia ornament appears more often in Italy than in either Greece or the Balkans, it does so no earlier there than on Cyprus, and Kalopissi-Verti and Frinta both conclude that it is a Byzantine technique that moved westward from the Holy Land with Cyprus playing a particularly visible role in its transmission.[39] The elaboration of the holy figures' clothing, finally, exemplified here by the Virgin's heavy veil, appears in mural and panel painting throughout the Byzantine periphery from Southern Italy to Moscow around 1200, including but by no means exclusively in the West.[40] Thus it seems more judicious to say simply that the icons reflect sources of inspiration other than those behind the major mural cycles, presumably sources closer to home. That Cypriot painters should have turned abruptly in 1191 to overtly Western sources is hard to believe. They may well, on the other hand, have relied more heavily on contacts with the Syro-Palestinian mainland. But the mainland upon which they relied had by 1200 seen several generations of artistic upheaval, importation, and amalgamation in the wake of the Crusades. Its art embraced a range of mingled and imported elements. Reverberations of these interminglings would have been felt in Cyprus. These, rather than direct Western imports, must lie behind the unfamiliar forms in the early thirteenth-century icons.

[36] See the icon from Asinou, now in the Byzantine Museum in Nicosia, Papageorghiou (1992a: pl. 35); the icon from Moutoullas, now in the Museum of the Holy Monastery of Kykkos, Papageorghiou (1992a: pl. 28); and the Hodegetria icon at Sinai, Mouriki (1990: pl. 60).
[37] Mouriki (1985–1986: 26, 32, 56) on red backgrounds, clothing, and *pastiglia*— that is, raised gesso patterns—respectively, with extensive earlier bibliography.
[38] Stylianou and Stylianou (1997: 507–10, pl. 303); Boyd (1974: 321, note 191).
[39] Soteriou (1933); Kalopissi-Verti (1986); Frinta (1981; 1986).
[40] Of many reflections on the veil of the Virgin, see recently Carr (2004a: 131, note 20); Hadermann-Misguich (1992). On the clothing of the Christ Child, see in particular Corrie (1996).

Striking in the icons on Cyprus is their coherence as a group. Whether this coherence emerged as abruptly as our attributions suggest or had a longer incubation reaching back into the twelfth century, and whether it reflects a coherence that had evolved already in mainland workshops or one that was evolved in and eventually radiated from Cyprus, are open questions. The focal message of the icons is that the continuity felt in the mural paintings produced around 1200 was just part of the picture. Just as the domestic paintings described by Wilbrand had conditioned the impression of French identity implied in the Lusignan cathedral, suggesting a greater continuity with the mingled habits of the Crusader mainland, so the icons of the Orthodox population condition the impression of fidelity to metropolitan traditions given by the mural cycles, suggesting heightened responsiveness to the local Christian traditions of the mainland.

What makes the ensuing developments on Cyprus so interesting—and so difficult—is the fact that Franks as well as Eastern Christians had artistic roots in the mainland. What happened as these two traditions of indebtedness converged on Cyprus becomes visible in the final third of the century, when Lusignan possession of the crown of Jerusalem stabilized and Cyprus absorbed large numbers of refugees, both Eastern Christian and Frankish, from the mainland Crusader States. Crusader patrons of figural art emerge on the island at this point, as Folda emphasizes;[41] at the same time, local patronage accelerates once again, yielding both portable and monumental painting. Along with isolated wall paintings at St Nicholas tis Stegis, St Kerykos and Ioulitta at Letympou, the Chryseleousa at Emba, and in the apse and narthex at Asinou,[42] four major cycles survive: at St Herakleidios in the monastery of St John Lampadistes at Kalopanagiotis (ca. 1265–80; Fig. 18); at the little monastic church of the Panagia in Moutoullas of 1280, published by Doula Mouriki (Fig. 23); at the as-yet unpublished Transfiguration church of Sotira in the Famagusta district (ca. 1280–1300); and in the dome of the triconch Chryseleousa church, Strovolos (ca. 1275–1300), studied by Athanasios Papageorghiou.[43] The cycles are heterogeneous in both style and iconography.

---

[41] Folda (1995: passim and esp. 221–2).
[42] Stylianou and Stylianou (1997: 65–6 for Kakopetria, 126, 138–40, and figs. 65, 71 for Asinou); Papageorghiou (1996: pls. 70–1).
[43] Stylianou and Stylianou (1997: 295–8) and Young (1983: 144–245) (St Herakleidios); Mouriki (1984) and Stylianou and Stylianou (1997: 323–30) (Moutoullas); *RDAC 1989* (1990), 29–30, pls. 11, 12 (two images of Sotira); Papageorghiou (1999b) (Chryseleousa).

One notes especially their unconventional iconographic programmes. Nothing attests more sharply to the discontinuity with Byzantium than the disruption of the traditional Middle Byzantine cycles seen in these churches. The murals at Strovolos repeat closely those in the dome of St Themonianos, Lysi, and so adhere to tradition, but the other three cycles depart sharply from the organization of imagery seen in twelfth and early thirteenth-century churches, and in two cases— Kalopanagiotis and Sotira—verge on the incoherent. Nikolaos Gioles has associated the Etoimasia without a Gospel Book and the enthroned Christ of the Ascension in St Herakleidios with the Western *Filioque* doctrine, but he offers no explanation for their errant placement in the south arm of the church (Fig. 18);[44] the programme at Sotira, in turn, presents the first of a series of Last Judgments from Lusignan Cyprus,[45] coupled with very oddly distributed Christological scenes. The programme at Moutoullas, on the other hand, announces a new organizational system. The only fully preserved thirteenth-century cycle on Cyprus, Moutoullas is also the earliest surviving instance of a single-naved, wood-roofed church with a frescoed interior. Though probably known earlier, the gabled naos became usual only in the Frankish period.[46] The way in which it is frescoed at Moutoullas, with a band of Gospel scenes unrolling around the naos above a taller register with saints, would become a recurrent pattern in later Cypriot painting. It indicates the emergence of a new, locally rooted canon.

The acceleration of Greek artistic activity that is signaled by the resumption of wall painting is seen more sharply in panel painting: in contrast to the eight published panels from the beginning of the century, some thirty-four are known from the second half of the century, of which fifteen (marked with an asterisk) are from Marathasa, the same Troodos valley that houses Moutoullas and Kalopanagiotis. A list follows:

From the third quarter of the century:
*The Koimesis from Pedoulas, now Byzantine Museum, Nicosia [Papageorghiou (1992a: pl. 23)];
*Elijah from Kalopanagiotis, now Byzantine Museum, Nicosia [Ibid., pl. 24];

---

[44] Gioles (1986).
[45] The Last Judgment is represented notably often in medieval Cyprus: see De Cholet (1984: 110); Garides (1985); Nicolaides (1995); Emmanuel (1997); Duba (2000).
[46] Maravalaki and Prokopiou (1998); Stylianou and Stylianou (1996: 1239).

Ascension of Elijah from St Theodoros Agrou [Ibid., pl. 25];
Timotheos and Mavra in Koilani [Ibid., pl. 19];
Eleousa from Karonos [Ibid., pl. 20];
Mother of God at St Theodoros [Sophocleous (1994: pl. 22)];
Mother of God at Fasoula [Ibid., pl. 23];
Crucifixion at Pelendri [Ibid., pl. 24];
Mother of God from Anogyra [Papageorghiou (1996: pl. 96)];
Anonymous saint [Ibid., pl. 97];
Crucifixion at Korakos [*Holy Metropolis of Morphou* (2000: no. 10)];
*St Basil from Moutoullas [Ibid., no. 2];
Enthroned Virgin with SS Luke and Lazarus [Spanou (2002: no. 3)].

From the last quarter of the century:
*Christ from Moutoullas [Papageorghiou (1992a: pl. 29)];
* Mother of God from Moutoullas [Ibid., pl. 28];
Virgin of the Carmelites, now Byzantine Museum, Nicosia [Ibid., pl. 31];
Fig. 6: *Vita* icon of St Nicholas tis Stegis, Kakopetria, now Byzantine Museum, Nicosia [Ibid., pl. 32];
St Paul from the Chrysaliniotissa church, Nicosia, now Byzantine Museum, Nicosia [Ibid., pl. 33];
**Vita* icon of St Marina from Pedoulas, now Byzantine Museum, Nicosia [Ibid., pl. 34];
Fig. 8: Mother of God from Asinou, now Byzantine Museum, Nicosia, often called 'Kykkotissa' [Ibid., pl. 35];
*Templon, St John Lampadistes, Kalopanagiotis [Ibid., pl. 36];
*Eleousa from Kalopanagiotis [*Holy Metropolis of Morphou* (2000: no. 132)];
Bilateral icon with Mother of God surrounded by scenes of her life; Crucifixion, SS Joachim and Anna, Kaliana [Ibid., no. 3];
**Vita* icon of St John Lampadistes, St John Lampadistes, Kalopanagiotis [Ibid., no. 4];
**Vita* icon of St John Lampadistes, St John Lampadistes, Kalopanagiotis [Ibid., no. 5];
Mother of God, SS Barnabas and Hilarion, Peristerona [Ibid., no. 6];
*Templon, St John Lampadistes, Kalopanagiotis [Ibid., no. 7];
* Fig. 9: Panagia Voreine, Pedoulas [Ibid., no. 11];
St Mamas from Pelendri [Sophocleous (1994: pl. 27)];
*Dexiokratousa from Moutoullas [Vocotopoulos (1999: pl. 10)];
*Hodegetria from Moutoullas [Ibid., pl. 11];

*John the Baptist with John Moutoullas [Ibid., pl. 12];
Mother of God, Zoodochos Pege, Zoopigi [Sophocleous (1990, II: 326; III: pls. 192–3)];
Mother of God, Panagia Amasgou, Monagri [Ibid., II: 346; III: pl. 209].

Icons of this manner on Sinai:
Eleousa [Mouriki (1990: pl. 59)];
Crucifixion [Ibid., pl. 58)];
Fig. 7: Mother of God in the pose of the Hodegetria [Ibid., pl. 60)].

Many of the icons retain the broad forms, red and green colour scheme, and pastiglia ornament that had struck historians as exceptional in the early thirteenth century and that we have associated with Syro-Palestinian conventions; Doula Mouriki groups them as the *maniera Cypria*.[47] They comprise at least two significant stylistic clusters. One, exemplified by the 'Kykkotissa' at Asinou (Fig. 21), the *vita* icon of St Nicholas from Kakopetria (Fig. 19), the *vita* icon of St Marina from Pedoulas, and the Eleousa from Kalopanagiotis, echoes the conventions seen at St Themonianos, Lysi,[48] iterating the importance given to Lysi by the repetition of its iconography at Strovolos, and recalling the painterly technique of twelfth-century Byzantine art. The elegance of these images has made them favourites among the icons of the period. Their Byzantine character stands out so clearly that Jaroslav Folda could single out the figure of St Nicholas in the great *vita* icon from St Nicholas tis Stegis as the work of a Cypriot painter (Fig. 19).[49] He assigned the scenes of St Nicholas' *vita*, on the other hand, to a Frankish shop or painter. The patron of the panel, portrayed by the painter of St Nicholas but in the Latin posture of prayer, was a Frankish knight of the Raven[d]el family. The presence of the Latin knightly patron has been extensively discussed; the likely presence of a Latin painter was brought out only recently by Folda. The contrast between Frankish and Orthodox was not initially striking. In figural arts, in fact, surviving works of Frankish patronage rarely contrast sharply with those of local sponsorship. This is equally true of the second cluster of icons.

[47] Mouriki (1985–1986: 35).
[48] See parallels in Carr and Morrocco (1991: 104–8).
[49] Folda (1995: 219).

The other stylistically consistent cluster of icons of the *maniera Cypria* is characterized by its linearity (Figs. 22–23). It includes a number of icons both on Cyprus itself, where it is exemplified especially by panels like the Panagia Voreine from Pedoulas (Fig. 22) and the Hodegetria at Mount Sinai (Fig. 20). Especially in the rendition of women saints the close kinship of the icons on Cyprus and Sinai is striking: see the St Marina from Pedoulas, the figures of Marina, Catherine, and Kyriake in St Herakleidios and Moutoullas, and the same figures in icons of the Crusader period on Sinai.[50] The icons on Cyprus are closely akin in style to the mural paintings of 1280 at Moutoullas, and given their numerical concentration in the Marathasa Valley (signaled by an asterisk in the list) they are often labeled the 'Moutoullas School'. The name suggests a locally rooted, regional tradition. Two factors challenge this conception, however. One of these is the bond between the Cypriot paintings and those of the Syro-Palestinian mainland. This is seen well in the works commissioned by John Moutoullas, patron of the mural cycle of 1280. Along with the wall paintings, we still have an icon of the Baptist that bears John Moutoullas' portrait. It may have been produced by a painter personally conversant with the icons at Sinai, for it repeats both the iconography and the lengthy inscriptions seen on a Comnenian panel that is preserved there.[51] If so, however, it was not as models of Comnenian Byzantinism that John's painter valued Sinai's panels: his forms reflect instead the curving, calligraphic linearity of the contemporary Crusader works, assigned most plausibly to local Orthodox painters.[52] It is in Bahdeidat in Lebanon and Qara, Syria, in turn, that the ornamental motifs of Moutoullas can best be paralleled.[53] More than the Byzantine, it was contemporary Eastern Christian forms that seem most to have affected the *maniera Cypria* in Marathasa. Certainly Eastern Christians immigrated to Cyprus in large numbers during the thirteenth century, swelling the artisan population, as Jean Richard has shown.[54]

The second factor that conditions an essentially regional assessment of the Marathasa manner is the fact that—as the icons at Sinai

[50] Mouriki (1984); Weitzmann *et al.* (1982: 235); Weitzmann (1966: figs. 46, 47, 50). Very similar again is the beautiful St Kyriake from Ormedeia: Spanou (2002: pl. 26).
[51] Vocotopoulos (1999: 167–71, pl. 12, figs. 7–12).
[52] Hunt (1991).
[53] Dodd (2004: pl. 19.12, C5); Carr and Morrocco (1991: figs. 36–8).
[54] Richard (1979: 171–3).

show—Frankish patrons had themselves adopted these same Eastern Christian forms, and had left their stamp upon them. On Sinai itself this is exemplified especially poignantly by the small icon of St Sergios with a kneeling Frankish lady studied by Lucy-Anne Hunt. Hunt attributes it persuasively to a Syrian painter; nonetheless, its donor is portrayed with a dynamic presence that is exceptional in Orthodox art and suggests a Latin inflection. Such mingled forms are also seen on Cyprus. This is illustrated well by the paintings at Sotira. These, too, are in the 'Marathasa' style. But the facial structure and coiffeur of key figures like King David and the crowned warrior saint on the southeast pier are thoroughly French, and the huge mounted warrior on the north wall curbs his horse with the same 'B'-shaped bit that is seen on the Crusader icons of mounted warriors at Sinai, including that of St Sergios with the kneeling lady.[55] Clearly this manner was appealing to Frankish patrons and acquired Frankish inflections, inflections that persisted even into an Orthodox cycle like that of Sotira. The margin of convergence between Frankish and Orthodox could be remarkably broad. Franks clearly espoused the Orthodox use of icons enthusiastically, and the resulting panels could be strikingly oecumenical in their address. This is exemplified by the icon most unequivocally belonging to the *maniera Cypria* on Sinai, the Hodegetria cited in the list above (Fig. 20). Painted in the manner seen in Marathasa, it is labeled in the same maroon paint as both 'Meter Theou' and 'Mater Domini'.[56] Presumably, its figure of Mary was as available to the prayers of Latin as of Greek Christians.

The presence of the 'Marathasa' manner far from the mountains, in Sotira, challenges the assumption that the *maniera Cypria* was a product of isolated, solidly Orthodox mountain villages. The Marathasa Valley itself may reinforce this challenge. Its artistic vitality implies that it flourished in the thirteenth century, presumably because it interacted effectively with its Frankish overlords. Testimony to such effective interaction seems to survive in the lavish decoration in the church of St Herakleidios in the monastery of St John Lampadistes, Kalopanagiotis. Rampant lions, a heraldic device of the Lusignans, stud the intricate thirteenth-century templon here and adorn the shield of Longinus, suggesting an allegiance to the Lusignans.[57] Other

---

[55] Hunt (1991); Evans (2004: nos. 229–30).
[56] Evans (2004: no. 213).
[57] Stylianou and Stylianou (1997: fig. 182; 1996: figs. 148–56).

elements of the imagery belong to the mainland. The scene of the Crucifixion repeats the distinctive style and gestures seen in Crusader works like the Latin Perugia Missal produced in Acre and icons at Sinai, while the figures in the scenes of the Sacrifice of Isaac, the Raising of Lazarus, the Entry into Jerusalem, and the Ascension, look Syrian.[58] Even the figure of St Paraskeve, seen here for the first time holding an image of the Man of Sorrows in a way distinctive to Cyprus, may have emerged in response to the Latin term 'Holy Friday' (Ἁγία Παρασκευή) rather than the Greek 'Great Friday' (Μεγάλη Παρασκευή), for the day of the Passion, as Triantaphyllopoulos suggests.[59] Far from being insular, then, the *maniera Cypria* reflects, and flourished in environments shaped by, the Crusader mélange of cultures.

The imagery in St Herakleidios raises the question of the role of the Greek monasteries in the mixed culture of the Lusignans. Had the monastery, like Neophytos' Enkleistra, simply endorsed the king as its *epitropos* and so placed his arms on its templon; or do the rampant lions and hybrid imagery imply that Latin lords had actually adopted the monastery as a *pied à terre*, as the kings would later do at Makhairas Monastery? The Gothic parekklesion containing the funerary plaque of Simone Guers (†1302) at the Panagia Angeloktisti, Kiti, and the portrait of a Latin lady in the narthex at Asinou indicate that, presumably in the absence of Latin parishes, Latin Christians availed themselves of Greek churches for the inevitable exigencies of death. Latin parish churches were few and mostly limited to the cities, as Jean Richard has argued.[60] On the other hand, neither the Frankish images in the narthex at St Nicholas tis Stegis nor the lions at St Herakleidios are funerary, and suggest that the Franks may have made more quotidian use of Orthodox monasteries and their churches. Whether by means of such overt sharing or by less conscious slippages of usage, the Franks' longstanding familiarity with mingled imagery on the mainland and the Cypriots' yet longer-standing interchange with the mainland produced a singularly complicated interpenetration of artistic habits in late thirteenth-century Cyprus.

How to read the patterns of life in these habits of artistic usage remains difficult. But it seems clear that an underlying formal matrix

---

[58] Carr and Morrocco (1991: 89–92, on the basis of Young (1983: 144–245).
[59] Triantaphyllopoulos (2001: 628).
[60] Makhairas, I, §§67–77 (Makhairas); Enlart (1987: 334–5) (Kiti); note 12 above and, on its likely funerary context, Grivaud (forthcoming) (Asinou); Richard (1979: 162).

of the kind offered on Cyprus during the twelfth century by Comnenian art was displaced in the thirteenth century by a community of form embracing Cyprus and the Syro-Palestinian mainland. The mainland had been stimulated and complicated since the advent of the Crusaders by the movement of peoples and groups, and ethnically determined boundaries were complex. Quite without 1191, Cyprus in the wake of 1204 may well have reflected much the same mélange of mainland forms in the thirteenth century that it did as a Frankish state. As it was, Franks and local Christians alike found variously inflected ways of using that common mélange, and both communities seem to have contributed to the steady flow of patronage that sustained artistic productivity on Cyprus.

The convergence of Cyprus' multiple communities upon a common fund of conventions is underscored by the fact that two artistic forms incubated on the Crusader mainland took exceptionally sturdy root in Cyprus. One is the *vita* icon: the icon of a saint framed by a sequence of small scenes of his or her life. No area preserves so many *vita* icons, displaying the lives of so many different saints, as medieval Cyprus does. Nancy Patterson Ševčenko has argued that the *vita* icon was developed on Mount Sinai around 1200 to serve the polyglot confluence of pilgrims who gathered there.[61] Examples on Cyprus begin to appear in the ensuing century and then burgeon, buttressing Ševčenko's hypothesis of their particular relevance to mixed societies. The spectacularly polyglot St Nicholas tis Stegis that Folda attributed to both a Greek and a Frankish hand (Fig. 19) was accompanied over the ensuing century by this exceptional roster:

Vita icon of the Virgin Mary on the obverse of the bilateral icon at SS Joachim and Anna, Kaliana [*Holy Metropolis of Morphou* (2000: no. 3)];

Vita icon of the Virgin Mary shown in the pose of the Kykkotissa, Byzantine Museum, Nicosia [Papageorghiou (1969: pl. 48)];

The Virgin of the Carmelites, Byzantine Museum, Nicosia [Papageorghiou (1992a: pl. 31)];

Vita icon of St Marina on the reverse of the icon of St George from Philousa, Byzantine Museum in Paphos, for which a thirteenth-century date is now proposed [Ibid., pl. 2];

---

[61] Patterson Ševčenko (1999).

Vita icon of St Marina from Pedoulas, Byzantine Museum, Nicosia
   [Ibid., pl. 34];
Vita icon of St Stephen, St Stephen, Agros [Gerasimos and Papaioakim
   (1997)];
Vita icon of St George, Byzantine Museum, Pedoulas [*Holy Metropolis
   of Morphou* (2000: no. 13)];
Vita icon of St Mamas, Museum of the Holy Monastery of Kykkos
   [Ibid., no. 15];
Vita icon of St John Lampadistes, monastery of St John Lampadistes,
   Kalopanagiotis [Ibid., no. 4];
Vita icon of St John Lampadistes, monastery of St John Lampadistes,
   Kalopanagiotis [Ibid., no. 5].

Of these, the Virgin with the Carmelites stands out not only for its
Latin patrons but its theme. It is a *vita* icon not of Mary herself but
of a golden image of her, perhaps a golden statue venerated by the
Carmelite community portrayed at the figure's feet. Only in post-
Byzantine times would Orthodox miracle-workers acquire such *vita*
icons. The Carmelite panel seems to be the precocious precipitate
of compounded traditions: the *vita* icon on the one hand, the venerated statue on the other. The icon of St Philip, in turn, may have
served the cult that developed in Arsos around a relic of that saint
sent as a gift by the Latin emperor of Constantinople, as proposed
by Ioannes Eliades.[62] Recurrently, then, the *vita* icons seem to address
the very kind of mingled context that Ševčenko proposed for them.
The second powerful implantation is the Italianate version of the
Crucifixion with the striped loincloth. It is seen often: in mural paintings at Moutoullas, St Herakleidios in Kalopanagiotis, and St Nicholas
tis Stegis, Kakopetria; on the reverse of the *vita* icon at Kaliana, the
Pelendri icon, and the icon of the Crucifixion from Sinai cited in
our list just above; and with almost overwhelming force in the bilateral icon in the Panagia Eleousa, Korakos.[63] In view of the power
of Byzantine Passion imagery in Italy, it is striking to see the force
of Italian Crucifixion imagery here in Cyprus.

---

[62] Eliades (2004a). The carpentry of this huge panel is complex, and the broad
frame bearing the *vita* scenes is an addition, perhaps added in response to the relics'
successful cult. Certainly the scenes differ in style from the portrait.

[63] Hein *et al.* (1996: fig. 93) (Moutoullas); Papageorghiou (1972: fig. XXI, 1) (St
Herakleidios); Hein *et al.* (1996: fig. 46) (St Nicholas); *Holy Metropolis of Morphou*
(2000: no. 10) (Panagia Eleousa).

The picture offered here, of a convergence of both locally Cypriot and Frankish usage upon a shared body of Eastern Christian conventions, leaves three important questions unanswered. The first question concerns priority: to what extent was this convergence of traditions a product of Cyprus itself, and to what extent was it a reflection of developments in the fertile ateliers of the mainland, i.e. in Sinai itself, Acre, and/or the Eastern Christian communities of Tripoli and Syria?[64] It remains unclear whether Cyprus was a dissemination point—as Doula Mouriki, Valentino Pace, and Maria Aspra-Varvadakis propose—supplying panels to sites throughout the Mediterranean, or whether it was a gathering point, as Kotoula suggests, where immigrant artisans and artifacts collected as the mainland became more troubled.[65]

The second question concerns personnel. Doula Mouriki was surely right that the majority of the painters of these works were Eastern Christians. They very probably included Syrians as well as Cypriots, though. Moreover, the Frankish facial types at Sotira show that these people were intimately acquainted with the work of Frankish painters, just as the conjunction of Frankish and Orthodox manners on the icon of St Nicholas (Fig. 19) shows that some—at least—of the Frankish artisans practiced the techniques of panel painting.

The third question, finally, concerns patronage. Works like the icon of St Nicholas (Fig. 19) make it clear that Orthodox forms need not imply an Orthodox patron, just as the Crucifixion at St Herakleidios and the murals in Sotira show that the presence of Frankish forms need not imply Frankish patrons. It is still unclear, however, how broadly representative these examples are. In particular, one wonders whether the reliance on local painters that one sees in the surviving works of Frankish patronage is due precisely to the fact that these works were commissioned for Orthodox churches and not Latin ones. Valuable evidence in this regard is offered by the panel of the enthroned Virgin with Carmelite monks.[66] Nearly identical in size and technique to the icon of St Nicholas (Fig. 19) and similar to it in style, this panel seems to portray a distinctive, miracle-working

---

[64] On developments in the region between Tripoli and Damascus, see Immerzeel (2003).

[65] Compare Mouriki (1987), Aspra-Varvadakis (1999), and Pace (1980; 1982a; 1982b; 2000: 426, pls. 214, 216) with Kotoula (2004) and Bacci (1997).

[66] Papageorgiou (1992a: pl. 31).

figure of the Virgin Mary whose golden garb recalls the gilded statues of the Latin West.[67] Surely made for a Latin community, it supports the belief that Frankish patrons did adopt Eastern Christian forms and media even in their own churches. But the question remains if, in their own churches, the Franks would not have called upon more overtly European painters. In their urban commissions, would they not, too, have drawn upon more overtly cosmopolitan painters conversant with the high styles of the international courts?

Tantalizing answers have been offered to the question of whether the Frankish cities generated artistic alternatives more sophisticated than those of the *maniera Cypria*. Jaroslav Folda has proposed that the Mellon Madonna in the National Gallery, Washington, D.C., might have been painted in one of Cyprus' Frankish cities.[68] This icon has proved famously hard to localize. It displays the bright, red and blue colour scheme and strong chrysography seen in Crusader panels at Sinai and again in muted form in the icon of St Nicholas tis Stegis on Cyprus (Fig. 19). But it uses them in conjunction with a delicate facial modeling and a round, Colosseum-like throne that are far more sophisticated than the Crusader icons. Since details of its imagery like the red scroll of the Christ Child recur in Cypriot panels, Folda wondered whether this icon might reflect the urban face of Frankish art on Cyprus, a face more fluently *au courant* of Constantinopolitan developments than village commissions like the panel of St Nicholas tis Stegis. To date, no concrete comparandum has emerged on Cyprus to confirm Folda's attribution and it remains no more than an idea. It brings with it, however, a fundamentally important admonition: the paintings preserved in the villages may be no more than provincial Frankish art. Perhaps more sophisticated traditions existed in the late thirteenth-century cities, only to be destroyed between 1373 and 1571.

More fraught than Folda's attribution of the Mellon Madonna is the belief, first espoused by George Soteriou and defended recently by Maria Aspra-Varvadakis, that the diptych with the 'Kykkotissa' and St Prokopios at Sinai was made in Cyprus, albeit as a gift for Sinai (Fig. 17).[69] The focal argument lies with the figure of Mary, associated by both scholars with the great icon of Kykkos Monastery. In fact, the figure is not a 'Kykkotissa'; it is, however, closely akin

---

[67] Folda (1995: 218–21).
[68] Folda (2002: esp. 135–9; 2001).
[69] Evans (2004: no. 214) with earlier bibliography; Aspra-Varvadakis (2002).

to two other icons on Cyprus that show the Virgin with an embroidered red veil and a lolling Child whose left foot rests on his mother's arm: the Virgin in SS Barnabas and Hilarion, Peristerona, and perhaps more particularly the Virgin Theoskepaste in Paphos (Figs. 15–16),[70] which is paired with a warrior saint as the Virgin of the diptych is. What makes the diptych's attribution significant is its combination of styles. The frame exhibits the deeply coloured, volumetric style and crisply incised chrysography seen on the very finest of the Sinai icons made for Crusader patrons.[71] If the diptych can indeed be assigned to Cyprus, then much of the finest Crusader icon painting, too, could be assigned there, a possibility long espoused by David Jacoby. The main figures, by contrast, display a different manner, with bright, broadly painted fabrics, narrow eyes, and bulbous circles of flesh marking the brow. Precisely these two styles—that of the central figures and that of the frame—are found joined together not in Crusader art but in the manuscripts made for the Armenian Queen Keran and Prince Vasak at Sis in Cilicia. It may have been for a member of their court that the diptych was produced. Cilicia, Cyprus, and Jerusalem were sibling kingdoms whose ruling families were intimately intermarried and whose language of cultural display was similarily interwoven.[72] Given this courtly interconnection, the attribution of the diptych cannot be cavalierly addressed. Were it to be attributed to Cyprus, it would bring a very significant body of art with it. One searches eagerly on the island for echoes of its distinctive styles, indicating that such fine Crusader painting was in fact practiced on Cyprus. Significantly, none has emerged so far.

Two works of slightly later date intimate the production not of hybrid but of high styles in Lusignan Cyprus around 1300. One is the antependium of Othon of Grandson (Bern, Historisches Museum), a length of cherry-coloured silk embroidered in elegant Byzantine style in gold but incorporating, as the icon of St Nicholas had, the portrait of its Frankish knightly patron.[73] Rich textiles figure recurrently in Latin texts about Cyprus, implying the production of pat-

---

[70] *Holy Metropolis of Morphou* (2000: no. 6); Papageorghiou (1992a: pls. 15a, 15b).
[71] Especially the Crucifixion; see Evans (2004: no. 224) with earlier bibliography.
[72] Der Nersessian (1993, II: figs. 641, 647, both in colour); Carr (1995c: 96–8; 1995a: esp. 240–1).
[73] Muthesius (2004: 240–1); Bacci (2000: 373–4, fig. 43) with earlier bibliography. Othon of Grandson was in Cyprus in 1291–92 after the fall of Acre.

terned silks there. A papal inventory of 1295 lists 21 'Cyprian' fabrics of silk with gold and patterns in the Vatican, and Pope Benedict XII thanked the Archbishop of Nicosia Elias of Nabinaux in 1338 for a gift of 'clothes from Outremer of various colours and fringed with gold'.[74] If, as legend attests, Othon had the antependium made in Cyprus, it would speak to a very high level of both style and execution on the island. The other intimation of high style on Cyprus is offered by the bilateral icon already mentioned in the church of SS Joachim and Anna at Kaliana.[75] Its overpainted obverse retains in its frame an extensive cycle of the life of the Virgin Mary in a bright, Byzantinizing style; its reverse, on the other hand, is painted on a soft red ground with a haunting scene of the Crucifixion that blends elaborate Greek inscriptions with facial types and an emotive sensibility that are Gothic. It offers a lone and alluring intimation that Gothic as well as Frankish and Eastern Christian paintings existed in late thirteenth-century Cyprus.

By the time we reach the four objects just discussed, we stand on the brink of the fourteenth century. All four pose the challenge of attributing to Cyprus a style or artifact for which there are no visual comparanda on the island. By far the most compelling attribution of this kind is Michele Bacci's study of a vast altar cloth of white silk embroidered with gold and colours that was given in 1325 to the Duomo in Pisa by the eminent Pisan Dominican, the Archbishop of Nicosia John of Conti (1312–32).[76] The forms of the fabric's many scenes are Gothic, but they bear no resemblance whatever to the Gothic conventions of contemporary Italian embroidery, and rather than to Pisa, Bacci assigns the creation of the piece to John's see in Cyprus. It is a compelling argument. John was major art patron, who is known to have given three such embroidered textiles to his own cathedral church in Nicosia. He takes us over the threshold and into the full flush of fourteenth-century art. As such, it is significant to see how thoroughly his antependium differs from that of Othon of Grandson. Neither style nor technique is traditionally Byzantine, and the imagery is Gothic. It indicates that we have entered a new era.

---

[74] *Synodicum Nicosiense*, no. X.53.2. For textiles, see especially the rich bibliography assembled by Bacci (2000: 368–81); for the inventory, see Muthesius (2004: passim and 247–9).
[75] *Holy Metropolis of Morphou* (2000: no. 3).
[76] Bacci (2000).

The sense of crossing into a new era is confirmed by a pair of manuscript illuminations that adorn the legal codex, Paris. gr. 1391.[77] The fact that these are miniatures in a manuscript deserves note in itself, for they are the only illuminations securely attributable to Cyprus in the medieval period. The extent to which manuscript illumination was practiced on Cyprus is extremely problematic, due partly to the improbably large number of late twelfth and thirteenth-century 'decorative style' books with links to Cyprus,[78] and partly to the improbably small cluster of three radically disparate books that can be associated with the island in the fourteenth century. Of these, the so-called Hamilton Psalter (Berlin, Staatliche Museen, Kupferstichkabinett 78 A 9) has attracted the most scholarly attention.[79] Produced in around 1300, the Hamilton Psalter is a composite of Greek and Latin texts including a bilingual psalter illuminated with a Byzantine marginal psalter cycle; it belonged in the fifteenth century to Queen Charlotte of Cyprus. Its numerous marginal illuminations are poorly painted over delicate and accomplished drawings; the frontispiece illuminations on the other hand display a superb Palaeologan Renaissance style, the sole example of this style associated with Cyprus. The rarity of illuminated bilingual books, the costliness of the long psalter cycle, and the high style of the frontispiece make the Hamilton Psalter thoroughly exceptional. Its litany suggests that it was made for use in Famagusta. If it could be shown to have been made there, it would open a glimpse not only into an otherwise fraught medium of artistic production, but into an otherwise unattested realm of cost and cultivation. Elegantly illuminated Armenian manuscripts tinged with Gothic style were being illuminated in Famagusta in the first two decades of the fourteenth century,[80] and it would be attractive to be able to add a comparably elegant codex from the Greek and Latin communities. To date, however, no tangible bond links its miniatures

---

[77] Constantinides and Browning, *Dated Greek Manuscripts*, 127–32, pls. 165–6.

[78] Carr (1987). Some 22 of the 113 'decorative style' codices have associations with Cyprus: see Carr (1987–1988); Constantinides and Browning, *Dated Greek Manuscripts*, 45.

[79] See Evans (2004: no. 77), with earlier bibliography, Buchthal (1975: 149–52, figs. 10–12), and esp. Havice (1984). The book is inscribed on fol. 1v: *Isto libro la Regina Charlotta de Jerousalem de Chipre et Armenia.*

[80] Der Nersessian (1993, I: 134–9) with earlier bibliography, citing: Jerusalem, Library of the Armenian Archbishopric MS 1033 of 1306, MS 1714 of 1308, and MS 1946 of 1310; Erevan, Matenadaran MS 7691 of 1307 and MS 104 of 1311; and Cluj-Napoca, State Archives MS 15.

with Cyprus. Moreover, the closely contemporary illuminated Gospel Book of 1304/5, London, British Library, Additional MS 22506,[81] is almost certain to have originated outside the island. Absent these two major manuscripts, the very likelihood that books were illuminated on Lusignan Cyprus has been questioned.

It is here that the two miniatures of Paris. gr. 1391 prove invaluable. Given the prominence of legal work in the literature of medieval Cyprus, it is striking that the one tangible proof of manuscript illumination on the island should occur in a legal volume, and a volume produced in the much neglected Paphos district, at that. The miniatures depict Byzantine law-giver emperors: Justinian I in one image; Constantine I and Leo VI in the other. They adorn a volume of legal texts composed partly in Cypriot dialect, produced around 1300 in the Paphos district and still on Cyprus in the sixteenth century. The images are clearly contemporary with the text, possibly painted by the rubricator himself, and the fact that the book was produced in and remained on Cyprus makes it certain that they were painted on the island. Their style is compatible with the date around 1300 proposed for the text. Slender and assured, with classically proportioned faces and graceful stance, wearing golden loroi and scarlet boots, the figures look more elegant and confidently metropolitan than anything encountered in the thirteenth century. Yet their firmly traced eyes are those of the Crusader 'Acre School', while their curious, mitre-like hats and flairing crown without *prependoulia*, their capes thrown back in dashing folds from the shoulders like those of Frankish kings, and their scarlet and blue colour schemes all reveal a conception of the imperial person that is as Frankish as it is Constantinopolitan. Bound in their imagery of rulership to a Frankish context, they are at the same time more conversant with Constantinopolitan conventions than the thirteenth-century works, and signal a new phase in Cyprus' art.

The Fourteenth Century

Earlier in this chapter we pondered when the thirteenth century should be said to have begun. The antependium of John of Conti and the miniatures of Paris. gr. 1391 suggest that the fourteenth century began

---

[81] Constantinides and Browning, *Dated Greek Manuscripts*, 134–35.

very close to 1300. The year 1300 is not singled out in histories of
Cyprus; King Henry II, who had been crowned in 1286, perhaps
with the magnificent illuminated Crusader *Histoire universelle* as a gift,[82]
was still king in 1324. Yet outside Cyprus two major changes had
taken place: the Crusader States on the mainland had ceased to
exist, and Constantinople had resumed its traditional place as the
cultural metropolis of the Eastern Christian world. These changes
affect the interpretation of visual art on Cyprus deeply. They bring
to an end the discontinuities on the external scene that had made
it so difficult in the thirteenth century to give internal consistency
either to Latin or to Eastern Christian artifacts, or to give meaning
to the cases of interchange between them. Traditions of form become
clearer, and with this it becomes easier to perceive the identities of
those who adopt them. Thus the fourteenth century assumes a clarity lacking in the copious but contradictory thirteenth.

Orthodox patronage is reflected most extensively in mural cycles.
Here, a degree of stylistic coherence unites a whole sequence of
paintings running through the first two thirds of the century. Anticipated
in the simply coloured, strongly contoured paintings of 1317 in St
Demetrianos, Dali, and the fourteenth-century naos figures and icon
at the Panagia Amasgou, Monagri,[83] this manner emerges with particular clarity in the narthex paintings of 1332/33 at Asinou (Fig.
24).[84] It synthesizes the two dominant modes of the *maniera Cypria*
that had been pointed out earlier. At the same time, it exhibits a
new volume and energy, with forms that hearken back to the dynamic,
late Comnenian repertoire of postures and ropy drapery folds. It is
not modern scholars alone who have seen a classic quality in the
late twelfth-century murals of Cyprus. The fourteenth-century painters,
too, drew heavily upon these images in both style and iconography,
relying on them as if tapping back to their own classic tradition. As
this artistic current develops further in the slightly later naos paintings at Asinou (Fig. 25),[85] the narthex paintings at Lagoudera,[86] and

[82] London, British Museum, Add. 15268. On its association with Henry II's coronation in Tyre, see Buchthal (1957: 86).
[83] Stylianou and Stylianou (1997: 425–7) (Dali); Boyd (1974: 323–7, figs. 54–64,
67) (Asinou).
[84] Stylianou and Stylianou (1997: 134–7); Seymer *et al.* (1933: 335–40). An icon of
the Mother of God at the church of the Hodegetria in Arediou seems from the
published photograph to belong to the same group: see Loulloupis (1991: 18, pls. 1–2).
[85] Stylianou and Stylianou (1997: 126–34); Seymer *et al.* (1933: 340–5).
[86] Winfield and Winfield (2003: figs. 8, 300–3).

just after mid-century in the naos of the Holy Cross, Pelendri (Fig. 26),[87] it becomes looser and more colouristic, with a decorative play of linear highlights in the drapery, and ornate, light-spangled architectural and landscape motifs in the backgrounds. The play upon light and landscape probably reflects Palaeologan developments ultimately, but little in the forms is identifiably Palaeologan, and the exuberantly patterned architecture recalls that of the contemporary Cilician Armenian miniaturist, Sargis Pidzak.[88] It is a local, not a metropolitan, style. The colour schemes, decorative patterns, and facial conventions seen in these works carry on then, both in the less energetic murals in the cave of St Sozomenos, and in the portions of the cycle at St Catherine, Pyrga, that Spanou believes predate the better-known scenes of 1421. The standing saints from the late fourteenth century at St Nicholas tis Stegis, Kakopetria, finally, serve as a coda, schematizing this manner.[89]

The sense of continuity conferred by the style in these paintings is reassuring after the diversity of the thirteenth-century cycles. But it serves to mask both the erratic experimentalism of their programmes and the syncretism of their iconography. The narthex at Asinou makes imaginative use of the Last Judgment (Fig. 24), a theme widespread in medieval Cyprus; the iconography of the naos paintings (Fig. 25), on the other hand, is radically composite, embracing elements drawn from the initial, early twelfth-century cycle, the classic late Comnenian models, the Passion imagery disseminated from Jerusalem in the Crusader era, and such novel Palaeologan themes as the prefigurations of the Virgin.[90] The programme at the Holy Cross, Pelendri, is even more intricate. Levantine, Byzantine, and Italian imagery mingle in the bema in an extended post-Passion cycle that spills out into an uneasy blend of Passion and Marian cycles in the naos (Fig. 26). The extraordinarily complicated pedigree of the scenes in Pelendri, which echo contemporary Armenian

---

[87] Stylianou and Stylianou (1997: 223–32). The church of the Holy Cross was painted by a cluster of workshops, of which two seem to have been active somewhat earlier at Asinou, one in the narthex and one in the naos.

[88] Der Nersessian (1993, I: 142–52; II: figs. 595–609) for Erevan, Matenadaran 5786 of 1336 (Gospels of priest Andreas) and Jerusalem, Library of the Armenian Patriarchate 1973 of 1346 (Gospels of Queen Mariun).

[89] Papageorghiou (1999a: 47–52) (St Sozomenos); Spanou (2002: 49–50) (Pyrga); Stylianou and Stylianou (1997: 72–5) (Kakopetria).

[90] The paintings at Asinou will be examined closely in Nicolaides and Carr (forthcoming).

as well as earlier Frankish, Italian, and Byzantine forms, has been beautifully illuminated by Ioanna Christoforaki;[91] one can only hope she will continue her work on this crucial and immensely complex monument. Its importance is compounded, as will emerge below, by the contemporary but stylistically distinct dome programme and the scenes in the north aisle. Painted in high Palaeologan style and incorporating both the arms of John of Lusignan (†1375), brother of King Peter I (1359–69), and the portraits of a Frankish couple, the dome and north aisle raise significant questions of local Greek and Latin components in fourteenth-century patronage.

Artistic patronage on the part of the Latin populace continues to be most visible in architecture and sculpture. As of about 1300, in fact, buildings begin to survive in fair numbers, and though it remains difficult to align the remaining structures with institutions named in texts, it is possible to assess their features. As in the thirteenth century, so now the forms are dominantly French, but their Frenchness no longer begs comparison with forms developed in the mainland Crusader States: rather than a variant of a living tradition on the Frankish mainland, the buildings on Cyprus are a genre in their own right, responsive to Cypriot conditions. Of the surviving Gothic churches in Nicosia—the cathedral of St Sophia, the Armenian church (Our Lady of Tortosa), St Catherine, the Yeni Mosque, the Omerieh Mosque, and the Bedestan—the one with the most nuanced scholarship so far is the cathedral (Fig. 14). Its nave, dedicated on 7 November 1326 by Archbishop John of Conti, introduced the rayonnant mullions that would also characterize the windows of the Armenian church and in time those of Bellapais' cloister and St Nicholas in Famagusta; here, too, the florid, decorative foliage motifs evolved that became so distinctive to Cypriot sculpture.[92] The cathedral's construction culminated in the elaborate porch that so distinguishes the building today. John of Conti, encountered already as the patron of a great embroidery for the cathedral of Pisa, clearly considered his own cathedral's splendour to be important, and he gifted it lavishly: he installed two bells, a marble font, and a rich marble sanctuary screen; had the ceiling painted blue with golden stars like that of the Sainte-Chapelle in Paris; added a chapel dedicated to and painted with the life of

---

[91] Christoforaki (2000; 1996; 1997).
[92] Enlart (1987: 105–15); Rivoire-Richard (1996: 1436); Boase (1977: 170).

St Thomas Aquinas; endowed the institution with three great silken altar panels, two in white and one in green; and gave it rich vestments and an episcopal throne embroidered with the Transfiguration.[93] Wealthy and powerful, he clearly conceived his cathedral as a counterpart to those of Europe, and his yards must have been crucial training sites for both sculptors and masons; full-length episcopal figures found in both Nicosia and Famagusta suggest the presence of an immigrant Parisian master-sculptor on Cyprus, while the imposing Christ in the Pancyprian Gymnasium and the archivolt figures still *in situ* in the cathedral porch bespeak local sculptors trained to French forms.[94]

That Gothic was the language of both Church and State in Lusignan Cyprus seems clear enough: not only the cathedrals of Nicosia, Famagusta,[95] Limassol,[96] and Paphos, but the churches of the Franciscan Order in Famagusta and Paphos, and the residences of urban immigrants and royal family alike were Gothic.[97] In what voice the Gothic actually spoke is more intricate, for the State did not always speak with the voice of the Church. This is addressed in Justine Andrews' analysis of the sculpture in the porch of St Sophia (Fig. 28). The sculptural programme was completed under Hugh IV (1324–59) with a theme of coronation that is still overt in the crown-bearing hands above the niches flanking the doors. Already Camille Enlart had compared the arcades and panels of the central portal of the porch to the interior western wall of Reims Cathedral, the coronation church of France as Nicosia's was of the Kingdom of Cyprus.[98] Reims, in turn, is yet more overtly the archetype of the cathedral of St Nicholas in Famagusta (Fig. 29), again a coronation church, now of Cyprus' rulers as kings of Jerusalem. Begun in 1300, St Nicholas was as fundamental to the evolution of Gothic in Famagusta as St Sophia was in Nicosia. Nicola Coldstream assigns both St George of the Greeks and the annexed chapel of the Franciscan church to the workshop of St Nicholas.[99] But St Nicholas is, by comparison with St Sophia,

---

[93] Bacci (2000: 361–4).

[94] Vaivre (2001); Solomidou-Ieronymidou (1988); Boase (1977: 170–1).

[95] Enlart (1987: 222–45); Rivoire-Richard (1996: 1418–19).

[96] Of Limassol almost nothing survives, though it may be identical with the thirteenth-century church beneath the castle; see Prokopiou (1997: 294) and Boase (1977: 181).

[97] Enlart (1987: 262–7, 355–8, 390–415); Maier and Wartburg (1985) on the royal manor at Kouklia.

[98] Andrews (1999); Enlart (1987: 125).

[99] Coldstream (1975). On the rapid development of Famagusta in the later thirteenth century, see in particular Jacoby (1984a) and Balard (1985).

Gothic-by-the-yard. It has a single-minded homogeneity that St Sophia
does not. St Sophia's western face is a composite, its message inflected
(Fig. 28). Its tympanum was most probably crowned with the Transfiguration, one of late Byzantium's most theologically sensitive scenes;[100]
its jambs were occupied by panel paintings rather than statues; its
foliage ornament was multiform and of varied origin; and its panel-
like niches perhaps reflected the similar, shallow niches in the Spanish
Gothic cathedral of Tarragona. Where St Nicholas, Andrews proposes, speaks in the purity of its form to the European theatre of
kingship in which the crown of Jerusalem retained its greatest significance, St Sophia's porch speaks to the Kingdom of Cyprus, a kingdom that Hugh IV clearly recognized was a religious and ethnic
composite.[101] Gothic, then, could become a locally inflected language.

With this, we stand on the brink of a fundamental shift in the
story of Cypriot artistic expression. It is signaled initially by the church
of St George of the Greeks in Famagusta (Fig. 30). Incorporating in
its south wall like a virtual relic an earlier Orthodox church, possibly
the earlier cathedral, St George was surely built *ab initio* as the Orthodox cathedral. Debate over its date has been resolved by Catherine
Otten-Froux's publication of documents citing its construction in the
1360s.[102] Its magnificent scale must have been planned to evoke the
grandeur of Famagusta's see, the see of Salamis/Constantia and for
centuries the archiepiscopal seat of Cyprus.[103] Strikingly in view of
its symbolic role in the history of the Church of Cyprus, it is a rib-
vaulted Gothic building: a Gothic building conceived not in the quilly
mold of St Nicholas' 'fretful porpentine' next door, but as a smooth,
vaulted skin over an ample interior clothed with painted and stained
glass colour.[104] Its paintings, now painfully abraded, were of superb quality and high Palaeologan style, and immensely important (Fig. 31).

---

[100] This was the Transfiguration, central in debates over Hesychast spirituality.
This controversy was felt in Cyprus; partisans of both sides came to the island,
though the most notable Cypriot participant, George Lapithes, learned friend of
Hugh IV, was a partisan of the anti-Palamites, and Cypriot sentiment seems to
have been dominantly anti-Palamite; see Kyrris (1961; 1962) and Grivaud and
Schabel in this volume.
[101] Andrews (1999: 74). On Hugh IV and the churches, see Grivaud (2001b).
[102] Otten-Froux (2003: 42, 46). Enlart (1987: 253–8) had dated the building in
the 1360s, a date later questioned by Coldstream (1975), Boase (1977: 178–9), and
Rivoire-Richard (1996: 1423).
[103] Kyrris (1993: 164–5, 176–7); Nicolaou-Konnari (1999: 332–4).
[104] Mogabgab (1934–1936: 104) reports on the discovery of fragments of stained
glass at St George of the Greeks.

It is impossible to overestimate the significance of the study of the building planned by Thierry Soulard. In both its Gothic form and its Palaeologan paintings, St George marks a fundamental shift in visual rhetoric. Imported architecture of cosmopolitan quality on the one hand, imported painting of cosmopolitan excellence on the other, displace locally specific forms as the voice of the Greek-rite community. Famagusta was home to Eastern Christians of immense wealth: the nearby church of SS Peter and Paul, closely akin to St George in date and plan, is reputed to have been built entirely from his own wealth in the reign of King Peter I (1359–69) by a merchant whom Boase, on the basis of a Syrian inscription in the building, suggests was Nestorian.[105] If he is right, Greek-rite and Nestorian Christians would both have been using artistic forms as an index not to their native ethnicity, origin, or creed, but to their high social standing. Nicosia, too, had an Orthodox cathedral after 1260, at first St Barnabas and then at some point a church dedicated to the Hodegetria (or, in Stephen of Lusignan's words, the Chrysotheistria).[106] Whether it was built in Gothic style is debated: consensus labels the domed and rib-vaulted Bedestan as Hodegetria, but this is speculative and the Bedestan may have been erected only in the fifteenth century.[107] It is St George in Famagusta that illustrates most clearly the shift to align styles with class. With this, new patterns of perception appear.

The Latin nobility, too, valued cosmopolitan excellence over creed. This is the clearest way to understand the surviving evidence of the patronage of the Lusignan kings themselves.[108] For centuries already, eminence as a court had lain in the capacity to become a cross-roads of excellence, where the splendors of the world both came, and—with prodigal generosity—also went. In just this way we hear of St Louis during his sojourn in Cyprus receiving as a gift from

---

[105] Boase (1977: 177–8).

[106] Papageorghiou (1995b: 280, note 15).

[107] Enlart (1987: 136–46), identifying the Bedestan as the church of St Nicholas; Boase (1977: 175). Papageorghiou (1995b: 276 and esp. 280, note 15) defends the Bedestan's identity as the cathedral and its existence already in the fourteenth century, because a note in Paris. gr. 1589, fol. 269v, implies the existence of an Orthodox cathedral in Nicosia at this date. Willis (1986) says flatly that the Bedestan goes back no earlier than the fifteenth. Sources confirm that in the fifteenth century the cathedral was dedicated to the Hodegetria; see Nicolaou-Konnari (1999: 332, 335 and note 238, 350 and note 302, 361 and note 357) and Otten-Froux (2002: 120).

[108] Carr (1995b).

the king of Armenia a pavilion that the king in turn had received as a gift from a vassal of the sultan of Iconium.[109] In the family of Hugh IV we see the Lusignans adopting much the same standard. Certainly, as the sculpted porch of St Sophia and the cathedral of Famagusta show, the ecclesiastical settings for their formal rituals of state were given every dignity of Gothic grandeur. Hugh's son Peter exhibited the same standard in his personal behaviour when he captivated his hosts during travels in Europe.[110] Paintings of comparably European pedigree must have been produced on Cyprus, too, for a small group of fourteenth-century icons, including those from the templon the Antiphonetes church, adopt the type of punchwork used in the workshops of Pietro Lorenzetti and Simone Martini, and seen on Cyprus in the tiny Gothic panel of an otherwise unidentified St Andrew once preserved at Kyrenia.[111]

Often when the patronage of painting was at issue, however, the Lusignans seem to have turned to the high style of the late Byzantine courts, the Palaeologan style. One sees this at the church of the Holy Cross at Pelendri. Pelendri is a complicated church, painted apparently in fairly short order by a number of different painters or shops. Two of them had worked already at Asinou and their work has figured in our earlier discussion of fourteenth-century Orthodox painting (Figs. 25–26). The painter of the dome, on the other hand, was a Palaeologan master of truly exceptional skill and currency (Fig. 27). His style was imitated by the main hand of the north aisle, which contains the crest of John of Lusignan (†1375) and portraits of a couple dressed as Latins, possibly though not certainly John himself and his wife.[112] From its location outside the village, it seems likely that the Holy Cross was a funerary church, and it may have been for this purpose that its Latin lord annexed its north aisle. If so, two factors stand out strongly in his patronage. One is his participation in the decoration not of the north aisle only but of the church as a whole, since its adornment must have begun with the dome; the other is the style he sponsored, for it was he who introduced the metropolitan style of Byzantium to its adornment. His class is signaled by the superbness, not the westernness, of his participation. Along with the Gothic and Palaeologan,

---

[109] John of Joinville, ch. 31.
[110] Carr (1995b: 342) with earlier bibliography.
[111] Carr (1995a: 244, fig. 9); Frinta (1998: nos. 199, 243, 244, 460).
[112] Christoforaki (1996: fig. 4); Carr (1995b: fig. 10 and 345, fig. 11). John was the lord of Pelendri: see *Synodicum Nicosiense*, no. X.55.1.

yet a third strand in the eclectic skein of Lusignan patronage enters when one turns to metalwork. King Hugh himself is identified as the owner—whether patron or recipient—of damascened vessels comparable to those of the Mamluk court.[113] What unites these works is not their form; it is their cosmopolitan excellence: high Gothic, high Palaeologan, high Mamluk.

When and by what means Palaeologan art reached Cyprus is not clear. A careful analysis of the murals at St George of the Greeks will be extremely helpful here (Fig. 31). Their iconography is distinct from that of both Macedonia and Mystras; their style has not been identified or dated. On Cyprus their style is most nearly akin to that of the sixteenth-century Italo-Byzantine murals at the Panagia Podithou, but the painter of Podithou was a master of retrospection and probably based his own work on that of St George. The ebullient energy of the paintings at St George almost necessitates a date in the fourteenth century. The earliest dated work of Palaeologan painting that survives on Cyprus—the famous, slender funerary panel in the Byzantine Museum in Nicosia recording the death of Maria, daughter of Manuel and Euphemia Xeros, in 1356 (Fig. 32)[114]—is probably not far distant from the frescoes at St George. Both are the product of local, Orthodox patronage. The avenue of the royal family's access to Palaeologan painters, on the other hand, may be illuminated by the kinship of the forms at Pelendri with those of the Perivleptos church in Mystras. The exceptionally gifted painter of Pelendri might have been brought to Lusignan attention by Isabella of Lusignan, wife of the Despot of Mystras, Manuel Cantacuzenos (1348–80). Isabella and her husband are likely to have been the patrons of the Perivleptos, which bears on two decorative slabs the motif of the rampant lion;[115] they also hosted King Peter II when he visited Mystras in 1371, and Isabella herself came to Cyprus.[116]

The currents of courtly interchange between Mystras and Nicosia create a persuasive context for the visual kinship of Cypriot art to

---

[113] Makariou (2000); Carr (1995a: 246–50) with earlier bibliography. One anticipates eagerly Dr. Makariou's promised monograph on these objects.

[114] Papageorghiou (1992a: pl. 38.).

[115] Chatzedakes (1985: 73). Thus it may be they who are portrayed as donors there; see Evgenidou and Albani (2001: pl. on p. 144). See also the fine entry by Evi Katsara on a gold finger ring found in Mystras with the same rampant lion, Evgenidou and Albani (2001: 162–3, no. 17).

[116] Runciman (1980: 56).

that of Mystras. Certainly the Palaeologan manner took firm root in
Cyprus. Beautiful icons in Palaeologan style from the later fourteenth
century survive from the churches of the Chrysaliniotissa and the
Phaneromene in Nicosia, from the Antiphonetes church in Kalogrea,
and from the churches of Kalopanagiotis. Especially interesting among
those at Kalopanagiotis is a pair of splendid icons—a templon beam
with 22 feast scenes, and a double-sided icon of the Mother of God
Athanasiotissa and Deposition[117]—that may have belonged together
as a unit in one of Kalopanagiotis' churches. The Deposition (Fig. 33)
is close in style to the dome at Pelendri (Fig. 27) and—given what
seem to be the Lusignan connections at Kalopanagiotis—may be
related to the painter of Pelendri. It raises again the likelihood that
the dissemination of the Palaeologan style may have been due not
only to local Orthodox patrons, but also to Frankish lords with bonds
to the courts of Constantinople and Mystras. Meanwhile, Palaeologan
conventions were joining with modes of local usage, a marriage illustrated vividly by the twin icons of the Panagia Paramythia in Paphos
and the Virgin in the Icon Museum at Peristerona of Polis, with
their succulent Palaeologan style and heavy carpet of Cypriot sil-
vered pastiglia on Mary's veil.[118]

The stability enabled by the coexistence in the fourteenth century
of clearly distinct metropolitan traditions—Gothic and Palaeologan—
permitted the emergence of artistic conventions that were to prove
fundamental to the future of Cyprus' history. Three examples can
represent them. The first is the adoption on the part of Cypriot
builders of the dressed stone masonry and cross-vaulted construction
that had been brought to the island by the Gothic master builders.
Along with the Orthodox cathedral of Famagusta and the Bedestan
in Nicosia, Papageorghiou notes especially St Nicholas of the Greeks
and St Zoni in Famagusta, St Mamas in Sotira, the church of the
Archangel in Lakatamia, St Nicholas of the Cats, and St James in
Trikomo. The rib-vaulted church at Stazousa, long assumed to have
been a Latin-rite building, has recently been assigned by Christopher
Schabel to the Orthodox, instead.[119] These buildings are ambigu-

---

[117] Papageorghiou (1992a: pls. 44–6, Chrysaliniotissa, pl. 47, Mother of God,
Phaneromene); Papageorghiou (1969: pl. on p. 53) and Papanikola-Bakirtzis and
Iacovou (1998: no. 54) (Kalogrea); Papageorghiou (1992a: pls. 55a–551 and 49) and
Holy Metropolis of Morphou (2000: pl. on p. 139) (Kalopanagiotis).
[118] Papageorghiou (1996: pl. 101); Tsiknopoullos (1971: pl. 372).
[119] Papageorghiou (1995b: 275); Schabel (2002: 406).

ously dated, but if they spill into the ensuing century, this serves simply to underscore the fact that dressed stone structures with cross-vaults became a durable part of Orthodox building, and continued to be constructed into the sixteenth century when outstanding structures like the Katholikon of St Neophytos monastery and St Mamas at Morphou capitalized upon that tradition.

A second tradition with roots in the fourteenth century is that of the funerary icon. Death is usually regarded in scholarship as a site of deep conservatism in which traditional habits of religious and ethnic behavior assume compelling power. But the sheer inevitability of death may in fact have made it especially demanding of accommodation. We have seen an intimation of this already in the association of Frankish burial with Greek churches: among the earliest examples of Latin presence in a Greek church is the north aisle added to the Panagia Angeloktisti at Kiti, containing the tomb slab of Simone Guers (†1302).[120] The portrait of a Latin lady at Asinou and the Latin presence in the north aisle at Pelendri, too, may reflect funerary needs of Latin Christians, for Latin parish churches were rare outside the major cities. The funerary icon may offer another insight into the patterns of funerary practice.[121] The Franks had brought with them the practice of indoor inhumation, and with it a vigorous tradition of sculpted funerary effigies, on stone sarcophagi or—more often—in the form of incised floor slabs with full-length figures of the deceased.[122] The conception of the church that such burial habits implied—as a large, urban, indoor cemetery—was alien to Greek practice in the twelfth century so far as we know, but St George of the Greeks was fitted along its nave walls with funerary niches of the same sort seen in contemporary Latin churches, and funerary slabs with Greek inscriptions imply Orthodox use of such images, too. Then over time, it seems, a distinctive form of icon was evolved to function in these settings. The slender icon recording the death of the virgin daughter of the Xeros family in 1356 may well be the first of these (Fig. 32).[123] It portrays Maria in much the posture of the funerary slabs, apparently reflecting their imagery, and identifies her

---

[120] Enlart (1987: 334–5).

[121] Carr (2005b) on funerary icons.

[122] On sculpted sarcophagi, see Imhaus (1998). On the incised slabs, see *Lacrimae Nicossienses* and since then Greenhill (1976).

[123] Papageorghiou (1992a: pl. 38); Carr (2001).

with a declarative inscription dating her death that is fundamentally unlike the votive formulae usually found on Orthodox icons. Nor is it alone: it stands at the beginning of a slowly growing number of icons that include both a portrait and an inscription recording the death of the person portrayed. Fifteen published icons of this type survive:

Fig. 19: The icon of the Xeros family from the Chrysaliniotissa church, Nicosia; Byzantine Museum, Nicosia [Papageorghiou (1992a: pl. 38)];

A now fragmentary copy of that icon, Byzantine Museum, Nicosia [Carr (2001: 604, fig. 9)];

Icon of St Euthymios with three kneeling deceased figures including a male and two females from the Chrysaliniotissa church, Nicosia; Byzantine Museum, Nicosia [Papageorghiou (1992a: pl. 39)];

Panel of the fifteenth century with a kneeling family before the Virgin and Child and the enlarged frontal figure of a deceased woman, Byzantine Museum, Nicosia [Papageorghiou (1969: pl. on p. 39)];

Fifteenth-century panel of the Mother of God Kamariotissa [Ibid., pl. on pp. 68–69].

Anastasis from the Chrysaliniotissa church, Nicosia; Byzantine Museum, Nicosia [Talbot Rice (1937: no. 23); also in Papageorghiou (1969: pl. on p. 102)];

Icon of the Mother of God with SS Nicholas and George from St George, Vatyle; Byzantine Museum, Nicosia [Talbot Rice (1937: no. 57); also in Papageorghiou (1969: pl. on p. 74)];

Icon of St George from St Cassianos, Nicosia, of 1599; Byzantine Museum, Nicosia [Talbot Rice (1937: no. 82)];

Sixteenth-century panel of St Mamas from the church of the Chrysaliniotissa with the family of a priest with a funerary inscription naming his first wife; Byzantine Museum, Nicosia [Ibid., no. 78];

Icon of John the Baptist of 1529 from the Panagia Amasgou in Monagri, now in the Bishop's Palace, Limassol, with a kneeling donor named Kyriakos Kazartos [Papanikola-Bakirtzis and Iacovou (1998: no. 145); Sophocleous (1994: 101, no. 49)];

Icon of Christ and donors from the Church of the Virgin at Emba [Talbot Rice (1937: no. 95)];

Crucifix at Kokkinotrimithia of 163 × 161 cm, dated 1567 [Papageorghiou (1992a: pl. 149)];

Sanctuary door of 1568 from the monastery of the Virgin Amirou,

Apsiou, showing St John the Baptist with a kneeling portrait of
one Fotios Vareskos [Sophocleous (1994: 103–4, no. 54)];
Icon of 1568 showing Christ as the Great Judge with a couple
flanking his feet [Papanikola-Bakirtzis and Iacovou (1998: no. 150)];
Panel of the Virgin and Child with a tiny kneeling figure claimed
by the inscription to have been killed unjustly in 1566 [Talbot
Rice (1937: figs. 127–28)].

The early examples are of architectural scale and very slender, as if
designed to fit a slender Gothic setting, perhaps akin to the steep
niches that flanked the tomb of Eschiva of Dampierre in the convent of Our Lady of Tortosa. The painted panels placed within the
sculpted molding of the tomb of St Mamas, Morphou,[124] suggest that
Orthodox families may have made a custom of placing not sculpted
plaques, but painted panels, at the tombs of their dead. The icon
of the Virgin Kamariotissa in Nicosia has an arched top, as though
echoing an architectural form in just the way the panels at Morphou
do. The later funerary icons, by contrast, are quite conventional in
both their size and shape. Apparently, as the custom of funerary
icons spread from the cities to the smaller churches of the villages
where indoor inhumation was not practiced, the accommodation of
the icon's shape to the architectural shape of the tomb ceased to be
necessary. Funerary icons must now have been accommodated simply in the places traditional for icons. But they proclaimed in their
commemorative inscriptions the new custom of funerary panels developed in the cities. In their number and persistence, the funerary icons
remain distinctive to Cyprus, a tradition incubated in the fourteenth-
century Lusignan cities.

A third tradition that becomes visible in the fourteenth century is
the iconographically identifiable icon of the Kykkotissa.[125] While the
history of the icon of Kykkos is complex, the image that would define
it for its ensuing centuries of prominence appears fully fledged for
the first time in a cluster of four large and extremely beautiful icons
of the later fourteenth century found in the villages of Marathasa

---

[124] For Tortosa, see Enlart (1987: 368, fig. 332). For St Mamas, see drawing in
Enlart (1987: 369, fig. 333); partial views in colour in *Holy Metropolis of Morphou*
(2000: pl. on p. 234); Hein *et al.* (1996: 142, pl. 145); full photograph in Carr (forthcoming: fig. 4).
[125] Carr (2004a).

and far western Cyprus; they are listed just below. The icon's signature miracle occurred in 1365, when it preserved itself from a fire that destroyed the monastery. Presumably in the wake of the fame associated with this event, a particularly clear and potent conception of the icon's form became current. This conception took tenacious hold, becoming the single most frequently repeated image of Mary after the Hodegetria in late medieval Cyprus. Fifteen panels of this type from before the Ottoman occupation are known.[126]

From the fourth quarter of the fourteenth century:
The Panagia Theoskepaste from the shrine of that name in Kalopanagiotis, now at St Herakleidios, Kalopanagiotis [*Holy Metropolis of Morphou* (2000: no. 20)];
Icon from the Panagia Theotokos church, Kalopanagiotis, now in the Icon Museum at St John Lampadistes [Evans (2004: no. 91)];
Double-sided Athanasiotissa cited above, now in the Byzantine Museum, Nicosia [*Holy Metropolis of Morphou* (2000: no. 139)];
The Panagia Galoktistes in Kato Pyrgos [Ibid., no. 19, entry by Stylianos Perdikes].

From the fifteenth and sixteenth centuries:
Vita icon in the Byzantine Museum, Nicosia [Papageorghiou (1969: pl. on p. 48)];
Icon in the Virgin's Church, Lemythou [Sophocleous (1993b: figs. 10–12)];
Close replica of the Lemythou icon in the village of Salamiou (in restoration with Savvas Papadopoulos in Yeroskipou);
Fresco icon in the closed apse window at the Panagia Chryseleousa, Lyso [Sophocleous (1993b: pl. 13)];
Mural icon at St Kerykos and Ioulitta, Letympou [Ibid., pl. 9];
Icon labeled with the name of 'He Kikiotisa' from St Paraskeve, Moutoullas, now in the Museum of the Holy Monastery of Kykkos [Perdikes (1997: fig. 55)];
Icon labeled with the same name in the church of the Panagia Kivotos at St Theodoros tou Agrou [Sophocleous (1993b: figs. 1–6)];
Icon labeled with the same name now in the Byzantine Museum in Pedoulas [Evans (2004: no. 93)];

[126] It is possible that the newly published Panagia Mesogitissa in the church of the Panagia in Mesoge, Papageorghiou (2004: 51, figs. 7–8), could also predate 1570.

Icon from St Sergios, Kalopanagiotis, now in the Icon Museum at
  St John Lampadistes (unpublished);
Icon of the Mesogitissa in Mesoge [Papageorghiou (2004)].
Icon once covered by the gilded plaques on the icon in the
  Chryseleousa church, Praitori, now overpainted or replaced
  [Papageorghiou (1992a: pl. 17)];
Icon recorded in a drawing of the templon of the Archangel church
  in Pedoulas by S. Phrankoulides [Soteriou (1935: pl. 148)].

Most are large; many are of high quality; but they vary in style, and
rather than implying deliberate dissemination from a central point,
as the Kykkotissa's images would in the Ottoman period, they seem
rather to have been made at the instigation of varied patrons and
villages. Half are from Marathasa; the rest trace a geography that moves
not eastward to the major cities but westward from the Troodos into
the fertile plains of Polis. One yearns to understand better the forces
that bound the icon's first, explosive success to the centuries of Latin
rule. Economic patterns, but also the habits of religious devotion and
display nurtured by the Lusignan regime must have played their role
in the robust life of Cyprus' miracle-working icons in the fourteenth
and fifteenth centuries;[127] while there is no question but that the
Kykkotissa's potent cult was a Greek phenomenon, it is also clear
that the Cyprus of Hugh IV and Peter I was finely attuned to holy
objects, holy wars, and holy happenings, and it could even be that
Frankish as well as Orthodox Christians found the Kykkotissa compelling. Dangerous as it is to equate a style with its patron's ethnicity, the gilded icon cover for a Kykkotissa that survives at Praitori
is remarkably Gothic in both the technique of its translucent enamel
medallions and style of the kneeling figure near the Virgin's head.
Here once again, an image crystallized in the fourteenth century
became formative for the island's later art.

　　The fourteenth century stands out for its strong base in well artic-
ulated metropolitan traditions—Gothic on the one hand, Palaeologan
on the other. This dual allegiance to metropolitan forms persisted
in the ensuing century. As cut stone became a widespread medium
for architecture, Palaeologan style became virtually pervasive for
painting. The Palaeologan style expands from the cities in this period

---

[127] Carr (2004b).

to permeate the full geography of the island. Icons, though fewer in number than in either of the preceding centuries, are of stable, often accomplished late Byzantine style; monumental painting develops a range of modes but all rooted in more or less current late Byzantine conventions. For the first time since the twelfth century it makes sense to speak of a coherent stylistic matrix on Cyprus.

Dating fourteenth-century monuments with precision is difficult. It remains hard to see the crucial dates of 1348 or 1373 with any clarity in the pattern of artistic production, or to see whether 1373 was followed by the kind of 'post-traumatic splendor' that followed the crises of 1191 and 1204. The murals at Pelendri seem to lie between 1348 and 1373. Though the sturdy sequence of frescoed churches that had punctuated the decades up to Pelendri weakens thereafter, other traditions like that of the funerary icons accelerate, and some of the finest panel paintings of the Lusignan era, like those from the Chrysaliniotissa church in Nicosia and the icons from Kalopanagiotis, are attributed to the later years of the century.

Looking backward from the perspective of the fifteenth century, however, it is clear by the time of the battle of Khirokitia in 1426 that the fourteenth century had closed. New patterns of artistic production had emerged, and those of the fourteenth century were taking their own shape in history. Three shifts stand out. First, it becomes far more difficult in the fifteenth century to follow the patronage of the court. Characteristically the rulers are represented by the tiny chapel at Pyrga dedicated in 1421 to the Passion and now dedicated to St Catherine.[128] The ribs of its single bay blazoned with the Lusignan arms and its apseless eastern wall displaying the kneeling portraits of the ruling couple, Janus (1398–1432) and Charlotte, the chapel is unquestionably a courtly one. Its architecture is without distinction, however; its iconography is opaque; and its style is disjunct, with some scenes still rooted in the fourteenth-century manner of Asinou and Pelendri,[129] and others in a Palaeologan volume style that hovers between mannerism and maladroitness. The scenes in the latter style are labeled in vernacular French, a unicum on Cyprus, and four portraits of contemporary people participate as actors in them, a convention so rare in both Byzantium and the West that it is hard

---

[128] Christoforaki (1997: 95–6); Stylianou and Stylianou (1997: 428–32); Papageorghiou (n.d.; 1982: 221–2, pls. XLIX, 4 and L, 1–4); Enlart (1987: 325–34).
[129] See note 80 above.

to know whether to call it *au courant* or simply odd.[130] Scholars cite the chapel to prove that Latin-rite patrons had adopted well-defined Byzantine styles, but that had been obvious since Pelendri (Fig. 27). They cite it, too, to prove the king's impoverishment, for it is a modest thing, especially by comparison with the paintings at Pelendri.

The paintings at Pyrga are, in fact, so modest that they should be regarded only reservedly as representative of the courtly culture. The Ferrarese Duke Niccolò d'Este was impressed by the amenities of Janus' court during a sojourn on Cyprus in 1412, and the remarkable musical manuscript, Torino, Biblioteca nazionale, J.II.9, reveals an extremely high level of musical culture in the royal chapel.[131] Both the music and the illuminations in the Torino manuscript are excellent, quite outstripping Pyrga. That work of far higher quality than Pyrga was available to Latins of discernment is seen in the bilateral icon of the Panagia Ieroskipiotissa at St Paraskeve, Yeroskipou. The Panagia Ieroskipiotissa was fully embraced by Orthodox Christians, who replicated it some decades later for the Chryseleousa church at Emba.[132] But the audience it addressed was not only or even primarily Greek: its dominant labels are in Latin and its elegant style hovers in a delicate balance between Palaeologan and Gothic. More than Pyrga, the Ieroskipiotissa shows the elegance with which Latin patrons could cultivate Byzantine artistic traditions. It is informative to compare the Ieroskipiotissa with the bilateral icon from the end of the thirteenth century at Kaliana. Both follow the Byzantine tradition of placing a Crucifixion on the reverse of an image of the Hodegetria, and in each case the Crucifixion reflects Western sensibility. What differentiates them is not the convergence of two traditions, which they share, but the extreme refinement of the models from both traditions at Yeroskipou. The internalization of high styles from both Byzantium and the West is precisely what the fourteenth century had brought. Patronage of great elegance, then, cannot be assumed simply to have degenerated. But the court no longer stands out. Artistic production in the fifteenth century was widespread, without the concentration in the cathedral cities that had characterized the fourteenth century.

---

[130] On the inclusion of donors in Gospel scenes see Carr (1995b: 347).
[131] *Excerpta Cypria Nova*, no. 1, 43–9; Finscher and Günther (1995) with extensive bibliography.
[132] Papageorghiou (1992b: pls. 63a, 63b, 87).

Throughout the island, in the second place, the dominant stylistic mode in painting is the Palaeologan. As a coherent stylistic matrix emerged, it did so not on the basis of the local manner that had flourished in the frescoed churches of the fourteenth century, but on the basis of what in the fourteenth century had been the elite style characteristic of the court and the cathedral cities. The high style now became pervasive. No other mural paintings quite equal the accomplished elegance of those in the enigmatic 'old Enkleistra' of St Euphymios near Kouklia,[133] but the scenes at St Andronikos in Liopetri and the Holy Cross in Anogyra, illustrated in colour by Christoforaki,[134] the vast expanse of Christological and eschatological imagery cloaking the earlier, cruciform church of St Kerykos and Ioulitta in Letympou,[135] the Last Judgment and Jesse Tree in the church of Christ Antiphonetes, Kalogrea,[136] and above all the murals from the very end of the century at the Katholikon of St Neophytos are of impressive quality.[137] Even a modest popular shrine like that of Hagia Mavre near Koilani has a late Byzantine edge of sophistication. Unpretentious as it seems, it adopts Palaeologan mannerisms of form and takes up in its iconography the theme of Old Testament prefigurations of the Virgin so elegantly elaborated in fourteenth-century Constantinople and Serbia, displaying over its entry Jeremiah looking to the Virgin as a tower. The shift to a predominantly Palaeologan manner is often linked to an influx of patrons and craftspeople after 1453. In fact, the evidence of change in the wake of 1453 is meagre. The adoption of Palaeologan conventions had far earlier roots. It was the fourteenth century that reoriented Cyprus to the Byzantine rather than the Syro-Palestinian mainland.

A third shift occurs in the Western elements of Cypriot imagery. As Christoforaki shows, if the pervasive dissemination of late Byzantine style is one of the period's features, the pervasive insemination of Cypriot imagery with Western European elements is another: they

[133] Stylianou and Stylianou (1997: 397–403); Papageorghiou (1999a: 57–9).
[134] Christoforaki (1997: figs. 5–6).
[135] Stylianou and Stylianou (1997: 414–18); Christoforaki (1997: 90) with a mid-century date; Karageorghis (1990: 33–4) with a date at the end of the century.
[136] Stylianou and Stylianou (1997: 476–85). Stolen after the 1974 Turkish invasion, the Jesse Tree from the south wall is now in shattered fragments in the Byzantine Museum in Nicosia.
[137] Stylianou and Stylianou (1997: 369–81); Christoforaki (1997: 94); Constantinides (1999: 281–3).

range from devices of form, especially a fascination with the creation of three-dimensional space boxes, through aspects of clothing
and costume to iconographic conventions, some mere motifs like the
angel guiding the Magi but some full scenes like the *Noli me Tangere*.[138]
These are elements derived not from the Crusader Holy Land, but
from a range of contemporary Western European developments. If
the thirteenth century had bewildered the effort to create boundaries
between groups, and the fourteenth had impressed by the ease with
which clearly defined categories like Palaeologan, Mamluk, or Gothic
could cross ethnic and creedal boundaries when social class invited
it, the fifteenth century impresses for its intricate 'speckling' of late
Byzantine forms with contemporary features drawn from Western
Europe.

Together, these exemplify what the fourteenth century had brought.
It had turned Cyprus from a Levantine to a Mediterranean culture,
drawing it from its focus on the Syro-Palestinian mainland to engage
once again the crosscurrents of Byzantium and the West. As the
fourteenth century itself slipped into the past, the components it left
to the fifteenth—seen throughout Cyprus—were those of the international high styles, Palaeologan, Gothic, and, slowly, the Renaissance.

---

[138] Christoforaki (1997: 90 and passim).

ILLUSTRATIONS

Fig. 1. Lusignan coat of arms. Photo by Chris Schabel.

Fig. 2. St Hilarion Castle, view from SE. Photo by Chris Schabel.

Fig. 3. Buffavento Castle, view from summit to SW. Photo by Chris Schabel.

Fig. 4. Kantara Castle, view from south. Photo by Chris Schabel.

Fig. 5. Kyrenia Castle, view from SE. Photo by Chris Schabel.

Fig. 6. St Hilarion Castle, window in residential quarters. Photo by Chris Schabel.

Fig. 7. Kolossi Castle, view from west. Photo by Chris Schabel.

Fig. 8. Kolossi Castle, window seat. Photo by Chris Schabel.

Fig. 9. Pyla Tower, from west. Photo by Chris Schabel.

Fig. 10. Silver gros, James II.

Fig. 11. White bezant, Henry I, type 3A.

Fig. 12. The channel and aqueduct carrying water to the mill of Archangelos, near Potamia. Photo courtesy of Benoît Garros.

Fig. 13. Water mill of Palaeomylos, near Potamia: the upper side of the water tower. Photo courtesy of Benoît Garros.

Fig. 14. Nicosia, Cathedral of St Sophia. Photo by Annemarie Weyl Carr.

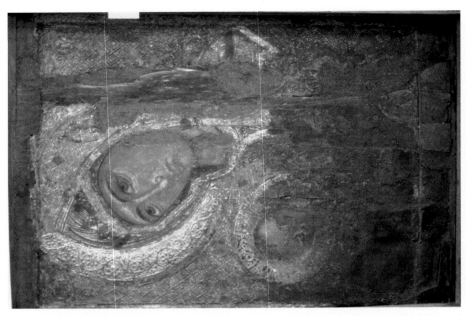

Fig. 16. Paphos, Byzantine Museum. Panagia Theoskepaste, obverse of Fig. 15. Photo by Annemarie Weyl Carr.

Fig. 15. Paphos, Byzantine Museum. Military Saint, reverse of Fig. 16. Photo by Annemarie Weyl Carr.

Fig. 17. Mount Sinai, Monastery of St Catherine. Diptych with Mother of God and St Prokopios.
Photo: By permission of the Michigan, Princeton, Alexandria expedition to Mount Sinai.

Fig. 18. Kalopanagiotis, St Herakleidios. View from south entrance. Photo by Gerard L. Carr.

Fig. 19. Nicosia, Byzantine Museum. *Vita* icon of St Nicholas. Photo: Byzantine Museum.

Fig. 21. Nicosia, Byzantine Museum. Mother of God. Photo: Byzantine Museum, Nicosia.

Fig. 20. Mount Sinai, Monastery of St Catherine. Mother of God. Photo: By permission of the Michigan, Princeton, Alexandria expedition to Mount Sinai.

Fig. 23. Moutoullas, Church of the Panagia. Mother of God, south wall, detail. Photo by Annemarie Weyl Carr.

Fig. 22. Pedoulas, Byzantine Museum. Panagia Voreine. Photo: By permission of the Bishop of Morphou.

Fig. 24. Asinou, Panagia Phorviotissa. Narthex vault. Photo by Gerard L. Carr.

Fig. 25. Asinou, Panagia Phorviotissa. Naos vault. Photo by Gerard L. Carr.

Fig. 26. Pelendri, Church of the Holy Cross. Naos vault. Photo by Annemarie Weyl Carr.

Fig. 27. Pelendri, Church of the Holy Cross. Pendentive: St Luke. Photo by Annemarie Weyl Carr.

Fig. 28. Nicosia, Cathedral of St Sophia, Porch. Photo by Annemarie Weyl Carr.

Fig. 29. Famagusta, Cathedral of St Nicholas. Photo by Gerard L. Carr.

Fig. 30. Famagusta, St George of the Greeks. Photo by Gerard L. Carr.

Fig. 31. Famagusta, St George of the Greeks. Betrayal of Judas. Photo by Annemarie Weyl Carr.

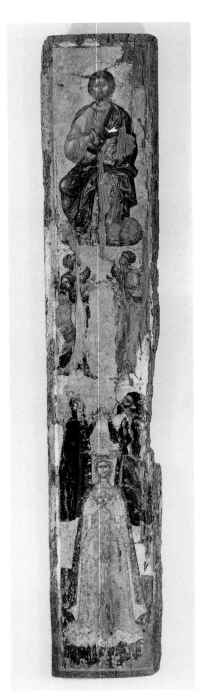

Fig. 32. Nicosia, Byzantine Museum. Funerary icon of 1356.
Photo: Byzantine Museum.

Fig. 33. Nicosia, Byzantine Museum. Deposition. Photo: Byzantine Museum.

BIBLIOGRAPHY

Abbreviations

AOL = *Archives de l'Orient latin.*
BEC = *Bibliothèque de l'École des chartes.*
BEFAR = Bibliothèque des Écoles françaises d'Athènes et de Rome.
BF = *Byzantinische Forschungen.*
BMGS = *Byzantine and Modern Greek Studies.*
BZ = *Byzantinische Zeitschrift.*
CICO = Pontificia commissio ad redigendum codicem iuris canonici orientalis, Fontes, Series III, 15 vols. (Rome, 1943–).
CSFS = Collana storica di fonti e studi, general ed. G. Pistarino (Genoa, 1969–).
DOP = *Dumbarton Oaks Papers.*
EHR = *English Historical Review.*
MAHEFR = *Mélanges d'archéologie et d'histoire de l'École française de Rome.*
MEFR = *Mélanges de l'École française de Rome.*
MHR = *Mediterranean Historical Review.*
PG = *Patrologiae cursus completus. Series Graeca,* ed. J.P. Migne, 161 vols. (Paris, 1857–1866).
PL = *Patrologiae cursus completus, Series Latina,* ed. J.P. Migne, 221 vols. (Paris, 1844–1864).
RDAC = *Report of the Department of Antiquities, Cyprus.*
REB = *Revue des études byzantines.*
RHC = *Recueil des historiens des croisades,* ed. Comte A. Beugnot, 16 vols. (Paris, 1841–1906).
RHC Arm. = *RHC Documents arméniens,* 2 vols. (Paris, 1869–1906).
RHC Lois = *RHC Lois: Les Assises de Jérusalem,* I. *Assises de la Haute Cour* (Paris, 1841). II. *Assises de la Cour des Bourgeois* (Paris, 1843).
RHC Occ. = *RHC Historiens Occidentaux,* 5 vols. (Paris, 1844–1895).
RHDFE = *Revue historique de droit français et étranger.*
ROL = *Revue de l'Orient latin.*
RS = *Rerum Britannicarum Medii Aevi Scriptores* (Rolls Series), 251 vols. (London, 1858–1896).
TSHC = Texts and Studies in the History of Cyprus, Cyprus Research Centre.

ΕΕΒΣ = *Επετηρίς Εταιρείας Βυζαντινών Σπουδών.*
ΕΚΕΕ = *Επετηρίς Κέντρου Επιστημονικών Ερευνών (Κύπρου).*
ΕΚΜΙΜΚ = *Επετηρίδα Κέντρου Μελετών Ιεράς Μονής Κύκκου.*
ΚΣ = *Κυπριακαί Σπουδαί.*
ΠΑ΄ΔΚΣ = *Πρακτικά του Πρώτου Διεθνούς Κυπρολογικού Συνεδρίου* (Nicosia, 1969), 3 vols. (Nicosia, 1972–1973).
ΠΒ΄ΔΚΣ = *Πρακτικά του Δευτέρου Διεθνούς Κυπριολογικού Συνεδρίου* (Nicosia, 1982), 3 vols. (Nicosia, 1985–1987).
ΠΓ΄ΔΚΣ = *Πρακτικά του Τρίτου Διεθνούς Κυπρολογικού Συνεδρίου* (Nicosia, 1996), 3 vols. (Nicosia, 1996–2001).

Documents and Collections of Sources

Acta Clementis V = Acta Clementis papae V (1303–1314), ed. A.L. Tautu [CICO 7/i] (Vatican City, 1955).
Acta Clementis VI = Acta Clementis papae VI (1342–1352), ed. A.L. Tautu [CICO 9] (Vatican City, 1960).
Acta Gregorii XI = Acta Gregorii papae XI (1370–1378), ed. A.L. Tautu [CICO 12] (Rome, 1966).
Acta Honorii III et Gregorii IX = Acta Honorii papae III (1216–1227) et Gregorii papae IX (1227–1241), ed. A.L. Tautu [CICO 3] (Vatican City, 1950).
Acta Innocentii III = Acta Innocentii papae III (1198–1216), ed. T. Haluscynskyj [CICO 2] (Vatican City, 1944).
Acta Innocentii IV = Acta Innocentii papae IV (1243–1254), ed. T. Haluscynskyj and M. Wojnar [CICO 4/i] (Rome, 1962).
Acta ab Innocentio V ad Benedictum XI = Acta Romanorum Pontificum ab Innocentio V ad Benedictum XI (1276–1304), ed. F.M. Delorme and A.L. Tautu [CICO 5/ii] (Vatican City, 1954).
Acta Innocentii VI = Acta Innocentii papae VI (1352–1362), ed. A.L. Tautu [CICO 10] (Vatican City, 1961).
Acta Ioannis XXII = Acta Ioannis papae XXII (1317–1334), ed. A.L. Tautu [CICO 7/ii] (Vatican City, 1952).
Acta Urbani V = Acta Urbani papae V (1362–1370), ed. A.L. Tautu [CICO 11] (Rome, 1964).
Aristeidou, *Ragusa = Ανέκδοτα έγγραφα της κυπριακής ιστορίας από το αρχείο της Ραγούζας (ΙΣΤ′ αι.)*, ed. E. Aristeidou [TSHC VII] (Nicosia, 1980).
Assegurances a Barcelona = Assegurances y Canvis Maritims Medièvals a Barcelona, ed. A. Garcia y Sanz and M.T. Ferrer Mallol (Barcelona, 1983).
Bullarium Cyprium = Bullarium Cyprium. Papal Letters Involving Cyprus 1196–1316, ed. C. Schabel and J. Richard [TSHC] (Nicosia, forthcoming).
Byzantinischen Kleinchroniken = Die byzantinischen Kleinchroniken, ed. P. Schreiner, 3 vols. (Vienna, 1975–1978).
Le Cartulaire du chapitre du Saint-Sépulcre de Jérusalem, ed. G. Bresc-Bautier (Paris, 1984).
Cartulaire général de l'Ordre des Hospitaliers = Cartulaire général de l'Ordre des Hospitaliers de S. Jean de Jérusalem (1100–1310), ed. J. Delaville le Roulx, 4 vols. (Paris, 1894–1905).
Cartulary = The Cartulary of the Cathedral of Holy Wisdom of Nicosia, ed. N. Coureas and C. Schabel [TSHC XXV] (Nicosia, 1997).
Christodoulou and Ioannides, *Cypriot Folk Songs = Κυπριακά δημώδη άσματα*, ed. M.N. Christodoulou and K.D. Ioannides [Publications of the Cyprus Research Centre X] (Nicosia, 1987), I.
Comandas Commerciales Barcelonesas = Comandas Commercials Barcelonesas de la Baja Edad Media, ed. J.M. Madurell y Marimon and A. Garcia y Sanz (Barcelona, 1973).
Constantinides and Browning, *Dated Greek Manuscripts* = C.N. Constantinides and R. Browning, *Dated Greek Manuscripts from Cyprus to the Year 1570* [Dumbarton Oaks Studies 30—TSHC XVIII] (Nicosia, 1993).
Délibérations des assemblées vénitiennes = Délibérations des assemblées vénitiennes concernant la Romanie, ed. F. Thiriet, 2 vols. (Paris–The Hague, 1966–1971).
Documenti del commercio veneziano = Documenti del commercio veneziano nei secoli XI–XIII, ed. R. Morocco della Rocca and A. Lombardo, 2 vols. (Rome–Turin, 1940).
Documenti sulle relazioni delle città toscane coll'Oriente = Documenti sulle relazioni delle città toscane coll'Oriente cristiano e coi Turci fino all'anno MDXXXI, ed. G. Müller (Florence, 1879).
Documents chypriotes des archives du Vatican = Chypre sous les Lusignans. Documents chypriotes des archives du Vatican (XlV^e et XVe siècles), ed. J. Richard (Paris, 1962).
Donato di Chiavari = *Notai Genovesi in Oltremare. Atti rogati a Chio da Donato di Chiavari (17 febbraio–12 novembre 1394)*, ed. M. Balard [CSFS 51] (Genoa, 1988).

Excerpta Cypria = *Excerpta Cypria. Materials for a History of Cyprus*, English trans. C.D. Cobham (Cambridge, 1908; repr. Nicosia, 1969).

Excerpta Cypria Nova = *Excerpta Cypria Nova*, I, *Voyageurs occidentaux à Chypre au XVème siècle*, ed. G. Grivaud [TSHC XV] (Nicosia, 1990).

Federico di Piazzalunga = *Notai Genovesi in Oltremare. Atti rogati a Laiazzo da Federico di Piazzalunga (1274) e Pietro di Bargone (1277, 1279)*, ed. L. Balletto [CSFS 53] (Genoa, 1989).

Giovanni de Rocha = *Notai Genovesi in Oltremare. Atti rogati a Cipro: Lamberto di Sambuceto (31 marzo 1304–19 luglio 1305. 4 gennaio–12 luglio 1307), Giovanni de Rocha (3 agosto 1308–4 marzo 1310)*, ed. M. Balard [CSFS 43] (Genoa, 1984).

Greek Texts = *Greeks Texts of the Fourth to Thirteenth Centuries*, English trans. H.A. Pohlsander [Sources for the History of Cyprus VII] (Albany, 1999).

Gregory IX, *Decretales*, ed. E. Friedberg, in *Corpus Iuris Canonici*, II (Leipzig, 1881; repr. Graz, 1956).

Lacrimae Nicossienses = *Lacrimae Nicossienses. Recueil d'inscriptions funéraires la plupart françaises existant encore dans l'île de Chypre*, ed. Major T.J. Chamberlayne (Paris, 1894).

Lamberto di Sambuceto, *1296–1299* = *Notai Genovesi in Oltremare. Atti rogati a Cipro da Lamberto di Sambuceto (11 ottobre 1296–23 giugno 1299)*, ed. M. Balard [CSFS 39] (Genoa, 1983).

Lamberto di Sambuceto, *1299–1301* = 'Actes passés à Famagouste de 1299 à 1301 par devant le notaire génois Lamberto di Sambuceto', ed. C. Desimoni, *AOL*, II (Paris, 1884), 3–120 and *ROL*, I (Paris, 1893), 58–139, 275–312, 321–53.

Lamberto di Sambuceto, *1300–1301* = *Notai Genovesi in Oltremare. Atti rogati a Cipro da Lamberto di Sambuceto (3 luglio 1300–3 agosto 1301)*, ed. V. Polonio [CSFS 31] (Genoa, 1982).

Lamberto di Sambuceto, *1301* = *Notai Genovesi in Oltremare. Atti rogati a Cipro da Lamberto di Sambuceto (6 luglio–17 ottobre 1301)*, ed. R. Pavoni [CSFS 32] (Genoa, 1982).

Lamberto di Sambuceto, *1302* = *Notai Genovesi in Oltremare. Atti rogati a Cipro da Lamberto di Sambuceto (gennaio–agosto 1302)*, ed. R. Pavoni [CSFS 49] (Genoa, 1987).

Lamberto di Sambuceto, *1304–1307* = *Notai Genovesi in Oltremare. Atti rogati a Cipro: Lamberto di Sambuceto (31 marzo 1304–19 luglio 1305. 4 gennaio–12 luglio 1307), Giovanni de Rocha (3 agosto 1308–4 marzo 1310)*, ed. M. Balard [CSFS 43] (Genoa, 1984).

Lettres de Benoît XII = *Lettres communes du pape Benoît XII*, ed. J.-M. Vidal [BEFAR 3rd Series], 3 vols. (Paris, 1903–1911).

Lettres de Clément VI = *Lettres closes, patentes et curiales du pape Clément VI se rapportant à la France*, ed. E. Déprez *et al.* [BEFAR 3rd Series], 3 vols. (Paris, 1901–1961).

Lettres d'Innocent VI = *Lettres secrètes et curiales du pape Innocent VI*, ed. P. Gasnault *et al.* [BEFAR 3rd Series], 4 vols. (Paris, 1959–).

Lettres de Jean XXII = *Lettres communes du pape Jean XXII analysées d'après les registres dits d'Avignon et du Vatican*, ed. G. Mollat *et al.* [BEFAR 3rd Series], 16 vols. (Paris, 1904–1947).

Lettres d'Urbain V = *Lettres secrètes et curiales du pape Urbain V se rapportant à la France*, ed. P. Lecacheux and G. Mollat [BEFAR 3rd Series] (Paris, 1902–1955).

I libri commemoriali = *I libri commemoriali della repubblica di Venezia. Regesti*, ed. G. Predelli, 8 vols. (Venice, 1876–1914).

Livre des remembrances = *Le Livre des remembrances de la secrète du royaume de Chypre (1468–1469)*, ed. J. Richard with the collaboration of Th. Papadopoullos [TSHC X] (Nicosia, 1983).

Mansi = *Sacrorum Conciliorum nova et amplissima collectio*, ed. J.D. Mansi, 31 vols. (Florence–Venice, 1759–1798; repr. Graz, 1960).

Mas Latrie, *Histoire* = L. de Mas Latrie (ed.), *Histoire de l'île de Chypre sous le règne des princes de la maison de Lusignan* (Paris, 1852–1855), II–III.

Mas Latrie, 'Nouvelles preuves (1871)' = L. de Mas Latrie (ed.), 'Nouvelles preuves de l'histoire de Chypre sous le règne des princes de la maison de Lusignan', *BEC*, 32 (1871), 341–78.

Mas Latrie, 'Nouvelles preuves (1873)' = L. de Mas Latrie (ed.), 'Nouvelles preuves de l'histoire de Chypre sous le règne des princes de la maison de Lusignan', *BEC*, 34 (1873), 47–87; repr. with other documents as vol. IV of Mas Latrie, *Histoire* (Famagusta, 1970), 1–79.

Mas Latrie, 'Nouvelles preuves (1874)' = L. de Mas Latrie (ed.), 'Nouvelles preuves de l'histoire de Chypre sous le règne des princes de la maison de Lusignan', *BEC*, 35 (1874), 81–140; repr. with other documents as vol. IV of Mas Latrie, *Histoire* (Famagusta, 1970), 81–140.

Memorias Historicas = *Memorias Historicas sobre la Marina, Comercio y Artes de la Antigua Ciudad de Barcelona*, ed. A. Capmany de Montpalau, 4 vols. (Madrid, 1779).

Nicola de Boateriis = *Nicola de Boateriis, notaio in Famagosta e Venezia (1355–1365)*, ed. A. Lombardo (Venice, 1973).

Papsturkunden = *Papsturkunden für kirchen im Heiligen Lande*, ed. R. Hiestand (Göttingen, 1985).

Pietro di Bargone = *Notai Genovesi in Oltremare. Atti rogati a Laiazzo da Federico di Piazzalunga (1274) e Pietro di Bargone (1277, 1279)*, ed. L. Balletto [CSFS 53] (Genoa, 1989).

Regesta Regni Hierosolymitani (1097–1291), ed. R. Röhricht (Innsbruck, 1893) (= vol. I); *Additamentum* (Innsbruck, 1904) (= vol. II).

Regesta Clementis V = *Regesta Clementis papae V*, editum cura et studio monachorum Ordinis S. Benedicti, 8 vols. (Rome, 1885–1892).

Regesta Honorii III = *Regesta Honorii papae III*, comp. P. Pressutti, 2 vols. (Rome, 1888–1895).

Les Registres de Boniface VIII, ed. G. Digard *et al.* [BEFAR 2nd Series], 4 vols. (Paris, 1884–1939).

Les Registres de Grégoire IX, ed. L. Auvray *et al.* [BEFAR 2nd Series], 4 vols. (Paris, 1890–1955).

Les Registres d'Innocent IV, ed. E. Berger [BEFAR 2nd Series], 4 vols. (Paris, 1881–1921).

Sathas = Μεσαιωνική Βιβλιοθήκη–*Bibliotheca Graeca Medii Aevi*, ed. C. Sathas, 7 vols. (Venice–Paris, 1872–1894; repr. Athens, 1972).

Supplementary Excerpts on Cyprus = *Supplementary Excerpts on Cyprus, or Further Materials for a History of Cyprus*, ed. Th.A.H. Mogabgab, 3 vols. (Nicosia, 1941–1945).

Synodicum Nicosiense = *The Synodicum Nicosiense and Other Documents of the Latin Church of Cyprus, 1196–1373*, ed. C. Schabel [TSHC XXXIX] (Nicosia, 2001).

Syntagma = Σύνταγμα βυζαντινών πηγών κυπριακής ιστορίας. 4ος–15ος αιώνας, ed. V. Nerantzi-Varmazi [TSHC XXIII] (Nicosia, 1996).

Narrative and Legal Sources

'Abrégé' = 'Abrégé du livre des Assises de la cour des Bourgeois', in *RHC Lois*, II, 227–352.

Akindynos, *Letters* = Gregory Akindynos, *Letters of Gregory Akindynos*, ed. and English trans. A.C. Hero (Dumbarton Oaks, Washington D.C., 1983).

'Amadi' = 'Francesco Amadi', *Chronique d'Amadi*, ed. R. de Mas Latrie, in *Chroniques d'Amadi et de Strambaldi* (Paris, 1891–1893; repr. Nicosia, 1999), I.

Anales de Tierra Santa, in A. Sanchez Candeira, 'Las cruzadas en la historiografia española de la epoca. Traducción castellana de una redacción desconocida de las "Anales de Tierra Santa"', *Hispania*, 20 (1960), 325–67 (text on pp. 338–67).

Annales de Terre Sainte, in R. Röhricht and G. Raynaud, 'Annales de Terre Sainte', *AOL*, II (1884), Documents, 427–61 (text on pp. 429–61).

Anonymous OP, *Contra Graecos*, in *PG*, CXL, cols. 487–574.

Ασίζαι = Ασίζαι του βασιλείου των Ιεροσολύμων και της Κύπρου, in Sathas, VI.

Assises de la Cour des Bourgeois, in *RHC Lois*, II, 1–226.

Assizes = *The Assizes of the Lusignan Kingdom of Cyprus*, English trans. N. Coureas [TSHC XLII] (Nicosia, 2002).
The Assizes of King Roger, English trans. G.A. Loud from F. Brandileone (ed.), *Il Diritto Romano nelle leggi normanno e Sveve del Regno di Sicilia* (Turin, 1884; repr. 1982), On-Line Leeds. Medieval History Texts in Translation [www.leeds.ac.uk/history/weblearning/MedievalHistoryTextCentre/medievalTexts.htm].
'Bans et ordonnances des rois de Chypre', in *RHC Lois*, II, 354–79.
'Benedict of Peterborough' = *Gesta Regis Henrici Secundi Benedicti Abbatis*, ed. W. Stubbs [RS 49], 2 vols. (London, 1867).
Bertrandon de la Broquière = *Le Voyage d'Outremer de Bertrandon de la Broquière*, ed. C. Schefer (Paris, 1892).
Boustronios, Georgios, *Τζώρτζης (Μ)Ποστρούς (Γεώργιος Βο(σ)τρ(υ)ηνός ή Βουστρώνιος), Διήγησις Κρονίκας Κύπρου*, ed. G. Kehayioglou [TSHC XXVII] (Nicosia, 1997).
Choniates, Nicetas, *Historia*, ed. J.A. van Dieten, 2 vols. (Berlin–New York, 1975).
'La Clef des Assises' = 'La Clef des Assises de la Haute Cour du royaume de Jérusalem et de Chypre', in *RHC Lois*, I, 575–600.
Continuation de Guillaume de Tyr = *La Continuation de Guillaume de Tyr (1184–1197)*, ed. M.R. Morgan (Paris, 1982).
Cydones = Démétrius Cydonès, *Correspondance*, ed. R.-J. Loenertz, 2 vols. (Vatican City, 1956–1960).
The Cyprus Passion Cycle, ed. A.C. Mahr (Notre Dame, Ind., 1947).
'Document relatif au service militaire', in *RHC Lois*, II, 425–34.
Ephraem Aenius = *Εφραίμ Αινίου, Χρονική Ιστορία—Historia Chronica*, ed. O. Lampsides (Athens, 1990).
'Ernoul' = *Chronique d'Ernoul et de Bernard le Trésorier*, ed. L. de Mas Latrie (Paris, 1871).
'Estoire de Eracles' = 'L'Estoire de Eracles empereur et la conqueste de la Terre d'Outremer', in *RHC Occ.*, II.
Étienne de Lusignan, *Chorograffia* = Estienne de Lusignan, *Chorograffia e breve historia universale dell'isola de Cipro principiando al tempo di Noè per il fino al 1572* (Bologna, 1573; repr. Famagusta, 1973; repr. Nicosia, 2004).
Étienne de Lusignan, *Chorography* = Estienne de Lusignan, *Lusignan's Chorography and Brief General History of the Island of Cyprus (A.D. 1573)*, English trans. O. Pelosi [Sources for the History of Cyprus X] (Altamont, NY, 2001).
Étienne de Lusignan, *Description* = Estienne de Lusignan, *Description de toute l'isle de Cypre* (Paris, 1580; repr. Famagusta, 1968; repr. Nicosia, 2004).
Florio Bustron, *Chronique de l'île de Chypre*, ed. R. de Mas Latrie [Collection des documents inédits sur l'histoire de France, Mélanges historiques 5] (Paris, 1886); repr. as *Historia over Commentarii di Cipro* (Nicosia, 1998)
'Formules', in *RHC Lois*, II, 380–9.
Francesco Attar, 'Mémoire sur l'île de Chypre', extracts in Mas Latrie, *Histoire*, III, 519–36.
Francesco Balducci Pegolotti, *La pratica della mercatura*, ed. A. Evans (Cambridge, Mass., 1936; repr. New York. 1970).
Geoffrey Chaucer, *The Complete Works of Geoffrey Chaucer*, ed. F.N. Robinson (London, 1957²).
Geoffrey Le Tor, 'Livre de Geoffroy Le Tort', in *RHC Lois*, I, 433–50.
George of Cyprus, 'Γρηγορίου του αγιωτάτου και μακαριωτάτου οικουμενικού πατριάρχου περί του καθ' εαυτόν βίου ως απ' άλλου προσώπου', in W. Lameere (1937: 176–91).
Germanos II, Patriarch of Constantinople, 'Letter 1', in Sathas, II, 5–14.
Germanos II, Patriarch of Constantinople, 'Letter 2', in Sathas, II, 14–19.
Les Gestes des Chiprois, ed. G. Raynaud (Geneva, 1887).
Les Gestes des Chiprois, ed. R. de Mas Latrie, G. Paris, and C. Kohler, in *RHC Arm.*, II, 653–872.

Giorgio de Nores, *Discorso* = Giorgio de Nores, *Discorso sopra l'isola di Cipri con le ragioni della vera successione in quel Regno*, ed. A. Nicolaou-Konnari [TSHC] (Nicosia, forthcoming).

Giovanni Boccaccio, *The Decameron*, English trans. G.H. McWilliam (Penguin, 1995²).

Giovanni Boccaccio, *Genealogia* = Giovanni Boccaccio, *Genealogia deorum gentilium*, ed. V. Zaccaria, 2 vols. (Milan, 1998).

Gregoras, *Correspondance* = Nicephoros Gregoras, *Correspondance de Nicéphore Grégoras*, ed. R. Guilland (Paris, 1927).

Gregoras, *Epistulae* = Nicephoros Gregoras, *Nicephori Gregorae Epistulae*, ed. P.A.M. Leone (Matino, 1982).

Guillaume de Machaut, *The Capture of Alexandria*, English trans. J. Shirley and introduction P.W. Edbury (Aldershot, 2001).

Guillaume de Machaut, *La Prise d'Alixandre (The Taking of Alexandria)*, ed. and English trans. R.B. Palmer (New York–London, 2002).

Guillaume de Rubrouck, *Voyage dans l'Empire mongol*, ed. C. and R. Kappler (Paris, 1985).

James of Ibelin, 'Livre de Jacques d'Ibelin', in *RHC Lois*, I, 451–68.

James of Verona, *Liber peregrinationis*, in R. Röhricht, 'Le pèlerinage du moine augustin Jacques de Vérone (1335)', *ROL*, 3 (1895), 155–302 (text on pp. 163–302).

John of Ibelin, *Le Livre des Assises*, ed. P.W. Edbury (Leiden, 2003).

John of Joinville, *L'Histoire de Saint Louis*, ed. N. de Wailly (Paris, 1868).

John of Journy, *La Dîme de pénitance* = Jean de Journy, *La Dîme de pénitance, altfranzösisches Gedicht verfasst im Jahre 1288 von Jehan von Journi*, ed. H. Breymann (Stuttgart, 1874).

'Les Lignages d'Outremer', in *RHC Lois*, II, 435–74.

Lignages d'Outremer, ed. M.-A. Nielen (Paris, 2003).

Le Livre au Roi, ed. M. Greilsammer (Paris, 1995).

Ludolph of Sudheim, 'Voyage en Terre Sainte', extracts in Mas Latrie, *Histoire*, II, 210–17.

Makhairas, Leontios, *Recital concerning the Sweet Land of Cyprus entitled 'Chronicle'*, ed. R.M. Dawkins, 2 vols. (Oxford, 1932).

Makhairas, *Diplomatic Edition* = Λεοντίου Μαχαιρά, *Χρονικό της Κύπρου. Παράλληλη διπλωματική έκδοση των χειρογράφων*, ed. M. Pieris and A. Nicolaou-Konnari [TSHC XLVIII] (Nicosia, 2003).

Manuel Palaeologos, *Letters* = *Lettres de l'empereur Manuel Paléologue*, ed. É. Legrand (Paris, 1893).

Marino Sanudo Torsello, *Liber secretorum fidelium crucis*, in J. Bongars (ed.), *Gesta Dei per Francos* (Hanover, 1611), II, 1–281; repr. with an introduction by J. Prawer (Toronto, 1972).

Marsilio Zorzi, *Der Bericht des Marsilio Zorzi. Codex Querini-Stampalia IV 3 (1064)*, ed. O. Berggötz [Kieler Werkstücke, ser. C: Beiträge zur europäischen Geschichte des frühen und hohen Mittelalters] (Frankfurt-am-Main, 1991) (the section on Cyprus, on pp. 184–91, may also be found in Papadopoulou (1983: 309–15)).

Martyrion Kyprion, in Th. Papadopoullos, 'Μαρτύριον Κυπρίων', *Τόμος αναμνηστικός επί τη πεντηκονταετηρίδι του περιοδικού Απόστολος Βαρνάβας* (Nicosia, 1975), 307–38 (text on pp. 320–38).

Maruhn = J.E. Maruhn (ed.), 'Eine zyprische Fassung eherechtlicher Titel der Epitome', *Forschungen zur byzantinischen Rechtsgeschichte*, 7 (1981) [Fontes Minores 4], 218–55 (text on pp. 226–55).

Mouzalon, Nicholas, 'Στίχοι Νικολάου μοναχού του Μουζάλωνος, του γεγονότος αρχιεπισκόπου Κύπρου, εν τη παραιτήσει αυτού γενόμενοι', in S. Doanidou, 'Η παραίτησις Νικολάου του Μουζάλωνος από της Αρχιεπισκοπής Κύπρου. Ανέκδοτον απολογητικόν ποίημα', *Ελληνικά*, 7 (1934), 109–50 (text on pp. 110–41).

Neilos, *Rule*, in *The Foundation Rules of Cypriot Medieval Monasteries: Makhairas and St Neophytos*, English trans. N. Coureas [TSHC XLVI] (Nicosia, 2003), 57–128.

Neilos, *Τυπική Διάταξις*, ed. I.P. Tsiknopoulos, in *Κυπριακά Τυπικά* (Nicosia, 1969), 1–68.

Neophytos the Recluse, Συγγράμματα = Αγίου Νεοφύτου του Εγκλείστου, Συγγράμματα, I–IV so far [Holy Monastery of St Neophytos] (Paphos, 1996, 1998, 1999, 2001).

Neophytos the Recluse, Catecheseis = Βίβλος των Κατηχήσεων, ed. B.K. Katsaros, in Neophytos the Recluse, Συγγράμματα, II, 71–431.

Neophytos the Recluse, Panegyric A = Πανηγυρική, ed. N. Papatriantafyllou-Theodoridi and Th. Yiangou, in Neophytos the Recluse, Συγγράμματα, III.

Neophytos the Recluse, De calamitatibus Cypri = Περί των κατά χώραν Κύπρου σκαιών, in Excerpta Cypria, 10–13.

Neophytos the Recluse, Enkomion for the Holy Cross = Εγκώμιον εις τον τίμιον και ζωοποιόν σταυρόν . . ., in Neophytos the Recluse, Panegyric A, 167–81.

Neophytos the Recluse, First Sunday Homily = Κατήχησις Α΄, Κυριακή των Αγίων Πάντων, in Neophytos the Recluse, Catecheseis, Book II, 306–10.

Neophytos the Recluse, Homily against the Jews = Λόγος αντιρρητικός προς τους λέγοντας Ιουδαίους. . ., in Neophytos the Recluse, Panegyric A, 514–38.

Neophytos the Recluse, Homily Concerning the Holy Fathers at the Council of Nicaea = Κατήχησις ΙΕ΄ Περί των εν Νικαία αγίων πατέρων. . ., in Neophytos the Recluse, Catecheseis, Book I, 269–72.

Neophytos the Recluse, Homily Concerning the Presentation of the Virgin = Λόγος εις την παναγίαν Κόρην και Θεομήτορα, οπηνίκα υπό των αυτής γονέων επεδόθη εις τα ῾Αγια των Αγίων τριετίζουσα, in E.M. Toniolo, 'Omelie e Catechesi mariane inedite di Neofito il Recluso (1134–1220 c.)', Marianum, 36 (1974), 184–315 (text on pp. 210–37).

Neophytos the Recluse, Sixth Sunday Homily = Κατήχησις Στ΄, Περί όρκου και φιλαργυρίας και περί τούτων γραφικαί μαρτυρίαι, in Neophytos the Recluse, Catecheseis, Book II, 327–31.

Neophytos the Recluse, Rule, in The Foundation Rules of Cypriot Medieval Monasteries: Makhairas and St Neophytos, English trans. N. Coureas [TSHC XLVI] (Nicosia, 2003), 129–68.

Neophytos the Recluse, Typike Diatheke = Τυπική Διαθήκη, ed. I.E. Stephanes, in Neophytos the Recluse, Συγγράμματα, II, 1–69.

Oger of Anglure, Le Saint Voyage de Jherusaleme du Seigneur d'Anglure, ed. F. Bonnardot and A. Longnon (Paris, 1878).

'Ordenemens de la court dou vesconte', in Les livres des assises et des usages du reaume de Jérusalem, ed. E.H. Kausler (Stuttgart, 1839), I, 403–24.

Philip of Mézières, Peter Thomae = Philippe de Mézières, The Life of Saint Peter Thomae, ed. J. Smet (Rome, 1954).

Philip of Mézières, Songe = Philippe de Mézières, Le Songe du vieil pelerin, extracts in Mas Latrie, Histoire, II, 381–5.

Philip of Novara, Guerra = Filippo da Novara, Guerra di Federico II in Oriente (1223–1242), ed. and Italian trans. S. Melani (Naples, 1994).

Philip of Novara, 'Livre' = 'Livre de Philippe de Navarre', in RHC Lois, I, 469–571.

Philip of Novara, Les quatre âges de l'homme = Philippe de Novare, Les quatre âges de l'homme, ed. M. de Fréville (Paris, 1888).

Pietro Valderio, La guerra di Cipro, ed. G. Grivaud and N. Patapiou [TSHC XXII] (Nicosia, 1996).

Processus Cypricus, ed. K. Schottmüller, in Der Untergang des Templer-Ordens (Berlin, 1887), II.

Ramon Lull, Liber de natura, in Ramon Lull, Opera Parva (Palma, 1744), II; repr. in Opuscula, with an introduction by E.-W. Platzeck (Hildesheim, 1971), I.

Ramon Lull, Rhetorica Nova = Ramon Lull's New Rhetoric, text and English trans. M.D. Johnston (Davis, Calif., 1994).

Riccold de Monte Croce, Pérégrination en Terre Sainte et au Proche-Orient. Lettres sur la chute de Saint-Jean-d'Acre, ed. and French trans. R. Kappler (Paris, 1997).

Roger of Howden = Roger of Hoveden, Chronica, ed. W. Stubbs [RS 51], 4 vols. (London, 1868–1871).

Simon = D. Simon (ed. and German trans. with the collaboration of V. Fidora, H.R. Lug, J.E. Maruhn, and H. Mondorf), *Zyprische Prozessprogramme* [Münchener Beiträge zur Papyrusforschungen und antiken Rechtsgeschichte, 65. Heft] (Munich, 1973) (text on pp. 12–73).
Skoutariotes, Theodore, *Σύνοψις Χρονική*, in Sathas, VII, 1–156.
'Spaneas' = 'Σπανέας', in Lampros (1917: 359–80).
The Templar of Tyre, *Cronaca = Cronaca del Templare di Tiro (1243–1314). La caduta degli Stati Crociati nel racconto di un testimone oculare*, ed. and Italian trans. L. Minervini (Naples, 2000).
The Templar of Tyre, *The Deeds of the Cypriots* = The Templar of Tyre, *Part III of 'The Deeds of the Cypriots'*, English trans. P. Crawford (Aldershot, 2003).
Thomas Aquinas, *De regimine principum* = Thomas d'Aquin, *De regimine principum ad regem Cypri*, ed. J. Mathis (Turin, 1948).
Thomas Aquinas, *Du gouvernement royal* = Thomas d'Aquin, *Du gouvernement royal*, ed. and French trans. C. Roguet (Paris, 1931²).
The Trial of the Templars in Cyprus = The Trial of the Templars in Cyprus. A Complete English Edition, English trans. A. Gilmour-Bryson (Leiden–Boston–Cologne, 1998).

Secondary Works

Abulafia (1987a): D. Abulafia, *Italy, Sicily and the Mediterranean, 1100–1400* [Variorum Reprints] (Aldershot, 1987).
—— (1987b): D. Abulafia, 'Ancona, Byzantium and the Adriatic, 1155–1173', in Abulafia (1987a: art. IX).
—— (1987c): D. Abulafia, 'Marseilles, Acre and the Mediterranean, 1200–1291', in Abulafia (1987a: art. XV).
—— (1993a): D. Abulafia, *Commerce and Conquest in the Mediterranean (1100–1400)* [Variorum Reprints] (Aldershot, 1993).
—— (1993b): D. Abulafia, 'The Levant Trade of the Minor Cities in the Thirteenth and Fourteenth Centuries: Strengths and Weaknesses', in Abulafia (1993a: art. XI).
—— (1993c): D. Abulafia, 'The Anconitan Privileges in the Kingdom of Jerusalem and the Levant Trade of Ancona', in Abulafia (1993a: art. XIII).
—— (1994): D. Abulafia, *A Mediterranean Emporium, The Catalan Kingdom of Majorca* (Cambridge, 1994).
Acheimastou-Potamianou (1992): M. Acheimastou-Potamianou (ed.), *Ευφρόσυνον. Αφιέρωμα στον Μανόλη Χατζηδάκη*, 2 vols. (Athens, 1992).
Aerts (1986): W. Aerts, 'Leontios of Neapolis and Cypriot Dialect Genesis', in *ΠΒ΄ΔΚΣ*, II, 379–89.
Agapitos (2004): 'Από την Περσία στην Προβηγκία: Ερωτικές διηγήσεις στο ύστερο Βυζάντιο', in E. Grammatikopoulou (ed.), *Το Βυζάντιο και οι απαρχές της Ευρώπης* [Εθνικό Ίδρυμα Ερευνών] (Athens, 2004), 119–53.
Agapitos and Pieris (2002): P. Agapitos and M. Pieris (eds.), *'Τ' αδόνιν κείνον που γλυκά θλιβάται', Εκδοτικά και ερμηνευτικά ζητήματα της δημώδους ελληνικής λογοτεχνίας στο πέρασμα από τον Μεσαίωνα στην Αναγέννηση (1400–1600)* [Acts of the Fourth International Conference *Neograeca Medii Aevi* (Nicosia, November 1997)] (Herakleion, 2002).
Airaldi and Kedar (1986): G. Airaldi and B.Z. Kedar (eds.), *I comuni italiani nel Regno Crociato di Gerusalemme* (Genoa, 1986).
Alexiou (1979): S. Alexiou, *Ακριτικά* (Herakleion, 1979).
Andrews (1999): J. Andrews, 'Santa Sophia in Nicosia: The Sculpture of the Western Portals and Its Reception', *Comitatus*, 30 (1999), 63–80.
Arbel (1979): B. Arbel, 'The Jews in Cyprus: New Evidence from the Venetian Period', *Jewish Social Studies*, 41/1 (1979), 23–40; repr. in Arbel (2000: art. X).

—— (1989): B. Arbel, 'The Cypriot Nobility from the Fourteenth to the Sixteenth Century: a New Interpretation', in B. Arbel, B. Hamilton, and D. Jacoby (eds.), *Latins and Greeks in the Eastern Mediterranean after 1204* (London, 1989), 175–97; repr. in Arbel (2000: art. VI).

—— (1993): B. Arbel, 'Slave Trade and Slave Labor in Frankish Cyprus (1191–1571)', *Studies in Medieval and Renaissance History*, 14 (1993), 151–90; repr. in Arbel (2000: art. IX).

—— (1995): B. Arbel, 'Greek Magnates in Venetian Cyprus: The Case of the Synglitico Family', *DOP*, 49 (1995), 325–37; repr. in Arbel (2000: art. VII).

—— (2000): B. Arbel, *Cyprus, the Franks and Venice, 13th–16th Centuries* [Variorum Reprints] (Aldershot, 2000).

Aristeidou (1978): E. Aristeidou, Ἐμπορικές σχέσεις μεταξύ Κύπρου και Αγκώνας από το ΙΓ΄ ως το ΙΣΤ΄ αιώνα', *ΚΣ*, 42 (1978), 47–58.

—— (1987): E. Aristeidou, 'Το προξενείο της Ραγούζας στην Κύπρο τον 18ο αιώνα', in *ΠΒ΄ΔΚΣ*, III, 47–52.

—— (2004): E. Aristeidou, Ἡ Εκκλησία σε σκοτεινές εποχές: Λατινοκρατία', *Χρονικό*, no. 136 [Supplement of the daily newspaper *Πολίτης*] (Nicosia, 11 January 2004).

Asdraha (1994): C. Asdraha, 'Les Lusignan à Chypre: langue et osmose culturelle', in Mutafian (1994: 11–15).

Ashtor (1976): E. Ashtor, 'The Venetian Cotton Trade in Syria in the Later Middle Ages', *Studi Medievali*, 17 (1976), 675–715.

—— (1983): E. Ashtor, *Levant Trade in the Later Middle Ages* (Princeton, N.J., 1983).

Aslanoff (1997): C. Aslanoff, 'Récit historique et discours poétique dans l'Estoire de la guerre des Ibelins contre les Impériaux de Philippe de Novare', *Le Moyen Age*, 103/1 (1997), 67–81.

Aspra-Varvadakis (1999): M. Aspra-Varvadakis, 'Three Thirteenth-Century Sinai Icons of John the Baptist Derived from a Cypriot Model', in Patterson Ševčenko and Moss (1999: 179–93).

—— (2002): M. Aspra-Varvadakis, 'Observations on a Thirteenth-Century Sinaitic Diptych Representing St. Procopios, the Virgin Kykkotissa and Saints Along Its Border', in M. Vassilaki (ed.), *Byzantine Icons: Art, Technique, and Technology* (Herakleion, 2002), 89–104.

Bacci (1997): M. Bacci, 'Due tavole della Vergine nella Toscana occidentale del primo Duecento', *Annali della Scuola normale superiore di Pisa*, 4/2 (1997), 1–59.

—— (2000): M. Bacci, 'Tra Pisa e Cipro: La committenza artistica di Giovanni Conti (†1332)', *Annali della Scuola normale superiore di Pisa*, 5/2 (2000), 343–81.

Balard (1978): M. Balard, *La Romanie génoise (XIIe–début XVe siècle)*, 2 vols. (Genoa–Rome, 1978).

—— (1985): M. Balard, 'Famagouste au début du XIVe siècle', in J. Heers (ed.), *Fortifications, portes de villes, places publiques dans le monde méditerranéen* (Paris, 1985), 279–300.

—— (1987): M. Balard, 'Péra au XIVe siècle: documents notariés des archives de Gênes', in M. Balard, A.E. Laiou, and C. Otten-Froux (eds.), *Les Italiens à Byzance. Édition et présentation de documents* (Paris, 1987), 9–78.

—— (1995): M. Balard, 'Οι Γενουάτες στο μεσαιωνικό βασίλειο της Κύπρου', in Papadopoullos (1995a: 259–332).

Balard and Ducellier (1995): M. Balard and A. Ducellier (eds.), *Coloniser au Moyen Age* (Paris, 1995).

Balard *et al.* (2001): M. Balard, B.Z. Kedar, and J. Riley-Smith (eds.), *Dei gesta per Francos. Études sur les croisades dédiées à Jean Richard. Crusade Studies in Honour of Jean Richard* (Aldershot, 2001).

Balletto (1998): L. Balletto, 'I Toscani nel Mediterraneo: L'Occidente, l'Africa, Cipro', in S. Gensini (ed.), *La Toscana nel secolo XIV, caratteri di una civiltà regionale* (Pisa, 1998), 251–69.

Banescu (1913): N. Banescu, *Deux poètes byzantins inédits du XIIIe siècle* (Bucharest, 1913).

Bartlett (1993): R. Bartlett, *The Making of Europe. Conquest, Colonization and Cultural Change 950–1350* (London, 1993).

Baud-Bovy (1959): S. Baud-Bovy, 'The strophe of rhymed distichs in Greek songs', in B. Rajeczky and L. Vargyas (eds.), *Studia memoriae Belae Bartok sacra* (Budapest, 1959), 359–76.

—— (1975): S. Baud-Bovy, 'Le théâtre religeux, Byzance et l'Occident', *Ελληνικά*, 28 (1975), 337–49.

Beaton (1989): R. Beaton, *The medieval Greek romance* (Cambridge, 1989).

Beck (1974): H.G. Beck, 'Die griechische volkstümliche Literatur des 14. Jahrhunderts. Eine Standortsbestimmung', in *Actes du XIVe Congrès International des Études Byzantines* (Bucharest, 1974), I, 125–38.

Beihammer (forthcoming): A. Beihammer, 'Byzantine Chancery Tradition in Frankish Cyprus: the Case of the Vaticanus MS Palatinus Graecus 367', in Fourrier and Grivaud (forthcoming).

Bertolucci Pizzorusso (1988): V. Bertolucci Pizzorusso, 'Testamento in francese di un mercante veneziano (Famagosta, gennaio 1294)', *Annali della Scuola Normale Superiore di Pisa, Classe di Lettere e Filosofia*, 18/3 (1988), 1011–33.

Bertram (1977): M. Bertram, 'Johannes de Ancona: Ein Jurist des 13. Jahrhunderts in den Kreuzfahrerstaaten', *Bulletin of Medieval Canon Law*, 7 (1977), 49–64.

Blijnuk (1991–1992): S.V. Blijnuk, 'Die Venezianer auf Zypern in 13. und in der erste Hälfte des 14. Jahrhunderts', *BZ*, 84–85 (1991–1992), 441–51.

Boase (1977): T.S.R. Boase, 'The Arts in Cyprus, A. Ecclesiastical Art', in Setton (1955–1989, IV (1977): 165–95).

Boehlke (1966): F.J. Boehlke, *Pierre de Thomas, Scholar, Diplomat, and Crusader* (Philadelphia, 1966).

Borg (1985): A. Borg, *Cypriot Arabic: a historical and comparative investigation into the phonology and morphology of the Arabic vernacular spoken by the Maronites of Kormakiti village in the Kyrenia district of north-western Cyprus* (Stuttgart, 1985).

Boulton (1987): D'A.J.D. Boulton, *The Knights of the Crown. The Monarchical Orders of Knighthood in Later Medieval Europe, 1325–1520* (Woodbridge, 1987).

Boutière and Schutz (1973): J. Boutière and A.H. Schutz, *Biographies des troubadours. Textes provençaux des XIIIe et XIVe siècles* (Paris, 1973²).

Boyd (1974): S. Boyd, 'The Church of the Panagia Amasgou, Monagri, Cyprus, and Its Wallpaintings', *DOP*, 28 (1974), 277–328.

Brayer (1947): É. Brayer, 'Un manuel de confession en ancien français conservé dans un manuscrit de Catane (Bibl. Ventimiliana 42)', *MAHEFR*, 59 (1947), 155–98.

Breillat (1938): P. Breillat, 'La Table Ronde en Orient. Le poème grec du Vieux Chevalier', *MAHEFR*, 55 (1938), 308–40.

Bromiley (1998): G.N. Bromiley, 'Philippe de Novare: Another epic Historian?', *Neophilologus*, 82 (1998), 527–41.

Browning (1978a): R. Browning, 'The Language of Byzantine Literature', in S. Vryonis Jr. (ed.), *The Past in Medieval and Modern Greek Culture* (Malibu, 1978), 103–33; repr. in Browning (1989: art. XV).

—— (1978b): R. Browning, 'Literacy in the Byzantine World', *BMGS*, 4 (1978), 39–54; repr. in Browning (1989: art. VII).

—— (1987–1988): R. Browning, 'Notes on Greek Manuscripts of Cypriot Provenance or Connection in the Libraries of Great Britain' [First International Symposium on Mediaeval Cypriot Palaeography (Nicosia 1984)], *EKEE*, 17 (1987–1988), 113–22.

—— (1989): R. Browning, *History, Language and Literacy in the Byzantine World* [Variorum Reprints] (Northampton, 1989).

Bryer and Georghallides (1993): A.A.M. Bryer and G.S. Georghallides (eds.), *The Sweet Land of Cyprus* [Papers Given at the Twenty-Fifth Jubilee Spring Symposium of Byzantine Studies (Birmingham, March 1991)] (Nicosia, 1993).

Buchthal (1957): H. Buchthal, *Miniature Painting in the Latin Kingdom of Jerusalem* [Warburg Institute] (London, 1957).

—— (1975): H. Buchthal, 'Toward a History of Palaeologan Illumination', in *The Place of Book Illumination in Byzantine Art* (Princeton, N.J., 1975), 143–78.

Cahen (1963): C. Cahen, '`A propos des coutumes du marché d'Acre', *RHDFE*, 41 (1963), 287–90.

Canart (1977): P. Canart, 'Un style d'écriture livresque dans les manuscrits chypriotes du XVIᵉ siècle: La chypriote "bouclée"', *La Paléographie grecque et byzantine* [Colloques Internationaux du Centre Nationale de la Recherche Scientifique 559] (Paris, 1977), 303–21.

—— (1987–1988): P. Canart, 'Les écritures livresques chypriotes du XIᵉ au XVIᵉ siècle' [First International Symposium on Mediaeval Cypriot Palaeography (Nicosia 1984)], *EKEE*, 17 (1987–1988), 27–53.

Cardini (2002): F. Cardini, *In Terrasanta. Pellegrini italiani tra Medioevo e prima età moderna* (Bologna, 2002).

Carile (1970): A. Carile, 'Aspetti della cronachistica veneziana nei secoli XIII e XIV', in A. Pertusi (ed.), *La storiografia veneziana fino al secolo XVI. Aspetti e problemi* (Florence, 1970), 75–120.

Carr (1987): A.W. Carr *Byzantine Illumination, 1150–1250. The Study of a Provincial Tradition* (Chicago, 1987).

—— (1987–1988): A.W. Carr, 'Cyprus and the "Decorative Style"' [First International Symposium on Mediaeval Cypriot Palaeography (Nicosia, 1984)], *EKEE*, 17 (1987–1988), 123–67.

—— (1995a): A.W. Carr, 'Art in the Court of the Lusignan Kings', in Coureas and Riley-Smith (1995: 239–74); repr. in Carr (2005a: art. VII).

—— (1995b): A.W. Carr, 'Byzantines and Italians on Cyprus: Images from Art', *DOP*, 49 (1995), 339–57; repr. in Carr (2005a: art. XI).

—— (1995c): A.W. Carr, 'Icon-Tact: Byzantium and the Art of Cilician Armenia', in T.F. Mathews and R. Wieck (eds.), *Treasures in Heaven: Armenian Art. Religion, and Society* (New York, 1995), 73–102; repr. in Carr (2005a: art. VIII).

—— (1998–1999): A.W. Carr, 'Correlative Spaces: Art, Identity and Appropriation in Lusignan Cyprus', *Modern Greek Studies Yearbook*, 14–15 (1998–1999), 59–80; repr. in Carr (2005a: art. VI).

—— (2001): A.W. Carr, 'A Palaiologan Funerary Icon from Gothic Cyprus', in *ΠΓ΄ΔΚΣ*, II, 599–619; repr. in Carr (2005a: art. IX).

—— (2004a): A.W. Carr, 'Reflections on the Life of an Icon: The Eleousa of Kykkos', *EKMIMK*, 6 (2004), 103–64.

—— (2004b): A.W. Carr, 'The Holy Icons: A Lusignan Asset?', in D.H. Weiss and L. Mahoney (eds.), *France and the Holy Land. Frankish Culture at the End of the Crusades* (Baltimore–London, 2004), 313–35.

—— (2005a): A.W. Carr, *Cyprus and the Devotional Arts of Byzantium in the Era of the Crusades* [Variorum Reprints] (Aldershot, 2005).

—— (2005b): A.W. Carr, 'Cypriot Funerary Icons: Questions of Convergence in a Complex Land', in S. Hayes-Healy (ed.), *Medieval Paradigms: Essays in Honor of Jeremy DuQuesnay Adams* (Boston, 2005), I, 153–73.

Carr and Morrocco (1991): A.W. Carr and L.J. Morrocco, *A Byzantine Masterpiece Recovered, The Thirteenth-Century Murals of Lysi, Cyprus* (Austin, Texas, 1991).

Cattin (1995): G. Cattin, 'The texts of the Offices of Sts. Hylarion and Anne in the Cypriot Manuscript Torino J. II. 9', in Finscher and Günther (1995: 249–301).

Catto (1976): J. Catto, 'Ideas and Experience in the Political Thought of Aquinas', *Past and Present*, 71 (1976), 3–21.

Charpentier (1989): H. Charpentier, 'Histoire, droit et morale du lignage dans l'œuvre de Philippe de Novare', in *Les relations de parenté dans le monde médiéval* [Centre Universitaire d'Études et de Recherches Médiévales] (Aix-en-Provence, 1989), 325–34.

Chatzedakes (1985): M. Chatzedakes, *Mystras. The Medieval City and Its Castle* (Athens, 1985).
Chatziioannou (1964): K.P. Chatziioannou, 'The Beginning of the Modern Greek Cypriote Dialect As It appears in the Greek Text of the Assizes, in the 13th Century A.D.', *Communications et rapports du Premier Congrès International de Dialectologie Générale* (Leuven, 1964), I, 296–309; repr. in K.P. Chatziioannou, *Τα εν διασπορά Α΄, 1933–1969* (Nicosia, 1990), 509–23.
Chatzipsaltes (1955): C. Chatzipsaltes, 'Εκκλησιαστικά δικαστήρια Κύπρου επί Φραγκοκρατίας', *ΚΣ*, 19 (1955), 23–34.
—— (1958): C. Chatzipsaltes, 'Εκ της ιστορίας της Εκκλησίας Κύπρου κατά την Φραγκοκρατίαν. Α. Τρόπος εκλογής Ελλήνων επισκόπων. Β. ΄Ελληνες επίσκοποι Λευκάρων (= Αμαθούντος, Νεμεσού και Κουρίου)', *ΚΣ*, 22 (1958), 11–26.
—— (1964): C. Chatzipsaltes, 'Η Εκκλησία Κύπρου και το εν Νικαία Οικουμενικόν Πατριαρχείον αρχομένου του ΙΓ΄ μ.Χ. αιώνος. Συνοδική πράξις του Πατριαρχείου Κωνσταντινουπόλεως σχετικώς προς την εκλογήν και την αναγνώρισιν του Αρχιεπισκόπου Κύπρου Ησαΐου', *ΚΣ*, 28 (1964), 135–68.
Cheynet (1994): J.-C. Cheynet, 'Chypre à la veille de la conquête franque', in Mutafian (1994: 67–77).
De Cholet (1984): D. de Cholet, 'Fresques du Jugement dernier dans l'église de Saint-Héraclide au monastère de Saint-Jean Lampadistis à Chypre', *Cahiers Balkaniques*, 6 (1984), 107–15.
Christodoulou and Perdikes (2001): M.N. Christodoulou and S.K. Perdikes (eds.), Πρακτικά συμποσίου 'Η ιερά Μονή Κύκκου στη βυζαντινή και μεταβυζαντινή αρχαιολογία και τέχνη' [Nicosia, 14–16 May 1998] (Nicosia, 2001).
Christoforaki (1996): I. Christoforaki, 'Cyprus between Byzantium and the Levant: Eclecticism and Interchange in the Cycle of the Life of the Virgin in the Church of the Holy Cross at Pelendri', *EKEE*, 21 (1996), 215–55.
—— (1997): I. Christoforaki, 'Η Τέχνη στην Κύπρο την εποχή του Μαχαιρά και του Βουστρώνιου', in Loizou-Chatzigabriel (1997: 87–96).
—— (1999): I. Christoforaki, *Patronage, Art and Society in Lusignan Cyprus, c. 1192–c.1489* [unpublished Ph.D. Thesis (University of Oxford, 1999)].
—— (2000): I. Christoforaki, 'An Unusual Representation of the Incredulity from Lusignan Cyprus', *Cahiers archéologiques*, 48 (2000), 71–87.
Ciggaar (1993): K. Ciggaar, 'Robert de Boron en Outremer? Le culte de Joseph d'Arimathie dans le monde byzantin et en Outremer', in H. Hokwerda, E.R. Smits, and M.M. Woesthuis (eds.), *Polyphonia Byzantina. Studies in Honour of Willem J. Aerts* (Groninguen, 1993), 145–59.
—— (1994): K. Ciggaar, 'Le royaume des Lusignans: terre de littérature et de traditions, échanges littéraires et culturels', in Mutafian (1994: 89–98).
—— (1996): K. Ciggaar, 'Manuscripts as Intermediaries. The Crusader States and Literary Cross-Fertilization', in Ciggaar *et al.* (1996: 131–51).
Ciggaar *et al.* (1996): K. Ciggaar, A. Davids, and H. Teule (eds.), *East and West in the Crusader States* (Leuven, 1996).
Claverie (1998): P.-V. Claverie, 'L'Ordre du Temple au coeur d'une crise politique majeure: la *Querela Cypri* des années 1279–1285', *Le Moyen Age*, 104 (1998), 495–511.
—— (forthcoming): P.-V. Claverie, *L'Ordre du Temple en Terre Sainte et à Chypre au XIIIᵉ siècle* [TSHC] (Nicosia, forthcoming).
Coldstream (1975): N. Coldstream, 'The Church of St George the Latin, Famagusta', *RDAC 1975* (1976), 147–51.
—— (1987): N. Coldstream, 'Introduction. Camille Enlart and the Gothic Architecture of Cyprus', in Enlart (1987: 1–10).
—— (1993): N. Coldstream, *Nicosia–Gothic City to Venetian Fortress* [Third Annual Lecture, The Leventis Municipal Museum of Nicosia (22 October 1992)] (Nicosia, 1993).

—— (1998): N. Coldstream, 'Gothic architecture in the Lusignan Kingdom', in Papanikola-Bakirtzis and Iacovou (1998: 51–60).

Collenberg (1977a): W.H. Rudt de Collenberg, 'Les Dispenses matrimoniales accordées à l'Orient latin selon les registres du Vatican d'Honorius III à Clément VII (1223–1385)', *MEFR*, 89 (1977), 10–93.

—— (1977b): W.H. Rudt de Collenberg, 'L'Héraldique de Chypre', *Cahiers d'héraldique*, 3 (1977), 86–157 and tables.

—— (1977–1979): W.H. Rudt de Collenberg, 'Les Ibelin aux XIII^c et XIV^c siècles. Généalogie compilée principalement selon les registres du Vatican', *EKEE*, 9 (1977–1979), 117–265; repr. in W.H. Rudt de Collenberg., *Familles de l'Orient latin XIIe–XIVe siècles* [Variorum Reprints] (London, 1983), art. IV.

—— (1979): W.H. Rudt de Collenberg, 'État et origine du haut clergé de Chypre avant le Grand Schisme d'après les Registres des papes du XIII^c et du XIV^c siècle', *MEFR*, 91/1 (1979), 197–332.

—— (1979–1980): W.H. Rudt de Collenberg, 'Les Lusignan de Chypre', *EKEE*, 10 (1979–1980), 85–319.

—— (1982a): W.H. Rudt de Collenberg, 'Le Royaume et l'Église de Chypre face au Grand Schisme (1378–1417) d'après les Registres des archives du Vatican', *MEFR*, 94/2 (1982), 621–701.

—— (1982b): W.H. Rudt de Collenberg, 'Le Déclin de la société franque de Chypre entre 1350 et 1450', *KΣ*, 46 (1982), 71–83.

—— (1983): W.H. Rudt de Collenberg, 'Recherches sur quelques familles chypriotes apparentées au pape Clément VIII Aldobrandini (1592–1605): Flatro, Davila, Sozomenoi, Lusignan, Bustron et Nores (selon les fonds de l'Archivio Segreto Vaticano, de la Biblioteca Vaticana et de l'Archivio Doria-Pamphili)', *EKEE*, 12 (1983), 5–68.

—— (1984): W.H. Rudt de Collenberg, 'Études de prosopographie généalogique des Chypriotes mentionnés dans les Registres du Vatican 1378–1471', *Μελέται και Υπομνήματα*, 1 (1984), 523–678.

—— (1993): W.H. Rudt de Collenberg, 'Les premiers Podocataro. Recherches basées sur le testament de Hugues (1452)', *Θησαυρίσματα*, 23 (1993), 130–82.

—— (1995): W.H. Rudt de Collenberg, 'Δομή και προέλευση της τάξεως των ευγενών', in Papadopoullos (1995a: 785–862).

Constantinides (1982): C.N. Constantinides, *Higher Education in Byzantium in the Thirteenth and Early Fourteenth Centuries (1204–ca 1310)* (Nicosia, 1982).

—— (1984–1987): C.N. Constantinides, 'Ο γραφέας του ευαγγελισταρίου Λευκάρων', *EKEE*, 13–16/1 (1984–1987), 627–46.

—— (1991): C.N. Constantinides, 'Ρόδιοι βιβλιογράφοι στη λατινοκρατούμενη Κύπρο', *Δωδώνη*, 20/1 (1991), 305–28.

—— (1995): C.N. Constantinides, 'The Copying and Circulation of Secular Greek Texts in Frankish Cyprus', *EKEE*, 21 (1995), 15–32.

Constantinides (1999): E. Constantinides, 'Monumental Painting in Cyprus during the Venetian Period, 1489–1570', in Patterson Ševčenko and Moss (1999: 263–300).

Corrie (1996): R.W. Corrie, 'Coppo di Marcovaldo's Madonna del bordone and the Meaning of the Bare-legged Christ Child in Siena and the East', *Gesta*, 35 (1996), 43–65.

Coureas (1994): N. Coureas, 'Η Μονή Αγίου Γεωργίου των Μαγγάνων επί Φραγκοκρατίας', *Επιστημονική Επετηρίς της Κυπριακής Εταιρείας Ιστορικών Σπουδών*, 2 (1994), 275–86.

—— (1995a): N. Coureas, 'Lusignan Cyprus and Lesser Armenia, 1195–1375', *EKEE*, 21 (1995), 33–71.

—— (1995b): N. Coureas, 'Cyprus and the Naval Leagues, 1333–1358', in Coureas and Riley-Smith (1995: 107–24).

—— (1995c): N. Coureas, 'The Cypriot Reaction to the Establishment of the Latin

Church. Resistance and Collaboration', *Sources Travaux Historiques*, 43–44 (1995), 75–84.

—— (1996): N. Coureas, 'The Orthodox Monastery of Mt. Sinae and Papal Protection of its Cretan and Cypriot Properties', in M. Balard (ed.), *Autour de la Première Croisade* (Paris, 1996), 475–84.

—— (1997): N. Coureas, *The Latin Church in Cyprus, 1195–1312* (Aldershot–Brookfield, Vermont, 1997).

—— (1998): N. Coureas, 'Conversion on Latin Cyprus: A New Faith or a New Rite?', *EKEE*, 24 (1998), 77–86.

—— (2000a): N. Coureas, 'Christian and Muslim Captives on Lusignan Cyprus: Redemption or Retention?', in G. Cipollone (ed.), *La liberazione dei 'Captivi' tra Cristianità e Islam* (Vatican City, 2000), 525–31.

—— (2000b): N. Coureas, 'Latin Provincial Synods of the Thirteenth Century as a Means of Promoting Ecclesiastical Discipline and Doctrinal Uniformity', *Annuarium Historiae Conciliorum*, 32/1 (2000), 82–105.

—— (2000c): N. Coureas, 'The Latin Elite on Cyprus: Trying to Keep Apart', *Journal of Mediterranean Studies*, 10 (2000), 31–45.

—— (2001a): N. Coureas, 'Non-Chalcedonian Christians on Latin Cyprus', in Balard *et al.* (2001: 349–60).

—— (2001b); N. Coureas, 'The Provision of Charity and Hospital Care on Latin Cyprus', *EKEE*, 27 (2001), 33–50.

Coureas and Riley-Smith (1995): N. Coureas and J. Riley-Smith (eds.), *Cyprus and the Crusades* [Papers Given at the International Conference 'Cyprus and the Crusades' (Nicosia, 1994)] (Nicosia, 1995).

Coureas *et al.* (forthcoming): N. Coureas, G. Grivaud, and C. Schabel, 'The Capital of the Sweet Land of Cyprus: Frankish and Venetian Nicosia', in Michaelides (forthcoming).

Couroupou and Géhin (2001): M. Couroupou and P. Géhin, 'Nouveaux documents chypriotes', *REB*, 59 (2001), 147–64.

Danezis (1986–1987): G. Danezis, Ὁ Σπανέας καὶ οἱ πολιτικοί στίχοι τοῦ Γεωργίου Λαπίθη', *Δίπτυχα*, 4, (1986–1987), 413–25.

—— (1987): G. Danezis, *Spaneas: Vorlage, Quellen, Versionen* (Munich, 1987).

Darrouzès (1950): J. Darrouzès, 'Manuscrits originaires de Chypre à la Bibliothèque Nationale de Paris', *REB*, 8 (1950), 162–96; repr. in Darrouzès (1972: art. XI).

—— (1951a): J. Darrouzès, 'Évêques inconnus ou peu connus de Chypre', *BZ*, 44 (1951), 97–104; repr. in Darrouzès (1972: art. XVIII).

—— (1951b): J. Darrouzès, 'Un obituaire chypriote: le Parisinus graecus 1588', *ΚΣ*, 15 (1951), 23–62; repr. in Darrouzès (1972: art. XIII).

—— (1953): J. Darrouzès, 'Notes pour servir à l'histoire de Chypre (premier article)', *ΚΣ*, 17 (1953), 81–102; repr. in Darrouzès (1972: art. XIV).

—— (1956): J. Darrouzès, 'Notes pour servir à l'histoire de Chypre (deuxième article)', *ΚΣ*, 20 (1956), 31–63; repr. in Darrouzès (1972: art. XV).

—— (1957): J. Darrouzès, 'Autres manuscrits originaires de Chypre', *REB*, 15 (1957), 131–68; repr. in Darrouzès (1972: art. XII).

—— (1958): J. Darrouzès, 'Notes pour servir à l'histoire de Chypre (troisième article)', *ΚΣ*, 22 (1958), 221–50; repr. in Darrouzès (1972: art. XVI).

—— (1959a): J. Darrouzès, 'Notes pour servir à l'histoire de Chypre (quatrième article)', *ΚΣ*, 23 (1959), 25–56.

—— (1959b): J. Darrouzès, 'Lettre inédite de Jean Cantacuzène relative à la controverse palamite', *REB*, 17 (1959), 7–27; repr. in Darrouzès (1972: art. XVII).

—— (1970): J. Darrouzès, *Recherches sur les offikia de l'Église byzantine* (Paris, 1970).

—— (1972): J. Darrouzès, *Littérature et histoire des textes byzantins* [Variorum Reprints] (London, 1972).

—— (1979): J. Darrouzès, 'Textes synodaux chypriotes', *REB*, 37 (1979), 5–122.

Dédéyan (1994): G. Dédéyan, 'Les Arméniens à Chypre de la fin du XIe au début du XIIIe siècle', in Mutafian (1994: 122–31).

Delaville Le Roulx (1886): J. Delaville Le Roulx, *La France en Orient au XIVe siècle. Expéditions du Marechal Boucicaut*, 2 vols. (Paris, 1886).

Delisle (1906): L. Delisle, 'Maître Jean d'Antioche, traducteur, et frère Guillaume de Saint-Étienne, Hospitalier', *Histoire Littéraire de la France*, 33 (1906), 1–40.

Dentakis (1977): V.L. Dentakis, Ιωάννης Κυπαρισσιώτης ο σοφός και φιλόσοφος (Athens, 1977).

Derbes (1989): A. Derbes, 'Siena and the Levant in the Later Dugento', *Gesta*, 28 (1989), 190–204.

Dodd (2004): E. Cruikshank Dodd, *Medieval Painting in the Lebanon* (Wiesbaden, 2004).

Duba (2000): W. Duba, 'The Afterlife in Medieval Frankish Cyprus', *EKEE*, 26 (2000), 167–94.

Duckworth (1900): H.T.F. Duckworth, *The Church of Cyprus* (London, 1900).

Edbury (1975–1977): P.W. Edbury, 'Latin Dioceses and Peristerona: A Contribution to the Topography of Lusignan Cyprus', *EKEE*, 8 (1975–1977), 45–51; repr. in Edbury (1999: art. XXI).

—— (1978): P.W. Edbury, 'The "Cartulaire de Manosque": A Grant to the Templars in Latin Syria and a Charter of King Hugh I of Cyprus', *Bulletin of the Institute of Historical Research*, 51 (1978), 174–81.

—— (1980): P.W. Edbury, 'The Murder of King Peter I of Cyprus (1359–1369)', *Journal of Medieval History*, 6 (1980), 219–33; repr. in Edbury (1999: art. XIII).

—— (1983): P.W. Edbury, 'John of Ibelin's Title to the County of Jaffa and Ascalon', *EHR*, 98 (1983), 115–33; repr. in Edbury (1999: art. VII).

—— (1986): P.W. Edbury, 'Cyprus and Genoa: The Origins of the War of 1373–1374', in *ΠΒ΄ΔΚΣ*, II, 109–26; repr. in Edbury (1999: art. XIV).

—— (1989): P.W. Edbury, 'La classe des propriétaires terriens franco-chypriotes et l'exploitation des ressources rurales de l'île de Chypre', in M. Balard (ed.), *État et colonisation au Moyen Age* [CNRS Conference (Reims, April 1987)] (Lyons, 1989), 145–52; trans. in English in Edbury (1999: art. XIX).

—— (1990): P.W. Edbury, 'The "Livre" of Geoffrey le Tor and the "Assises" of Jerusalem', in M.J. Peláez (ed.), *Historia administrativa y ciencia de la administración comparada. Trabajos en hamenaje a Ferran Vails i Taberner*, XV (Barcelona, 1990), 4291–8; repr. in Edbury (1999: art. X).

—— (1991): P.W. Edbury, *The Kingdom of Cyprus and the Crusades, 1191–1374* (Cambridge, 1991).

—— (1995a): P.W. Edbury, 'Η πολιτική ιστορία του μεσαιωνικού βασιλείου από τη βασιλεία του Ούγου Δ΄ έως τη βασιλεία του Ιανού (1324–1432)', in Papadopoullos (1995a: 51–158).

—— (1995b): P.W. Edbury, 'Famagusta in 1300', in Coureas and Riley-Smith (1995: 337–53); repr. in Edbury (1999: art. XVI).

—— (1995c): P.W. Edbury, 'Le régime des Lusignan en Chypre et la population locale', in Balard and Ducellier (1995: 354–8, 364–5); trans. in English in Edbury (1999: art. XX).

—— (1996): P.W. Edbury, 'Law and Custom in the Latin East: *Les Letres dou Sepulcre*', in B. Arbel (ed.), *Intercultural Contacts in the Medieval Mediterranean. Studies in Honour of David Jacoby* (London, 1996) [= *MHR*, 10, 1995], 71–9; repr. in Edbury (1999: art. IX).

—— (1997a): P.W. Edbury, *John of Ibelin and the Kingdom of Jerusalem* (Woodbridge, 1997).

—— (1997b): P.W. Edbury, 'Famagusta Society ca. 1300 from the Registers of Lamberto di Sambuceto', in H.E. Mayer (ed.), *Die Kreuzfahrerstaaten als multikulturelle Gesellschaft. Die Rolle der Einwanderer in Kirche, Staat, Verwaltung, Wirtschaft und Kultur* (Munich, 1997), 87–95; repr. in Edbury (1999: art. XVII).

—— (1997c): P.W. Edbury, 'The Genoese Community in Famagusta around the

Year 1300: A Historical Vignette', in L. Balletto (ed.), *Oriente e occidente tra medioevo ed età moderna. Studi in onore di Geo Pistarino* (Genoa, 1997), 235–44; repr. in Edbury (1999: art. XVIII).

—— (1997d): P.W. Edbury, 'John of Jaffa and the Kingdom of Cyprus', *EKEE*, 23 (1997), 15–26; repr. in Edbury (1999: art. VIII).

—— (1997e): P.W. Edbury, 'The Lyon *Eracles* and the Old French Continuation of William of Tyre', in B.J. Kedar, J. Riley-Smith, and R. Hiestand (eds.), *Montjoie. Studies in Crusade History in Honour of Hans Eberhard Mayer* (Aldershot, 1997), 139–53.

—— (1998a): P.W. Edbury, 'The *Livre des Assises* by John of Jaffa: The Development and Transmission of the Text', in J. France and W.G. Zajac (eds.), *The Crusades and Their Sources: Essays Presented to Bernard Hamilton* (Aldershot, 1998), 169–79.

—— (1998b): P.W. Edbury, 'Fiefs, vassaux et service militaire dans le royaume latin de Jérusalem', in M. Balard and A. Ducellier (eds.), *Le Partage du monde. Échanges et colonisation dans la Méditerranée médiévale* (Paris, 1998), 141–50.

—— (1999): P.W. Edbury, *Kingdoms of the Crusaders. From Jerusalem to Cyprus* [Variorum Reprints] (Aldershot, 1999).

—— (2001a): P.W. Edbury, 'The De Montforts in the Latin East', in M. Prestwich, R. Britnell, and R. Frame (eds.), *Proceedings of the Durham Conference 1999, Thirteenth Century England*, 8 (2001), 23–31.

—— (2001b): P.W. Edbury, 'Philip of Novara and the *Livre de forme de plait*', in *ΠΓ΄ΔΚΣ*, II, 555–69.

—— (2002): P.W. Edbury, 'Latins and Greeks on Crusader Cyprus', in D. Abulafia and N. Berend (eds.), *Medieval Frontiers: Concepts and Practices* (Aldershot, 2002), 133–42.

—— (forthcoming): P.W. Edbury, 'A New Text of the *Annales de Terre Sainte*', in *Festschrift Kedar* (forthcoming).

Edbury and Rowe (1988): P.W. Edbury and J.G. Rowe, *William of Tyre, Historian of the Latin East* (Cambridge, 1988).

Efthimiou (1987): M.B. Efthimiou, *Greeks and Latins on Cyprus in the Thirteenth Century* (Brookline, Mass., 1987).

Eideneier (1987): H. Eideneier, 'Μεσαιωνική ποίηση και οι απολήξεις της σε νεώτερα κυπριακά τραγούδια', in *ΠΒ΄ΔΚΣ*, III, 415–23.

Eliades (2004a): I.A. Eliades, 'Η προσκυνηματική εικόνα του Αγίου Φιλίππου στο ΄Αρσος Λεμεσού', in *Ορθόδοξη μαρτυρία*, 74 (2004), 9–12.

—— (2004b): I.A. Eliades, *Guide to the Museum of the Byzantine Heritage of Palaichori* (Nicosia, 2004).

Emilianides (1938): A.C. Emilianides, 'Η εξέλιξις του δικαίου των μικτών γάμων εν Κύπρω', *ΚΣ*, 2 (1938), 195–236.

Emmanuel (1997): M. Emmanuel, 'Ο ναός της Παναγίας στο Μουτουλλά της Κύπρου. Οι τοιχογραφίες της μεταβυζαντινής εποχής', *ΚΣ*, 6 (1997), 107–37.

Englezakis (1980): B. Englezakis, 'Cyprus as Stepping-Stone between West and East in the Age of the Crusades. The Two Churches', in *XVᵉ Congrès International des Sciences Historiques, Rapports, II, Section chronologique* (Bucharest, 1980), 216–21.

—— (1995): B. Englezakis, 'St Neophytos the Recluse and the Beginnings of Frankish Rule in Cyprus', in B. Englezakis, *Studies on the History of the Church of Cyprus, 4th–20th Centuries*, English trans. N. Russell (Nicosia 1995), 151–205.

Enlart (1899): C. Enlart, *L'Art gothique et la renaissance en Chypre*, 2 vols. (Paris, 1899).

—— (1987): C. Enlart, *Gothic Art and the Renaissance in Cyprus*, English trans. and ed. D. Hunt (London, 1987).

Evans (2004): H.C. Evans (ed.), *Byzantium. Faith and Power* [Exhibition Catalogue, The Metropolitan Museum of Art (New York, 23 March–4 July 2004)] (New Haven, 2004).

Evgenidou and Albani (2001): D. Evgenidou and J. Albani (eds.), *The City of Mystras* [Exhibition Catalogue (Mystras, August 2001–January 2002)] (Athens, 2001).

Fabris (1942): G. Fabris, 'Professori e scolari greci all'Università di Padova', *Archivio Veneto*, 5th ser., 30–31 (1942), 124–34.

Fedalto (1995): G. Fedalto, Ἡ Λατινική Ἐκκλησία στο μεσαιωνικό βασίλειο', in Papadopoullos (1995a: 667–732).
Finscher and Günther (1995): L. Finscher and U. Günther (eds.), *The Cypriot-French Repertory of the Manuscript, Torino J. II. 9.* [Report of the International Musicological Congress (Paphos, 20–25 March 1992)] (Neuhausen–Stuttgart, 1995).
Fleet (1999): K. Fleet, *European and Islamic Trade in the Early Ottoman State* (Cambridge, 1999).
Flinn (1963): J. Flinn, *Le Roman de Renart dans la littérature française et dans les littératures étrangères au Moyen Age* (Paris–Toronto, 1963).
Folda (1973): J. Folda, 'Manuscripts of the *History of Outremer* by William of Tyre: a Handlist', *Scriptorium*, 27 (1973), 90–5.
—— (1976): J. Folda, *Crusader Manuscript Illuminations at Saint-Jean d'Acre, 1275–1291* (Princeton, 1976).
—— (1995): J. Folda, 'Crusader Art in the Kingdom of Cyprus, c. 1275–1291: Reflections on the State of the Question', in Coureas and Riley-Smith (1995: 209–37).
—— (2001): J. Folda, 'Reflections on the Mellon Madonna as a Work of Crusader Art: Links with Crusader Art on Cyprus', in Balard *et al.* (2001: 361–71).
—— (2002): J. Folda, 'Icon to Altarpiece in the Frankish East: Images of the Virgin and Child Enthroned', in V. Schmidt (ed.), *Italian Panel Painting in the Duecento and Trecento* (Washington, D.C., 2002), 123–45.
Forey (1995): A. Forey, 'Cyprus as a Base for Crusading Expeditions from the West', in Coureas and Riley-Smith (1995: 69–79).
Fourrier and Grivaud (forthcoming): S. Fourrier and G. Grivaud (eds.), *Actes du Colloque 'Identités croisées en un milieu méditerranéen: le cas de Chypre'* [Université de Rouen (Rouen, 11–13 March 2004)] (Rouen, forthcoming).
Frankoudes (1890): G.S. Frankoudes, Κύπρις (Athens, 1890).
Frigerio-Zeniou (1998): S. Frigerio-Zeniou, *L'art 'italo-byzantin' à Chypre au XVIe siècle. Trois témoins de la peinture religieuse: Panagia Podithou, la Chapelle Latine et Panagia Iamatikè* [Bibliothèque de l'Institut hellénique d'études byzantines et post-byzantines de Venise 20] (Venice, 1998).
—— (2000–2001): S. Frigerio-Zeniou, 'Notes sur trois églises de la fin du 16e–début du 17e siècle à Chypre', ΚΣ, 64–65 (2000–2001), 351–71.
Frinta (1981): M.S. Frinta, 'Raised Gilded Adornment of the Cypriot Icons, and the Occurrence of the Technique in the West', *Gesta*, 20 (1981), 333–47.
—— (1986): M.S. Frinta, 'Relief Decoration in Gilded Pastiglia on the Cypriot Icons and Its Propagation in the West', in ΠΒ΄ΔΚΣ, II, 539–44.
—— (1998): M.S. Frinta, *Punched Decoration on Late Medieval Panel and Miniature Painting, Part I: Catalogue* (Prague, 1998).
Galatariotou (1991): C. Galatariotou, *The Making of a Saint: The Life, Times and Sanctification of Neophytos the Recluse* (Cambridge, 1991).
Gallais (1970): P. Gallais, 'Robert de Boron en Orient', in *Mélanges offerts à Jean Frappier* (Geneva, 1970), I, 313–9.
Gamillscheg and Harlfinger (1989): E. Gamillscheg and D. Harlfinger, *Repertorium der griechischen Kopisten 800–1600. 1. Teil. Handschriften aus Bibliotheken Grossbritanniens* (Vienna, 1989).
Garides (1985): M.-M. Garides, *Études sur le jugement dernier post-byzantin du XVe à la fin du XIXe siècle. Iconographie–esthétique* (Thessalonike, 1985).
Garzya (1983): A. Garzya, 'Matière de Bretagne a Bisanzio', in *Letterature comparate: problemi e metodo. Studi in onore di Ettore Paratore* (Bologna, 1981), III, 1029–41; repr. in A. Garzya, *Il Mandarino e il Quotidiano: Saggi sulla Letteratura Tardoantica e Bizantina* (Naples, 1983), 263–81.
Gaspares (1997): Ch. Gaspares, Η γή και οι αγρότες στη μεσαιωνική Κρήτη 13ος–14ος αιώνας (Athens, 1997).
Gerasimos and Papaioakim (1997): C. Gerasimos and K. Papaioakim, Ο Άγιος Φίλιππος. Η μεγάλη εικόνα του αγίου στον Αγρό (13ου αιώνα) (Larnaca, 1997).

Gerstel (2001): S.E.J. Gerstel, 'Art and Identity in the Medieval Morea', in A.E. Laiou and R.P. Mottahedeh (eds.), *The Crusades from the Perspective of Byzantium and the Muslim World* (Dumbarton Oaks, Washington, D.C., 2001), 263–85.

Gill (1977): J. Gill, 'The Tribulations of the Greek Church in Cyprus 1196–c. 1280', *BF*, 5 (1977), 73–93.

Gilson (1974): É. Gilson, *Saint Thomas moraliste* (Paris, 1974²).

Gioles (1986): N. Gioles, 'Οι λειτουργικές πηγές της Ανάληψης στο ναό του Αγίου Ηρακλειδίου της μονής του Αγ. Ιωάννη του Λαμπαδιστή', in *ΠΒ΄ΔΚΣ*, II, 513–21.

—— (2003): N. Gioles, *Η Χριστιανική Τέχνη στην Κύπρο* (Nicosia, Museum of the Holy Monastery of Kykkos, 2003).

Golubovich (1906–1927): G. Golubovich, *Biblioteca bio-bibliografica della Terra Santa e dell'Oriente francescano*, 5 vols. (Quaracchi, Florence, 1906–1927).

Gonis (1986): D.B. Gonis, 'Ειδήσεις για την Εκκλησία της Κύπρου κατ' ανέκδοτη επιστολή πατριάρχου Κω/πόλεως (μέσα ΙΔ΄ αι.)', in *ΠΒ΄ΔΚΣ*, II, 333–50.

Gounarides (1986): P. Gounarides, 'Η *διήγησις* του μαρτυρίου των μοναχών της Καντάρας και η Εκκλησία της Κύπρου', in *ΠΒ΄ΔΚΣ*, II, 313–32.

Graboïs (1997): A. Graboïs, 'La bibliothèque du noble d'*Outremer* à Acre dans la seconde moitié du XIIIᵉ siècle', *Le Moyen Age*, 103/1 (1997), 43–66.

Grandclaude (1923): M. Grandclaude, *Étude critique sur les livres des Assises de Jérusalem* (Paris, 1923).

—— (1926): M. Grandclaude, 'Classement sommaire des manuscrits des principaux livres des Assises de Jérusalem', *RHDFE*, 5 (1926), 418–75.

—— (1929): M. Grandclaude, 'Les particularités du *De regimine principum* de saint Thomas', *RHDFE*, 8 (1929), 665–6.

Greenhill (1976): F.A. Greenhill, *Incised Effigial Slabs: A Study of Stone Memorials in Latin Christendom c. 1100–c. 1700*, 2 vols. (London, 1976).

Grégoire and Lüdeke (1939): H. Grégoire and H. Lüdeke, 'Nouvelles chansons épiques des IXᵉ et Xᵉ siècles. *Ο Αζγουρής*', *Byzantion*, 14 (1939), 235–63.

Greilsammer (1999): M. Greilsammer, 'Anatomie d'un mensonge: le *Livre au Roi* et la révision de l'histoire du royaume latin par les juristes du XIIIᵉ siècle', *Tijdschrift voor Rechtsgeschiedenis*, 67/3–4 (1999), 239–54.

Grivaud (1991): G. Grivaud, 'Formes byzantines de la fiscalité foncière chypriote à l'époque latine', *EKEE*, 18 (1991), 117–27.

—— (1992): G. Grivaud, '*Ordine della Secreta di Cipro*. Florio Bustron et les institutions franco-byzantines afférantes au régime agraire de Chypre à l'époque vénitienne', *Μελέται και Υπομνήματα*, 2 (1992), 533–92.

—— (1993): G. Grivaud, 'Sur le *comerc* chypriote de l'époque latine', in Bryer and Georghallides (1993: 133–45).

—— (1994): G. Grivaud, 'Les Lusignan et leurs archontes chypriotes (1192–1359)', in Mutafian (1994: 150–8).

—— (1995): G. Grivaud, 'Éveil de la nation *chyproise* (XIIᵉ–XVᵉ siècles)', in *'Kyprios character'. Quelle identité chypriote? Sources travaux historiques*, 43–44 (1995), 105–16.

—— (1996): G. Grivaud, 'Ο πνευματικός βίος και η γραμματολογία κατά την περίοδο της Φραγκοκρατίας', in Papadopoullos (1996: 863–1227).

—— (1998a): G. Grivaud, 'Formes et mythe de la *strateia* à Chypre', in P. Odorico (ed.), *Matériaux pour une histoire de Chypre (IVᵉ–XXᵉ s.)*, Études Balkaniques, Cahiers Pierre Belon, 5 (1998), 33–54.

—— (1998b): G. Grivaud, 'Villages désertés à Chypre (fin XIIᵉ–fin XIXᵉ siècle)', *Μελέται και Υπομνήματα*, 3 (1998), 1–604.

—— (2000): G. Grivaud, 'Les minorités orientales à Chypre (époque médiévale et moderne)', in Y. Ioannou, F. Metral, and M. Yon (eds.), *Chypre et la Méditerranée orientale* (Lyons, 2000), 43–70.

—— (2001a): G. Grivaud, 'Peut-on parler d'une politique économique des Lusignan?', in *ΠΓ΄ΔΚΣ*, II, 360–8.

—— (2001b): G. Grivaud, *Grecs et Francs dans le royaume de Chypre (1191–1474): les voies de l'acculturation* [unpublished Dissertation for the *Habilitation à diriger des recherches* (Université de Paris I Panthéon–Sorbonne, 2001)].

—— (2001c): G. Grivaud, 'Une petite chronique chypriote du XVᵉ siècle', in Balard *et al.* (2001: 317–38).

—— (2003); G. Grivaud, 'Pèlerinages grecs et pèlerinages latins dans le royaume de Chypre (1192–1474): concurrence ou complémentarité?', in C. Vincent (ed.), *Identités pèlerines* (Rouen, 2003), 67–76.

—— (forthcoming): G. Grivaud, 'Fortune et infortune d'une petite fondation monastique', in Nicolaides and Carr (forthcoming).

Guéret-Laferté (1994): M. Guéret-Laferté, *Sur les routes de l'empire Mongol. Ordre et rhétorique dans les relations de voyage aux XIIIᵉ et XIVᵉ siècles* (Paris, 1994).

Gunnis (1936): R. Gunnis, *Historic Cyprus* (London, 1936).

Hackett (1901): J. Hackett, *History of the Orthodox Church of Cyprus* (London, 1901).

Hackett—Papaioannou (1923–1932): J. Hackett, Ιστορία της ορθοδόξου Εκκλησίας της Κύπρου, Greek trans. and additions Ch. Papaioannou, 3 vols. (Athens–Piraeus, 1923–1932).

Hadermann-Misguich (1992): L. Hadermann-Misguich, 'La Vierge Kykkotissa et l'eventuelle origine latine de son voile', in Acheimastou-Potamianou (1992, I: 197–204).

Halkin (1942): F. Halkin, 'La légende de saint Antoine traduite de l'arabe par Alphonse Bonhome, O.P.', *Analecta Bollandiana*, 60 (1942), 143–212.

Hamilton (1980): B. Hamilton, *The Latin Church in the Crusader States: The Secular Church* (London, 1980).

Hamilton Bleakley (1999): H. Hamilton Bleakley, 'The art of ruling in Aquinas' *De Regimine Principum*', *History of Political Thought*, 20/4 (1999), 575–602.

Havice (1984): C. Havice, 'The Marginal Miniatures in the Hamilton Psalter (Kupferstichkabinett 78.A.9)', *Jahrbuch der berliner Museen*, 26 (1984), 79–142.

Hein *et al.* (1996): E. Hein, A. Jakovljević, and B. Kleidt, *Zypern–byzantinische Kirchen und Klöster. Mosaiken und Fresken* (Ratingen, 1996).

Herrin *et al.* (2001): J. Herrin, M. Mullett, and C. Otten-Froux (eds.), *Mosaic. Festschrift for A.H.S. Megaw* [British School at Athens Studies 8] (Athens, 2001).

Hill (1940–1952): Sir G. Hill, *A History of Cyprus*, 4 vols. (Cambridge, 1940–1952).

Hinterberger (1999): M. Hinterberger, *Autobiographische Traditionen in Byzanz* (Vienna, 1999).

Hocquet (1979): J.-C. Hocquet, *Le sel et la fortune de Venise*, I: *Production et monopole*, II: *Voiliers et commerce en Méditerranée* (Lille, 1979).

Hoepffner (1961): E. Hoepffner, *Le troubadour Peire Vidal. Sa vie et son œuvre* (Paris, 1961).

Holy Metropolis of Morphou (2000): Ιερά Μητρόπολις Μόρφου. 2000 Χρόνια Τέχνης και Αγιότητος [Exhibition Catalogue, Bank of Cyprus Cultural Foundation (Nicosia, 2000)] (Nicosia, 2000).

Hoppin (1968): R.H. Hoppin, *Cypriot Plainchant of the Manuscript Torino, Biblioteca Nazionale J.II.9* (Rome, 1968).

Hubatsch (1955): W. Hubatsch, 'Der Deutsche Orden und die Reichslehnschaft über Cypern', *Nachrichten der Akademie der Wissenschaften in Göttingen I. Philologisch-Historische Klasse*, 8 (1955), 245–306.

Hunt (1991): L.-A. Hunt, 'A Woman's Prayer to St. Sergios in Latin Syria: Interpreting a Thirteenth-Century Icon at Mount Sinai', *BMGS*, 15 (1991), 96–145.

Imhaus (1998): B. Imhaus, 'Tombeaux et fragments funéraires médiévaux de l'île de Chypre', *RDAC 1998* (1998), 225–31.

—— (2001): B. Imhaus, 'Un monastère féminin de Nicosie: Notre-Dame de Tortose', in Balard *et al.* (2001: 389–401).

Immerzeel (2003): M. Immerzeel, 'Divine Cavalry. Mounted Saints in Middle Eastern Christian Art', in K. Ciggaar and H. Teule (eds.), *East and West in the Crusader States. Context—Contacts—Confrontations* [Orientalia Lovaniensia Analecta 125] (Leuven–Dudley, Ma., 2003), III, 265–86.

Ioannides (2000): G.A. Ioannides, 'La *Constitutio* o *Bulla Cypria Alexandri Papae IV* del *Barberinianus graecus 390*', *Orientalia Christiana Periodica*, 66/2 (2000), 335–71.

Iorga (1896): N. Iorga, *Philippe de Mézières (1327–1405) et la croisade au XIVe siècle* (Paris, 1896; repr. London, 1973).

Irmscher and Troumbeta (2002): J. Irmscher and S. Troumbeta, 'Το τραγούδι της Ζωγγραφούς', in Agapitos and Pieris (2002: 337–45).

Irwin (1995): R. Irwin, 'Οι εισβολές των Μαμελούκων στην Κύπρο', in Papadopoullos (1995a: 159–76).

Jacoby (1977): D. Jacoby, 'Citoyens, sujets et protégés de Venise et de Gênes en Chypre du XIIIe au XVe siècle', *BF*, 5 (1977), 159–88; repr. in D. Jacoby, *Recherches sur la Méditerranée orientale du XIIe au XVe siècle* [Variorum Reprints] (London, 1979), art. VI.

——— (1984a): D. Jacoby, 'The Rise of a New Emporium in the Eastern Mediterranean: Famagusta in the Late Thirteenth Century', *Μελέται και Υπομνήματα*, 1 (1984), 145–79; repr. in Jacoby (1989: art. VIII).

——— (1984b): D. Jacoby, 'La littérature française dans les états latins de la Méditerranée orientale à l'époque des croisades: diffusion et création', in *Essor et fortune de la Chanson de geste dans l'Europe et l'Orient latin* [Actes du IXe Congrès International de la Société Rencesvals pour l'étude des époques romanes (Padua–Venice, 1982)] (Modena, 1984), 617–46; repr. in Jacoby (1989: art. II).

——— (1986a): D. Jacoby, 'Knightly Values and Class Consciousness in the Crusader States of the Eastern Mediterranean', *MHR*, 1 (1986), 158–86; repr. in Jacoby (1989: art. I).

——— (1986b): D. Jacoby, 'A Venetian Manual of Commercial Practice from Crusader Acre', in Airaldi and Kedar (1986: 403–28).

——— (1989): D. Jacoby, *Studies on the Crusaders States and on Venetian Expansion* [Variorum Reprints] (London, 1989).

——— (1995): D. Jacoby, 'Το εμπόριο και η οικονομία της Κύπρου', in Papadopoullos (1995a: 387–454).

——— (1999): D. Jacoby, 'Cretan Cheese: A Neglected Aspect of Venetian Medieval Trade', in E. Kittell and T.F. Madden (eds.), *Medieval and Renaissance Venice* (Urbana–Chicago, 1999), 49–68.

Joubert Amari Perry (1981): A. Joubert Amari Perry, *La Passion des jongleurs* (Paris, 1981).

Kahane and Kahane (1982): H. Kahane and R. Kahane, 'The Western Impact on Byzantium: the Linguistic Evidence', *DOP*, 36 (1982), 127–53.

Kahane, Kahane, and Tietze (1958): H. Kahane, R. Kahane, and A. Tietze, *The Lingua Franca in the Levant. Turkish Nautical Terms of Italian and Greek Origin* (Urbana, 1958).

Kalopissi-Verti (1986): S. Kalopissi-Verti, 'Διακοσμημένοι φωτοστέφανοι σε εικόνες και τοιχογραφίες της Κύπρου και του ελλαδικού χώρου', in *ΠΒ΄ΔΚΣ*, II, 555–60.

Karageorghis (1990): V. Karageorghis, *The A. G. Leventis Foundation and the Cultural Heritage of Cyprus* [Leventis Foundation] (Nicosia, 1990).

Karpozilos (1981–1982): A. Karpozilos, 'Η Ησυχαστική έριδα και η Κύπρος', *EKEE*, 11 (1981–1982), 491–8.

Katsaros (2000): V. Katsaros, 'Ιωσήφ Βρυεννίου, *Τα Πρακτικά της Συνόδου Κύπρου* (1406)', *Βυζαντινά*, 21 (2000), 21–56.

Kazhdan and Wharton Epstein (1985): A.P. Kazhdan and A. Wharton Epstein, *Change in Byzantine Culture in the Eleventh and Twelfth Centuries* (Berkeley–Los Angeles–London, 1985).

Kedar (1985): B.Z. Kedar, 'Ecclesiastical Legislation in the Kingdom of Jerusalem: The Statutes of Jaffa (1253) and Acre (1254)', in P.W. Edbury (ed.), *Crusade and Settlement* [Papers Read at the First Conference of the Society for the Study of the Crusades and the Latin East and Presented to R.C. Smail] (Cardiff, 1985), 225–30; repr. in B.Z. Kedar, *The Franks in the Levant, 11th to 14th Centuries* [Variorum Reprints] (Aldershot, 1993), art. XVII.

Keen (1984): M.H. Keen, *Chivalry* (New Haven–London, 1984).
Kevorkian (1996): R.H. Kevorkian (ed.), *Arménie entre Orient et Occident. Trois mille ans de civilisation* (Paris, 1996).
Kirmitses (1983): P.I. Kirmitses, 'Η Εκκλησία Κύπρου επί Φραγκοκρατίας', *ΚΣ*, 47 (1983), 1–108.
Kotoula (2004): D. Kotoula, '"Maniera cypria" and Thirteenth-Century Icon Production on Cyprus. A Critical Approach', *BMGS*, 28 (2004), 89–100.
Kourites (1907): P.I. Kourites, *Η Ορθόδοξος Εκκλησία εν Κύπρω επί Φραγκοκρατίας* (Athens, 1907).
Krékić (1961): B. Krékić, *Dubrovnik (Raguse) et le Levant au Moyen Age* (Paris, 1961).
—— (1980a): B. Krékić, *Dubrovnik, Italy and the Balkans in the Late Middle Ages* [Variorum Reprints] (London, 1980).
—— (1980b): B. Krékić, 'Four Florentine Commercial Companies in Dubrovnik (Ragusa) in the First Half of the Fourteenth Century', in Krékić (1980a: art. I).
—— (1980c): B. Krékić, 'The Role of the Jews in Dubrovnik (Thirteenth—Sixteenth Centuries)', in Krékić (1980a: art. XXI).
Kriaras (1967): E. Kriaras, 'Diglossie des derniers siècles de Byzance: naissance de la littérature néo-hellénique', in *Actes du XIIIe Congrès International des Études Byzantines* (Oxford, 1967), 283–99.
Kristeller (1952): P.O. Kristeller, 'Petrarch's "Averroists". A Note on the History of Aristotelianism in Venice, Padua and Bologna', *Bibliothèque d'Humanisme et Renaissance*, 14 (1952) [= *Mélanges Augustin Renaudet*], 59–65.
Kügle (1995): K. Kügle, 'The Repertory of Manuscript Torino, Biblioteca Nazionale J. II. 9, and the French Tradition of the 14th and Early 15th Centuries', in Finscher and Günther (1995: 151–81).
Kyrris (1961): C.P. Kyrris, 'Ο κύπριος Αρχιεπίσκοπος Θεσσαλονίκης Υάκινθος (1345–6) και ο ρόλος του εις τον αντιπαλαμιτικόν αγώνα', *ΚΣ*, 5 (1961), 89–122.
—— (1962): C.P. Kyrris, 'Η Κύπρος και το Ησυχαστικόν ζήτημα κατά τον XIV αιώνα (εισαγωγή)', *ΚΣ*, 26 (1962), 19–32.
—— (1985): C.P. Kyrris, *History of Cyprus. With an introduction to the Geography of Cyprus* (Nicosia, 1985).
—— (1989–1993): C.P. Kyrris, 'Some Aspects of Leontios Makhairas' Ethnoreligious Ideology, Cultural Identity and Historiographic Method', *Στασίνος*, 10 (1989–1993), 167–281.
—— (1990–1991): C.P. Kyrris, 'L'organisation de l'église orthodoxe de Chypre pendant les deux premiers siècles de l'occupation franque', *EEBΣ*, 48 (1990–1991), 327–66.
—— (1993): C.P. Kyrris, 'Η οργάνωση της Ορθοδόξου Εκκλησίας της Κύπρου κατά τους δύο πρώτους αιώνες της Φραγκοκρατίας', *EKMIMK*, 2 (1993), 149–86.
Laiou (1972): A.E. Laiou, *Constantinople and the Latins. The Foreign Policy of Andronicus II 1282–1328* (Cambridge, Mass., 1972).
Lameere (1937): W. Lameere, *La tradition manuscrite de la correspondance de Grégoire de Chypre, Patriarche de Constantinople (1283–1289)* (Brussels–Rome, 1937).
Lampros (1908): S.P. Lampros, *Νέος Ελληνομνήμων*, 5 (1908).
—— (1916): S.P. Lampros, *Νέος Ελληνομνήμων*, 13 (1916).
—— (1917): S.P. Lampros, *Νέος Ελληνομνήμων*, 14 (1917).
—— (1921): S.P. Lampros, *Νέος Ελληνομνήμων*, 15 (1921).
Langlois (1908): C.-V. Langlois, *La vie en France au Moyen Age d'après quelques moralistes du temps* (Paris, 1908).
Lassithiotakis (1999): M. Lassithiotakis, 'Le personnage du "chevalier errant" dans la littérature byzantine de langue vulgaire', in Pioletti and Rizzo Nervo (1999: 189–205).
Laurent and Richard (1951): M.-H. Laurent and J. Richard, 'La bibliothèque d'un évêque dominicain de Chypre en 1367', *Archivum Fratrum Praedicatorum*, 21 (1951), 451–4; repr. in Richard (1976b: art. VI).

Lécuyer (2004): N. Lécuyer, 'Le territoire de Potamia aux époques médiévale et moderne: acquis récents', *Cahier, Centre d'Études Chypriotes*, 34 (2004), 11–30.

—— (forthcoming): N. Lécuyer, 'Marqueurs identitaires médiévaux et modernes sur le territoire de Potamia–Agios Sozomenos', in Fourrier and Grivaud (forthcoming).

Le Goff (1996): J. Le Goff, *Saint Louis* (Paris, 1996).

Leone (1981): P. Leone, 'L'encomio di Niceforo Gregora per il re di Cipro (Ugo IV di Lusignano)', *Byzantion*, 51 (1981), 211–24.

Leventis (2003): P. Leventis, *Nicosia, Cyprus, 1192–1570: Topography, Architecture, and Urban Experience in a Diversified Capital City* [unpublished Ph.D. Dissertation (McGill University, 2003)].

Livi (1918): R. Livi, 'Guido da Bagnolo, medico del re di Cipro', *Atti e memorie della R. deputazione di Storia Patria per le provincie Modenesi*, ser. 5, 11 (1918), 45–91.

Llinares (1963): A. Llinares, *Raymond Lulle philosophe de l'action* (Grenoble, 1963).

Lodge (1903): E.C. Lodge, 'Serfdom in the Bordelais', *EHR*, 18 (1903), 417–38.

Loenertz (1937): R.J. Loenertz, *La Société des Frères Pérégrinants. Études sur l'Orient dominicain* (Rome, 1937).

—— (1948): R.J. Loenertz, 'Fr. Philippe de Bindo Incontri O.P. du couvent de Péra, inquisiteur en Orient', *Archivum Fratrum Praedicatorum*, 18 (1948), 265–80; repr. in R.J. Loenertz, *Byzantina et franco-graeca* (Rome, 1978), II, 29–37.

—— (1957): R.J. Loenertz, 'Gregorii Acindyni Epistulae Selectae IX. Ex Codice Veneto Marciano 155', *EEBΣ*, 27 (1957), 89–109.

Loizou-Chatzigabriel (1997): L. Loizou-Chatzigabriel (ed.), *Λεόντιος Μαχαιράς – Γεώργιος Βουστρώνιος. Δυο χρονικά της μεσαιωνικής Κύπρου* [Πρακτικά Συμποσίου (Nicosia, 21 September 1996)] (Nicosia, 1997).

Loomis (1939): R.S. Loomis, 'Chivalric and dramatic imitations of Arthurian romance', in W.R.W. Koehler (ed.), *Medieval studies in memory of A. Kingsley Porter* (Cambridge Mass., 1939), I, 79–97.

Löseth (1890): E. Löseth, *Le Roman en prose de Tristan, le Roman de Palamède et la Compilation de Rusticien de Pise d'après les manuscrits de Paris* (Paris, 1890; repr. Paris, 1974).

Loulloupis (1991): M. Loulloupis (ed.), *Annual Report of the Department of Antiquities for the Year 1991*, 18 (Nicosia, 1991).

Luke (1924): H.C. Luke, 'Excerpta Cypria', *Κυπριακά Χρονικά*, 2 (1924), 7–11.

Luttrell (1972): A.T. Luttrell, 'The Hospitallers in Cyprus after 1291', in *ΠΑ΄ΔΚΣ*, II, 161–71; repr. in Luttrell (1978: art. II).

—— (1974): A.T. Luttrell, 'Crete and Rhodes (1340–1360)', in *Πρακτικά του Γ΄ Διεθνούς Κρητολογικού Συνεδρίου* (Herakleion, 1974), II, 167–75; repr. in Luttrell (1978: art. VI).

—— (1975): A.T. Luttrell, 'The Hospitallers at Rhodes (1306–1421)', in Setton (1955–1989, III (1975): 278–313); repr. in Luttrell (1978: art. I).

—— (1978): A.T. Luttrell, *The Hospitallers in Cyprus, Rhodes, Greece and the West, 1291–1440* [Variorum Reprints] (London, 1978).

—— (1986): A.T. Luttrell, 'The Hospitallers in Cyprus: 1310–1378', *ΚΣ*, 50 (1986), 155–84.

—— (1993a): A.T. Luttrell, 'Sugar and Schism. The Hospitallers in Cyprus from 1378 to 1386', in Bryer and Georghallides (1993: 157–66).

—— (1993b): A.T. Luttrell, 'The Greeks of Rhodes under Hospitaller Rule, 1306–1421', *Rivista di Studi Bizantini e Neoellenici*, 29 (1993), 193–223; repr. in A.T. Luttrell, *The Hospitaller State on Rhodes and Its Western Provinces, 1306–1462* [Variorum Reprints] (Aldershot, 1999), art. IV.

—— (1996): A.T. Luttrell, 'The Sugar Industry and Its Importance for the Economy of Cyprus during the Frankish Period', in V. Karageorghis and D. Michaelides (eds.), *The Development of the Cypriot Economy. From the Prehistoric Period to the Present Day* (Nicosia, 1996), 163–73.

—— (2003): A.T. Luttrell, *The Town of Rhodes: 1306–1356* (Rhodes, 2003).

Magoulias (1964): Rev. H.J. Magoulias, 'A Study in Roman Catholic and Greek Orthodox Church Relations on the Island of Cyprus between the Years A.D. 1196 and 1360', *The Greek Orthodox Theological Review*, 10 (1964), 75–106.

Mahé (1996): J.-P. Mahé, 'Connaître la Sagesse: le programme des anciens traducteurs arméniens', in Kevorkian (1996: 40–61).

Maier and Wartburg (1985): F.-G. Maier and M.-L. von Wartburg, 'Excavations at Kouklia-Palaepaphos. Fourteenth Preliminary Report: Season 1985', *RDAC 1985* (1985), 55–62.

Makariou (2000): S. Makariou, *Two Objects from the Louvre made for the Lusignans of Cyprus* [Exhibition Flyer, The Leventis Municipal Museum of Nicosia (19 May–31 July 2000)] (Nicosia, 2000).

Maltezou (1990): Ch.A. Maltezou, *Η Κρήτη στη διάρκεια της περιόδου της Βενετοκρατίας (1211–1669)* (Herakleion, 1990).

—— (1995): Ch.A. Maltezou, 'Έλληνες και Λατίνοι: Η εικόνα του άλλου στον πρώτο αιώνα φραγκικής κυριαρχίας στην Κύπρο', in Coureas and Riley-Smith (1995: 47–57).

Mango (1976): C. Mango, 'Chypre carrefour du monde byzantin', *XVᵉ Congrès International d'Études Byzantines, Rapports et Co-Rapports, V. Chypre dans le monde byzantin, 5. Chypre carrefour du monde byzantin* (Athens, 1976), 1–13; repr. in C. Mango, *Byzantium and Its Image. History and Culture of the Byzantine Empire and Its Heritage* [Variorum Reprints] (London, 1984), art. XVII.

Mango and Hawkins (1966): C. Mango and E.J.W. Hawkins, 'The Hermitage of Saint Neophytos and Its Wall Paintings', *DOP*, 20 (1966), 119–206.

Maravalaki and Prokopiou (1998): E. Maravalaki and P. Prokopiou, 'Οι ξυλόστεγοι ναοί της Κύπρου', *ΚΣ*, 61 (1998), 139–244.

Mas Latrie (1861): L. de Mas Latrie, *Histoire de l'île de Chypre sous le règne des princes de la maison de Lusignan* (Paris, 1861), I.

—— (1888): L. de Mas Latrie, 'Texte officiel de l'allocution adressée par les barons de Chypre au roi Henri II de Lusignan pour lui notifier sa déchéance', *Revue des questions historiques*, 43 (1888), 524–41.

Mayer (1972): H.E. Mayer, *Marseilles Levantehandel und ein akkonensisches Fälscheratelier des 13. Jahrhunderts* (Tübingen, 1972).

—— (1996): H.E. Mayer, *Die Kanzlei der lateinischen Könige von Jerusalem* (Hannover, 1996), II.

Meersseman (1940): G. Meersseman, 'La chronologie des voyages et des œuvres de frère Alphonse Buenhombre O. P.', *Archivum Fratrum Praedicatorum*, 10 (1940), 77–108.

Megaw (1977): A.H.S. Megaw, 'The Arts in Cyprus, B. Military Architecture', in Setton (1955–1989, IV (1977): 196–207).

—— (1982): A.H.S. Megaw, 'Saranda Kolones 1981', *RDAC 1982* (1982), 210–16.

Megaw and Hawkins (1977): A.H.S. Megaw and E.J.W. Hawkins, *The Church of the Panagia Kanakaria at Lythrangomi in Cyprus. Its Mosaics and Frescoes* (Dumbarton Oaks, Washington, D.C., 1977).

Megaw (1994): Peter (A.H.S.) Megaw, 'A Castle in Cyprus Attributable to the Hospital?', in M. Barber (ed.), *The Military Orders: Fighting for the Faith and Caring for the Sick* (Aldershot, 1994), 42–51.

Menardos (1921): S. Menardos, 'Το τραούδιν της Ζωγγραφούς', *Λαογραφία*, 8 (1921), 181–200; repr. in K. Pilavakes and M.N. Christodoulou (eds.), *Σίμου Μενάρδου Τοπωνυμικαί και λαογραφικαί μελέται* (Nicosia, 1970), 348–64 (text on pp. 357–64).

Mercati (1917): S.G. Mercati, 'Intorno a Μιχαήλ Γραμματικός ο Ιερομόναχος', *Bessarione*, 21 (1917), 199–207; repr. in Mercati (1970, I: 114–20).

—— (1920–1921): S.G. Mercati, 'Macaire Coloritès et Constantin Anagnostès', *Revue de l'Orient chrétien*, 22 (1920–1921), 181–93; repr. in Mercati (1970, I: 227–35).

—— (1922): S.G. Mercati, 'Osservazioni alle poesie del codice Vaticano Palatino greco 367 edite in *Νέος Ελληνομνήμων* 16 (1922), p. 39–59', *Studi Bizantini*, 2 (1927), 276–92; repr. in Mercati (1970, I: 406–25).

—— (1931): S.G. Mercati, *Notizie di Procoro e Demetrio Cidone, Manuele Caleca e Teodoro Meliteniota ed altri appunti per la storia della teologia e della letteratura bizantina del secolo XIV* (Vatican City, 1931).

—— (1970): S.G. Mercati, *Collectanea Byzantina*, 2 vols. (Rome, 1970).

Metcalf (1983): D.M. Metcalf, *Coinage of the Crusades and the Latin East in the Ashmolean Museum Oxford* (London, 1983).

—— (1995a): D.M. Metcalf, *Coinage of the Crusades and the Latin East in the Ashmolean Museum Oxford* (London, 1995²).

—— (1995b): D.M. Metcalf, 'The Iconography and Style of Crusader Seals in Cyprus', in Coureas and Riley-Smith (1995: 365–75).

—— (1996–2000): D.M. Metcalf, *Corpus of Lusignan Coinage* [TSHC XXI, XXIX, XXXV], 3 vols. (Nicosia, 1996–2000).

Metcalf and Pitsillides (1992): D.M. Metcalf and A.G. Pitsillides, 'Studies of the Lusignan Coinage', *EKEE*, 19 (1992), 1–104.

Meyendorff (1959): J. Meyendorff, *Introduction à l'étude de Grégoire Palamas* (Paris, 1959).

—— (1983): J. Meyendorff, *Byzantine Theology. Historical Trends and Doctrinal Themes* (New York, 1983²).

Michaelides (forthcoming): D. Michaelides (ed.), *A History of Nicosia* (Nicosia, forthcoming).

Minervini (1995): L. Minervini, 'Tradizioni linguistiche e culturali negli Stati Latini d'Oriente', in A. Pioletti and F. Rizzo Nervo (eds.), *Medioevo romanzo e orientale. Oralità, scrittura, modelli narrativi* [II Colloquio Internazionale (Naples, 17–19 February 1994)] (Messina, 1995), 155–72.

—— (1996a): L. Minervini, 'La lingua franca mediterranea. Plurilinguismo, mistilinguismo, pidginizzazione sulle coste del Mediterraneo tra tardo medioevo e prima età moderna', *Medioevo romanzo*, 20/2 (1996), 231–301.

—— (1996b): L. Minervini, 'Les contacts entre indigènes et croisés dans l'Orient latin: le role des drogmans', in J. Lüdtke (ed.), *Romania arabica. Festchrift für Reinhold Kontzi zum 70. Geburstag* (Tübingen, 1996), 57–62.

—— (1999): L. Minervini, 'Produzione e circolazione di manoscritti negli stati crociati: biblioteche e scriptoria latini', in Pioletti and Rizzo Nervo (1999: 79–96).

—— (2001): L. Minervini, 'Outremer', in P. Boitani, M. Mancini, and A. Vàrvaro (eds.), *Lo spazio letterario del Medioevo. 2. Il Medioevo volgare*, vol. 1, *La produzione del testo* (Rome, 2001), II, 611–48.

—— (2002): L. Minervini, 'Modelli culturali e attività letteraria nell'Oriente latino', *Studi medievali*, 43/1 (2002), 337–48.

Mogabgab (1934–1936): Th.A.H. Mogabgab, 'Excavations and Improvements in Famagusta', *RDAC 1934–1936* (1939), 103–5.

Monfrin (1964): J. Monfrin, 'Humanisme et traductions au Moyen Age', in A. Fourrier (ed.), *L'humanisme médiéval dans les littératures romanes du XIIe au XIVe siècles* (Paris, 1964), 217–46.

Morgan (1973): M.R. Morgan, *The Chronicle of Ernoul and the Continuations of William of Tyre* (Oxford, 1973).

Mouriki (1984): D. Mouriki, 'The Wall Paintings of the Church of the Panagia at Moutoullas, Cyprus', in I. Hutter (ed.), *Byzanz und der Westen. Studien zur Kunst des europäischen Mittelalters* (Vienna, 1984), 171–213.

—— (1985–1986): D. Mouriki, 'Thirteenth-Century Icon Painting in Cyprus', *The Griffon*, New Series 1–2 (1985–1986), 9–112.

—— (1987): D. Mouriki, 'A Thirteenth-Century Icon with a Variant of the Hodegetria in the Byzantine Museum of Athens', *DOP*, 41 (1987), 403–14.

—— (1990): D. Mouriki, 'Icons from the 12th to the 15th Century', in K.A. Manafes (ed.), *Sinai, Treasures of the Monastery* (Athens, 1990), 102–23.

Mutafian (1994): C. Mutafian (ed.), *Les Lusignans et l'Outre Mer* [Actes du colloque de Poitiers-Lusignan (20–24 October 1993)] (Poitiers, 1994).

Muthesius (2004): A. Muthesius, 'Introduction to Silk in Medieval Cyprus', in A. Muthesius, *Studies in Silk in Byzantium* (London, 2004), 237–55.

Naumann (1994): C. Naumann, *Der Kreuzzug Kaiser Heinrichs VI* (Frankfurt-am-Main, 1994).

Nepaulsingh (1997): C.I. Nepaulsingh, *Pero Tafur and Cyprus* (New York, 1997).

Nerantzi-Varmazi (2001): V. Nerantzi-Varmazi, 'Το Ρηγάτο του Ούγου Δ´ Λουζινιάν μέσα από τα κείμενα του Νικηφόρου Γρηγορά', in *ΠΓ´ΔΚΣ*, II, 353–60.

Der Nersessian (1993): S. der Nersessian, *Miniature Painting in the Armenian Kingdom of Cilicia from the Twelfth to the Fourteenth Century*, 2 vols. (Dumbarton Oaks, Washington, D.C., 1993).

Nicholson (2001): H. Nicholson, *Love, War and the Grail: Templars, Hospitallers and Teutonic Knights in Medieval Epic and Romance, 1150–1500* (Leiden, 2001).

Nicolaides (1983): A. Nicolaides, 'Les ktitors dans la peinture au XIIᵉ siècle à Chypre: une remise au point', in *Artistes, artisans et production artistique au moyen-âge* [Abstracts] (Université de Haute Bretagne, Rennes, 1983), I, 679–86.

——— (1995): A. Nicolaides, 'Le Jugement dernier de l'église de la Panagia de Moutoullas à Chypre', *Δελτίον της Χριστιανικής Αρχαιολογικής Εταιρείας*, 18 (1995), 71–7.

——— (1996): A. Nicolaides, 'L'église de la Panagia Arakiotissa à Lagoudera, Chypre: Étude iconographique des fresques de 1192', *DOP*, 50 (1996), 1–138.

Nicolaides and Carr (forthcoming): A. Nicolaides and A.W. Carr (eds.), *Asinou. The Church and Paintings of the Panagia Phorviotissa* (forthcoming).

Nicolaou-Konnari (1985): A. Nicolaou-Konnari, 'Αροδαφνούσα', *Μεγάλη Κυπριακή Εγκυκλοπαίδεια*, II (Nicosia, 1985), 322–4.

——— (1995): A. Nicolaou-Konnari, 'Η Γλώσσα στην Κύπρο κατά τη Φραγκοκρατία (1192–1489)—Μέσο έκφρασης φαινομένων αλληλεπίδρασης και καθορισμού εθνικής ταυτότητας', *Βυζαντιακά*, 15 (1995), 349–87.

——— (1998): A. Nicolaou-Konnari, 'La *Chronique* de Léontios Machéras: Historicité et identité nationale', in P. Odorico (ed.), *Matériaux pour une histoire de Chypre (IVᵉ–XXᵉ s.), Études Balkaniques, Cahiers Pierre Belon*, 5 (1998), 55–80.

——— (1999): A. Nicolaou-Konnari, *The Encounter of Greeks and Franks in Cyprus in the Late Twelfth and Thirteenth Centuries. Phenomena of Acculturation and Ethnic Awareness* [unpublished Ph.D Thesis (University of Wales, College of Cardiff, 1999)].

——— (2000a): A. Nicolaou-Konnari, 'The Conquest of Cyprus by Richard the Lionheart and Its Aftermath: A Study of Sources and Legend, Politics and Attitudes in the Year 1191–1192', *EKEE*, 26 (2000), 25–123.

——— (2000b): A. Nicolaou-Konnari, 'Literary Languages in the Lusignan Kingdom of Cyprus in the Thirteenth-Century', *Μολυβδοκονδυλοπελεκητής* 7 (2000), 7–27.

——— (2000–2001): A. Nicolaou-Konnari, 'Ethnic Names and the Construction of Group Identity in Medieval and Early Modern Cyprus: The Case of *Κυπριώτης*', *Κυπριολογία. Αφιέρωμα εις Θεόδωρον Παπαδόπουλλον*, ΚΣ, 64–65 (2000–2001), 259–75.

——— (2002a): A. Nicolaou-Konnari, 'Η διασκευή του χειρογράφου της Ραβέννας της *Εξήγησης* του Λεοντίου Μαχαιρά και η *Narratione* του Διομήδη Strambali', in Agapitos and Pieris (2002: 287–315).

——— (2002b): A. Nicolaou-Konnari, 'Strategies of Distinction: The Construction of the Ethnic Name *Griffon* and the Western Perception of the Greeks (Twelfth–Fourteenth Centuries)', *Byzantinistica. Rivista di Studi Bizantini e Slavi*, 2nd Series, 4 (2002), 181–96.

——— (forthcoming a): A. Nicolaou-Konnari, 'Η ονοματολογία στα χειρόγραφα του *Χρονικού* του Λεοντίου Μαχαιρά', in E.M. Jeffreys and M. Jeffreys (eds.), *Αναδρομικά και Προδρομικά* [Acts of the Fifth International Conference *Neograeca Medii Aevi* (Oxford, 15–18 September 2000)] (Oxford, forthcoming).

—— (forthcoming b): A. Nicolaou-Konnari, 'L'Identité en diaspora: vies et œuvres de Pierre (avant 1570 (?)-après 1646) et Georges de Nores (1619–1638)', in Fourrier and Grivaud (forthcoming).

Nielen-Vandevoorde (1995): M.-A. Nielen-Vandevoorde, 'Un livre méconnu des *Assises de Jérusalem: Les Lignages d'Outremer*', *BEC*, 153 (1995), 103–30.

D'Olwer (1926): N. d'Olwer, 'Els Catalans a Xipre', *Expansio*, 71/2 (1926), 163–76.

Otten-Froux (1986): C. Otten-Froux, 'Les Pisans en Chypre au Moyen-Age', in *ΠΒ´ΔΚΣ*, II, 127–43.

—— (2002): C. Otten-Froux, 'Les investissements financiers des Chypriotes en Italie', in Ch. Maltezou (ed.), *Πρακτικά του Διεθνούς Συμποσίου 'Κύπρος—Βενετία. Κοινές ιστορικές τύχες'* (Venice–Athens, 2002), 107–34.

—— (2003): C. Otten-Froux, 'Un notaire vénitien à Famagouste au XIVᵉ siècle. Les actes de Simeone, prêtre de San Giacomo dell'Orio (1362–1371)', *Θησαυρίσματα*, 33 (2003), 15–159.

Pace (1980): V. Pace, 'La pittura delle origini in Puglia (secc. IX–XIV)', in P. Belli d'Elia *et al.*, *La Puglia fra Bisanzio e l'Occidente* (Milan, 1980), 317–400.

—— (1982a): V. Pace, 'Icone di Puglia, della Terra Santa e di Cipro: Appunti preliminari per un'indagine sulla ricensione bizantina nell'Italia meridionale duecentesca', in H. Belting (ed.), *Il Medio Oriente e l'Occidente nell'arte del XIII secolo* [Acts of the XXIVth International Congress of Art History (Bologna, 1979)] (Bologna, 1982), II, 181–91.

—— (1982b): V. Pace, 'Pittura bizantina nell'Italia meridionale', in G. Cavallo (ed.), *I Bizantini in Italia* (Milan, 1982), 429–94.

—— (2000): V. Pace, 'Between East and West', in M. Vassilaki (ed.), *Mother of God. Representations of the Virgin in Byzantine Art* [Exhibition Catalogue, Benaki Museum of Athens (20 November 2000–20 January 2001)] (Milan, 2000), 425–32.

Papacostas (1999a): T.C. Papacostas, *Byzantine Cyprus. The Testimony of Its Churches, 650–1200* [unpublished Ph.D. Thesis, 2 vols. (University of Oxford, 1999)].

—— (1999b): T.C. Papacostas, 'Secular Landholding and Venetians in 12th-Century Cyprus', *BZ*, 92/2 (1999), 479–501.

—— (forthcoming): T.C. Papacostas, 'Byzantine Nicosia', in Michaelides (forthcoming).

Papadakis (1997): A. Papadakis, *Crisis in Byzantium. The* Filioque *Controversy in the Patriarchate of Gregory II of Cyprus (1283–1289)* (Crestwood, NY, 1997).

Papadopoullos (1964): Th. Papadopoullos, 'Ιστορικαί περί Κύπρου ειδήσεις εκ του Χρονικού του Ερνούλ και του Βερνάρδου του Θησαυροφύλακος', *ΚΣ*, 28 (1964), 39–114.

—— (1976): Th. Papadopoullos, 'Chypre: Frontière ethnique et socio-culturelle du monde byzantin', *XVᵉ Congrès International d'Études Byzantines, Rapports et Co-Rapports, V. Chypre dans le monde byzantin, 5. Chypre carrefour du monde byzantin* (Athens, 1976), 1–51.

—— (1984): Th. Papadopoullos, 'Κυπριακά Νόμιμα', *Μελέται και Υπομνήματα*, 1 (1984), 3–142.

—— (1995a): Th. Papadopoullos (ed.), *Ιστορία της Κύπρου*, IV, *Μεσαιωνικόν βασίλειον—Ενετοκρατία*, part 1 [Archbishop Makarios III Cultural Foundation] (Nicosia, 1995).

—— (1995b): Th. Papadopoullos, 'Πρόλογος', in Papadopoullos (1995a: ix–xv).

—— (1995c): Th. Papadopoullos, 'Η Εκκλησία Κύπρου κατά την περίοδο της Φραγκοκρατίας', in Papadopoullos (1995a: 543–666).

—— (1996): Th. Papadopoullos (ed.), *Ιστορία της Κύπρου*, V, *Μεσαιωνικόν βασίλειον—Ενετοκρατία*, part 2 [Archbishop Makarios III Cultural Foundation] (Nicosia, 1996).

Papadopoulou (1983): E. Papadopoulou, 'Οι πρώτες εγκαταστάσεις Βενετών στην Κύπρο', *Σύμμεικτα του Κέντρου Βυζαντινών Ερευνών*, 5 (1983), 303–32 (text on pp. 309–15).

Papageorghiou (1969): A. Papageorghiou, *Icons of Cyprus* (Geneva–London, 1969).
—— (1972): A. Papageorghiou, Ἰδιάζουσαι βυζαντιναί τοιχογραφίαι του 13ου αιώνος εν Κύπρω', in *ΠΑ΄ΔΚΣ*, II, 201–12.
—— (1974): A. Papageorghiou, 'Κύπριοι ζωγράφοι του 15ου και 16ου αιώνα', *RDAC 1974* (1975), 195–208.
—— (1982): A. Papageorghiou, 'L'art byzantin de Chypre et l'art des croisés. Influences réciproques', *RDAC 1982* (1982), 217–26.
—— (1990): A. Papageorghiou, 'Η Εκκλησία του Αρχαγγέλου, Κάτω Λεύκαρα', *RDAC 1990* (1990), 189–230.
—— (1992a): A. Papageorghiou, *Icons of Cyprus* (Nicosia, 1992).
—— (1992b): A. Papageorghiou, 'Η αμφιπρόσωπη εικόνα της εκκλησίας της Παναγίας Θεοσκέπαστης στην Πάφο', in Acheimastou-Potamianou (1992, II: 484–90).
—— (1995a): A. Papageorghiou (ed.), *Η αυτοκέφαλος Εκκλησία της Κύπρου. Κατάλογος της έκθεσης. The Autocephalous Church of Cyprus. A Catalogue of the Exhibition* [Exhibition Catalogue, Byzantine Museum in Nicosia, Archbishop Makarios III Cultural Foundation (15 September–15 October 1995)] (Nicosia, 1995).
—— (1995b): A. Papageorghiou, 'Crusader Influence on the Byzantine Art of Cyprus', in Coureas and Riley-Smith (1995: 275–94).
—— (1996): A. Papageorghiou, *Ιερά Μητρόπολις Πάφου: Ιστορία και τέχνη. 1950 χρόνια από την ίδρυσή της* (Nicosia, 1996).
—— (1999a): A. Papageorghiou, 'Λαξευτά ασκητήρια και μοναστήρια της Κύπρου', *ΕΚΜΙΜΚ*, 4 (1999), 33–96.
—— (1999b): A. Papageorghiou, 'The Paintings in the Dome of the Church of the Panagia Chryseleousa, Strovolos', in Patterson Ševčenko and Moss (1999: 147–60).
—— (2004): A. Papageorghiou, 'Μία ανέκδοτη διήγηση για την εικόνα που ζωγράφισε, κατά την παράδοση, ο Απόστολος Λουκάς και την ίδρυση της Μονής Κύκκου', *ΕΚΜΙΜΚ*, 6 (2004), 9–60.
—— (n.d.): A. Papageorghiou, *Βασιλικό Παρεκκλήσι' Πυργά. Οδηγός* (Nicosia, n.d.).
Papaioannou (1912–1913): Ch.I. Papaioannou, 'Τακτικόν, ήτοι αρχιερατικόν ευχολόγιον της επισκοπής Καρπασέων και Αμμοχώστου', *Εκκλησιαστικός Κήρυξ*, 2 (1912), 443–56, 489–94, 511–17, 588–95, 623–31, 668–74, and 3 (1913), 115–19, 239–43.
Papanikola-Bakirtzis (1988): D. Papanikola-Bakirtzis, 'Χρονολογημένη κεραμική 14ου αιώνα από την Πάφο', *RDAC 1988* (1988), 245–8.
—— (1989): D. Papanikola-Bakirtzis, *Medieval Cypriot Pottery in the Pierides Foundation Museum* (Larnaca, 1989).
—— (1993): D. Papanikola-Bakirtzis, 'Cypriot Medieval Glazed Pottery: Answers and Questions', in Bryer and Georghallides (1993: 115–30).
—— (1996a): D. Papanikola-Bakirtzis, 'Η εφυαλωμένη κεραμική', in Papadopoullos (1996: 1409–13).
—— (1996b): D. Papanikola-Bakirtzis, *Μεσαιωνική εφυαλωμένη κεραμική της Κύπρου. Τα εργαστήρια Πάφου και Λαπήθου* (Thessalonike, 1996).
Papanikola-Bakirtzis and Iacovou (1998): D. Papanikola-Bakirtzis and M. Iacovou (eds.), *Byzantine Medieval Cyprus* [Exhibition Catalogue, Byzantine Museum in Thessalonike, Bank of Cyprus Cultural Foundation (Thessalonike, 1997)] (Nicosia, 1998).
Paravicini Bagliani (1999): A. Paravicini Bagliani, 'Ages de la vie', in J. Le Goff and J.-C. Schmitt (eds.), *Dictionnaire raisonné de l'Occident médiéval* (Paris, 1999), 7–19.
Patterson Ševčenko (1999): N. Patterson Ševčenko, 'The *Vita* Icon and the Painter as Hagiographer', *DOP*, 53 (1999), 149–65.
Patterson Ševčenko and Moss (1999): N. Patterson Ševčenko and C. Moss (eds.), *Medieval Cyprus. Studies in Art, Architecture, and History in Memory of Doula Mouriki* (Princeton, N.J., 1999).
Pavlides (1992): A. Pavlides, *Ιστορία της νήσου Κύπρου* (Nicosia, 1992), III.
Payen (1967): J.-C. Payen, *Le motif du repentir dans la littérature française médiévale* (Geneva, 1967).

Pedersen (2002): F.S. Pedersen, *The Toledan Tables. A Review of the Manuscripts and the Textual Versions with an Edition*, 4 vols. (Copenhagen, 2002).

Perdikes (1997): S.K. Perdikes, *Οδηγός Επισκεπτών Μουσείου Ιεράς Μονής Κύκκου* (Nicosia, 1997).

Pérez Martín (1996): I. Pérez Martín, *El patriarca Gregorio de Chipre (ca. 1240–1290) y la transmisión de los textos clásicos en Bizancio* (Madrid, 1996).

Pertusi (1962): A. Pertusi, 'Leonzio Pilato a Creta prima del 1358–1359. Scuole e cultura a Creta durante il secolo XIV', *Κρητικά Χρονικά*, 16 (1962), 363–81.

—— (1970): A. Pertusi, 'La poesia epica bizantina e la sua formazione: problemi sul fondo storico e la struttura letteraria del Digenis Akritas', in *Atti del Convegno Internazionale sul tema: la Poesia epica e la sua formazione* [Accademia Nazionale dei Lincei (Rome, 28 March–3 April 1969)] (Rome, 1970), 481–537.

Petkov (1997): K. Petkov, 'The Rotten Apple and the Good Apples: Orthodox, Catholics, and Turks in Philippe de Mézières' Crusading Propaganda', *Journal of Medieval History*, 23/3 (1997), 255–70.

Philippou (1875): G. Philippou, *Ειδήσεις ιστορικαί περί της Εκκλησίας Κύπρου* (Athens, 1875; repr. Nicosia, 1975).

Pieris (2003): M. Pieris, 'Cronaca e poesia popolare: Arodafnusa e Zuana l'Aleman. Interrogativi e problemi', in A. Proiou and A. Armati (eds.), *La presenza femminile nella letteratura neogreca* [Atti del VI Convegno Nazionale di Studi Neogreci, Università di Roma 'La Sapienza' (Rome, 19–21 November 2001)] (Rome, 2003), 49–62.

Pieris and Nicolaou-Konnari (1997): M. Pieris and A. Nicolaou-Konnari, 'Λεοντίου Μαχαιρά, *Εξήγησις της γλυκείας χώρας Κύπρου η ποία λέγεται κρόνικα τουτέστιν χρονικόν.* Βιβλιογραφικός Οδηγός', *EKEE*, 23 (1997), 75–114.

Pijper (1909): F. Pijper, 'The Christian Church and Slavery in the Middle Ages', *American Historical Review*, 14 (1909), 675–95.

Piltz (1986): E. Piltz, 'Saint Bridget and Byzantium. In View of her Cyprian Revelations', in *ΠΒ΄ΔΚΣ*, II, 45–60.

Pingree (1976): D. Pingree, 'The Byzantine Version of the Toledan Tables. The Work of George Lapithes?', *DOP*, 30 (1976), 85–132.

Pioletti and Rizzo Nervo (1999): A. Pioletti and F. Rizzo Nervo (eds.), *Medioevo romanzo e orientale. Il viaggio dei testi* [III Colloquio Internazionale (Venice, 10–13 October 1996)] (Messina–Venice, 1999).

Plana i Borràs (1992): J. Plana i Borràs, 'The Accounts of Joan Benet's Trading Venture from Barcelona to Famagusta: 1343', *EKEE*, 19 (1992), 105–68.

Platzeck (1964): E.W. Platzeck, *Raimund Lull. Sein Leben, seine Werke, die Grundlagen seines Denkens (Prinzipienlehre)*, 2 vols. (Düsseldorf, 1964).

Poirion (1978): D. Poirion, *Le Poète et le prince: l'évolution du lyrisme courtois de Guillaume de Machaut à Charles d'Orléans* (Geneva, 1978).

Poncelet (1934): E. Poncelet, 'Compte du domaine de Gautier de Brienne au royaume de Chypre', *Académie Royale de Belgique. Bulletin de la commission royale d'histoire*, 98 (1934), 1–28.

Poulle (1984): E. Poulle, *Les Tables Alphonsines avec les canons de Jean de Saxe* (Paris, 1984).

Prawer (1980): J. Prawer, *Crusader Institutions* (Oxford, 1980).

Pringle (1986): D. Pringle, 'Pottery as Evidence of Trade in the Crusader States', in Airaldi and Kedar (1986: 449–76).

Prokopiou (1997): E. Prokopiou, 'Λεμεσός Οδός Ζικ-Ζακ. ᾿Εκθεση αποτελεσμάτων σωστικής ανασκαφικής έρευνας', *RDAC 1997* (1997), 285–322.

Pryor (1984): J.H. Pryor, '*Commenda*: The Operation of the Contract in Long-Distance Commerce at Marseilles during the Thirteenth Century', *Journal of Economic History*, 13 (1984), 397–440.

Puchner (1983): W. Puchner, 'Θεατρολογικές παρατηρήσεις για τον ῾Κύκλο των Παθών᾿ της Κύπρου', *EKEE*, 12 (1983), 87–107.

—— (2004): W. Puchner, *Η Κύπρος των σταυροφόρων και το θρησκευτικό θέατρο του Μεσαίωνα* (Nicosia, 2004).

Rein (1915): E. Rein, 'Die Florentiner Briefsammlung (Codex Laurentianus S. Marco 356)', *Suomalaisen Tiedeakatemian Toimituksia* (= *Annales Academiae Scientiarum Fennicae*), B ser., 14/2 (1915), 1–150.

Richard (1947): J. Richard, 'Le Casal de Psimolofo et la vie rurale en Chypre au XIV⁰ siècle', *MAHEFR*, 59 (1947), 121–53; repr. in Richard (1977c: art. IV).

—— (1950): J. Richard, 'Un évêque d'Orient latin au XIV⁰ siècle. Guy d'Ibelin O.P., évêque de Limassol, et l'inventaire de ses biens (1367)', *Bulletin de Correspondance hellénique*, 74 (1950), 98–133; repr. in Richard (1977c: art. V).

—— (1952): J. Richard, 'La révolution de 1369 dans le royaume de Chypre', *BEC*, 110 (1952), 108–23; repr. in Richard (1976b: art. XVI).

—— (1953): J. Richard, 'Colonies marchandes privilégiées et marché seigneurial. La fonde d'Acre et ses droitures', *Le Moyen Age*, 59 (1953), 325–32; repr. in Richard (1976b: art. X).

—— (1963): J. Richard, 'La Fauconnerie de Jean de Francières et ses sources', *Le Moyen Age*, 69 (1963), 893–902; repr. in Richard (1977c: art. XXIII).

—— (1967–1968): J. Richard, 'L'ordonnance de décembre 1296 sur le prix du pain à Chypre', *EKEE*, 1 (1967–1968), 45–51; repr. in Richard (1976b: art. XX).

—— (1969–1970): J. Richard, 'L'Abbaye cistercienne de Jubin et le prieuré Saint-Blaise de Nicosie', *EKEE*, 3 (1969–1970), 63–74; repr. in Richard (1976b: art. XIX).

—— (1972): J. Richard, 'La situation juridique de Famagouste dans le Royaume des Lusignans', in *ΠΑ΄ΔΚΣ*, II, 221–9; repr. in Richard (1976b: art. XVII).

—— (1976a): J. Richard, 'Le Droit et les institutions franques dans le royaume de Chypre', *XV⁰ Congrès International d'Études Byzantines, Rapports et Co-Rapports, V. Chypre dans le monde byzantin, 3. Droit et institutions franques du Royaume de Chypre* (Athens, 1976), 1– 20; repr. in Richard (1983b: art. IX).

—— (1976b): J. Richard, *Orient et Occident au Moyen Age: contacts et relations (XII⁰–XIV⁰ siècles)* [Variorum Reprints] (London, 1976).

—— (1977a): J. Richard, 'Une économie coloniale? Chypre et ses ressources agricoles au Moyen-Age', *BF*, 5 (1977), 331–52; repr. in Richard (1983b: art. VIII).

—— (1977b): J. Richard, *La Papauté et les missions d'Orient au Moyen Age (XIII⁰–XV⁰ siècles)* (Rome, 1977).

—— (1977c): J. Richard, *Les relations entre l'Orient et l'Occident au Moyen Age* [Variorum Reprints] (London, 1977).

—— (1979): J. Richard, 'Le Peuplement latin et syrien en Chypre au XIII⁰ siècle', *BF*, 7 (1979), 157–73; repr. in Richard (1983b: art. VII).

—— (1981): J. Richard, 'Une famille de "Vénitiens blancs" dans le royaume de Chypre au milieu du XV⁰ siècle: les Audeth et la seigneurie du Marethasse', *Rivista di studi bizantini e slavi*, 1, *Miscellanea Agostino Pertusi*, 1 (1981), 89–129 bis; repr. in Richard (1983b: art. X).

—— (1983a): J. Richard, *Saint Louis* (Paris, 1983).

—— (1983b): J. Richard, *Croisés, missionnaires et voyageurs. Les perspectives orientales du monde latin médiéval* [Variorum Reprints] (London, 1983).

—— (1984–1987): J. Richard, 'Les Comptes du collecteur de la Chambre apostolique dans le royaume de Chypre (1357–1363), *EKEE*, 13–16/1 (1984–1987), 1–47; repr. in Richard (1992b: art. XV).

—— (1985): J. Richard, 'Agriculture in the Crusader States', in Setton (1955–1989, V (1985): 251–94).

—— (1986a): J. Richard, 'Un monastère grec de Palestine et son domaine chypriote: le monachisme orthodoxe et l'établissement de la domination franque', in *ΠΒ΄ΔΚΣ*, II, 61–75; repr. in Richard (1992b: art. XIV).

—— (1986b): J. Richard, 'Les Turcoples au service des royaumes de Jérusalem et de Chypre: Musulmans convertis ou Chrétiens orientaux?', *Mélanges Dominique Sourdel, Revue des études islamiques*, 56 (1986), 259–70; repr. in Richard (1992b: art. X).

—— (1986c): J. Richard, 'La diplomatique royale dans le royaume d'Arménie et de Chypre (XIIe–XVe siècles)', *BEC*, 144 (1986), 69–86; repr. in Richard (1992b: art. XIX).

—— (1987): J. Richard, 'La cour des Syriens de Famagouste d'après un texte de 1448', *BF*, 12 (1987), 383–98; repr. in Richard (1992b: art. XVII).

—— (1991–1992): J. Richard, 'Culture franque, culture grecque, culture arabe, dans le royaume de Chypre au XIIIe et au début du XIVe siècle', *Annales du Département des Lettres Arabes de la Faculté des Lettres et Sciences Humaines de l'Université Saint-Joseph*, 6 B (1991–1992), 235–45; repr. in Richard (2003: art. XXI).

—— (1992a): J. Richard, 'Le paiement des dîmes dans les états des croisés', *BEC*, 150 (1992), 71–83; repr. in Richard (2003: art. XVII).

—— (1992b): J. Richard, *Croisades et États latins d'Orient* [Variorum Reprints] (London, 1992).

—— (1995a): J. Richard, 'Η σύσταση και οι βάσεις του μεσαιωνικού βασιλείου (1192–1205)', in Papadopoullos (1995a: 1–19).

—— (1995b): J. Richard, 'Οι πολιτικοί και κοινωνικοί θεσμοί του μεσαιωνικού βασιλείου', in Papadopoullos (1995a: 333–74).

—— (1995c): J. Richard, 'Το δίκαιο του μεσαιωνικού βασιλείου', in Papadopoullos (1995a: 375–86).

—— (1996): J. Richard, '`A propos de la 'Bulla Cypria' de 1260', *BF*, 22 (1996), 19–31; repr. in Richard (2003: art. XIX).

—— (1997): J. Richard, 'Les Révoltes chypriotes de 1191–1192 et les inféodations de Guy de Lusignan', in B.Z. Kedar, J. Riley-Smith, and R. Hiestand (eds.), *Montjoie. Studies in Crusade History in Honour of H.E. Mayer* (Leicester, 1997), 123–8; repr. in Richard (2003: art. XVI).

—— (1999): J. Richard, 'La levée des décimes sur l'église latine de Chypre. Documents comptables de 1363–1371', *EKEE*, 25 (1999), 11–18; repr. in Richard (2003: art. XX).

—— (2001a): J. Richard, 'Un but de pèlerinage: Notre-Dame de Nicosie', in Herrin *et al.* (2001: 135–8).

—— (2001b): J. Richard, 'La succession de l'évêque de Famagouste de la remise en ordre de la collectorie de Chypre (1365–1374)', *MEFR, Moyen Age*, 113 (2001), 637–61.

—— (2003): J. Richard, *Francs et Orientaux dans le monde des croisades* [Variorum Reprints] (Aldershot, 2003).

Riley-Smith (1967): J. Riley-Smith, *The Knights of St. John in Jerusalem and Cyprus c. 1050–1310* (London, 1967).

—— (1973): J. Riley-Smith, *The Feudal Nobility and the Kingdom of Jerusalem* (London, 1973).

—— (1995): J. Riley-Smith, 'The Crusading Heritage of Guy and Aimery of Lusignan', in Coureas and Riley-Smith (1995: 31–45).

Rivoire-Richard (1996): M. Rivoire-Richard, 'Η γοτθική τέχνη στην Κύπρο', in Papadopoullos (1996: 1415–54).

Rizopoulou-Igoumenidou *et al.* (2002): E. Rizopoulou-Igoumenidou, D. Myriantheus, and Ph. Chatzichristophi, 'Ο νερόμυλος στον Πύργο Λεμεσού', *RDAC 2002* (2002), 381–400.

Rizzo Nervo (1985): F. Rizzo Nervo, 'Il "Mondo dei Padri" nella metafora del Vecchio Cavaliere', *Studi di filologia bizantina*, 3 (1985), 115–28.

Runciman (1980): S. Runciman, *Mistra. Byzantine Capital of the Peloponnese* (London, 1980).

Sacopoulo (1975): M. Sacopoulo, *La Théotokos à la Mandorle de Lythrankomi* (Paris, 1975).

Savvides (1993): A.G.C. Savvides, 'Late Byzantine and Western historiographers on Turkish mercenaries in Greek and Latin armies: the Turcoples/Tourkopouloi', in R. Beaton and C. Roueché (eds.), *The Making of Byzantine History. Studies dedicated to Donald M. Nicol* (London, 1993), 122–36.

Schabel (1998): C. Schabel, 'Elias of Nabinaux, Archbishop of Nicosia, and the Intellectual History of Later Medieval Cyprus', *Cahiers de l'Institut du Moyen-Age grec et latin*, 68 (1998), 35–52.

—— (2000a): C. Schabel, 'Archbishop Elias and the *Synodicum Nicosiense*', *Annuarium historiae conciliorum*, 32/1 (2000), 61–81.

—— (2000b): C. Schabel, 'Frankish Pyrgos and the Cistercians', *RDAC 2000* (2000), 349–60.

—— (2002): C. Schabel, 'Ο Camille Enlart και οι Κιστερκιανοί στον Πύργο', *RDAC 2002* (2002), 401–6.

—— (2002–2003): C. Schabel, 'Etienne de Lusignan's *Chorograffia* and the Ecclesiastical History of Frankish Cyprus: Notes on a Recent Reprint and English Translation', *Modern Greek Studies Yearbook*, 18–19 (2002–2003), 339–53.

—— (2004a): C. Schabel, 'The Latin Bishops of Cyprus, 1255–1313, with a Note on Bishop Neophytos of Solea', *EKEE*, 30 (2004), 75–111.

—— (2004b): C. Schabel, 'Hugh the Just: The Further Rehabilitation of King Hugh IV Lusignan of Cyprus', *EKEE*, 30 (2004), 123–52.

—— (forthcoming a): C. Schabel, 'The Status of the Greek Clergy in Early Frankish Cyprus', in J. Chrysostomides and Ch. Dendrinos (eds.), *'Sweet Land . . .', Cyprus through the Ages: Lectures on the History and Culture of Cyprus* (Camberley, Surrey, forthcoming).

—— (forthcoming b): C. Schabel, 'The Myth of Queen Alice and the Subjugation of the Greek Clergy on Cyprus', in Fourrier and Grivaud (forthcoming).

Schryver (2005): J.G. Schryver, *Spheres of Contact and Instances of Interaction in the Art and Archaeology of Frankish Cyprus, 1191–1359* [unpublished Ph.D. Dissertation (Cornell University, 2005)].

Setton (1955–1989): K.M. Setton (ed.), *A History of the Crusades*, 6 vols. (Philadelphia–Madison, 1955–1989).

—— (1975): K.M. Setton, 'The Catalans in Greece, 1311–1380', in Setton (1955–1989, III (1975): 167–224).

Ševčenko (1974): I. Ševčenko, 'Society and Intellectual Life in the Fourteenth Century', in *Actes du XIVe Congrès International des Études Byzantines* (Bucharest, 1974), I, 69–92; repr. in I. Ševčenko, *Society and Intellectual Life in Late Byzantium* [Variorum Reprints] (London, 1981), art. I.

Seymer et al. (1933): V. Seymer, W.H. Buckler, and Mrs. W.H. (Georgina) Buckler, 'The Church of Asinou, Cyprus, and Its Frescoes', *Archaeologia*, 83 (1933), 327–50.

Sinkewicz (1981): R.E. Sinkewicz, 'The Solutions addressed to Georges Lapithes by Barlaam the Calabrian and their philosophical context', *Mediaeval Studies*, 43 (1981), 151–217.

Smets (forthcoming): A. Smets, 'Le "prince guérisseur" ou le *Livre du Prince* par Molopin et Michelin', in *II Congreso Internacional: La caza en la Edad Media. Los libros de caza* [Tordesillas, 21–23 October 2004] (forthcoming).

Solomidou-Ieronymidou (1988): M. Solomidou-Ieronymidou, "À propos d'un relief gothique inédit', *RDAC 1988* (1988), 249–53.

—— (2001): M. Solomidou-Ieronymidou, 'Οι αρχαιολογικές ανασκαφές στους μεσαιωνικούς ζαχαρόμυλους Επισκοπής-Σεράγια και Κολοσσίου', in *ΠΓ´ΔΚΣ*, II, 1–11.

Sophocleous (1990): S. Sophocleous, *Le patrimoine des icônes dans le diocèse de Limassol, Chypre, 12e–16e siècle*, 3 vols. [unpublished Ph.D. Thesis (Université des sciences humaines de Strasbourg, 1990)].

—— (1993a): S. Sophocleous, 'Some Recently Discovered Medieval Cypriot Icons', in Bryer and Georghallides (1993: 431–2).

—— (1993b) S. Sophocleous, Ἡ Εικόνα της Κυκκώτισσας στον ῞Αγιο Θεόδωρο του Αγρού', *ΕΚΜΙΜΚ*, 2 (1993), 329–47.

—— (1994): S. Sophocleous, *Icons of Cyprus, 7th–20th Century* (Nicosia, 1994).

—— (2000): S. Sophocleous (ed.), *Cyprus the Holy Island. Icons through the Centuries, 10th–20th Centuries* [Exhibition Catalogue, The Hellenic Centre in London (1 November–17 December 2000)] (Nicosia, 2000).

Soteriou (1933): G.A. Soteriou, Ἡ εικών της Παμμακαρίστου', *Πρακτικά της Ακαδημίας Αθηνών*, 8 (1933), 359–68.

—— (1935): G.A. Soteriou, *Τα Βυζαντινά Μνημεία της Κύπρου* (Athens, 1935).

Spadaro (1986): G. Spadaro, Ἡ κυπριακή παραλλαγή του Σπανέα', in *ΠΒ΄ΔΚΣ*, II, 407–17.

Spanou (2002): Ch. Spanou (ed.), *Η κατά Κίτιον αγιογραφική τέχνη* (Larnaca, 2002).

Starr (1942): J. Starr, 'Jewish Life in Crete under the Rule of Venice', *Proceedings of the American Academy for Jewish Research*, 12 (1942), 59–114.

—— (1949): J. Starr, *Romania. The Jeweries of the Levant after the Fourth Crusade* (Paris, 1949).

Stern (1995): E. Stern, 'Exports to the Latin East of Cypriot Manufactured Glazed Pottery in the 12th–13th Century', in Coureas and Riley-Smith (1995: 325–35).

Stöckly (1995): D. Stöckly, 'Le transport maritime d'état à Chypre. Complément des techniques coloniales vénitiennes (XIIIᵉ–XVᵉ siècle): l'example du sucre', in Balard and Ducellier (1995: 131–41).

Stylianou and Stylianou (1985): A. Stylianou and J.A. Stylianou, *The Painted Churches of Cyprus. Treasures of Byzantine Art* (Nicosia, 1985²).

—— (1996): A. Stylianou and J.A. Stylianou, Ἡ Βυζαντινή τέχνη κατά την περίοδο της Φραγκοκρατίας (1191–1570)', in Papadopoullos (1996: 1229–407).

—— (1997): A. Stylianou and J.A. Stylianou, *The Painted Churches of Cyprus. Masterpieces of Byzantine Art* (Nicosia, 1997).

Svoronos (1956): N. Svoronos, 'Sur quelques formes de la vie rurale à Byzance. Petite et grande exploitation', *Annales Économies Sociétés Civilisations*, 11 (1956), 325–35; repr. in Svoronos (1973: art. II).

—— (1959): N. Svoronos, 'Recherches sur le cadastre byzantin et la fiscalité aux XIᵉ et XIIᵉ siècles: Le cadastre de Thèbes', *Bulletin de Correspondance hellénique*, 83 (1959), 1–166; repr. in Svoronos (1973: art. III).

—— (1973): N. Svoronos, *Études sur l'organisation intérieure, la société et l'économie de l'Empire byzantin* [Variorum Reprints] (London, 1973).

—— (1976): N. Svoronos, 'Questions sur la situation économique, sociale et juridique des Grecs Chypriotes pendant la domination franque', *XVᵉ Congrès International d'Études Byzantines, Rapports et Co-Rapports, V. Chypre dans le monde byzantin, 3. Droit et institutions franques du Royaume de Chypre* (Athens, 1976), 1–18.

Talbot Rice (1937): D. Talbot Rice, *The Icons of Cyprus* (London, 1937).

Ter-Vardanian (1996): G. Ter-Vardanian, 'La littérature des milieux uniteurs (XIIᵉ–XVᵉ siècle)', in Kevorkian (1996: 62–4).

Thiriet (1959): F. Thiriet, *La Romanie vénitienne au Moyen Age. Le développement et l'exploitation du domaine colonial vénitien (XIIᵉ–XVᵉ siècles)* (Paris, 1959).

Thomas (1923): A. Thomas, 'Notice sur le manuscrit latin 4788 du Vatican contenant une traduction française, avec commentaire par Maître Pierre de Paris, de la *Consolatio Philosophiae* de Boèce', *Notices et extraits des manuscrits de la Bibliothèque Nationale et autres bibliothèques*, 41 (1923), 29–90.

Tierney (1964): B. Tierney, *The Crisis of Church and State, 1050–1300* (Englewood Cliffs, N.J., 1964).

Tihon (1977): A. Tihon, 'Un traité d'astronomie chypriote du XIVᵉ siècle', *Janus, Revue internationale de l'histoire des sciences, de la médecine, de la pharmacie et de la technique*, 64 (1977), 279–308; repr. in Tihon (1994: art. VII).

—— (1979): A. Tihon, 'Un traité d'astronomie chypriote du XIVᵉ siècle', *Janus, Revue internationale de l'histoire des sciences, de la médecine, de la pharmacie et de la technique*, 66 (1979), 49–81; repr. in Tihon (1994: art. VII).

—— (1981): A. Tihon, 'Un traité d'astronomie chypriote du XIVe siècle', *Janus, Revue internationale de l'histoire des sciences, de la médecine, de la pharmacie et de la technique*, 68 (1981), 65–127; repr. in Tihon (1994: art. VII).

—— (1994): A. Tihon, *Études d'astronomie byzantine* [Variorum Reprints] (Aldershot, 1994).

Topping (1975): F. Topping, 'The Morea, 1311–1364', in Setton (1955–1989, III (1975): 104–40).

Triantaphyllopoulos (2001): D.D. Triantaphyllopoulos, 'Η τέχνη στην Κύπρο από την άλωση της Κωνσταντινουπόλεως (1453) έως την έναρξη της Τουρκοκρατίας (1571): Βυζαντινή/Μεσαιωνική/Μεταβυζαντινή;', in *ΠΓ΄ΔΚΣ*, III, 621–50.

Tsiknopoulos (1969): I.P. Tsiknopoulos, 'Τα ελάσσονα του Νεοφύτου πρεσβυτέρου, μοναχού και εγκλείστου', *Byzantion*, 39 (1969), 318–419.

—— (1971): I.P. Tsiknopoulos, *Ιστορία της Εκκλησίας Πάφου* (Nicosia, 1971).

Tsolakis (1964): E.Ch. Tsolakis, 'Ο Γεώργιος Λαπίθης και η ησυχαστική έριδα', *Ελληνικά*, 18 (1964), 84–96.

Vaivre (2001): J.B. de Vaivre, 'Sculpteurs parisiens en Chypre autour de 1300', in Balard *et al.* (2001: 373–88).

Vocotopoulos (1999): P.L. Vocotopoulos, 'Three Thirteenth-Century Icons at Moutoullas', in Patterson Ševčenko and Moss (1999: 161–77).

Vogt (1931): A. Vogt, 'Études sur le théâtre byzantin', *Byzantion*, 6 (1931), 37–74, 623–40.

Walz (1962): A. Walz, *Saint Thomas d'Aquin* (Leuven–Paris, 1962).

Wartburg (1995): M.-L. von Wartburg, 'Production de sucre de canne à Chypre: un chapitre de technologie médiévale', in Balard and Ducellier (1995: 126–31, 151–3).

—— (2001): M.-L. von Wartburg, 'Earthquakes and Archaeology: Paphos after 1222', in *ΠΓ΄ΔΚΣ*, 127–45.

Weisheipl (1974): J.A. Weisheipl, *Friar Thomas d'Aquino. His Life, Thought and Work* (New York, 1974).

Weitenberg (1996): J.J.S. Weitenberg, 'Literary Contacts in Cilician Armenia', in K. Ciggaar *et al.* (1996: 63–72).

Weitzmann (1966): K. Weitzmann, 'Icon Painting in the Crusader Kingdom', *DOP*, 20 (1966), 51–83.

—— (1975): K. Weitzmann, 'A Group of Early Twelfth-Century Sinai Icons Attributed to Cyprus', in G. Robertson and G. Henderson (eds.), *Studies in Memory of David Talbot Rice* (Edinburgh, 1975), 47–63.

Weitzmann *et al.* (1982): K. Weitzmann, G. Alibegašvili, A. Volskaja, M. Chatzedakes, G. Babić, M. Alpatov, and T. Voinescu (eds.), *The Icon* (New York, 1982).

Wharton (1988): A.J. Wharton, *Art of Empire. Painting and Architecture of the Byzantine Periphery. A Comparative Study of Four Provinces* (University Park, Pennsylvania, 1988).

Willis (1986): M.D. Willis, 'Byzantine Beginnings of the Bedestan', *ΚΣ*, 50 (1986), 185–92.

Winfield and Winfield (2003): D. Winfield and J. Winfield, *The Church of the Panaghia tou Arakos at Lagoudhera, Cyprus: The Paintings and their Painterly Significance* (Dumbarton Oaks, Washington, D.C., 2003).

Wistedt (1967): R. Wistedt, *Le livre de fauconnerie de Jean de Francières. L'auteur et ses sources* (Lund, 1967).

Young (1978): S. Hatfield Young, 'The Date and Iconography of the Wall Paintings at Ayia Solomoni, Paphos, Cyprus', *Byzantion*, 48 (1978), 91–111.

—— (1983): S. Hatfield Young, *Byzantine Painting in Cyprus during the Early Lusignan Period* [unpublished Ph.D. Dissertation (Pennsylvania State University, 1983)].

Zaccaria (2001): V. Zaccaria, *Boccaccio narratore, storico, moralista e mitografo* (Florence, 2001).

Zachariadou (1983): E.A. Zachariadou, *Trade and Crusade. Venetian Crete and the Emirates of Menteshe and Aydin, 1300–1415* (Venice, 1983).

Zannetos (1910–1912): Ph. Zannetos, *Ιστορία της νήσου Κύπρου από της Αγγλικής κατοχής μέχρι σήμερον. Μετά εισαγωγής περιλαμβανούσης βραχείαν περιγραφήν της όλης ιστορίας αυτής*, 3 vols. (Larnaca, 1910–1912; repr. Nicosia, 1997).

Zepos (1976a): P.I. Zepos, 'Droit et institutions franques du Royaume de Chypre', *XVe Congrès International d'Études Byzantines, Rapports et Co-Rapports, V. Chypre dans le monde byzantin, 3. Droit et institutions franques du Royaume de Chypre* (Athens, 1976), 1–9.

—— (1976b): P.I. Zepos, 'Το δίκαιον της Κύπρου επί Φραγκοκρατίας', *Επετηρίς του Κέντρου ερεύνης της ιστορίας του ελληνικού δικαίου*, 23 (1976), 123–41.

Zink (1985): M. Zink, *La subjectivité littéraire. Autour du siècle de saint Louis* (Paris, 1985).

INDEX

Abbreviations: abp: archbishop; bp: bishop; k: king; cath: cathedral; ch: church; mon: monastery; MS: manuscript.
Names before 1571 are by Christian name first.

abbeys, *see* monasteries
abbots,
    Georgian, 164
    Greek, 157, 164, 205, 209, 245
    Latin, 175, 211
    Maronite, 166
    Syrian, 169, 170
Abbyssinians, *see* Ethiopians
Abraynus, 101
'Abrégé', 22, 30, 256
    also see 'Livres du Plédéant et du
    Plaidoyer'
absenteeism, 177, 229
absolution, 177
abuses, clerical, 176, 177, 178, 179,
    202, 209
accountants, 225
acculturation (cultural contacts and
    exchanges), 50, 58–62 passim, 86,
    158, 181–3, 210, 212–18 passim,
    219, 220–5 passim, 229, 232, 237,
    255, 275, 277, 280, 286–8, 295,
    301, 302, 303, 307, 311, 320, 322,
    324, 326, 327–8
Achaea, principality of, 69, 79
Achilléide, 278
acolytes, Latin, 173
Acre, 17, 66, 67, 72, 73, 77, 99, 100,
    101, 104, 115, 117, 121, 125, 127,
    128, 132, 134, 139, 179, 230, 231,
    237, 241, 250, 251, 252, 253, 261,
    270, 279, 302, 305
    art school in, 310
    bps of, 110
    fall of (1291), 2, 3, 15, 16, 68, 73,
        93, 95, 100, 111, 119, 128, 138,
        168, 179, 182, 215, 231, 243,
        244, 253, 254
Acrotiri Peninsula, 201
Adam, creation of, 241
administration, ecclesiastical, Greek, 7,
    24–6, 37, 55–7
    royal and seigneurial, 7, 21, 25, 26,
        36–7, 40, 53–5, 58, 60, 117, 129,
        220–1, 225–6

administrators, *see* officials
admirals of Cyprus, 85
Adriatic Sea, 109, 133, 135, 144, 145,
    147
adultery, 209, 264, 265
Aegean Sea, 73, 109, 133, 152, 155
Agathangelos, 275
agreements of 1220–22, 169, 187, 191,
    192, 193, 194, 195, 200, 202, 203,
    205, 206
agriculture, 8, 9, 69, 103–15, 145,
    156, 162
Agros, 201, 202, 298, 304, 323
Aimery of Lusignan, lord and k of
    Cyprus, 1, 19, 27, 65, 67–8, 71, 72,
    77, 87–8, 90, 111, 116, 117, 120,
    122, 171, 180, 246, 249–50
Aimery Barlais, *bailli* of Cyprus,
    260
Aimery of Milmars, 241
Akaki, 81
Akanthou, 111
Akhelia, 111, 290
Akko, *see* Acre
Akritic poetry, 220, 236, 237, 281–2
Alaminos, 81
Alan, chancellor of Cyprus, abp of
    Nicosia, 173
L'Aleman, surname, 63
    also see Garnier, Joan
Aleppo, 141
Alexander IV, pope, 16, 169, 190,
    199, 203, 205, 207, 208, 210
Alexandre le Grand, 266
Alexandria, 107, 109, 124, 129, 138,
    143, 149, 150, 151
    sack of (1365), 3, 73, 85, 97, 98
Alexios I Comnenos, Byzantine
    emperor, 115
Alexios III Angelos, Byzantine
    emperor, 290
Alfonso Buenhombre, OP, 163, 231–2,
    237
Alice of Champagne, queen of Cyprus,
    2, 88, 123, 169, 173, 187, 192